Special Edition
Using
Macromedia®
Director® 7

Gary Rosenzweig

A Division of Macmillan Computer Publishing, USA

201 W. 103rd Street

Indianapolis, Indiana 46290

CONTENTS AT

SPECIAL EDITION USING MACROMEDIA® DIRECTOR® 7

Copyright © 1999 by QUE® Corporation

All rights reserved. No part of this book shall be reproduced, stored in a retrieval system, or transmitted by any means, electronic, mechanical, photocopying, recording, or otherwise, without written permission from the publisher. No patent liability is assumed with respect to the use of the information contained herein. Although every precaution has been taken in the preparation of this book, the publisher and author assume no responsibility for errors or omissions. Neither is any liability assumed for damages resulting from the use of the information contained herein.

International Standard Book Number: 0-7897-1957-6

Library of Congress Catalog Card Number: 99-61027

Printed in the United States of America

First Printing: May 1999

01 00 99   4   3   2   1

TRADEMARKS

All terms mentioned in this book that are known to be trademarks or service marks have been appropriately capitalized. Que cannot attest to the accuracy of this information. Use of a term in this book should not be regarded as affecting the validity of any trademark or service mark.

Authorware, Backstage, Director, Extreme 3D, Flash, Fontographer, FreeHand, Lingo, Macromedia, the Macromedia logo, the Made With Macromedia logo, Power Applets, SoundEdit, Shockwave, xRes, and Xtra are all trademarks of Macromedia.

WARNING AND DISCLAIMER

Every effort has been made to make this book as complete and as accurate as possible, but no warranty or fitness is implied. The information provided is on an "as is" basis. The author and the publisher shall have neither liability or responsibility to any person or entity with respect to any loss or damages arising from the information contained in this book or from the use of the CD, or programs accompanying it.

Publisher
John Pierce

Executive Editor
Beth Millett

Acquisitions Editor
Karen Whitehouse

Development Editor
Kezia Endsley

Managing Editor
Tom Hayes

Project Editor
George E. Nedeff

Copy Editor
Margo Catts

Indexer
Sandy Henselmeier

Proofreader
Maryann Steinhart

Technical Editor
Allison Kelsey

Software Development Specialist
Adam Swetnam

Additional Illustrations
William Follett

Interior Design
Ruth Lewis

Cover Designers
Dan Armstrong
Ruth Lewis

Copy Writer
Eric Borgert

Layout Technicians
Brian Borders
Susan Geiselman
Amy Parker
Mark Walchle

TABLE OF CONTENTS

About The Author

Gary Rosenzweig is the Chief Engineer, founder, and owner of CleverMedia, a game and multimedia development company in Denver, Colorado. This is his third book on Director.

Before the multimedia industry started, he was a computer science student at Drexel University in Philadelphia. There, he took a greater interest in journalism than computers. After working for years in various positions at the student newspaper, he eventually rose to the position of Editor-In-Chief.

Gary followed his journalistic interests to the University of North Carolina at Chapel Hill, where he earned a master's degree. As an undergraduate, he found that he was someone who knew a lot about publishing at a school where everyone was a computer expert. In graduate school, he found that he was someone that knew a lot about computers at a school where everyone was involved in publishing.

While in school he got his first taste of a scripting language with Hypercard 1.0. Although class projects were done in Pascal, C, and other "serious" programming languages, Gary found that he was able to build programs for freelance jobs with Hypercard in a fraction of the time.

After school, rather than enter one field or another, Gary combined both and began freelancing for publications to build multimedia products. Shortly thereafter, he moved to Denver to take a job at Ingenius, an educational news service partially owned by Reuters. It was there that he began using Director all day, every day.

Being a serious developer, Gary went to bookstores to find books on Director. Seeing none, he decided to write one. He then published the book, for free, on the Internet. Soon after that, he was paid to rewrite and update the book as *The Comprehensive Guide to Lingo*.

After the book was published, Gary left Ingenius and started his own development company, CleverMedia. This was made possible because of Shockwave, which gives users the capability to play Director movies on the Web. Demand for Shockwave applets rose and CleverMedia was hired by many companies, both large and small, to build Shockwave applets. Today, CleverMedia owns two of the largest Shockwave game sites on the Web, and creates games for many of the others.

Gary lives in Denver, Colorado, with his soon-to-be wife, Debby, and a cat named Lucy. Other than computers and the Internet, he also enjoys film, camping, classic science fiction, and writing.

Personal Home Page: `http://clevermedia.com/rosenz/`

Email: `http://clevermedia.com/email-usingd7.html`

Dedication

To my fiancée, Debby Bach Thomsen.

Acknowledgments

Very special thanks goes to William Follett, CleverMedia's Art Director, who helped me run CleverMedia while I was busy writing. Also, thanks to John Nyquist for ideas and encouragement, and to Lee Allis-Hayes, without whom I wouldn't have written this book. Thanks also to the team at Que: Karen Whitehouse, Kezia Endsley, and George Nedeff; and thank you to my tech editor, Allison Kelsey. Thanks to my family for their continuing lifetime of support: Jacqueline, Jerry, and Larry Rosenzweig; Rebecca Jacob; Barbara and Richard Shifrin.

The most thanks goes to my fiancée, Debby, for her love and support.

Music is a very important part of my writing environment. Here are a few of the artists that I listened to while writing. I recommend them all: Ludwig van Beethoven, Big Bad Voodoo Daddy, Cowboy Junkies, Hole, Madonna, Liz Phair, Sleater-Kinney, That Dog, and the soundtrack to the movie *Bandits* (Germany, 1997).

TELL US WHAT YOU THINK!

As the reader of this book, *you* are our most important critic and commentator. We value your opinion and want to know what we're doing right, what we could do better, what areas you'd like to see us publish in, and any other words of wisdom you're willing to pass our way.

As the Executive Editor for the Web development team at Que, I welcome your comments. You can fax, email, or write me directly to let me know what you did or didn't like about this book—as well as what we can do to make our books stronger.

Please note that I cannot help you with technical problems related to the topic of this book, and that due to the high volume of mail I receive, I might not be able to reply to every message.

When you write, please be sure to include this book's title and author as well as your name and phone or fax number. I will carefully review your comments and share them with the author and editors who worked on the book.

Fax: 317-581-4666

E-mail: desktop_pub@mcp.com

Mail: Beth Millett
          Graphics and Design
          Que Corporation
          201 West 103rd Street
          Indianapolis, IN 46290 USA

FOREWORD

A large community of Director users has developed over the past few years. People from diverse backgrounds have learned, experimented, and grown with Director to be able to make a living doing what they enjoy. A few in the Director community have gone beyond this and shared their expertise or pushed the boundary of what was thought possible with Director. Gary Rosenzweig has done both to a unique degree.

I first became aware of Gary's educational efforts back in 1994 when I saw his book on Director that he had self published online. At that time the Director book market had not yet proven itself and it was hard to convince a publisher to stand behind a Director title. Gary did not let this deter him and he provided a valuable service to aspiring Director users by making his first book available online for no charge.

My next early encounter with Gary was through his web site, `www.clevermedia.com`, where he provided many Director Shockwave movies that could be enjoyed by all. As early as 1995 Gary had innovative and imaginative titles such as, "Pretty Good Golf," which packs a lot of activity into a very small size; "CleverChess," the very first real multiplayer Internet game in Shockwave; "Space Pirate," a multiplay game so popular it was elevated to its own private site.

Eventually, Gary and I met in person at a Macromedia Developer User Conference, where developers from around the world come to learn more about Macromedia tools and to exchange ideas. I was pleased to find out that he and I share a strong interest in education and gaming. We continued chatting on these topics as we met over the years at other conferences. In addition to informal discussions with other developers, Gary has shared his extensive expertise at these conferences as a presenter.

While many of you may not get a chance to meet Gary at a conference, you do have this excellent book. It's a big book because it covers just about everything you might choose to do in Director—from basic animation to beginning and advanced Lingo programming. The Director community is fortunate to have one of its most innovative developers willing to share his knowledge so that you can benefit from his many years of experience.

John (JT) Thompson

Chief Architect of Lingo

INTRODUCTION

I love working with Director. By education, I am a computer scientist and a journalist. By nature, I am a problem solver. I love using both logic and imagination. Director requires me to use all these things.

If you have a job where you work all day with Director, consider yourself lucky. You probably already do. In fact, you have probably said to yourself before: "I can't believe I get paid for this!"

Director is a great tool for creating software. On the one hand, you can quickly bring to life your ideas. On the other hand, Director is an environment that inspires new ideas as you explore it.

The possibilities for animators are incredible, even if they never choose to do any programming. Director also has built-in programs called behaviors that expand the possibilities a thousand times for those looking to make interactive presentations.

If you are willing to go on to learn Lingo, the programming language of Director, the possibilities for your creations become virtually limitless. There are more than 800 Lingo keywords and all standard programming language structures. This makes Lingo every bit as powerful as languages such as C++, Pascal, and Java. In some cases, it is even more powerful.

The results of your work can be easily distributed to the world. You can create standalone applications to send over the Internet or burn into CD-ROMs. You can embed your creations into HTML pages for the Web to see. You can even create a Java applet.

Many people in the computer industry still think of Director as it was in version 3: an animation tool with a simple scripting language. However, each version since then has added a huge array of powerful features. It is now the most advanced animation tool ever, with the one of the most advanced programming languages.

Anyone who says, "You can't do that in Director," doesn't really understand the power or depth of Director 7.

WHO IS THIS BOOK FOR?

Chapter 1 of this book assumes that you have never used Director before. However, it does not assume that you are an idiot, either.

The first two chapters move quickly through the basics. Those chapters, like the rest of this book, state concepts and techniques clearly, and never assume you know something about Director before it is taught in the book.

The idea is to not waste time by walking you step-by-step through basic and simple tasks. Instead, this book assumes that you are motivated learner, wanting to read, absorb, understand, and then move on to the next piece of information.

If you are an animator, or are simply using Director to create presentations, Chapters 1 through 11 are for you. They go into detail about making animations and presentations without using any Lingo programming.

If you want to learn Lingo, Chapters 12 and on teach you from the ground up. Like Chapters 1 and 2, these chapters do not assume you know anything about Lingo or programming in advance. However, they move quickly, and will have a motivated learner programming Lingo in a matter of hours.

If you are interested in advanced Lingo techniques, the later chapters are filled with high-level Lingo programs. I have continued the practice of my earlier books in providing more advanced Lingo concepts than any of the other books on the market.

Finally, if you are seeking a good reference book on Director, this book will beat or rival any other. I have tried to cover all topics, even ones that other books do not explore. In addition, I have made the reference section comprehensive. It features a full Lingo dictionary and many other useful appendixes.

THIS BOOK IS ABOUT DIRECTOR 7

One thing to note is that this book is really for Director 7, not earlier versions of Director. In the past, many people have bought my Director 6 book and tried to use it to learn Director 5. They, of course, ran into problems.

The difference between Director 6 and Director 7 is huge. Macromedia is definitely not one of those companies that fixes a few bugs and calls it an upgrade. It has added a huge number of new features, and changed the way you write programs. Other companies should take a lesson from Macromedia about creating upgrades that are really worth the upgrade price.

If you consider yourself a serious developer, you should be using Director 7 by the time you read this. Director 6 is a great tool, but Director 7 is fantastic. It will empower you to create better products.

WHERE DID THIS BOOK COME FROM?

After writing a book on Director 5 and another on Director 6, there was little question in my mind that I would be working on one again when Director 7 was announced. The question was: who would I be writing for?

My old publisher was sadly no longer in business. So I put the word out to other publishers.

The result was that I was contacted by Macmillan (QUE) about updating the "Inside Director" series. The former author had declined to do an update, but was a friend of mine and recommended me.

After talking with the publisher, it was decided that a new direction was needed. The "Inside Director" books were very successful, but the material would be hard to update. Besides, I was up for writing a whole new tome myself.

So the idea came up to write a new book under the "Using, Special Edition" series. This series, which can be found in bookstores everywhere, is very well known and respected.

If you own one of the Inside Director books, you may recognize a sentence, paragraph, or phrase here and there. Probably 95% of this book is my own writing, but in a few cases the old Inside Director text stated something so well that I felt it was best to reuse it.

Writing for this book began during the Director 7 beta cycle, but I was able to work with the final version of Director 7 for the last month of writing. Hopefully, this will result in an error-free book that covers all the bases.

HOW TO USE THIS BOOK

You can read this book through, or use it for random access reference. If you are just learning Director, or are looking to expand your skills, you can pick a point in the book that seems to match your current skill level and start reading there.

Each chapter makes the general assumption that you know the basics of the material in the previous chapters. However, there is enough context in each chapter to allow you to fill gaps in your knowledge as you go along. There are "See Also" markers throughout the book that will refer you both forward and backward in the book to places where a similar topic is covered.

Chapters 1 and 2 are meant to teach the basics, from using Director as an animation tool to using Director as a presentation tool. Chapters 3 through 11 then add to those basics with information about each media type and some more advanced techniques. No Lingo knowledge is required or taught during these chapters.

Chapters 12 through 14 teach Lingo basics. Then, Chapters 15 through 20 build on that knowledge by showing how Lingo can control various types of media. Chapters 21 through 26 are about even more advanced Lingo techniques.

Chapters 27 to 32 are very different from the rest of the book, and from material found in other books. They provide examples of Director movies. An explanation of what each movie does and how it does it, plus the source code for each movie, is given. These are examples that you can use to see how Lingo code is put to use in real-life situations. These chapters also include suggestions for how you can alter and adapt them to make your own movies.

The rest of the chapters have information useful for completing a project, such as debugging, performance issues, and building Projectors and Shockwave pages.

To round out the book as a reference guide, I have added a complete Lingo quick reference section and many tables and charts as appendixes.

CONVENTIONS USED IN THIS BOOK

The following conventions are used to differentiate Lingo keywords from user-defined keywords and any other text with special emphasis:

- Italics—Used for official Lingo keywords. This includes handlers, commands, properties, and anything found in the official Macromedia documentation. Examples: *on mouseUp*, *on exitFrame*, *puppetSprite*, and *the ticks*.

- Quotation marks:

  Anything made up by the programmer or the author. These keywords can't be found in the official documentation, because they don't exist until the programmer creates them. Examples: "on myHandler" and "myVariable".

  Messages. A message is an invisible thing that is sent through the director environment. They have names only as a way to relate to the reader what is going on. Examples: "mouseUp" and "exitFrame". They look like official keywords, but are not.

  Values. When I want to say something such as: the value of this variable is "hello world", the value returned is shown in quotes.

- Monospace—Lines of code and commands that the programmer is asked to type into Director appear in monospace, regardless of keyword type. For example: `put 41+1`.

This formatting reflects the importance of showing the difference between official Lingo keywords and made-up words.

At the end of most chapters you will find two sections: "Troubleshooting" and "Did You Know?" The first presents some common problems that developers face and how to avoid them. This is in addition to troubleshooting advice found throughout many chapters.

The "Did You Know?" section is something a little different. It contains extra information about the topic. Sometimes the information is a little more advanced than the level of the chapter. Other times it highlights little-known facts or undocumented Lingo. On occasion it simply contains an idea for an interesting application of the information taught in the chapter. In addition, "Tips" placed throughout the chapters provide interesting ideas and methods you may not have considered.

BEFORE YOU BEGIN...

There are several ways that I recommend beginning to use this book. The first suggestion is for first-time Director users. Play with Director first. Just open the program and play with it. Try all the menu commands and look at some of the tutorials that come with Director.

Another thing that beginners should do is check out as many Shockwave movies on the Web as you can. These give you an idea of what is possible. If you need a place to start, try `http://clevermedia.com`, a site created by my company CleverMedia and me.

Getting grounded by playing with Director and surfing the Web will give you some context as you start reading this book.

If you are a Director user who has just upgraded to Director 7, you should check out Appendix A. It has a list of most of the features new to Director 7.

There are so many new features that I honestly recommend that even an experienced Director 6 user start this book at Chapter 1. However, such a user would be able to move through most of the early chapters quickly.

Another way to use this book is to simply place it next to you computer as a reference. Need to know about using the Behavior Inspector? Chapter 11. Need to remember the basics for creating a behavior? Chapter 14. Need to create or alter a vector shape? Chapter 20. Want to make a game? Chapter 32. You get the idea.

All in all, there is a lot in this book for every level of Director user. I hope you enjoy reading this book as much as I enjoyed writing it!

DIRECTOR BASICS

CHAPTER 1

ANIMATION WITH DIRECTOR

In this chapter

Macromedia Director 7 is a complete environment for the creation of multimedia. Think of it as an artist's canvas. Or, to use the metaphor that Director follows, a stage.

You can fill this stage with your own production. Any element in the production is called a *cast member* or simply a *member*. The computer screen where the action takes place is a window called the *Stage*.

The rest of the elements in Director also follow a theater/film metaphor, although some element names follow it better than others.

AN INTRODUCTION TO DIRECTOR

Assume that you have an image drawn in another program that you want to place in Director.

When you import this image into Director, it becomes a *cast member*. The *cast window* displays a list of all the cast members. This list is called the *cast library* or sometimes simply the *Cast*. Members can be of different types: bitmap images, text, sounds, shapes, and so on. In this case, you have a bitmap image, commonly called a *bitmap*.

You can take this bitmap and place it on to the Stage. (I'll go into specifics about how to do this later.) It actually appears on both the Stage and in the Score. The *Score* is a chart that shows which members appear on the Stage at which times. A moment in time is called a *frame*. The Score shows which members appear in which frames. The Stage shows the positions of each member on the Stage during a particular frame.

The user only sees the Stage when you are finished with your project. The cast window and Score window are tools used only by you, the author of the Director project.

A member that is in the Score is called a *sprite*. The term does not describe the member, but rather the combination of the member and its placement in the Score and on the Stage. A member is simply a bitmap or other media element, whereas a sprite is the description of which member is being used, what frame of the Score it is in, where it is located on the Stage, as well as many other properties. For instance, a member might be a picture, and a sprite is that member when placed on the Stage.

A Director production is called a *movie*. This term is more accurately used to describe the file that contains all your work. A Director project can actually contain many movies, or just one. A movie can have many cast members, but generally only one Score.

Understanding Director's terminology is the first step toward learning to use the program:

- Movie—The primary Director file; contains one or more cast libraries and a Score. It is the only Director file you need for most productions.
- Cast—The list of cast members used in a movie.
- Member—A single element such as a bitmap, some text, a sound, a shape, a vector drawing, or a piece of digital video.

- Score—A chart showing what members appear on the Stage at what times.
- Frame—An instant of time in Director. While you are working on a movie, the Stage shows a single frame. While the movie is animating, the Stage moves through frames to create the visual effect of animation.
- Channel—A numbered position in the Score. The Score has channels 1 through 1000, as well as a few special channels at the top. Which channel a sprite is in determines whether it gets drawn over or under another sprite.
- Sprite—The description of which member is shown, where it is in the Score, where it appears on the Stage, and many other properties.

Using only the preceding elements, you can create animations with Director. They are the primary parts of the program and are used in the simplest of movies as well as in the most complex.

However, several other important elements are required to create anything but the simplest projects in Director. The most critical is *scripts*.

If you want to stick with the theater/film metaphor, a *script* is like stage direction. Using a programming language in Director called *Lingo*, you can tell sprites what to do. Although it is possible to animate a sprite using only the Stage and Score, more complex movements and interaction with the user require you to learn and use Lingo. You'll learn more about using Lingo in Chapter 12, "Learning Lingo," and Chapter 13, "Essential Lingo Syntax."

A Lingo script that is attached to a sprite in the Score is called a *behavior*. This type of script shows a sprite how to behave under different circumstances. A script attached to a whole frame is called a *frame script*, and a script that controls the entire movie is called a *movie script*. You'll find more information about scripts and scripting later in the book.

These terms will become important to you after you have mastered the basic skills of Director and begin to make professional projects. Here is a review of some more advanced Director terms:

- Script—A set of Lingo commands that controls sprites and other elements of the movie.
- Lingo—The programming language of Director.
- Behavior—A script that controls a sprite.
- Frame Script—A script that controls a frame.
- Movie Script—A script that controls the entire movie.
- Projector—A standalone application program created from a Director movie.
- Shockwave—Technology that enables users to play Director movies in Web browsers.

PLAYBACK OPTIONS

After you have created a movie and want to make a standalone computer application, you create a *projector*. This is simply a program that can be distributed to your users. It runs your Director movie without requiring Director 7.

Another way to distribute your finished Director movie is to embed it in Internet Web pages. People without Director can use Shockwave to play your movies. They can view your original Director movie file, or a special protected and compressed version of it. Shockwave most commonly comes in the form of a Web browser plug-in for Netscape Navigator and Microsoft Internet Explorer.

When a Director movie plays, it begins by displaying frame 1 on the Stage. Which members are shown on the Stage is determined by what is in the Score. The positions of the members on the Stage are determined by how you placed them there. After frame 1 is displayed, Director waits an appropriate amount of time, usually a fraction of a second, and then displays frame 2.

If frame 1 and frame 2 look the same, you will see no difference. However, if the locations of the sprites change, they appear to move. As the movie goes from one frame to the next, changes in the locations of sprites create the illusion of movement.

As the movie progresses, each sprite starts and ends. Some sprites exist throughout the entire movie, whereas others begin at a certain frame and end at another. Some sprites may only appear for one frame.

When the last frame is reached, the movie stops. You may want to simply have the movie loop back to the beginning and start again. However, you also can use Lingo to have the movie jump to any other frame.

MOVIE EXAMPLE

A simple example will help you understand how Macromedia movies are made. It includes three bitmap cast members and 28 frames of animation. Figure 1.1 shows the cast window with all three members. You can open the cast window by choosing Window, Cast in the menu bar. The shortcut for this is Command+3 on the Mac and Ctrl+3 in Windows.

Figure 1.1
The Internal Cast window with three bitmap members. The name of the window refers to the name of the Cast: Internal (the default name for the main Cast).

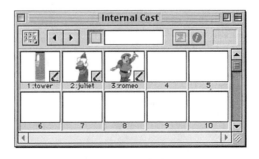

Note in Figure 1.1 that I have also named these three members. You can name members by selecting a member and editing its name in the text area at the top of the cast window. The cast window shows miniature images of each bitmap, which are called *thumbnails*.

Take the first member, the tower, and place it on the Stage by clicking and dragging the thumbnail from the cast window to the Stage window. The image was drawn to be placed on the right side of the Stage, so you would put it there.

Placing the member on the Stage also places it in the Score in the first available channel, which in this case is channel 1. Figure 1.2 shows the Stage with the member placed, as well as the Score window on top of it. More details about all these windows can be found later in the chapter. Right now, just notice that the sprite appears in channel 1 and stretches from frame 1 to frame 28.

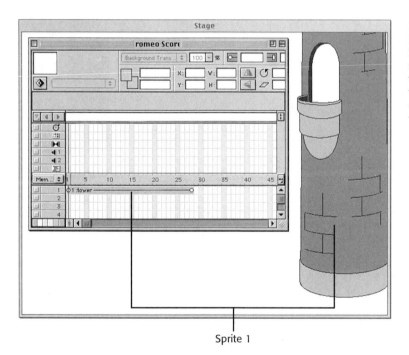

Figure 1.2
Both the Stage and the Score window are shown. The bitmap of the tower corresponds to the sprite shown in channel 1, from frames 1 to 28.

Sprite 1

The Stage window contains the bitmap from member 1. The Score shows a sprite that will display member 1 from frames 1 to 28.

If you play the movie now, not much happens. You will see an indicator in the Score window move from frame 1 to 28. The bitmap stays in the same place on the Stage because you have not told it to do otherwise.

Now add a second element to the movie. Drag the picture of the woman onto the Stage. It then appears in channel 2 in the Score. If you move the woman over to the tower, you see an interesting result. Figure 1.3 shows the woman and the tower on the Stage as well as in the Score. The woman appears to be outside the tower. Her sprite is drawn after the tower's sprite because it appears in a higher Score channel.

Figure 1.3
The Stage shows two members: a woman and a tower. The woman is drawn on top of the tower because her sprite is in a higher Score channel.

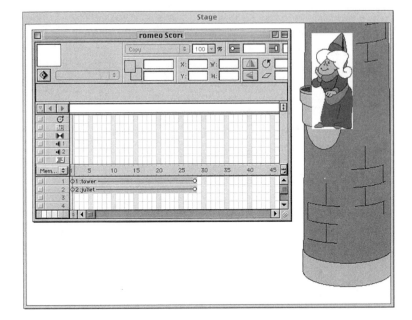

You can fix this problem by swapping the two sprites. If you move the woman's sprite to channel 1 and the tower's sprite to channel 2, the tower then covers the woman rather than the other way around. You can swap the sprites by simply dragging them around the Score window. Move the tower to channel 3, the woman to channel 1, and then the tower back to channel 2.

The desired effect, however, is not to completely cover the woman with the tower, but instead to have her show through the tower window. You can do this by applying an ink to the sprite.

Sprites are more than just a member, a Stage location, and a frame range. They also have properties such as inks. An *ink* determines how a sprite is drawn on the Stage. The default ink is *copy*, which means that a bitmap member blocks out everything under its rectangular boundaries. This is what you have been using, which is why the woman is completely obscured by the tower.

However, if you set the ink of the tower sprite to *Background Transparent*, the tower sprite draws differently. This ink setting causes all pure white pixels in the drawing to appear as transparent, so that the sprites behind them show through. Setting the tower sprite to Background Transparent gives you the result seen in Figure 1.4.

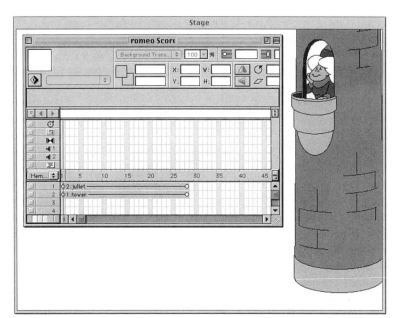

Figure 1.4
Now the woman shows through the window of the tower on the Stage. This effect is achieved by having the tower sprite set to use the Background Transparent ink.

Now you have a movie with two sprites, but it still does not include animation. Drag the bitmap of the man on the Stage and place him somewhere toward the bottom. You want to have him slide in from the left. For now, he appears as sprite 3, which spans the same frames as the other two sprites.

Take a close look at the sprites as represented in the Score. Notice that a dot appears in the very first frame of each sprite and another dot appears in the last frame. These marks signify *keyframes*, which describe frames where the graphic is locked into a position on the Stage.

In any frame of a sprite that does not include a keyframe, Director positions the sprite on the Stage relative to the last and next keyframe. This process is known as *tweening*. With it you can define simple animations by just showing Director the starting and ending points of a sprite.

For instance, suppose you have a sprite that is three frames long. The first frame is always a keyframe, otherwise Director would not know where to start the animation. In most cases the last frame is also a keyframe, so Director knows where to end the animation. If you position the sprite on the left side of the screen in frame 1, and the right side of the screen in frame 3, you have set the locations of both keyframes.

Director then determines that for frame 2 the sprite needs to be in the middle of the Stage, directly between the first and last locations. You never have to show Director where to place the sprite in frame 2; it just figures it out by looking at the keyframes before and after it.

You can position the man's sprite over to the left of the Stage in frame 1, and then place him closer to the tower in frame 28. Do this by using the Score window to select which frame to edit. Just click anywhere in that frame's column to move to that frame. Move to frame 1 and position the man, and then move to frame 28 and position him again.

The result is that he will animate from frame 1 to 28, moving across the Stage from left to right. Figure 1.5 shows this animation somewhere in the middle.

Figure 1.5
Sprite 3 moves from left to right, which results from having different settings for the initial and final keyframes of the sprite in the Score.

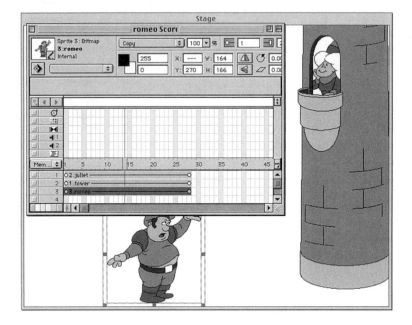

Later in this book, you will find out how to add more than one keyframe to a sprite, how to use many different inks, and even how to make sprites move in directions other than straight lines and constant speeds.

→ **See** "Sprite Ink," Chapter 10, "Properties of Sprites and Frames," for more information about inks

THE CAST

Recall that when you import an image into Director, it becomes a cast member. The cast window displays a list of all the cast members. This list is called the *Cast*. Members can be of different types: bitmap images, text, sounds, shapes, and so on. This section discusses in more detail the various types of cast members.

TYPES OF CAST MEMBERS

The most basic elements of any Director movie are the cast members. You can't do any work in the Score or on the Stage without first having some members to work with.

In the last section, you saw examples of bitmap members. You can also use many more types of members. Basically, any form of media can be represented in Director as a cast member.

Each type of cast member has either its own editing window, or its own Properties dialog box, or both. For instance, the paint window enables you to edit a bitmap member. It resembles a standalone image editing application, but with an emphasis on editing the bitmap for use in Director.

In some cases, you can assign external editors to cast member types. You can use Adobe Photoshop to edit bitmap members if you want.

Every cast member also has a name and a number. The number corresponds to its position in the Cast. The name is anything you want it to be.

Tip

It is always a good idea to assign every cast member a unique name. This will come in handy when you begin scripting with Lingo.

Figure 1.1 showed a typical cast window. It is really just one continuous list of members. You can stretch or shrink the window to display more or fewer members at a time.

You already know that you can add a member to the Score or Stage by simply dragging from the cast window. You can edit a member by double-clicking it. A single click on a member selects it, and then you can click the information button in the cast window to view its properties.

Note

The information button—a blue box with a lowercase "i"—appears in the upper-right corner of many windows in Director. Clicking it shows you the properties of the selected cast member. Sometimes you can edit important properties of the member this way.

Cast member types vary greatly. Some can be created and edited in Director. Others need to be created in programs such as video or sound editing tools and then imported. The following list summarizes most of the possible member types. Chapter 3, "Bitmap Members," provides more details.

- Bitmaps—A bitmap is essentially a graphic or image. It can be a drawing, photograph, or even an image generated by a 3D program. You can use the paint window to edit most bitmaps in Director.

- Text—A text member contains formatted characters. You can create them in Director with the text-editing window, or you can import files created in word processing programs. Director has the capability to display very graphically pleasing anti-aliased text. This means that the edges of characters are smooth rather than jagged. Director 7 also enables you to create text members that use fonts that don't need to be on the user's machine to display properly.

- Fields—These are like text members, but date back to earlier versions of Director where fields were the only text display option. Although they can't be anti-aliased and you cannot import word processing files as fields, they have other advantages. Mostly, they take up less file space and are more suited to general text use where file size is important.

- Sounds—Director can import many different types of sound formats, but does not really have the capability to create or edit sounds. Sounds can be quick, simple buzzes and beeps or long music pieces.

- Shapes—Director has a few special cast member types called *shapes*. You can draw lines, ovals, rectangles, and rounded rectangles. All but lines can be either filled or outlines. You can use these shapes to add quick graphic elements to your movies without having to create bitmaps for them.

- Vectors—You can also create unique, complex shapes called *vectors*. These are similar to the media created with programs such as Macromedia Freehand and Adobe Illustrator. A vector member is one long line that can be bent and curved. A closed loop in a vector member can be filled. Vector members can be scaled to any size and still maintain their shape and clarity.

- Buttons—You can make quick, simple buttons in Director. These buttons have a very generic look and feel. They are mostly useful for prototyping and pre-release versions of your project. You will eventually want to replace them with bitmaps that act as buttons.

- Digital Video—Video members can come in a variety of sources but are usually in Apple QuickTime format or Windows AVI format. Most of the time these members are merely links to external files that contain the real media. This category can be extended to hold a variety of QuickTime formats such as QuickTime VR and MIDI files.

- Scripts—cast members that hold scripts appear to be similar to field members. They hold the Lingo instructions that control the elements of the movie.

- Xtra Members—Macromedia and third parties develop extensions to Director that add or enhance functionality. These are called *Xtras*. Some of these xtras enable you to have new types of cast members such as cursor cast members or 3D graphics.

As you explore Director's different cast members you will find that they relate to each other in many ways. For instance, most cast members can have a script attached to them. The script is not a separate cast member, but a property of that single cast member. You can therefore create a bitmap image that has a script in it. That script enables it to react to the user clicking it. But you could also use that bitmap without any script attached to it. Instead you would attach a separate script member, known as a behavior, to the same sprite in the Score.

CAST WINDOW PROPERTIES AND SETTINGS

The cast window is one of your primary tools for using Director. Some customizable features may help you better organize your work. First, take a look at the toolbar area of a cast window. Figure 1.6 shows an Internal Cast window with some members. You can see several icon buttons in the toolbar.

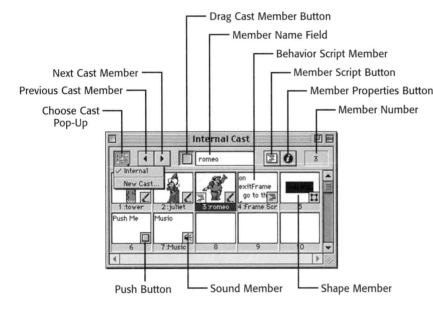

Figure 1.6
An Internal Cast window with several sample members. There are three bitmaps, a behavior script, a shape, a button, and a sound.

The first button on the left, the Choose Cast Pop-Up, enables you to browse the various cast libraries contained in, or attached to, the movie. You can have many internal and external Casts. More information about this feature appears later in the chapter.

> **Tip**
>
> You can select one or many cast members in the cast window. Using the Shift key, you can select a set of continuous members. Using the Command key on the Mac and the Ctrl key in Windows, you can add single members to what you have already selected.

The rest of the buttons are pretty simple. The arrows enable you to select the next or previous member in the Cast. The square is a button that you can click and drag to the Stage or Score. Doing so places the selected cast member or members there. The Member Script button enables you to add or edit a script to most members. For script members it simply opens the script editing window. The Member Properties button, as you have seen before, shows you the Properties dialog box for the selected member or members.

In addition to these buttons, the toolbar shows you the name and number of the cast member. Within the toolbar you can edit the name of the member.

Now look at the members in this Cast. Every member shown has a thumbnail representation of the contents of the member. In the case of a bitmap, it is simply a resized version of the image. In other cases, such as with scripts and buttons, the text is displayed. In addition to this image, an icon appears in the lower-right corner of each box that tells you what type the member is. A little paintbrush shows you that it is a bitmap.

Another icon sometimes appears in the lower-left corner of each box. This icon, seen in member 3 of Figure 1.6, tells you that a script is attached to this member.

You can customize cast windows to an extent. Choose File, Preferences, Cast to bring up the Cast Window Preferences dialog box. Figure 1.7 shows this dialog box for the Internal Cast window.

Figure 1.7
The Cast Window Preferences dialog box enables you to customize the appearance of the cast window.

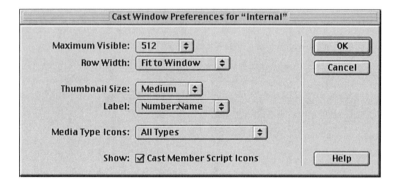

The various settings in this dialog box are pretty self-explanatory. You can use the row width setting to fix the number of members shown on each row regardless of the present size of the window. You can also set the thumbnail size, label display, and icon display options.

Tip

Setting the row width option to "10 thumbnails" can sometimes help you organize your cast members. However, if you set the window width on the screen to be less than 10 members across, you will not be able to see a continuous set of members. For instance, you may see members 1 to 8, 11 to 18, 21 to 28, and 31 to 38. A few times I have lost time looking for lost members that are simply outside the viewable window area.

MULTIPLE CAST LIBRARIES

In the days of Director 4, all cast members had to be contained in one Cast. This sometimes meant a huge Cast with hundreds of cast members. The only option for sharing members between movies was to have one specially labeled movie that acted as a shared Cast. Director 5 introduced the idea of *multiple cast libraries*. The main advantage is that you can better organize the members.

Each cast library has a name. Each movie must have at least one cast library. This first cast library is named "Internal" by default, but you can change that.

Use the cast icon that appears as the leftmost button in the cast window toolbar to create a new Cast. You are then prompted for its name.

Tip

> If you are using multiple cast libraries, you may find it necessary to look at more than one Cast at a time. You can do this by holding down the Option key on the Mac or the Alt key in Windows and selecting the second Cast from the list presented when pressing the cast icon on the left side of the cast window toolbar. A second cast window opens. You can drag members between windows.

Organizing your members into multiple Casts is a requirement for some developers, whereas others still prefer to use just one Cast. In practice, it really depends on the type of project you are working on.

If you are creating a simple, linear animation that has only a few members, it is probably best to keep your movie to one Cast. However, multiple casts really help when you have more than a few dozen members.

Some developers organize their casts by member type, placing bitmaps in one Cast, scripts in another, sounds in another, and so on. Others mix member types in a Cast, but place items according to when they are used, such as placing members that are part of an introduction screen together and members that are in the main animation together.

EXTERNAL CAST LIBRARIES

Not all your Casts have to be contained inside a single movie. You can have Casts that exist as their own files—these are called *external cast libraries*.

Note

> In Windows, dot-three extensions are still necessary to enable the operating system to tell what files contain. Director movies use a .dir extension. External Cast libraries use a .cst extension. You can make protected versions of either type of file so that other developers cannot see your code. These files have .dxr and .cxt extensions. If you compress the files for internet delivery, the extensions are .dcr and .cct. Projectors, of course, are executable applications and use the .exe extension. Even if you are developing on a Mac, it is useful to name your files this way to avoid problems when making a cross-platform version of your project.

By their very nature, these external Casts have some interesting properties. For one, they can be shared by multiple movies. For instance, you can have a series of photographs in an external Cast. One movie can use some of these members in a slide-show presentation. A totally separate movie can use these same images in a puzzle game. The cast library needs to be included only once even though it is being used twice.

The inverse of this property of external Casts is that you can easily switch Casts in one movie without editing the movie. For instance, a Cast called images.cst might contain pictures of famous buildings in New York. A movie called slideshow.dir can use these images in a slide show presentation. If you take another cast file also called images.cst and replace the first one with it, you could have a slide show of famous buildings in San Francisco instead.

External Cast libraries also make it easier for multiple people to work on a project together. You could have an artist working on one cast file, a sound engineer on another, and a multi-media author on the main movie. When the artist and engineer are done, you can plug the new cast libraries right in.

THE STAGE

The Stage is the only window that the end user will actually see. It is where all the visual action of a movie takes place, at least until you start using some very advanced techniques.

During authoring, the main purpose of the Stage is to show you a preview of what the user will see. While the movie is stopped you see a frozen moment in time: one single frame of the movie.

The Stage also acts as your primary placement tool. You can drag cast members to either the Stage or the Score to use them on the Stage. However, only on the Stage can you position them. With the Score and other tools, you are limited to positioning the sprites by tweaking numbers. On the Stage, you can position sprites by dragging them with the mouse.

Tip

> The Stage in Director 7 is a separate window. You can make the window temporarily disappear by pressing Command+1 on the Mac or Ctrl+1 in Windows. You can make it reappear the same way.

The size of the Stage can be changed in the Movie Properties dialog box. To access this dialog box, Choose Modify, Movie, Properties. You can change the size of the Stage as well as its position on the screen.

A common Stage size is 640 pixels wide and 480 pixels high, because that screen size was the standard for personal computers for a long time. Today, 800×600 seems to be the most common size, but enough people still use 640×480 screens that it is the default size of multimedia presentations.

Stage size depends on what you expect your users to have. It also depends on other factors. For instance, if your movie will end up on the Web and be played with Shockwave, take into account the window borders of the Netscape and Internet Explorer windows. You will examine this more closely when you read about projectors and Shockwave in Part VII, "Using Director to Create Professional Applications."

Note You do not have to decide on a Stage size at the beginning of a project. Just keep in mind that the top left corner of the Stage stays still if you readjust the Stage size. Only the width and height from this top left corner can change.

Another property of the Stage is its background color. You can set the background color of the Stage by using the same Movie Properties dialog box. The default is white and the second most common setting is black, but you can use any color.

→ **See** "Movie Preferences," Chapter 9, "The Director Environment," for more information about the Movie Preferences dialog box

THE SCORE

The real heart and soul of a movie is the Score. As you can see in Figure 1.8, it really is just a chart of the contents of the movie. Time, represented by frames, goes across the Score, whereas sprite channels and other elements are listed as rows in the chart.

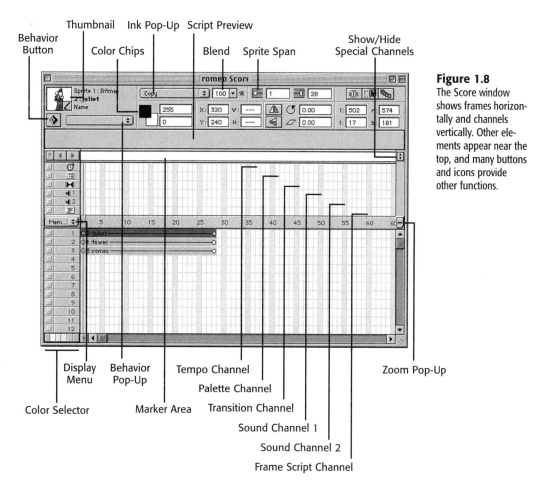

Figure 1.8
The Score window shows frames horizontally and channels vertically. Other elements appear near the top, and many buttons and icons provide other functions.

ELEMENTS OF THE SCORE WINDOW

The Score window is much more complex than the cast window. Notice that the toolbar at the top contains dozens of items. Each item corresponds to a property of the selected sprite or sprites.

Moving from left to right across the top, you can see the thumbnail of the sprite's cast member, a pop-up menu for the ink setting, a percentage for a property called the *blend*, the starting and ending frames of the sprite, and three sprite properties known as *editable*, *movable*, and *trails*. You can find out more about these properties in Chapter 4, "Text and Field Members."

Starting on the left across the bottom of the toolbar you can see a button and a pop-up menu that relate to any behavior scripts attached to the sprite. Next are the foreground and background colors for the selected sprite. Most of the rest of the settings correspond to the position and size of the sprite on the Stage. You can also see buttons for flipping, skewing, and rotating the sprites. For simple animation, most of this information can be ignored, so don't let it overwhelm you right now.

Below the toolbar is an area that would show a script preview if you had selected a sprite with a script. In Figure 1.8, this is simply a blank space. Clicking this space is a shortcut for adding or editing a script.

> **Note**
>
> Sprites can have more than one behavior script attached to them. In this case the behavior-related elements in the Score window are not very useful. Another window, called the Behavior Inspector, enables you to manipulate multiple behaviors. You will learn more about it in Chapter 11, "Advanced Techniques."

Under the script preview area is the marker area. You can mark special frames in your movie with text called *labels*. A typical marker label may be "introduction" or "main animated loop." You add a marker by simply clicking in the marker area. The small down arrow button on the left enables you to see a list of markers or even open a dialog box that lists all the markers. The two other arrows enable you to jump between frames that have markers.

> **Note**
>
> Markers can be used to organize your project. When you begin programming with Lingo, markers are even more important because you can refer to them in your code.

Under the marker area are some rows that contains special channels. Like the sprite channels below them, some of these channels refer to cast members. For instance, the two sound channels, marked with little sound speaker icons, can refer to sound cast members that are supposed to play during those frames.

■ The first channel, the one with the clock icon, is the *tempo channel*. You can use this channel to specify the speed at which the movie moves through this frame. Double-clicking this row brings up a dialog box. You can specify the rate at which this movie should be progressing in frames per second (fps). This setting persists until another frame contains a new setting to override it.

You can also set the tempo channel to pause for a certain number of seconds. This is useful for slow animations, such as automatic slide shows. Other settings include having the movie stop altogether until the mouse is clicked, and having the movie wait for a sound or video cue point.

→ **See** "Waiting for Sounds and Cue Points," Chapter 5, "Sound Members," for more information about using the tempo channel to wait for sounds

■ Palettes are controlled by the *palette channel*. Color palettes, discussed in Chapter 3, "Bitmap Members," are sets of 256 colors that the computer uses to display graphics. If a computer is capable of displaying only 256 colors, a palette defines which 256 colors can be used at one time. You can use the palette channel of the Score to set which palette is used in which frame. There are also a few palette special effects that can be performed.

Because most home computers can now support more than 256 colors, it is becoming more common to ignore palettes and simply work in a thousands- or millions-of-colors mode. Director 7 is the first version of Director to support the use of millions of colors as the basis for the movie's color scheme, as opposed to requiring you to select a palette.

■ The next channel is the *transition channel*. Director has a number of predefined visual transitions that can be applied to a frame. The transition defines how that frame appears as the movie goes from the preceding frame to the current one. For instance, you can have the screen wipe from left to right, or you can have one frame dissolve into the next.

■ The two *sound channels* enable you to overlap sounds. You can have background music playing in sound channel 1, and voice narration in sound channel 2. With Lingo, you can use even more sound channels.

■ The last special channel is the *frame script channel*. Here, you can place Lingo script members that are meant to control that specific frame, the sprites on it, and the entire Director environment so long as the movie is passing through that frame.

The rest of the Score shows the numbered sprite channels. You can have from 1 to 1000 channels in a movie. The number of channels depends on the setting in the movie properties dialog box.

> **Tip**
>
> It is best to stick to the lowest number of channels that you can. Some overhead is involved with processing all the channels in every frame, and Director may perform better if you set your channel limit as low as possible. The default setting of 120 channels is a good start.

CUSTOMIZING THE SCORE WINDOW

You can customize the Score window in several ways. Some involve buttons and menus incorporated into the window itself, and others involve setting Director preferences.

The display menu is a little pop-up menu that appears just under the script channel and all the way to the left. It offers a variety of ways to label the sprites in the Score. In the earlier figures that contained the Score window, you saw this setting set to "Member." This means that it will display the member number and name in the sprite channel. Here is a rundown of all the possible settings:

- Member—Shows the cast member of the sprite. The default setting shows the number of the cast member followed by the name if there is room in the span. To change this setting so that the name of the cast member is displayed, select Cast from the Preferences sub-menu of the File menu and change the Label pop-up to Name.
- Behavior—Displays the behavior number associated with the sprite, if a script is attached.
- Location—When the cursor is over a particular sprite span, displays the horizontal and vertical coordinates of the sprite in the frame in which you currently have the cursor.
- Ink—Displays the ink applied to the sprite span from the Ink pop-up menu to the right of the sprite thumbnail at the top of the Score.
- Blend—Displays the blend percentage as set in the Blend pop-up menu just to the right of the Ink menu in the Score or under Sprite Properties in the Modify menu.
- Extended—Displays the cast member number, the behavior, the location, the ink, and the blend, as well as changes in the X and Y location. To customize the extended display options, choose File, Preferences, Score.

Directly across from the Display Options menu, on the right side of the window, is the Zoom Pop-Up. You can use this to adjust the width of frame columns in the display. Larger sizes might make it easier for you to examine the contents of individual frames. With smaller sizes, you can see more frames at one time in the window.

> **Note**
>
> If you are dealing with animations that span more than 20 frames at a time, a zoom of 100% or less is easier to work with.

Also on the right side, directly next to the marker area, is a button that enables you to show or hide most of the special sprite channels. Clicking it toggles between showing and not showing the tempo, palette, transition, and sound channels. When you get into creating interactive applications, you will find that it is more important to see more sprite channels below than these special channels at the top. The frame script window is always displayed, regardless of this setting.

Another useful feature of the Score window is the Color Selector. You can use these little chips of color, located at the very bottom left corner of the window, to add color to the Score. This has absolutely no effect on movie playback. It is simply there to help you better organize your Score. To use it, first select a sprite, and then click a color chip to change its color.

SCORE WINDOW PREFERENCES

Figure 1.9 shows the Score Window Preferences dialog box. You can bring this up by choosing File, Preferences, Score. This dialog box has only a few settings.

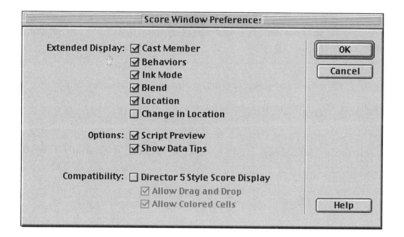

Figure 1.9
The Score Window Preferences dialog box enables you to customize sprite display or change the Score to appear like the Director 5 Score.

> **Tip**
>
> You can quickly select the Sprite Preferences dialog box by pressing the Control key and clicking on the Mac or by right-clicking in Windows on any empty space in the Score window toolbar and selecting Score Preferences.

The first part of this dialog box enables you to specify what properties of a sprite display when you select "Extended" in the Display Options of the Score. For instance, you can decide that you want to see both the member name and the ink. The default for this option is to show almost all the available information.

Next, you can choose to show or hide the script preview area. The script preview is handy not only because you can see the first few lines of code of a behavior script, but because you can click on it to create or edit the script. If this is not important to you and you would rather have the extra space in the window, turn this off.

Data tips are those little yellow-boxed labels that appear over sprites when you hover the cursor over them. They are mostly useful when you have small, single-frame sprites. In this case there is not enough room in the Score window to display the member number and name. Instead, you can just roll the cursor over the sprites and see the information you want as data tips. The preferences dialog box enables you to turn this function off if you want.

The last set of options gives you the chance to make the Score appear like a Director 5 Score. This was useful for developers who became attached to the way Director 4 and 5 displayed the Score information. However, using the Director 5 Score option is not recommended. The Director 6/7 Score window displays more information in a way closer to how things are actually represented in Director. For those more familiar with the Director 5 Score, it can be a hard transition to the next Score window. However, when that transition is complete you will find that you have more control and are able to accomplish tasks faster.

Tip

You can quickly switch between the Director 7 and Director 5 Scores by right-clicking (Control-clicking on Macs) any empty space in the Score window toolbar and selecting Director 5 Style Display.

➔ **See** "Preferences," Chapter 9, for more information about Score window preferences

SPRITE PREFERENCES DIALOG BOX

Choosing File, Preferences, Sprite brings up the Sprite Preferences dialog box, as shown in Figure 1.10. Because sprites and the Score window go hand in hand, it should be discussed here.

Figure 1.10
The Sprite Preferences dialog box enables you to alter the default settings for sprites.

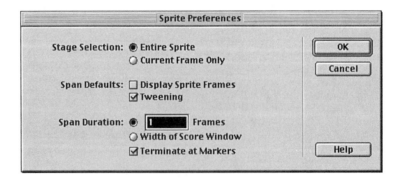

Tip

You can quickly select the Sprite Preferences dialog box by pressing Control and clicking on the Mac or by right-clicking in Windows on any empty space in the Score window toolbar and selecting Sprite Preferences.

The first option, Stage Selection, enables you to specify what happens when you click a sprite on the Stage. The first choice is to have this action select the entire sprite in the Score, including the frames before and after the current one, if any. If you choose the second option, however, clicking the sprite on the Stage selects only that one frame of the sprite in the Score.

The Display Sprite Frames option enables you to set the default setting for adding keyframes to a sprite. A sprite can be set to add keyframes automatically whenever you change something about the sprite in a single frame. Or, the sprite can be set to require you to use the Insert, Keyframe menu option to create a new keyframe.

You can switch between these options for any sprite by using the Edit Sprite Frames and Edit Entire Sprite options in the Edit menu. Checking this option in the Sprite Preferences dialog box makes every new sprite you create start out as if the Edit Sprite Frames option was turned on.

The Tweening option works in a similar way. Sprites have various tweening options set by the Tweening dialog box that you will examine later in this chapter. Checking the Tweening option in the Sprite Preferences dialog box makes all new sprites use tweening for size and position by default.

The last set of options enables you to specify the length of a new sprite. The default in Director is to set sprites to be 28 frames long. However, you can change this to a specific number or have the new sprites fill the Score window. As a further modification, you can limit the size of new sprites to always end just before the next marker in the Score.

Tip

I always use a default span duration of one. I find it to be more convenient to start with a small sprite and stretch it to the length I need.

OTHER SCORE AND SPRITE SETTINGS

The following settings are helpful for using Director:

- The View menu holds a few more items that change the way the Score looks and works.

- The Sprite Toolbar option enables you to choose whether Director will show or hide the entire toolbar area of the Score. The only advantage to hiding it is if you really need the screen space to display more sprites at one time. Access the Sprite toolbar by choosing Windows, Toolbar.

- The Keyframes menu item offers an option to show or hide the little dots in the sprite spans that signify keyframes. When you turn this off, the sprite number is usually repeated at the end of the sprite span rather than with the final keyframe dot. Access the keyframes item by choosing View, Keyframes.

■ The Sprite Labels submenu enables you to specify how often you want the label of the sprite to be displayed in the Score. You can have it display in only the first frame, every keyframe, only where changes occur, every single frame, or not at all. The label information depends on your settings in the Score Preferences dialog box. Access the Sprite Labels submenu by choosing View, Sprite Labels.

OTHER CONTROLS

Several other control windows round out the Director interface. The Control Panel enables you to move the playback head and control some other functions. The Tool Palette enables you to quickly create cast members and sprites. The Sprite Inspector enables you to examine and change some properties of a sprite without using the Score window.

THE CONTROL PANEL

The Control Panel is small and simple. It has all the functions available to manipulate the playback head. Choose Control Panel from the Window menu or press Command+2 on the Mac, or Ctrl+2 in Windows. Figure 1.11 shows all the Control Panel functions.

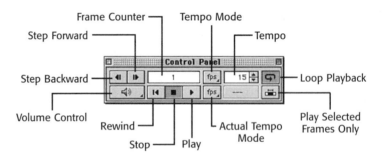

Figure 1.11
The Control Panel is used to move the playback head, to start and stop your movie, and to get information about the frame rate.

Starting at the top left of the panel, the functions are as follows:

■ Step Backward and Step Forward buttons—These two buttons move the playback head forward or backward one frame. Holding down either button scans the movie quickly in the corresponding direction.

■ Frame Counter—Displays the current position of the playback head. Entering a number in the frame counter and pressing Return advances you to that frame. Dragging the mouse in the frame counter, Option-dragging on the Mac, or Alt-dragging in Windows moves the playback head quickly forward or backward.

■ Tempo Mode pop-up—Determines how the tempo is displayed. The choices are frames per second (fps) or seconds per frame (spf).

- Tempo—This is the area to the right of the Tempo Mode and left of the Loop Playback button. This is the assigned speed of the selected frame in either fps or spf. Entering a new tempo into the field and pressing Return or clicking the arrow buttons changes the tempo.

- Loop Playback button—Sets the movie to play again after the last frame or to play only once.

- Volume Control—This pop-up menu sets the volume for the entire movie. It can be overridden by Lingo commands.

- Rewind button—Rewinds the movie to frame 1. You can also select Rewind from the Control menu or press Command+Option+R on the Mac or Ctrl+Alt+R in Windows.

- Stop button—Stops the movie on the current frame. Select Stop from the Control menu or press Command+. (period) on the Mac or Ctrl+. (period) in Windows.

- Play button—Plays the movie from the current frame. Select Play from the Control menu or press Command+Option+P on the Mac, Ctrl+Alt+P in Windows.

- Actual Tempo Mode—This pop-up list sets the display mode of the actual tempo to the right of this setting. The choices are frames per second (fps), seconds per frame (spf), Running Total, and Estimated Total. Running Total is the elapsed time since the start of the movie. Estimated Total is a more accurate, although slower, calculation of elapsed time.

- Actual Tempo display—This number shows the actual tempo that Director is achieving in the current frame. Depending on how much activity is taking place on the Stage, the actual tempo could be less than the assigned tempo on slower machines. It never exceeds the assigned tempo.

- Play Selected Frames Only button—Toggle this button on or off to set the movie to play only the selected frames in the Score window. A green line at the top of the Sprite channels indicates the selected frames. If the movie is looped, only the selected frames play over and over.

THE TOOL PALETTE

The Tool Palette contains a variety of buttons. Most of them enable you to quickly create both a cast member and a sprite at the same time by placing a new element on the Stage. To open or close the Tool Palette, press Command+7 on the Mac or Ctrl+7 in Windows.

The topmost two tools in the Tool Palette are the selection tool and the rotate/skew tool. Picking the selection tool enables you to select sprites on the Stage with the arrow cursor.

Usually, clicking a sprite once selects it and enables you to move it around the Stage. If a sprite is editable, as a bitmap sprite is, double-clicking brings up the editing window. Some sprites, such as text members, can be edited directly on the Stage.

Selection Tool ——— ——— Rotate Tool

Figure 1.12
The Tool Palette has
buttons that enable
you to create cast
members and sprites
at the same time,
as well as tools for
altering the color of
sprites.

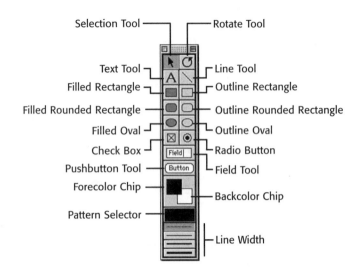

Text Tool —| |— Line Tool
Filled Rectangle —| |— Outline Rectangle
Filled Rounded Rectangle — |— Outline Rounded Rectangle
Filled Oval —| |— Outline Oval
Check Box —| |— Radio Button
Pushbutton Tool — |— Field Tool
Forecolor Chip —
|— Backcolor Chip
Pattern Selector —
|— Line Width

Note

The rotate/skew tool is new to Director 7. It enables you to grab certain types of sprites and rotate them at any angle. You can also grab the corners of sprites and pull them to distort the image. This does not change the cast member at all, just its appearance on the Stage as that particular sprite.

The main set of tools in the Tool Palette changes the cursor to signal you that clicking on the Stage creates a new member and sprite. When you select one of these tools and click on the Stage, a new member is added in the Cast in the new available spot. In addition, this member is automatically placed on the Stage and in the Score in the form of a sprite.

Two tools enable you to create text. The first is represented by the letter *A*. This button enables you to create text cast members. Text members can be anti-aliased and can use a variety of formatting.

The button with the word *Field* enables you to create field members. Field members are more basic than text members, but have a few special features of their own. In Chapter 3 you can read more about the difference between text and field members.

Many of the buttons in the Tool Palette are there to let you create simple shapes. There are tools for lines, ovals, rounded rectangles, and rectangles. The last three have both filled and outline options.

Three buttons enable you to create control items. These are the radio button, the check box, and the button. The first two require some Lingo programming to work properly. The button cast member creates a standard Director-style button to which Lingo scripts can be attached.

Below all these tools are the color chips. These represent the foreground and background colors of the selected sprite or sprites. You can change these colors by clicking and holding over one of the chips. Doing so brings up a small color palette from which you can pick a new color.

Changing colors works for only those sprites that have active foreground and background color properties. You can change the color of all shapes, for instance, or for 1-bit (black-and-white) artwork. You can change only the background color of fields, but you must select the field and edit it first.

Note

Use the foreground color chip to change the color of a shape or 1-bit bitmap. You can drag the same shape member to the Score multiple times and apply a different color to each one. The result is that you can have many different-colored shapes on the Stage, but use only one cast member.

Below the color chips is an area that is usually plain black. Clicking it enables you to select a pattern for the sprite. Patterns are tiled bitmap images that repeat over the duration of the sprite area. You can use them only on filled shape sprites.

The last item on the toolbar is the line width selector. You can set the line width of any line or outlined shape. The options here are limited, but Lingo enables you to use other sizes as well.

THE SPRITE INSPECTOR

The Sprite Inspector window, shown in Figure 1.13, is exactly the same as the top toolbar of the Score. However, with the rest of the Score window left behind, you have a compact sprite editing tool.

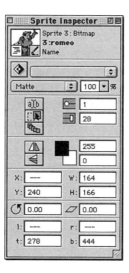

Figure 1.13
The Sprite Inspector is similar to the top portion of the Score window.

The Sprite Inspector shows you many of the properties of the selected sprite or sprites. You can edit these properties, or watch them change as you drag, rotate, or skew a sprite.

This little tool actually has three versions. By clicking and dragging the bottom-right corner of the Sprite Inspector you can make it a long, horizontal box; a tall, thin box; or something in between. This way you can fit the window around the others you are currently working on.

SPRITE OVERLAYS

The Sprite Overlay tool is one you either love or hate. The Sprite overlay is a gray box below each sprite that enables you to access sprite information. It contains some information about the sprite, such as which member it uses, as well as a few buttons to quickly bring up more windows. Figure 1.14 shows a Stage with sprite overlays turned on for all sprites.

Figure 1.14
Sprite Overlays show you some sprite information right on the Stage.

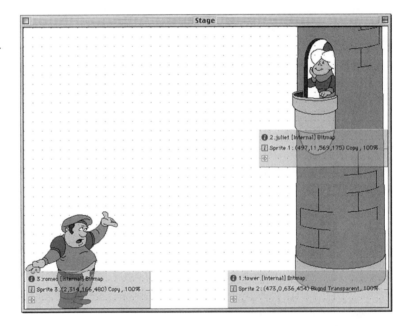

You can turn on sprite overlays, as well as change settings, by choosing View, Sprite Overlay. The settings are pretty self-explanatory. You can choose where the overlays appear: either on every sprite, on only selected sprites, or on only sprites that are under the cursor. You can also choose the color of the text if black is not readable because of the colors on your Stage.

In addition to member and sprite information, sprite overlays give you three small buttons. You can use them to quickly bring up the member information dialog box, the sprite information dialog box, and the Behavior Inspector. You will be introduced to behaviors in the next chapter.

> **Tip**
>
> Sprite overlays are sometimes useful to quickly track down information on a single frame. If you want to quickly turn on and off Sprite Overlays, use Command+Shift+Option+O on the Mac and Ctrl+Shift+Alt+O in Windows.

Another aspect of sprite overlays is their capability to show animation paths. An animation path is a curve on the screen that shows the complete animated path of a sprite. You find out more about this later in this chapter.

THE TOOLBAR

Although many windows in Director have toolbars at the top, "the toolbar" refers to a long strip of buttons that appears just under the menu bar at the top of the screen. It contains various buttons that correspond to menu items and controls. No functions are found in the toolbar *only*. All the buttons on the toolbar act merely as shortcuts. You can quickly show and hide the toolbar using Command+Shift+Option+B on the Mac and Ctrl+Shift+Alt+B in Windows.

Some developers never use the toolbar. Others cannot live without it. It all depends on what you are comfortable with. Because many Director functions have window or palette buttons, menu items, and keyboard shortcuts, you can operate in different ways.

ANIMATING WITH THE CAST, STAGE, AND SCORE

You can use members in the Cast, frames in the Score, and positions on the Stage to animate graphics over time. There are several methods to create these animations.

STEP RECORDING

The easiest type of animation is called *step recording*. It enables you to specify the position of a sprite in every frame.

To perform step recording, you first have to open the correct windows and prepare a sprite to animate. Create or import a bitmap member and place it on the Stage. Make sure that the sprite covers many frames in the Score. If not, stretch it so that it does.

Now close the cast window and move the Score window out of the way of the area on the Stage where the sprite is to animate. Make sure you can see the Control Panel. Although it is not necessary, turn on the Sprite Overlay, Show Paths function by choosing View, Sprite Overlay, Show Paths. This enables you to see the animation path as you create each step.

To begin animating, select the first frame of the sprite in the Score. Then choose Control, Step Recording. Now you are ready to begin.

The position of the sprite is probably where you want it to be for frame 1, so proceed to frame 2. Click the Step Forward button in the control panel. The Score should reflect that you are now working in frame 2.

Click and drag the sprite on the Stage. A line should form from the center of the original placement of the sprite to the current placement as you drag. This is the Sprite Overlay showing you the animation path.

Drop the sprite where you want it to be in frame 2. Click the Step Forward button again to go to frame 3. Set the third position for the sprite. You will see that the sprite overlay feature shows you all the locations of the sprite in each frame. Your screen should look a lot like Figure 1.15.

Figure 1.15
The Sprite Overlay feature reflects a step animation in progress.

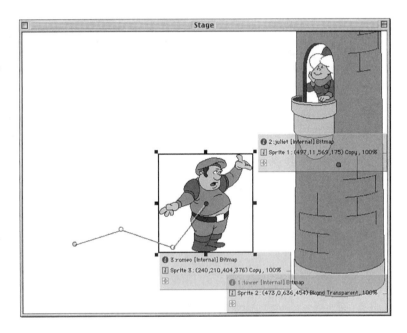

You can continue this way, advancing one frame at a time, until your animation is complete. You can delete any leftover sprite cells by selecting those frames and deleting them. You can also go back and edit the animation positions on each frame by using the Step Forward and Step Backward buttons or just clicking in the Score. Doing so halts the step recording process and you will have to reselect the menu item later to continue.

Tip

When you are editing an animation path, simply clicking and dragging the sprite result in your dragging the entire animation sequence. Clicking and dragging the Sprite Overlay circle for each frame enables you to move just that one frame of animation.

After you are finished with step recording, or any animation technique, you can go back and animate other sprites relative to the ones you have completed. As you step through the frames, you will see the sprites you have already worked with move through their paths.

REAL-TIME RECORDING

Step recording is good for small animation sequences. However, if you want to animate 200 frames, it can take a long time. For cases such as this, you should use real-time recording.

You set up a real-time recording session in the same way as a step-recording session. After the first frame of the sprite is selected, you can start. Choose Control, Real-Time Recording from the menu. Nothing happens until you click the sprite on the Stage again.

> **Note**
>
> In both step recording and real-time recording, the sprite automatically grows in the Score if you add more frames of animation than the sprite was originally sized to hold.

What you want to do is click and hold down the mouse on the sprite. The movie starts going and the frame indicator on the Score moves with it. Drag the sprite around the Stage to change its position. This all happens pretty quickly.

> **Tip**
>
> Real-time recording happens at the speed of the tempo of the movie. Adjust this in the Control Panel. It is a good idea to lower the tempo for real-time recording, perform your animation in slow motion, and then reset the tempo to play it back. This gives you better control over the placement of each step.

When you are finished, the result is similar to step recording. You can go back and edit individual frames of animation. After some practice, you can even combine step and real-time animation techniques to make precisely the animations you want.

SPACE TO TIME

An animation technique that is not used much anymore is called *space to time*. You can place several sprites in the same frame, but in different channels, to represent different steps in the animation. The sprites can use the same cast member, and very often do. You should arrange them so that each step is placed in descending order with the first step in the lowest sprite channel.

When you have all the sprites in place, select them in the Score. This can be done by clicking the first sprite, holding down the Shift key, and clicking the last sprite. Then choose Modify, Space To Time. This menu item is active only if you have properly selected consecutive, single-framed sprites in the Score.

You are then prompted by a dialog box asking you how far apart you want the sprites placed. This simply adds extra frames in the Score between each animation keyframe.

The result of a space to time operation is that all the selected sprites are removed from the Score. They are replaced with a horizontal animated sequence consisting of the member and position of each sprite. This sequence exists in one sprite channel.

Uses for this technique are limited. Because you must place each sprite individually first, it is not ideal for long animations. However, because you can quickly place sprites that use different members, it is good for multiple-member animation.

For example, you may want to animate a bird flying using three different drawings. You can see each step of the animation on one frame, and easily swap members for some steps before using the space to time command. You can create the same animation using any other animation technique as well, but some people may find it easier to use space to time.

CAST TO TIME

A similar technique to space to time is *Cast to time*. Here, you can use the cast window rather than the Score to set up the animation.

To start, place an animated sequence of members in the Cast in consecutive members. For instance, if you have a seven-member sequence that shows a man walking, place each member in member slots 1 through 7. Looking at the cast window thumbnails should give you a preview of what the animation will look like, as if it were laid out on individual sheets of paper.

Select all those cast members and then open the Score window. Select the sprite channel and frame where you would like the animation to start. Now, choose Control, Cast To Time to place the animation.

This technique is mostly useful for animations where each and every step uses a different cast member.

TWEENING

Each of the preceding techniques relies on each step of the animation being represented by a specific location on the Stage. If you have a 30-frame animation, you will have 30 keyframes, each with a specific location as a property.

However, there is a better way to make animations. With *tweening* you set two positions in the animation and have Director automatically fill in the rest. The result is that each frame in between the two positions will show one step in the progression of movement from the first point to the last.

Figure 1.16 shows the Stage and the Score with the simplest of tweening animations. In fact, this is the same example you saw earlier in this chapter. The only difference is that sprite overlay paths have been turned on.

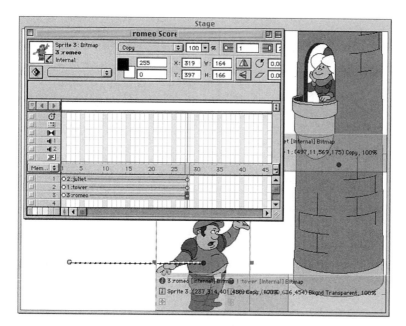

Figure 1.16
A simple animation that uses two keyframes and tweening.

The Sprite Overlay animation line shows you exactly what is going on here. The two large dots show the two keyframes: the first frame and the last frame. The line between them is the animation path. The small dots on the line show the positions that the sprite will occupy during each frame of the animation. You didn't have to set any of these positions because the tweening function does it for you.

What makes tweening so powerful is that you can reposition any keyframe point and the rest of the animation adjusts automatically. If you move the position of the sprite in the last frame up to the top of the screen, the animation line will go from the initial point up to the top of the screen. All the intermediate points will reposition themselves as expected.

You can even lengthen or shorten the sprite span. The example in Figure 1.16 shows an animation 28 frames long. The first and last frame are keyframes and there are 26 intermediate frames. If you were to drag the end of the sprite out to frame 40, there would be 38 intermediate frames. The animation would take longer, but it would run smoother because smaller steps would be involved.

But the power of tweening doesn't end there. You can do more than just straight lines. You can actually use tweening to define a curve with three or more points.

Figure 1.17 shows an animation with three keyframe points. The first keyframe starts the animation on the left side of the screen and in frame 1. The last keyframe puts the sprite on the right side of the screen and a little lower. A third keyframe is at frame 10. The position of the sprite at this keyframe is higher and to the right of both the start and finish points.

Figure 1.17
A three-keyframe sprite animation. Tweening is used to interpolate the points in between.

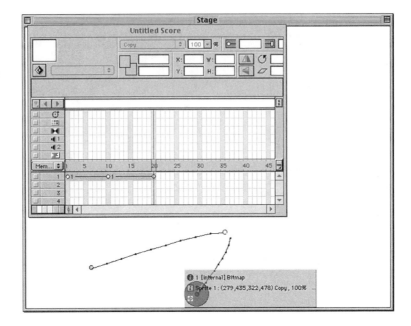

Tip

To create a keyframe, click a specific frame in a sprite span in the Score. The red line drawn vertically in the Score shows you precisely which frame of the sprite is selected. To create a keyframe, choose Insert, Keyframe from the menu bar or Command+Option+K on the Mac or Ctrl+Alt+K in Windows.

As Figure 1.17 shows, the result is not a straight line between the keyframes. Instead, Director interprets a natural curve for you. But this doesn't mean that you cannot make the path a straight line. Nor does it mean that you are stuck with the curve shape shown.

Tweened animations have a variety of settings that can be adjusted for each sprite. You can change these settings by choosing Modify, Sprite, Tweening, or by pressing Command+Shift+B on the Mac and Ctrl+Shift+B in Windows. Figure 1.18 shows the dialog box that appears.

At the top of the Tweening Sprite dialog box is a set of check boxes. You can use these to decide which sprite properties are tweened. The examples so far have used only position tweening. However, because you have not changed the size or other properties of the sprite in any keyframe, the other options could be turned on and would have no effect.

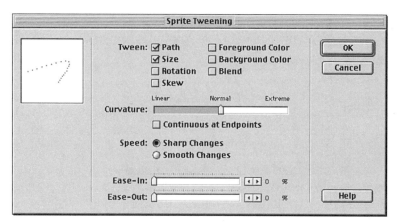

Figure 1.18
The Sprite Tweening dialog box enables you to control what properties of a sprite are tweened and how.

Tweening the other properties has the obvious result. For instance, if you stretch the sprite in the last keyframe, the sprite stretch is applied gradually from the second-to-last keyframe. Rather than becoming a new size suddenly, the sprite would change size over time. You can get the same result by tweening the rotation or skew of a sprite. Changing the forecolor or backcolor of a sprite affects only sprites where color changes can change the appearance of the sprite, as in a 1-bit bitmap sprite. Changing the blend gradually alters the blend property of the sprite, something you can read more about in Chapter 4.

Below the check boxes is a slider bar that enables you to alter the curvature of the tween. The further to the left you position the slider, the closer the path will come to being a straight line. Placing the slider at the middle setting gives you Director's best curved path. If you want a more unusual curve, adjust the slider toward Extreme. The effect varies according to the positions and number of keyframes. In general, you should have at least three keyframes to create curved paths.

Note

As you adjust the curvature slider, a preview window in the dialog box shows you approximately what the path will look like when you are finished.

The Continuous at Endpoints option is primarily for circular paths. If you have the animation move through a circle and end at the same point that it began (first and last keyframes have the same position), turn this option on to create a smoother transition between one cycle and the next.

The ease-in and ease-out sliders enable you to alter the apparent speed of the sprite as it moves through the animation. All it really does is space the path points slightly differently to create the illusion of acceleration or deceleration. The two sliders are related to each other, so they cannot add up to more than 100%. If you try to adjust a slider too far, the other adjusts itself automatically to compensate.

The two options for the speed of the tween affect how abrupt the changes are when the sprite is traveling between keyframes. In most animations, it is hard to tell the difference. The most dramatic effect is when you are using ease-in or ease out. Try both speed settings and see which one you like best.

WORKING WITH SPRITES

The five animation techniques that Director 7 offers are not the only ways to create moving objects on the Stage. You can also force animation by placing new sprites on each frame and manually building each frame.

It wouldn't make sense to build an entire animation this way, but it sometimes does make sense to mix this strategy in with the other techniques. You may have 100 frames of tweened animation, another 100 frames of animation built with real-time recording, and a few manually constructed frames in between.

To construct frames of animation manually, you should become familiar with a few Director commands. The Insert menu, for instance, not only enables you to insert and remove keyframes in a sprite, but it enables you to insert and remove frames for all sprite channels. Inserting a frame stretches a sprite span that crosses that frame. Any tweening adjusts automatically to reflect this extra frame.

The Modify menu enables you to split and join sprite spans. Splitting a sprite enables you to break free from a previous tweened path and start with a fresh keyframe point. Joining sprite spans automatically tweens their properties provided that those tweening options are turned on for the new sprite.

You can also extend a sprite by selecting the sprite, and then selecting a frame in the Score that is beyond the current sprite span. Choosing Modify, Extend Sprite brings the last frame of the sprite out to the new location.

A variety of other tools exist to help you position sprites on the Stage. The Modify menu contains access to the align and tweak tools. The align tool enables you to line up sprites horizontally or vertically, according to their sides, registration points or centers. The tweak tool is a small window that enables you to specify an exact amount of movement for the sprite. You can set horizontal and vertical numbers, in pixels, and then execute this movement for any sprite or group of sprites.

Note

Any tools that enable you to position sprites work while you are using step recording. They can give you more precise control over your animations.

Similar to these tools is Director's grid function. You can find this by choosing View, Grids. You can set horizontal and vertical amounts for the grid, and then specify whether you want to have sprites snap to the grid. This is very useful if you want to quickly lay out items in precise positions relative to each other.

Suppose you want to place five sprites on the Stage and position them exactly 60 pixels apart vertically, aligned an inch or so from the left side of the Stage. Figure 1.19 shows the desired result.

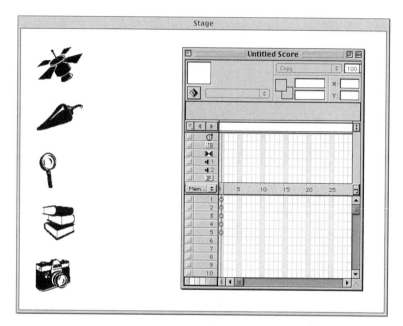

Figure 1.19
A Stage with five sprites. These sprites were precisely placed by using tools such as align, tweak, and grids.

First, try to place these sprites by just dragging them to the Score. This places all five members into sprites that are positioned at the exact center of the Stage.

To space out the sprite vertically, open the tweak tool. Type -60 into the vertical change field. Select the first sprite in the Score. Click the tweek button twice. This moves the first sprite up 120 pixels. Select the second sprite in the Score and click the tweak button once to move it up 60 pixels. Now change the vertical setting in the tween tool to be 60 pixels (remove the negative sign). Use tweak to move the fourth sprite down 60 pixels and the fifth sprite down 120. Now the sprites are vertically spaced 60 pixels apart.

Tip

A common shortcut for moving sprites is to use arrow keys along with the Shift key. Doing so moves the sprite 10 pixels at a time. Therefore, you could have gotten the same result by selecting a sprite and hitting the up arrow key six times while holding the Shift key, rather than using the tweak tool set to –60 vertical change.

A minor detail is that the sprites are still horizontally aligned to the center of the Stage. You can align the left sides of the sprites with each other, instead, by using the align tool. Bring it up and set the second pop-up menu to Align Lefts. Click the Align button to make the change. You will see some of the sprites shift.

Dragging all the sprites at once to the left of the Stage is one way to complete the example. However, there are some other ways of doing this.

For instance, you can simply turn on grids. You can set the vertical grid to 60 pixels and space each sprite by just dragging it until it locks onto a grid line. You can position them all to a vertical grid line as well, which accomplishes the left side alignment.

You can also use the Sprite Inspector or the toolbar at the top of the Score to manually set the locations of all the sprites. Although this sounds complex, it actually takes about the same amount of time.

All in all, there are many ways to move sprites around in Director. The idea of having more than one way to do something is present throughout Director, from simple animation to complex Lingo scripts. Director almost always gives you two or more ways to accomplish a task. This makes Director a very easy-to-learn and flexible environment.

EXPORTING ANIMATIONS

After you finish creating an animation, you can do three things with it: you can make a projector, you can make a Shockwave movie, or you can export it to a variety of file types. The last section of the next chapter introduces projectors and Shockwave files. Exporting, however, is usually used with animation only.

To export an animation, first check to see which elements in your movie cannot be exported. You cannot export scripts, for instance, because file formats such as PICS files and Video for Windows cannot do anything with them. Basically, you can export only pictures of the Stage, frame for frame.

To export, choose File, Export. This brings up the Export dialog box shown in Figure 1.20.

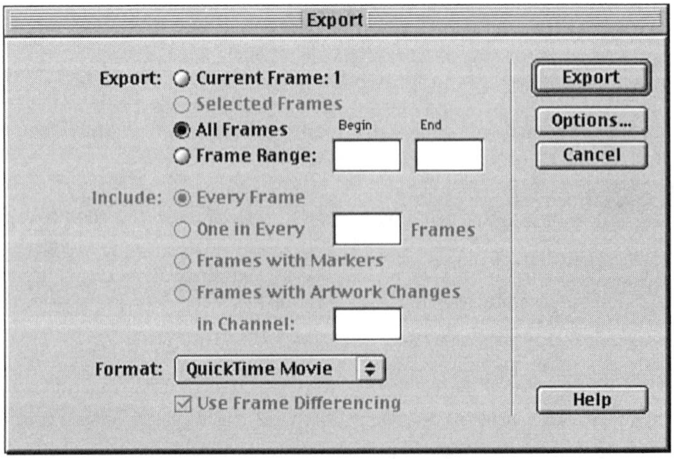

Figure 1.20
The Export dialog box on the Macintosh (shown here) has different format options than Export in Windows.

The primary option is the format of the exported file or files. This option is at the bottom of the dialog box. Here is a rundown of the types of files you can export:

- PICT—The standard image file for Macs, choosing this option gives you a numbered series of PICT files. Available on the Mac only.

- Scrapbook—If you choose this option, Director outputs a Macintosh scrapbook file, similar to the one found in the system folder. Some video programs can import this type of file. Available on the Mac only.

- PICS—A single file that contains multiple images. This type of file can be imported into a variety of programs. It can also be imported into Director as a film loop and series of members. Available on the Mac only.

- QuickTime—The standard video format for Macs and also used by about 50% of all Windows machines. This is the only option that will preserves some of the tempo changes in your animation. Available as an export option on Macs only.

- DIB File Sequence—A single file that contains a series of images. Available in Windows only.

- Video For Windows—The video format built in to Windows. Sometimes called AVI files. Available in Windows only.

Most of the formats you can export to are useful only if you plan on bringing the file into another editing program. QuickTime and Video For Windows, however, can be played by small video players on most computers and can be used by other presentation software.

The export for each of these formats is basically the same. Director moves though the frames you specify and takes a snapshot of the Stage each time. Each image is incorporated into the export as the next file or the next portion of the file. In most cases, scripting, tempo changes, and transitions are not considered.

The export to QuickTime capability, however, is a little more powerful. You can specify a variety of settings by using the additional QuickTime Options dialog box. Figure 1.21 shows this dialog box.

Most of the options in the QuickTime Options dialog box are self-explanatory. Note that the compression options depend on the version of QuickTime you are using and any additional compression algorithms you may have added to QuickTime on your machine.

The frame rate option determines how the frames are written out to the QuickTime movie. If you set it to Real Time, the export becomes much more complex. It is essentially recording the progress on the screen as the movie plays. This means it is taking changes in tempo into account. Otherwise, you just get a frame-by-frame dump of the movie as a QuickTime file.

Figure 1.21
The QuickTime
Options dialog box is
available only on
Macintosh versions of
Director.

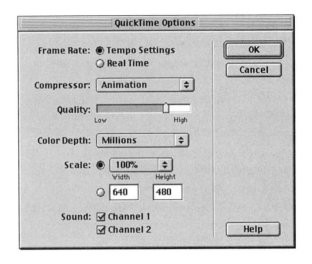

In Windows, the export to Video For Windows (.avi) files is not as flexible. You cannot capture in real-time mode. However, you can set the frame rate independent of the movie's tempo, and you can set the quality and compression technique.

Even these built-in export options may not give you what you want. If, for instance, you have scripts that move the movie about in a nonlinear fashion, or you want user-initiated events recorded, you can always record the video directly from your computer's output. Many computers come with a video outfeed that can be plugged into standard and S-video video tape recorders. Or, you could always have one computer capture a screen directly from another computer playing a Director movie. This is, of course, providing they both have appropriate video capabilities.

Another approach is to use a screen capture utility that takes a snapshot of the screen automatically every fraction of a second. In practice, to play an animation and record it at the same time is a heavy task for even a production machine.

TROUBLESHOOTING ANIMATION

- It is not uncommon for a developer to create an animation with real-time recording or tweening and not get it quite right the first time. This is what the delete key is for. Just select the sprites, delete, and start again.

- If tweening does not seem to be working, check the sprite properties by choosing Modify, Sprite, Tweening. Tweening may simply be turned off for that sprite.

- If you are exporting animation and are also using more advanced techniques such as behaviors and other scripting, the changes made by Lingo may not be reflected in the exported animation. Exporting is really just for Score animation, not Lingo animation.

- Getting little white edges around images set to Background Transparent or Matte ink? These appear when the image is anti-aliased around the edges to white, which happens very often. You can either manually edit these pixels out of the image, or use PhotoShop to create images with an alpha-channel that will properly anti-alias the edges.

- Does your animation play too fast on some machines or too slow on others? Choose a frame rate that your target user machine can handle. Many older PCs cannot handle more than a few frames per second when many bitmaps with different inks are used.

DID YOU KNOW?

- If you are upgrading from Director 5 to Director 7, and really like the Director 5 look and feel for the Score, you can switch to the Director 5 Style display in the Score window preferences.

- If you are having trouble making your first movie, try to open a simple example movie first, such as one somewhere on the Director 7 CD-ROM or one on this book's CD-ROM. Play around with it first before trying to create your own movie.

- You can export a single frame of a movie to an image by selecting only that one frame as the export range and an image format as opposed to a video format.

- Grids always start in the very upper-left corner. If you want to have a grid that starts a little farther in, such as a 20×20 grid that starts at 10, 10, you can just use the 20×20 grid as-is, and then move all the sprites over and down by 10 pixels when you are done. This way your grid starts at 10 horizontally and vertically, and it continues to 30, 50, 70, and so on.

2

PRESENTATIONS WITH DIRECTOR

In this chapter

It is easy to create presentations in Director. A typical presentation appears much like a slide show, wherein a variety of screens are displayed on the monitor, all containing sequential information of some sort. A simple presentation shows a series of ordered slides, whereas a complex one includes navigation buttons so that the contents can be browsed by the user. This chapter covers all types of presentations, including linear and nonlinear ones. The first step to every presentation is designing the screens.

DESIGNING SCREENS

A presentation can be broken up into a number of screens. Each screen presents some information, usually through text and graphics. Before designing an entire presentation, you should put some thought into how you plan to design your screens.

In Director, a screen appears as a frame in the Score. A simple way to organize this is to have frame 1 be your first screen, frame 2 your second, and so on. You might also decide to space frames farther apart—say every five frames—if this is easier for you to manage.

On the Stage, sprite positions are measured in pixels. A pixel is equal to exactly one "dot" on the screen; it is the smallest graphic element on computer screens. When one reads that the Stage is 640 by 480, for example, this means that the Stage is 640 pixels across and 480 pixels down. The pixel at the top-left corner of the Stage is pixel 0, 0.

Note

It might help you to know that an inch usually comprises 72 pixels. This is an arbitrary standard; the size of a pixel depends on the size of a user's monitor and other settings. To confuse things further, some computer documentation refers to an inch as 96 pixels.

PLANNING A CONSISTENT DESIGN

Before starting to build the presentation, think about what you want on each screen. Will background elements appear on every screen? Will a title appear across the top on every screen? Will all the screens have a similar design or will they vary greatly?

Figure 2.1 shows a typical presentation design. It has a title across the top, a matching graphic element across the bottom, a picture on the right, and text on the left.

This layout has six elements. They correspond to six sprites in the Score. Figure 2.2 shows the Score for this layout. Sprite 1 contains a solid-colored box that is used as the backing for the title area. Sprite 2 is a text member that contains the title. Sprite 3 contains the same cast member as sprite 1. It is the same box, but this time it is positioned at the bottom of the Stage and is a little smaller. Sprite 4 is a bitmap image of an arrow. You can use this as the button to enable the user to go to the next screen.

Tip

To create screens that are equivalent to one frame in the Score, set your sprite preferences to use a default width of 1. Choose File, Preferences, Sprite to adjust this setting.

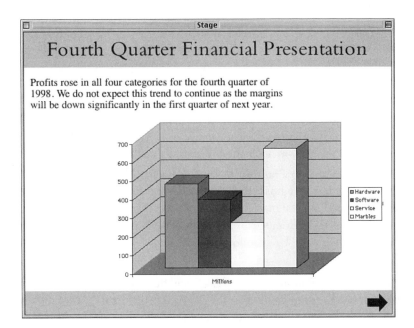

Figure 2.1
A typical presentation screen. It is good to decide on one layout and use it, or versions of it, throughout the presentation.

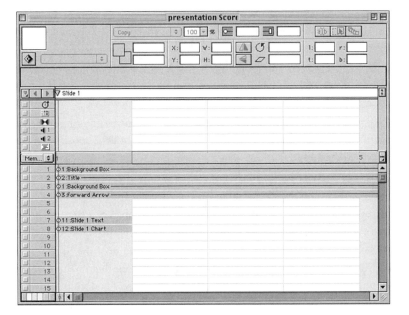

Figure 2.2
The Score shows six sprites being used to make the screen shown in Figure 2.1.

After sprite 4 are two empty sprite channels. This is just a way to better organize the Score. Everything above these channels appears in every frame. Everything below these channels appears in only one screen.

> **Tip**
>
> It is a good idea to use empty channels to help visually divide your Score. Otherwise, you end up with all your sprites in consecutive channels, which can make it hard to find a specific sprite quickly.

Sprite 7 contains the text for this one screen and sprite 8 contains the image. These elements will change on every screen. On some screens, you might add additional sprites after sprite 8. For instance, if a screen has more than one image or if an arrow graphic is needed to point something out in an image, you need to add sprites to that specific screen for those elements.

TOOLS FOR SCREEN DESIGN

When designing your screens, take advantage of some of the tools that you learned about in Chapter 1, "Animation with Director." The following list includes the most useful tools for screen design:

- Grids—You can position your sprites more precisely and quickly if you use grids. Use the grids in visible mode to see guidelines on the Stage. Use the Snap To feature to line up items quickly. Choose View, Grids to access the grids options.

- Sprite Inspector—If you like sprites to be at precise locations, the Sprite Inspector enables you to manually edit the horizontal and vertical locations, as well as the width, height, rotation, and other properties. Choose Windows, Inspectors, Sprite to bring up the Sprite Inspector.

- Sprite overlays—This tool shows you sprite information and enables you to gain access to the Properties windows without having the Score and cast windows open. Choose View, Sprite Overlay to access the sprite overlay options.

- Align tool—You can select groups of sprites and align them horizontally or vertically based on their left, right, top, bottom, center, or registration points. Choose Modify, Align to bring up the Align tool.

- Tweak tool—This tool enables you to move a sprite or group of sprites a precise number of pixels in any direction. Choose Modify, Tweak to bring up the Tweak tool.

- Arrow keys—You can move any sprite or group of sprites one pixel at a time with the arrow keys. Hold the Shift key down and you can move sprites 10 pixels at a time.

- The Score window—The Score window combines all the elements of the Sprite Inspector and Sprite Overlays, plus much more. It is the only tool that enables you to move sprites up and down in the sprite channels, and thereby over and under other sprites. Choose Window, Score to bring up the Score window.

→ **See** "Customizing the Score Window," Chapter 1, for more information about the Score window
→ **See** "Score Window Preferences," Chapter 1, for more information about the Score window
→ **See** "Sprite Overlays," Chapter 1, for more information about sprite overlays
→ **See** "The Sprite Inspector," Chapter 1, for more information about sprites

LINEAR PRESENTATIONS

The simplest type of presentation is a linear presentation. Linear presentations are sometimes referred to as "slide shows" because they resemble the process of showing visuals with a slide projector.

The objective of a linear presentation is to present screens of information in a defined sequence. The movie should move from one screen to the next either automatically, after a period of time, or after some input such as a keyboard press or a mouse click. You may even want to give the user the capability to back up one screen, just as a slide projector would.

CREATING YOUR PRESENTATION

To start, create your presentation, screen for screen. Each screen should be in a different frame. If you are not using every frame, it is a good idea to name each screen frame with a label in the markers area of the Score. This will help you later. Label frames by clicking in the marker area directly above the tempo channel in the Score.

If some elements are used in more than one frame, you do not need to place them in every frame individually. Instead, stretch them so that their sprite spans cover all the screen frames. For example, sprites 1 through 4 of the example in Figure 2.2 can be stretched to cover all the frames of the movie, which places the title bar, bottom bar, and forward button on every screen.

Tip

There are several ways to stretch a sprite span. You can grab the keyframe, shown as a large dot in the last frame, and pull it. You can also select the sprite, click in the frame number area in the frame to which you want to stretch it, and press Command+B on the Mac or Ctrl+B in Windows. Or, you can use the Start Frame and End Frame fields in the Score window.

Arrangement in the Cast is another matter. In the example presentation, you will end up with a few cast members that represent graphics used in every screen: the title bar text, the boxes, and the forward button. The rest of the cast members are graphics that appear in only one frame.

You could have one cast library for the reused graphics, and one cast library for the text and images. Or, you could have everything in one Cast. If the screens were more complex and had dozens of members, you might even want to consider a new cast library for every frame. However, schemes such as this can cause problems when you want to use a member in more than one frame, such as a photo of the company headquarters that is used on both the introduction screen and the corporate summary screen of a financial presentation.

Whichever way you decide to arrange your Cast, keep in mind that you may be adding graphics and text for each screen. If you have 100 screens in your presentation, you will have a lot of members.

> **Tip**
> Cast arrangement is something you can worry about later. You can drag and drop cast members within the cast window, or open a second cast window and drag and drop between them. This second window can be another cast library or even another view of the same cast library.

ADJUSTING THE TEMPO

Running the movie now results in anything but a nice presentation. If you have all your screens in consecutive frames, the whole presentation flies by as quickly as Director can display it. If you skipped frames, the presentation flashes by, alternating screens and blank stages.

You need the movie to pause on each frame. The simplest way to do this is to use the tempo channel. First, make sure that the special Score channels are visible in the Score window. Click the Hide/Show Score button on the right side of the Score to make them visible. It contains two arrows pointing up and down at each other.

The first channel is the tempo channel. It is marked with a small clock icon. Double-click the tempo channel in the current frame to bring up the Frame Properties: Tempo dialog box shown in Figure 2.3. You can see that one of the options is Wait For Mouse Click or Key Press. Select that option and close the dialog box.

Figure 2.3
The Frame Properties: Tempo dialog box enables you to stop the movie until a key is pressed.

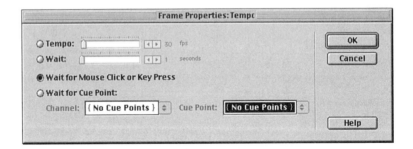

The tempo channel now says "Click" to remind you of your choice. When you play the movie now, Director pauses on that frame until the you click the mouse. The cursor changes to an animated cursor which indicates to the user that a mouse click is needed.

> **Tip**
> You can copy, cut, and paste in the Score just as you can in a word processor or spreadsheet program. For example, after selecting a tempo channel setting for one frame, you can copy and paste this setting into any other channel. You can also hold down the Option key on the Mac or the Alt key in Windows and click and drag the tempo channel to stretch that setting over several frames.

This way of pausing the movie and enabling the user to control the forward movement of the presentation works very well. However, it is very generic in that it contains no options or alternatives for the way in which it works or the cursor that is used. Additionally, the little "click now" cursor animation can be distracting to the viewers.

Another way is to pause the movie on that frame and then use the forward button to go to the next screen. To do this you must use some scripting. Fortunately, you do not have to do the scripting yourself. Director comes with many behaviors ready to be dragged and dropped into the Score.

To access the behaviors in the libraries, choose Window, Library Palette. Figure 2.4 shows the Library palette.

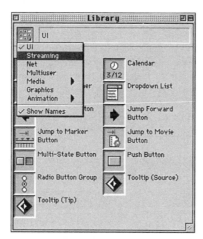

Figure 2.4
The Library palette contains some behaviors built in to Director 7.

To use a behavior from the Library palette, first select the library from the pop-up menu at the upper left corner of the window. Then drag and drop the appropriate behavior onto the Score. If you want the behavior applied to the frame, drop it in the frame script channel. Otherwise, drop it on top of a sprite.

To use a behavior from the Library Palette, follow these steps:
1. Choose Window, Library Palette.
2. Using the pop-up menu in the upper left corner, shown in Figure 2.4, choose the library name.
3. Click the behavior you need and drag it onto a sprite on the Stage or in the Score.
4. If the behavior needs more information, it prompts you with a dialog box.

Tip

The Library palette can also contain other behaviors that you can get from third-party companies, or ones that you write yourself.

To get the movie to pause on a frame, select the Navigation category in the Library Palette and drag and drop the behavior named "Hold on Current Frame" onto one of the screen frames in the Score. You can drag and drop it onto each one of the frames you use, use Copy and Paste to spread it around to all the frames, or simply stretch its sprite span to encompass all the frames.

Now you have a presentation that pauses correctly over each frame. The next step is to activate the Forward button so that the user can go to the next frame. You can use another behavior from the library to do this. Just drag and drop the Go Next Button behavior onto the forward arrow sprite.

The Go Next Button behavior causes the action to be initiated when the user completes a click on the sprite. Make sure that you have just one sprite for the forward button that covers all the frames in your movie. When you apply the behavior to it, the behavior works throughout the entire sprite span.

> **Tip**
>
> When you select a behavior from the library, it copies that behavior from the library to your Cast. The behavior that you are using then actually comes from your own movie's Cast. This way, you don't have to provide the library to the end user with the rest of your project.

The Go Next Button behavior makes the movie jump forward to the next frame that has a marker label. For it to work, you need to label each frame that is used as a screen. The behavior skips any frame that has no label, even if sprites are on it.

The presentation now behaves as desired. It begins at frame 1 and waits. When the user clicks the Forward button, the movie advances to the next labeled frame and waits again.

This simple presentation design can be used for anything from showing your vacation photos to presenting your company's financial data. But it is only the tip of the iceberg as far as Director's capabilities are concerned. The next section discusses how nonlinear presentations are accomplished in Director.

NONLINEAR PRESENTATIONS

The next step in creating advanced presentations is to give users the capability to navigate throughout the presentation in any direction. The previous presentation only moves forward. What if users want to go back one screen? Or what if they want to return to the beginning?

ADDING BACK AND HOME BUTTONS

Creating a button that enables the user to move back in the presentation is easy. You saw how to create a button that moved the user forward, which was done with the Go Next Button behavior. There is also a behavior called Go Previous Button. All you need to do is create a new bitmap, add it to the Score, and place the Go Previous Button behavior on it from the Library palette. Figure 2.5 shows the addition of the Go Previous button.

Figure 2.5 also shows a button labeled "Home" that takes the user back to the first frame. The behavior you need to use to accomplish this is the Go to Frame X Button behavior also found in the Library palette. When you drag it to the sprite with the bitmap you've created for the new button, you can specify a frame number. You can enter a number or a name. You should type the name of the first frame of your presentation here.

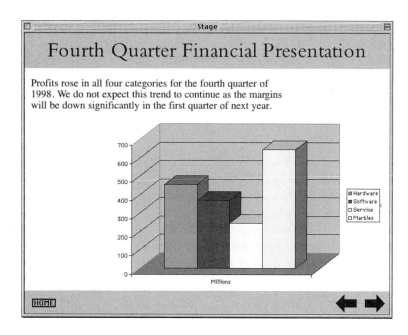

Figure 2.5
The presentation screen now includes a back (Go Previous) and a home button.

Now that you know how to add a button that moves the presentation to any frame, you can add buttons as necessary. If your presentation is easily broken into three main sections, you can have buttons that take the user to the first frame of each section.

Also, remember that you don't necessarily have to have the same buttons on each frame. If you have multiple sections in your presentation, you can have buttons that take the user forward or back to the next or previous section.

To do this, use the same cast member buttons, but create separate sprites that cover each section. If the first section covers frames 1 to 17 and the second section covers frames 20 to 34, place one sprite from frame 1 to 17 and a second sprite from frame 20 to 34. You can use the same sprite channel, but make sure that the sprites are not joined to each other.

When you apply the Go to Frame X Button behavior to each sprite, just input a different frame for each. You can specify that the Next Section button for section 1 is to take the user to the first frame of section 2. The Next Section button in section 2 takes the user to the first frame of section 3. You need to have only one cast member and use only one behavior for this. The only difference between the sprites is the destination frame property of the behavior.

Note You can leave the Next Section button off in the last section. Or, you can place a new cast member, such as a dimmed or grayed version of the button, in its place. Don't place any behavior on this sprite, so that nothing happens if the user tries to click it. The same can be done for the Previous Section button in the first section.

ADDING A MENU SCREEN

One name for the area at the bottom of the example presentation is the *toolbar*. It contains elements such as the forward and back buttons. After you start adding buttons that take the user to a specific section, it becomes more like a menu.

If you want to add a table of contents to the presentation, the toolbar or menu area might start to get a little crowded. If you have 100 frames of screens and eight sections, you can have a lot of buttons. Rather than crowd this area with buttons, you may want to consider adding a menu screen, otherwise known as a table of contents screen.

With a menu screen, you can have just a few buttons in the toolbar: Forward, Back, and New Menu. The New Menu button takes users to the menu screen. From there, they can navigate to any section of the presentation. Because you have an entire screen to dedicate to this, you can be more descriptive about each section, rather than try to simplify the sections into a single button.

Figure 2.6 shows an example of a menu screen. The title bar remains, but the toolbar is not necessary. You may decide otherwise when designing your presentation. Notice that no buttons are on the screen. Instead, what appears to be a text member shows a list of the sections. This is actually not one text member, but five. Each line is its own member. This enables you to place a separate behavior on each line.

You can create these text members by simply selecting the text tool (not the field tool), which looks like the letter *A*, in the Tools palette, and clicking on the Stage. Be sure to check the Score afterward to make sure that the sprites have been placed in channels that make sense. Move them around and group them together if you want.

Drag the Hold on Current Frame behavior from the library palette onto each of these sprites separately. This enables you to enter the destination frame for each sprite. This is all it takes to set up your menu screen. You will want to arrange the sprites and probably use the grid or align tool to set them up on the Stage.

→ **See** "Text Members," Chapter 4, "Text and Field Members," for more information on using text in your presentations

Note If you enter the wrong destination frame, or want to edit it later, you can access the sprite's behavior properties by bringing up the Behavior Inspector. A button for this is on the left side of the Score toolbar or on the Sprite Inspector. It looks like a diamond-shaped beveled box icon.

You can also press Command+Option+(semicolon) on the Mac or Ctrl+Alt+(semicolon) in Windows. When the Behavior Inspector appears, you see the list of behaviors applied to the sprite. Use the Parameters button, which looks like a diamond with an equal sign in the middle, to change the properties. Chapter 11, "Advanced Techniques," describes the Behavior Inspector in more detail.

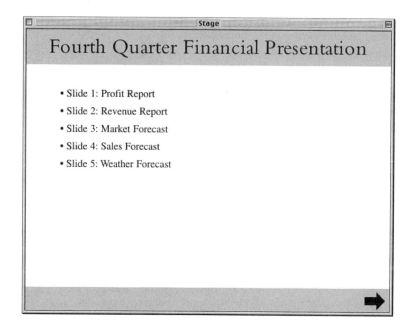

Figure 2.6
A presentation menu. Each line of text is a separate member and sprite.

PART

I

CH

2

A presentation with a set of toolbar buttons and a menu screen can be used for almost any purpose. This sort of movie can even be used to prototype software, whereby you show each screen of the software and enable users to browse its functions in a nonlinear fashion.

→ **See** "Building Your Own Behaviors," Chapter 11, for more information about behaviors

ADVANCED PRESENTATIONS

You can add functionality to your presentations in many ways without learning Lingo. You can make your buttons a little nicer, use the cursor to guide the user, and even add sounds and transitions.

PLAY AND RETURN

Suppose you want to have a side topic referenced in your presentation. For example, if you present a list of products that your company sells, you can have a button that links to a screen with more information about those products.

In this example, you may not want to have the presentation leap to a new frame. You might want it to remember where it came from, and return to that frame when the user is finished. This way, you can have the presentation jump to a frame from several places, and then a button on the destination frame returns the user to the original frame.

You can do this with the Play Frame X behavior from the library palette. This behavior causes the presentation to jump to a frame, just as the Go to Frame X behavior does. However, it remembers the frame it came from. When a button with a Play Done behavior is clicked, the presentation returns to the original frame.

BUTTON HIGHLIGHTS

Chapter 14, "Creating Behaviors," describes how to make complex button behaviors such as buttons that have rollover and down states. For now, you can learn a simple way to provide the users with some feedback when they press a button.

Select any bitmap from the Cast. For example, select the forward arrow button bitmap. Click the information button at the top of the cast window, which looks like a white *i* with a blue circle around it. This information button brings up the cast member's properties. The first property is Highlight When Clicked. When this property is turned on, the bitmap appears highlighted when it is clicked by the user. It is a very generic effect, but much better than having none at all.

Turn this option on for all your presentation buttons. Ideally, you want to define the down state of a button with another bitmap entirely. This enables you to customize the look of the button as it is pressed. For now, however, this behavior suffices. Unfortunately, you can use this option only on bitmaps. Your text members used in the menu screen do not change appearance as they are pressed.

CURSOR CHANGES

Cursor changes work on any cast member type. The idea is to have the cursor change when the user positions it over a button. The behavior for this is called the Rollover Cursor Change.

Upon dragging and dropping this behavior from the library palette onto a sprite, you are prompted by the behavior's parameter box. You need to worry about only one property of the behavior. The first property enables you to choose from some standard cursors that are built in to Director 7. The best choice for this purpose is probably the "finger" cursor. It is similar to the cursor used by Web browsers when the user rolls over a hypertext link. The rest of the properties are used when you want to make your own cursor.

Note

If you need to remove behaviors from a sprite, bring up the Behavior Inspector by choosing Window, Inspectors, Behavior. This shows you all the current behaviors and enables you to select and delete any of them. You can also use the behavior pop-up menu in the Score to clear all the behaviors and start over.

→ **See** "A Simple Button Behavior," Chapter 14, for more information on button behaviors

→ **See** "A Complex Button Behavior," Chapter 14, for more information on button behaviors

→ **See** "Cursors," Chapter 21, "Controlling the Director Environment," for more information about using cursors

TRANSITIONS

The next step in jazzing up your presentations is adding some transitions. Up until now, the frames advanced in an abrupt manner, whereby the new frame suddenly replaced the old. You can soften these changes by using *transitions*, which are designs such as dissolves and wipes that change one screen into another.

PART

I

CH

2

Transitions are applied by using the transitions channel at the top of the Score, directly under the tempo and palette channels. Double-clicking this channel on a frame presents you with a list of transitions and a few options. You become more familiar with the different types of transitions in Chapter 10, "Properties of Sprites and Frames." For now, use any Dissolve transition with its default settings.

> **Tip**
>
> When you add a transition to the Score for the first time, it creates a transition cast member automatically. You can then use this cast member again by dragging it to a new position in the transition channel of the Score window. If you double-click the transition channel again, it creates another new cast member, even if the transition is exactly the same as the one you previously created. The advantage to having one transition cast member and applying it throughout the Score is that you have to change that one member's settings only once to change all of the transitions.

A transition on a frame occurs as the movie enters the frame. This means that the dissolve occurs between the preceding frame that the movie displayed and the new one. It does not matter whether the preceding frame was the frame directly before the new one in the Score. Transitions work just fine even if you jump from frame 45 to frame 23, as long as the transition is on frame 23.

You cannot, however, simply add transitions such as this to a frame when you have placed a Hold on Current Frame behavior in the frame script channel of that frame. This is because that behavior actually sends the movie back to the current frame when the frame is done. It is, in effect, looping on one single frame. Therefore, if you had a transition on that frame, the transition would be repeated over and over again.

Assume, for example, that a button took the user from frame 12 to frame 14, and there was a dissolve transition and a "Hold on Current Frame" on frame 14. The Stage would first show a dissolve from frame 12 to frame 14 and then repeat a dissolve from frame 14 to frame 14. The result would be a slow-down of the movies reaction time, such as mouse click reactions, as the complex dissolve transition was performed over and over.

Note

A repeated dissolve transition would not actually be visible because the movie is dissolving from one screen to an identical screen. A transition such as a Push Left, however, would be clearly visible.

Avoiding this pitfall is easy. You need to create two frames for each presentation screen. All the sprites in each frame should be the same. However, the first frame features the transition in the transition channel. It has no frame script, and so the movie flows naturally from that frame to the next. The second frame does not contain any transition, but does have the Hold on Current Frame behavior. The marker label should appear on the first frame of the pair. Figure 2.7 shows an example.

Transition Frames

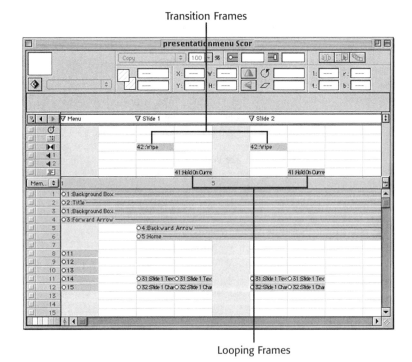

Figure 2.7
The Score shows a dual-frame setup for each presentation screen. The first frame of each pair has the marker and transition. The second frame uses the Hold on Current Frame behavior.

Looping Frames

Note that you don't need to actually create a whole separate set of sprites to make this second frame. Instead, you can stretch all the sprites of one frame. Do this by selecting all the first frame, moving the playback head of the movie forward one frame, and then choosing Modify, Extend Sprite.

ADDING SOUNDS

You can add sounds to your presentations in a few simple ways. First you need to import some sounds into the Cast. Choose File, Import to bring in a sound.

Note

> You can create sounds with Macromedia's SoundEdit 16 or Peak LE on the Mac or SoundForge in Windows or with many other sound editing programs. Many are available as shareware on the Internet.

Try adding sounds to the buttons. It is sometimes nice to have the button actually make a noise when the user clicks it. The Play Sound Member behavior enables you to do this.

This behavior prompts you for a sound, channel, and initializing event. Choose the sound from the pop-up menu. It should list all the sound cast members available. Keep the channel at 1, and choose "mouseDown" as the initializing event. You need to do this because the event "mouseUp" is already being used by one of the other behaviors that you have assigned to the button sprites.

→ **See** "Building Your Own Behaviors," in Chapter 11, for more information about messages and behaviors

The buttons now play a sound when the user clicks them. You can define different sounds for each type of button if you like.

Note

> Notice that there is also a Sound Beep behavior in the Media: Sound library. This behavior plays the system beep instead of a cast member sound. This is not recommended, because many users have customized their system sounds. You never really know what sounds will play on various machines.

Another way to use sounds is to have a sound play when the presentation enters a new frame. Adding sounds such as this is even easier. All you need to do is place a sound in the sound channel of any frame. You can double-click the sound channels and add sounds the same way you add transitions. Or, you can drag a sound from the Cast to the Score. You can even drag and drop a sound member onto the Stage to have it added to the Score.

An extension of this is to add a background sound to a frame. Background sounds look the same as any other sound to Director, but they are typically longer pieces with music or some sort of ambient noise such as wind. Often these background sounds are built so that they loop. When the sound ends, it can start playing again in a manner that makes the loop seem seamless.

When you have a looping sound, you want to tell Director what it is. Do this by editing the properties of a sound cast member. The only available option is to let Director know that it is a looping sound. Director then plays the sound continuously as long as it appears in the sound channel of the frame currently playing.

Add a background sound to the Score in the same way that you added the previous sound to the Score. Be sure that you are not using this sound channel for anything else. For instance, if you have a button sound that plays in sound channel 1, place the background sound in channel 2. Otherwise, the button sound interrupts the background sound.

→ **See** "Using Sound In Director," Chapter 5, "Sound Members," for more information on using sound

PART

I

CH

2

ADDING ANIMATION IN PRESENTATIONS

Don't forget that Director is a fantastic animation tool. Just because you are creating a slide show-like presentation doesn't mean that you can't have moving objects. The two frames per screen design that has been shown in the previous examples can easily be expanded to include animation.

To make an animated presentation screen, just create your animated sequence in a set of frames. Label the first frame, but not any others. Do not place any frame scripts in any of the animation frames except the last. In the last frame, use the Go Loop behavior as the frame script. This causes the movie to return to the first frame in the animation when the last frame is reached. The movie continues to loop until the user breaks the pattern by using a button to jump to another set of frames. Figure 2.8 shows this sort of setup.

Figure 2.8
The Score shows an animated presentation screen. The playback head will move from the frame label "Slide 1" to the end of that animation sequence and then loop back.

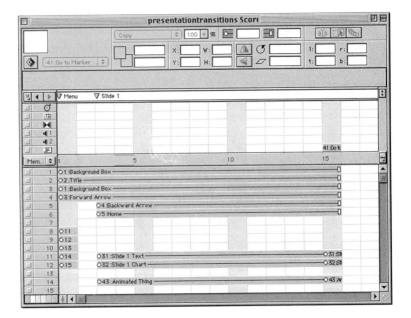

You could also have the screen animate until it reaches a certain point and then stop. To do this, simply use a Hold on Current Frame behavior in the last frame. This means that the animation will not loop, but instead play itself out and then pause on the last frame.

Adding animation to a presentation can really spice it up. You can have elements slide into the screen, or even have animated characters that introduce the next screen.

→ **See** "Animating with the Cast, Stage, and Score," Chapter 1, for more information about animation

SHOWING YOUR PRESENTATION

After you have completed a presentation, you have basically three options for presenting the final product. You can use Director to present it, create a stand-alone projector, or compress the movie for use on the Internet or an intranet. Each of these options is discussed in the following sections.

USING DIRECTOR TO SHOW YOUR PRESENTATION

This option makes sense only for presentations meant to be shown at a certain time and place, such as a business meeting or a sales pitch. To show a raw movie, you must have Director present on the machine. If you plan to show the presentation yourself, this poses no problem. Otherwise, make sure the person showing the presentation has the same version of Director that you do and that you test it on the playback machine. Slight differences in computers can cause the presentation to look different. They could be missing fonts or have their monitors set to different bit depths.

PART

I

CH

2

Note

> If you are sending the Director movie to someone else, remember that he can see all your source code, the Score, cast members, and so on.

The advantage to showing a movie in Director is that you don't have to spend time building and testing projectors. You can also edit the presentation seconds before showing it, or even while it is playing.

CREATING A STANDALONE PROJECTOR

This is the most common way of showing a presentation project. A projector is a standalone application that other people can play on their computers without having Director. Issues such as fonts and monitor settings are still valid, but if the movie is authored correctly it should run fine on all similar computer systems.

Note

> Director cannot create a cross-platform projector. There is no such thing. A Mac version of Director can create a Mac projector and a Windows version of Director can create a Windows projector. You'll have to buy two copies of Director to create projectors on both platforms.

To create a projector, follow these steps:

1. Choose File, Create Projector. This brings up the Create Projector dialog box shown in Figure 2.9.

2. Specify which file or files you want to incorporate in the projector. The Create Projector dialog box prompts you to add movie and cast files. Do this by selecting the files and clicking the Add button. In most cases you will be adding only one movie file. However, you can have a projector play several movie files sequentially by adding more than one.

3. Decide on the projector options by clicking the Options button to go to the Projector Options dialog box, shown in Figure 2.10.

Figure 2.9
The Create Projector dialog box is the first step in making stand-alone applications from Director movies. This is the Macintosh version of the dialog box. The Windows version is slightly different, but offers the same settings.

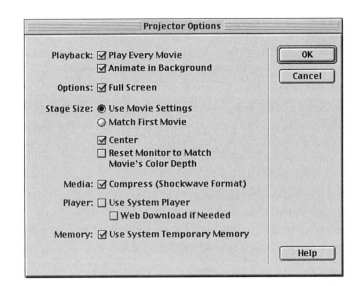

Figure 2.10
The Mac version of the Projector Options dialog box. The Windows version is similar.

The Projector Options dialog box has the following options to choose from:

- Play Every Movie causes the projector to play each movie in the list sequentially. If this option is not selected, only the first movie is played. The other movies included in your list can still be called from Lingo.

- The Animate in Background option determines whether the movie continues to play if it is not the front-most application on the computer. If this option is not turned on and a user clicks on another application, or uses the Windows Alt-Tab function, the movie pauses. Unless your movie is a straightforward animation, you should turn this option on.

- With the Full Screen option, you can choose to have your movie take over the full screen when the projector runs. This means that the rest of the screen will be blanked out, using the background color of the stage. If you are creating a presentation or an animation, this is a desired option. However, if you are creating something that you want to look like a normal Mac or Windows application, don't use this option.

- The two Stage Size options enable you to decide how the projector handles multiple movies that are different sizes. If you have two movies in your projector, for instance, and the first is 640 by 480 and the second is 320 by 240, choosing the Match First Movie option forces the second movie to be contained in a larger, 640 by 480 Stage. The other option resizes the stage when the other movie starts.

- The Center option should always be selected unless you want the Stage to appear at a specific location on the user's monitor. If it is not selected, the stage appears at the same location as it does when you are authoring in Director. This can be dangerous if you are not sure what size monitor the playback machine will have.

- The Reset Monitor to Match Movie's Color Depth is only available for Mac projectors. On the Mac, a program such as a projector can automatically adjust the monitor itself. This means that you can switch the monitor to thousands or millions of colors, if that is what your movie requires.

- You have several options that affect the size of the final projector. You can choose to have Director compress media for you before placing the movie in the projector. This uses the same compression technique that you use when you create a Shockwave movie.

  You can also choose to make a compact projector that relies on the user's computer system having certain files. The user would get these files from Macromedia's Web site. The files basically contain the meat of a projector. If the end users have installed these files, they can run the smaller, compact projectors. You even have the option to make the projector automatically prompt the users to get these files if they do not already have them.

> **Note**
>
> This compact projector is a new feature of Director 7. At the time of this writing it is not clear how successful Macromedia will be at distributing the player. If it becomes a standard part of Mac and Windows operating systems, full projectors could become a thing of the past.

- The Use System Temporary Memory option is available only on the Mac. It enables the projector to steal memory not being used by other programs. It is not used if virtual memory is turned on, so it is not likely to be a factor in most cases. However, it might give a large presentation a speed boost on some machines.

When you finish with the options, the only thing left to do is choose a filename. The result is an application program on the Mac and an .exe file on Windows. Chapter 36 goes into more detail about creating projectors.

→ **See** "Making Projectors," Chapter 36, "Delivering the Goods," for more information about building projectors

CREATING A SHOCKWAVE MOVIE

The big misconception about Shockwave movies is that you have to "shock" (compress) them. This is not true. You can take a normal Director movie file and play it back in a Web browser with Shockwave.

What is normally referred to as "shocking a movie" is actually just compressing it. The new file is a copy of the movie with images, text, sounds, and Score information compressed. The difference is usually very large; often the file is less than half the size of the original. This makes it much easier for Internet users to download Director movies, especially when they are using modems.

> **Note**
>
> Compressing a Director movie also protects it from being opened by other people who have Director. Otherwise, they could steal your code and media.

Shockwave movies, as these compressed files are called, always have .dcr as a file extension. Web servers use this extension to identify them as Shockwave movies and tell the browser to use the Shockwave plug-in to play them.

The process for placing Shockwave movies on your Web server depends on your file transfer protocol (FTP) software. In most cases, you have the option to upload the file in text or binary format. You *must* select binary for the file to be properly transferred.

To place the Shockwave movie inside a Web page, you can use the "embed" tag. This is the correct way of doing so for Netscape browsers. For Microsoft Internet Explorer Users, the correct way is the much more complex "object" tag. Chapters 23, "Object Oriented Programming," and 36 go into detail about that. Here is an example of how you would embed the movie into a page for Netscape:

```
<EMBED SRC="mymovie.dcr" WIDTH=320 HEIGHT=240>
```

There are actually many more options for the "embed" tag that are explained in Chapters 23 and 36. For now, this gets your movies up and running for a large part of the Internet community.

→ **See** "Making Shockwave Movies," Chapter 36, for more information about building Shockwave movies

TROUBLESHOOTING DIRECTOR

- Be sure to set your Span Duration to 1 if you plan on placing a lot of single-frame sprites. Do this by choosing File, Preferences, Sprite.
- If a sprite or frame is behaving strangely, use the Behavior Inspector to ensure that only the behavior(s) you want are present. You can also use it to check the behavior's parameters.
- Remember to reuse transitions that have been added to the Cast when you can, rather than creating a new transition member each time.
- Always check your Projector options before making a projector.
- Don't assume that a playback computer will have compatible fonts, monitor size, and other options. Always test projectors on the playback machine, or on as many machines as possible.

DID YOU KNOW?

- When you add a behavior from the library, a copy is placed in your Cast. You can open this script and examine the code and comments if you are interested.

- You can import PowerPoint presentations into movies that will then look very much like the examples described here. Just choose Xtras, Import PowerPoint File.

- In addition to the transitions built in to Director, you can purchase third-party Xtras that add more transitions.

- If you always use the Play behavior rather than the Go behavior to go to a frame, a Play Done button acts just like a Back button in a Web browser, taking the users back through their navigation paths.

PART II

MEMBERS IN DETAIL

BITMAP MEMBERS

In this chapter

Images, graphics, illustrations, photographs, and renderings: these are all different names for the same thing as far as Director is concerned. They are all bitmaps: arrangements of colored pixels in computer format. For such content, Director has the bitmap member type.

You can create bitmaps in a variety of programs, and then you can bring these images into Director by importing from a variety of standard formats. You can also create and edit bitmaps by using Director's Paint window. This chapter is dedicated to explaining the bitmap member type and the tasks that Director can do with it.

TYPES OF BITMAPS

The biggest difference between types of bitmaps is that they can be of different bit depths. There are five different bit depth settings. *Bits* refer to the amount of information stored for each pixel of a graphic. A One-bit image has only one piece of information: on or off. An 8-bit image has eight pieces of information, which corresponds to 256 possible combinations. This means that every pixel can have 256 possible colors. Here is a rundown of some of the possible bit-depths.

- A 1-bit bitmap contains only black-and-white pixels. It is small, as only "on" or "off" data has to be stored for each pixel, not a color value. 1-bit bitmaps can be very useful because you can define the colors of the two types of pixels in them to different colors depending on the sprite. So a single 1-bit member can be used multiple times to display graphics with different colors.

- A 4-bit bitmap contains 16 colors. On the Macintosh, you can customize these 16 colors. In Windows, you can use only one 16-color palette: the Microsoft VGA palette. If you are making your Director movie for a 4-bit machine and intend to distribute it cross-platform, you will want to use the Windows VGA palette.

- An 8-bit bitmap contains 256 colors. These 256 colors correspond to a color palette. This palette contains black, white, a small range of grays, and a general selection of basic colors. You can customize an 8-bit palette both on the Macintosh and in Windows. Director ships with a number of built-in 8-bit palettes. You also can import custom 8-bit palettes into your Director movie either with images that use them, or on their own in the standard palette format (PAL). They are then stored as cast members.

- The 16-bit, or thousands of colors, color depth contains 65,536 colors. This color depth was created to closely match the color values of a normal television set. This color depth does not have a palette associated with it.

- The 24/32-bit, or millions of colors, color depth contains 16,777,216 colors. This is the maximum numbers of colors that can be viewed on a computer monitor. This number is actually overkill because a person with normal vision can only perceive about nine million colors. This color depth does not have a palette associated with it.

  The notation 24/32 may seem a bit odd. The 32 refers to total bits of information: 24 bits for everyday colors and 8 bits that deal with alpha channel information or other special effects. You can't, however, work in 24 bits; when 24-bit terminology is used, it actually means a 32-bit resolution.

Using 8-bit images wherever possible is a good idea. An 8-bit image draws faster than a 16- or 32-bit image because the computer can process the smaller 8-bit image faster than a larger one. However, if your movie requires better color, use a higher setting.

An 8-bit bitmap can use only 256 colors at one time. However, a technique known as dithering can make the color range look wider. *Dithering* is the process of approximating a color by placing pixels of different, but similar, colors next to each other.

Using Palettes

You can use Director and bitmaps without knowing much at all about palettes, but it helps to understand them. Several palettes are built into Director. These include the Mac system palette and the Windows system palette. Each acts as a default palette for Director running on the system.

Strangely enough, these palettes are not the same. This is where a lot of trouble begins. If you decide to make your movie work with 8-bit graphics, you must choose a palette in the Movie Properties dialog box. But which standard palette do you use? The Mac palette displays fine on Macs, but not on some Windows machines, and vice versa.

In fact, if a user has a monitor set to use 16- or 32-bit color, the palette issue will never arise. This monitor has enough colors available to display any palette. However, if a computer is set to use an 8-bit monitor setting, it means that it can display only 256 colors at one time.

Showing a movie that uses a palette that differs from the one the system uses causes the computer to adjust and shift to your movie's palette. This is fine as long as the movie takes over the entire computer screen. However, if a window of another application or the desktop shows through, it will display in the wrong colors.

In addition, showing two 8-bit images that use different palettes also causes problems. Two totally different palettes would mean that you are asking the computer to display 512 colors at one time. Because it can't do this, some of the colors shift.

> **Tip**
>
> If you want to use 8-bit images and you don't need to stick to a standard palette, it may be a good idea to create a new palette that is optimized to display your collection of graphics as best as possible. This palette can be imported as a cast member and referred to just like the built-in palettes. Programs like DeBabelizer on the Mac and Brenda in Windows can create custom palettes for you. Also, the PhotoCaster Xtra can import a series of Photoshop images and create a new palette at the same time.

Using graphics that are 16- or 32-bit also causes problems for users with only 8-bit displays. The graphics probably use far more than 256 colors, so Director attempts to compromise when displaying them. The result may be that your graphics do not look very good.

CHOOSING THE BIT DEPTH

You should think about palettes and bit depth before starting your project. What will your users be using? If they all have 32-bit monitors, you know that you have the option to use 32-bit graphics. If many have only 8-bit capability, 8-bit may be your only option.

If your project is focused on deep, complex images such as photographs, you may want to consider 16- or 32-bit graphics if possible. However, remember that they are two or four times larger than 8-bit bitmaps. If your movie has only hand-drawn cartoon images, anything above 8-bit might be overkill.

If you know that most of your users use either Macs or Windows, the choice of a palette is obvious. Otherwise, consider that one is appropriate for both platforms or perhaps construct a new one. If your movie will end up as a Shockwave movie on a Web site, using Director's built in Web palette might be the answer. It displays well on both Mac and Windows.

> **Tip**
>
> The Web palette uses only 216 colors that are shared by both palettes. The rest of the colors are not used, but are reserved to enable the system to display the desktop and other elements.

The options can be confusing. If you are just learning Director, stick to using the default palette of your system for now.

→ **See** "Color Palettes," Chapter 8, "Other Member Types," for more information on palettes

→ **See** "Developing for Both Mac and Windows," Chapter 35, "Cross-Platform Issues," for more information on cross-platform development

IMPORTING BITMAPS

Even though there is only one bitmap member type, a variety of formats can be imported into this bitmap member type. You can import any one of these types of formatted files:

- BMP—A common Windows graphic format.
- GIF —A format originally used by CompuServe known as the Graphic Interchange Format. It is now one of the two standard image formats of the Internet.
- JPEG —Defined by the Joint Photographers Experts Group as a high-quality compressed image format. It is the other of the two standard image formats of the Internet.
- LRG —The native format of Macromedia's xRes image editor.
- Photoshop —The native format of Adobe Photoshop.
- MacPaint —An older Macintosh image format.
- PNG —Portable Network Graphics format. There is some momentum behind this format to be the new standard for the Internet.

- PICT —Originally defined for the Apple Lisa computer, now a standard Macintosh image format.

- Targa —Also known as the .tga format. Targa was the name of the Truevision graphics card that first used the .tga format.

- TIFF —Tag Image File Format.

After you import any of these file formats into Director as a bitmap, it no longer matters what the original format of the document was; it is now a bitmap cast member. By default, however, JPEG and GIF files retain their original file data inside Director until you edit them.

To import a bitmap image, choose File, Import. This brings up Director's Import dialog box. Figure 3.1 shows this complex window. You can import most media from here, including sound and video.

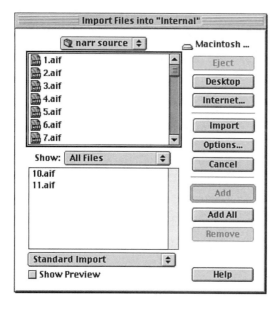

Figure 3.1
This is the Macintosh Import dialog box. It looks slightly different on the Windows platform, but the functions are basically the same.

PART
II
CH
3

You can choose one or more images and add them to your import list. When you are done, click Import to bring them in. If the graphics are set to the same bit depth as the monitor, and use the same palette as the movie does, they are immediately brought in. Otherwise you are prompted with the Import Options dialog box shown in Figure 3.2.

In the Import Options dialog box, you are given the choice of bringing in the bitmap using its bit depth or palette, or converting it to the bit depth of the movie. Selecting the dither option smoothes over any color changes that need to be made. The final option enables you to bypass this dialog box for the rest of the images that you have selected in that single import.

Figure 3.2
The Import Options dialog box enables you to specify how to translate images that use a different bit depth or palette than the movie.

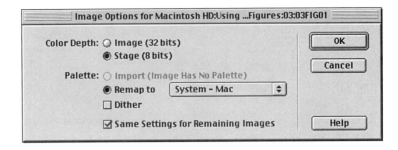

Tip

It is always best to convert your graphics to the desired bit depth and palette in the program that you originally used to create them. Photoshop, for instance, generally does a better job of converting and dithering an image down to 8-bit than Director can.

After you have imported a bitmap, you can still change its bit depth or palette. Just select a bitmap or bitmaps in the Cast and choose Modify, Transform Bitmap. This command also enables you to resize the image.

USING THE PAINT WINDOW

Some people love the Paint window and others hate it. Those who dislike it point to its weakness when compared with programs such as Photoshop, plus its odd quirks and idiosyncrasies. Those who love it, myself included, point to its speed, ease of use, and its unique tool set.

You can open the Paint window by double-clicking a bitmap cast member or choosing Command+5 on the Mac or Ctrl+5 in Windows. Figure 3.3 shows an empty Paint window. Notice that it has a toolbar both on the top and on the left side of the window. It also has a typical set of buttons and the name field at the top of the window.

The tools on the left side of the window are used to edit or add to the bitmap. Notice that some of them have a small arrow at the right bottom corner of the button. This means that you can click and hold over that button to see a small pop-up list of tool options.

SELECTION TOOLS

The first two tools, the Lasso and Marquee tools, are the selection tools. They enable you to select an area of the image to manipulate, move, or delete. The Lasso tool has three options and the Marquee tool has four, as follows:

- Marquee, Shrink—On selection of an element, the selection marquee shrinks to the outside edges of the artwork to create a rectangular selection. All white pixels contained within this selection are seen as opaque white.

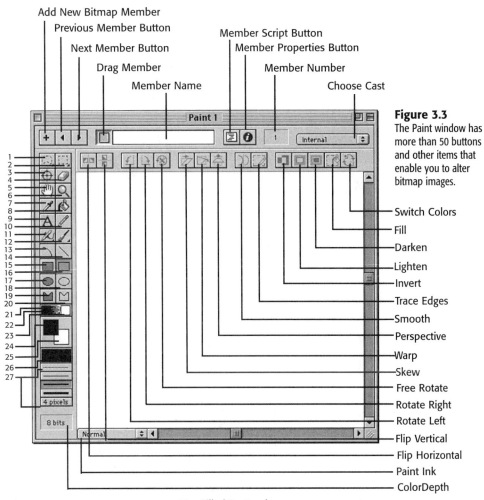

Add New Bitmap Member
Previous Member Button
Next Member Button
Drag Member
Member Name

Member Script Button
Member Properties Button
Member Number
Choose Cast

Figure 3.3
The Paint window has more than 50 buttons and other items that enable you to alter bitmap images.

Switch Colors
Fill
Darken
Lighten
Invert
Trace Edges
Smooth
Perspective
Warp
Skew
Free Rotate
Rotate Right
Rotate Left
Flip Vertical
Flip Horizontal
Paint Ink
ColorDepth

PART

II

CH

3

1	Lasso	15	Filled Rectangle
2	Marquee	16	Rectangle
3	Registration Point	17	Filled Ellipse
4	Eraser	18	Ellipse
5	Hand	19	Filled Polygon
6	Magnifying Glass	20	Polygon
7	Eyedropper	21	Foreground Color
8	Paint Bucket	22	Gradient
9	Text	23	Destination Color
10	Pencil	24	Foreground Color
11	Air Brush	25	Background Color
12	Brush	26	Pattern
13	Arc	27	Line Size
14	Line		

- Marquee, No Shrink—On selection of an element, the selection marquee remains in the dragged position as a rectangular selection. All white pixels contained within this selection are seen as opaque white.

- Marquee, Lasso—On selection of an element, the color of the pixel where the drag was started and all same-colored touching pixels are ignored. All other colors within the selection are selected within a flat-sided selection. All white pixels contained within this selection are seen as opaque white.

- Marquee, See Thru Lasso—This option behaves the same as Marquee, Lasso except all white pixels contained within this selection are seen as transparent (no value).

- Lasso, No Shrink—The area drawn with the Lasso tool retains its shape and selects all its content. All white pixels contained within this selection are seen as opaque white.

- Lasso, Lasso—On selection of an element, the color of the pixel where the drag was started and all same-colored touching pixels are ignored. All other colors within the selection are selected within the drawn area. All white pixels contained within this selection are seen as opaque white.

- Lasso, See Thru Lasso—This option behaves the same as Lasso, Lasso, except that all white pixels contained within this selected area are seen as transparent (no value).

REGISTRATION POINT TOOL

The next tool, shown as a target sight, can be used to view or reset the registration point of a member. A *registration point* is a location in the bitmap that the Stage uses to decide the placement of the sprite. By default, the registration point is at the center of the image. A bitmap displayed at location 50, 120 on the Stage, would then be centered at 50, 120. However, you can use the registration point tool to shift that point from the center of the image, and thus have it displayed according to the new registration point.

Note

Bitmap members use the center of the bitmap as the default registration point. However, text and field members use the upper left corner of the sprite as their registration points. You can't change the registration points of text or field members.

Why would you want to do this? If you are animating something that requires a series of members, say a man jumping, you would expect the center of the graphic to change as the animation progresses. In the middle of the jump, for instance, the center of the man would be higher than at the start. You can move that portion of the sprite higher on the Stage when creating the animation.

Tip

If you open a bitmap member where the registration point is not in the center, you can double-click the registration point tool button to re-center it.

However, by using different registration points, you can have each and every bitmap in the animation stay at the same Stage location, and let the offset of registration points do the movement for you. It will then be easy to reuse this set of cast members as an animation without having to reposition each and every sprite.

ERASER TOOL

Next to the registration point button is the eraser tool. You can choose this to paint white pixels on the bitmap. This has the same effect as using the paintbrush tool with the color set to white, except that the eraser paints in a different shape. Double-clicking this tool button erases the entire image in the window.

HAND TOOL

The Hand tool is one way to move artwork around in the Paint window. It does the same job as the window's scroll bars. You can quickly access the Hand tool by pressing the spacebar.

Tip

> The Paint window has no real boundaries, so it is very easy to move the paint object so far away from the center of the visible window that you can't find it again. In this situation, simply close and reopen the Paint window and the artwork will again appear in the middle.

PART

II

CH

3

ZOOM TOOL

The capacity of the Paint window to enable you to zoom in on artwork is one of its best features. You can edit your graphic's pixels much more easily this way. You can zoom up to 800%.

The Paint window changes somewhat when you zoom in. The upper right corner of the window contains an actual-size version of what you see in the main, zoomed area of the window. When you make changes to the bitmap, both images update. Because the number of pixels that fit in the Paint window changes as you zoom, this actual-size area also shrinks as you zoom in. The result is that at 200% zoom, one quarter of the window shows the actual-size view. At 400%, only one sixteenth of the window is occupied by it. This makes editing at 400% and 800% much more effective than at 200%. You can click the actual-size area to immediately zoom all the way back out again. Figure 3.4 shows the Paint window with a zoom of 400%.

A few shortcuts enable you to zoom in and out in the Paint window. You can press the Photoshop familiar Command+(plus) and Command+(minus) on the Mac, or Ctrl+(plus) an Ctrl+(minus) in Windows to quickly zoom in and out. While using most Paint window tools, you can also hold the Command key on the Mac and the Control key in Windows and click in the Paint window to zoom in. The Command+Shift keys on the Mac and the Ctrl+Shift keys in Windows enable you to zoom back out.

Figure 3.4
The Paint window here is zoomed 400%. The upper right corner shows the same image, but actual size.

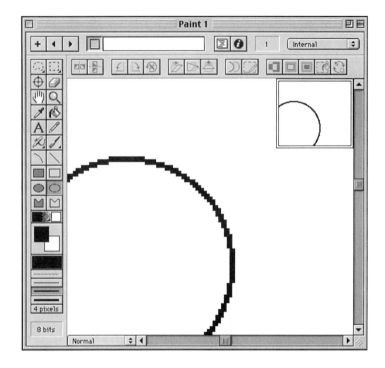

EYEDROPPER TOOL

The Eyedropper tool enables you to select a color in the Paint window to use as the foreground color. If you hold the Shift key, that color becomes the background color. If you hold the Option key on the Mac or the Alt key in Windows, that color becomes the gradient destination color.

As in other drawing programs, you can hold the Option key on the Mac or the Alt key in Windows to temporarily use the eyedropper tool without selecting it from the tool area. You can also hold the Shift key down at the same time to grab a background color.

PAINT BUCKET TOOL

This tool enables you to fill an area with the foreground color. The fill begins at the hot spot of the fill cursor, which is the very tip of the pouring paint. The fill changes the color of the selected pixel and all pixels of that color that surround it. Double-clicking the paint bucket button brings up the Gradient Settings dialog box.

TEXT TOOL

You can paint text into a bitmap member with the text tool. Selecting this tool changes the cursor to a text insert cursor. You can then click in the Paint window to set the start position of the text. A blinking cursor appears and you can start to type. While typing, you can double-click the text tool button to bring up the Font dialog box, with which you can change the font, size, and style of the text you are inserting.

After you have clicked another tool, or clicked in the Paint window to start typing another piece of text, the text you type becomes a permanent part of the image. You can, however, undo to restore the bitmap to its preceding state.

Note

Text entered into the Paint window is not anti-aliased, nor is it editable. To create members that are purely text, use the text member type instead.

PENCIL TOOL

This tool is the simplest, and yet the most useful tool in the Paint window. You can draw one pixel at a time with this tool, something that is not easy to do in Photoshop or other image editing programs. Pixel editing is a must for creating precise graphics to be displayed on the computer screen.

PART

II

CH

3

Tip

Holding the Shift key before clicking the screen constrains the pencil tool to drawing a straight line, eitherhorizontally or vertically.

AIR BRUSH TOOL

The effect the Air Brush tool creates, at first, might not look like paint being sprayed out of an air brush. To get a very smooth spray, the pixels must be smoothed out or anti-aliased, something you generally don't want to do in a Director animation. The Air Brush tool can create some fun patterns despite its limitations. This tool has five fixed settings, ranging from small to large, and a custom setting dialog box to set up your own air brush pattern. Click the Air Brush tool to activate the pop-up menu. Choose Settings or double-click the Air Brush tool to open the Air Brush Settings dialog box.

The following settings are available for the Air Brush tool:

- Flow Rate—How fast the paint comes out of the gun. The higher the setting, the quicker the paint dots come out of the gun.
- Spray Area—How much area the dots can cover for each click of the mouse. If the mouse is clicked and held in one place for a period of time, the paint dots eventually fill the entire spray area.
- Dot Size—Size of the paint dots that hit the canvas.

The Air Brush options are as follows:

- Uniform Spray—Sprays an even amount of paint from the tool.

- Random Sizes—Sprays paints dot of random sizes.
- Current Brush—Sets the paint dot to the shape of the Brush tool. Double-click the Brush tool to set this option.

BRUSH TOOL

The Brush tool is for freehand drawing. It uses one of five brush settings. Click and hold the tool button to choose which setting you want to use, or open the Brush Settings dialog box.

You can preset up to five brushes in the Paint window at any one time. Figure 3.5 shows the Brush Settings dialog box, which includes of some standard brush shapes and a brush editing area. You can get to this dialog box by double-clicking the Brush tool in the Paint window. This dialog box enables you to edit the currently selected brush.

Figure 3.5
The Brush Settings dialog box enables you to set the shape of one of five brushes.

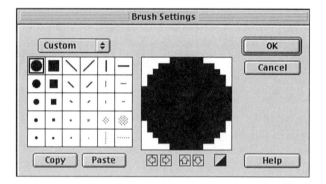

In the Brush Settings dialog box, you can choose one of the preset Standard brush tips. These brush tips appear in a box on the left in the dialog box. You can also access the brush tips by clicking the pop-up menu at the top of the dialog box to customize one of the Standard settings.

The palette of standard brush settings is fully customizable via the Custom Brush Settings window. With the Custom Brush Settings open, select an area outside the dialog box and a black-and-white image of what is under the cursor is placed in the custom brush creation canvas, shown in the box on the right side of the Brush Settings dialog box.

Within the Custom Brush Settings dialog box, pixels can be added or removed from the enlarged brush creation canvas. You can use the move arrow buttons below the brush creation canvas to shuffle the pixels up, down, right, and left one pixel. The pixels in the blown-up area can also be swapped or inverted: white to black or black to white. In addition, brushes can be copied to or from the clipboard.

ARC TOOL

The Arc tool draws an arched line on the canvas the thickness of the line set in the line weight selection area of the Tool palette. Pressing the Shift key when an arc is created causes the arc to constrain to a circular radius.

LINE TOOL

The Line tool creates straight lines. The width of a line in the Paint window can be between 1 and 64 pixels. Click the default one-, two-, and three-pixel line width settings, or double-click the Other Line Width setting to select a larger width. Pressing the Shift key before starting to draw a line causes the line to constrain to a 45° angle.

SHAPE TOOLS

The rectangle and ellipse tools create basic shapes on the canvas. These bitmapped shapes can be filled or unfilled, depending on which tool you select. The line weight of the shape is set with the line weight selectors.

Pressing the Shift key as the bitmapped rectangle or ellipse is being created constrains the shape to square or circular, respectively.

The Polygon tools create both filled and outlined polygons. Each click you make on the Paint window with the Polygon tool becomes a corner of the desired shape. The shape can be finished by either double-clicking to close the shape or by clicking the last position over the top of the first position.

PART

II

CH

3

COLOR CHIPS

Four color chips are in the left-side tool area of the Paint window. They correspond to the foreground color, the gradient destination color, the foreground color, and the background color. You will notice that two color chips represent the foreground color. They behave as you might expect, with a change made to one of these two affecting both. So despite the four color chips, there are really only three color settings.

The foreground color is used by just about all the tools as the primary painting color. The background color is used if you are drawing or filling an area with a pattern. It is also used as the background color when you are drawing text in the Paint window. The gradient destination color is used when you are filling or painting with a gradient, rather than a solid color.

To change any of these colors, click and hold the chip. A color palette appears, in which the current color is selected. You can drag the cursor to the new color and release. This little palette selector also includes a group of "favorite" colors and a color picker tool option for selecting 32-bit colors. Figure 3.6 shows what this palette selector looks like.

Figure 3.6
The palette selector enables you to choose a color. It, as well as many other Director tools, is used in the Paint window.

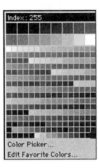

GRADIENTS

Between the first foreground color chip and the gradient destination color chip is a small area in which you can specify a gradient for use with the paint bucket tool and some others. You can select options such as Top to Bottom, Bottom to Top, Left to Right, Right to Left, Directional, Shape Burst, and Sun Burst. You can also choose to bring up the Gradient Settings dialog box, shown in Figure 3.7.

Figure 3.7
The Gradient Settings dialog box enables you to choose many options. Experimentation is the best way to understand them all.

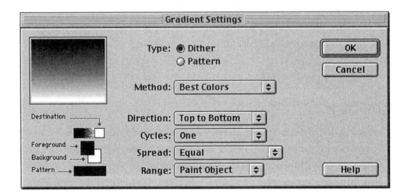

After you have set the gradient options, you still need to select Gradient as your ink effect for a specific tool. To do this, select the tool you want, such as the paint bucket, and then select Gradient from the pop-up menu at the bottom of the Paint window. You can find out more about this pop-up a little later in this chapter.

PATTERNS

Most of the time you will want to draw and fill with solid colors. However, Director includes a set of patterns that you can use instead. Clicking the area directly below the background color chip brings up the palette of patterns shown in Figure 3.8. The patterns should display using your current foreground and background colors.

Figure 3.8
The pattern selector enables you to specify a pattern with which to paint and fill.

After you select a pattern, tools such as the paint brush and the paint bucket will use that pattern, with the current colors, to draw. The pencil tool remains a single-pixel editing tool, however.

LINE WEIGHT SETTINGS

Five choices for line weights are given at the bottom left corner of the Paint window. The first is to have no line. The others are widths 1 through 3. The last line width choice is a custom setting. Double-clicking it brings up the Paint Window Preferences dialog box, where you can set it.

PAINT WINDOW INKS

A small pop-up menu at the bottom of the Paint window usually reads "Normal." This pop-up enables you to set the ink of a drawing tool, such as the paint brush or the rectangle shape. These are different from sprite inks in that they apply only to the result of editing in the Paint window. Not all inks are available to all painting tools. The inks options are as follows:

- Normal—The default ink draws with the foreground color or selected pattern.

- Transparent—When used with a pattern, this ink draws only the foreground color and leaves the background areas (white pixels) of the pattern with their existing colors.

- Reverse—This reverses the color of anything drawn over. If used with a pattern, only the black pixels of the pattern reverse the pixels under them.

- Ghost—This draws with the current background color. If you are using black and white, white pixels will be drawn in such a way that they will show up over a black background.

- Gradient—This uses the gradient settings and draws appropriately. Use with the paint bucket tool or a shape drawing tool.

- Reveal—This unusual ink uses the image of the previous bitmap member in the Cast. As you paint, you are actually painting with colors from that member, mapped onto the current bitmap.

- Cycle—This ink causes the paintbrush to cycle though colors in the palette as you draw. It starts with the foreground color and cycles through all the colors until it reaches the background color. It can then repeat the sequence or move through the sequence in reverse, depending on your setting in the Paint Window Preferences dialog box.

- Switch—This ink causes any pixels that use the foreground color to switch to the destination color. You should have your monitor set to 8 bits for this to work properly.

- Blend—This will enables you to blend the foreground color with the color of the pixels underneath it. It works best with 16- or 32-bit bitmaps.

- Darkest—This ink draws the foreground color only if it is darker than the pixels you are drawing over.

- Lightest—This ink draws the foreground color only if it is lighter than the pixels you are drawing over.

- Darken—This ink darkens the pixels as you paint over them.

- Lighten—This ink lightens the pixels as you paint over them.

- Smooth—This ink smoothes differences between adjoining pixels. The current color settings have no affect on the operation of this ink.

- Smear—This ink creates an effect similar to smearing paint across the image. The current color settings have no affect on the operation of this ink.

- Smudge—This ink is similar to smear, but the colors do not carry as far.

- Spread—This ink is similar to using the eyedropper tool and then painting. Each time you click in the Paint window, the spread ink picks up the color under the brush and uses it to paint that stroke. It even works when several different colors are under the paint brush. It just repeats that pattern as you draw.

- Clipboard—This ink draws with the clipboard image as the paint brush shape and color pattern.

PAINT WINDOW PREFERENCES

The Paint Window Preferences dialog box, shown in Figure 3.9, enables you to set a variety of options. In the middle, you can see the custom line width setting, mentioned previously. Most of the rest of the options deal with the different inks.

The first two options enable you to specify whether you want Director to remember the last color set and ink used with each brush. The Interpolate by option determines whether the Cycle ink is to cycle between colors in the palette or real colors.

The Paint window also has a ruler that you can turn on or off. You can do this by choosing View, Rulers. After rulers are turned on, you can click a small area in the upper left corner of the Paint window to change the type of units that the ruler displays.

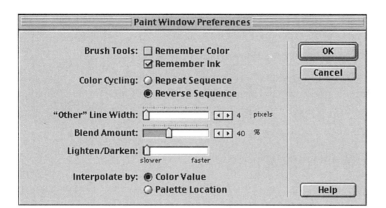

Figure 3.9
The Paint Window Preferences dialog box can be found by choosing File, Preferences, Paint or by double-clicking the custom line width tool.

You can also hide or show the Paint window tools in the View menu. The tools still work, but you won't be able to change them unless you use keyboard shortcuts.

THE EFFECTS TOOLBAR

Above the paint area is another toolbar space with a few buttons that represent certain tools. To use these tools, first select an area in the bitmap.

- Flip—The Flip Horizontal and Flip Vertical tools flip a selected element across a horizontal or vertical axis.

- Rotate—Selected elements can be rotated 90° clockwise or counterclockwise. The Free rotate tool enables the selected element to rotate freely around its center. The selection places handles on each of the element's corners. Drag these handles to a new position to produce the rotation.

- Distort—The next three buttons can create interesting effects. The Skew tool skews selected elements by slanting the sides of an element equally, leaving the top and bottom of the element perpendicular to one another. The Warp tool enables handles of the selected element to be pulled around to create a smashed or twisted effect. The Perspective tool shrinks or expands the edges of the selected element to give the illusion of depth.

- Smooth—This enables smoothing of pixels within a selected area of artwork. The smoothing effect functions only when the bit depth of the cast member is set to 8 bits.

- Trace Edges—This creates a new 1-pixel thick line around the edges of the original pixels of the artwork, leaving the original pixels white.

- Invert—When clicked, Invert causes the selection to change its black pixels to white and white pixels to black. Colors in the active 8-bit palette flip to the opposite side of the palette. To see the exact place a color occupies in a palette, open the Color Palettes window from the Window menu. If an image has a color depth higher than 8-bit, the Invert button replaces the colors with their RGB complement colors.

■ Lighten and Darken—Selected elements grow lighter or darker in their palette of colors. This command is unavailable in a 16-bit color space.

■ Fill—Fills any selected area with the current foreground color or pattern.

■ Switch Colors—Changes the color of identically colored pixels in a selected area. Pixels that match the foreground color are changed to the destination color. Switch color works only when the cast member is set to a palette of 256 or fewer colors.

BITMAP MEMBER PROPERTIES

Bitmaps have a few options that can be set in the Bitmap Cast Member Properties dialog box, shown in Figure 3.10. You bring up this dialog box by pressing the "i" button at the top of the bitmap Paint window. The first option, Highlight When Clicked, was mentioned in Chapter 2, "Presentations with Director." It enables you to have the bitmap automatically invert itself when the user clicks it. This can be used to make quick-and-dirty buttons that react to mouse clicks.

Figure 3.10
The Bitmap Cast Member Properties dialog box enables you to set dithering and alpha channel options.

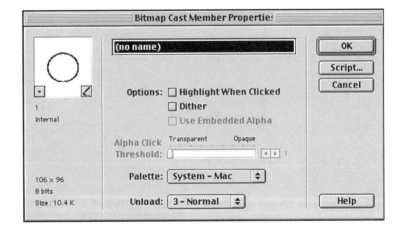

The next option, Dither, comes into play if you scale or rotate the image. The image may display better with a dither, but dithering may hurt your animation speed.

A new feature of Director 7 is the capability for 32-bit images to use the alpha channel data. *Alpha channels* are a fourth channel of image data. The others are the red, green, and blue channels. The alpha channel defines how transparent each pixel is. If you create a 32-bit image with an alpha channel, you can anti-alias the edges of the image, or make some of it transparent. You can use the Use Embedded Alpha option to make graphics that are semi-transparent or have edges that blend nicely with any background.

The Alpha Click Threshold defines how much of a role the alpha channel plays in defining where the user can click the image. If the image is set to transparent, the alpha channel is used to define the clickable area.

The palette pop-up is active only when the bitmap is set to 8-bit. It enables you to change the palette for the member without actually transforming it. The new palette is applied, regardless of the changes to the colors of the pixels.

ONION SKINNING

Director operates on the principle that you have not just one image, but many images. It is a rare movie that has only one bitmap. Very often bitmaps relate to each other. If you are drawing a man jumping, for example, the second step of the jump animation would probably be based on the first step. This is where onion skinning comes into play.

In cases such as this, it is useful to be able to see two bitmap members at once. You can do this by using the Option key on the Mac or the Alt key in Windows to open two Paint windows. However, all you see is the two members in different parts of your screen. Onion Skinning enables you to see two or more members in the *same* Paint window. You can draw on only one of those members, but the others remain visible for reference.

PART

II

CH

3

To turn on onion skinning, first open the Onion Skin tool by choosing View, Onion Skin. A small tool window, shown in Figure 3.11, appears. It includes a few buttons and two number settings. You should also have the Paint window open, because it is the only window in which the Onion Skin tool works.

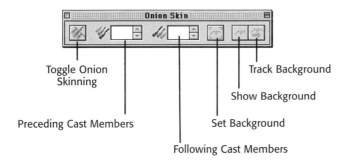

Toggle Onion
Skinning

Track Background

Show Background

Preceding Cast Members

Set Background

Following Cast Members

Figure 3.11
The Onion Skin tool enables you to see more than one member in the Paint window at one time.

You must have at least two bitmap members for the Onion Skin tool to work. You then need to turn onion skinning on by pressing the left-most button in the tool (Toggle Onion Skinning).

The default settings for the Onion Skin tool are to show a single preceding bitmap member. You can actually show many more and even show many following bitmaps. The two number settings in the tool enable you to set this. Each bitmap shown appears dimmed slightly and always behind the paint image of the bitmap you are editing. If you are showing more than one bitmap in the background, each image is successively dimmed. Figure 3.12 shows this effect.

Figure 3.12
This Paint window is using onion skinning to show the two preceding members.

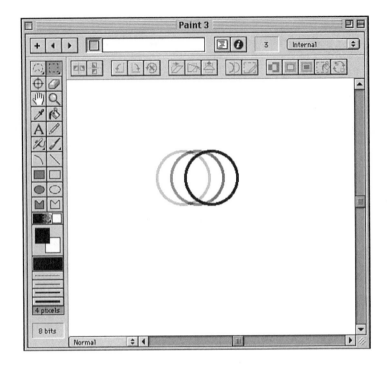

The point of showing these images is so that you can draw on top of them and create artwork that is relative to another member. You can also adjust the registration point of the current member to match it to the background image.

> **Note**
>
> Try using onion skinning while painting with the Reveal ink. It enables you to preview the image that is being revealed before you draw.

In addition to using the standard method for onion skinning, you can also use the tool to set a fixed background image. This image remains in the background no matter which other member you edit. Use this tool by first selecting the background bitmap. Click the Set Background button in the Onion Skin tool. To use that background image as your background, turn on onion skinning, set both numbers to zero, and then click the Show Background button. You will see that background image used as the background of any bitmap that you edit.

You can also combine background onion skinning with regular onion skinning and have several background images. While normal onion skinning images will change as you move from bitmap to bitmap, the background image will remain the same.

In addition, you can turn on background tracking and have the background image used by the Paint window change relative to the bitmap you are editing. For instance, if you choose member 20 as your background, and then edit member 35, you will see member 20 act as the background to member 35, member 21 act as the background to member 36, and so on. Onion skinning is a very powerful tool and one you will need to experiment with for a while before you become proficient with it.

PHOTOSHOP FILTERS

Although not all the features of programs such as Photoshop are available in the Paint window, one very powerful feature, *filters*, can be borrowed. If you are a Photoshop user, you probably already know about filters and what they can do. From a simple blur to a complex rendering, filters can alter a whole graphic or part of one. They are really just special effects for still images.

In Photoshop, you place filters in a plug-ins folder and access them through the Filter menu. You can apply the transformation, such as a blur effect, to the whole image, or to just an area.

PART
II
CH
3

Director can borrow these Photoshop filters and use them on cast members or in the Paint window. First, you need to tell Director where the filters are. This can be as easy as making an alias or shortcut to your Photoshop filters folder and placing it in the Director Xtras folder. You can also copy filters or folders of filters into the Xtras folder.

In addition to the filters that come with Photoshop, several third-party companies make filters that work with both Photoshop and Director.

The simplest way to use filters is to apply them to a whole single cast member. Select that cast member in the Cast and choose Xtras, Filter Bitmap. This brings up the Filter Bitmap dialog box, which organizes the filters into categories. Figure 3.12 shows an example of this dialog box.

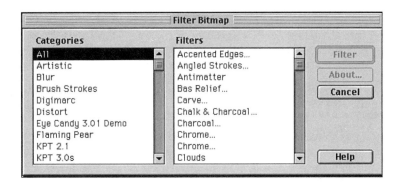

Figure 3.13
The Filter Bitmap dialog box looks different depending on which filters you have available.

If no filters show up in your dialog box, it means that you have no filters in your Xtras folder, or the filters that you do have are not compatible with Director. You also might be missing the PhotoShop Filters Xtra, which should have been installed when you initially installed Director.

To use a filter, simply select it and click the Filter button. If the filter has its own dialog box, as most do, you see that dialog box first and can then choose your options. The filter is then applied to the cast member.

Note

If you are looking for some good special effects filters, check out Kai's Power Tools from MetaCreations, Inc. It is one of the most powerful and popular filter sets available.

A very powerful feature of using filters with Director is that you can apply a filter to more than one cast member at a time. Simply select multiple cast members in the cast window and filter. Each of the members gets the same filter, with the same settings, applied to it.

You can also use filters by selecting an area in the Paint window. In that case, the filter is applied to only that area in that one bitmap.

Tip

If you don't get as nice an effect as you expected, check the bit depth settings of the bitmap. Most filters only work well with 32-bit images. If you have an 8-bit image that you want to filter, convert it first to 32-bit, filter it, and then convert it back to 8-bit.

Director also has an auto filter function. Choose Xtras, Auto Filter to use it. Its purpose is to create a series of bitmaps based on a filter that changes slightly over time. However, very few filters are built to have a filter-over-time function. The dialog box that appears lists only the filters that do. Do not be disappointed if no filters are shown. Hopefully, more filters will be written in the future to take advantage of this feature.

When working with filters, use a lot of caution. Filters are written by third-party companies that rarely test their filters on Director. Some filters do not work, others work in strange ways, and some will crash Director. It is always a good idea to save your movie and Casts just before trying to apply a filter. If a filter does not work at first, add more memory to the Director application and try again.

TROUBLESHOOTING BITMAP IMAGES

- The Paint window has always had a few quirks. It got an overhaul in Director 7, which removed many of the older quirks and created some new ones. At the time of this writing it is hard to determine which quirks will stick around and which might get fixed in version 7.0.1. Just don't worry so much if something doesn't seem to work quite as it should. There are many ways to perform the same task in the Paint window.

- If you are trying to use a PhotoShop filter and Director crashes, it is probably because the filter is not compatible with Director. Most filter developers test their products only on PhotoShop, and they may not be 100% compatible with Director. Make a note when a filter doesn't work so that you do not crash again.

- Director imports JPEGs and GIFs in their native format, which is not editable. When you first try to edit on of these images, Director asks you first whether you want to convert it to a bitmap. This is normal. However, if you want to keep using the JPEG or GIF image, you must edit the image in an external application such as PhotoShop or Fireworks, and re-import the changed file.

- If you need to edit a 1-bit member in the Paint window, note that the pencil tool does not always switch black to white and white to black as it should. However, converting the image to 8-bit and editing it there works fine; then you can convert back to 1-bit when you are done.

DID YOU KNOW?

- You can cut, copy, and paste between the Paint window and other image programs.

- On the Mac, you can drag and drop a graphics file from the desktop to the cast window.

- After you use the one of the Distort tools in the Paint window, you can then choose Xtras, Auto Distort. This creates new cast members that are copies of the original image, but include the distortion you last used. So if you rotate the image about 10 °, and use Auto Distort to create six new members, the new members will be rotated 10, 20, 30, 40, 50, and 60°.

- You can convert a color image to black and white by using Transform Bitmap and then changing the color depth to 8-bit and the color palette to Grayscale. You can then convert it to another palette if you need to.

- You can create a selected area in one bitmap member and then select that same area in another member. First, use the lasso to select the area. Then copy it. Go to the second bitmap image. Choose Edit, Paste, and then immediately choose Edit, Undo. The pasted image goes away, but the selection lasso remains.

- If you really don't like the Paint window, you can set Director so that it launches another application, such as PhotoShop or Fireworks, every time you go to edit a bitmap. Just choose File, Preferences, Editors. You can even opt to have an external application launch for certain types of bitmaps.

TEXT AND FIELD MEMBERS

In this chapter

Director 7 uses two types of text members. One is simply referred to as a *text member* and the other is called a *field*. Fields have been around in Director for a long time. Text members are relatively new, first appearing in Director 5.

Until Director 7, the difference between text and field members has been clear: text members are anti-aliased, use fonts without requiring that those fonts be present on the user's system, and are not editable, whereas fields use the user's system's fonts, are not anti-aliased, but are editable.

One of the powerful new features in Director 7 is the capability of text members to be edited. This blurs the line between text and field members. Differences, however, still exist, and there definitely are some good reasons to use field members whenever possible.

USING TEXT MEMBERS

Text members are complex, involving lots of options and features. However, you can create a simple one without much trouble. Just select the text tool, which looks like a letter *A*, in the tool palette, and click the Stage. This creates a text cast member and at the same time places that member on the Stage and in the Score. You are then in edit mode, and can type text into this member on the Stage. Figure 4.1 shows this type of procedure in action.

Figure 4.1
You can simply click the Stage with the text tool and start typing text. This text actually goes into the new text member.

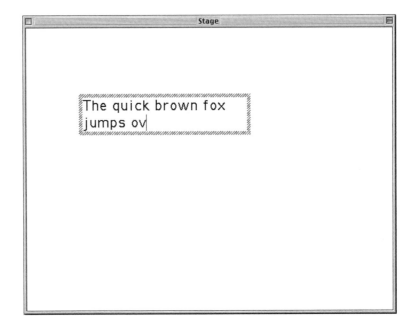

After you finish typing your text, you can click elsewhere on the Stage to deselect the text member. There are actually two ways to select a text member. The first, achieved by simply clicking it, enables you to drag the sprite around the Stage. You can also stretch and shrink the sprites Stage area. If you double-click the sprite, you can once again edit the text inside it. In this mode, you cannot move or resize the sprite.

TEXT EDITING

Although editing on the Stage is quick and easy, it doesn't give you as much control over the text as editing the member in a text window. You can open the member in a text window by double-clicking it in the Cast. You can also Control+Click on the Mac or right-click in Windows on the sprite to bring up a context menu. From here you can select Edit Cast Member.

Figure 4.2 shows the text editing window with typical options. A simple toolbar at the top of the window gives you tools to change the font, size, style, alignment, line spacing, and kerning of any selection. A standard text ruler also enables you to add and adjust tabs.

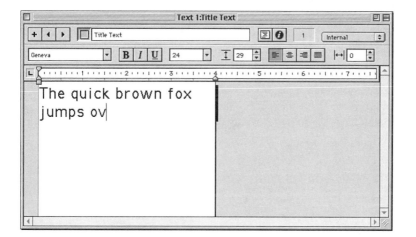

Figure 4.2
The text window has functions similar to that of a simple word processor.

The tools in this toolbar are pretty self-explanatory. Line spacing enables you to set how many pixels apart each line begins. Kerning is an adjustment that you can make to the spacing of each character. Although each character has a different width, *m* being wider than *l* for instance, you can add or subtract from the width of each character space. This does not change the actual shape of the character, only the amount of space between that character and the next.

Note

Justified text, the last option of the four justification buttons, aligns both the left and right sides of lines of text. This is commonly used in newspapers. Although this technique looks nice at first, it can be distracting to the reader if the text columns are too narrow. Make sure you use it only for wide columns of text where many words appear on each line.

Using the tabs in the ruler is pretty simple as well. Click the tab button, which appears to the left of the ruler, to change the type of tab you want. You can have tabs that left justify, right justify, and center text. You can also have a decimal tab that lines up columns of numbers on their decimal points. To add a tab, click in the ruler. To remove a tab, click and drag that tab away from the ruler.

Tip

When setting any text property, whether it is font, size, tabs, or indents, remember that |the property affects only the selected text, or the text in the paragraph where the cursor is located. If you mean to have the change affect the whole member, select all first.

You can specify left, right, and first line indents for paragraphs in the ruler as well. The thick markers along the top and bottom of the ruler can be dragged left and right. You can also grab the black bar to the right of the text area to stretch or shrink the page width. This bar brings the right margin along with it.

Figure 4.3 shows a text member with some complex formatting.

Figure 4.3
This text member uses tabs and various fonts and sizes to create a complex table.

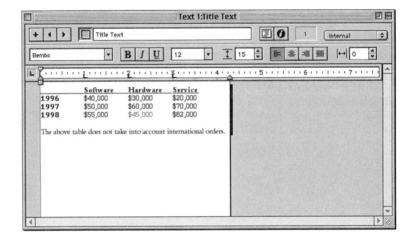

TEXT IMPORTING

Although the text window is great for editing text, larger pieces of text are likely to come from an outside source such as a word processor. You can easily import text of various formats into Director. It can even remember most of the various styles and settings of that text.

Three primary file formats can be read by Director: text, rich text (RTF), and hypertext markup language (HTML). The first type of file does not have any formatting; it is just a simple stream of characters. You can still style these characters after they are in a text member, but they have no styling when they first arrive.

The other two formats can contain a variety of styles and formats. Rich text contains a very similar set of styles and formatting options to the text editing window. There are more advanced forms of RTF files, but the basic idea behind rich text is to accommodate different fonts, sizes, styles, and paragraph formatting. As long as your RTF files stick to these basics you should be able to import them completely.

Some RTF files, such as those created from complex Microsoft Word documents, can include tables, images, and drawings. Director skips these elements when it imports the RTF file because the text member type does not support these options. All in all, rich text is your best bet for importing general text that uses only some formatting.

A new feature in Director 7 is its capability to import HTML files. You can create these with some modern word processors, but they are commonly created with HTML editing programs. Netscape Communicator also enables you to create and edit HTML.

Director cannot import all the elements and formats used in modern HTML, but it does a fairly good job with those it can. Standard styles, font size changes, paragraphs, line breaks, and the most basic tags are all supported. Director even goes as far as importing tables. This is probably the most powerful aspect of the HTML import.

After the HTML text has been imported, you can edit it in the text editor window. However, because HTML is more complex than the features of the window, you might be better off editing the original HTML document in an HTML editor. Of course, if your text is only a few lines of plain paragraphs, it doesn't matter.

TEXT MEMBER OPTIONS

You can set a variety of options to change the appearance of your text member. To get to the Text Cast Member Properties dialog box, click the information button in the text editing window, or use the context menu on the Stage. The dialog box appears as shown in Figure 4.4.

PART

II

CH

4

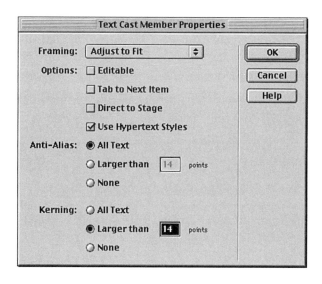

Figure 4.4
You can use the Text Cast Member Properties dialog box to make decisions about how the member will look on the Stage.

The first option is framing. You can decide to have the sprite's size adjust to automatically fit the amount of text in it. This adjustment is made with only the height of the box, because the width of the box is determined by the width of the member. Another choice is to have the size of the sprite fixed. Fixing the sprite size enables you to manually stretch or shrink the sprite, and the text in it is cropped if it cannot fit. This is very useful if you plan on doing exact screen layouts and you want to make sure that the text will never overlap another element. Of course the drawback is that this sprite might not display some text if there is too much to fit.

The third framing choice is to use a scrolling frame, which enables you to set the exact size of the text sprite. If the text doesn't fit, the scrolling bar on the sprite becomes active and the user can scroll through the text.

The next option enables you to make the text editable. This feature is new to Director 7. Previously, text members were akin to bitmaps after a projector or Shockwave movie was created. They could not be edited in any way except in the authoring environment. Making the text editable means that the user can change the text in the member while viewing a frame with that sprite. These changes do not affect the file, or anything else for that matter, unless you use Lingo to read and interpret the changes.

If you make a text member editable, you can also use the Tab to Next Item property to instruct Director to accommodate a common text editing technique. This property enables the user to use the Tab key to move from editable text member to editable text member on the Stage. Mac and Windows applications, including Web browsers, work this way. Turn this option on if you plan on having more than one text member on the Stage at a time.

The Direct to Stage option speeds up the presentation of the text by ignoring other sprites drawn under it. If you are using background transparent ink, turning this option on will block out underlying sprites. If you are using the Copy ink, however, then you are already blocking the appearance of sprites underneath, so you should turn this option on.

The Use Hypertext Styles option works only when you have imported HTML to create your member. Any links in the hypertext then appear as blue and underlined, just as they typically do in a Web browser. When the user clicks on them, they turn to a purple color to signify that they have already been used. You can find out how to use hypertext in Chapter 16, "Controlling Text."

→ **See** "HTML and Hypertext," Chapter 16, for more information on hypertext

The next set of options enables you to determine when Director is to anti-alias the text in the field. For those unfamiliar with anti-aliased text, look at Figure 4.5 to see the difference it can make.

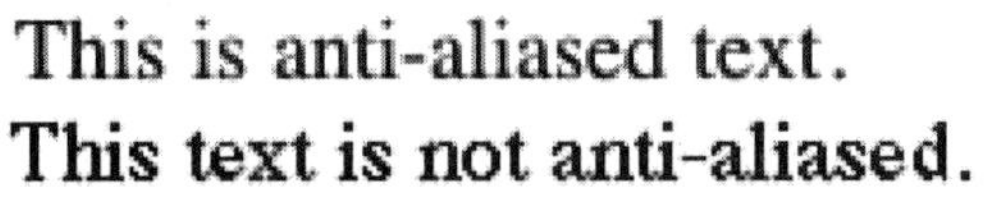

This is anti-aliased text.
This text is not anti-aliased.

Figure 4.5
The anti-aliased text shown on the top appears smoother than the jagged characters below. The image is magnified 400 percent to show detail.

You might be tempted to use anti-aliasing all the time. However, it has a few disadvantages. First, anti-aliased text takes up much more disk space than plain text. If you are making a size-sensitive Shockwave movie, you must consider this effect. Also, some fonts and sizes just don't look very good anti-aliased. However, titles that use large font sizes are good places to use anti-aliased text. At the same time, very small text, such as 9-point Arial, is more readable anti-aliased.

> **Tip**
>
> A good rule is to use anti-aliased text for small text portions and use plain text for longer text that the user will have to *read,* as opposed to *glance* at. But this rule can be applied on only a case-by-case basis. Experimentation usually reveals the best method.

You can use the options in the Text Properties dialog box to specify whether you want all text anti-aliased, no text anti-aliased, or only text that is above a certain point size. This setting affects only the selected cast member.

You can assign the same set of conditions to *text kerning.* Kerning is spacing between individual characters. This could come in handy if you have set kerning universally throughout the text member, but really want only larger font sizes affected.

THE TEXT INSPECTOR

Although the text window's toolbar contains just about everything you need to style and format text, it is not always convenient to have this window open. Instead, you can edit text directly on the Stage, as shown previously, and use the Text Inspector to make some style and format changes. Figure 4.6 shows the Text Inspector. You can access it by choosing Windows, Inspectors, Text.

In addition to the style and format tools, the Text Inspector has two color chips. You can use the foreground color chip to change the color of any selected text. The background color chip text works on the entire text member that is being edited. A text member can have only one background color. This color is ignored if you are displaying the sprite in a background transparent ink.

You can also use the Text Inspector to add hyperlinks. For now, this just colors and underlines the text for you. When you read about the Lingo involved in hyperlinks, you will see how this can be usedtext for navigation and control.

Figure 4.6
The Text Inspector can be used to style and format text in text members, fields, scripts and even in the Paint window.

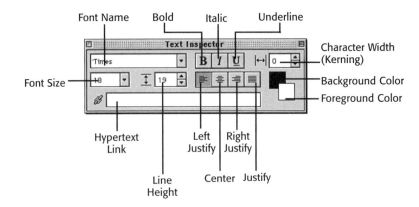

THE FONT DIALOG BOX

Although you can change fonts with either the text editing window toolbar or the Text Inspector, you can also bring up a Font dialog box that contains detailed information about your selected text. Figure 4.7 shows this dialog box.

Figure 4.7
The Font dialog box is accessed by choosing Modify, Font. You can also use Command+Shift+T on the Mac or Ctrl+Shift+T in Windows.

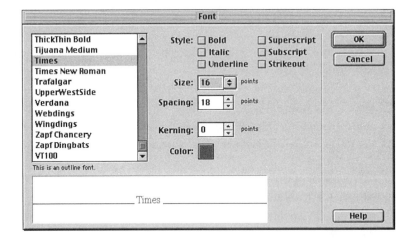

You have three more style choices in the Font dialog box: superscript, subscript, and strike-out. The first two adjust the vertical position of the selected text. The last places a line through the center of the text.

You also have a much nicer font selection method in the Font dialog box. The scrolling list is easier to look through than the pop-up menu. In addition, the Font dialog box can tell you which fonts are capable of displaying anti-aliased. Bitmapped fonts cannot be anti-aliased, whereas TrueType fonts can.

THE PARAGRAPH DIALOG BOX

The Paragraph dialog box, shown in Figure 4.8, enables you to set the left, right, and first line indents. Unlike the actual text editing window, the Paragraph dialog box enables you to set these indents to precise numbers. You will find that this comes in handy when you are trying to match settings between two or more text members. Clicking and dragging the indent tabs does not give you precise enough control.

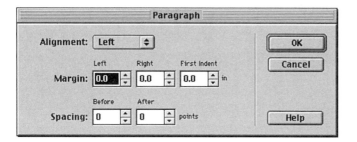

Figure 4.8
The Paragraph dialog box is accessed by choosing Modify, Paragraph. You can also use Command+Shift+Option+T on the Mac or Ctrl+Shift+Alt+T in Windows.

You can also use the Paragraph dialog box to set extra space between paragraphs. Specified in points, you can set these two items so that paragraphs are spaced farther apart than normal lines of text. This is a technique sometimes used to increase the readability of large text blocks.

→ **See** "Text Members and Fields," Chapter 16, for more information on formatting text

PART

II

CH

4

USING FIELD MEMBERS

Once the only text option in Director, field members are still very useful for a variety of tasks. For one, they take up much less file space than text members. A text member with *This is a test* placed in it is about 1600 bytes, whereas a field containing the same text is only about 700 bytes. The difference is even more dramatic when you use anti-aliased text in the text member.

A field member editing window, shown in Figure 4.9, looks different than a text member editing window. For one thing, the ruler is gone. Field members do not have the capability to recognize indents or tabs. However, you can still adjust the width of the field.

You also cannot fully justify text; only left, center, and right justification is possible. The justify button is inactive.

Fields cannot be imported. Instead you have to copy and paste text into the field editing window if you want to use text generated by an outside program. You can't anti-alias text within fields either. As a matter of fact, the field relies totally on the computer's fonts to display the text. So if you use a font that is available on your machine, but not the user's machine, Director will have to use another font to display the field. This is usually not a problem, however, when you stick to common fonts that are included on the operating system, such as Geneva on the Mac or Arial in Windows.

Figure 4.9
The field member editing window is similar to the text member editing window, except fewer options are available.

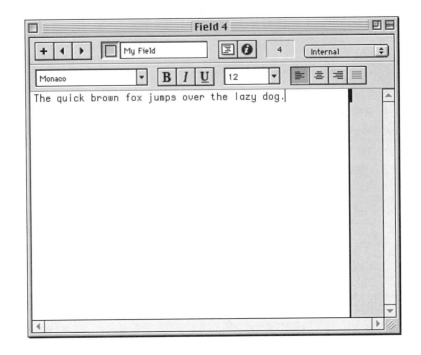

Note

Developers can use fontmap.txt to have more control over how fonts are mapped on other machines, across platforms. See "Developing for Both Mac and Windows," Chapter 35, "Cross-Platform Issues," for more information.

Figure 4.10 shows the Field Cast Member Properties dialog box. You do not have as many options available as you do with text members. However, you have an additional frame choice: Limit to Field Size. This option is useful only when you make the field editable. In that case, the user is restricted to typing only as much text as can fit into the field. Otherwise, the user can continue to type beyond the field's capability to display all the text on the screen. Both of these options are useful; you just need to decide which one to use depending on your needs.

Figure 4.10
The Field Cast Member Properties dialog box offers different options than the Text Cast Member Properties dialog box.

Another unique field option is Word Wrap. This option is on by default. Turning it off means that the text displays a new line only when there is a return character. The result is that each paragraph uses exactly one line, no matter how long it is. If a paragraph is too long, it simply disappears past the right of the field rather than wrapping to the next line. This is actually very useful when you begin to use Lingo to place text into fields.

With the Word Wrap option off, you can be assured that no text will wrap, no matter the length of the lines or the font used to display them. If you are displaying tabular data, this is often the lesser of two evils.

You can take advantage of four settings to add border-like elements to fields. You can find these by choosing Modify, Borders when you have the field selected on the Stage or in the cast. The available border settings are Border, Margin, Box Shadow, and Text Shadow. Each one offers six options: None and the numbers 1 through 5.

The first setting enables you to add a plain black border around the field. You can add a border that is any size from one to five pixels wide. You can use the second option to add a margin inside the field. This places extra pixels between the border and the area that contains the text.

Tip

If you are using a border, you should always use a margin. One of the most common mistakes that Director developers make is to not include a margin on their fields. This makes the text bump right up against the border which makes it look unprofessional. A two- or three-point margin should be used.

PART

II

CH

4

The Box Shadow option places a black shadow to the bottom and right of the field. This classic computer display effect can help make fields stand out, but can also be easily overused.

The Text Shadow option comes in handy when you are trying to display text over a background that makes the text hard to read. Figure 4.11 shows how this might work. The field is displayed with the background transparent ink so the image shows through. The 1-point text shadow places a black shadow behind the text and helps it to stand out.

→ **See** "Text Members and Fields," Chapter 16, for more information on field members

Figure 4.11
Using a text shadow
can help fields stand
out when they are
placed on top of a
background image.

KNOWING WHEN TO USE TEXT AND FIELDS

When deciding whether to use text or field members, you must take a variety of factors into account. Table 4.1 may help you decide. In most cases, you will find reasons to use both types. To choose which to use, you must decide which factor is a priority.

TABLE 4.1 FACTORS IN DECIDING BETWEEN TEXT AND FIELD MEMBERS

Factor	Use
Must look smooth	Text
Must display quickly and cleanly	Field
Must not add too much to the file size	Field
Must be editable by the user	Either
Must be editable, but also limit the user's input	Field
Must be capable of displaying indents	Text
Must be capable of displaying tables	Text
Must be capable of receiving imported RTF and HTML files	Text
Must be able to add borders and margins easily	Field
Must be able to add a text shadow easily	Field
Must be able to add hypertext links easily	Text

Factor	Use
Must be able to work with Lingo easily	Field
Must be able to display large amounts of text	Field
Must never change appearance from platform to platform	Text

A good rule of thumb is to use a field unless you need to use one of the features of a text member. You will find your movies are lighter and run more smoothly without the extra baggage.

USING FONT MEMBERS

A new feature of Director 7 is the capability to import fonts as cast members. This feature is very powerful because it enables you to use fonts in your movies that the users do not have on their machines. Previously, you had to use non-editable text members to display special fonts, or stick to fonts that you knew the users would have on their machines.

To import a font, choose Insert, Media Element, Font. What this does is create a new font cast member. The Font Cast Member Properties dialog box, shown in Figure 4.12, is immediately displayed. In this dialog box you can choose the font that this cast member will display. The only fonts listed are those compatible with your machine.

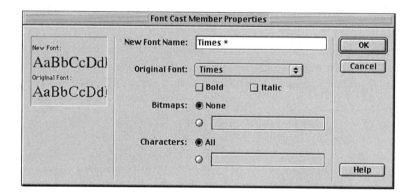

Figure 4.12
The Font Cast Member Properties dialog box enables you to set the options for a font member.

You can choose any font to be represented by that cast member. After import, the font thereafter appears in font pop-up menus as a font with the same name, but followed by an asterisk. The asterisk signifies that this is a font internal to this movie. Director immediately converts all the field and text members that use the original font to now use the new internal font. When you create new field and text members, you can select the new internal font.

Note

According to Macromedia, no legal issues are involved in distributing fonts inside a Director movie. There is no way for users to export and then redistribute them as fonts again. So as long as you have the right to display the fonts on your authoring machine, you should be allowed to use them in your movies.

Director also enables you to decide how much of that font to import. If you want only the basic font, leave the bold and italic check boxes off. However, if you do want these versions of the font, check them. This increases the size of the font cast member. These members are compressed in Shockwave movies and compressed projectors, but it is a good idea to leave out whatever you don't use.

You can also specify the exact characters you want to import. This can further help shrink the size of the font member. Another option enables you to choose to include bitmap versions of fonts. Many fonts include them to display perfect text at certain sizes. Include these by typing in font sizes separated by commas.

Tip

After you have a font member and are using it in text members and fields, do not try to delete or replace the font member. This will confuse your text and field members.

A good way to use imported fonts is to decide which fonts you want to use before authoring the movie. Import all your fonts first. You can also create external cast libraries that hold a variety of font members. You can then copy and paste these members into your current movie. This saves you from having to have these fonts on your system.

Another useful side-effect of using font members is that you can have custom-built fonts that display a variety of simple images. Using a program such as Macromedia Fontographer, you can create a vector graphic disguised as a font and import it into Director. You can then have text members that use these images. It's like having dozens of vector graphics embedded in a single member.

TROUBLESHOOTING TEXT AND FIELD MEMBERS

- If you are trying to import an .rtf file or an HTML file and you are not getting the results you want, it is probably because the file uses an RTF or HTML feature that Director does not support. Try eliminating that part of the text or converting it to a simpler layout.

- Using fields means that the spacing between lines will differ on Mac and Windows. You will learn how to set the line spacing of fields in Chapter 16, but it is a good idea to use text members rather than fields if line spacing is important.

- There are a lot of cross-platform issues with fonts. Even the same font can differ on Mac and Windows, especially when it comes to special characters. See Chapter 35 for information about font mapping.

Did You Know?

- Some fonts, such as Courier and Courier New, are monospaced, which means that each character is the same width. You can use these fonts to create simple tables in which each column lines up exactly.

- In most fonts, all the number characters are monospaced.

- A common design mistake in Director is to use a field with a border, but not to set a margin. Any field that uses a border should have at least a 2-pixel margin.

- Because you can import fonts and specify which characters you need to keep, you can use the special Dingbats font and keep only one or two members. Then use these members in text member sprites as graphics. They take up very little space, and are scalable by setting the font size.

SOUND MEMBERS

In this chapter

There are many reasons to include sounds in your movies. Sounds can be small button feedback noises, background music, audio narration, animation soundtracks, special effects, and more. Remember, this is called "multimedia" because it is more than just images.

SOUND FILE FORMATS

Like images, sound files come in a variety of formats. Director can import a large number of these formats. Inside each sound file the sound is represented in a variety of different sample rates and bit depths.

The Audio Interchange File Format   (AIFF) is the most common format used on Macs. It is also used in the digital music recording industry. You will see these files on both Mac and Windows machines, usually represented as an .aif file.

The .wav or wave file is a Windows file format. It is widely supported by most Windows and Mac programs. Both the AIFF and wave files can be imported into Director with no problems. You can also import System 7 sounds on the Mac and even MP3 (MPEG 3) formatted sounds.

If a sound file comes in another format, it is usually easy to find a program that will convert it to either an AIFF or wave file. You can even convert CD audio tracks to AIFF files by using a program such as Macromedia's SoundEdit 16 on the Mac.

After you have your sound files formatted properly, you can use them in three ways in Director. The first is to import them as cast members by choosing File, Import. You can place the members in the Score's sound channels by dragging them to the Score, or you can use Lingo. Although sound members can be large, when you save the movie as a compressed Shockwave file or projector, Director can compress them for you.

Another way to use sound files in Director is as external files. You can import sound files using the Link to External File option, which is a check box in the Import Dialog. This action creates a cast member that contains no data, but represents the external file. You can place this member in the Score as well. Director accesses the external file as needed. You can also play external sound files with a Lingo command, even if the sound is not represented by a member.

You can also create what are called Shockwave audio files. You create these files by exporting a file from your sound editing program in Shockwave audio format. The resulting files are pre-compressed external files that can be called with Lingo. These files can also be *streamed*, meaning that Director can play them over the Internet as the files are downloaded. Shockwave audio files can be created on the Mac inside SoundEdit 16. In Windows, you can use a Director Xtra that converts wave files to Shockwave audio files.

FREQUENCY AND BIT DEPTH

Two measurements are used to set the quality of a sound file: sample frequency and bit depth. *Sample frequency* is the measurement of how often the samples of the sound are taken and stored as digital data. *Bit depth* is the range of information stored in each sample.

The rate at which audio is sampled is like the resolution of a scanned image, and defines how many samples are to be taken in a given time or space. The sample rate defines the detail of the sound wave. More samples can accommodate more detail, which means higher pitched sounds can be recorded. Natural sounds contain a wide range of frequencies from low to high. The capability to record high-pitched sounds adds to the clarity of the overall sound. Examples of common sample rates include 44.1KHz, 22.05KHz, and 11.025KHz.

The depth at which the samples are measured is like the color depth of an image: 256 colors (8-bit), thousands of colors (16-bit), and millions of colors (32-bit). Digital audio can be commonly sampled at 16 bits per sample or 8 bits per sample. Lower bit depths are unacceptable and unpleasant to listen to due to the lack of clarity. *Bit depth* controls the signal-to-noise ratio, measured in decibels (dB), and refers to the number of times the quietest sound must be amplified to match the loudest sound.

The relationship between sample rate and sample depth can be varied to accommodate differing quality and playback requirements. A 11.025KHz audio file that uses 8 bits, for example, sounds like a scratchy telephone line. The same rate used with 16 bits improves the dynamics of the sound but not the clarity. The 8-bit file, however, requires half the storage space that a 16-bit file does. The best results come from using the highest sample rate with the largest bit depth, which creates the largest file size. The trade-off between quality and memory requirements is a familiar one, which applies to many aspects of multimedia and computer work in general.

Use the following guidelines when sampling or resampling audio for multimedia.

- 5.564KHz—Poor quality, speech only. Intended for voice annotations rather than multimedia. Voice annotations are sound files attached to documents intended for comments, memos, and so on. The file sizes are very small (suitable for floppy disks and slow networks), but the quality is less than a pocket dictation machine.

- 7.418KHz—The lowest recommended quality for speech (Macintosh only). Very small file sizes, although ShockWave audio can provide similar sizes in powerful machines.

- 11.025KHz (CD)—A good choice for playback on older Windows and Macintosh computers. Some distortion and background noise (equivalent to a telephone line). Use for low-quality music or medium-quality speech.

- 11.127KHz—This was the original standard frequency for older Macintosh computers. New Macs have adopted the IBM 11.025KHz frequency. This frequency is not recommended if you are producing a cross-platform production. Some PC sound cards will not play this frequency.

PART

II

CH

5

- 22.050KHz—The most popular choice for Macintosh and Windows. Good quality music and narration, similar to a strong AM radio broadcast.

- 22.225KHz—The old, high-quality Macintosh standard. Suffers compatibility problems on Windows machines.

- 44.100KHz—Standard compact disc (CD) audio rate.

It is a good idea to record sound at the highest level possible, 44.1KHz and 16 bits, for example, and then *downsample* to the quality that you need in your Director movie. This results in a better quality sound. In addition, it gives you the high quality sound to fall back on if you want to re-import your sounds at a different quality later. You have to do this downsampling in your sound editing program because Director has no way of doing it. By downsampling, you are just converting the sound to a lower quality, and thus smaller file size.

Tip

A recommended quality setting for sounds imported into Director is 22.050KHz and 16 bits. This is half the size of a 44.1KHz sound, but the quality is nearly the same. Although this is much larger than a 11.025KHz 8-bit sound, Shockwave audio compression can be used when you make your Shockwave movie or projector to compress the sound further.

→ **See** "Sound Commands," Chapter 17, "Controlling Sound," for more information on sounds

INTERNAL SOUND MEMBERS

You can import sounds into Director with the same import function used for bitmaps and text. Choose File, Import, and select the sound file or files you want to import.

After the sound is in the Cast, the Sound Cast Member Properties dialog box, shown in Figure 5.1, has only one available option. It enables you to tell Director whether the sound is a looping one or not.

→ **See** "Importing Bitmaps," Chapter 3, "Bitmap Members," for more information about importing

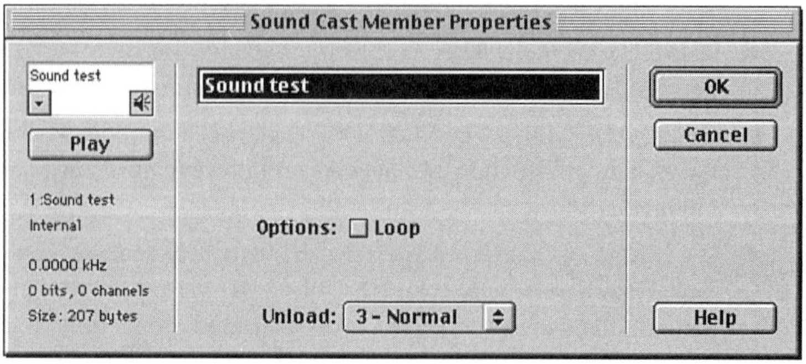

Figure 5.1
In the Sound Cast Member Properties dialog box you can preview the sound and set looping.

If looping is turned on, Director plays this sound over and over again as long as the sound is in one of the sound channels in the Score. As soon as you jump to a frame that does not have this sound, it stops.

You can record sounds in Director only on the Mac. If you choose Insert, Sound, a Mac system sound recording dialog box appears that enables you to record a sound from the current sound source, usually the microphone. No editing options are available, so this technique has use only as a way to create temporary placeholder sounds.

EXTERNAL SOUNDS

Sounds tend to be very large and add significantly to the file size of a Director movie. For this reason, you may want to consider keeping sounds as external files and creating a linked cast member that uses this external sound. You can create a linked sound member by choosing File, Import to get the Import dialog box, and then selecting Link to External File instead of Standard Import.

Another method for using an external sound involves no cast member at all, but simply playing a file directly with a Lingo command. You will learn about sound-related Lingo commands in Chapter 17.

An even more compelling reason to use external sounds is that internal sounds need to be completely loaded into memory before being played. If a sound is one megabyte in size, and the user's machine does not have the extra memory to store it, the sound simply does not play. However, an external sound does not have to be completely loaded to start playing. This may be your only option for playing larger sounds.

Starting speed is another issue. A large sound inside the Director movie may take some time to load and begin playing. However, an external file may also take some time to start because hard drives and CD-ROM drives have to search for the beginning of the sound file.

PART

II

CH

5

Note

If you are expecting instant starts to sounds, prepare to be disappointed. Most Windows machines handle sound very poorly. Even on what could be considered a fast machine, sounds sometimes take several seconds to begin playing, an issue called *latency*. Updates in hardware and operating systems continue to promise improvements, but sound performance in Windows still is not what can be expected on Macs. See the troubleshooting section of this chapter for one workaround.

→ **See** "Sound Commands," Chapter 17, for more information on controlling sounds

SHOCKWAVE AUDIO

For audio to stream over a network, the data rate has to be small and regular. This means that the size of the file devoted to the first second of sound and the second second of sound have to be exactly the same. This is known as the *bit rate* of the sound.

A typical streaming sound may be 16 kilobits per second (Kbps), or 16 times 1024 bytes of information. A file with this bit rate can be streamed over a 28.8 modem that gets data at 28.8Kbps. However, a 32Kbps sound cannot stream smoothly.

Even a 24Kbps sound will probably not stream smoothly over a 28.8 modem because a 28.8 modem rarely gets a continuous stream of data at 28.8Kbps. The measurement is really telling you the maximum that the modem can receive.

Shockwave audio is typically produced by SoundEdit 16 or Bias Peak on the Mac and the Shockwave converter Xtra in Director on Windows. You can choose from a range of bit rates between 8 and 128Kbps. The following list will help you decide which to use:

- 8Kbps: Limited use for voice-only sounds when you need maximum compression.
- 16Kbps: The only real choice for any type of audio that needs to stream over 28.8 modems. Sound quality supports voice, music, and sound effects.
- 32Kbps: Should be used only when users are using 56K modems or better. Good quality, although still mono.
- 48Kbps: Enables you to use stereo sounds, but at a relative 24Kbps per channel rate. Users must have fast connections. This rate and higher can also be used for streaming sounds from the hard drive or CD-ROM.
- 64Kbps: At this rate you can do good quality stereo sound.
- 96 and 128Kbps: Accommodates excellent quality audio. This rate is usually overkill unless you have a need for the absolute best quality of sound, such as a CD-ROM version of a symphony orchestra recording.

If you want to get an idea of which bit rate settings match which sample frequency settings, 8Kbps uses 8KHz output sample rate, 14 and 24Kbps use 16KHz output sample rate, 32Kbps and above try to use the same sample rate as the original sound file. However, if the sound file was at 44.1KHz and the Shockwave audio compression is set to be less than 48Kbps for mono and 96Kbps for stereo, it is forced to use 22.050KHz.

You cannot import a Shockwave audio sound completely into Director, but you can create a cast member that links to it. Choose Insert, Media Element, Shockwave Audio. This brings up the SWA Cast Member Properties dialog box shown in Figure 5.2.

Figure 5.2
The SWA Cast Member Properties dialog box enables you to link to an external Shockwave audio file.

You can type a full or relative path for the SWA file. The path can be a file on your hard disk or CD-ROM, or a Web address. Use the browser button to quickly get the path of a local file.

You can also set the volume and sound channel for the sound. Choosing Any for the sound channel means the machine will attempt to play the sound in the first unused channel.

You can also set the preload time of the sound. The *preload time* determines how many seconds of sound have to load before the sound starts. Smaller numbers mean that the sound can begin sooner. However, a larger number reduces the chance that a streaming sound will be interrupted if the user has a bad connection. This occurs because Director buffers that many seconds of sound at the start. If Director buffers five seconds of sound, there needs to be only a five-second interruption in the transmission for the Shockwave audio to need to pause and wait for more data. With a ten-second buffer, Director can take a ten-second interruption, or even two five-second interruptions before it needs to pause the sound.

➔ **See** "Shockwave Audio," Chapter 17, for more information on controlling Shockwave Audio

Using Sound in Director

Without using Lingo, there are four ways to make a sound play in Director: use the Score, use a Play Sound Member behavior from the library, use a Play Sound File behavior from the library, or use another behavior that uses a sound effect. A button behavior, for instance, may ask for a sound that plays when the user clicks. In Chapter 11, "Advanced Techniques," you will see how to construct behaviors that use sound in a variety of ways. In Chapter 17, you will get the full rundown on what is possible with sounds and Lingo.

Using the Score to Play Sound

Using the Score is the simplest method to produce sound. Just drag and drop a sound cast member, either internal or linked, onto one of the two sound channels in the Score. The sound starts playing when the playback head reaches the first frame with this sound. The sound continues to play while it exists on the current frame or until it is done playing. If the sound is set to loop, the sound continues to play until you get to a frame that is out of the sound's current sprite span.

You can play two sounds at once in the Score by using the two sound channels. Because most Windows machines really are capable of playing only one sound at a time, Director mixes the sounds before sending them to the sound card. This can cause delays. A sound scheduled to come in on frame 27 of an animation may not be heard until several frames later. It might be a good idea to pre-mix sounds with sound editing software in cases such as this. That way, you can ask your computer to play only one sound rather than two. See the troubleshooting section of this chapter for another workaround.

USING LIBRARY BEHAVIORS TO PRODUCE SOUND

A second way to play sounds it to use some Lingo commands. Fortunately, the Play Sound Member behavior in the library enables you to do this without writing code. You just attach it to a sprite or frame and choose when you want the behavior to play.

> **Tip**
>
> If you already have another behavior attached to a sprite, you will want to experiment when the sound plays. If a button behavior uses the On MouseUp message to do an action, it might interfere with the On MouseUp that the sound behavior expects to get to play the sound. Sometimes, swapping the order of the behaviors for that sprite in the Behavior Inspector fixes the problem.

Another behavior, Play Sound File enables you to specify a sound filename to play. It enables you to play sounds that may be too large to store and use internally to the movie.

In both behaviors mentioned, you get to choose the sound channel where the sound should play. You can type any number you want, although you should stick to numbers 1 through 8 to ensure compatibility with all machines. In fact, it is a good idea to use channels above channel 2 to ensure that the sound channel never interferes with channels 1 and 2, which can be used by the Score.

→ **See** "External Sounds," Chapter 17, for more information about playing external sounds

WAITING FOR SOUNDS AND CUE POINTS

You can also make your movie wait for a sound to complete. To do this, use the tempo channel in the Score. First, place a sound in either sound channel. Then double-click the temp channel to bring up the Frame Properties: Tempo dialog box. The last option is to Wait For Cue Point. Select that option and then use the two pop-up menus to set its parameters.

First, select the sound channel that this tempo command should be watching. Then, select the cue point that it should be looking for. Always present here are the {Next} and {End} options. Choose {End} to make the movie wait on that frame until the sound ends.

If you want, you can set cue points in a sound file with SoundEdit 16 or Bias Peak on the Mac. Similar functionality is possible with Sound Forge 4.0 in Windows. Figure 5.3 shows a sound file opened in SoundEdit 16 with some cue points placed. Save the file as an AIFF file when you are finished.

Figure 5.3
SoundEdit 16 enables you to place cue points in sound files. These cue points can then be used in Director.

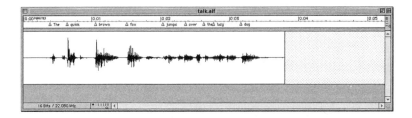

After you import a sound file that has some cue points, the second pop-up menu of the Wait For Sound option will list these cue points. You can then tell any frame to wait for a certain cue point before moving to the next frame. The {Next} option does not wait for any specific cue point, but the next one that the sound passes. With cue points, you can synchronize sound and animation.

TROUBLESHOOTING SOUNDS

- Although Windows machines are still not capable of mixing more than one sound without a latency effect, Macromedia Apple has come to the rescue. Director movies can use QuickTime 3, if it is installed on the Windows machine, to mix sounds. This produces much better results. You need to run one Lingo command: the soundDevice = "QT3Mix". This should be done when the movie starts.

- If a sound created on the Mac does not work on Windows, make sure it is in a format that Windows can recognize, such as 16-bit and 22.050Khz, for instance. Using an odd setting can result in an unplayable sound in Windows.

- Does a sound seem to wait a while to start, even when no other sounds are playing? It could simply be that the sound has a second or so of silence at the start. Many sounds that come from CD-ROM sound collections have this. It is recommended that you check all your sounds in a sound-editing program before importing them.

- If a large internal sound does not work in a projector, it may simply mean that not enough memory is available to play it. Mac users can increase the amount of memory allocated to a Projector by choosing File, Get Info. Otherwise, you may want to consider downsampling large sounds to something that will take up less space, or use them as external sounds.

DID YOU KNOW?

- You can create Shockwave audio compressed files and then import them into Director as internal cast members. You can create sounds that are compressed all the way down to 8Kbps in this way. However, watch to make sure you don't lose too much quality.

- You can't export sounds out of Director normally, but you can copy a sound cast member and then paste it into another sound program. You can also choose an external editor through the File, Preferences, Editors menu and save the sound that is referenced when you launch the editor.

- Just because a Shockwave audio file sits on an Internet server doesn't mean that the movie must, also. A Director movie can be run as a Projector, or even in Director, and can still play Shockwave audio over the Internet as long as a connection exists.

CHAPTER **6**

DIGITAL VIDEO

In this chapter

Like animation, digital video presents successive frames of graphics to create a moving image. Video is typically real-life recordings, but can also be rendered animations. You can use various digital video formats with Director.

USING DIGITAL VIDEO FORMATS

There are many aspects to digital video. File type is only one issue to consider. Compression is another. Because digital video files tend to be huge, uncompressed video is almost unheard of. Whatever type of file you choose to store and play back the video, you should also choose a video compression algorithm to use with this file type.

FILE TYPES

Director authors primarily use two digital video formats. The most common is QuickTime: a cross-platform multimedia format created by Apple. The other is the Video for Windows (AVI) format, which is built into Windows 95, 98, and NT.

QuickTime is more than just digital video. It actually consists of tracks of media, including video, sound, MIDI, text, controls, transitions, and even 3D objects. A subject like QuickTime deserves a book all to itself. This chapter discusses just Director's capability to use QuickTime.

> **Note**
>
> It is important to realize that QuickTime underwent a major transformation in 1998. With the release of QuickTime 3, major improvements were made. This chapter discusses only QuickTime 3 because that is what Director 7 primarily supports.

Digital video files that are just video and sound include a variety of format and compression settings. You can use at least a dozen different types of compression with QuickTime Pro. Each one compresses in a different way, some better or worse for different types of video.

Digital video doesn't have to be video camera-recorded material. You can also render images such as computer animations as digital video. Plus, video footage of a basketball game differs greatly from video footage of a college professor lecturing. Therefore, the types of compression that work well with each vary as well.

Like sounds, digital video can use different sample rates and bit depths. It gets even more complex as you are trying to compress both images and sound.

→ **See** "Exporting Animations," Chapter 1, "Animation with Director," for more information on digital video

COMPRESSION

Digital video is actually a series of images. Like a child's flip-book, the images are shown in rapid succession to give the illusion of animation.

If you have an image that is 320 by 240 pixels and in 32-bit, that image will be 300K in size ($320 \times 240 \times 32$ bits / 8 bits per pixel / 1024 bytes per kilobyte = 300K). Imagine if you have some digital video that runs at 24 frames per second. Five seconds of it will contain 120 images. That's 36,000K or about 35 megabytes. All for five seconds of quarter-screen video!

The secret to digital video is that it compresses each image to bring this file size down. It also compares consecutive images to determine whether it really needs to store all the data for each image. If one image is 90% the same as the preceding image, only the 10% percent that is different should be needed.

This type of compression is called *temporal* compression, or *delta change* compression. This technique records the changes between images, rather than the images themselves. It works well for some situations, such as when you have a talking head with a static background, but doesn't work well at all in cases such as a panning image where the whole scene is changing constantly.

Spatial compression is a technique that looks at the images themselves. It tries to recognize "runs" of colors. For instance, it would scan the image from left to right and recognize lines of pixels that are the same color as a single piece of data. So an image that has a solid white background would compress well using this algorithm. This is how JPEG compression works.

In order to really get digital video down to sizes that make sense, *lossy* compression needs to be applied. Lossy compression includes algorithms that attempt to summarize the images rather than represent them exactly as they are. Some of these compression techniques average the colors of adjacent pixels. Others apply mathematical formulae to a series of pixels to estimate the appearance. It is called lossy compression because the original image can never be restored from the compressed video. After it has lost some of its quality to become smaller, the file can never show details that were once there. For that reason, you should save your original files before compressing them when you use this technique.

With lossy compression, you can usually specify how much compression you want. A video compressed to 2:1 may not lose enough detail to be noticeable. However, a video compressed 100:1 may barely be recognizable.

Almost all compression algorithms that you will use are lossy compression algorithms. As you might expect, there are also *lossless* video compression techniques used for archiving and storage. Here, there is no loss of quality at all, and the original video file can be recreated from the compressed one. However, the compression is not as dramatic as with lossy compression. Sometimes the compression is only 2:1 and it is rarely as high as 10:1.

DATA RATE

Another important factor in digital files is the data rate. The *data rate* is the amount of data that exists for each second of video. Because digital video needs to play in real time, and the files tend to be huge, the data streams off the hard drive, CD-ROM, or the Internet. Because each of these can transfer data at only a certain rate, the digital video data rate must be less that the originating media. A single-speed CD-ROM drive can stream video at only 150K per second. And because CD-ROM drives are not perfect, it is reasonable to expect only 90K per second.

> **Note** Few people have single-speed CD-ROM drives, but a lot do still have double-speed CD-ROMs. They can read data at a theoretical 300K per second, but you should consider 180K per second to be the actual speed in practice.

If you are streaming video from the Internet, your options are very limited. Even with a poor-quality 90K per second data rate, you are exceeding what a standard 28.8 modem can be expected to handle. However, if your access is across a reliable T1 line or local network, streaming video becomes possible.

IMPORTING DIGITAL VIDEO

Both QuickTime and Video for Windows can be imported into Director as cast members. In Windows you can have either a QuickTime member or a digital video cast member. On Macs, QuickTime is the only option. In both cases, the cast members are linked to the external video file. Unfortunately, there is no way to import a video file completely in Director; you always have to rely on the external file.

To import a digital video file, just choose File, Import and select a digital video file in the same way you would select an image file or a sound.

If you import a QuickTime movie as a QuickTime cast member, you need to include the QuickTime 3 Xtra with your projector, or rely on this Xtra being on a user's machine already or automatically downloaded in the case of Shockwave. A digital video member, however, is handled without any Xtras. You still need to have Video For Windows on a machine to handle AVI members and QuickTime 2.x on machines to handle QuickTime movies imported as digital video. This may change in future upgrades of Director.

→ **See** "Importing Bitmaps," Chapter 3, "Bitmap Members," for more information about importing

DIGITAL VIDEO SETTINGS

After a digital video member or a QuickTime member is in the Cast, you can set a variety of important settings in the Digital Video Properties dialog box shown in Figure 6.1. To bring up this dialog box, just double-click the member in the Cast, click the Info button in the digital video's window, and finally click the Options button.

The first two items in the Properties dialog box enable you to specify whether you want to hide or show the video or sound portions of the video. In case you are using video that does not have one of these two elements, you can turn it off. For instance, if you have a QuickTime movie that contains only a MIDI track, you can turn off the video portion. Or, if you have a video that has both video and sound, you might want to turn off the sound in a situation where it is not needed.

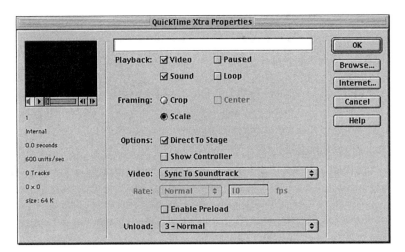

Figure 6.1
The Digital Video Properties dialog box enables you to set a number of options.

With the Paused option you can specify whether you want the movie to begin playing automatically, as soon as it appears on the Stage. If you want it to show up paused on the first frame, be sure to include the controller so the user can start the video. Alternatively, you can use some Lingo to kick off the video.

With the next item (Loop) you can tell the movie whether it should automatically loop. If set, this causes the movie to start at the beginning again as soon as it is finished.

You can use the Framing options to determine what happens if you stretch the sprite on the Stage. Because the size of the sprite will no longer equal the original size of the digital video, Director needs to know what to do in this case. The first option is to crop the video. Of course if you are stretching the sprite, a crop will not occur, but neither will the video stretch to fill the space. If you choose crop, the Center option tells Director whether it should automatically center the video in the sprite rectangle.

If you select the "Scale" option, Director forces the video to fill the sprite rectangle, even if it is larger or smaller than the original digital video. You can distort the video this way. Note that a digital video member playing back in a stretched sprite requires more processor power than one playing back at the original size.

You can even move and change the size of the digital video sprite over time with the same tweening effects mentioned in Chapter 1. The digital video adjusts while it is playing!

→ **See** "Sprite Preferences Dialog Box," Chapter 1, for more information about setting sprite preferences

The Direct to Stage option enables the video to be placed over all other sprites in the frame. This means that Director is telling the QuickTime or Video for Windows portion of the operating system to ignore other sprites. The result is a faster, smoother playback. If you are not trying to blend the video in with any other sprites or perform any special effects with the sprites, use this option.

PART

II

CH

6

The Show Controller setting tells Director to place the standard video controller bar under the digital video. This controller is not a part of Director, but a part of QuickTime and Video for Windows.

Another option in the Digital Video Properties dialog box (Sync To Soundtrack) enables you to tell Director to ignore the video timing in the digital video movie, and instead display each frame at a constant frame rate. When you do this, the sound for the video is disabled. This is useful for digital video files that contain simple, silent animation. You can present this video at a speed different than intended in the original file.

The last option is the Enable Preload option, which tells Director to load as much of the video into memory as it can before it starts playing. Although this might cause a pause at the start of the video, it allows for smoother playback because Director continues to load and store sections of the video in memory while the video plays. Otherwise, the entire video will be played from disk.

→ **See** "Digital Video Commands," Chapter 19, "Controlling Video," for more information about controlling video

WORKING WITH DIGITAL VIDEO

To use a digital video member, all you need to do is drag it to the Score or Stage. A sprite will contain the video member and automatically size itself to the proportions of the video. If you selected the video controller option, it displays below the sprite.

If you are using the video in a presentation, you are likely to want it to appear on a frame that has a "Hold On Current Frame" behavior placed on it. This keeps the playback head steady and enables the video to be played back.

You can use the same "Wait for Cue Point" tempo setting with QuickTime movies that you can with sounds. Many editing tools enable you to place cue points in video and export the video as QuickTime. You can use the {End} setting to have the movie pause on a frame and wait for the video to end. You would use this, of course, for cases in which you are not using the video controller and have the movie not be paused when it appears.

QuickTime 3 videos are cross-platform, so the same files work on both Macs and Windows, provided that the computer has QuickTime 3 installed.

→ **See** "Digital Video Commands," Chapter 19, for more information about controlling video

CUSTOM VIDEO CONTROLS

If you prefer not to use the video controller that QuickTime or Video For Windows uses, you can make your own. Simply select the option to not have this controller appear in the Digital Video Member Settings dialog box. Then you need to create your own buttons. Figure 6.2 shows a video sprite and some sample buttons.

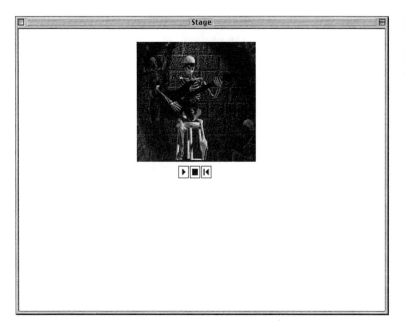

Figure 6.2
The Stage has a video sprite and several bitmaps that act as video controls.

You can create the bitmaps to have any appearance that you want. To make them control something about the video, look in the library palette for some digital video control behaviors. QuickTime Control Buttons will take care of most of your needs. Attach these to the sprites and choose the function you want them to perform. You will also have to specify which sprite the video is in.

TROUBLESHOOTING DIGITAL VIDEO

- Just because the QuickTime 3 Xtra is included with your projector doesn't mean that QuickTime movies will play on any machine. It is a common mistake for developers to assume that the user has it installed. You can point the user to the Apple Web site (`http://www.apple.com/quicktime/`) to download and install QuickTime 3 for free.

- Digital video is a very processor-intensive medium. Newer computers handle it with ease, but older machines may just not have the power to display video of any decent quality.

- If you are having a problem playing digital video in Director, the first place to look is always the Digital Video Properties dialog box. Is it set to Paused? Are both the sound and video tracks enabled? You might try Direct To Stage if all else fails.

- In the past, QuickTime movies with sound have not relinquished the sound channels back to Director immediately after playing on Windows. If sound doesn't seem to work immediately after a QuickTime movie plays, try having the movie jump to a frame

PART

II

CH

6

without either QuickTime or a Director sound. Then, have it proceed to the frame with sound. If that fails, try using the Lingo *sound stop* command from Chapter 17, "Controlling Sounds."

Did You Know?

- Using QuickTime movies that contain only a MIDI track is an easy way to use MIDI inside Director. You can convert any standard MIDI file to a QuickTime movie with the QuickTime MoviePlayer application. Simply open a MIDI file with it, and it prompts you to convert the MIDI file to QuickTime format.
- You can use cue points in QuickTime movies in Director in the same way that you can use sound cue points. If a QuickTime movie is present in a frame, you can double-click the Tempo channel and select Wait For Cue Point. In addition to any sound channels, you can see any QuickTime sprites lists. You can choose a cue point or {Next} or {End}.

CHAPTER 7

Vector Members

In this chapter

You can divide still-image computer formats into two groups: bitmaps and vectors. A *bitmap* is a collection of colored pixels that stores an image. A *vector* is a description of lines, curves, fills, colors, and other information that can be used to construct an image.

Bitmaps can be used for all sorts of images, but have one main drawback: they are already set to a certain size. You can shrink bitmaps without much trouble, but enlarging them results in a loss of quality. With vector graphics, on the other hand, you can stretch the image to any size without changing the level of detail. Vector graphics are not very useful for complex images, however, such as photographs. The descriptions of such images would make the file huge and a burden for the computer to interpret.

Although bitmap images are stored pixel for pixel, with color data recorded for each pixel, vector graphics are stored as a description. This description typically states positions, colors, and curves of lines, rather than information on specific pixels.

For those of you familiar with graphics programs, bitmaps are typically created with such applications as PhotoShop, Fireworks, Painter, and other image-editing software. Vector graphics are typically created with applications such as Macromedia Freehand and Adobe Illustrator.

In Director, you can use three types of vector graphics. The first is a group of simple shapes, such as circles and lines, that are built into Director as special cast members. Second, you can create simple vector graphics as vector shape cast members. Third, you can import and use images and animations created with Macromedia's Flash tool.

SHAPE MEMBERS

There are eight different kinds of shape members: two kinds of lines, and filled and unfilled ovals, rectangles and rounded rectangles. You can create all these shape members with the tool palette shown in Figure 7.1. If this tool palette is not already present, choose Window, Tool Palette, and then select the tool and draw on the Stage. This creates a cast member with that shape and a sprite that contains it. After you have a cast member for a shape, you can drag that member from the cast window to the Stage or Score to reuse it in another sprite. You can even stretch or shrink it differently in different sprites.

Note

Director sometimes refers to round shape members as "ellipses" and sometimes as "ovals." They are, in fact, the same thing.

The ovals, rectangles, and rounded rectangles are pretty straightforward. You can set their color by selecting the forecolor chip in the tool palette. This changes the color of the whole shape in the case of filled shapes. However, it will change the color of only the outline in the case of non-filled shapes. The background color chip has no effect.

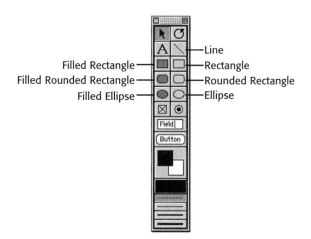

Figure 7.1
The tool palette enables you to create all eight types of shape members using just seven different buttons.

If you want to create an area that is both filled with a color and uses an outline of a different color, you need to create both shapes, filled and non-filled, and change their colors separately. The shapes cannot share the same cast member, either, because one cast member must be filled and the other not.

Filled is a member property, whereas the dimensions, line size, and color of shapes are sprite properties. This means that you can change these properties to be different for different sprites, but all those sprites can use the same cast member. You can therefore have four different sprites—a small blue oval outline, a small black oval outline, a large green oval outline, and a large green oval outline with a thick border—that all use one single cast member. However, if you want an oval outline and a filled oval, you need two separate cast members.

The Filled member property can be changed in the Shape Cast Member Properties dialog box shown in Figure 7.2. To get to this dialog box, select the member in the Cast and press the Info button in the cast window. Within this dialog box you can actually change the type of member to another shape type. Although it doesn't make sense to change a line into an oval, having the capability to change a rectangle to a rounded rectangle might be very useful at some point.

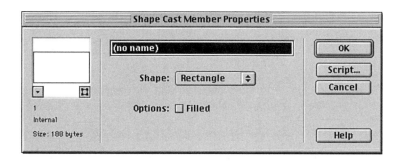

Figure 7.2
The Shape Cast Member Properties dialog box enables you to determine whether the shape is filled or outlined, and enables you to change the shape type.

PART

II

CH

7

Line shapes don't have a filled and non-filled version, of course. The Filled property of a line member must always be turned on for the line to be visible. However, there are still two types of line members: lines that draw from the upper left to the lower right, and lines that draw from the upper right to the lower left.

If you think about it, you can see why these two types are needed. A sprite is placed on the screen at a certain position and with a certain rectangular area. This is all that is needed for a rectangle shape to be drawn, but a line shape does not automatically sense which diagonal *direction* to use to fill the sprite's shape. When you first draw a line, it uses your drawing motion to determine which type of line to create.

The danger is not immediately apparent. If you draw a line on the Stage from upper left to bottom right, and then use that same cast member in another sprite for a second line, you will have one cast member and two sprites. If you then alter one of the sprites to draw from the upper right to the lower left, the change is made to the *cast member* itself. This means that your first sprite will also flip! The solution is to use two different cast members, one for each type of line. Or, you can simply use a new line member each time if you don't mind the extra members.

Most uses for lines are not sensitive to this problem, however. If you draw a straight horizontal or vertical line, as you might use in a presentation screen layout to separate elements, it doesn't matter which line type is used.

VECTOR MEMBERS

Vector members are a new and very powerful feature of Director 7. You can create common lines and shapes that can be scaled, anti-aliased, and modified on-the-fly. These shapes also take up a relatively small amount of file space, making them ideal for Internet delivery.

VECTOR SHAPE EDITING WINDOW

To create a vector member, choose Insert, Media Element, Vector Shape to bring up the Vector Shape editing window shown in Figure 7.3. Like the Paint window, it includes two toolbars. Most of the tools are on the left, whereas you use the top toolbar to set fills.

A vector shape is essentially only a long curve built around two or more points. Some points also contain curvature information. If the image is *closed*, the first and last points are connected and a fill may be applied to the enclosed area.

Note

Unlike vector graphics in Freehand, Illustrator, and Flash, you cannot have more than one curved line in a member. You will be surprised, however, at how complex a single curve can be.

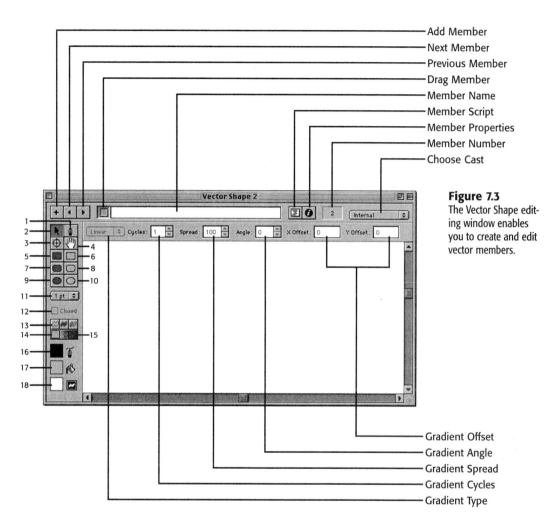

Figure 7.3
The Vector Shape editing window enables you to create and edit vector members.

1 Pen	10 Oval
2 Arrow	11 Stroke Width
3 Registration Point	12 Close Shape
4 Hand	13 Gradient
5 Filled Rectangle	14 Gradient Start Color
6 Rectangle	15 Gradient End Color
7 Filled Rounded Rectangle	16 Stroke Color
8 Rounded Rectangle	17 Fill Color
9 Filled Oval	18 Background Color

PART

II

CH

7

To create a vector shape, choose the Pen tool. Click in the window to create the first point of the vector shape. If you click and hold the mouse button down, you can set the curvature amount, or *handles*, of the point. You can then place other points in different locations. A quick click adds a point with no handles, while a prolonged click and hold enables you to set the curve of the line.

Figure 7.4 shows a vector shape in the middle of its creation. The user has clicked to create several points. You can see the two handles of the last point created. You can also see the second handle of the next-to-last point because that handle affects the curve drawn between the two points. Any of these handles shown can be grabbed and moved to change the curve of the line.

Figure 7.4
While you create a vector graphic, you see not only the points you have created so far, but also the handles of your current point and the second handle of the preceding point. The handles define the amount of curve from one point to the next.

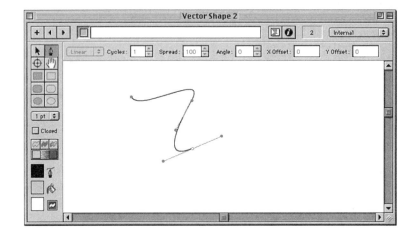

Note

Curves defined by points and handles are also known as *Bezier* curves. The first handle of any point determines how the line curves into the point, whereas the second handle determines how the line curves away from a point. So any section of the curved line will curve depending on the second handle of the preceding point and the first handle of the next point. If neither point has these handles, the line is drawn straight from one to the other.

The last point in any curve is very important. If you match that last point up to the first point in the vector shape, you then have the option to set the vector to Filled. If the two points do not match, the shape can be used only as a curved line.

After you finish drawing, you can edit any point by selecting it with the arrow tool. After you select one point, you can edit its location and the locations of its handles. You can also continue the curve by selecting the pen tool again and clicking to create another point. To insert a new point between two points that already exist, use the pen tool with the Option key held down on the Mac or the Alt key held down in Windows.

Six shapes are also shown in the toolbar. The only time you can use these is before you have drawn anything else. You can use them to make some standard shapes. Because these shapes all exist in Director as regular shape members, there is no point to using them here to create plain shapes. Instead, you can use them to create a starting point for a shape that still needs to be edited to get the result you want. For instance, you can use the rectangle shape to create a rectangle that you will edit and to which you will add other points.

Another reason to use these standard shapes is that you may want to take advantage of the fill techniques available to vector shapes but not standard shapes. By having a closed shape and turning on the Closed setting, you can apply a fill. Select the type of fill from the left toolbar. You can have no fill, a solid fill, or a gradient.

If you select a solid fill, you must also select the fill color from the collection of color chips on the left toolbar. The first is the color of the line. The line color does not matter if you set the line to be zero pixels wide. The second is the color of a solid fill. Having these as two separate colors means that you can have a vector graphic that has one color for the outline and another for the fill. The last color chip enables you to set the color of the background. This color comes into play only if you set the sprite that uses the vector member to copy ink.

If you set the fill type to be a gradient, you can also set the destination color with a color chip arrangement that is similar to what is used in the Paint window. A host of settings in the top toolbar define the type of gradients.

You can use a linear or radial gradient and set the number of cycles, or the number of times that the gradient is to travel between the initial and destination colors. The Spread setting enables you to restrict the fill to only a small portion of the image, or enlarge it so that only a portion of the gradient fits into the shape. You can also change the angle and offset location of the gradient. This gives you an incredible amount of control over where the gradient is placed and how it looks.

→ **See** "Building Vectors with Lingo," Chapter 20, "Controlling Vector Graphics," for more information about creating vector shape members

VECTOR SHAPE PROPERTIES

In addition to the vector shape editing window, the Vector' Shape Properties dialog box, shown in Figure 7.5, has a few settings you can establish. You can access it when you are editing the vector shape by pressing the Info button.

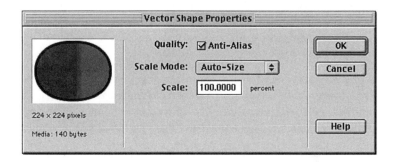

Figure 7.5
The Vector Shape Properties dialog box enables you to define what happens when a sprite containing this member is stretched.

PART

II

CH

7

The first setting is whether the shape is drawn using anti-aliasing. Anti-aliasing uses shading to smooth out the line. This type of line is slower to draw, of course, but looks much better than a ragged line of pixels.

The Scale Mode pop-up menu enables you to choose what will happen when the member is stretched on the Stage. Here are the options:

- Show All—The vector shape keeps the same dimensions, stretching only when it can still fit the entire shape in the sprite.
- No Border—The vector shape keeps the same dimensions, but scales to fill the sprite area, even if it means cutting off some of the shape horizontally or vertically.
- Exact Fit—The vector scales to the new dimensions of the sprite, stretching horizontally and vertically as needed.
- Auto Size—The sprite's rectangle changes shape to fit the entire member as you rotate, skew, or flip it.
- No Scale—The vector does not scale when the sprite is stretched. This keeps the vector looking the same size, even if it means that the shape is cropped if the sprite is shrunk.

The last setting in the Vector Shape Properties dialog box enables you to scale the cast member. This is independent of any scaling on the Stage. The latter is sprite scaling and affects only each sprite, whereas the former is member scaling and will affect all instances of the member in a sprite.

Note

Unfortunately, you cannot import vectors from other programs such as Freehand and Illustrator. Vectors created with these programs are usually much more complex than vector cast members. Chapter 20, however, teaches you how to import some vector graphics files.

VECTOR SHAPE TECHNIQUES

The number of uses for vector shapes grows every day as developers experiment with this new member type. You can now create everything from little arrows to vector maps. Because they can be rotated and resized on the Stage, a single vector member can be used over and over in different ways. Figure 7.6 shows a single vector shape member that has been used in a variety of ways in different sprites. Some of the sprites are rotated, some are skewed, and others are stretched.

You can use fills to perform a variety of effects. If, for instance, you want to place a gradient over the whole stage as a background, you can make a simple rectangular vector shape, apply a gradient fill, and place it in sprite 1. Figure 7.7 shows this technique. The vector shape editing window shows a small, simple member, and the Stage shows that member in sprite 1, stretched to encompass the whole Stage. With Director 6, you had to create a huge bitmap member to get the same result.

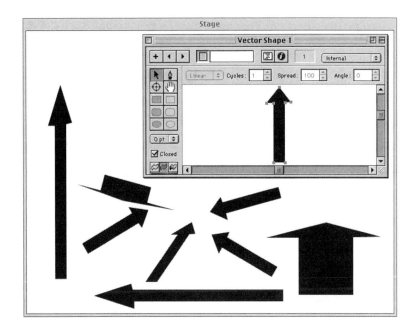

Figure 7.6
The Vector Shape editing window shows a single vector shape member. The Stage shows this member used in a variety of sprites.

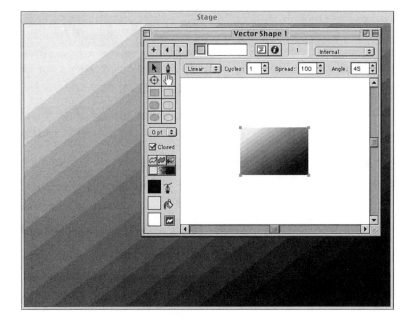

Figure 7.7
A simple vector shape can be used to create a gradient background.

The most powerful thing about this type of background gradient is that you can change your mind about the colors as often as you want. To change the colors, all you have to do is double-click the sprite, which brings up the Vector Shape editing window, and then use the color chips.

PART

II

CH

7

Fills can also be used in creative ways to make the vector shapes seem more complex than just a single curve. Turning the line width to zero is the first step. This "hides" the actual position of the curved line. Instead, only the fill is visible. Figure 7.8 shows such a shape. It actually consists of a single vector line with a fill, but part of the shape is so thin that it doesn't appear.

Figure 7.8
The Vector Shape edit-
ing window shows a
single vector shape,
but one that uses a
very thin area and a
line width of zero to
hide the bridge
between what looks
like two shapes.

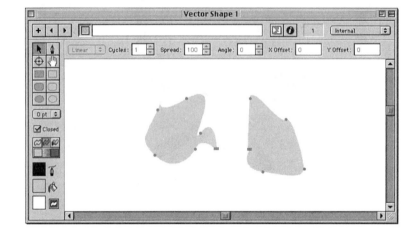

Another technique enables you to create some areas that are filled and others that are not. If you cross a line while drawing the curve in your vector shape, the cross-over area is treated as a non-filled area. Figure 7.9 demonstrates this technique. The star is created by overlapping five lines. The center area is then covered more than once by the area made by the lines. Therefore, the center area is blank, rather than filled.

Figure 7.9
The vector's lines
cross each other and
create an area that is
transparent rather
than filled.

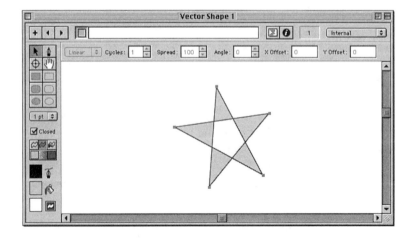

→ **See** "Vector Shape Lingo," Chapter 20, for more information about vector shape properties

FLASH MEMBERS

Another type of vector graphic that needs mentioning is the Flash member. Macromedia Flash is a stand-alone tool for creating vector graphics and animations for Web pages. It uses vectors, rather than bitmaps, to create very small files that can do a lot.

Starting with Director 6.5, developers have had the capability to import Flash members into Director as cast members. A Flash movie can be as simple as a single frame with a vector drawing on it. In this case, you can use them like vector shape members. The advantage is that you can have multiple vector curves showing in one cast member.

Flash movies can also be animations, so you can use Flash members as you use digital video. The movie can play once, loop, or even contain interactivity tools such as simple buttons.

> **Note**
>
> You can also import bitmaps and sounds into Flash movies, but because Director can already use bitmaps and sounds as members, there is little point. However, if you have graphic artists who are used to working in Flash, you can easily import their animations.

Many Lingo commands can also be used to control Flash movies. Chapter 20 will show you how to control Flash movie playback.

→ **See** "Flash Member Lingo," Chapter 20, for more information about Flash member properties

TROUBLESHOOTING VECTOR MEMBERS

- If you make a mistake when you are creating a vector shape member in the editing window, you can just delete the whole thing and start again, rather than try to adjust everything.

- If you are trying to create a very small or very large circle with the vector shape editor, it is better to create a medium-sized one and scale it on the Stage. Small ones, less than 50 pixels in diameter, and large ones, more than 300 pixels in diameter, start to look distorted because they are drawn with just four points. Drawing one about 100 pixels in diameter and then stretching it on the Stage produces a near-perfect circle.

- Remember that there are two types of line shapes: ones that draw from the upper left to lower right and ones that draw from the upper right to lower left. If you use one line member on the Stage and try to make it go in different directions for different sprites, all the sprites that use that line will turn out to be the same type.

PART

II

CH

7

DID YOU KNOW?

- You can change the fill color of a vector shape member as a sprite on the Stage. Just take a filled vector shape, place it on the Stage, and use the foreground color ship in the Tool Palette. You can also tween the fill color over a series of frames. You cannot, however, change the line color.

- You can create an invisible line by turning off the Filled property of a line shape member.

CHAPTER **8**

OTHER MEMBER TYPES

In this chapter

Although the last few chapters have covered the most common cast member types, there are actually many more. In fact, with Xtras, you can keep adding cast member types as long as Macromedia and third parties keep developing more Xtras. This chapter summarizes some of the minor cast member types and their uses.

CREATING PUSHBUTTONS

Director pushbuttons are easy to create and use, but lack a professional appearance, which makes them useless in real-world situations. However, they can be useful for quick prototypes or as placeholders until you get around to making the final buttons.

Figure 8.1 shows a typical pushbutton on the Stage. It is a black-bordered rounded rectangle with some text in it. It is reminiscent of buttons used in Hypercard on the Mac.

Figure 8.1
Examples of Director's standard pushbutton cast member.

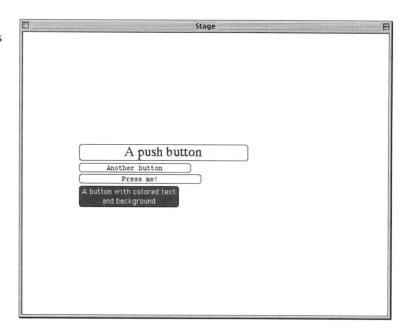

To place a pushbutton on the Stage, use the Tool Palette, select the pushbutton tool, and then draw the pushbutton on the Stage. After you finish, you can adjust the size of the pushbutton by grabbing the corners. You can also double-click and type text into the pushbutton.

You can do a few things to standardize the pushbutton. For one, you can change the font and style of the text inside it. As a matter of fact, if you double-click the member, you can edit it directly on the Stage. If you choose to edit it from the Cast, you do so in an editing window that looks just like the field editing window. You can select any font, style, and even right, left, or center justify the text.

Pushbuttons really are like fields insofar as how they handle text. They use the system's installed fonts, so make sure that any font you use in them is available on all machines that are expected to run the movie. The text is not anti-aliased.

Tip

You can use text members as buttons. In fact, any member can be placed on the Stage and used as a button if the proper behavior is attached. One way you can get a text member to actually look more like a button is to set its background color to something other than white and center the text inside it.

You can customize pushbuttons by setting the foreground and background colors of the text. To do this, you must be editing the text, not just the sprite. Then use the color chips to set the background color of the button and the foreground color of the text.

The behavior of the pushbutton is similar to the behavior of a bitmap member with the Hilite When Clicked option turned on. When the user presses the button, the colors reverse. When the user releases the mouse, the action usually occurs. You can use any standard library behavior that reacts to a mouse click.

→ **See** "A Simple Button Behavior," Chapter 14, "Creating Behaviors," for more information on creating buttons

CREATING CHECK BOXES

If you examine a pushbutton's member properties, you can see that you can change its type. You can examine the properties by selecting the member in the Cast and pressing the Info button. You can choose either a pushbutton, check box, or radio button. All three of these button types are the same cast member, but with different settings. You can choose the other two types from the Tool Palette as well.

The check box is a small square that the user can click to signify a true or false value. You see them all the time in other software programs and even in Director's own dialog boxes.

The check box cast member, however, is like the pushbutton cast member in that it shows a fairly old-fashioned version of a check box that is not used in either Mac or Windows operating systems anymore. Figure 8.2 shows some Director check boxes.

With the pushbutton, it is better to use a series of bitmaps to represent a multiple-state button such as a check box. However, using the built-in check box member provides an ease-of-use benefit. See Chapter 15, "Graphic Interface Elements," for more advanced check boxes that use bitmaps.

→ **See** "Using Check Boxes," Chapter 15, for more information on using check boxes

The check box also uses a text editor similar to that of the field member. Adding a background color, however, is fairly useless because the color wraps around the check box area and you are not offered any option for setting a margin or border.

Figure 8.2
Director's built-in check box member is a bit old-fashioned for today's applications.

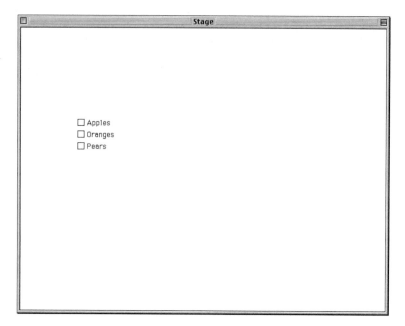

After a check box member is on the Stage as a sprite and the movie is running, you can click it to turn the check on or off. This value is then available for Lingo commands to interpret.

CREATING RADIO BUTTONS

Radio buttons are similar to check boxes. They have some text next to an on-off switch. The visible difference is the type of switch. Whereas check boxes have a box with an *x* in them to signify whether the switch is on or off, radio buttons are circles that have a dot in them to signify whether they are on or off. Figure 8.3 shows some radio buttons on the Stage.

The term *radio button* comes from the old-style car radios that had a row of pushbuttons on the front. If you pressed down one button, the others would automatically pop up. In fact, you could only have one button down at a time. This made sense, because you could listen to only one radio station at a time.

The same is true for computer radio buttons. In any one group of radio buttons, only one should be selected at any time. They are usually used to offer a choice between many options. If you want the user to choose one color from three, for instance, pressing the button for one color immediately turns off any other selection.

For this reason, radio buttons are grouped together. In any one group, only one can be selected at any time. Another rule is that one *must* be selected. So you have to start the user with a default setting.

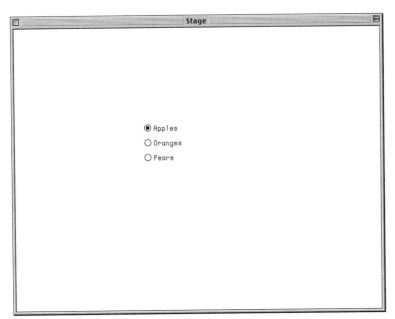

Figure 8.3
Director radio buttons.

You need Lingo to interpret radio button selections, and to make them work properly. Included in the Macromedia Director library is a behavior that enables you to group radio buttons together.

To make this behavior work, first create two or more radio buttons and place them on the Stage. Then drag the behavior to the first radio button. You are then prompted to assign a group name to the button. The group name should be exactly the same for the other buttons you wish to group together. You also need to select the Initially Selected option for exactly one of the radio buttons. Drag the behavior and set the parameters for each of the other buttons.

Now when you run the movie, each of these buttons will control how the others are set. Only one can be selected at a time. You can always add more radio buttons to a group, or start another group on the same frame.

Note

Both radio buttons and check boxes rely on the cast member to determine whether the button is on or off. For this reason, you cannot reuse a cast member, even if it appears exactly the same, in two sprites. Clicking one of the sprites affects any others that use the same member.

Chapter 16, "Controlling Text," goes into how to interpret the results of a radio group with Lingo. You will also learn how to make radio buttons from bitmap members, so that you can customize them in many ways.

→ **See** "Radio Buttons," Chapter 15, for more information in using radio buttons

USING PALETTE MEMBERS

Typically, a palette is a set of 256 colors. Palettes are used in situations where the computer does not have enough power to display the thousands of colors visible to the eye. Instead, the computer is instructed to use 256 colors.

Palettes can also be applied to bitmaps to make them smaller. Rather than having each pixel of a bitmap represent one of thousands or millions of colors, it can represent just one of 256 colors from a palette. This means the image might not look as nice, but it will take up less file space.

If a computer is using a 256-color palette, it must define what those 256 colors are. Macs and Windows machines have a different idea about what these colors should be. The result is two standard palettes: the Mac system palette and the Windows system palette.

Because these palettes were designed for a wide range of uses and are used by the operating systems, they are the most common palettes. They contain a variety of colors that can be used for almost any image.

Another common palette is the Web palette. This palette actually contains only 216 colors. The rest of the color slots are empty. The 216 colors used are found in both the Mac and Windows system palettes. The other 40 colors change depending on the system. This means that a graphic created using the Web palette can be displayed on either system without having to swap out colors. Web browsers are built to handle this special Web palette.

You can also build your own custom palettes. You may want to do this for a variety of reasons. Suppose, for instance, that you are doing a project about Mars. All the images you have use a lot of reds and oranges, but few other colors. The space in the palette used by greens, blues, and other colors are never used. You can make a palette that is mostly reds, giving your images the capability to show a wide range of reds. The other colors are not missed because no images use them.

You can make your own palette in Director. Simply choose Insert, Media Element, Color Palette. This brings up the Color Palette editing window shown in Figure 8.4.

A variety of tools are in this window, some above the color chart and some below. The pop-up menu enables you to select the palette you are working on. All of Director's built-in palettes are displayed, as well as any cast member palettes you have created. If you select a built-in palette and then edit it, Director automatically creates a new cast member with the new palette.

The tools across the top are used to reserve, select, and move colors in the palette. The first button enables you reserve colors. First, select some colors in the palette. Use the Shift key to select multiple consecutive colors and Command on the Mac or Ctrl in Windows to add to the selection. Then press the button to reserve colors. These colors now cannot be used by any bitmaps being converted to this palette. They are reserved for use for things such as color cycling, which you will learn about in Chapter 11, "Advanced Techniques."

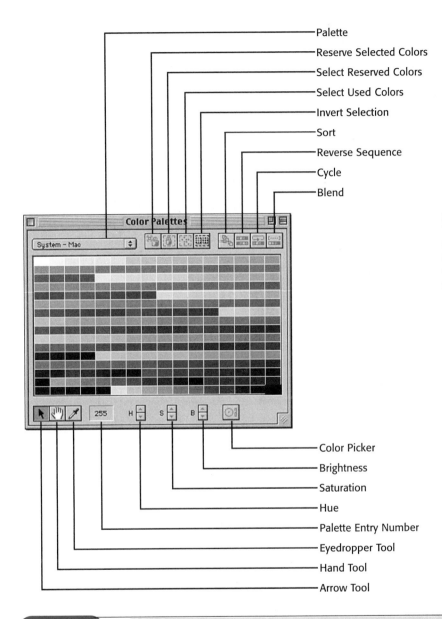

Palette
Reserve Selected Colors
Select Reserved Colors
Select Used Colors
Invert Selection
Sort
Reverse Sequence
Cycle
Blend

Color Picker
Brightness
Saturation
Hue
Palette Entry Number
Eyedropper Tool
Hand Tool
Arrow Tool

Figure 8.4
The Color Palette
editing window
allows you to
examine palettes
or build your own.

Tip

To convert any bitmap to use a palette you create, select the member and choose Modify, Transform Bitmap. You can choose whether you want to dither the colors or re-map them color for color.

Another button, called the Select Used Colors button, on the toolbar enables you to select all the colors used by the currently selected member in the Cast. This member must be set to 8-bit color. This is very useful if you want to alter a palette but do not want to edit any colors used by a certain member. You can also select several members in the Cast and use this button to determine which colors are used by any of the members. This can help you develop new palettes based on which colors are most important.

The Sort, Reverse Sequence, Cycle, and Blend buttons enable you to alter the color values of a series of colors that you have selected. The Sort button sorts them by color. The Reverse Sequence button reverses the color positions. The Cycle button moves them all by one position and places the last color as the first. The Blend button creates a new series of colors based on the first and last color selected.

You can choose from three tools on the lower-left side of the color palette. The first is the standard selection tool. The second, the Hand tool, enables you to drag colors around the chart. The third tool, the eyedropper, enables you to select a color based on where the cursor is located on the Stage. To use the eyedropper, first select it. Then click and hold down on any color in the chart. While holding, drag the cursor over to the Stage. The selection in the color palette then reflects the closest one to the color that the cursor is over.

The rest of the Color Palette editing window enables you to specify the exact color of the selected color. You can either play with the hue, saturation, and brightness of the color, or you can click the color wheel button to bring up your computer system's color options.

Color palettes give you more control over what your movie is doing. Very complex movies can be made without any special color palettes. However, learning how to use them might enable you to do things more easily and make your movies look better.

→ **See** "Developing for Both Mac and Windows," Chapter 35, "Cross-Platform Issues," for more information on developing cross-platform movies

ADDING CURSORS

Three types of custom cursors are available in Director: built-in cursors, custom bitmap cursors, and animated cursors.

BUILT-IN CURSORS

The Director's built-in cursors include the arrow, the hand, the crosshairs, and a clock. The following is a list of some of the most common built-in cast members and their numbers. Use their numbers to refer to them in behaviors that ask for a cursor type.

- 0—Revert to system default
- −1—Arrow cursor
- 1—I-beam cursor
- 2—Thin crosshair cursor
- 3—Thick crossbar cursor
- 4—Watch cursor
- 200—Blank cursor
- 280—Finger cursor

If you are using the "Rollover Cursor Change" behavior from Director's built-in library, you don't even have to remember the number of the cursor. Instead, you can choose from a list of names that the behavior parameters dialog box provides.

CUSTOM BITMAP CURSORS

You can also build your own cursors. The easiest way to do this is to create a single bitmap member that contains a 1-bit image that is no larger than 16 pixels wide and 16 pixels high. Figure 8.5 shows the Paint window with a bitmap member that is destined to be used as a cursor. The zoom is turned on to show detail.

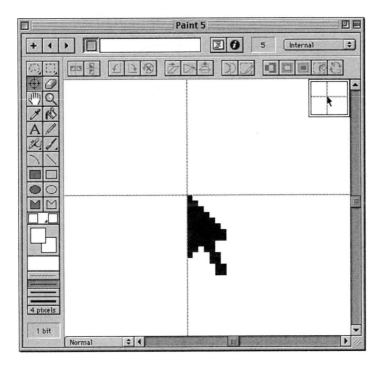

Figure 8.5
The Paint window can be used to create 1-bit bitmaps to be used as custom cursors.

Notice the registration point in Figure 8.5. This point is used to determine the control point of the cursor. Even though cursors can be 16 by 16, only one point (the *control point*) is the actual clicking area. In an arrow cursor, it is usually the tip of the arrow; in a paint bucket cursor it is usually the bottom tip of the falling paint.

You can use cursors such as this in the Rollover Change Pointer behavior of the library. Just select the member as the Custom Image for the effect. Note that you can also provide a *mask image* for the cursor. This is another 1-bit image that shows the cursor where it should be opaque.

ANIMATED CURSORS

A third way to create a custom cursor is to use the special cursor Xtra. Choose Insert, Media Element, Cursor to add one of these cast members to your movie. The Cursor Properties Editor (shown in Figure 8.6) appears.

Figure 8.6
The Cursor Properties Editor dialog box enables you to create color and animated cursors.

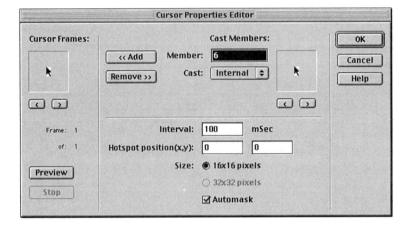

You can add and remove bitmap members from the animated cursor sequence. The members can be in color, not just 1-bit, but they must use 8-bit color. You can add only one bitmap to the cursor if you want it to remain a static cursor. Adding more than one makes the cursor animate between the two or more members that make it up. You can set the interval time between the frames of the animation.

The last option in the Cursor Properties Editor dialog box enables you to determine whether the cursor should use a mask that fits around the cursor just as the matte ink fits around sprites. Turning this off masks the entire cursor rectangle. You cannot make custom masks for animated cursors.

Like the other custom cursor type, you set the control point of the cursor by setting the registration point of the members involved.

→ **See** "Using Cursors," Chapter 21, "Controlling the Director Environment," for more information on using cursors

USING ANIMATED GIFS

Director 7 comes complete with an Xtra that enables you to add animated GIFs as cast members. When you import a file that is in GIF format, Director prompts you as to whether you want to import it as a bitmap or an animated GIF member.

As you can imagine, animated GIF members have a special dialog box (see Figure 8.7) to handle their properties. You can access it by selecting the member in the cast window and pressing the Info button. You then need to press the Options button in the dialog box that appears.

Figure 8.7
The Animated GIF
Asset Properties dialog
box enables you to
determine how an ani-
mated GIF member is
played on the Stage.

You can choose to have the animated GIF file embedded in the Cast, or to have it linked to an external file. You can also choose Direct To Stage for faster playback when you don't need to use special inks.

You have three choices as to how you want the animated GIF to keep pace. The first is for it to use the same tempo that it would if it were presented on the Web. The second is to throw away its built-in tempo information and have it move at a consistent rate that you can define. The third method, Lock Step, ties the $I~animated GIFs>tempo of the GIF to the tempo of the movie.

USING QUICKTIME VR

QuickTime virtual reality (VR) files are often considered another media type. In fact, with QuickTime 3, they are treated in Director just like any other QuickTime media file. The main difference is that the control strip for a QuickTime VR movie has different controls.

There are two types of QuickTime VR. The first is a panoramic image. Here, the user can use the cursor to swing the image left, right, up and down, and enjoy a 360-degree view. You can even zoom in and out of such images. Real-life images must be captured with a special camera and stitched together with special software. Some 3D rendering tools enable you to create modeled panoramic scenes.

The second type of QuickTime VR file is an object file. This is a series of pictures or ren-derings of an object from every direction. Using controls, the user can view the object from any angle.

QuickTime VRs can contain one or more panoramic objects. Quite often, several scenes are combined into one file and linked together with *hotspots* that the user can click on to go from scene to scene. These combined scenes are called QuickTime VR tours.

Before QuickTime 3, you needed a special Xtra and lots of Lingo code to use QuickTime VR files in Director. Now, you can simply import them as QuickTime 3 media and place them on the Stage.

ADDING NEW CAST MEMBER TYPES WITH XTRAS

Xtras enable third-party companies to develop programs that add to the functionality of Director. Sometimes they add new Lingo commands. Other times they add the possibilities for new types of cast members. Many times they add both.

Xtras that enable you to use new types of cast members are called *asset* Xtras. Some of the cast members that you may think are built into Director are actually made possible by asset Xtras that come preinstalled with Director. Examples are QuickTime 3 members, Flash members, cursor members, and even vector shape members.

Other Xtras enable you to add even more types of members. You just need to download or purchase them from the companies that make them and then follow their installation instructions. For instance, the AlphaMania Xtra from Media Lab enables you to import anti-aliased images and perform special effects on them. See Appendix H, "Guide to Xtras," for a listing of where you can find some asset xtras.

TROUBLESHOOTING OTHER MEMBER TYPES

- Because the vertical size of pushbuttons is determined by the type, size, and amount of text in them, the size can differ from platform to platform. Be sure to test these, or use a more advanced type of button such as the ones described in Chapter 15.

- Both radio buttons and check boxes also have text associated with them. Not only can the size of the text differ across platforms, but the text usually doesn't line up with the check box or radio button graphic. Use more advanced radio buttons such as the ones in Chapter 15 for more precise results.

- Custom cursors that refer to members that are not 1-bit do not work. This is the first thing to check if you are having problems. Also, animated cursors need to use 8-bit members.

- Check box and radio button members actually change when you click them while the movie is running. Make sure you reset them all to their starting values before you save the movie.

DID YOU KNOW?

- You can change the background color of a pushbutton by selecting the text in it and then using the background color chip in the Tool Palette. This creates more interesting buttons.

- Even if you are working in 16-, 24-, or 32-bit color, palettes are still useful. If you have a large image of trees, for instance, you can save it from Photoshop as an 8-bit image with an "adaptive" palette. This palette contains the 256 colors that best represent the colors in the image. When you import the image, you will also import that palette in another member. This makes the image more compact in the file, but ensures that it still looks good on the Stage. Plus, you can have many images using many different palettes on the Stage at the same time when you are above 8-bit color.

AUTHORING IN DIRECTOR

CHAPTER 9

THE DIRECTOR ENVIRONMENT

In this chapter

Director is a customizable working environment. This means that there are many ways to display and position windows and many ways that the contents of these windows can look. Understanding all the options is the first step to customizing your work environment. In addition, there are many ways to organize your work. A whole book can be written on the subject, but this chapter presents a brief summary of ways to work.

WAYS TO WORK IN DIRECTOR

If you are creating a small project, one where only you are involved and you expect to finish the work in a few days, it probably doesn't matter how you organize your work. However, if the project will takes months and involve many people with different talents, a systematic approach will help.

Such a system should involve careful planning, documentation, division of labor, a hardware network, and lots of teamwork.

PLANNING YOUR ATTACK

Diving right into a project may work for small programs, but does not work for large projects when more than one person is involved. Sometimes the most important work is done before the first image is generated or the first line of code is written. Planning your strategy can include steps such as creating an outline, determining your specifications, and setting up a schedule.

THE OUTLINE

There are many ways to plan a project. One is to outline. Creating a list of contents and ordering it can reveal the true scope of the project and act as a checklist later on. For a presentation, each line can represent a screen. For an animation, each line can represent a different scene. For larger projects the outline should also represent a hierarchy with small parts of the project organized under larger headings.

The outline doesn't necessarily have to present the project in a linear fashion. It can divide the project up into media types or production deadlines. However, it should include *everything* in the project: art, sounds, code, and the like.

THE FLOWCHART

Similar to an outline, a flowchart is a step closer to describing exactly how the project should work. Arrows and lines define the possible flow of navigation from screen to screen or function to function.

YOUR SPECIFICATIONS

A specification document, or *spec*, tells you exactly what the project should look like when it is finished. If you are working for a client, it is always a good idea to get the client to write up a detailed spec so you know what is expected of you. The same goes for management within your own company. It is best that all parties agree on what the project will be when complete before you start.

THE SCHEDULE

After you know what the project needs to look like when you are finished, the next step is to determine *when* everything needs to be done. You need to think about early steps, such as research, as well as later steps, such as testing. Try to build some extra time into the schedule to allow for unforeseen events or difficulties. Also, consider what would happen if a critical piece of content were not delivered on time by the client or someone outside of your control.

CREATING DOCUMENTATION

After work begins, you need to take into account more than just the work itself. When a task is done, it might not necessarily be *done*. Three months later you may have to go back into your code and change something. If you take the time to document what you are doing while you are doing it, the editing process becomes easier.

Also, take into account that someone else may one day have to open your movie and alter it. If all the markers are named "marker01" and the cast members have names like "a button," it will be very difficult to make changes later.

YOUR NAMING SCHEME

Name your cast members and movies intelligently. There is no excuse for an unnamed cast member. Since Director 7 doesn't work on Windows 3.1, you have no reason to ever use filenames such as cfr99.dir. Use real names like Corporate Financial Report.dir.

Name media files with the same amount of detail. Images, sounds, video, text files, and so on, should all have names that make it obvious what is in the file without requiring you to check inside it. It is a hassle to have to launch PhotoShop just to see whether a file is what you think it is.

You should also come up with a naming convention for all your files. This way, different people will name files in a way that everyone can understand. If your project has chapters and sections, a naming convention could be something like including the chapter and section numbers in the file name: 6-2 golden gate bridge, for example, for a picture of the golden gate bridge in Chapter 6, Section 2.

DOCUMENTS

All users who are responsible for a portion of the project should take the time to document their procedures. For instance, if the person in charge of sounds is running all the sounds through a filter and downsampling them to 22KHz, he should prepare a document that says just that. If someone needs to take over that job or later alter those files, she has everything she needs to know in that document. It could save a temporary employee a few hours of work in the morning; it could help if the person doing the work leaves the position; or if that same person returns to the project after months away from it.

CODE COMMENTS

When writing Lingo code, it is important to comment as much as necessary to make the text readable by another programmer who may come along later. More frequently, you will find, it is important to comment so that *you* remember what a line or handler was supposed to do. That first line of code may seem obvious when you write it, but three months and 100,000 lines of code later, it might look like a foreign language.

To add comments in Lingo, just use a double dash, "--". You can place a comment on a line by itself, or on the same line as code by using the double dash to signify that everything on that line that follows it is a comment.

DIVISION OF LABOR

If more than one person is on your team it will be very important to decide who does what *before* anyone starts working. The biggest mistake is letting one person do too much. That step can become a bottleneck and others can waste time waiting for the overworked individual to finish his or her job.

Are all team members doing things suited to their skill sets? Are they all enthusiastic about what they are doing? Does anyone have too much to do, or feel that way? Too little? It is important to address all these issues up front and continually as the project progresses.

HARDWARE NETWORK

An integral part of the work environment for multimedia production is the hardware network. What computers are people using? Are peripherals such as scanners and printers accessible by the people who will need them? Do all team members have the types of computers that they need?

Look at your equipment and determine whether you have everything you need to finish the job. If you are developing a cross-platform project, do you have both Mac and Windows machines available to use for creation and testing? How will people working together share files: a network, the Internet, swapping disks?

Software is also a very important part of the network. Do the team members have what they need to complete their work? How about what they need to do a really good job and beat the competition?

TEAMWORK

The underlying theme for any team project should be teamwork. If people are not working well together, their efforts will cancel each other, work will suffer, and deadlines will be missed.

Consider the structure of the project. Is there a clear project leader? Who has the final say over decisions? Who runs the project from day to day? Do these responsibilities belong to the same person? If not, how do these people work together?

SETTING PREFERENCES

After all the organizational details of a project have been decided, you can get down to work. If your job is working in Director 7 all day, you're the lucky one. Now you just have to organize your working environment.

Director has several preference dialog boxes that you can use to change the Director environment. There are no correct or incorrect ways to set these preferences; it is all a matter of personal taste. The best approach is experimentation to find what suits you best.

GENERAL PREFERENCES

You can bring up most of the preferences dialog boxes by choosing File, Preferences, and then the appropriate category. The General Preferences dialog box is shown in Figure 9.1. It contains some settings similar to those seen when creating a projector.

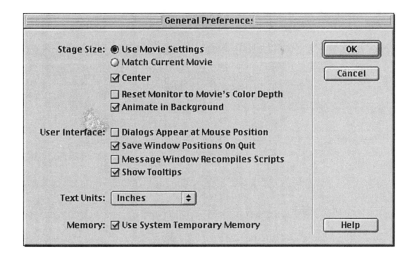

Figure 9.1
The General Preferences dialog box enables you to specify a few general options. Some options are not necessary in Windows.

The first set of options has to do with the Stage size and position. You can set it to either use the settings of each movie that is opened, or match only the current movie. You can have it automatically center when a new movie is opened and force the monitor to change color depths for each movie. You can also tell Director to keep playing the movie even when Director is not the frontmost application with the Animation in Background option.

You have four user interface options:

- Dialogs Appear at Mouse Position—Determines whether dialog boxes appear at the mouse position or centered on the monitor.

- Save Window Positions On Quit—Tells Director to remember the window positions when you quit, so that when you return to Director the next time, they are in the same places.

- Message Window Recompiles Scripts—Automatically recompiles all scripts when you enter something in the message window. Although it makes sense to always do this, if you are working on a movie that is filled with errors, you cannot use the message window for much until you fix the errors.

- Show Tooltips—Turns on or off tooltips. Tooltips are the little yellow boxes that appear as you hover the mouse over buttons in the interface. They can be useful, but you may find them annoying.

The General Preferences dialog box also enables you to set the ruler measurement for windows that use a ruler. You can select inches, centimeters, or pixels.

The last option (Memory) enables Mac users to tell Director to use memory outside its normal memory block. It doesn't work with virtual memory turned on, however.

NETWORK PREFERENCES

The Network Preferences dialog box enables you to set the network preferences for Director. Figure 9.2 shows this dialog box. It has settings similar to those found in a Web browser.

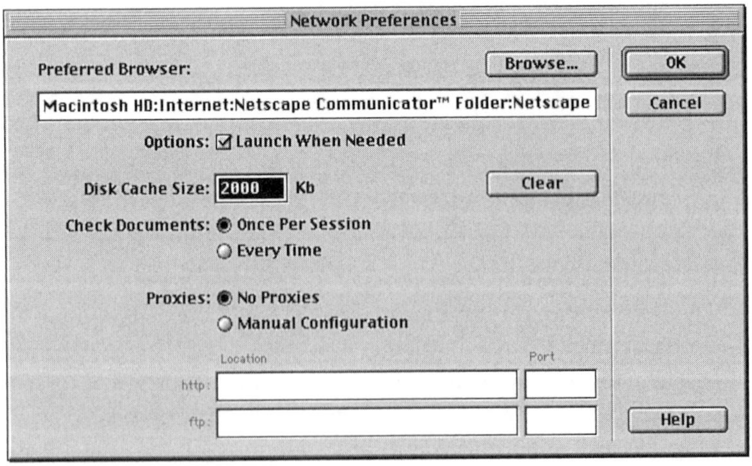

Figure 9.2
The Network Preferences dialog box enables you to set the default browser and cache options.

The first option sets the default browser used by Director. Primarily, this comes into play only when you use a gotoNetPage Lingo command. It is also used when you choose File, Preview In Browser to check how your movie works in Shockwave.

You can also define the size of the disk cache. Like browsers, Director movies can access files from the Internet and store them in a cache for later retrieval. You can set Director to check the file on the Internet for new versions every time or only once per session. Choosing once per session, which I recommend, means that if a document on the Internet is updated after you access it once, you may get the older copy of it when accessing it the second time during the same session.

For those who have to work inside a firewall of some sort, the rest of the options enable you to set proxies to get files through the firewall. Consult your network administrator about these settings if you need them.

EDITORS PREFERENCES

If you double-click a bitmap member, it brings up the Paint window to enable you to edit the bitmap. However, you can have it launch PhotoShop instead by associating bitmaps with PhotoShop. You can edit that member in PhotoShop and then save the changes back into the cast member.

The Editors Preferences dialog box, shown in Figure 9.3, enables you to select different editors for different cast types. You can access this dialog box by choosing File, Preferences, Editors. You can also choose some options for some Director-only member data.

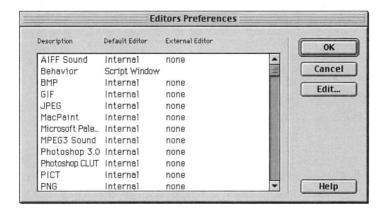

Figure 9.3
The Editors Preferences dialog box enables you to choose external editors for some cast member types.

For example, a common setting is to use SoundEdit 16 to handle sound members. You can point Director to your copy of that application using this window. Then, when you double-click a sound member, you will launch SoundEdit 16.

Certain member types have special settings. Behaviors, for instance, enable you to pick between opening the behavior inspector or the script window.

You can even tell Director to scan your computer for applications that can be used to edit a type of file. You will be presented with a list and asked to choose your preferred editor.

SCRIPT WINDOW PREFERENCES

The last preference dialog box listed in the File menu enables you to set a few options for the script editing window. Figure 9.4 shows the Script Window Preferences dialog box.

Figure 9.4
The primary use of the Script Window Preferences dialog box is to control coloring.

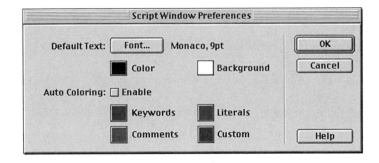

With the first option you pick a default font for the script window. You are still able to change the font of any script; this option just establishes the font to be used when a new script is created.

The rest of the settings are for script colorization. Director 7 automatically colors your scripts to make them easier to read. These settings determine what colors you want Director to use. You can also turn this option off and color the scripts on your own.

MOVIE PROPERTIES

The Movie Properties dialog box can be reached by choosing Modify, Movie, Properties. The settings here affect only the current movie. Figure 9.5 shows this dialog box.

The first group of settings lets you to change the size and location of the Stage. You can also set the background color of the Stage.

The color selection option is very important. If you select RGB, the movie does not use a specific color palette, but instead displays with thousands or millions of colors. A selection of Palette Index, however, enables you to specify a default movie palette. These settings affect mostly Lingo commands that need to specify color numbers.

The Remap Palettes When Needed setting enables Director to display a bitmap image on the Stage with the best possible colors even when the bitmap's palette and the Stage's palette are different.

The Maintain Outdated Ink Mode Limitations option makes the sprite inks work exactly as they did in Director 6. The difference is that some inks that ignored blend numbers in Director 6 obey those numbers in Director 7. If you are converting a Director 6 movie that used blends with inks that didn't recognize them, the sprites may now look different.

You can also set the number of Score channels that are used in the movie. You can go up to 1000 channels, but a smaller number gives you better performance. Unless you really need it, keep the number of sprites to 120 channels.

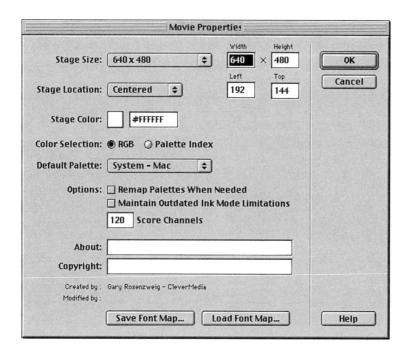

PART

III

CH

9

Figure 9.5
In the Movie Properties dialog box you can change the size, location, and color of the Stage.

You can use the last two options to set an information message and a copyright line in the Director movie. This will be embedded in the file and seen by people looking for more information about the movie from within some playback methods. The Created by and Modified by options are set by Director according to the registration of the Director application.

The buttons at the bottom of the dialog box enable you to define a font map for the movie. A *font map* is a small text file that you can save out from this dialog box and edit. After it is edited, it can be re-imported into the movie with this same dialog box.

The font map was once very important. It tells Director, Shockwave, or a projector, exactly how to deal with fonts when the movie is played back on a different platform: Mac or Windows. The file is well-commented and easy to edit. It is no longer very important because text members can use fonts that are embedded into the movie as cast members.

→ **See** "Developing for Both Mac and Windows," Chapter 35, "Cross-Platform Issues," for more information on developing cross-platform movies

MOVIE PLAYBACK PROPERTIES

The Movie Playback Properties dialog box, shown in Figure 9.6, offers even more movie settings.

The first setting, Lock Frame Durations, enables the movie to remember the speed at which it played back on your machine. Every frame that is played remembers how long it was on the screen. When the movie is on another computer, it plays back at the same speed, no matter how much the speed may differ from frame to frame. This setting enables you to prevent faster computers from playing your movie back too fast, but it does not enable your movie to gain any extra speed on slower machines.

Figure 9.6
The Movie Playback Properties dialog box gives you control over streaming and Shockwave menu settings of a movie.

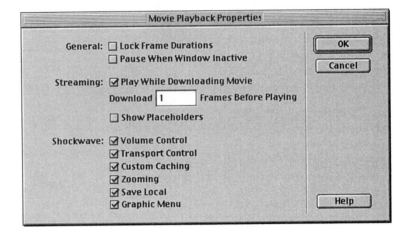

The next setting, Pause When Window Inactive, determines whether the movie keeps playing when it is a movie in a window (MIAW) and it is not the frontmost MIAW. A MIAW is a Director movie that is run in a separate window rather than the Stage. You can read more about them in Chapter 24, "Movies in a Window and Alternatives."

The next set of options has to do with streaming movies over the Internet. The first option (Play While Downloading Movie) enables streaming. The second option (Download X Frames Before Playing) enables the machine to download a specified number of frames before the movie begins playing. The last option (Show placeholders) enables you to show placeholders, usually boxes, in place of media that has not yet been loaded. When the graphics arrive, the boxes will be replaced with them.

The last set of options has to do with Shockwave playback. A future version of the Shockwave player might allow users to adjust the volume, zoom, and cache settings for a movie. Users might even be able to download and save a local copy of the movie on their hard drives. You can enable or disable any of these options with the settings here. If you disable them, the user will not be allowed to control those aspects of the movie.

SHOCKWAVE FOR AUDIO SETTINGS

The Shockwave for Audio Settings dialog box, shown in Figure 9.7, is often overlooked, but is very important. It enables you to turn on sound compression for internal sound members. You can specify the bit rate and quality. You can access this dialog box by choosing Xtras, Shockwave for Audio Settings.

It is very common to forget about the settings in this dialog box. Check it before you make a Shockwave movie or a Projector. Otherwise, your sounds will be compressed according to the preferences that you chose the last time, which may not be the ones you want now.

Figure 9.7
The Shockwave for Audio Settings dialog box enables you to set the compression rate for internal sounds.

PART

III

CH

9

MEMORY INSPECTOR

Although not really a settings dialog box, the Memory Inspector is an important part of the Director environment. Choose Window, Inspectors, Memory to bring it up. You can take a look at it in Figure 9.8. It tells you how much memory each part of Director is using and enables you to purge memory when things are tight.

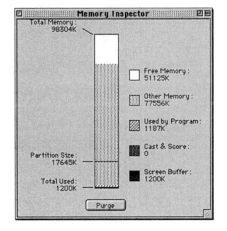

Figure 9.8
The Mac version of the Memory Inspector, shown here, looks different than the Windows version.

Although purging memory when there are problems might seem like just what you need, in practice only quitting and restarting Director really gets you back to square one.

→ **See** "Making Projectors," Chapter 36, "Delivering the Goods," for more information on movie settings

USING THE DIRECTOR LIBRARY

New to Director 7 is the library. It is a folder in your Director folder named *Libs*. In it are cast files that contain behaviors and other media. You can drag items from the library into your current movie or Cast.

Although Director comes with a nice selection of behaviors in the library, you can add and edit Casts in the folder to include your own behaviors or media. A collection of commonly used graphics or sounds can make a fine library. In addition, you may be able to download or purchase third-party library files that enable you to use new behaviors or media.

To add a library, just place the library file, which is really just a plain external cast file, in the Libs folder of your Director folder. That library then becomes available in the Library palette. You can access your libraries by choosing Window, Library Palette.

→ **See** "Behavior Libraries," Chapter 26, "Developing for Developers," for more information on using the behavior library

Using Xtras

Like the library, Xtras have their own special folder named *Xtras*. Xtras add functionality to Director, such as a new type of cast member or some new Lingo commands.

A large number of Xtras already come with Director, but even more can be added. To add one, follow that Xtra's installation instructions. Installation usually results in the Xtra just being placed in the Xtras folder.

The following list includes some Xtras that are most likely to be included with Director 7 in its final release:

■ Photocaster—This Xtra enables you to import a single layer of a Photoshop document rather than the entire image. If you buy the full version, you can actually import all the layers of the document with matching registration points.

■ Print-o-Matic Lite—The lite version of Print-o-Matic enables you to print out text or many types of cast members, such as bitmaps. You can bring up the Page Setup and Print dialog boxes and specify a lot of print options.

■ Beatnik Lite—Plays specially formatted music files.

■ Flash Asset—Enables you to include whole Macromedia Flash movies as single cast members in Director.

■ PowerPoint Importer—You can import Microsoft PowerPoint presentations. This Xtra places all the elements into the Cast and builds a Score that resembles the original presentation.

■ Save As Java—You can export some of your Director movies to cross-platform Java applets.

→ **See** Chapter 25, "Xtras," for more information about using Xtras

Getting Help

Director comes with a full-featured online help application. Although the manuals and this book contain just about everything you need to know, sometimes the online help is the quickest way to find out the details of a feature. You will find the Director help files to be informative and comprehensive.

To access help, use the Help menu. Or, on most computers, you can press Alt+H.

In addition, a lot of information is available at Macromedia's Web site (http://www.macro-media.com). It has a Tech Notes section that includes a variety of helpful tips and tricks. When you are having a problem and you think, "I bet I'm not the first one to run into this!," check the Tech Notes. They are compiled by Macromedia tech support from common and interesting support calls.

Also, many other Web sites offer information, tips, and developer forums. See Appendix C, "Online Resources," for more information and a list of places to start.

TROUBLESHOOTING THE DIRECTOR ENVIRONMENT

- Some preferences, such as cast window thumbnail sizes, do not persist across movies. If you change this preference, and then open an old movie, the cast window reflects the preferences set for that movie.

- If you get an error when you start Director that claims a duplicate Xtra is in the Xtras folder, the only way to determine which Xtra is a duplicate is to make an educated guess. If you don't find two of the same name, it might be two of similar names, such as "sound xtra" and "sounds xtra." You may have to use trial and error to find the culprit.

- When you use an item from the library, a copy is made and placed in your current Cast. If you need to use that item again, use the version from your Cast, not the library, to avoid a chance that a second instance of the library item might be added. This is especially true if you change the library item once it is in your Cast. Even if you change the name of the item, Director does not recognize that the item already exists in your Cast.

DID YOU KNOW?

- If you ever want to reset your preferences to the default settings, and you are using a Mac, just throw away the "Director 7.0 Preferences" file in the Preferences folder in your system folder. In the past, this has been the only way to retrieve a window that is lost from sight.

- You can also set the font type, size, and style of text in the Message window. This is not a preference, but you can select the text in the Message window and change it. New text placed in the Message window picks up the font used where the cursor in the Message window is located.

- You can place any cast library in the Libs folder to create a library. It can include members of any type, including scripts, bitmaps, sounds, and so on.

- Mac users can also set how much memory is available in Director. Select the Director application in the Finder and Choose File, Get Info. Under the Memory category, you can set the Preferred Size much larger. I prefer at least 20MB. This helps when you are working with large images or importing many images at a time.

CHAPTER **10**

PROPERTIES OF SPRITES AND FRAMES

In this chapter

Simple animations and presentations can be created with plain sprites and ordinary frames. However, a large number of special settings can do everything from changing the speed of the movie to the color of a bitmap. Some of these properties are part of the special channels in the Score. Other properties are applied directly to individual sprites. This chapter covers all these types of settings.

FRAME TEMPO

The special tempo channel in the Score enables you to control the forward flow of the movie. All settings are performed through the Frame Properties: Tempo dialog box shown in Figure 10.1. To access it, just double-click the tempo channel in the Score.

Figure 10.1
The Tempo settings dialog box is the only place to control the tempo channel in the Score.

The Tempo button determines how long the movie waits on a frame. You can set this to one of four different options. The first is the most common, and causes the movie to wait for a fraction of a second on a frame.

This standard tempo is measured in frames per second (fps). You can set the movie to run from one to 999 frames per second. The movie attempts to run at this speed, but is restricted by the speed of the computer on which it is running. Director displays every single frame, never skipping any. So if a frame contains a lot of graphic changes, and the computer takes a full half a second to draw it, the relative fps will be 2fps, even if you are set to run at 15fps.

The Wait button enables you to have the frame *wait* for between 1 and 60 seconds. This is sort of an extension of the last option. Rates such as these are too slow for real animation. However, for an automatic slide show that changes images every few seconds, this is perfect. It is also commonly used at the end of an animation to pause the movie on the last frame for a few seconds before continuing to whatever is next.

The Wait for Mouse Click or Key Press button was discussed in Chapter 2, "Presentations with Director." It pauses the frame until the mouse is clicked or the keyboard is used. This is a simple, non-behavior and non-Lingo way to make presentations.

Note

> The Wait for Mouse Click or Key Press option does not currently work with Shockwave movies. Use behaviors instead.

The Wait for Cue Point setting ties the tempo of the movie to a sound or QuickTime sprite. You can make the movie wait on a frame until a point in the sound is reached. To use it, you need to have one of these two sprites in the Score on that frame. The names of all the channels with cue points appears in the Channel pop-up menu. Select which one you want to use. Then select the cue point in the next pop-up.

In addition to sounds and QuickTime sprites, you always have the standard {Next} and {End} choices. They enable you to have the frame end when the next cue point is hit, or when the sound or video is done playing.

The {End} choice is very useful, because you can have any frame wait until a sound or video clip is done playing. Chapter 5, "Sound Members," has information about how to add cue points to sounds.

→ **See** "Waiting for Sounds and Cue Points," Chapter 5, for more information on sound cue points

FRAME PALETTES

Under the tempo channel is the palette channel. This enables you to set the palette for each frame in a movie. To access the Frame Palette dialog box, double-click the palette channel in the Score. Whereas some developers can go their whole lives without this feature, others use it constantly.

Suppose that you are making an educational CD-ROM about the planets in our solar system. You want to display the best possible images of each planet, but the movie must run on machines that use 256-color monitors. You can display a very nice image of Mars by using a palette with lots of reds. However, an image of Saturn should have lots of yellows. You can make custom palettes for each of these and then display them in frames that use these palettes. The palette should be assigned both the bitmap and the frame it is on.

When you use multiple palettes in a movie, one of the problems you are faced with is how to switch between them. Performing a simple switch shows only one or more images in the old palette before switching to the new one. It looks like a screen flash.

The simple solution is to go to a frame that is all black or all white before switching palettes. Because all palettes contain both black and white, the screen will not appear to change. Then, you can go to the new frame knowing that the movie has already switched palettes. The Frame Properties: Palette dialog box, shown in Figure 10.2, enables you to perform even more complex palette transitions.

Figure 10.2
The Frame Properties dialog box for palettes is reached by double-clicking the palette channel in the Score.

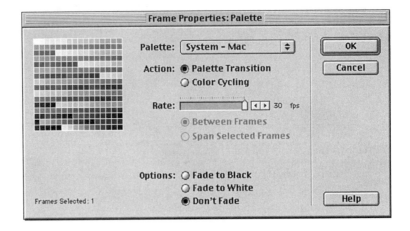

You can choose three types of transitions: one that gradually takes the movie from one palette to another, one that fades to black between changes and one that fades to white between changes. You can choose which option you prefer at the bottom of the dialog box. To choose any of them you must have the Palette Transition button selected. "Color Cycling" is another palette technique that you will learn about in the next chapter.

→ **See** "Color Cycling," Chapter 11, "Advanced Techniques," for more information on color cycling

Using the fade option turns the entire monitor black or white, even the area outside the Stage. The actual palette change takes place as soon as the screen is completely blank. You can control the speed of the fade with the rate setting in the dialog box.

Note
Palette changes and transitions have no real effect when the monitor is set to thousands or millions of colors. In that case, the computer is not using palettes at all. Therefore, make sure the playback monitor is set to 256 colors before you begin your presentation or your palette transitions will not appear.

If you choose the "Don't Fade" option, one palette transitions into the other. You can also use the rate setting to control the speed of this change. If you select "Between Frames," the movie pauses between the last frame and the first frame with the new palette. During this pause, the palette transition occurs. Every color gradually changes to the new color used in that position in the palette. If you select Span Selected Frames, you can actually have this transition occur while the movie is going forward and sprites are animating.

→ **See** "Types of Bitmaps," Chapter 3, "Bitmap Members," for more information on color palettes

FRAME TRANSITIONS

Frame transitions are effects that help usher in a new frame. When placed in the transitions frame channel, they control the change from the preceding frame to the current one.

Figure 10.3 shows the Frame Properties: Transition dialog box. Most of it is used to select the type of transition. You can also control the duration, smoothness, and changing area of a transition.

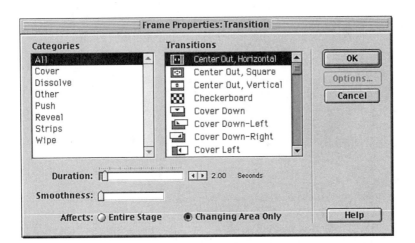

Figure 10.3
The Frame Properties dialog box for transitions comes up when you double-click the transitions channel in the Score.

Seven transition categories are listed. If you were to add an Xtra that adds some new transitions, those categories would appear as well. Selecting All in the Categories list on the left shows all the available transitions in the Transitions list on the right.

Not all the transitions enable you to set the duration, smoothness, and change area. For those that do, the duration setting is self-explanatory. Note that a transition might actually take longer to complete than the set time if the computer is having trouble making it happen.

Note

Setting a transition on a frame that loops is a bad idea. The transition will occur every time the frame loops, even if this does not make a visible change after the first time. The result will be sluggish performance and maybe a blinking cursor.

The Smoothness setting can be used to help in situations where the transition is taking too long to complete. Moving the smoothness slider to the right makes the steps in the transition more dramatic. Keeping the slider all the way to the left ensures that the transition uses the smallest steps possible. You should move the slider as far left as possible while ensuring that the transition is still occurring quickly enough for you.

The Affects radio buttons at the bottom of the transition properties dialog box enable you to decide whether the transition affects the whole Stage or just the changing area. It really makes no difference for dissolve-like transitions. However, for any transition that actually *moves* images around the Stage, such as the Push category, it matters. If you have changed only one area of the Stage between frames and use a Push transition with Changing Area Only turned on, the push will happen only in that rectangle of the Stage that was changed. Figure 10.4 shows a Stage in mid-transition that uses this technique.

Figure 10.4
The Stage is in the middle of a transition using a Push Down. Because Changing Area Only is selected in the Transitions Properties dialog box , only the changing area exhibits the transition.

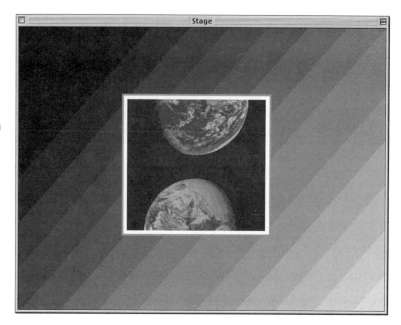

After you have set a transition in the Score, Director creates a transition cast member in the Cast. You can access the properties of this transition through the Score again, or by double-clicking the cast member. Any changes will be applied to the member, which will in turn affect how the transition plays in the Score.

You can create a new cast member for every frame transition by double-clicking in empty transition channel cells in the Score. Or, you can reuse transitions by dragging the member from the Cast onto the Score, or by copying and pasting it around in the Score. If you use a transition member in more than one place in the Score, remember that the transition in each frame is affected by any changes to that one cast member.

This can be a great time-saving technique. If you use a certain transition in several places in the Score, having it as one member enables you to adjust the duration, smoothness, and even the transition type itself in one place and have it affect the whole movie.

→ **See** "The Score," Chapter 1, "Animation with Director," for more information on the Score

→ **See** "Advanced Presentations," Chapter 2, "Presentations with Director," for more information on transitions

SPRITE INKS

Any sprite is drawn on the Stage according to the rules set by the sprite's ink. The ink takes into account the image itself, often the Any sprite is drawn on the Stage according to the rules set by the sprite's ink. images and Stage color behind it, and sometimes the sprite's foreground and background colors.

The most common inks are Copy, Matte, and Background Transparent. Anything else can be considered a special effect. However, sometimes a special effect is just what you need to make things work the way you want them to.

You can set the ink of a sprite in many ways. The Score and Sprite Inspector windows have pop-ups for setting inks. You can also Command+Click the Mac or Ctrl+Click in Windows directly on the Stage to bring up an instant pop-up menu.

The following list includes descriptions of all the inks. The last two inks, Darken and Lighten, are new to Director 7:

- Copy—Displays the cast member as is. The rectangular bounding box of the image appears as white.

- Matte—Sets the white pixels within a bounding box of a sprite to transparent.

- Background Transparent—Sets all the white pixels within an image to transparent.

- Transparent—Makes all the colors in a sprite transparent.

- Reverse—Reverses all color in the sprite, and sets white pixels to transparent.

- Ghost—Changes black to white and white to transparent. Works best on 1-bit cast members.

- Not Inks—These ink effects are based on the immediately preceding four ink effects. First, a reverse effect is applied to all colors in the sprite and then the Copy, Transparent, Reverse, or Ghost ink effect (previously mentioned) is reapplied to the selected sprite.

- Mask—Uses the next cast member in the cast window to block or unblock background colors. Rules for a Mask are as follows: must be the same size as the masked cast member, must be the next cast member position in the cast window, and must be 1-bit.

- Blend—Applies a blend to the sprite. The amount used in the blend is set in Sprite Properties from the Modify menu or in the Score or Sprite Inspector.

- Darkest—Compares pixels of the foreground and background colors. The Darkest ink effect displays only the darkest pixel found in the background and foreground colors.

- Lightest—Compares pixels in the foreground and background colors. The Lightest ink effect displays only the lightest pixel found in the background and foreground colors.

- Add—Creates a new color. The values of the background and foreground colors are added to one another. The sprite displays the combined values. If the color value exceeds the maximum visible color, the color wraps around the color scale.

- Add Pin—The same as Add with the exception that if the color value exceeds the maximum visible color, the maximum color is used.

- Subtract—The opposite of Add with the exception that the minimum values are used. If the new value is less than the minimum visible color, the color wraps around the color scale from the top.

- Subtract Pin—The same as Subtract with the exception that if the color value is less than the minimum visible color, the minimum color is used.

- Darken—Takes the background color and uses it like a color filter. The foreground color is applied to the sprite as if you were shining a light of that color on it.
- Lighten—The background color changes the brightness of the sprite: lighter colors make the sprite darker. The foreground color is applied to the sprite as if you were shining a light of that color on it.

The real power of inks can only be appreciated by experimentation. Figure 10.5, for instance, shows a creative use of the lightest ink. In this example, a member is placed on the Stage in two places. The sprite to the left uses Copy ink. The sprite on the right uses Lightest ink. Under the sprite on the right is a black circle. Because the image is lighter than the black circle, it shows over it. However, the rest of the image is over only the white Stage, which is lighter than the sprite.

Figure 10.5
A member is placed on the Stage in two places.

→ **See** "Controlling Sprite Properties," Chapter 13, "Essential Lingo Syntax," for more information on using inks

SPRITE BLEND

In addition to inks, you can use blends to modify the appearance of a sprite. Blends enable you to mix the sprite with whatever is behind it. You control the percent of the blend, with 100% being totally opaque.

To use blends, you should set the ink of the sprite to Blend. Director enables you to use other inks, but the use of Blend overrides them. The Blend ink is similar to Matte in that Director creates a mask to fit the shape of the image. You can also use Copy ink if you want no mask, or use Background Transparent ink if you want all the white pixels to be transparent. Both these inks work as expected in addition to having the blend.

One effective use of blends is to take images and use them in both the normal way and as background images. You can do this by taking the image and stretching it to the size of the Stage, while at the same time reducing its blend to somewhere around 50%. Figure 10.6 shows this type of effect.

Figure 10.6
Two sprites are used to show the same image. One is stretched and faded with a blend.

The Stage in Figure 10.6 shows two sprites. The first one is selected and then stretched on the Stage to cover the whole Stage area. Then its ink is set to Blend. Finally, the blend of that sprite is set to 50 percent. Both the ink and blend settings can be controlled in the Score or the Sprite Inspector. The second sprite is at normal size with Copy ink.

→ **See** "Controlling Sprite Properties," Chapter 13, for more information on using blends

SPRITE COLOR

You can also set the foreground and background colors of your sprites. You can change these by selecting the color chips in the Score window, Sprite Inspector, or Tool Palette. The defaults are to have the foreground black and the background white.

By changing the colors of sprite, you ask Director to perform a type of tint. Changing the foreground color causes all pixels to be tinted to that color, except for black. All back pixels simply become that color. With the background color, all pixels are tinted except for white, which then becomes that color.

One way to use this color is to set 1-bit bitmap colors. Because 1-bit bitmaps contain only black and white pixels, you are essentially changing the two colors from black and white to whatever you want. The display of the sprite also depends on the ink used.

Figure 10.7 shows three sprites that use the same member. All three sprites are 1-bit bitmaps that have their foreground color set to black and their background color set to gray.

The first sprite is using the Copy ink, so all pixels within the rectangle are affected. The second sprite uses the Matte ink, so all pixels within the automatically generated mask are affected and the rest are transparent. The last sprite uses a Background Transparent ink, so only the foreground pixels are shown, and the rest are transparent.

Figure 10.7
The three sprites are 1-bit members with a gray background color and three different inks.

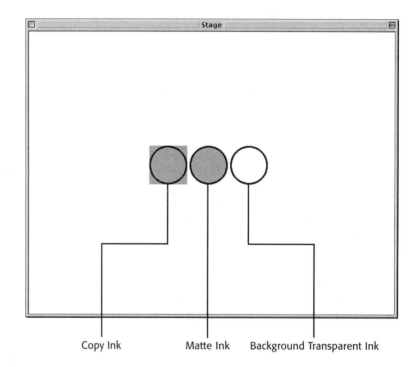

Copy Ink   Matte Ink   Background Transparent Ink

→ **See** "Controlling Sprite Properties," Chapter 13, for more information on altering sprite colors

SPRITE SHAPE

In addition to changing the appearance and color of pixels in a sprite, you can also distort the sprite in a variety of ways. You can stretch, shrink, rotate, and skew many types of sprites.

To stretch a sprite, select it on the Stage and pull one of the four corners or four sides. You can make the sprite wider or taller, or hold down the Shift key and drag one of the corners to maintain proportions. You can always reset the sprite by choosing Modify, Sprite, Properties, and clicking the Restore button.

Tip

You can also set the rectangle of a sprite through the number fields at the top of the Score or in the Sprite Inspector.

Sprites can be resized over time with the same tweening techniques used in Chapter 1, "Animation with Director." You can reuse cast members for sprites that need the same image, but at a different size.

→ **See** "Animating with the Cast, Stage, and Score," Chapter 1, for more information on stretching sprites

You can also rotate bitmap sprites. Choose the Rotate tool in the tool palette and then click and drag a sprite to pull it around its registration point. Some member types, such as fields and simple shapes, cannot be rotated.

Tip

You can also set the rotation of a sprite, a group of sprites, or a single frame in a sprite animation with the toolbar at the top of the Score or with the Sprite Inspector.

Figure 10.8 shows two sprites that use the same cast member, but one is presented normally, whereas the other is rotated.

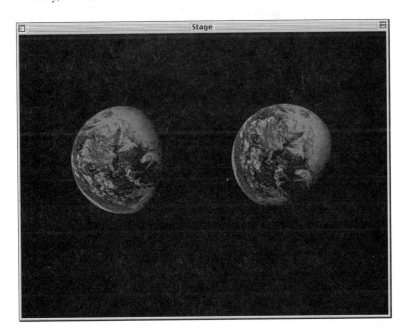

Stage

Figure 10.8
Both sprites use the same cast member, but the second has been rotated.

You can also rotate with tweening. You can have a sprite that rotates a full 360 degrees. The result is that the sprite spins around its registration point.

You can also use the rotation tool to grab the sides of sprites to skew them. You can pull one side of the sprite rectangle independent of the other three sizes. Figure 10.9 shows the same sprite skewed in a number of ways.

Figure 10.9
A single member is
used in several sprites
with different skewing.

While you are using the rotate tool, you can also pull on the four corners or four sides. You can use this method to stretch the sprite just as you can with the selection tool, but you can go even further. If you pull the left side of the sprite past the right side of the sprite with the rotation tool, the new image is shown flipped. The same is true for all four sides, in fact.

Flipping can be accomplished this way, or by simply using the Flip buttons in the toolbar portion of the Score or in the Sprite Inspector. With flipping, you can cut down on the number of images you need at times. For instance, if you want to have a spaceship in a game fly both left and right, you can use a "fly right" member for flying right and then flip that member horizontally to show it flying left.

Figure 10.10 brings together the concepts of flipping and rotating to create a whole series of sprites. All these sprites use just one cast member. With earlier versions of Director, you would have had to create a separate cast member of each image.

→ **See** "Distorting Sprites," Chapter 18, "Controlling Bitmaps," for more information on rotating sprites

Figure 10.10
A single member is used to create a variety of sprites through sprite flipping, rotation, and skewing.

OTHER SPRITE PROPERTIES

Several other sprite properties are used to control how a sprite looks or acts. You can find them all at the top right side of the Score window.

EDITABLE PROPERTY

This property determines whether a text or field member can be edited by the user. Both types of members also have a cast member property of the same name.

If you turn on the Editable property for the members, they are editable even if the sprite property is not switched on. Otherwise, you can make a non-editable sprite editable in the Score with this switch.

The sprite property enables you to make a field or text member editable in some instances and not others. If you ask the users to enter their names at the start of a movie, you can still display that field later without worrying about them editing it.

MOVEABLE PROPERTY

The Moveable property "unlocks" the sprite from the position recorded in the Score, and enables the user to click and drag it anywhere on the Stage. You can add interactivity to the movie this way without programming a line of Lingo.

The behavior library includes some behaviors that enable you to do similar, but more complex, functions. In truth, it is better to use Lingo or library behaviors rather than the moveable property. The latter provides only limited functionality. Lingo, however, enables you to control when and where the sprite is moveable and also enables you to relate that movement to other sprites.

TRAILS PROPERTY

Not all visible elements on the Stage have to be sprites. With the Trails option turned on, the sprite leaves a copy of itself on the Stage wherever it is placed. To demonstrate, use both the Trails and Moveable property at the same time. As you drag the sprite around the Stage, it leaves a visible trail. Figure 10.11 demonstrates this property.

Figure 10.11
You can use the Moveable and Trails properties together to enable someone to draw on the Stage.

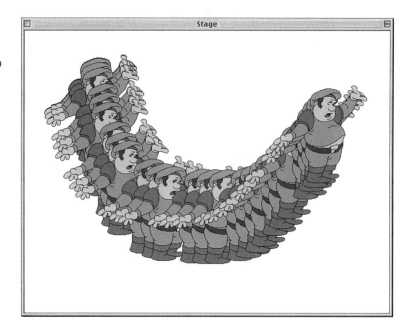

Note

The trailing images are only temporary. They are erased by the first sprite that crosses their path.

You can even use trails with regular animation. If you move the sprite from left to right across the Stage, and Trails is turned on for that sprite, the sprite leaves an image with each step. Figure 10.12 shows an animation that uses both trails and a blend.

→ **See** "Drawing," Chapter 27, "Educational Applications," for more information on using trails

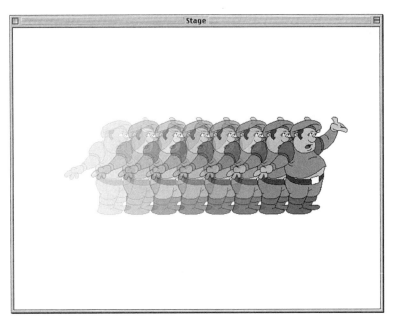

Figure 10.12
The sprite is animated with tweening from left to right. The blend is also tweened from 0 to 100%. Trails is turned on so that the animation leaves pieces behind.

PART

III

CH

10

TROUBLESHOOTING PROPERTIES OF SPRITES AND FRAMES

- Setting the frame tempo below four frames per second is not recommended. Doing so means that some behaviors and other Lingo will react very slowly. Instead, keep the frame rate higher and increase the length of your animation. After all, a 30-second animation can be 30 1fps frames or 240 4fps frames.

- Switching from one palette to the next without a palette transition might cause the user's monitor to flicker.

- Some transitions, such as dissolves, are processor-intensive. A fast machine, like the one on which you may be developing, might handle it fine, but even a slightly slower computer might take far longer. Decrease the Smoothness property as much as you can to counteract this.

- Background Transparent inks and Matte inks look great for some images, and not so great for others. Try using a 32-bit image with an alpha channel for more control over transparency.

- When you change a bitmap sprite's shape, you make it much harder for Director to draw it. This can slow down animation considerably.

DID YOU KNOW?

- You can use the Darken ink, combined with applying a color other than black or white as the foreground color, to simulate color saturation in an image. PhotoShop users can do this with the Hue, Saturation, and Brightness tool. However, in Director you can tween color values to animate it!

CHAPTER **11**

Advanced Techniques

In this chapter

The previous 10 chapters have covered just about all the basic elements of Director. To perform most of the more advanced operations, you need Lingo. However, some advanced techniques don't require Lingo knowledge. This chapter examines these techniques, and the next introduces Lingo.

BUILDING YOUR OWN BEHAVIORS

Until now, you have been using behaviors that were part of this book's library or the ones installed with Director. You will soon be able to make your own behaviors by writing Lingo. However, you can create your own behaviors by simply using the Behavior Inspector. To access the Behavior Inspector, choose Window, Inspector, Behavior.

The Behavior Inspector window, shown in Figure 11.1, contains three text lists and some buttons above each. In the top list you can add and remove behaviors to a sprite. You can use the behavior pop-up at the upper left to create a new behavior.

Figure 11.1
The Behavior Inspector enables you to build custom behaviors without any coding.

If you already have behaviors assigned to a sprite, you can see them listed here. You can select and remove any behavior with the Delete key. You can also change the order in which the behaviors execute by selecting one behavior and using the up and down arrow buttons.

When you create a new behavior, Director asks you to name it. Because all you are doing is creating a new cast member, you can easily edit this name later in the cast window.

Under the top text list is a set of two thinner text lists. If you don't see them, it may be because you have closed that section of the window. You can expand the window using the tiny expand buttons on the left side.

The left text list is for events and the right list is for actions. An *event* is something that happens, such as a mouse click. An *action* is something that you create to react to an event.

Start by selecting one event. Use the event pop-up menu to do this. You can choose from among a number of events, but for now choose Mouse Up. This event corresponds to the completion of a mouse click by the user. It is typically used as the primary way to have a button perform an action.

> **Note**
>
> Why not use the "Mouse Down" event? User interface standards for Mac and Windows machines specify that actions take place only after the user clicks down and then lifts up again. Otherwise, users can click and hold and the action can happen while they are still holding. It's not a big deal for simple Director projects, but because a standard has been set, it's best to use it.

After you have selected at least one event, you apply an action to it. Use the action pop-up button to select an action. A number of categories appear in the menu list. Under Sound, choose the Beep action.

Figure 11.2 shows the Sprite Inspector window with the event and action added. You now have a cast member that is a behavior. When placed on a sprite, this behavior will play a system beep when the sprite is clicked.

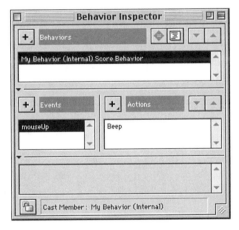

Figure 11.2
The Behavior Inspector window shows a simple behavior that plays a system beep when the user clicks.

PART

III

CH

11

Not only can you rename the behavior now, but you can also edit it. Just open the cast member and the Behavior Inspector appears again. You can add, alter, and delete events and actions.

CREATING MORE COMPLEX BEHAVIORS

These behaviors, of course, can get a lot more complex. Suppose you want to create a button behavior. The goal is to have a button that changes when the user rolls over it, and also changes when the user presses down. When the user lifts the button up, it should return to its rollover state, because the mouse is still over the sprite. It should also then perform an action, such as going to another frame.

To do this, first create some bitmaps that you can use. You need a normal state of the button, a rollover state, and a down state. Figure 11.3 shows the cast window with these three members.

Figure 11.3
The cast window shows three states of the same button.

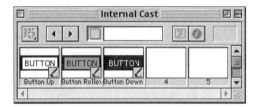

Create a new behavior with the Sprite Inspector. The first event you need to handle is a Mouse Enter event. This is the event that occurs when the user moves the cursor into the rectangle or shape of the sprite. The rectangle of the sprite is used if the sprite is set to Copy ink. The shape of the sprite is used if the ink is set to Matte.

Now, assign the Change Cast Member action to the Mouse Enter event. You can find this action under the Sprite category. Director asks you for a cast member name. Assign the rollover state cast member to this action.

The sprite now changes to a rollover bitmap when the user moves the mouse over it. To turn this off when the user leaves the sprite, add a Mouse Leave event. To this event, add another Change Cast Member action. This time, assign the original, normal state of the button.

The next event is the Mouse Down event. Add this one and assign yet another Change Cast Member action. This is where you use the down state of the button. This bitmap appears on the Stage briefly, in between the user pressing down and lifting up.

The last event is the Mouse Up event. First, add a Change Cast Member action that uses the rollover bitmap member. When the user lifts up, the cursor is still over the sprite, so you don't want to change to the normal bitmap. In addition to this action, also add a second action. This is the action that corresponds to the actual function of the button. If the behavior reaches this point, it means that the user has rolled over the sprite, clicked down, and then lifted up.

Add the Go To Marker action with the Next option selected. You can find this action under the Navigation category. The result of this button is that the movie will then move forward to the next marker, just as one of the examples in Chapter 1, "Animation with Director," showed.

Figure 11.4 shows a Behavior Inspector window with this behavior set. You can see all four events listed, plus the actions for the Mouse Up event.

Figure 11.4
The Behavior
Inspector shows
a typical custom
button behavior.

ADDING EVENTS TO BEHAVIORS

You can choose from many more actions and events when you create behaviors with the
Behavior Inspector. The following is a list of all the events and when they are triggered:

- Mouse Up—The user releases the mouse button while the cursor is positioned over the
  sprite.

- Mouse Down—The user clicks down on the mouse button while the cursor is positioned over the sprite.

- Mouse Enter—The user brings the cursor over the sprite from some position outside
  the sprite's area.

- Mouse Within—Occurs once per frame or frame loop as long as the cursor is within
  the sprite's rectangle or shape.

- Mouse Leave—The user brings the cursor to a position away from the sprite after it
  has just been inside the sprite. For each Mouse Leave event there must have been a
  Mouse Enter.

- Key Up—Used for fields and text members; this event occurs when the user lifts up
  from pressing a key on the keyboard.

- Key Down—Used for fields and text members; this event occurs when the user presses
  down on a key on the keyboard.

- Right Mouse Up—Like Mouse Up, but with the right mouse button in Windows or a
  Control+Click on the Mac.

- Right Mouse Down—Like Mouse Down, but with the right mouse button in Windows
  or a Control+Click on the Mac.

- Prepare Frame—This event occurs every frame or frame loop. It happens before the sprite is actually drawn on the Stage, so you can use it to change the appearance of a sprite before it is shown.

- Exit Frame—This event occurs every frame or frame loop. It happens after the sprite is drawn and all other events have taken place.

ADDING ACTIONS TO BEHAVIORS

You can also choose from plenty of actions. The following is a complete list of actions:

- Navigation, Go To Frame—You must enter a frame number. This action makes the movie jump to that frame.

- Navigation, Go To Marker—You must choose Next, Previous, or Loop. The first two move the movie forward or backward a marker. The last one will causes the movie to loop back to the current marker.

- Navigation, Go To Movie—You must enter a movie file name. Director takes the user to the first frame in that movie.

- Navigation, Go To Net Page—With Shockwave, this causes the user's browser to jump to a specific Web page. While in Director or a projector, this causes the user's default browser to launch and go to that page.

- Navigation, Exit—This causes projectors to quit and Shockwave movies to stop playing. While in Director, it simply stops the movie.

- Wait, On Current Frame—The movie loops on the current frame. Different from using the Go To Marker action with the Loop option, because that action loops back to the frame with the current marker.

- Wait, Until Click or Keypress—This is the same as setting the tempo channel to the equivalent setting.

- Wait, For Time Duration—This is similar to setting the tempo channel to wait for a number of seconds.

- Sound, Play Cast Member—The behavior plays a cast member sound.

- Sound, Play External File—The behavior plays an external sound file.

- Sound, Beep—This action plays the system beep.

- Sound, Set Volume—You must choose a sound level between zero and seven. The action then sets the volume to that level. You can make a series of buttons to set the volume to all different levels, or just one to set the volume to zero.

- Frame, Change Tempo—This enables you to set a new tempo. If you are animating at 30fps (frames per second), for instance, a button can be created to jump up the rate to 60fps.

- Frame, Perform Transition—This enables you to select a transition to be performed during the next frame change. Add this before a navigation action to create transitions into the next screen.

- Frame, Change Palette—You can select a new palette to which the movie should change.

- Sprite, Change Location—You can specify a new location for the sprite. Use the format "point(x,y)" where x and y are numbers that represent the horizontal and vertical position.

- Sprite, Change Cast Member—You can pick a new cast member to be used by the sprite.

- Sprite, Change Ink—You can choose a new ink to be used by the sprite.

- Cursor, Change Cursor—You can pick a new cursor from a standard list. Useful for rollovers.

- Cursor, Restore Cursor—This releases control of the cursor so that it again appears as a standard arrow, or whatever cursor is appropriate.

Note that in addition to the events and actions listed here, you can also define your own actions with the New Action and New Event choices. However, you have to learn about Lingo programming to do that.

FILM LOOPS AND LINKED MOVIES

Although you already know about many different types of bitmap members, did you know that you can have a member that contains an entire Director movie?

Such members are called *film loops*. When a film loop cast member links to an external file, it is sometimes called a *linked movie*.

The simplest use of a film loop member is when it captures an entire animated sequence and places it in one sprite. Doing this is literally as easy as copying and pasting it.

First, create an animation in the Score. You can use as many different sprites and members as you want. Place them across as many different frames as needed. Use any area on the Stage, but make sure there is nothing else on the Stage in those frames.

To create a film loop of this sequence, first select the entire sequence, every sprite and every frame, in the Score. Then copy it. Now, open the cast window, select an empty slot, and paste it. The new film loop member appears after you give it a name.

Now you can go back to the Score and erase the entire animation sequence. In place of it, put the single film loop member. The result on the Stage is the same as your original animation even though the Score shows something much simpler.

Another way to create a film loop is to drag and drop the Score selection from the Score Window to the cast window. A third way is to save the animation all by itself in a separate movie. Then you can import the movie the same way you would import any other media. The result is a film loop member.

A film loop member relies on any other members that were used in constructing the animation. If you copy and paste or drag and drop to create the film loop, you already have the members. However, if you import a Director movie, it also brings any of the cast members from that movie that are needed in the film loop. Other members, those that are not used in the Score, are not imported.

Tip

If you import a movie and select Link To External File, only a single film loop member will be created. All the other members are accessed directly from the linked file. This way, you can section off your project into smaller movies that appear in the main one. If your project contains three main animations, an animator can work on these as three separate files, and you can import them as linked movies into the main movie file later on.

Essentially, a film loop is an entire Director Score stored as a member. Even scripts and markers are included in a film loop.

You can choose several options for film loop members. They are accessed from the Film Loop Cast Member Properties dialog box shown in Figure 11.5. When you import a linked movie, you are shown a Linked Director Movie Cast Member Properties dialog box. They are the same, except that the second has a File Name property and an Enable Scripts check box.

Figure 11.5
The Film Loop Cast Member Properties dialog box enables you to determine what happens when the sprite is stretched and enables you to turn sound and looping on or off.

The two framing options for film loops are Crop and Scale. The Crop option keeps the film loop's images at the same size, no matter how you stretch the sprite. If you shrink the sprite, the images may be cropped. When you select this option, you can also check Center to have the film loop center itself in the sprite rectangle.

The Scale option scales the film loop, including bitmaps in it, to fit the sprite rectangle. Elements that are not scalable, such as fields, change position as the sprite is stretched.

You can choose to have the film loop play any sounds that were in the sound channels of the movie or Score selection that was used to create the film loop. If you created the film loop by copying and pasting a Score selection, you needed to include the sound channels to have them be a part of the film loop. You can also decide whether a film loop is to loop or play only once.

In addition to these options, a linked movie has the Enabled Scripts option. This option enables any behaviors attached to sprites inside the film loop to operate. It also includes any frame scripts. With this functionality, you can really include entire Director movies, with scripts and all, as a single sprite in the Score.

→ **See** "Linked Movies," Chapter 24, "Movies in a Window and Alternatives," for more information about linked movies

COLOR CYCLING

Color cycling is an old technique that relies on palettes to shift the colors of an image. A *palette* is a list of 256 colors that an image uses to display its pixels. See "Using Palette Members," in Chapter 8, "Other Member Types," to learn how to create and modify palettes.

Because each pixel in an image is assigned a color from the palette, Director remembers only the number assignment of that color, not what the actual color is. In other words, if a pixel uses color 57 from the palette, Director doesn't care what color 57 is: red, yellow, green, whatever. Instead, when it comes time to draw that pixel on the Stage, it looks up the actual color that position 57 represents and uses it to draw the pixel.

This means that you have the opportunity to tell Director that color 57 is actually something different than what was originally used in the image. When you do this, all the pixels that use that color from the palette will change. So if color 57 was originally a yellow, and you change it to green, all the yellow pixels in the image will change to green pixels.

PART

III

CH

11

> **Tip**
>
> Although each bitmap image uses a palette, the actual palette used to display all the sprites on the Stage can be set with the palette channel in the Score. This works only when the monitor is set to 8-bit or 256 colors.

One way to do this is to prepare two palettes, each with different colors in different positions. When you want to switch colors, simply switch palettes. The images on the Stage obey the color settings for the new palette in place of the old.

Color cycling provides a way to alter the palette used. You can select a range of colors in the palette and make them move through a cycle. To demonstrate, bring up the Frame Properties: Palette dialog box (see Figure 11.6) by double-clicking the Palette channel in the Score.

First, choose Color Cycling. Then you can select a range of colors in the small palette on the left side of the dialog box. It also includes options for the rate of the cycle, how many cycles occur on one frame, and whether the cycle loops back to the beginning or reverses direction when it reaches the end of the cycle.

The way the color cycle proceeds is that each color moves down one position. If you select colors 11 to 19 to cycle, Director's first step is to take the color in position 12 and place it in position 11, the color in position 13 is placed in 12, and so on. The color in position 11, meanwhile, is placed in position 19. The colors move through the selected range until they are back in their original positions.

Figure 11.6
The Frame Properties: Palette dialog box enables you to select a range of colors to use in a color cycle.

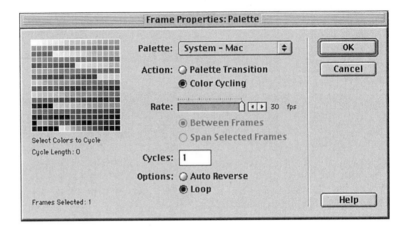

> **Note**
>
> The number one mistake made when trying to use color cycling is doing so with a monitor set to something other than 8-bit or 256 colors. Be sure to adjust this setting before you begin working with color cycling.

One way to use this unusual technique is to create all your images with this effect in mind. Decide that you want to *not* use a group of colors in the palette, such as colors 11 to 19. Then, make all your images with these colors set to "reserved" in your custom palette.

The one image that you want to be affected by color cycling then uses these colors. The result is that when the cycle happens, all the other sprites show no change because they don't use these color positions. Meanwhile, the one sprite that does use them shows the cycle.

> **Note**
>
> Changing the palette through color cycling affects the entire screen, not just the Stage. So if the desktop shows through in your movie, the user may see some of those colors change as well.

A good example is an image that has a flying saucer. You have one or more sprites that make up a background. These sprites use bitmaps that don't use the colors in the palette that you want to cycle. The one sprite that has the saucer uses these colors, and perhaps only these colors. Then, when the cycle occurs, the saucer changes colors and the background stays the same.

Using color cycling requires you to be an expert in using Director's color palettes and creating images with palettes. Director 7 gives you a number of options that make most color effects much easier to accomplish and give you more control over them than earlier versions did. For example, you can use the Lighten or Darken inks with a gradual change to the foreground or background colors.

SHOCKWAVE STREAMING

With the introduction of cable modems, digital subscriber lines, and other modes of fast Internet access, people are able to download and view larger and larger pieces of media over the Internet. However, even at these high speeds, the loading process is still much slower than from a hard drive or CD-ROM drive. Plus, many people will continue to use 33.6Kbps or 56Kbps modems for a long time to come.

For these reasons, you may want to consider streaming your Shockwave movies rather than asking the user to download the entire movie before it begins playing. This is especially useful for linear animations, where the first frames of animation need only a few images.

Note

Streaming is the process whereby a movie begins before all the media is loaded through the network. The movie starts with a minimum amount of media, and then adds more as it continues. This enables the movie to start sooner, rather than requiring users to wait for the entire movie to download first.

However, you do not want to use streaming unless you have a good reason. If you expect the whole movie to load quickly, for instance, there is no advantage to streaming and it may cause an undesirable effect because images appear at random on the first few frames as they are being loaded. In my experience, streaming also increases non-reproducible bug reports from your users, including crashes and such, especially if you are using a lot of Lingo.

Streaming your Director movies is as easy as selecting that option in the Movie Playback Properties dialog box, shown in Figure 11.7. You can access this dialog box by choosing Modify, Movie, Playback. From there, just choose Play While Downloading Movie.

You can also choose to have the movie wait until a certain number of frames are downloaded before the animation begins. This helps the movie play more smoothly. If you have a one-minute movie at 15fps, you may decide that you want 300 frames (one third of the movie) to download before playing. Shockwave makes sure that all the members it needs for those frames are present before it begins playing.

Tip

You can also place some more members in these first frames, but position them off the Stage, to make sure that they download before the movie begins.

When the movie continues past a point where it has all the media it needs, it simply does not show the images it does not yet have. You can choose to "Show Placeholders" to place a rectangle in place of the not-yet-loaded members.

Figure 11.7
The Movie Playback Properties dialog box has the main streaming settings.

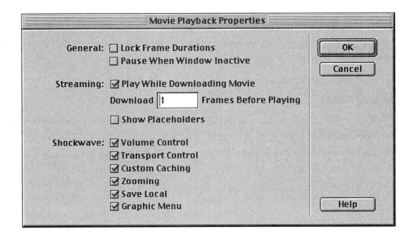

You can also use a number of behaviors to control streaming. Director's included library has a whole set of streaming behaviors. Most of them wait on the frame until some other media is ready. You can specify a certain frame or a specific piece of media that you want to make sure has been loaded before continuing.

A typical way to use these behaviors is to have an opening animation sequence. Set the movie to start playing only when that many frames have been loaded. Then, at the end of this loop, use a behavior to have the movie wait until all the members used by the last frame in the next sequence have been loaded. Because Director loads members in the order that they are used in the Score, you can be sure that the whole animation sequence is available when the last frame in the sequence has been loaded.

→ **See** "Improving Performance" Chapter 34, "Performance Issues," for more information about Shockwave file size and streaming

TROUBLESHOOTING ADVANCED TECHNIQUES

- In the Behavior Inspector, you can use the little padlock button at the bottom-left corner to lock the contents of the window to the currently selected sprite. Then you can use the Score and Stage to look at other sprites without changing the Behavior Inspector.

- It is easy to add multiple behaviors to a sprite by accident. Keep that in mind and check for it if you see strange things happening to a sprite.

- If you want film loops to be Background Transparent, you must set the individual sprites to use Background Transparent ink before you copy and paste or drag them to the Cast to create a film loop. The same is true for other inks, such as Matte.

DID YOU KNOW?

- If you want to use streaming and you want to make sure that some members get loaded before the movie starts, just place these members in frame 1, but position them off-screen. Then set the movie to begin playing only after frame 1 has been loaded.

- Film loops can include multiple sprites. They can even include other film loops!

- When you use a behavior from the library, it is imported into your Cast. You can use the Behavior Inspector to edit these behaviors, although some are too complex for you to alter without knowing Lingo.

USING BASIC LINGO

LEARNING LINGO

In this chapter

Director is much, much more than an animation or presentation tool. You can make full applications, Web applets, and software utilities. You can build games, educational software, and business applications. Just about anything that can be done with software can be done in Director.

The key to writing powerful software with Director is Lingo, Director's programming language. Lingo started out as a simple set of scripting commands used to control animation. Now it is a complete object-oriented language rivaling traditional ones such as C and Pascal, as well as new languages such as Java. Chapter 13, "Essential Lingo Syntax," continues this discussion with a more complete list of all the important Lingo commands with which you should be familiar.

WHAT IS LINGO?

Lingo is a programming language. It is a way of speaking to the computer by giving it commands and asking it questions. In Director, you can speak to the Director environment: the Score, the Cast, and the Stage.

Lingo is an English-like programming language. A line of Lingo code can actually be read out loud and interpreted by the English definitions of the words. All the commands, functions, and other keywords in Director are English words, groups of words, or abbreviations. This makes Lingo easier to learn than other languages.

Lingo is a cast member type, which means that when you create the Lingo code that controls your movie, it is stored in cast members called *scripts*. *Scripts* are cast members that contain a piece of text that is valid Lingo code. They exist alongside the bitmaps, sounds, and shapes of your Director movie in the Cast. In some cases, they are also placed in the Score.

Lingo is power. Out of all the possible things that Director can do, only a handful of them can be done without using Lingo. Almost any project that has been done with software can be accomplished using Lingo and Director. In some cases it is not the best tool for the job, but in other cases Lingo can be used to program a piece of software with less effort than traditional methods.

Learning Lingo is the key to using Director fully. Unless you stick to bare-bones, PowerPoint-like presentations or linear animations, you need to learn Lingo to use Director.

Fortunately, Lingo is easy to learn. Hundreds of Lingo keywords are in the language, but you need only a few to get started. You can start with the Lingo Message window.

FIRST STEPS WITH THE MESSAGE WINDOW

Although Lingo scripts are usually stored in cast members, you can also run short, one-line programs in something called the *Message window*. Open the Message window by choosing Windows, Message, or by pressing Command+M on the Mac or Ctrl+M in Windows.

The Message window is very plain, with just a large area to type and view text. When you type while the Message window is open, the characters appear there. It is doing more than just echoing text. The Message window is, in fact, a Lingo interpreter. It takes Lingo commands and evaluates them in the same way as the scripts you will soon learn how to write.

Type put 42 into the Message window. When you press Return/Enter, the Message window will interpret what you just typed and return -- 42 on the next line. Figure 12.1 shows how the Message window now looks.

Figure 12.1
The Message window enables you to type single lines of Lingo code and see the results.

The double dash, a "--", appears before lines that Director returns to you in the Message window. Later, you will learn how to use the double dash to comment your code.

Now you know your first Lingo command: *put*. The *put* command is actually used to place text into the Message window. It has some other uses that you will learn much later.

You asked Director to *put* the number 42 into the Message window. It did just that. But it did more than just echo a number back at you. It actually understood what you meant by 42. To prove it, try this:

```
put 42+1
-- 43
```

Now you see that Director can add. It doesn't merely spit back "42+1," but instead understands that these are numbers and that the plus symbol means that they should be added together.

You can do other things with Lingo besides math. Try this in the Message window:

```
beep
```

You should hear your computer's default system beep. (If you don't, it is probably because your volume is turned down or your system beep is turned off.) Notice that the Message

PART
IV

CH

12

window does not return anything in the next line, because you didn't ask it to. The command *beep* simply plays the system beep. It does not place anything in the Message window as the *put* command does.

The Message window is nice for taking your first Lingo steps, and it continues to be useful as you learn new Lingo commands. Even expert Lingo programmers use the Message window constantly to program in Lingo.

→ **See** "Integers and Floats," Chapter 13, "Essential Lingo Syntax," for more information about using numbers in Lingo

UNDERSTANDING SCRIPT TYPES

The Message window enables you to type and interpret one line of Lingo code at a time, but you need to string together many lines of Lingo code at a time to make programs. You store these lines of Lingo code in cast members called *scripts*. There are three different types of script members: *movie scripts*, *behavior scripts*, and *parent scripts*. In addition, other cast members, such as bitmaps, can have scripts embedded inside themselves. These are usually referred to as *cast scripts*.

The difference between all these script types is not in what they look like or how they behave, but it is in *when* they act.

A movie script, for instance, is a global presence in a movie. If a movie script is written that produces a system beep whenever the mouse is clicked, this script sounds the beep whenever the mouse is clicked *anywhere* in the movie. Thus the name "movie" script: it acts on the entire movie.

A behavior script is similar in concept to the behaviors that you read about in Chapter 2, "Presentations with Director." It does nothing until it is placed on a sprite or in a frame script channel. If it is placed on a sprite, the Lingo commands inside the script are active only as far as the sprite is concerned. If you have a behavior that plays a beep when the mouse is clicked, and you apply that behavior to a sprite, the beep sounds only when the user clicks on that sprite. Behavior scripts are sometimes called Sprite or Score scripts for this reason. They act only on a sprite in the Score to which they are assigned.

Behavior scripts can also be assigned to the frame script channel of the Score. When they are, they act like movie scripts, but only for the frame or frames to which they are assigned. Behaviors used this way are sometimes called Score scripts.

Parent scripts are a much more advanced type of script. They actually don't do anything until you use some object-oriented programming Lingo commands to tell them how and when they are to be used.

Cast scripts, on the other hand, are easy to use. You can create one by selecting a member, such as a bitmap, and pressing the script button at the top of the cast window. This will opens the Script window and enables you to add a script to that particular member.

Cast scripts act only on that one cast member. If you place a script with a cast member that makes the system beep when the user clicks the mouse, that action affects only that one cast member when it is on the Stage. If you use that cast member more than once in the Score, the script with it is active in all those places.

Cast scripts are not used with modern Lingo programming. Behaviors can accomplish the same tasks and are much more flexible. Cast scripts are rarely used in this book.

To create a script, select an empty location in the cast window and press Command+0 (zero) on the Mac or Ctrl+0 in Windows. The Script window appears. It is a fairly simple window, but has a few tricks hidden in the buttons at the top. The Script window also appears when you edit the script of another type of cast member. Figure 12.2 shows the Script window.

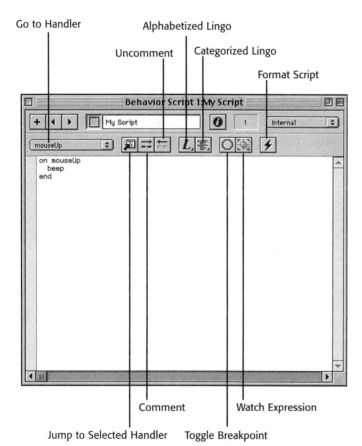

Figure 12.2
The Script window enables you to edit movie scripts, behaviors, and parent scripts.

PART

IV

CH

12

The very top of the Script window has the typical Director cast member buttons that take you forward and backward in the Cast, enable you to add a new cast member, and enable you to switch cast libraries. The rest of the buttons deal with more advanced Lingo functions such as handlers and debugging. You will learn about them as you learn about those functions.

The two buttons called Alphabetized Lingo and Categorized Lingo enable you to hunt for and automatically insert any Lingo keyword into your script. They come in handy when you just can't remember the name of a command, but you have a good idea of how it starts or under which category it falls. They are also handy in refreshing your memory as to the proper syntax for using Lingo commands.

Tip

Holding the Option key down on the Mac or the Alt key in Windows while using the Alphabetized Lingo and Categorized Lingo pop-ups instantly brings up the help entry for that command.

A script cast member also has a Script Cast Member Properties dialog box, shown in Figure 12.3. Script cast members have only two properties: the name of the member and the type of script it holds. The three options, of course, are Movie, Behavior, and Parent.

Figure 12.3
The Script Cast Member Properties dialog box enables you to change the script's type.

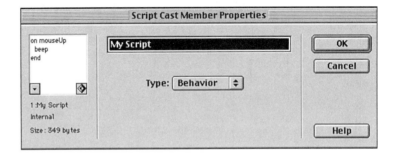

USING MESSAGES AND HANDLERS

The Script window shown in Figure 12.3 contains a very small, very simple script. It states

```
on mouseUp
   beep
end
```

You may recognize the mouseUp message from your work with behaviors in Chapter 11, "Advanced Techniques."

A *message* is a signal sent by an event. When the user clicks the mouse button down and then releases it, a "mouseUp" message is sent. Similarly, the initial click down sends a "mouseDown" message.

Messages such as these get sent to any Director object that is related to the action itself. A "mouseUp" message, for instance, is sent to the sprite that was clicked. If the user clicks a bitmap that happens to be sprite three on the Stage, that sprite gets a "mouseUp" message.

If a behavior happens to be attached to that sprite, Director checks to see whether that behavior handles a "mouseUp" message.

A behavior, or any script, handles a message such as this by defining a *handler*. Handlers start with the word *on*. In the preceding example, the first line of the handler is *on mouseUp*. This simply means that the handler is to handle any "mouseUp" messages sent to that sprite.

The contents of the handler, in this case the lone command *beep*, are the Lingo commands that are to be executed if the handler is triggered by the message. The series of commands ends with *end*, which signifies the end of the handler.

Note

Many times programmers like to place the name of the handler after the *end*. So the last line of Figure 12.3 would read "end mouseUp." Lingo doesn't require this, but some programmers use it anyway.

You can place more than one handler in a script. So, for instance, you can have an *on mouseUp* and an *on mouseDown* handler both in one behavior. They are triggered by different messages, so they won't get in each other's way.

→ **See** "Simple Behaviors," Chapter 14, "Creating Behaviors," for more information about creating behaviors

TYPES OF MESSAGES

There are many more types of messages besides *on mouseUp* and *on mouseDown*. They all correspond to some event that takes place in Director. The follow list includes some of the most common events and messages:

- mouseDown—The user clicks the mouse button. On Windows, this corresponds to the left mouse button.
- mouseUp—The user lifts up the mouse button. Every "mouseUp" message is preceded by a "mouseDown" message, although they don't necessarily have to be on the same sprite.
- mouseEnter—The cursor enters the area of a sprite.
- mouseLeave—The cursor leaves the area of a sprite.
- mouseWithin—A message sent continuously, once per frame, as long as the cursor is over a sprite.
- mouseUpOutside—,A message sent when the user clicks down in a sprite, but moves the cursor away and then releases the mouse button.
- beginSprite—A message sent once when the sprite is first encountered by the playback head in the Score.
- prepareFrame—A message sent when each new frame starts, before the frame is drawn on the Stage.

- enterFrame—A message sent when each new frame starts, after the frame is drawn on the Stage.

- exitFrame—A message sent when a frame is done and the movie is about to move on to the next one.

- prepareMovie—A message sent before the first frame of the movie is drawn.

- startMovie—A message sent immediately after the first frame of a movie is drawn.

- stopMovie—A message sent when the movie ends.

- idle—A message sent continuously while the movie is advancing from the start of a frame to the end of a frame. The number of times it is sent depends on how slow the tempo is and how fast the computer is.

- keyDown—A message sent when the user presses a key on the keyboard.

- keyUp—A message sent when the user releases a key on the keyboard.

MESSAGE HIERARCHY

In addition to the many different messages that events in Director can send, it is important to understand where these messages go. A mouseUp message, for instance, can be received by a behavior attached to the sprite that was clicked. However, if the sprite has no behavior with an *on mouseUp* handler in it, the message continues to look for a receiving handler.

The next place it looks is in the cast member. It checks to see whether an *on mouseUp* handler has been placed in the cast script. If not, it checks the behavior in the frame script channel. Finally, if that fails, it looks for an *on mouseUp* in a movie script member.

If it still cannot find a handler to receive the message, the message is simply not used. The following list is a run-down of where messages look for handlers:

- A behavior attached to the sprite acted on. If there is more than one behavior, it looks at them in the order that they appear in the Behavior Inspector.

- The cast script.

- A behavior in the frame script channel.

- Any movie script cast member.

In some cases, one or more of these steps will be skipped for obvious reasons. An *exitFrame* handler, for instance, does not act on any sprite, so Director skips directly to the frame script channel. A *startMovie* handler looks only in movie scripts.

CREATING YOUR OWN HANDLERS

The preceding list of messages shows you some of the events messages that are built into Director; you can actually create and send your own messages, too. In addition, you can create handlers to receive these messages.

Create a movie script and place a very simple handler inside it:

```
on playBeep
  beep
end
```

Make sure it is a movie script, and close the Script window. Now go to the Message window.

Note A Lingo convention is to use several words, such as "my number" or "play beep" to define a handler or a variable. But a handler name cannot contain spaces. To make these names easier to read, capitalize the first letter of each word after the first word. So "my number" becomes "myNumber" and "play beep" becomes "playBeep." Lingo does not actually care about capitalization, so this is merely for cosmetic purposes. ("myNumber" and "mynumber" are exactly the same to Lingo.)

Another function of the Message window is to enable you to send messages to the movie. Do this by typing the name of the message. If a movie script has a handler that deals with this message, the handler runs. Otherwise, an error message tells you that no handler is defined to receive the message.

When you type playBeep in the message window, your *playBeep* handler is executed and a beep is played.

USING VARIABLES

Another key element in Lingo, and every programming language, is variables. Variables are storage areas for values.

For instance, you can store the number 42 in a variable named "myNumber." To do this, simply assign this value with the "=" symbol. Try it in the Message window:

```
myNumber = 42
```

Note Before Director 7, you had to use the Lingo command *set* to assign values to variables. Director 7 does not require this, but can accommodate this old syntax for simple commands such as this one.

The syntax "myNumber" meant absolutely nothing to Director and Lingo before you typed this line. This line, however, told Director to create a variable called "myNumber" and store the numerical value 42 in it. You can now get this value back by using the *put* command to place it in the Message window.

```
put myNumber
-- 42
```

PART

IV

CH

12

Director remembered that you stored the value 42 in a variable called "myNumber." When you asked it to place "myNumber" in the Message window, it looked into its memory and found a variable called "myNumber" and placed its value in the Message window. You can do even more complex things with variables. Try this:

```
myNumber = 42+1
put myNumber
-- 43
```

Director performed the arithmetic before placing the value in the variable. You can even do arithmetic with variables that already have a value.

```
myNumber = 5
myOtherNumber = 3
put myNumber+myOtherNumber
-- 8
```

You can also change the value of a variable that already exists.

```
myNumber = 42
put myNumber
-- 42
myNumber = myNumber+1
put myNumber
-- 43
```

Numbers are not the only items that variables can store. They can also store characters. Try this:

```
myName = "Gary"
put myName
-- "Gary"
```

A series of characters is called a *string*. It is usually shown with quotation marks around it. Lingo, in fact, insists that these quotation marks be present. So a number, such as 42, can just be written as 42, but a string such as my name must be written with quotes: "Gary".

A string can actually be only one character long, or even zero characters long (""). There is no limit (except your computer's memory) to how long a string can be.

Variables can be used in handlers as well. For instance:

```
on playWithVariables
  myNumber = 5
  myNumber = myNumber+4
  myNumber = myNumber-2
  put myNumber
end
```

If you place this handler in a movie script, and then type playWithVariables in the Message window, you will see the number 7 placed in the Message window.

A variable used in this way is called a *local* variable. That means that it is used inside only one handler. It exists only when the handler is being used, and is disposed of when the handler ends. If the handler is called again, the variable is recreated from scratch.

If you created another handler that also used a variable named "myNumber," it would in fact be a different variable altogether. Each handler is like a little world all to itself. A local variable inside it belongs to it and no other handler.

You can create another type of variable, called a *global* variable, which is shared by more than one handler. Here is an example of a global variable. The following is the complete text of a movie script. It contains three handlers:

```
on initNumber
  global myNumber
  myNumber = 42
end

on addOneToNumber
  global myNumber
  myNumber = myNumber+1
end

on putNumberInMessageWindow
  global myNumber
  put myNumber
end
```

Note
Rather than declare the global variable with *global* commands in each and every handler, you can place one *global* command outside all the handlers, perhaps in the very first line of the script. This declares the global variable for every handler in that script member.

Because all three handlers use the command *global* to state that the variable "myNumber" is a global variable, they all share that variable. So you can now do the following in the Message window:

```
initNumber
putNumberInMessageWindow
-- 42
addOneToNumber
putNumberInMessageWindow
-- 43
```

This code demonstrates how each of the handlers is actually referring to the same variable. Try it without the *global* lines and see what happens.

Tip
You can use the *clearGlobals* command in the Message window or in a handler to erase all global variables. You can also use the *showGlobals* command in the Message window to see a list of all current globals and their values.

WRITING LINGO CODE

There are many ways to go about creating a Director movie with Lingo. Over time, you will adopt your own method.

For instance, some programmers create one movie script member to hold all their movie handlers. Others break them up into several script members by category. Some people even create one script member per handler.

If you do a lot of programming, you will find that your style adjusts over time. There is no right or wrong way to go about doing it. However, some basic programming guidelines can help you get started.

THE LINGO PROGRAMMER

Lingo programmers are really of two types. The first type is someone who has a background in computer science or engineering. These programmers probably know languages such as C or Pascal, and took courses such as "Data Structures" and "Linear Algebra" in college.

The second type is far more common. This is the graphic artist or multimedia producer. These programmers may have used presentation tools before, even Director, but have never used a programming language before. They are now ready to start learning Lingo.

For both types of programmers, starting to learn Lingo can be difficult. For experienced programmers, Lingo takes care of much of the tedious work that they were used to in the past, but gives them control over graphic elements and the user interface. For graphic artists, Lingo is lines and lines of text that stand between them and their end products.

The important point to remember is that programming *is* an art. Programming languages such as Lingo provide a wide canvas for programmers to express themselves. Two programmers given the same task are almost certain to write two different programs. Each one shows the programmer's own style.

For experienced programmers, this means that programming in Lingo provides another type of canvas on which they can create. As an experienced programmer myself, I will even venture to say that Lingo will enable them to be more creative than before.

For graphic artists, this means that Lingo is a new brush with which they can paint. The many artists that I have known who have become Lingo programmers have used it as a way to create the art they envision.

PROGRAMMING AS PROBLEM-SOLVING

Programming is just problem solving. If you want to make a Director movie that is a matching game, think of it as a problem. Your goal is to find a solution.

As with all problems, more than one step is usually needed to solve the problem. You have to examine the problem, take it apart, find out what you know and what you don't. Then, you need to come up with a plan for solving it.

To solve a programming problem, first define it. What, exactly, do you want to happen? Saying, "I want to animate a sprite" is not a well-defined problem. Saying "I want to move a sprite from the left side of the Stage to the right side" is better. What you really should be going for is something like "I want to move a sprite from position 50,200 to position 550,200 over the period of five seconds at the rate of 10fps."

After a problem has been defined, you can start to see how it can be solved. Imagine that your goal is to move a sprite 500 pixels in five seconds at 10fps. At 10fps, five seconds will be 50 frame loops. So you want to move the sprite 10 pixels per frame loop.

Only by clearly defining the problem can you start to envision a solution.

SMALLER PROBLEMS

The key to writing a program in any language is being able to break it down. You start off with a large concept, such as "A quiz that teaches children about geography." That's a pretty tall order. You can bet that Lingo has no *quizKidsOnGeography* command.

So you break it into smaller parts. Maybe you want to have each question of the quiz show a map of the world with one country lit up. Then, three choices are presented as to what the country might be. So now forget about the whole program and start to concentrate on just asking one question.

But this part is also too big to tackle all at once. However, it has smaller parts. How does the map display a country? How do the three choices appear? How do you make sure one of the three choices is correct?

A very small part of this might be just having a Lingo program that selects a random country out of a list of 100 names. Now that you have broken the problem down this far, you might begin to program. The result is a handler that selects a random country and outputs it to the Message window. You build it and test it and you've solved your first small problem.

Then, you continue to identify and solve other small problems in this way. Before you know it, you have a working program.

The concept of breaking big problems into smaller ones is the most important aspect of programming. If you ever get stuck while programming in Director it is likely to be because you have not broken the problem down into small enough pieces. Take a step back from what you are doing and decide how you can break it down before continuing.

SETTING UP YOUR SCRIPT MEMBERS

If you are creating a small applet or projector, a useful way to organize your scripts is to have one movie script member and several behavior members.

PART
IV

Ch
12

It may even be possible for you to not have any movie scripts at all. Well-written behaviors can eliminate the need for movie scripts.

If your movie requires mostly buttons, some behavior scripts can handle it all. Each behavior can be attached to a button and tell the movie what to do when it is pressed.

A larger Lingo project may require a few movie scripts. Movie scripts are needed for items placed in the *on startMovie* handler, for instance, where commands need to be executed when the movie is initially run.

Movie scripts can also hold handlers that are used by more than one behavior. If you want various behaviors to play a random sound, for instance, you may want them all to call your *on playRandomSound* handler that is stored in a movie script member. This saves you from having to include a similar handler in many different behavior scripts.

It is always a good idea to keep movie scripts together in the Cast. The same goes for behaviors. There are exceptions, of course. Sometimes, you may want to place behaviors near the bitmap members that they usually control.

WRITING YOUR CODE

Director 7 is equipped with an automatic script color function. This function adds color to different types of words in your scripts. The goal is to make it easier for you to read. You can also turn this function off in the Script Preferences dialog box. If you do, you can use the Text Inspector to color and style your code manually.

The most important task to complete when writing code is to remember to add comments. Comments are words, phrases, and even sentences that you can sprinkle throughout your code to help clarify what the code is doing. You can place comments on a new line, or at the end of a line with code. Use a double dash to tell Director that everything after it is a comment and should be ignored when the Lingo runs. Here is an example:

```
-- This handler output powers of 2 to the Message Window
on powersOfTwo
  n = 2 -- start with 2
  repeat with i = 1 to 100 -- output 100 numbers
    put n -- send to the Message window
    n = n*2 -- multiply by 2 to get the next number
  end repeat
end
```

Now compare that with the same exact handler that is not commented:

```
on powersOfTwo
  n = 2
  repeat with i = 1 to 100
    put n
    n = n*2
  end repeat
end
```

The first can be understood immediately. If you wrote the second one and then saved the file and came back to it a year later, would you be able to remember what it did immediately? Now imagine a 100-line handler that picks random geography quiz questions and modifies a map on the Stage.

In addition to straightforward commenting, you can also accomplish a lot by using sensible names for handlers and variables. You could name a handler "convTemp," for instance, but it would be better if it was named "convertTemperature." You could have variables in it called "f" and "c", but it would be much more readable code if they were named "fahrenheitTemp" and "centigradeTemp". Because you can use long variable names in Lingo, take advantage of it to make your code more readable. Because you can copy, cut, and paste in the Lingo scripting window, there's really no reason to use short, one-character, names.

Using colors and styles, comments, and realistic handler and variable names will save you time and frustration. Get used to using them now, from the beginning, and your work will go much more smoothly.

→ **See** "Writing Good Code," Chapter 33, "Debugging," for more information about code-writing practices

TROUBLESHOOTING LINGO

- Remember that a local variable is destroyed when a handler is done. The next time that handler begins, it will not have a value. If you want a variable to retain its value, you should use a global or a behavior property variable, which is introduced in Chapter 14, "Creating Behaviors."

- Even if you don't plan on using them all, you should familiarize yourself with the different messages and event handlers. You should not try to use an event handler name as a custom handler or a variable name. You should also avoid using any other Lingo syntax as handler names or variable names.

- Every Lingo programmer eventually runs into the problem of a movie script not working when it should. The code might seem perfect—the Score, Cast, and Stage are all set up as they should be—yet the script acts as if it is not even there. Sure enough, the simple solution is that the movie script is set to be a behavior script by mistake. Keep this in mind, because it will happen to you one day. To fix it, just use the member's Script Cast Member Properties dialog box to change it to the proper script type.

PART

IV

CH

12

DID YOU KNOW?

- You can change the font in the Message window by selecting text and using the Text Inspector. This is especially useful when you are teaching Lingo and need to show a class the Message window on a projection screen.

- Because the Message window can do math for you by using the *put* command, consider using it rather than launching a separate calculator program. I find it useful for computing data such as the midpoint between two locations on the screen.

- You can use the Lingo *scriptText* property to get the text of a script cast member. You can also set the text of a script with this property.

- You can use the Script Preferences dialog box to change the default font of the script window. You can also turn the auto-coloring function on or off. If you turn the auto-coloring function off, you can color in the text manually with the Text Inspector.

- Handler names can contain some symbols and punctuation marks. You can use a question mark or an exclamation point, for example. You can even have a handler called "on !". You can also use symbols in handler names or as variable names.

- Many Lingo programmers prefer to repeat the handler's name after the *end* statement at the end of a handler. This is common in other programming languages as well. It is just an alternate way of writing the code. Director doesn't require it.

CHAPTER **13**

ESSENTIAL LINGO SYNTAX

In this chapter

Although there are hundreds of Lingo keywords, few of them are used in day-to-day programming. Most have to deal with specific properties of cast members or events; the essential syntax is all you need to know to do most things.

The essential commands enable the program to make decisions, repeat actions, and manipulate variables. After you master those, you have mastered Lingo. The rest are just details.

This chapter goes through these essential commands, functions, and properties quickly, with the simplest of examples. When you are finished, you will have the knowledge to start building useful Lingo scripts.

USING NUMBER VARIABLES

You learned how Lingo performs simple math functions in the last chapter. However, there are many more ways to work with number variables. Lingo has a full set of commands and functions that work with numbers just as any other programming language does.

PERFORMING OPERATIONS

You can add, subtract, multiply, and divide numbers and variables. The symbols you use to do this are the +, -, * and /. The first symbol, the plus sign, is the only one that makes complete sense. The dash is used as a substitute for the minus symbol. An asterisk is used as a multiplication symbol. It is used in just about every programming language for this purpose. The forward slash is used in place of the division symbol, because a standard keyboard does not include a division character.

To use these operators, apply them to numbers as you would write them on paper. Here are some examples in the message window:

```
put 4+5
-- 9
put 7-3
-- 4
put 6*9
-- 54
put 8/2
-- 4
put 9/2
-- 4
```

INTEGERS AND FLOATS

Notice that the last operation, nine divided by two, returned a four. This is because Director is dealing here in *integers* only. An integer is a number, positive or negative, with no fractional value. Four is an integer. However, four-and-a-half, or 4.5, is not.

Numbers that have fractional parts are called *floating point numbers*. This name refers to the way in which the computer stores these values, using a more complex method than how it stores integers. The number 4.5 is a floating point number, or a *float*.

Be aware that floating point numbers include integers. A four is an integer and a floating point number. However, 4.5 is a floating point number but *not* an integer because it has a fractional component.

In Lingo, floating point numbers are always shown with a decimal point. This way, Director can tell the difference between the two types of numbers.

If Director is asked to interpret an operation such as 9/2, it looks at all the numbers involved and determines whether the result should be an integer or a float. In this case, because you are asking it to perform an operation on two integers, it returns an integer. To do this, it drops the fractional component of the number and returns only the integer component. So 9/2 returns a 4, not a 4.5.

Note

> Director does not round when dividing two integers such as these. Instead, the decimal portion is just dropped. So 7/4 returns a 1, not a 2.

You can force Director to return a floating point value by making one of the numbers in the calculation a floating point number. Try this in the Message window:

```
put 7/4
-- 1
put 7.0/4
-- 1.7500
put 7/4.0
-- 1.7500
put 7.0/4.0
-- 1.7500
```

You can also use two functions to convert back and forth between integers and floats. A *function* is a piece of Lingo syntax that usually takes one or more values and returns a value. Try this in the Message window:

```
put 7
-- 7
put float(7)
-- 7.0000
put 7.75
-- 7.7500
put integer(7.25)
-- 7
put integer(7)
-- 7
put integer(7.75)
-- 8
```

These two functions, *integer* and *float*, convert any number value, either integer or floating point, to the type you want. Notice in the example that applying the *integer* function to an integer value does not change it. Also, notice that the *integer* function rounds numbers. So a value of 7.75 produces an integer of 8.

You can use these commands on functions inside operations. Try this in the Message window:

```
put 8/5
-- 1
put float(8)/5
-- 1.6000
put float(8/5)
-- 1.0000
put integer(float(8)/5)
-- 2
```

Notice that the line put float(8)/5 behaves in the same way as put 8.0/5 would. Also notice that the third example returns what appears to be a wrong answer. It says that the floating point result of 8/5 is 1.000. This is because you are asking it to evaluate 8/5 first, before converting it to a floating point number. As the first example shows, the value of 8/5 is 1. So the line is simply converting a 1 to a 1.000.

The last example shows how you can use the two functions together to perform an operation and get a rounded result. The division returns a floating point number, which is then rounded to an integer with the *integer* function.

PRECEDENCE

These last two examples bring up an interesting topic: order of operations (also called precedence). When more than one operation is performed, or a combination of operations and functions, what gets performed first? Try this in the Message window:

```
put 5+3
-- 8
put 8*6
-- 48
put 5+3*6
-- 23
```

Five plus three is eight. Multiply eight times six and you get 48. However, if you try to do that all at once on the same line, you get 23. Why? Well, some multiplication and division operators take precedence over addition and subtraction. So in the statement 5+3*6, multiplication is evaluated first, and then the addition. Most programming languages work this way.

However, you can override precedence by specifying which operations you want to perform first. To do this, use parentheses to group together operations. Try this in the Message window:

```
put 5+3*6
-- 23
put (5+3)*6
-- 48
```

The use of parentheses ensures that the addition is performed first, and then the sum is multiplied by six. You can use multiple layers of parentheses if you need to.

```
put ((5+3)*6+(7-3)*4)*8
-- 512
```

OPERATIONS AND VARIABLES

Now that you have all the basic functions for math, the next step is to combine this knowledge with the use of variables. Variables used in mathematical operations are interpreted just as numbers were in the preceding examples.

```
myNumber = 5
put myNumber
-- 5
put myNumber+1
-- 6
put myNumber*7
-- 35
put (myNumber+2)*3
-- 21
```

You can also set a variable to be equal to the result of an operation.

```
myNumber = 7+4
put myNumber
-- 11
myNumber = (7+4)*2
put myNumber
-- 22
myNumber = 5
myOtherNumber = 6
mySum = myNumber + myOtherNumber
put mySum
-- 11
```

The last example shows you how one variable can be set to the result of an operation that involves two other variables. Performing operations on variables and storing the results in other variables is very common in Lingo and other programming languages. In this case, it is so obvious what the variable contains, that it almost makes more sense to just use the numbers instead. However, in a real program, the variable holds values that change, such as the score of a game or the age of the user.

FUNCTIONS

In addition to the *integer* and *float* functions, many other functions manipulate numbers. Table 13.1 lists these functions and what they do.

TABLE 13.1   LINGO MATH FUNCTIONS

Function	Description	Example
abs	Returns the absolute value of the number. It basically strips off the negative sign from numbers less than 0.	abs(-7) = 7
atan	Returns the arctangent of the number. It uses the radians system rather than degrees.	atan(1.0) = 0.7854
cos	Returns the cosine of the number. It uses the radians system rather than degrees.	cos(3.14) = -1.000
exp	Returns the natural logarithm base (2.7183) to the power of the number provided.	exp(3) = 20.0855
float	Converts the number to a floating point number.	float(4) = 4.000
integer	Converts a floating point number to an integer using rounding. Leaves integers the same.	integer(7.8) = 8
mod	Used to limit a number to a range. The limit always starts with 0, and goes up to the specified number.	4 mod 3 = 1.
sqrt	Returns the square root of the number. If given an integer, it rounds the result to the nearest integer. If given a float, it returns a float.	sqrt(4) = 2
sin	Returns the sine of the number. It uses the radians system rather than degrees.	sin(3.14/2) = 1.000

Many of these functions are based on trigonometry. Trig functions are very useful for defining curved and circular animation paths with Lingo, but are rarely used by anyone but advanced Lingo programmers. Don't worry if you can't remember your high school math class; you probably won't need it for most things.

→ **See** "Rotation," Chapter 18, "Controlling Bitmaps," for more information about using trigonometry functions

USING STRING VARIABLES

The other basic type of variable is the string, which stores a series of characters. Strings can be as simple as a single character, as complex as words, lines, or pages of text, or can even contain no characters at all. The following examples demonstrate different types of strings in the Message window:

```
myString = "A"
put myString
-- "A"
myString = "Hello"
put myString
-- "Hello"
myString = "Hello World."
put myString
-- "Hello World."
myString = ""
put myString
-- ""
```

CHUNK EXPRESSIONS

You can use Lingo to take strings apart and get single characters or groups of characters from them. A subset of a string is called a *chunk*. To define chunks, use keywords such as *char* and *word*. Try this in the Message window:

```
myString = "Hello World."
put char 1 of myString
-- "H"
put word 1 of myString
-- "Hello"
put char 2 to 4 of myString
-- "ell"
```

Using a chunk expression such as *char* in conjunction with the keyword *of* and the string is actually old-fashioned Lingo syntax. Director 7 enables you to do the same thing with the new *dot syntax*. It is called dot syntax because it uses dots, or periods, to formulate expressions.

```
myString = "Hello World."
put myString
-- "Hello World."
put myString.char[1]
-- "H"
put myString.word[1]
-- "Hello"
put myString.char[2..4]
-- "ell"
```

PART

IV

CH

13

There are more chunk expressions than just *char* and *word*. There are also *line* and *paragraph*. *Paragraph* is actually a new keyword in Director 7. However, it means the same thing as *line*. While *word* returns items based on where spaces are in the string, a *line* or *paragraph* returns whole lines, based on return characters in the string.

In addition, there is the *item* chunk expression. This returns segments of a string based on the location of commas in a string. Try this in the Message window:

```
myString = "apples,oranges,pears,peaches,bananas"
put item 2 of myString
-- "oranges"
put myString.item[3]
-- "pears"
```

As you can see, the *item* expression can be used with both the old syntax and the new dot syntax. In addition, you can change the character that the *item* expression uses as its delimiter. To do this, you need to set a value for a special variable called *the itemDelimiter*. The keyword *the* signifies that this is a special property in Director. Try this in the Message window:

```
myString = "walnuts;peanuts;sunflower seeds"
the itemDelimiter = ";"
put item 2 of myString
-- "peanuts"
put myString.item[3]
-- "sunflower seeds"
```

The best thing about chunk expressions is that they can all be used together. You can get a character of a word of a line, for instance. Try this in the Message window:

```
the itemDelimiter = ","
myString = "red,yellow,blue,green,light brown"
put myString.item[5]
-- "light brown"
put myString.item[5].word[2]
-- "brown"
put myString.item[5].word[2].char[4]
-- "w"
put char 4 of word 2 of item 5 of myString
-- "w"
```

MANIPULATING STRINGS

In addition to gettingpieces of strings, you can also add to or delete pieces of strings. The way to concatenate strings is to use the & (ampersand) character. Try this in the Message window:

```
myString = "Hello"
put myString&"World."
-- "HelloWorld."
myOtherString = "World."
put myString&myOtherString
-- "HelloWorld."
put myString&&myOtherString
-- "Hello World."
```

The first example used a string variable and a string *literal*, which describes values such as numbers and strings. When you use "&" to concatenate the string variable with the word "Hello" and the literal string "World." you get a result of "HelloWorld." When you use two variables instead, it returns the same thing. Finally, when you use two ampersands (&&) it inserts an extra space in the new string. The double ampersand is used for exactly that purpose: to concatenate two strings with an extra space. You can see how it comes in handy in the final line.

You can also use concatenation to create a new string and store it in a variable. Try this in the Message window:

```
myString = "Hello"
myOtherString = "World."
myNewString = myString&&myOtherString
put myNewString
-- "Hello World."
```

You can alter the contents of a string in still another way, which involves using the *put* command. When you use the *put* command by itself, it places something in the Message window. However, if you use the *put* command along with the keywords *after*, *before*, or *into*, it becomes something very different. It actually assigns a new value to a variable. Try this in the Message window:

```
myString = "Hello"
put "World." after myString
put myString
-- "HelloWorld."
put "I said " before myString
put myString
-- "I said HelloWorld."
```

You see that you can use the *put* command to add text to strings. You could have done the same thing by concatenating strings together and assigning them to a new (or the same) variable. However, this technique is something you should know about.

One special way to use this is to combine the *put* command with chunk expressions. You can actually insert text into a string.

```
myString = "HelloWorld."
put " " after myString.char[5]
put myString
-- "Hello World."
```

PART

IV

CH

13

The *into* keyword can also be used with the *put* command. It would replace the string. However, that would be the same as just stating the variable name followed by an = and the new value. But you can use *put* and *into* to surgically replace characters in the middle of a string.

```
myString = "Hello World."
put "Earth" into myString.char[7..11]
put myString
-- "Hello Earth."
```

In addition to the *put* command, there is also a *delete* command. This will remove a chunk from a string variable. Try this in the Message window:

```
myString = "Hello World."
delete myString.char[2]
put myString
-- "Hllo World."
```

Delete works with character spans, words, lines, and items as well.

→ **See** "Strings and Chunks," Chapter 16, "Controlling Text," for more information about strings

COMPARING VARIABLES

One of the tasks that you will want Lingo to do for you is to make decisions. For the computer to make decisions, it needs to have information. Information, to a computer, is binary: 1 or 0, on or off, true or false.

Lingo uses the idea of true or false in cases where it needs to make decisions. When you compare variables, for instance, you are asking, "Are they equal?" The answer can either be yes or no, which the computer shows as true or false.

Use the Message window to try an example. The operator = is the most common comparison operator. Try it out:

```
put 1 = 1
-- 1
put 1 = 2
-- 0
put "abc" = "def"
-- 0
put "abc" = "abc"
-- 1
```

You can see that when a comparison is true, Director returns a value of 1. When it is false, it returns a value of 0. The use of 1 and 0 as true and false is used so much that Director even recognizes the words true and false as those numbers.

```
put TRUE
-- 1
put FALSE
-- 0
```

Note

The words *TRUE* and *FALSE* are capitalized in the preceding example because they are constants. Constants are Lingo terms that always define the same thing, such as *TRUE* being 1. Because Lingo is not case-sensitive, you don't have to capitalize these terms, but it is a common convention that this book will follow.

Variables and literals can be compared in a lot of ways other than with the = operator. Table 13.2 shows all of Lingo's comparison operators.

TABLE 13.2 LINGO COMPARISON OPERATORS

Operator	Comparing Numbers	Comparing Strings
=	Are the two numbers equal?	Are the two strings the same?
<	Is the first number less than the second?	Does the first string come before the second alphabetically?
>	Is the first number greater than the second?	Does the first string come after the second alphabetically?
<=	Is the first number less than or equal to the second?	Does the first string come before the second alphabetically or match up exactly?
>=	Is the first number greater than or equal to the second?	Does the first string come after the second alphabetically or match up exactly?
<>	Is the first number different from the second? In other words, are they not equal?	Are the two strings different?

Here are some examples from the Message window:

```
put 1 < 2
-- 1
put 2 < 1
-- 0
put 2 <= 1
-- 0
put 2 <= 2
-- 1
put 2 <=3
-- 1
put 2 >= 2
-- 1
put 2 >= 1
-- 1
put 2 <> 1
-- 1
put "this" > "that"
-- 1
```

One important point to note is that when strings are compared, Director rules out capitalization. So "abc" and "Abc" are seen as equal. Also, remember not to accidentally place the comparison operator inside the quotation marks.

USING HANDLERS

In the last chapter you saw how to create handlers. Handlers are collections of Lingo statements brought together to perform a task. Handlers can be named with specific keywords to react to Director events. Handlers can also have custom names and can be called from other handlers you write. Sometimes, handlers can even return a value.

→ **See** "Writing Your Code," Chapter 12, "Learning Lingo," for more information about creating handlers

EVENT HANDLERS

A handler such as *on mouseUp* or *on exitFrame* is an event handler. It is built to respond to a message sent by a specific event in Director. Chapter 12 lists many types of events and gives some examples, such as when the user clicks the mouse or when a frame is done playing.

It is important to know what types of scripts use what types of handlers. An *on mouseUp* handler is typically found in a behavior script that is meant to be attached to a sprite that the user can click. An *on exitFrame* handler is usually meant for a frame script where an action is to be performed after the frame is drawn. These are typical locations for these handlers in scripts written by beginner Lingo programmers.

Most handlers can actually be placed anywhere. An *on mouseUp* behavior can be in a frame script or a movie script, as long as you want that handler to be called every time the user clicks and no other object is there to get the message. An *on exitFrame* script can be used on a sprite behavior script, as long as you want the handler to run every time a frame ends while the sprite is present.

Some handlers don't belong in some places. An *on keyDown* handler gets a message when the user presses a key on the keyboard. It can be used on an editable text member or field, in the frame script, or even in the movie script. However, if *on keyDown* is used in a behavior assigned to a bitmap sprite, it will never be called. This occurs because bitmaps, unlike editable text members or fields, do not accept or react to keystrokes.

Any Lingo code must always be called from an event handler. Even if you write your own custom handler to do something, that handler must be called from some event handler; otherwise, custom handlers sit idle until called. There are a few exceptions, such as typing a custom handler's name in the Message window, which will run the handler although no event handler was involved.

CUSTOM HANDLERS

When you write your own handler, it can have any name you want, as long as it is not the name of an event. You would typically place it in a movie script. That way, the handler is available to be called from any behavior or other movie script. A custom handler can be placed in a behavior, but then it can only be used by other handlers in that behavior. When you learn to write complex behaviors, you will be adding custom handlers to them, but they will all be called by other event handlers in that behavior.

The following example is a movie script. An *on startMovie* handler is called by an event message when the movie starts. It, in turn, calls a custom handler named "initScore." The word "score" refers to a game score, in this case, rather than the Director Score. This handler sets a few global variables:

```
on startMovie
  initScore
  go to frame "intro"
end

on initScore
  global gScore, gLevel
  set gScore = 0
  set gLevel = 0
end
```

You could have all the lines of the "initScore" handler included in the *on startMovie* handler. However, creating your own custom handler does a couple of things. First, it makes the code neater. The "initScore" handler takes care of one task and one task only. Second, it makes it so that the "initScore" handler can be called again later in the program. In this case, you might need to reset the score when the user starts a new game. If you were to place the same lines in *on startMovie*, you would be stuck executing unwanted lines, such as go to frame "intro" again, even though that may not be required the next time you want to reset the score.

FUNCTIONS

One type of custom handler is sometimes called a *function*. What makes this type of handler different is that it returns a value. It works in the same way as the math functions shown earlier in this chapter. The difference, of course is that you can define what the function does.

Two elements to a function are different than a simple handler: input and output. A function handler usually accepts one or more values as input, and sends one value back. The inputs are called *parameters* and the output is simply called the returned value.

For a handler to accept parameters, all you need to do is add the variable names to the handler declaration line. This is the line that begins with the word *on*. Here is an example:

```
on myHandler myNumber
  put myNumber
end
```

This example is not showing a real function, because it does not return a value. However, it is a valid handler. After you begin writing your own programs, it will be very common for you to write handlers that accept one or more parameters even if they do not return a value.

By placing the variable name "myNumber" in the declaration line of a handler, you are preparing the handler to receive its value when it is called. If you place this handler in a movie script and then type the following in the Message window, the handler executes:

```
myHandler(7)
-- 7
```

PART

IV

CH

13

You can see that the number 7 was sent back to the Message window. The line `put myNumber` is responsible for placing it there. When you called the handler "myHandler" with the number 7 as the parameter, the handler executed. Before any Lingo commands were performed, it placed the number 7 into the local variable "myNumber."

You can easily have more that one variable as a parameter. Just use commas to separate them in the declaration line as well as when you are calling the handler. Here is an example:

```
on myHandler myNumber, myOtherNumber
  mySum = myNumber + myOtherNumber
  put mySum
end
```

When you call this handler from the Message window, place two numbers after the handler name in the parentheses. The handler places both those numbers in the variables specified by the declaration line. In the case of our handler, it then adds them to create a new variable and then outputs that variable to the Message window.

```
myHandler(7,4)
-- 11
```

You are actually only one step away from turning this example into a real function. You need to have the handler return a value to do that. For this, simply use the *return* command. Here is the same handler without the *put* command, but with a *return* command:

```
on myHandler myNumber, myOtherNumber
  mySum = myNumber + myOtherNumber
  return mySum
end
```

Now, you can call this handler from the Message window in the same way that you called functions such as *integer* earlier in the chapter. Try this in the Message window:

```
set myNumber = myHandler(7,4)
put myNumber
-- 11
```

The handler "on myHandler" is now a self-contained unit that will take two numbers and return their sum. It would probably be more appropriate to assign names to the handler and the variables in it that are more suitable to their functions:

```
on addTwoNumbers num1, num2
  sum = num1 + num2
  return sum
end
```

This function can now be used in the Message window, as well as other handlers.

```
put addTwoNumbers(5,24)
-- 29
put addTwoNumbers(-7,2)
-- -5
put addTwoNumbers(4.5,2.1)
-- 6.6000
```

You can also use functions to compare variables. Rather than returning a new value, it can return a true or false value:

```
on isOneGreaterThan num1, num2
  return (num1 - 1) = num2
end
```

This function takes two numbers and compares them. It actually subtracts one from the first number and compares it to the value of the second. It returns a 1 if this is true and a 0 if it is not.

```
put isOneGreaterThan(5,4)
-- 1
put isOneGreaterThan(7,2)
-- 0
```

USING *IF...THEN*

Now that you know how to compare variables and get a true or false value, it would be useful to have some additional syntax to enable you to process these comparisons.

SIMPLE IF STATEMENTS

The *if* and *then* keywords can be used to process comparisons. Here is an example:

```
on testIf num
  if num = 7 then
    put "You entered the number 7"
  end if
end
```

You can probably guess what the result of trying this in the message window is:

```
testIf(7)
-- "You entered the number 7"
```

Any commands that you place between the line starting *if* and the line *end if* are executed if the value of the statement between the *if* and the *then* is true.

Note

You can also place the entire *if* statement on one line: `if num = 7 then put "You entered the number 7"`. This works only if you have one line of commands that needs to be inside the *if* statement.

A natural extension of the *if* statement is the *else* keyword. You can use this keyword to specify commands to be performed if the *if* statement is not true. Here is an example:

```
on testElse num
  if num = 7 then
    put "You entered the number 7"
  else
    put "You entered a number that is not 7"
  end if
end
```

Here is what happens when you test this function in the Message window:

```
put testElse(7)
-- "You entered the number 7"
put testIf(9)
-- "You entered a number that is not 7"
```

CASE STATEMENTS

If statements can actually get a little more complex. You can use the *else* keyword to look for other specific situations. For example:

```
on testElse2 num
  if num = 7 then
    put "You entered the number 7"
  else if num = 9 then
    put "You entered the number 9"
  else
    put "You entered another number"
  end if
end
```

Now you have a handler that deals with all sorts of different cases. In fact, Director has some special syntax that handles multiple condition statements like those in this handler. Here is a handler that does exactly the same thing:

```
on testCase num
  case num of
    7:
      put "You entered the number 7"
    9:
      put "You entered the number 9"
    otherwise:
      put "You entered another number"
  end case
end
```

The *case* statement is simply a neater way of writing multiple condition statements. It provides no extra functionality over the *if* statement.

In the *case* statement, you enclose the condition between the word *case* and the word *of* in the first line. Then, you order your commands under each value, followed by a colon. The *otherwise* keyword acts as a final *else* in an *if* sequence.

NESTED IF STATEMENTS

It is important to understand how dynamic commands in Lingo are. An *if* statement, for instance, can exist inside another *if* statement. Check out this example:

```
on nestedIf num
  if num < 0 then
    if num = -1 then
      put "You entered a -1"
    else
      put "You entered a negative number other than -1"
    end if
```

```
    else
      if num = 7 then
        put "You entered a 7"
      else
        put "You entered a positive number other than 7"
      end if
  end if
end
```

The preceding example first determines whether the number is less than 0. If it is, it does one of two things depending on whether the number is -1 or another negative number. If the number is not less than 0, it does another one of two things, one if the number is 7 and something else otherwise.

Although this nesting is not really necessary to achieve the desired result, it demonstrates using the *if* statement in a nested fashion. You could do this to make your code better fit the logic you have in mind, or you could do this because the logic requires nested *if* statements. You will encounter situations like this as you gain more programming experience.

The nests can even go further. You can go as many levels deep as you want. You can even embed *if* statements inside *case* statements and vice-versa.

LOGICAL OPERATORS

But what if you want to test more than one item at a time? Suppose you have a function that tests two numbers rather than one. Such a function would look like this:

```
on testTwoNumbers num1, num2
  if num1 = 7 then
    if num2 = 7 then
      put "You entered two 7s"
    end if
  end if
end
```

An easier way to do this is to use the logical operator *and*. It enables you to check multiple conditions in one *if* statement:

```
on testTwoNumbers2 num1, num2
  if num1 = 7 and num2 = 7 then
    put "You entered two 7s"
  end if
end
```

The second handler is much more compact and readable. You could also use the *or* operator to determine whether either of two conditions are true rather than both.

```
on testEither num1, num2
  if num1 = 7 or num2 = 7 then
    put "You entered at least one 7"
  end if
end
```

Another logical operator that you should know about is the *not* operator. This operator reverses the result of a comparison. A true value becomes false and a false value becomes true. This simple examples shows you how one is used:

```
on testNot num
  if not (num = 7) then
    put "You did not enter a 7"
  end if
end
```

These simple examples of logical operators only scratch the surface of their real uses. You can construct complex logical statements by using *and*, *or*, *not*, and parentheses.

USING REPEAT LOOPS

Computers are great at doing repetitive tasks. The way to ask a set of Lingo commands to repeat is to use the *repeat* command. You can have commands repeat a certain number of times, until a certain condition is met, or forever.

REPEAT WITH

If you want to make a Lingo program count to 100, all you need is a few simple lines. Here is an example:

```
on countTo100
  repeat with i = 1 to 100
    put i
  end repeat
end
```

The *repeat with* loop creates a new variable, in this case "i," and tells it where to start and where to end. Everything in between the *repeat* line and the *end repeat* are executed that many times. In addition, the variable "i" will contain the number of the current loop.

The result of this handler is to count from one to 100 and place each value in the Message window.

Tip

You can also have *repeat* loops count backward from a specific number by using *down to* rather than just *to*.

REPEAT WHILE

Another type of repeat loop is the *repeat while* loop. This operator repeats until a certain statement is true. Here is a handler that does exactly the same thing as the last example:

```
on repeatTo100
  i = 1
  repeat while i <= 100
```

```
      put i
      i = i + 1
   end repeat
end
```

This handler starts the variable "i" out as one, and then repeats over and over, each time outputting the number to the Message window and increasing it by one. Each time, before the repeat loop begins, the statement i <= 100 is checked to see whether it is true. When it is, the repeat loop ends.

This example is, of course, very simple. If you wanted to do this in real life, you would use the *repeat with* loop in the earlier example. The *repeat with* syntax is good for counting and the *repeat while* syntax is good for a lot of other things, such as in the following simple example. In this case, you are writing a handler that counts until the user holds the Shift key to stop it:

```
on countWhileNoShift
  i = 1
  repeat while not the shiftDown
    put i
    i = i + 1
  end repeat
end
```

This example uses a new property called *the shiftDown*. It returns a 1 when the Shift key is held down, and a 0 when it is not. When you run this handler in the Message window, the "i" variable starts counting. Press and hold the Shift key and it stops. The Message window contains the history of the count.

OTHER REPEAT COMMANDS

Suppose you want a handler that counts to 100, but can also be interrupted by the Shift key. The following might be one way to do that:

```
on countTo100orShift1
  i = 1
  repeat while (i <= 100) and (not the shiftDown)
    put i
    i = i + 1
  end repeat
end
```

This handler uses a *repeat while* loop that checks to make sure that two conditions are true: "i" is still less than or equal to 100 and the Shift key is not down. Another way to do this is to use the *exit repeat* command:

```
on countTo100orShift2
  repeat with i = 1 to 100
    put i
    if the shiftDown then exit repeat
  end repeat
end
```

This second handler is much neater. It uses a *repeat with* loop, which makes more sense for a loop that counts. One line of the loop checks whether the Shift key is down, and then the *exit repeat* command breaks Director out of that loop.

The *exit repeat* command works in both *repeat with* and *repeat while* loops. It acts as essentially a second way for the loop to end. The loops you are writing now are only a few lines long, but advanced Lingo programmers write loops that are much more involved. Sometimes an *exit repeat* command is the best way to break out of a loop when needed.

There is also a *next repeat* command that doesn't go quite as far as the *exit repeat*. Rather than end the loop, the *next repeat* prevents all the rest of the lines in that loop from executing and goes immediately back to the beginning of the loop. Here is an example:

```
on countTo100WithShift
  repeat with i = 1 to 100
    put "Counting..."
    if the shiftDown then next repeat
    put i
  end repeat
end
```

The preceding handler counts from 1 to 100 like a lot of the previous examples. Each time through the loop it sends a "Counting..." to the Message window. It then sends the number to the Message window. However, if you hold the Shift key down while it is running, the *next repeat* command prevents Director from continuing to the put i line. The result is that only "Counting..." goes to the Message window those times.

> **Note**
>
> Lingo is very fast—so fast, in fact, that it may be impossible to interrupt the previous handlers with the Shift key before they get the chance to finish. You may want to try them with 10,000 or an even higher number instead of 100.

REPEATING FOREVER

Sometimes, it may be necessary to construct a repeat loop that keeps going until an *exit repeat* command is executed. In that case, you don't want to use *repeat with*, because that command causes the loop to repeat only a certain number of times. Using *repeat while* demands that you also place a condition on when the repeat loop stops.

However, there is a tricky way to use *repeat while* without a condition, but instead basically tell it to repeat forever. Here is an example:

```
on repeatForever
  repeat while TRUE
    put "repeating..."
    if the shiftDown then exit repeat
  end repeat
end
```

This handler doesn't really repeat forever, it just repeats until the Shift key is pressed. However, an *exit repeat* and only an *exit repeat* can terminate the loop, because you have placed a *TRUE* as the condition on the *repeat while* loop. Because *TRUE* is always true, it repeats forever, or at least until the *exit repeat* command executes.

You need this kind of repeat loop in cases where you want the conditions that determine when the repeat loop ends to not be after the *repeat while* statement. You might want to have a loop like this when the condition is long and involved, or because several conditions exit the repeat loop and no one condition is more important than the other.

> **Tip**
>
> If you ever set up a repeat loop to repeat forever and don't give Director a way to get out of it, you can always press Command+. (Period) on the Mac or Ctrl+. (Period) in Windows to halt Director and Lingo. If you don't, Director may eventually crash.

Using Lingo Navigation Commands

Repeat loops, *if* statements, and handlers are ways to organize and control Lingo commands. But what about commands that actually *do* something?

The simplest commands in Director are the ones that move the playback head around the Score. You have total control over where the playback head goes next. You can jump to a frame number or marker, or even to another movie.

Go

You can make the movie jump to a frame number by simply telling it to *go*. Open the Score window and the Message window. The playback head should be on frame 1. Now, in the Message window, type go 5.

The playback head should proceed to frame 5. A more common form of this command is to use the full statement *go to frame 5*. This is a little more readable.

You can also tell the movie to go to the next marker. Create a marker label for frame seven simply called "intro". Then, in the Message window type go to frame "intro".

Table 13.3 shows all the variations of the *go* command.

PART
IV

CH

13

TABLE 13.3   THE MANY VERSIONS OF THE GO COMMAND

Version	Description	Example
go to frame X	The movie goes to frame number X.	go to frame 7
go to frame "X"	The movie goes to the frame labeled X.	go to frame "credits"

continues

TABLE 13.3   CONTINUED

Version	Description	Example
go to the frame	The movie begins the same frame over again.	go to the frame
go to the frame + X	The movie jumps ahead X frames	go to the frame + 1
go to the frame - X	The movie jumps back X frames	go to the frame - 1
go next	The movie jumps to the next labeled frame.	go next
go previous	The movie jumps to the labeled frame immediately before the currently labeled frame.	go previous
go loop	The movie jumps back to the currently labeled frame.	go loop
go marker(X)	The movie jumps forward X labeled frames.	go marker(2)
go marker(-X)	The movie jumps back X labeled frames.	Go marker(-2)

The most confusing concept is the difference between the current label and the previous label. Figure 13.1 shows the Score with some labeled frames. The playback head is between two of them in frame 9. Frame 7 is labeled "that", frame 3 is labeled "this", and frame 12 is labeled "other". If you were to execute a *go loop*, the movie would jump back to "that", because it is the closest marker just before the playback head. However, a *go previous* command takes the movie back to "this", which is considered the previous label.

Figure 13.1
The playback head is between two labeled frames. "That" is considered the current label and "this" is the previous one.

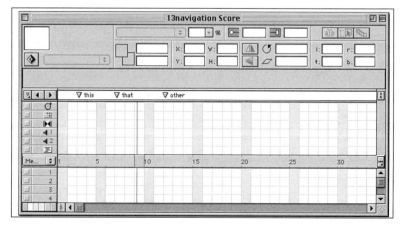

Some other Lingo elements are introduced in Table 13.3. The first is the property *the frame*. This property returns the current frame number. If you set the Score up as it is in Figure 13.1, you could do this in the Message window:

```
put the frame
-- 7
```

The function *marker* also gets information from the Score. It takes one number as a parameter. If that number is a 0, it returns the name of the current label marker. If it is a -1, it returns the name of the previous marker. A 1 returns the name of the next marker. Try this in the Message window with a Score like that shown in Figure 13.1:

```
put marker(0)
-- "that"
put marker(1)
-- "other"
put marker(-1)
-- "this"
```

So the Lingo command *go previous* is the same as saying go to `marker(-1)`. Also, *go next* and *go loop* match the other two lines in the preceding example.

You can even use the *marker* function to get or go to markers that are several markers after or before the current one. Just use a higher number, such as 2 or -2, to go to markers more than one away from the current marker.

Using Go

To use the *go* command to actually do something, all you need to do is place it in a simple behavior script. Here is an example:

```
on mouseUp
  go to frame 8
end
```

Make sure that you create this as a behavior script, not a movie script. Check this option using the Script Cast Member Properties dialog box. Use the Info button in the script window to access this dialog box.

After you have this behavior script, you can drag and drop it on any sprite to create a simple button. The script acts in the same way as a behavior created with the Behavior Inspector would act.

A more useful behavior would go to a frame label rather than a number. You can also use *go next* and *go previous* to create forward and backward buttons.

Another way to use the *go* command is in a frame script. This example is probably the most commonly written script in Lingo:

```
on exitFrame
  go to the frame
end
```

All that this frame script does is hold the movie on the current frame. Every time the frame ends, it simply starts over again. A behavior in the library called "Hold on Current Frame" does this as well. You use this script to hold the movie on a frame while the user selects buttons and performs actions.

You can also use the *go loop* command in this way to have the movie loop back to the current frame marker. While *go to the frame* loops on one frame, *go loop* can loop on a whole series of frames. This enables you to have looping animation present while still keeping elements such as buttons around for the user to select.

PLAY

A second way to navigate around a movie is to use the *play* command. The basic command works just like a *go*, but there is a major difference. *Play* actually remembers what frame the movie was on when the command was issued. That way, the *play done* command can be used to return the playback head to the original frame.

Suppose that you have three labels named "menu", "chapter1", and "chapter2" in the Score. A button on the frame labeled "menu" can issue a `play frame "chapter1"`. Then, another button on the frame labeled "chapter1" can issue a *play done* to have the playback head return to the frame "menu". The same *play done* button and behavior can be reused in the frame labeled "chapter2".

You could, in fact, issue the initial *play* command anywhere in the movie and Director remembers that frame and uses it with the *play done* command.

LEAVING THE MOVIE

Both *go* and *play* can be used to jump to another movie as well as a frame in the current movie. The syntax is simply an extension of what you have already read about.

Here is a behavior that opens another movie and starts playing it from frame 1:

```
on mouseUp
  go to movie "nextMovie.dir"
end
```

Note

Director is actually smart enough to assume the correct extension at the end of a movie name if you leave it off. This way, you don't have to worry about having a .dir extension on a Windows file and not on a Mac. It also solves the problem of changing the movie's filename to have a .dxr or a .dcr when you protect or compress it later.

If you don't want to have the movie start playing on frame 1, you can specify the frame by extending the command a bit:

```
on mouseUp
  go to frame "intro" of movie "nextMovie.dir"
end
```

You can use the same format with the *play* command. Here is actually where the power of the *play* command really shines. You can have a button that takes users to a completely separate movie and enables them to navigate there. When they are finished, they can press a button that executes a *play done* command and they will return to the previous movie. The *play done* command even returns users to the correct frame in that movie.

→ **See** "Nonlinear Presentations," Chapter 2, "Presentations with Director," for more information about movies and navigation

CONTROLLING SPRITE PROPERTIES

Besides navigation, the next most important task that a Lingo command can perform is to change the properties of a sprite. Properties are attributes of sprites that describe anything from their positions on the Stage to their ink types. Changing the sprites' properties is how you use Lingo to animate your sprites.

You will usually set sprite properties in the behavior scripts attached to the sprites, but for now you can examine some sprite properties in the Message window.

SPRITE LOCATION

For these examples, create a bitmap member and place it on the Stage and in the Score at sprite channel 1. Then open the Message window. Try this:

```
sprite(1).locH = 50
updateStage
```

You should see your sprite jump so that its registration point (usually the center) is 50 pixels from the left side of the Stage. It was the first line of the example that actually did this. It set the property *locH* of sprite 1 to the number 50. The *locH* property is the horizontal location of the sprite.

However, you didn't see any change on the Stage until the second command, *updateStage*. This is a special command that shows changes to sprite properties on the Stage while the movie is not playing. If the movie had been playing, and the change to the property had been inside a behavior script, the Stage would have updated automatically the next time a frame began. But for all the examples here, you need to use *updateStage* to see the sprite properties change.

The syntax sprite(1).locH is new to Director 7. Had you been programming in Director 6.5 or earlier, you would have actually typed this:

```
set the locH of sprite 1 = 50
updateStage
```

This older syntax still works for simple examples such as this one. However, it is best to get used to the new dot syntax. It is not only easier to type, but is required for features of Director that are new to this version.

You can also set the vertical location of a sprite. To do this, use the *locV* property.

```
sprite(1).locV = 100
updateStage
```

There is also a way to set both the horizontal and vertical locations of a sprite. This property is just called the *loc* of the sprite. However, it doesn't take a number value, but rather a *point*. A point is a special Lingo object that looks like this: *point(x,y)*. The two numbers in the parentheses represent a horizontal and vertical location. Here it is in use:

```
sprite(1).loc = point(200,225)
updateStage
```

You can also set many other sprite properties. Table 13.4 shows a partial list of them.

TABLE 13.4   PARTIAL LIST OF SPRITE PROPERTIES

Property	Description	Example Value
member	The member used by the sprite	member"myButton"
locH	The horizontal position of the sprite	50
locV	The vertical position of the sprite	50
loc	The position of the sprite	point(50,50)
rect	The rectangle of the sprite	rect(25,25,75,75)
ink	The sprite's ink	8
blend	The sprite's blend	100
trails	Whether the trails property is on or off	FALSE
color	The foreground color of a sprite	rgb("#000000")
bgcolor	The background color of a sprite	rgb("#FFFFFF")

SPRITE MEMBER

Setting the member of the sprite to something different than the original member is quite common. This way, rollover and down states for buttons can be different cast members than the normal state of the button, and animations can use different images.

To change the member that a sprite is using, just set the *member* property of that sprite. You cannot simply set it to the name or number of a member, but to an actual member object.

Member objects are simply ways of referring to a member that Lingo can understand. If there is a member called "button down state," you need to refer to it as member("button down state"). If that member is member number 7, you could also refer to it as member(7).

Create a movie with two bitmaps. They can be anything, even just scribbles in the Paint window. Name them "bitmap1" and "bitmap2". Place the first bitmap on the Stage, as sprite 1. Try this in the Message window:

```
sprite(1).member = member("bitmap2")
updateStage
sprite(1).member = member("bitmap1")
updateStage
```

You will see the sprite change and then change back with each *updateStage*. You could have also referred to the members by their numbers.

SPRITE RECTANGLE

The *rect* property also has a special Lingo object associated with it. In Table 3.4, the example "rect(25,25,75,75)" was used. This represents the position of the left, top, right, and bottom of the sprite respectively.

You can set the *rect* of a sprite to any size, regardless of how well this corresponds to the dimensions of the actual member. In cases where the member can be stretched, like bitmaps, the member is distorted on the Stage to correspond to the sprite's rectangle.

SPRITE INK

The *ink* property takes a number as its value. Unfortunately, you cannot set it to values such as Background Transparent. Refer to Table 13.5 for corresponding ink numbers.

TABLE 13.5   LINGO INK NUMBERS

Number	Corresponding Ink
0	Copy
1	Transparent
2	Reverse
3	Ghost
4	Not Copy
5	Not Transparent
6	Not Reverse
7	Not Ghost
8	Matte
9	Mask

PART

IV

CH

13

continues

TABLE 13.5   CONTINUED

Number	Corresponding Ink
32	Blend
33	Add Pin
34	Add
35	Subtract Pin
36	Background Transparent
37	Lightest
38	Subtract
39	Darkest
40	Lighten
41	Darken

SPRITE COLOR

Changing the *color* and *bgColor* of a sprite has an effect only some of the time. It depends on what type of sprite it is and what ink it is using. A 1-bit bitmap uses these two colors to set the color of the black and white pixels of the bitmap. Color bitmaps that use the Lighten and Darken inks use these colors to alter the appearance of the bitmap.

There are several ways to define colors. The first is to set them to the red, green, and blue values for the color. To do this, you need to use the *rgb* structure. Like the *point* and *rect* structure, *rgb* helps you to define an item that cannot be represented by a single number.

For these examples, create a 1-bit bitmap and place it on the Stage. It should be in sprite 1. It should appear black on the Stage as a default. Try this in the Message window:

```
sprite(1).color = rgb(0,0,255)
updateStage
```

The color of the black pixels in the bitmap should change to blue. The three numbers in the *rgb* structure represent red, green, and blue colors. The results of them being set to zero, zero, and 255 is that the color becomes pure blue. When defining *rgb* like this, keep in mind that the minimum value is zero and the maximum value is 255.

Another way to define a color with *rgb* is to use the hexadecimal string value for the color. This corresponds to the color values used in HTML. Here is an example:

```
sprite(1).color = rgb("#0000FF")
updateStage
```

This sets the color to pure blue just as the previous example did. The six digits in the string represent the three colors: a "00" is a 0 and a "FF" is a 255. If you are familiar with hexadecimal values, you can use this system. It also comes in handy if you are used to working with HTML colors. Otherwise, stick to the other version of the *rgb* structure.

Note

Before Director 7, you could define colors only according to the movie's color palette. These 256 colors were used for the *foreColor* and *backColor* properties. Both of these properties are now obsolete, but they still work in Director 7 if you really want to use them.

To refer to a color based on the color palette of the movie, use the *paletteIndex* structure. This enables you to use a palette color number rather than an *rgb* value:

```
sprite(1).color = paletteIndex(35)
updateStage
```

With both the Mac System palette and the Windows System palette, the color 35 is a red.

→ **See** "Controlling a Single Sprite," Chapter 14, "Creating Behaviors," for more information about sprite properties

CONTROLLING MEMBER PROPERTIES

As well as setting sprite properties, you can also set member properties. These properties depend on the member type.

One example is the shape member. It has a property of *shapeType*. You can set this to be #rect, #roundRect, #oval, or #line. Create a shape member on the Stage and make sure it is in cast member slot 1. Then try this:

```
member(1).shapeType = #rect
member(1).shapeType = #oval
member(1).shapeType = #roundRect
member(1).shapeType = #line
```

Notice that the shape changes without an *updateStage* command. This happens because this command usually updates sprite properties. Member properties, on the other hand, update as soon as the property changes. There are exceptions to this, as you'll discover later with more advanced Lingo.

PART
IV
CH
13

USING LIST VARIABLES

Every major programming language has the capability to store a series of variables. In some languages these are called *arrays*. In Lingo, they called *lists*. There are two types of lists: linear lists and property lists.

LINEAR LISTS

A linear list is a series of numbers, strings, or data of some other type that is contained in a single variable. Try this in the Message window:

```
myList = [4,7,8,42,245]
put myList
-- [4, 7, 8, 42, 245]
```

Now that you have created a list, you need a way to access each item in it. This is done with some special syntax:

```
put myList[1]
-- 4
put myList[4]
-- 42
```

Note

In Director 6 and before, you needed to use the function *getAt* to accomplish this task. This function still works, but the new syntax makes it unnecessary.

Lists can also hold strings. In fact, they can hold a combination of numbers and strings. They can even hold structures such as *points*, *rects*, and *rgb* values. Here are some examples of valid lists:

```
myList = ["apples", "oranges", "peaches"]
myList = [1, 2, 3, "other"]
myList = [point(50,50), point(100,100), point(100,125)]
myList = [[1,2,3,4,5], [1,2,3,5,7,9], [345,725]]
```

The last example shows a list that actually contains other lists. These come in handy in advanced Lingo. Here is an example of a list that holds a small database of names and phone numbers:

```
myList = [["Gary", "555-1234"], ["William", "555-9876"], ["John", "555-1928"]]
```

Here is a handler that shows a somewhat practical use for lists. The list contains a series of member names. When the handler is called, it uses the list to rapidly change sprite 1's member to these members:

```
on animateWithList
  myList = ["arrow1", "arrow2", "arrow3"]
  repeat with i = 1 to 3
    sprite(1).member = member myList[1]
    updateStage
  end repeat
end
```

The handler uses a *repeat* loop to take the variable "i" from 1 to 3. It then sets the member of sprite 1 to the member with the name used in each location of the list. An *updateStage* is used to make the change visible on the Stage.

Another way to create lists is to use commands that add or remove an item from them, rather than create the list all at once. The *add* command places an item in a list that already exists. A *deleteAt* command removes an item from a list. Try this in the Message window:

```
myList = []
add myList, 5
add myList, 7
add myList, 9
put myList
-- [5, 7, 9]
add myList, 242
put myList
-- [5, 7, 9, 242]
deleteAt myList, 3
put myList
-- [5, 7, 242]
```

The first line in this example creates an empty list. Then, you added three items to it. After taking a look at the contents, you added a fourth item. Finally, you deleted item number 3, which was a "9," from the list.

Another command you should know about is the *count* property of a list. It tells you how many items are currently in the list. Try this in the Message window:

```
myList = [5,7,9,12]
put myList.count
-- 4
```

In the preceding handler example, instead of having "i" go from 1 to 3, you could have had "i" go from 1 to "myList.count". This would have made it possible to add or remove items from the list later, without having to worry about changing the hard-coded number "3" in the script as well.

PROPERTY LISTS

One of the problems with linear lists is that you can refer to the items in the list only by position. A different type of list, called a *property list*, enables you to define a name for each item in the list. Here is a typical property list:

```
myList = [#name: "Gary", #phone: "555-1234", #employedSince: 1996]
```

Each item in a property list contains both a property name and a property value. For instance, the first item in the preceding list is the property #name, and its value is "Gary". The property name and the property value are separated by a colon.

To refer to a property in a list such as this, you can use the property name rather than the position. Try this in the Message window:

```
myList = [#name: "Gary", #phone: "555-1234", #employedSince: 1996]
put myList[#name]
-- "Gary"
```

Tip
> The properties in this list are called *symbols*. In Lingo, anything prefaced by a "#" charac-
> ter is a symbol. Anything referred to with a symbol can be accessed by Lingo very quickly.
> Symbols are ideal for property lists for this reason. However, you can use numbers and
> strings as property names in property lists as well.

You can add items to a property list with the *addProp* command, and you can also delete an
item in a property list with a *deleteProp* command.

```
myList = [:]
addProp myList, #name, "Gary"
addProp myList, #phone, "555-1234"
put myList
-- [#name: "Gary", #phone: "555-1234"]
deleteProp myList, #phone
put myList
-- [#name: "Gary"]
```

Notice that you use a "[:]" rather than a "[]" to create an empty property list. You cannot
use *addProp* with a linear list and you cannot use *add* with a property list.

FRAME SCRIPTS

Frame scripts are behaviors that occupy the frame script channel of a frame in the Score.
This chapter already had one example of a frame script. It looked like this:

```
on exitFrame
  go to the frame
end
```

This simple frame script is very important. It holds the movie on a single frame and enables
your other scripts to receive many *prepareFrame*, *enterFrame*, and *exitFrame* messages while
the user can explore the screen.

Without this type of frame script, the movie is obliged to move on to the next frame in the
Score. For straight animation this is fine, but for actually creating real programs, you need
the movie to loop on the frame.

Just about all the scripts in this book from this point on rely on an *on exitFrame* handlerthat
loops on the frame.

TROUBLESHOOTING LINGO SYNTAX

- Any time you place something inside quotes, it represents a string. So "4+2" is just 4+2,
  whereas 4+2 is 6.

- Remember that rounding works two different ways in Lingo. If you perform an operation on integers, such as 3/4, the fractional remainder is dropped, giving you a 3/4 = 0.
  However, if you use the *integer* function, the result is rounded. So integer(.75) = 1.

- A function that does not use a *return* command at the end, or instead uses an *exit* command to leave the handler, returns a value of VOID, which is interpreted by Lingo to
  be equal to FALSE.

DID YOU KNOW?

- You can set the default number of decimal places that Lingo is to use in floating point values with *the floatPrecision* system property. It starts with a value of 4.

- Using a function called *chars* is another way to extract a piece of a string. If you try `chars("abcdefdgh",3,5)`, you get the value "cde". Because chunk expressions cannot be used if you plan to export to a Java applet, *chars* is the only option for extracting characters from strings or fields.

- If you use an *if* statement on a single line, Director expects there to be an *else* statement on the very next line. If there is not, or if there is a blank line, Director assumes that there is no *else* statement to match the *if* statement. However, it is very easy to accidentally nest a one-line *if* statement inside another *if* statement that has an *else*. In that case, Director assumes that the *else* goes with the second *if*, not the first. This example shows how to fix this problem with a blank line:

```
if a = 1 then
  if b = 1 then c = 1
  -- need comment or blank line here
else
  c = 2
end if
```

- You can include more than one possible value as a condition of a case statement by simply placing a list of values before the colon separated by commas.

- Rectangles can be a series of four numbers, such as rect(10,20,50,60) or a series of two points, such as rect(point(10,20),point(50,60)).

- You can also use the function *list* to create a list. So list (4, 7, 8) is the same as [4, 7. 8].

Using Behaviors

CREATING BEHAVIORS

In this chapter

Even though behaviors were only introduced with Director 6, they have already become the standard way of getting things done with Lingo. Understanding behaviors—how to write them, how they work, and how to use them—is the key to powerful Lingo scripting.

CONTROLLING A SINGLE SPRITE

All that behaviors essentially do is control a single sprite. You write them, and then attach them to one or more sprites in the Score to have them "take over" that sprite.

As the name suggests, a behavior tells a sprite how to behave. For instance, an *on mouseUp* handler in a behavior tells the sprite how to behave when the user clicks on the sprite.

SPRITE MESSAGES

Many messages are sent to behaviors from different Director events. A "mouseUp" is a common example. A behavior script is the very first script to get such messages and so has the capability to use them before frame or movie scripts do.

Here is a complete list of messages that can be sent to behaviors. It is similar to the list in Chapter 12, "Learning Lingo," but only messages that behaviors can receive are included here:

- mouseDown—The user has pressed down the mouse button while the cursor is over the sprite.
- mouseUp —The user pressed down on the mouse button while the cursor was over the sprite and has now lifted the mouse button up while still over the sprite.
- mouseUpOutside —The user pressed down the mouse button while the cursor was over the sprite and has now lifted the mouse button up while no longer over the sprite.
- mouseEnter —The cursor enters the sprite's area. In the case of an ink such as Copy, the sprite area is the rectangle that bounds it. In the case of an ink such as Matte, the sprite is the masked area of the sprite.
- mouseLeave —The mouse leaves the sprite's area.
- mouseWithin —This message is sent with every frame loop if the cursor is within the sprite's area.
- prepareFrame —This message is sent with every frame loop just before the frame is drawn on the Stage.
- enterFrame —This message is sent with every frame loop just after the frame is drawn on the Stage.
- exitFrame —This message is sent with every frame loop just before the next frame begins.
- beginSprite —This message is sent when the sprite first appears or reappears on the Stage.

- endSprite —This message is sent just before the sprite leaves the Stage.

- keyDown —This message is sent when the user first presses a key on the keyboard. It is sent for editable text members or fields only.

- keyUp —The user pressed down on a keyboard key and has now lifted it up. It is sent for editable text members or fields only.

Each one of these messages can be handled in a behavior with a handler of the same name. In addition to these event handlers, several special functions can be added to behaviors. Each enables you to customize the behavior further.

- getBehaviorDescription —This gives you a chance to define a text description of a behavior. This is the text that appears in the bottom area of the Behavior Inspector window. It is a simple function where you are expected to create a string and use *return* to send it along.

- getPropertyDescriptionList —This function enables you to create a property list that contains the parameters for the behavior. Using this function allows the library behaviors to show a dialog box with parameter settings when the behavior is dragged to a sprite.

- runPropertyDialog —With this function you can use Lingo to automatically set the parameters of a behavior when it is dragged to a sprite.

- getBehaviorToolTip —Tool tips are those little yellow boxes of help text that appear when you roll over some screen elements. You can add this text to a behavior so that if it is added to your Library Palette, it displays that text as the tool tip.

PROPERTIES

A behavior is an object-oriented programming method. *Object-oriented* just means that both a program and data are stored in the same place. In the case of behaviors, the program is the handlers of the behavior. The data is the variables used by the behavior. These variables are called *properties*.

A property is something in between a local and a global variable. The first exists only inside a single handler. The second exists throughout the entire movie. A property, however, exists throughout the entire behavior script, accessible for all the handlers in the behavior, but not normally accessible outside of it.

You create properties like the way you create global variables. Rather than use a *global* command, you use a *property* command. The best place for this is in the first lines at the top of a behavior script.

Properties hold the data that is important to the behavior. For instance, if a behavior needs to move a sprite horizontally across the Stage, two properties might be "horizLoc" and "horizSpeed". They would correspond to the current horizontal location of the sprite and the number of pixels that the sprite moves each frame, respectively.

PART

V

CH

14

Although the first property, "horizLoc", might just start off from wherever the sprite begins, the second property, "horizSpeed", might be something that can be set when you drag the behavior to a sprite. In that case, "horizSpeed" might be referred to as a *parameter* as well as a *property*.

USING ME

Because behaviors are object-oriented, each handler in a behavior must have a reference to the object it is a part of as its first parameter. Sound confusing? It can be.

A behavior script by itself is just a bunch of text in a cast member. When you attach it to a sprite, it is still just a bunch of text with which the sprite knows it has a relationship. However, when you run the movie and the sprite appears on the Stage, an object is created.

The object, called an *instance* of the behavior, is sort of a copy of the behavior. The Lingo code is loaded into a new location of memory and the property variables are created. This instance is now attached to and controlling the sprite.

If the same behavior is attached to two different sprites, and they both appear on the Stage at the same time, they actually have two different instances of the behavior. Both instances have copies of the same handlers, and both have properties of the same names, but the values of these properties are stored in different locations and can have different values.

The idea of an instance needs to be present in your behavior code. Each handler needs to know that it is part of a behavior. To signify this in your code, you should place the parameter *me* as the very first parameter of all handlers in the behavior.

Create a new script member and set its type to be "Behavior". Now, add this simple script to it:

```
on mouseUp me
  put me
end
```

Name this behavior "Test Behavior" and attach it to any sprite on the Stage. A simple shape will do. Run the movie and click the sprite. You should see something like this appear in the Message window:

```
-- <offspring "Test Behavior" 4 33b1e64>
```

The actual numbers at the end of this line will vary. They are the memory locations of the instance of the behavior and are not important to your programming. However, the special variable *me* is important. Because it points to the actual instance of the object, having it as the first parameter of all the handlers in a behavior will indicate that the handlers are all meant to be a part of the behavior.

If you are still confused, think of it this way: The common first parameter *me* of the handlers in a behavior ties all those behaviors together. *me* is a reference to the behavior in the same way that *sprite* is a reference to a sprite, or that *member* is a reference to a member.

me has properties, the most useful of which is *spriteNum*. You can use it to get the sprite channel number of the sprite to which the behavior is currently attached:

```
on mouseUp me
   put me.spriteNum
end
```

If you do not place the *me* after the handler name, the script does not work. As a matter of fact, it gives you an error message when you try to close the script window because Director doesn't even know what *me* is supposed to refer to if it is not included after the handler name.

→ **See** "Creating an Object in Lingo," Chapter 23, "Object-Oriented Programming," for more information about object-oriented programming

CREATING SIMPLE BEHAVIORS

Simple behaviors can be no more than one handler with one Lingo command. Complex ones, on the other hand, can be hundreds of lines long with just about every event handler and many custom handlers.

NAVIGATION BEHAVIORS

A simple navigation handler is usually applied to a button or bitmap sprite. It uses the *on mouseUp* event to trigger a navigation command. Here is an example:

```
on mouseUp me
   go to frame 7
end
```

This handler is no more useful than one created with the Behavior Inspector. However, using a single property, you can create a behavior that can be used on many different buttons.

```
property pTargetFrame

on getPropertyDescriptionList me
   return [#pTargetFrame: [#comment: "Target Frame:",¬
          #format: #integer, #default: 1]]
end

on mouseUp me
   go to frame pTargetFrame
end
```

> **Tip**
>
> Notice the continuation character (¬) at the end of the first part of a long line in the first handler. Lines of Lingo can be as long as you like, whereas lines in a printed book cannot. So feel free to leave out this character and just type one long line. If you want to use the continuation character in Lingo, hold down the Option key and press Return on the Mac or the Alt key and press Enter in Windows. If you simply press Return or Enter, the line will actually become two lines and generate errors.

This behavior uses a property "pTargetFrame" to determine to which frame the button will cause the movie to jump. This property is used in the *on getPropertyDescriptionList* function to set things up so that the Parameters dialog box for this behavior will enable you to select the frame number.

> **Note**
>
> The property "pTargetFrame" can also easily be named just "targetFrame". However, sometimes it is useful to have your variable names provide a hint as to which type they are. Some programmers like to place a "p" as the first letter of property variables. "g" is a common prefix for global variables. Some developers prefer to place an "i" in front of property variables, to stand for "instance." These are not really part of Lingo, but just convenient conventions.

The list in the *on getPropertyDescriptionList* function is a property list that contains one or more other property lists. The property name for the first (and only, in this case) item of the list is the name of the property, turned into a symbol by adding a "#" in front of it. The list that is its property value contains three items. The first is the *#comment* property. This is the string that the Parameters dialog box will show for this parameter. The second item, the #format, tells the Parameters dialog box what types of values to accept for this parameter. The last item is a default value for this parameter.

When you drag and drop this behavior onto the Stage or Score, the Parameters dialog box appears with a field labeled "Target Frame:". This field takes any number as a value. It will at first show the default value of "1".

This behavior can now be attached to many sprites, but with a different target frame each time. This reusability is one of the powerful features of behaviors. You can have a movie filled with navigation buttons, but you need only this one behavior.

To complete this behavior, you should add an *on getBehaviorDescription* function to it. This function displays some informative text in the Behavior Inspector when the script is added to a sprite:

```
on getBehaviorDescription me
  return "Jumps to a frame number on mouseUp."
end
```

Figure 14.1 shows the Behavior Inspector when a sprite with this behavior is attached. Notice the description in the bottom area.

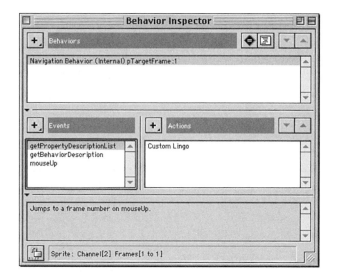

Figure 14.1
The Behavior
Inspector shows a
custom behavior with
a description.

ROLLOVER BEHAVIORS

A common behavior in Director is one that has a button or other graphic that changes appearance when the cursor is over it. This is commonly referred to as a *rollover*.

Rollover behaviors are easy to do with the *on mouseEnter* and *on mouseLeave* events. The bitmap should change when the cursor enters the sprite's area, and then change back when it leaves it. The behavior can be as simple as this:

```
on mouseEnter me
  sprite(1).member = member("button rollover")
end

on mouseLeave me
  sprite(1).member = member("button normal")
end
```

This behavior works fine as long as you use it only on a sprite in channel 1, and you use only the two members "button rollover" and "button normal" as the bitmaps. So it is not much of behavior because it can only be used in one specific instance.

The first thing that you can do to improve this behavior is to have it automatically figure out in which sprite it is used. The sprite number is a property of the behavior instance, which you know better as *me*. Rather than hard-coding the number "1" as the sprite, you can use the syntax *me.spriteNum*. This works as a variable that contains the number of the sprite channel that this sprite is using. If it happens to be in sprite 1, it will contain a 1; otherwise it will contain whatever sprite channel number it is in.

```
on mouseEnter me
  sprite(me.spriteNum).member = member("button rollover")
end

on mouseLeave me
  sprite(me.spriteNum).member = member("button normal")
end
```

PART

V

CH

14

Now you have a behavior that can be attached to any sprite in any channel. However, it still uses two hard-coded members as the normal and rollover states. You can easily figure out the normal state of a button because it is probably the member with which that button is set to begin. You can get that member and store it in a property in the *on beginSprite* handler.

```
property pMemberNormal

on beginSprite me
  pMemberNormal = sprite(me.spriteNum).member
end

on mouseEnter me
  sprite(me.spriteNum).member = member("button rollover")
end

on mouseLeave me
  sprite(me.spriteNum).member = pMemberNormal
end
```

The *on beginSprite* handler uses the sprite number, through *me.spriteNum*, to get the member that is assigned to the sprite in the Score. It stores this in the property variable "pMemberNormal" and then uses it in the *on mouseLeave* handler as the member of the normal state.

Now you have only one hard-coded element left: the member of the rollover state. It is set to always be the member named "button rollover" no matter which sprite and which normal state member are used.

Three techniques for completing this behavior are most commonly used. The first is to assume that the rollover member for the button is always in the very next cast slot over from the normal member. So if the normal member is number 67, the rollover member is 68.

```
property pMemberNormal, pMemberRollover

on beginSprite me
  pMemberNormal = sprite(me.spriteNum).member
  pMemberRollover = member(pMemberNormal.number + 1)
end

on mouseEnter me
  sprite(me.spriteNum).member = pMemberRollover
end

on mouseLeave me
  sprite(me.spriteNum).member = pMemberNormal
end
```

The *on beginSprite* handler gets the current member and places it in "pMemberNormal" as before. It also gets the number of that member and adds one to it to create a new member object. This member would always be the very next member in the Cast. It stores that in "pMemberRollover".

This behavior works only when the normal and rollover states of the sprite are placed in consecutive member slots. It is far more flexible than the previous script. However, you can use the member names to make it even more flexible. You can get the name of the normal member and append something to it, such as "rollover" for instance.

```
property pMemberNormal, pMemberRollover

on beginSprite me
  pMemberNormal = sprite(me.spriteNum).member
  pMemberRollover = member(pMemberNormal.name&&"rollover")
end

on mouseEnter me
  sprite(me.spriteNum).member = pMemberRollover
end

on mouseLeave me
  sprite(me.spriteNum).member = pMemberNormal
end
```

The only difference between the last two behaviors is how they set the "pMemberRollover" property. In the last example, the name of the normal state is taken and the word "rollover" is appended to it. The double ampersand is used to insert a space between the two. So if the normal member is named "button1" the rollover member must be named "button1 rollover". It doesn't need to be placed anywhere in particular in the Score as long as it is named appropriately.

Another way to determine what member is used in the rollover state is to set the property in the Parameters dialog box each time the behavior is applied. Use the *on getPropertyDescriptionList* handler to do this.

```
 property pMemberNormal, pMemberRollover

on getPropertyDescriptionList me
return [#pMemberRollover: [#comment: "Rollover Member:", ¬
         #format: #member, #default: VOID]]
end

on beginSprite me
  pMemberNormal = sprite(me.spriteNum).member
end

on mouseEnter me
  sprite(me.spriteNum).member = pMemberRollover
end

on mouseLeave me
  sprite(me.spriteNum).member = pMemberNormal
end
```

In the *on getPropertyDescriptionList* function, the format *#member* is used. This presents a pop-up menu list of all the current members in the Parameters dialog box for the behavior. You could have also used *#string* to enable yourself to enter a member name manually. Or, the value of *#bitmap* could have been used to restrict the dialog box pop-up to bitmap members only. Because no default really makes sense here, a value of *VOID* is used.

ANIMATION BEHAVIORS

Now that you know how to change the location of a sprite on the Stage, you can apply that to a behavior and have it animate a sprite without tweening it in the Score.

Three events occur regularly and send messages to sprite behaviors: "prepareFrame", "enterFrame", and "exitFrame". The "exitFrame" is the best general purpose animation handler, because it enables you to show the sprite untouched at first, and then altered by the commands in the *on exitFrame* handler the second time the frame loops. Here is a simple example:

```
on exitFrame me
   sprite(me.spriteNum).locH = sprite(me.spriteNum).locH + 1
end
```

This behavior simply takes the horizontal position of the sprite and adds one to it each time the frame loops. If you have a *go to the frame* command in the *on exitFrame* handler of the frame script, the playback head holds on the current frame and this behavior makes the sprite move one pixel every frame loop.

Instead of hard-coding a "1" as the number of pixels that the sprite moves every frame, you can create a property. You can use the *on getPropertyDescriptionList* function to have this property set when you drag the behavior to the sprite.

```
property pSpeed

on getPropertyDescriptionList me
   return [#pSpeed: [#comment: "Speed:", ¬
           #format: #integer, #default: 1]]
end

on exitFrame me
   sprite(me.spriteNum).locH = sprite(me.spriteNum).locH + pSpeed
end
```

This behavior now prompts you to enter a number for the speed of movement when you drop it on a sprite. The default is set to 1. Nothing is in the code that would prevent you from entering a negative number and making the sprite move to the left.

You can use another technique in the *on getPropertyDescriptionList* function that enables you to place a sliding bar in the Parameters dialog box rather than a plain typing field. All you need to do is add the property *#range* to #pSpeed's property list and add a small list with a *#min* and *#max* property in it. This determines the bounds of the sliding bar.

```
property pSpeed

on getPropertyDescriptionList me
   return [#pSpeed: [#comment: "Speed:", #format: #integer, ¬
           #default: 1, #range: [#min:-50, #max:50]]]
end

on exitFrame me
   sprite(me.spriteNum).locH = sprite(me.spriteNum).locH + 1
end
```

Figure 14.2 shows the Parameters dialog box with this slider in it. Sliders such as this are a great tool for controlling the range of values that a parameter can contain. You can also make it a pop-up menu rather than a slider by placing a linear list, such as [1,5,10,15,-5,-10] as the *#range* property. Those values would be the ones available in the pop-up menu for the "pSpeed" property.

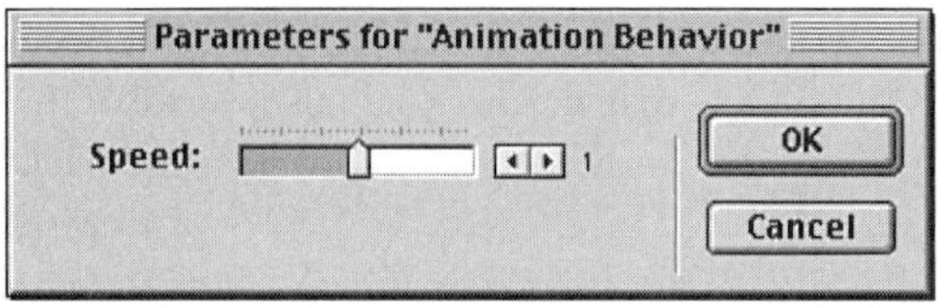

Figure 14.2
The Parameters dialog box can contain interface elements, such as a slider, rather than plain text boxes.

A SIMPLE BUTTON BEHAVIOR

A simple button behavior should do several things. First, it should enable you to have a different cast member as a down state when the button is pressed. Second, it should recognize the difference between the mouse being released above the sprite and it being released outside the sprite. This enables the user to click down, but then move the mouse so that it doesn't activate the button when it's released. Third, the button should perform a task, such as simple navigation, when there is a successful button press.

A behavior such as this should have two parameters. The first is a property that determines the down state of the button. The second defines what the navigation function of the behavior should be. Here is the *on getPropertyDescriptionList* handler for this behavior:

```
property pMemberNormal, pMemberDown, pTargetFrame

on getPropertyDescriptionList me
  list = [:]
  addProp list, #pMemberDown, [#comment: "Down State Member:", ¬
    #format: #member, #default: VOID]
  addProp list, #pTargetFrame, [#comment: "Target Frame Label:", ¬
    #format: #marker, #default: VOID]
  return list
end
```

First, notice that the variable "list" is built, property by property, and then returned. This makes the code easier to read than a one-line *return* command does.

Two special formats are used for the properties in the list. The first is *#member*, which presents a pop-up menu of all the available members. The second is *#format*, which presents a pop-up menu of available Score markers. It also adds markers *#next*, *#previous*, and *#loop* which can be used along with the *go to frame* command to go to the next, preceding, or current marker.

The *on beginSprite* handler gets just the starting member of the sprite, which is used for the normal button state member.

```
on beginSprite me
  pMemberNormal = sprite(me.spriteNum).member
end
```

The next three handlers refer to the three mouse button actions that are possible: "mouseDown", "mouseUp", and "mouseUpOutside". The difference between the *on mouseUp* and *on mouseUpOutside* handlers is that the first will also perform the action that the button is meant to do. The second will set the member of the sprite back to the normal state.

```
on mouseDown me
  sprite(me.spriteNum).member = pMemberDown
end

on mouseUp me
  sprite(me.spriteNum).member = pMemberNormal
  action(me)
end

on mouseUpOutside me
  sprite(me.spriteNum).member = pMemberNormal
end
```

Rather than just perform the action in the *on mouseUp* handler, the handler calls another handler called "action". This is a custom handler that you will create specifically for this behavior. It does not need to be called "action", but it seems like a sensible choice.

```
on action me
  go to frame pTargetFrame
end
```

This custom handler simply needs to execute the command "go to frame pTargetFrame". The property must contain either the name of a frame marker, or one of the special symbols that can be used by *go to frame*: *#next*, *#previous*, or *#loop*.

This completes the simple button behavior. Later in this chapter, you will see how to add a lot more functionality to it, including rollover states, actions other than navigation, sounds, and even different ways of deciding among the members for the down and rollover states.

USING COMPLETE BEHAVIORS

A behavior script has many parts. However, they are all optional. When you are writing quick behaviors to take care of a single action for a single sprite, you might use only one handler with one command. However, for complete behaviors, you will want to include all the optional functions.

Behavior Descriptions

The only use for a behavior description is to have something to appear in the bottom area of the Behavior Inspector. However, because it is in your script as the *on getBehaviorDescription* function, it can also act as commentary in your script.

All that the *on getBehaviorDescription* does to accomplish this task is to return a string. You can do this with one line:

```
on getBehaviorDescription me
  return "This behavior plays a sound when clicked."
end
```

Chances are, however, that you want to present more information than just seven words. You could expand that line to include as much information as you want, but a better way might be to construct the string in a variable first, and then return its value.

```
on getBehaviorDescription me
  desc = ""
  put "This behavior plays a sound when clicked."&RETURN after desc
  put "Choose a sound to play as the Sound paramater."&RETURN after desc
  put "Choose an action as the Action parameter." after desc
  return desc
end
```

This example is easier to write and edit, and will also be easier to read for someone editing the script.

The behavior description is also a good place to include your name or your company's name if the behavior is to be distributed in any way.

Behavior Property Description List

Although the behavior description is cosmetic, the behavior property description list is an essential element for behaviors that require customization. You can use the *on getPropertyDescriptionList* function to create a Parameters dialog box, for any behavior, that can contain a wide array of interface elements.

The property list that the *on getPropertyDescriptionList* returns contains a series of smaller lists. Each smaller list defines a single parameter. It does this through the use of four properties: *#comment*, *#format*, *#default*, and *#range*. Here is an example from earlier in the chapter:

```
on getPropertyDescriptionList me
  return [#pSpeed: [#comment: "Speed:", #format: #integer, ¬
          #default: 1, #range: [#min:-50, #max:50]]]
end
```

The main list contains the definition of one property: "pSpeed". In it, you can see each of the four properties needed to define it.

The comment property is only a short string that is used to label the parameter in the Behavior Parameters dialog box. It is nice to place a colon as the last character if you like that style.

The #format property can be set to one of many things. Many settings place a specific type of pop-up menu in the Parameters dialog box. The #member setting, for instance, places a pop-up that enables you to select any member used by the movie. Table 14.1 shows the different #format property settings.

TABLE 14.1   SETTINGS USED BY THE #FORMAT PROPERTY

Setting	Parameter Dialog Result	Possible Values
#integer	A text entry area	The value is converted to an integer
#float	A text entry area	The value is converted to a floating point number
#string	A text entry area	A string
#boolean	A check box	TRUE or FALSE (1 or 0)
#symbol	A text entry area	A symbol
#member	A pop-up with a list of all members	A member name
#bitmap	A pop-up with a list of bitmap members	A member name
#filmloop	A pop-up with a list of film loop members	A member name
#field	A pop-up with a list of field members	A member name
#palette	A pop-up with a list of palette members and built-in Director palettes	A string with the name of the palette
#sound	A pop-up with a list of sound members	A member name
#button	A pop-up with a list of pushbutton, radio button, and check box members	A member name
#shape	A pop-up with a list of shape members	A member name
#vectorShape	A pop-up with a list of vector graphic members	A member name
#font	A pop-up with a list of font members	A member name
#digitalVideo	A pop-up with a list of digital video members	A member name
#script	A pop-up with a list of script members	A member name
#text	A pop-up with a list of text members	A member name

Setting	Parameter Dialog Result	Possible Values
#transition	A pop-up with a list of built-in transitions	A transition member name
#frame	A text field	A frame number
#marker	A list of markers in the Score, plus "next", "previous", and "loop"	A string or the symbol #next, #previous, or #loop
#ink	A list of inks	An ink number

Most of the *#format* types result in a pop-up menu being placed in the Parameters dialog box. In cases when there are absolutely no values that can be used there, a text field appears instead. For instance, if one parameter is set to *#sound* and there are no sound members in the movie yet, a text field replaces the pop-up menu.

The #range property is optional at all times, but can be very useful for narrowing choices. There are two ways of using it: as a pop-up menu list of items or as a slider with minimum and maximum values.

A slider is created in the Parameters dialog box with the format [#min: a, #max: b]. The values of the slider go from a to b. When used with a linear list, such as ["a", "b", "c"], the values of that list are used as choices in the pop-up.

The #default property is required for any parameter. However, you can use values such as "" and 0 in cases where you really don't plan on using a default.

AUTOMATIC PROPERTY SETTING

In rare cases, you will want to create a behavior that sets its parameters semiautomatically, rather than requiring you to set them each time you apply the behavior. The *on runPropertyDialog* handler enables you to intercept the message that triggers the Parameters dialog box when you apply a behavior. You can use it to examine the properties and even change them. You can also decide whether the Parameters dialog box ever appears.

Here is an example behavior. It has both *on getPropertyDescriptionList* and *on runPropertyDialog* handlers. When the behavior is applied to a sprite, the *on runPropertyDialog* runs and sends a message using the *alert* command. It takes the property list for the behavior, which is passed in as a second parameter to the handler, and resets one of the properties. It then uses the *pass* command to signify that the "runPropertyDialog" message should pass on to open the Parameters dialog box as usual.

```
property pFrame, pBoolean

on getPropertyDescriptionList me
  list = [:]
  addProp list, #pFrame, [#comment: "Frame:", ¬
    #format: #integer, #default: 0]
  addProp list, #pBoolean, [#comment: "Boolean:", ¬
    #format: #boolean, #default: TRUE]
  return list
end
```

PART

V

CH

14

```
on runPropertyDialog me, list
  setProp list, #pFrame, the frame + 1
  alert "I will now set the pFrame property to the next frame."
  pass
  return list
end
```

The properties in the behavior are passed to the *on runPropertyDialog* handler through the second parameter, which is the variable "list". The variable should contain something like this: `[#pFrame: 0, #pBoolean: 1]`.

Tip

The *alert* command generates a plain dialog box with a string message and an OK button. It is a quick and easy way to show some information.

Because this is just a plain property list, the *setProp* command can be used to change the value of one of the properties in it. The "pBoolean" property is used only to color up the example a bit. The only property affected by the *setProp* command is "pFrame".

After the variable "list" holds a new value, you need to remember to return this value with the *return* command so that the changes can be applied to the behavior. The *pass* command can be placed anywhere in the handler, because it just tells Director that when the handler is done, the message that called it (in this case a "runPropertyDialog" message) should continue to be used. The result is that the message triggers the normal Parameters dialog box.

Without *pass*, the Parameters dialog box never appears. This is sometimes desired when the *on runPropertyDialog* handler is meant to set all the parameters and override any use of the Parameters dialog box.

TOOL TIPS

The only use for the *on getBehaviorTooltip* function is if you plan to use the behavior in the library palette. If so, placing this function there enables you to define what text appears in that little yellow box called a tool tip.

Here is an example. It basically works the same way as the *on getBehaviorDescription* handler. You need to simply return a string. In the case of tool tips, these should be as short as possible so that they fit on the screen nicely and don't cover up too much when they appear.

```
on getBehaviorTooltip me
  return "Button Behavior"
end
```

A Complete Button Behavior

Now you know enough to build a complex button behavior. This behavior needs to perform many tasks such as

- Changing state when the user presses down. There should be a choice of how the down state member is chosen: the next member in the Cast, or a member with the same name as the original member, but with the word "down" appended, or a specific member name.

- Changing state when the user rolls over it. There should be a choice of how the rollover state member is chosen: two members from the original in the Cast, or a member with the same name as the original member, but with the word "rollover" appended, or a specific member name.

- Playing a sound when the user presses down. The sound name is chosen from the current sound members in the Cast.

- Playing a sound when the user rolls over it. The sound name is chosen from the current sound members in the Cast.

- Changing the cursor when the user rolls over it. The cursor is chosen from the built-in cursors.

- Playing a sound when the button is successfully clicked.

- Taking the movie to another frame with a *go to* or *play* command when the button is successfully clicked. Also, a *play done* command can be executed.

- Calling a specific Lingo command or handler when the button is successfully clicked.

A behavior such as this is typical of what you need in a large movie. It take cares of all the different buttons that you may use. It even enables you to create non-button rollover sprites.

Creating the Parameters

To begin, create the *on getPropertyDescriptionList* handler. By making this handler, property by property, you can see how many properties are used and name them appropriately. You can then return to the beginning of the script and add the *property* declarations.

Start by creating the property list:

```
on getPropertyDescriptionList me
  list = [:]
```

Now, take care of the first item in the bullet list given at the beginning of this section: having a down state for the sprite.

PART

V

CH

14

In addition to the three choices listed in the bullet item, you should have a fourth choice: no down state. Here is the line of code that adds this property. The name of the property will be "pDownState" and a pop-up list will be used to let you choose the type of down state. You need to list these choices with the *#range* property.

```
addProp list, #pDownState, ¬
    [#comment: "Down State", #format: #string, ¬
    #range: ["No Down State", "Member + 1",¬
            "Append 'down'", "Name Down State"],¬
    #default: "No Down State"]
```

Notice that the default state is set to "No Down State". You need to set default states for all the properties.

One of the down state options is to name a down state member. You want to then have a pop-up menu for the name of this member as a parameter.

```
addProp list, #pDownMemberName, ¬
    [#comment: "Down Member", #format: #bitmap, #default: ""]
```

You need to provide similar functionality for a rollover state as you did for the down state. However, because you already have a way for the down state to be the next member in the Cast, it makes sense that the rollover state should be the second member after the current one. This way you can line up normal, down, and rollover bitmaps in the Cast if you want.

```
addProp list, #pRolloverState, ¬
    [#comment: "Rollover State", #format: #string, ¬
    #range: ["No Rollover", "Member + 2", "Append 'rollover'",¬
            "Name Rollover", "Cursor Change"],¬
    #default: "No Rollover"]
```

As with the down state, you want to provide a pop-up menu of bitmaps for use in case the "Name Rollover" choice is selected.

```
addProp list, #pRolloverMemberName, ¬
    [#comment: "Rollover Member", #format: #bitmap, #default: ""]
```

There is an extra option for rollovers: the cursor change. If that option is selected, you want to know which cursor has been chosen as the rollover cursor.

```
addProp list, #pRolloverCursor, ¬
    [#comment: "Rollover Cursor", #format: #cursor, #default: ""]
```

You also need to provide a way for sounds to play when the button is clicked down and when the button is rolled over. You need to provide a check box for whether the sound is played, and then a pop-up menu with a list of sounds.

```
addProp list, #pPlayDownSound, ¬
    [#comment: "Play Down Sound", #format: #boolean, #default: FALSE]

  addProp list, #pDownSound, ¬
    [#comment: "Down Sound", #format: #sound, #default: ""]
```

The same properties need to be present for the rollover action:

```
addProp list, #pPlayRolloverSound, ¬
    [#comment: "Play Rollover Sound", #format: #boolean, #default: FALSE]

  addProp list, #pRolloverSound, ¬
    [#comment: "Rollover Sound", #format: #sound, #default: ""]
```

All that is left now is to define what happens when the button is successfully clicked. The first option is to have some navigation. This could be either a *go to frame*, a *play frame*, or a *play done*. There should also be an option for no navigation, and that should be the default.

```
addProp list, #pActionNavigation, ¬
    [#comment: "Action Navigation", #format: #string, ¬
    #range: ["None", "go to frame", "play frame", "play done"],¬
    #default: "None"]
```

If either *go to frame* or *play frame* is selected, there needs to be a property that holds the name of that frame. A *play done* does not need a frame name.

```
addProp list, #pActionFrame,¬
    [#comment: "Action Frame", #format: #frame, #default: ""]
```

There should also be an option for a sound to be played when the button is successfully clicked. This requires two more properties, similar to the sound properties for down states and rollovers.

```
addProp list, #pPlayActionSound, ¬
    [#comment: "Play Action Sound", #format: #boolean, #default: FALSE]

  addProp list, #pActionSound, ¬
    [#comment: "Action Sound", #format: #sound, #default: ""]
```

The last property will be another action that takes place when there is a successful click. It is the name of a Lingo command or a custom handler. Using a special command named *do*, you can execute this command when the user presses the button. It can be something as simple as a *beep* or as complex as the name of a custom movie handler that does a variety of things. For the *on getPropertyDescriptionList* purposes, it just needs to be a string.

```
addProp list, #pActionLingo, ¬
    [#comment: "Action Lingo", #format: #string, #default: ""]
```

The *on getPropertyDescriptionList* is now complete. Just top it off with a `return list`. You should now go back and figure out what the property declarations for the behavior should be.

All the properties used in the *on getPropertyDescriptionList* handler should be present, as well as other properties that you can predict you will need. You should have properties to hold the normal, down, and rollover state member references. You will also need a property called "pPressed" that is true when a button press is in progress and false at all other times.

```
property pNormalMember, pDownMember, pRolloverMember, pPressed
property pDownState, pDownMemberName
property pPlayDownSound, pDownSound
property pRolloverState, pRolloverMemberName, pRolloverCursor
```

```
property pPlayRolloverSound, pRolloverSound
property pActionNavigation, pActionFrame
property pPlayActionSound, pActionSound, pActionLingo
```

> **Tip**
>
> You can use the *property* declaration on several different lines (as shown in the preceding example) or have one long line. The same is true of the *global* declaration.

WRITING THE EVENT HANDLERS

Now that all the preliminary steps have been taken to create the behavior, you can actually start writing the event handlers. A logical place to start is with the *on beginSprite* handler.

This handler should be used to set the properties that contain references to the three members used: "pNormalMember", "pDownMember", and "pRolloverMember". What they are set to depends on the parameter properties. For instance, if the "pDownState" is set to "Member + 1", you need to get the member number of the original member, add one to it, and get that member.

Here is the *on beginSprite* handler. It first gets the member currently used by the sprite, and stores it as the "pNormalMember". Then it looks at the "pDownState" property to determine what to place in the "pDownMember" property. The same thing is done for the "pRolloverState" and "pRolloverMember" properties.

```
on beginSprite me
  pNormalMember = sprite(me.spriteNum).member

  case pDownState of
    "No Down State":
      pDownMember = member pNormalMember
    "Append 'Down'":
      pDownMember = member(pNormalMember.name&&"Down")
    "Member + 1":
      pDownMember = member(pNormalMember.number + 1)
    "Name Down State":
      pDownMember = member pDownMemberName
  end case

  case pRolloverState of
    "No Rollover":
      pRolloverMember = pNormalMember
    "Cursor Change":
      pRolloverMember = pNormalMember
    "Append 'Rollover'":
      pRolloverMember = member (pNormalMember.name&&"Rollover")
    "Member + 2":
      pRolloverMember = member (pNormalMember.number + 2)
    "Name Rollover":
      pRolloverMember = member pRolloverMemberName
  end case

  pPressed = FALSE
end
```

The last thing that the *on beginSprite* handler does is set the "pPressed" property to FALSE. Note that properties such as "pDownState", "pDownMemberName", and "pRolloverMemberName" are not needed any more in the behavior. Their purpose was to determine what "pDownMember" and "pRolloverMember" are supposed to be.

Figure 14.3 shows the Parameters dialog box for this behavior. You can see each property listed in the *on getPropertyDescriptionList*.

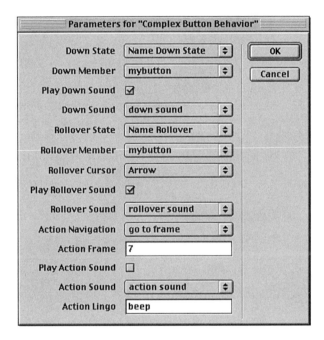

Figure 14.3
The Parameters dialog box for the complex button behavior shows the properties grouped together by function rather than in the order discussed in the text.

A comprehensive behavior such as this one requires you to use most of the basic event handlers: *on mouseDown*, *on mouseUp*, *on mouseUpOutside*, *on mouseEnter*, and *on mouseLeave*. The last two are used to determine when the sprite is being rolled over.

In the *on mouseDown* handler, you need to place the commands that get executed when the sprite is first clicked. Specifically, you need to set the member to the down state, play a sound if needed, and set the "pPressed" property.

```
on mouseDown me
  pPressed = TRUE
  sprite(me.spriteNum).member = pDownMember

  if pPlayDownSound then
    puppetSound pDownSound
  end if
end
```

The *on mouseUp* handler is the other end of the click. It is here that you want to call a custom handler that performs the button's actions. You also want to set the "pPressed" property to false. Because you can't assume that the action of the button will be to leave the current frame entirely, it is a good idea to set the member of the sprite back to a non-pressed state. Because the cursor must still be over the sprite when the button is released to get an *on mouseUp* message, you should set the sprite not to the normal state, but to the rollover state.

```
on mouseUp me
  pPressed = FALSE
  sprite(me.spriteNum).member = pRolloverMember
  doAction(me)
end
```

The companion to *on mouseUp* is *on mouseUpOutside*. If this handler is executed, it means that the user clicked the button when the cursor was over the sprite at first, but then moved off it before lifting up. This is a standard user interface way of backing out of an action. The user clearly does not want the action to take place, so you should not call the "on doAction" handler as in the *on mouseUp* handler. In addition, you know that the cursor is not over the sprite, so you can set the member back to the normal state.

```
on mouseUpOutside me
  pPressed = FALSE
  sprite(me.spriteNum).member = pNormalMember
end
```

The two rollover handlers, *on mouseEnter* and *on mouseLeave*, actually have a lot more to do. The first handler needs to set the member to the rollover member. However, if the user has already clicked and is holding down the mouse button, the down state member should be used instead.

In addition, the *on mouseEnter* handler needs to play a sound if required. If the "pRolloverState" property is set to "Cursor Change", the *cursor* command should be used to change the cursor.

```
on mouseEnter me
  if pPressed then
    sprite(me.spriteNum).member = pDownMember
  else
    sprite(me.spriteNum).member = pRolloverMember
  end if

  if pPlayRolloverSound then
    puppetSound pRolloverSound
  end if

  if pRolloverState = "Cursor Change" then
    cursor(pRolloverCursor)
  end if
end
```

Note

> The *cursor* command changes the cursor to one of many special built-in cursors. In this case, it gets the setting from the Parameters dialog box pop-up. You can also use numbers such as 280 for a hand or 4 for a clock/watch. The number 0 resets the cursor.

The companion *on mouseLeave* handler has to undo what the *on mouseEnter* handler does. It turns out this is pretty simple. It needs to set the member back to the normal state, and change the cursor back if needed.

```
on mouseLeave me
  sprite(me.spriteNum).member = pNormalMember

  if pRolloverState = "Cursor Change" then
    cursor(0)
  end if
end
```

That takes care of all the event handlers needed. Only the custom "doAction" handler is left. This handler needs to look at three possible values for "pActionNavigation" that need processing. In each case, it performs the necessary commands. Because a navigation command takes the movie immediately away from the current frame where the sprite is, it is a good idea to use *cursor(0)* to reset the cursor before that happens.

In addition to navigation, the "on doAction" handler figures out when a sound is needed. It also determines whether any Lingo command was entered as the "pActionLingo" property. It uses the *do* command to run that command or handler.

Also notice that rather than just using the "pActionFrame" as a marker name, the code checks to see whether it can be considered a number. It uses the *integer* function to do this. This function tries to convert the string to a number. If it is successful, it uses the number as a frame to jump to, rather than as a marker label string. The same can be done for the "play frame" option if you want.

```
on doAction me
  if pActionNavigation = "go to frame" then
    cursor(0)
    if integer(pActionFrame) > 0 then
      go to frame integer(pActionFrame)
    else
      go to frame pActionFrame
    end if
  else if pActionNavigation = "play frame" then
    cursor(0)
    play frame pActionFrame
  else if pActionNavigation = "play done" then
    cursor(0)
    play done
  end if

  if pPlayActionSound then
    puppetSound pActionSound
  end if
```

```
    if pActionLingo <> "" then
      do pActionLingo
    end if
end
```

This behavior is now a powerful multipurpose script that can be used over and over in your current movie and others. It is a good idea to gather any general purpose behaviors such as this and store them in your own behavior library for future use.

CREATING ANIMATION BEHAVIORS

With Lingo, animation does not have to take place over several frames anymore. Instead, it can exist on a single frame as the movie loops on that frame. The possibilities are limitless, but the following two examples show some of the possibilities.

BOUNCING OFF WALLS

Changing the position of a sprite is easy enough to do. Moving one in a straight line is no great feat, as the Score and tweening already enable you to do this easily. With Lingo, however, you can create a behavior that has a sprite react to its environment. For example, it can bounce off walls.

A behavior to do this is relatively simple. As usual, first create the *on getPropertyDescriptionList* handler. Three properties should be sufficient: the speed of movement in horizontal and vertical directions, plus a rectangle to bound the object.

```
property pMoveX, pMoveY, pLimit

on getPropertyDescriptionList me
  list = [:]
  addProp list, #pMoveX, [#Comment: "Horizontal Movement",¬
    #format: #integer, #range: [#min:-10,#max:10], #default: 0]
  addProp list, #pMoveY, [#Comment: "Vertical Movement",¬
    #format: #integer, #range: [#min:-10,#max:10], #default: 0]
  addProp list, #pLimit, [#Comment: "Limit Rectangle",¬
    #format: #rect, #default: rect(0,0,640,480)]
  return list
end
```

Using sliders for the horizontal and vertical movement is a good idea, because you probably don't want to be using far out values anyway. In this case, the properties are limited to plus or minus 10 pixels at a time.

Note

> The use of X and Y in variable names is common in Lingo and other languages. The X value is commonly used to denote horizontal positions and movement, whereas Y is commonly used to denote vertical positions and movement.

The "pLimit" property is supposed to be a *rect* structure. Using the format type *#rect* forces the value of the text entered for this property into a *rect*.

To make this behavior work, you need only one event handler. The *on exitFrame* handler is commonly used for animation such as this. You can take the current location of a sprite and add a point to it. *Points* and *rects* can be added and subtracted like other variables. Try this in the message window:

```
p = point(100,150)
p = p + point(40,20)
put p
-- point(140, 170)
```

This technique makes the coding very easy. You don't have to break the location of the sprite into horizontal and vertical components. Here is the handler:

```
on exitFrame me
  -- get the old location
  currentLoc = sprite(me.spriteNum).loc

  -- set the new location
  newLoc = currentLoc + point(pMoveX, pMoveY)

  -- set the sprite location
  sprite(me.spriteNum).loc = sprite(me.spriteNum).loc + ¬
    point(pMoveX, pMoveY)
end
```

You will also need to check the "pLimit" property to figure out whether the sprite has hit a side and should turn around. A *rect* structure, like the "pLimit" property, can be broken into four properties: *left*, *right*, *top*, and *bottom*. You must check the *left* and *right* to see whether a side was hit, and the *top* and *bottom* to see whether they were hit.

After a hit is determined, the movement in that direction, either the "pMoveX" or "pMoveY" property should be reversed. That is, a positive value turned to negative and vice versa.

To make sure the handler works correctly when the limiting rectangle is tight or the sprite starts outside the limit, each case is handled individually. When the sprite hits the right wall, the "pMoveX" property is taken as an absolute value and made a negative. When it hits the left wall, the absolute value is taken and kept positive. The result in most cases is that the sign of the property changes when a wall is hit.

```
on exitFrame me
  -- get the old location
  currentLoc = sprite(me.spriteNum).loc

  -- set the new location
  newLoc = currentLoc + point(pMoveX, pMoveY)

  -- check to see if it has hit a side of the limit
  if newLoc.locH > pLimit.right then
    pMoveX = -abs(pMoveX)
  else if newLoc.locH < pLimit.left then
```

```
        pMoveX = abs(pMoveX)
      end if

      -- check to see if it has hit top or bottom of the limit
      if newLoc.locV > pLimit.bottom then
        pMoveY = -abs(pMoveY)
      else if newLoc.locV < pLimit.top then
        pMoveY = abs(pMoveY)
      end if

      -- set the sprite location
      sprite(me.spriteNum).loc = sprite(me.spriteNum).loc + ¬
          point(pMoveX, pMoveY)
    end
```

You now have a behavior that causes a sprite to move at a constant rate and bounce off walls when necessary. The animation does not stop as long as the sprite is present on the Stage.

ADDING GRAVITY

The "bounce" behavior seems to act on a sprite as if it were in outer space in a perfect universe. When the sprite hits the side of the screen, it bounces back without losing any speed or being pulled down by gravity.

To create convincing animation, you sometimes need to include elements such as energy loss and gravity. After all, in real life a ball thrown against a wall will hit the wall, fall down to the ground, and bounce back.

Adding gravity is easy, but it always takes two properties. The first is the amount of force that you want gravity to exert on the sprite. The second is the speed at which the sprite is traveling downward.

When you release an object in real life, it begins falling down slowly at first, and then picks up speed as it continues, because gravity accelerates the object's speed toward the ground. Acceleration is a change in speed, rather than the speed itself.

This acceleration is your first property: "pGravity". In addition, there needs to be a "pSpeedDown" property that keeps track of how fast the sprite travels downward. For the energy loss feature of the behavior, all that is needed is a "pLoseEnergy" property that can be either true or false.

To create this behavior, you can just start with the "bounce" behavior just described. You need to add a few properties to the *property* declaration:

```
property pGravity, pSpeedDown, pMoveX, pMoveY, pLimit, pLoseEnergy
```

Now, you need to add two new parameters in the *on getPropertyDescriptionList* handler:

```
addProp list, #pGravity, [#Comment: "Gravity",¬
    #format: #integer, #range: [#min:0,#max:3], #default: 0]
  addProp list, #pLoseEnergy, [#Comment: "Lose Energy",¬
    #format: #boolean, #default: FALSE]
```

The "pGravity" property works best when it is set to 1, but the slider accommodates values up to 3. The 0 is used as the default, which results in no gravity effect.

The "pSpeedDown" property needs to be set when the sprite starts, so you need to create a *on beginSprite* handler.

```
on beginSprite me
  pSpeedDown = 0
end
```

Then, each time the *on exitFrame* handler runs, you want to increase the downward speed by the force of gravity.

```
pSpeedDown = pSpeedDown + pGravity
```

Also, this property must be reversed when the sprite hits the ground, according to Issac Newton. You can add one line after the line in the *on exitFrame* handler that reverses the "pMoveY" property.

```
pSpeedDown = -abs(pSpeedDown)-1
```

The -1 is added to the resulting speed to fix an inconsistency. When the sprite hits the ground and the "pSpeedDown" changed to negative, the location of the sprite will not be changed again until the next time through the *on exitFrame* handler. At that point, a 1 will be added to it before the location is changed again. So if the "pSpeedDown" is 22, and it hits bottom, it changes to a -22. Then, it goes through the handler again and gets 1 added, so now it is a -21.

The result is that the sprite moves 22 one time, and then -21 the next. It gains one pixel because of this. But, by adding a -1 to the "pSpeedDown", it evens out.

To create the energy loss, you first want to check to see whether "pEnergyLoss" is true. Then, you want to add 1 to the "pSpeedDown" when the sprite hits the ground. However, you want to be careful not to do this when the speed of the sprite is near 0, because it will slowly suck the sprite under the ground.

```
if pSpeedDown < -1 then pSpeedDown = pSpeedDown + 1
```

Here is the final behavior. Notice that the code that handles the ceiling hit has been taken out. This is because a ceiling hit is less likely now that gravity is involved. Plus, it would further complicate the code that handles the gravity. So this behavior acts as if there are walls on the sides and ground below, but only sky above.

```
property pGravity, pSpeedDown, pMoveX, pMoveY, pLimit, pLoseEnergy

on getPropertyDescriptionList me
  list = [:]
  addProp list, #pGravity, [#Comment: "Gravity",¬
    #format: #integer, #range: [#min:0,#max:3], #default: 0]
  addProp list, #pLoseEnergy, [#Comment: "Lose Energy",¬
    #format: #boolean, #default: FALSE]
  addProp list, #pMoveX, [#Comment: "Horizontal Movement",¬
    #format: #integer, #range: [#min:-10,#max:10], #default: 0]
  addProp list, #pMoveY, [#Comment: "Vertical Movement",¬
```

```
    #format: #integer, #range: [#min:-10,#max:10], #default: 0]
  addProp list, #pLimit, [#Comment: "Limit Rectangle",¬
    #format: #rect, #default: rect(0,0,640,480)]
  return list
end

on beginSprite me
  pSpeedDown = 0
end

on exitFrame me
  -- Accelerate due to gravity
  pSpeedDown = pSpeedDown + pGravity

  -- get the old location
  currentLoc = sprite(me.spriteNum).loc

  -- set the new location
  newLoc = currentLoc + point(pMoveX, pMoveY+pSpeedDown)

  -- check to see if it has hit a side of the limit
  if newLoc.locH > pLimit.right then
    pMoveX = -abs(pMoveX)
  else if newLoc.locH < pLimit.left then
    pMoveX = abs(pMoveX)
  end if

  -- check to see if it has hit top or bottom of the limit
  if newLoc.locV > pLimit.bottom then
    pMoveY = -abs(pMoveY)
    pSpeedDown = -abs(pSpeedDown)-1
    if pLoseEnergy then
      if pSpeedDown < -1 then pSpeedDown = pSpeedDown + 1
    end if
  end if

  -- set the sprite location
  sprite (me.spriteNum).loc = newLoc
end
```

COMMUNICATING BETWEEN BEHAVIORS

Behaviors do not have to control only their own sprites; they can actually send instructions and information to other sprites and behaviors as well. Two special commands are used for doing this.

The first is *sendSprite*, which sends a message to a specific sprite, along with additional information. For example:

```
sendSpritesprite(sprite 1, #myHandler, 5)
```

This line sends the message "myHandler" to sprite 1. If that sprite has a "on myHandler" handler, it runs. In addition, the number 5 is passed to it as the first parameter after *me*. It might look like this:

```
on myHandler me, num
  put "I got your message:"&&num
end
```

A more useful example might be to tie two sprites together so that when one is dragged by the mouse, the other follows in synch. The first sprite's behavior might look like this:

```
property pPressed

on beginSprite me
  pPressed = FALSE
end

on mouseDown me
  pPressed = TRUE
end

on mouseUp me
  pPressed = FALSE
end

on mouseUpOutside me
  pPressed = FALSE
end

on exitFrame me
  if pPressed then
    -- calculate move amount
    moveAmount = the mouseLoc - sprite(me.spriteNum).loc

    -- move this sprite
    sprite(me.spriteNum).loc = sprite(me.spriteNum).loc + moveAmount

    -- move another sprite
    sendSpritesprite(sprite 2,#move,moveAmount)
  end if
end
```

This is a pretty basic drag behavior. When the user clicks on it, the "pPressed" variable is set to TRUE. This enables three lines to run in the *on exitFrame* handler. Those three lines calculate the difference between the current location of the cursor and the current location of the sprite, move that sprite that amount so that it matches the cursor, and then send that movement amount to sprite number 2.

The second behavior should be attached to sprite 2 and it can simply be:

```
-- get message from another sprite to move
on move me, moveAmount
  sprite(me.spriteNum).loc = sprite(me.spriteNum).loc + moveAmount
end
```

This handler receives a message from the first sprite and uses the point included with the message to change its location. The result is that the two sprites move together when the first one is dragged.

Another way for behaviors to communicate is to use the *sendAllSprites* command. This is essentially the same as *sendSprite*, but it does not require the first parameter:

```
sendAllSprites(#myHandler, 5)
```

As you can probably guess, this command sends the message and information to all the sprites in the current frame. Any of them that have an "on myHandler" handler receive the message and use it. If a behavior does not have this handler, the message is ignored.

TROUBLESHOOTING CREATING BEHAVIORS

- Make sure that if you are creating a behavior, the script type is set to "Behavior". Otherwise, you won't even be able to attach the member to a sprite.

- Remember to use *return* at the end of the *getPropertDescriptionList* handler. Without returning the property list defined within, Director cannot make the Parameters dialog box.

- When you refer to a sprite with the sprite(x) syntax, the sprite number needs to be totally contained in the parentheses. The code `sprite(x)+1` is wrong, but `sprite(x+1)` is correct.

- When you build a list for a *getPropertyDescription* handler, each item must have a *#comment*, *#format*, and *#default* property. Even in cases where there is no logical *#default*, you need to put something there, such as a 0, VOID, or an empty string.

DID YOU KNOW?

- You can set a #min and #max to a range of values in a behavior parameter description, and also can include an #increment property that determines how much one click of the arrow keys next to the slider will change the value.

- The continuation character was more useful in Director 6 and earlier, when lines in script could only be a finite length before a wrap was forced. Make sure when you use the character that you don't place an extra Return after it, because Director just assumes that you mean to have two separate lines.

- If you have overlapping sprites and you want to make sure your rollover behaviors work only when you roll over a visible portion of the sprite, check to ensure that the rollover is the same as the number of the sprite before you set the member in the on *mouseEnter* handler.

■ When you are determining the wall, floor, and ceiling positions for the bounce behavior, you might want to compute them relative to the Stage size. Use *(the stage).drawRect* to get a rectangle with the Stage size. Use *(the stage).drawRect.width* and *(the stage).drawRect.height* to get the right wall and floor positions.

GRAPHIC INTERFACE ELEMENTS

In this chapter

Whether you are creating a simple presentation or a complex piece of software, it is primarily through user interface elements that the Director movie and the user interact. They can be as plain as pushbuttons, or as complex as slider bars. This chapter looks at the most common user interface elements and the behaviors that you need to use to create them.

CREATING DISPLAY ROLLOVERS

Chapter 14, "Creating Behaviors," contained a script that showed a simple rollover behavior. Typically, a rollover is a sprite that changes members when the cursor is over it. However, there is another type of rollover as well, one which leaves the rolled-over sprite alone, but instead changes another sprite.

A typical use for this interface element is to present a list of items and then show more information about them in another part of the screen when the user rolls over it. Figure 15.1 shows a screen that does this. Rolling over the three items on the left brings up three different text members in the sprite to the right.

Figure 15.1
The screen shows three sprites on the left and one on the right. The one on the right changes depending on which sprite on the left the cursor is over.

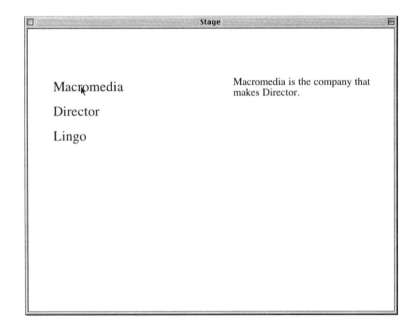

The behavior to do this is similar to the rollover behavior discussed in Chapter 14. Rather than change the same sprite, it must change a different one. It also needs to know which member to use. One last parameter should be a default member that should be displayed when the cursor is not over one of the rollover sprites. Here is the start of a behavior:

```
property pRolloverMember, pRolloverSprite, pDefaultMember

on getPropertyDescriptionList me
  list = [:]
  addProp list, #pRolloverMember, [#comment: "Rollover Member",¬
    #format: #member, #default: ""]
  addProp list, #pRolloverSprite, [#comment: "Rollover Sprite",¬
    #format: #integer, #default: 0]
  addProp list, #pDefaultMember, [#comment: "Default Member",¬
    #format: #member, #default: ""]
  return list
end
```

The default member should be the one in the rollover sprite on the Score. You can use *on mouseEnter* to change this sprite to the desired member. Then, when the cursor leaves the sprite, the *on mouseLeave* handler can switch it back to the default member.

```
on mouseEnter me
  sprite(pRolloverSprite).member = pRolloverMember
end

on mouseLeave me
  sprite(pRolloverSprite).member = pDefaultMember
end
```

As the cursor moves between the sprites, the "mouseEnter" and "mouseLeave" messages control which member the rollover sprite displays. Make sure that the sprites do not overlap, otherwise the order of the messages can create undesired results. For instance, if sprites 1 and 2 overlap, the cursor can enter sprite 2 before it leaves sprite 1. The result would be that the default member would be displayed rather than the member specified by sprite 2.

Because you can attach multiple behaviors to a sprite, you can add a button behavior to these same sprites. That way, the rollovers are handled by the rollover display behavior here, but a click is handled by the button behavior. You can have sprites that display preview information, such as "Click this button to go to the index" in one sprite, but also react to the click to go to another frame.

→ **See** "Creating Simple Behaviors," Chapter 14, for more information about creating rollover behaviors

Using Check Boxes

A check box is a button that has two states: on and off. Director has a check box member type that is a variant on the button member. You can use this built-in member as a check box, or build your own check boxes with two members per selection.

A behavior for the built-in check box member is almost not needed. The member reacts to a mouse click by itself, placing a mark in the box when clicked and then removing it on a second click. Figure 15.2 shows a small group of check box members.

Figure 15.2
A group of three
check box members.

☐ Apples

☐ Oranges

☐ Bananas

One thing that a behavior can do is make it easier to determine which check boxes are checked. You can get this as a simple Lingo property of the member. For instance, *(member "apple check box").hilite*. This *hilite* property returns true or false.

A behavior can use similar syntax, but because behaviors are assigned to sprites, not members, you can get the state of a check box according to the sprite number. Here is a simple behavior to do this:

```
on isChecked me
  return sprite(me.spriteNum).member.hilite
end
```

You can check the state of any check box by asking isChecked(sprite X), where "X" is the number of the sprite. Or you can do the same thing with sendSprite(sprite X, #isChecked). You get a TRUE or FALSE value from either of these. (A value of TRUE indicates that the check box has a mark in it, and a value of FALSE indicates that the box is empty.)

Because the built-in check boxes are rather limited in appearance, it is usually a good idea to create your own multi-state buttons with bitmaps. Figure 15.3 shows three such buttons, with the middle one being checked.

Figure 15.3
Three sprites are used
to hold bitmap repre-
sentations of check
boxes. Behaviors con-
trol these sprites.

Each sprite can contain one of two members: the on state and the off state. So Figure 15.3 has a total of six members. In this example, the on states look the same as the off states, except for the addition of a check mark next to them.

A behavior to handle these states needs to know what the on and off state members are. It also needs to know whether the sprite should start out in the on or off state. Three properties and parameters take care of this, as follows:

```
property pOnMember, pOffMember, pState

on getPropertyDescriptionList me
  list = [:]
  addProp list, #pOnMember, [#comment: "On Member",¬
    #format: #member, #default: ""]
  addProp list, #pOffMember, [#comment: "Off Member",¬
    #format: #member, #default: ""]
  addProp list, #pState, [#comment: "Initial State",¬
    #format: #boolean, #default: FALSE]
  return list
end
```

When the sprite begins, it should adjust itself to be the proper state, regardless of what is in the Score. This can be done by the *on beginSprite* handler. Because you will need to reuse the code that changes the member of the sprite according to the "pState" property, it is a good idea to create a custom handler to do that. The *on beginSprite* handler needs to call that custom handler.

```
on beginSprite me
  setMember(me)
end

on setMember me
  if pState = TRUE then
    sprite(me.spriteNum).member = pOnMember
  else
    sprite(me.spriteNum).member = pOffMember
  end if
end
```

The sprite needs to change state when the user clicks it. If it is on, it needs to go off, and vice versa. This can be done with one line using the *not* operator.

```
on mouseUp me
  pState = not pState
  setMember(me)
end
```

The *on mouseUp* handler calls the "on setMember" handler to change the member after the state changes.

One final handler can be a function that returns the state of the check box. This can be used by other Lingo handlers in movie scripts or other behaviors.

```
on isChecked me
  return pState
end
```

Note that you can also ask for this property directly in this manner: `sprite(X).pState`.

→ **See** "Questionnaires," Chapter 28, "Business Applications," for more information about using check boxes

USING RADIO BUTTONS

The topic of check boxes naturally leads into the topic of radio buttons. They are very similar to each other. Whereas check boxes enable users to select one or more items from a list, radio buttons enable users to select *only one* item from a list.

Director also has a built-in radio button member in the form of a button member variant. It works the same way as the check box in that it already accepts mouse clicks and turns itself on and off accordingly. Figure 15.4 shows a small group of radio buttons.

Figure 15.4
A group of three
radio buttons.

○ Apples
◉ Oranges
○ Bananas

Whereas check boxes don't really need any Lingo to work, radio buttons definitely require some. The reason is that at this point the radio buttons don't know of each other's existence. In the example in Figure 15.4, the "Apples" button and the "Oranges" button do not interact in any way. This means that the user can select *both* buttons, which goes against the whole point of radio buttons. The user should be able to select only "Apples," "Oranges," *or* "Bananas".

A simple behavior works to restrict the three buttons and get them to work together. To start, the behavior needs to know what other sprites are in its group. It also needs to know whether it begins as selected, which is the equivalent of TRUE.

```
property pState, pGroupList

on getPropertyDescriptionList me
  list = [:]
  addProp list, #pState, [#comment: "Initial State",¬
    #format: #boolean, #default: FALSE]
  addProp list, #pGroupList, [#comment: "Group List",¬
    #format: #list, #default: []]
  return list
end
```

The property "pGroupList" should contain a linear list of sprites in the group. For instance, if the example's three radio buttons are in sprites 1 to 3, "pGroupList" should be [1,2,3].

The "pState" property should also be set with care. One and only one of the radio buttons in the group should be set to true. Then, in the *on beginSprite* handler, the sprite needs to be set to the on member if its initial "pState" is set to true.

```
on beginSprite me
  if pState then turnMeOn(me)
end
```

The custom handler "on turnMeOn" is used to set the member of the sprite. Because these are radio buttons, this handler also has to make sure that the other sprites in this group are turned off.

```
on turnMeOn me
  pState = TRUE
  sprite(me.spriteNum).member.hilite = TRUE
  repeat with i in pGroupList
    if i <> me.spriteNum then
      sendSprite(sprite i,#turnMeOff)
    end if
  end repeat
end
```

The *repeat* command in this handler uses the form *repeat with* i *in*. This special form of the *repeat* command can be used only with lists. Instead of the variable "i" counting from one number to the next, it moves through the values of the list. If the list is [5,8,14], the loop runs three times and the value of "i" will be set to 5, 8, and 14 for those times though the loop.

The *sendSprite* command is used to send the message "#turnMeOff" to each of the sprites in the list. An *if* statement makes sure that this message isn't sent back to the current sprite. The "on turnMeOff" handler is a simple one:

```
on turnMeOff me
  pState = FALSE
  sprite(me.spriteNum).member.hilite = FALSE
end
```

Now that there is a handler to turn on the current radio button, a mouse click is easily handled. It just calls the "on turnMeOn" handler, which turns on the current sprite and turns off all the others.

```
on mouseUp me
  turnMeOn(me)
end
```

One last handler can be used to determine which sprite in the group is currently selected. This handler uses the same *repeat* loop as the "on turnMeOn" handler, but rather than change the sprite, it just finds one that is on and returns that value.

```
on selected me
  repeat with i in pGroupList
    if sprite(i).pState = TRUE then return i
  end repeat
end
```

This handler relies on the fact that one and only one sprite is turned on. There should never be a time when none, or more than one, are on. The handler also has the unusual capability to return the same answer no matter which sprite in the group is used to call it. If a radio button group is in sprites one to three, a selected(sprite 1) and a selected(sprite 2) should return the same answer because they should have the same "pGroupList" property value.

Although this behavior takes care of the complexity of the radio button group, it does not offer the opportunity to use custom bitmaps as radio buttons rather than the boring built-in radio button member. However, it can be easily modified to do so.

The first step is to add two new properties to represent the on and off state bitmaps. These look the same as they do in the check box behavior:

```
property pOnMember, pOffMember, pState, pGroupList

on getPropertyDescriptionList me
  list = [:]
  addProp list, #pOnMember, [#comment: "On Member",¬
    #format: #member, #default: ""]
  addProp list, #pOffMember, [#comment: "Off Member",¬
    #format: #member, #default: ""]
  addProp list, #pState, [#comment: "Initial State",¬
    #format: #boolean, #default: FALSE]
  addProp list, #pGroupList, [#comment: "Group List",¬
    #format: #list, #default: []]
  return list
end
```

Then, the "on turnMeOn" and "on turnMeOff" handlers need to be modified to set the member of the sprite, rather than the hilite property of the member:

```
on turnMeOn me
  pState = TRUE
  sprite(me.spriteNum).member = pOnMember
  repeat with i in pGroupList
    if i <> me.spriteNum then
      sendSprite(sprite i,#turnMeOff)
    end if
  end repeat
end

on turnMeOff me
  pState = FALSE
  sprite(me.spriteNum).member = pOffMember
end
```

The rest of the behavior can stay the same. Figure 15.5 shows what this screen may look like. The off members and the on member differ only in that the on member includes an arrow to the right of the picture to signify that it is selected.

→ **See** "Standardized Tests," Chapter 27, "Educational Applications," for more examples of using radio buttons

Figure 15.5
A set of custom-built radio buttons. A behavior controls which member is used depending on which item is selected.

DRAGGING SPRITES

Although dragging sprites is possible without Lingo (by setting the movable property of a sprite in the Score), Lingo enables you to add all sorts of functionality to dragging. Learning how to drag a sprite with Lingo is the first step, and then you will be ready to try some dragging applications.

SIMPLE DRAG SCRIPT

A drag script can be as simple as setting the sprite to constantly follow the cursor. However, a real drag behavior waits until the user clicks the sprite, and then follows the cursor around until the user releases the mouse button.

To do this type of drag, you don't even need any parameters. However, you do need one property to tell the behavior when the dragging is taking place. This should be set to false when the sprite begins.

```
property pPressed
```

```
on beginSprite me
  pPressed = FALSE
end
```

When the user clicks the sprite, the behavior needs to change this "pPressed" property to TRUE. When the user lifts up, it needs to be set to FALSE.

```
on mouseDown me
  pPressed = TRUE
end
```

```
on mouseUp me
  pPressed = FALSE
end
```

It is possible for the user to lift up the mouse button while the cursor is not over the sprite. The mouse location is updated in real time, whereas you will only be setting the location of the sprite every frame loop. To make sure that dragging stops whenever the mouse button is lifted, you need to also use the *on mouseUpOutside* handler.

```
on mouseUpOutside me
  pPressed = FALSE
end
```

Finally, the *on exitFrame* handler does all the heavy lifting. It checks to see whether the "pPressed" property is true, and moves the sprite to the mouse location if it is:

```
on exitFrame me
  if pPressed then
    sprite(me.spriteNum).loc = the mouseLoc
  end if
end
```

A BETTER DRAG BEHAVIOR

The main problem with the simple drag script is a cosmetic one. The sprite appears to snap to center itself on the cursor no matter where the user clicks. So if you click on the upper right side of the sprite, the sprite immediately shifts so that the center, or actually the registration point, is directly under the cursor.

Fixing this glitch in not a problem. When the initial click is made, the difference in location between the mouse and the center of the sprite can be recorded. This value can then be applied to every change in the sprite's location. The result is that the cursor and the sprite remain synchronized, wherever the user grabs the sprite. If the user grabs the sprite by the upper right corner, it then drags by the upper right corner.

To make this change, first add the property "pClickDiff" to the property declaration. Then, alter the *on mouseDown* handler to record the difference between the click location and the sprite location, as follows:

```
on mouseDown me
  pPressed = TRUE
  pClickDiff = sprite(me.spriteNum).loc - the clickLoc
end
```

Note

The property the clickLoc is similar to the mouseLoc. They both return a point as their value. However, the mouseLoc might change if the mouse moves between the time the click was made and the time that the line of Lingo code runs. The clickLoc gives the exact location of the last click in an on mouseDown or similar handler, whereas the mouseLoc is the current mouse position.

Now that the offset is stored in the "pClickDiff", it can be applied to the position of the sprite in the *on exitFrame* handler.

```
on exitFrame me
  if pPressed then
    sprite(me.spriteNum).loc = the mouseLoc + pClickDiff
  end if
end
```

If this is still confusing, seeing it in action will help; check the example on the CD-ROM.

CLICK, DRAG, AND LOCK

One application of dragging is using it to build a matching game or quiz. You have elements of one type on one side of the screen and elements of another type on another side. The game is essentially made up of matching pairs. It is up to the user to drag the sprites on the left over to the sprites on the right. Figure 15.6 shows what this might look like.

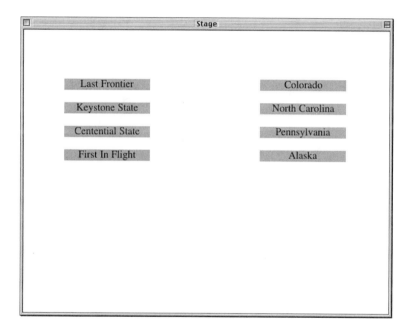

Figure 15.6
The screen shows four pairs of matching items. The user's task is to drag the ones on the right onto the correct ones on the left.

Although this can be done with the drag scripts already described, these scripts have no capability to tell the user whether the match is correct. A better way to do it would be to have a script that locks a sprite into position if it is near the place it belongs.

This requires some parameters. The first is the number of the sprite to which that the behavior's sprite should lock. The second should be the maximum distance that the dragged sprite can be from the destination sprite before it automatically locks.

Also, an option is needed to tell the behavior what to do in case the sprite is not close enough to its destination to lock. One option is for it to snap back to its original position. The other option is to leave it where it is.

In addition to these new properties, you will still want the old properties of "pPressed" and "pClickDiff". You will also need a property to store the original location of the sprite in cases where it needs to snap back.

```
property pPressed, pClickDiff, pLockToSprite, pOrigLoc, pLockDist, pSnapBack

on getPropertyDescriptionList me
  list = [:]
  addProp list, #pLockToSprite, [#comment: "Lock To Sprite",¬
    #format: #integer, #default: 0]
  addProp list, #pLockDist, [#comment: "Maximum Lock Distance",¬
    #format: #integer, #default: 25]
  addProp list, #pSnapBack, [#comment: "Snap Back If Not Locked",¬
    #format: #boolean, #default: TRUE]
  return list
end
```

The "pLockDist" is a key property for this behavior. Without it, the user would be required to lock the sprite exactly into position over the destination sprite.

The behavior needs to start off by initializing "pPressed" and also setting the "pOrigLoc" property.

```
on beginSprite me
  pPressed = FALSE
  pOrigLoc = sprite(me.spriteNum).loc
end
```

The mouse click handlers are the same as before, except that a custom handler is called from the *on mouseUp* and *on mouseUpOutside* handlers. This behavior has more to do than just setting the "pPressed" back to FALSE, so it is best to place it all in a custom handler rather than attempt to duplicate the code between *on mouseUp* and *on mouseUpOutside*.

```
on mouseDown me
  pPressed = TRUE
  pClickDiff = sprite(me.spriteNum).loc - the clickLoc
end

on mouseUp me
  release(me)
end

on mouseUpOutside me
  release(me)
end
```

The *on exitFrame* script is exactly as before.

```
on exitFrame me
  if pPressed then
    sprite(me.spriteNum).loc = the mouseLoc + pClickDiff
  end if
end
```

The custom "on release" handler has to do several things. First it sets the "pPressed" to FALSE. Then, it needs to determine whether the sprite is now close enough to its destination to lock into place. It calls yet another custom handler, "on distance", to do this. This function takes two points as parameters and returns the distance between them in pixels.

If the sprite is close enough, the new location of the sprite is set to exactly the location of the destination sprite. Otherwise, if the "pSnapBack" property is TRUE, the location snaps back to the original location. If not, the location remains where the user left it.

```
on release me
  pPressed = FALSE

  if distance(me,sprite(me.spriteNum).loc,sprite(pLockToSprite).loc) ¬
      < pLockDist then
    sprite(me.spriteNum).loc = sprite(pLockToSprite).loc
  else if pSnapBack then
    sprite(me.spriteNum).loc = pOrigLoc
  end if
end
```

The "on distance" function is a handy tool that is used in a lot of behaviors. It takes two points and uses the square root of the sum of the squares of the differences between horizontal and vertical locations. You might remember this formula from high school trigonometry:

$$\sqrt{((X_2 - X_1)^2 + (Y_2 - Y_1)^2)}$$

```
on distance me, point1, point2
  return sqrt(power(point1.locH-point2.locH,2)+ ¬
    power(point1.locV-point2.locV,2))
end
```

All that is left to do is apply the behavior to some sprites. In the example shown in Figure 15.6, the behavior should be applied to the sprites on the right. They are in higher sprite channels and appear above the sprites on the left. The "pLockToSprite" of each one of these sprites should be set to the matching item's sprite.

If you were really making a game of this, you could use this movie script to determine whether all the sprites were locked in place.

```
on checkGameDone
  done = TRUE
  repeat with i = 5 to 8
    if (sprite i).loc <> sprite(sprite(i).pLockToSprite).loc then
      done = FALSE
    end if
  end repeat
  if done then beep()
end
```

This movie handler assumes the game is done by setting the local variable "done" to TRUE. It then looks at sprites 5 through 8, which is where the dragging sprites are located, and compares their locations to the locations of their designated destination sprites. If they all match, "done" is never set to FALSE. In this case, the result is a simple *beep*. However, you could also make it jump to another frame or play a sound.

The perfect place for a call to this handler is in the "on release" handler of the behavior. It only needs to check this every time a sprite is locked, so place it after the `sprite(me.spriteNum).loc = sprite(pLockToSprite).loc` line.

→ **See** "Matching," Chapter 27, for an example of click, drag and lock behavior

DRAG AND THROW

Another way to apply a drag behavior is to enable the users to grab and throw a sprite. They click it and drag it around while the mouse is down, like the other drag behaviors, but then when they release it the sprite keeps going with some amount of momentum.

This is much more complex than a simple drag behavior. First, you have more than just pressed and non-pressed states. A third state is the state of being thrown. So the "pPressed" property should be replaced with a "pMode" property that is #normal, #pressed, or #throw.

In addition, you need to know how far and in which direction to throw the sprite when it is released. Measuring the distance between the position of the sprite upon release and the position of the sprite just before provides the appropriate information. However, it is not a good idea to take the position of the sprite exactly one frame prior to release, as that can be too short a period of time: it is only one sixtieth of a second if the frame rate is 60 fps. A better idea is to have a parameter that determines how many frames back to look to determine the momentum of the released sprite. A good default for this might be five. So if a sprite is clicked and dragged for 150 frame loops, and then released, the position in frame 145 and the position in frame 150 are compared to set the throwing momentum. A list is needed to record the last five positions at any given time. Here is the property list and *on getPropertyDescriptionList* for this behavior:

```
property pThrowSpan, pMode, pCurrentLoc, pLocList, pMoveAmount

on getPropertyDescriptionList me
  list = [:]
  addProp list, #pThrowSpan, [#comment: "Frame Span of Throw",¬
    #format: #integer, #range: [#min: 1, #max: 20], ¬
    #default: 5]
  return list
end
```

The sprite starts by setting the "pMode" to #normal.

```
on beginSprite me
  pMode = #normal
end
```

When the user clicks, the mode must change to #pressed and the list used to store the positions must be initialized:

```
on mouseDown me
  pMode = #pressed
  pLocList = []
end
```

Whenever the mouse button lifts, a custom handler called "on throw" runs. This calculates the momentum by taking the current mouse location and the first item in the "pLocList". It needs to divide that by "pThrowSpan" to get a relative per-frame movement amount. This way, if "pThrowSpan" is set to 5, the "pMoveAmount" is set to the current location of the sprite, minus the location of the sprite 5 frame loops ago, divided by 5:

```
on mouseUp me
  throw(me)
end

on mouseUpOutside me
  throw(me)
end

on throw me
  pMoveAmount = (the mouseLoc - pLocList[1])/pThrowSpan
  pMode = #throw
end
```

The *on exitFrame* handler must move the sprite whether it is being dragged or thrown. If being dragged, it needs to set the location of the sprite to the current mouse location. It also needs to record this location in "pLocList". If "pLocList" has more items than specified by "pThrowSpan", the oldest item is removed.

If the mode is #throw, the "pMoveAmount" is used to move the sprite. In addition, this property is multiplied by .9, thereby decreasing it by approximately 10%. This imitates a sort of friction that one would expect the sprite to exhibit when thrown. If you want, the .9 can be made into a property, say "pFriction", and altered at the movie author's whim.

```
on exitFrame me
  if pMode = #pressed then
    pCurrentLoc = the mouseLoc
    sprite(me.spriteNum).loc = pCurrentLoc
    pLocList.add(pCurrentLoc)
    if pLocList.count > pThrowSpan then pLocList.deleteAt(1)

  else if pMode = #throw then
    pCurrentLoc = pCurrentLoc + pMoveAmount
    sprite(me.spriteNum).loc = pCurrentLoc
    pMoveAmount = pMoveAmount * .9
  end if
end
```

Think of the possibilities of a behavior like this. Do you want to add code like that used in the bouncing behavior so it bounces off the sides of the screen? How about code that adds gravity? How about code that will lock the sprite to the position of another if it is close enough? Combine all three and you get something that resembles a basketball free-throw video game.

CREATING SLIDERS

Sliders are a familiar user interface element used in all major software programs. They offer the best way to enable the user to input a number within a small range. They are even used in behavior Parameter dialog boxes for this purpose.

Creating one with several bitmap members and a behavior can be fairly complex. A lot of actions must be taken into account, and more than one sprite is needed to form the elements of a slider.

Figure 15.7 shows what a slider should look like. This is just a straight imitation of the sliders used in the Director Preferences dialog boxes:

Figure 15.7
A typical slider
contains about six
parts.

A full slider element contains six parts: a marker, a shadow, a background graphic, two buttons, and a text field. However, you can start by creating the main three parts: the marker, the shadow, and the background graphic. The shadow is the dark coloring to the left side of the marker. It is the only non-bitmap element in this case; it uses a shape sprite instead.

You actually will need only one behavior script, attached to the marker sprite. Like the button and drag behaviors, this behavior needs a property to tell whether it is in the process of being pressed. It also needs to know how far to the left and right it can move, and what range of values it represents, such as 1 to 3, 0 to 100, or -500 to 500. A relationship with the shadow sprite is needed, so one property should hold that sprite number. Another property needs to record the current value of the slider, as follows:

```
property pPressed -- whether the sprite is being pressed
property pBounds -- the rect of the shadow sprite at start
property pMinimumValue, pMaximumValue -- use by the marker sprite only
property pShadowSprite -- the number of the shadow sprite
property pValue -- actual value of the slider

on getPropertyDescriptionList me
  list = [:]
  addProp list, #pShadowSprite, [#comment: "Shadow Sprite",¬
    #format: #integer, #default: 0]
addProp list, #pMinimumValue, [#comment: "Minimum Value",¬
    #format: #integer, #default: 0]
  addProp list, #pMaximumValue, [#comment: "Maximum Value",¬
```

```
      #format: #integer, #default: 100]
    addProp list, #pValue, [#comment: "Start Value",¬
      #format: #integer, #default: 50]
    return list
end
```

The *on getPropertyDescriptionList* needs to use only four of the properties as parameters: the minimum, maximum, and starting value of the slider, as well as the shadow sprite's number.

Although the minimum and maximum values are set by the behavior's parameter dialog box, the behavior also needs to know the physical screen locations of the minimum and maximum values. To determine these locations, a trick is used. The shadow sprite is set to mark the exact bounds of the marker sprite. Because the shadow sprite will be reset by the behavior when it starts anyway, using it to show the boundaries of the slider does not affect its future appearance. In the case of the slider shown in Figure 15.7, the shadow sprite is stretched all the way across the inner part of the background graphic. Its rect is recorded by the *on beginSprite* handler of the behavior. Then, it is set to display properly, as shown in Figure 15.7:

```
on beginSprite me
  pBounds = sprite(pShadowSprite).rect
  setMarker(me)
  setShadow(me)
end
```

The left and right physical limits of the slider could have been added to the *on getPropertyDescriptionList* handler, but this would mean that you would have had to determine the exact screen locations and type them in. Worse than that, if the slider were moved, even by one pixel, you would have to re-enter these numbers. Using the shadow sprite as a "template" of sorts saves you the trouble, and it is easily adjusted on the Stage.

The *on beginSprite* handler includes calls to the custom "on setMarker" and "on setShadow" handlers. These take the current value of the slider and set the position of these two sprites.

The "on setMarker" handler first figures out the value range of the slider. If the slider goes from 0 to 100, the range is 100 (not 101). It computes the value of the slider as a number between 0 and 1, regardless of the real range. It then takes this percentage and applies it to the physical screen range to get the location of the marker:

```
-- this sets the marker sprite
on setMarker me
  -- compute the value as a number between 0 and 1
  valueRange = pMaximumValue - pMinimumValue
  sliderPos = float(pValue)/float(valueRange)

  -- translate to a screen position
  sliderRange = pBounds.right-pBounds.left
  x = sliderPos*sliderRange + pBounds.left

  -- set marker
  sprite(me.spriteNum).locH = x
end
```

The "on setShadow" handler sets the shadow to its original rectangle, but with the right side adjusted to fall under the marker.

```
-- this handler lets the marker sprite set the shadow sprite
on setShadow me
  x = sprite(me.spriteNum).locH
  r = rect(pBounds.left, pBounds.top, x, pBounds.bottom)
  sprite(pShadowSprite).rect = r
end
```

These handlers accomplish the task of setting the slider to its starting position. Now you need some handlers to enable users to click and drag the marker:

```
on mouseDown me
  pPressed = TRUE
end

on mouseUp me
  pPressed = FALSE
end

on mouseUpOutside me
  pPressed = FALSE
end

on exitFrame me
  if pPressed then
    moveMarker(me)
    setMarker(me)
    setShadow(me)
  end if
end
```

The *on exitFrame* handler checks to make sure that "pPressed" is true, and then calls other handlers to handle the work. The "on setMarker" and "on setShadow" handlers are there, but called after an "on moveMarker" handler. This handler does the opposite of what the "on setMarker" handler does: it determines the value of the slider based on the mouse location.

In addition, it translates the value to an integer. If you want the slider to show floating point numbers instead, just removing that line does the trick:

```
-- this handler takes the mouse position and figures the
-- value of the slider
on moveMarker me
  -- compute the position as a number between 0 and 1
  x = the mouseH - pBounds.left
  sliderRange = pBounds.right-pBounds.left
  pos = float(x)/sliderRange

  -- translate to a value
  valueRange = pMaximumValue - pMinimumValue
  pValue = pos*valueRange + pMinimumValue
  pValue = integer(pValue)
```

```
  -- check to make sure it is within bounds
  if pValue > pMaximumValue then
    pValue = pMaximumValue
  else if pValue < pMinimumValue then
    pValue = pMinimumValue
  end if
end
```

The "on moveMarker" also makes sure that the new value of the slider falls within its range. Note that this handler's sole purpose is to set the "pValue" property. After it is called in the *on exitFrame* handler, the "on setMarker" and "on setShadow" handlers update the sprites.

Because the value of the slider is held in the "pValue" property, a handler that returns the value of the slider is quite simple. You can call this handler with *sendSprite* from other behaviors or movie scripts to get the current value of the slider, even while it is being dragged.

```
-- this handler returns the value of the slider
on getValue me
  return pValue
end
```

Several elements can be added to a slider to make it as complete as sliders found in other software. A text field can show the current value of the slider and two buttons can enable users to move the slider one value at a time.

Figure 15.8 shows all these elements. There are a total of eight cast members if you include down states for the buttons.

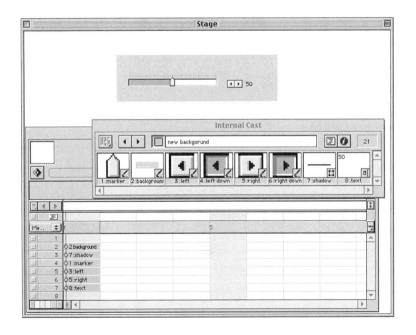

Figure 15.8
The cast window shows the eight elements of the slider. The Score shows the sprite placement of each. The Stage shows the assembled slider.

The first bit of extra functionality that you would want to add to a simple slider such as this is a text field that shows the value of the slider. To do this, create a text field and place it on the Stage. You need to tell the marker sprite where this text sprite is located. An extra parameter should do it. Add a "pTextSprite" property to the property declarations at the top of the behavior. Add this to the *on getPropertyDescriptionList* handler:

```
addProp list, #pTextSprite, [#comment: "Text Sprite",¬
    #format: #integer, #default: 0]
```

An "on setText" handler places the current value of the slider in this text field. Just in case no text sprite is used, this handler makes sure that the "pTextSprite" property is not 0. If it is, it assumes that there is no text sprite and does not place the text:

```
-- this handler sets the text of the text sprite
on setText me
  if pTextSprite <> 0 then -- is there a text sprite?
    sprite(pTextSprite).member.text = string(pValue)
  end if
end
```

Calls to "on setText" need to be added immediately after the calls to "on setShadow" in both the *on beginSprite* and *on exitFrame* handlers.

The next elements that the slider needs are the buttons that enable the user to move the slider one value in either direction. You need both normal and down states for these buttons, as was shown in Figure 15.8.

These buttons need their own behavior, but before you create that, a handler needs to be added to the marker behavior. This handler enables the marker to be moved one value in either direction. It should take one parameter that is either a #left or a #right depending on which direction the slider should move. It also needs to perform the same boundary check that the "on moveMarker" handler does to make sure that the slider doesn't go past its limits.

```
-- this handler moves the marker one value left or right
on moveMarkerOne me, direction
  if direction = #left then
    pValue = pValue - 1
  else if direction = #right then
    pValue = pValue + 1
  end if

  -- check to make sure it is within bounds
  if pValue > pMaximumValue then
    pValue = pMaximumValue
  else if pValue < pMinimumValue then
    pValue = pMinimumValue
  end if

  setMarker(me)
  setShadow(me)
  setText(me)
end
```

The "on moveMarkerOne" handler ends by calling the three handlers needed to update the slider. This makes it possible to call this one handler and have the slider changed and updated by the other three automatically.

A handler to take care of the two buttons is similar to any simple button handler. It mostly controls normal and down states for the button sprite. It also has to know where the marker sprite is so that it can send the "moveMarkerOne" message to it. A key parameter is the "pArrowDirection", which is set to #left or #right depending on which button is selected:

```
property pDownMember, pOrigMember -- down and normal states
property pPressed -- whether the sprite is being pressed
property pMarkerSprite -- the number of the marker sprite
property pArrowDirection -- 1 or -1 to add to slider

on getPropertyDescriptionList me
  list = [:]
  addProp list, #pMarkerSprite, [#comment: "Marker Sprite",¬
    #format: #integer, #default: 0]
  addProp list, #pDownMember, [#comment: "Arrow Button Down Member",¬
    #format: #bitmap, #default: ""]
  addProp list, #pArrowDirection, [#comment: "Arrow Direction",¬
    #format: #symbol, #range: [#left,#right], #default: #right]
  return list
end
```

The rest of the slider button behavior handles the mouse clicking and calls the "moveMarkerOne" handler in the marker behavior once per frame loop while the button is pressed:

```
on beginSprite me
  pOrigMember = sprite(me.spriteNum).member
end

on mouseDown me
  pPressed = TRUE
  sprite(me.spriteNum).member = member pDownMember
end

on mouseUp me
  liftUp(me)
end

on mouseUpOutside me
  liftUp(me)
end

on liftUp me
  pPressed = FALSE
  sprite(me.spriteNum).member = member pOrigMember
end

on exitFrame me
  if pPressed then
    sendSprite(sprite pMarkerSprite, #moveMarkerOne, ¬
    pArrowDirection)
  end if
end
```

With the eight members and two behaviors, you have all the functionality of the sliders used by other software programs. Even better, you can change the graphics used to anything you want in order to stylize your sliders to fit your design.

You have a lot of control over how the slider looks and behaves. You can alter your code to place an extra word behind the number in the text field. So rather than reading "50" it can read "50%" or "50 widgets". You can tweak the slider screen boundaries if the shadow sprite isn't working the way you want. You can even remove the shadow sprite.

There is nothing to stop you from taking all the references to horizontal locations and boundaries and converting them to vertical locations and boundaries to make a vertical slider. This is a good example of how much control Lingo behaviors give you as opposed to the drag-and-drop interface elements in other authoring programs.

→ **See** "Volume Controls," Chapter 30, "Sound Applications," for an example of a slider

CREATING PROGRESS BARS

Using some of the same techniques as the slider bar, you can create a progress bar behavior. A progress bar is a rectangle that enlarges to fill a space as a process is completed. An example is the progress bar the Director displays every time you choose File, Save.

If you have a Lingo process that takes more than a fraction of a second to complete, you may want to display a progress bar so that the users know that the computer is not frozen, but simply processing their requests.

Figure 15.9 shows a simple progress bar. It shows two sprites: a hollow rectangle shape and a filled rectangle. To make the progress bar look like others used in various pieces of software, the fill of the rectangle is set to a pattern, rather than a solid.

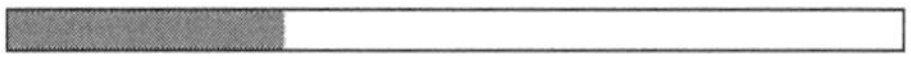

Figure 15.9
A simple progress bar showing a task about one-third done.

To create a progress bar, you will need a process to use to test it. Here are two movie handlers that work together to compute all the prime numbers between one and 1000. A prime number is a number divisible only by one and itself.

```
on findPrimeNumbers
  list = []
  repeat with i = 1 to 1000
    if isPrime(i) then add list, i
  end repeat
  return list
end

on isPrime n
  repeat with i = 2 to integer(sqrt(n))
    div = float(n)/float(i)
```

```
      if div = integer(div) then return FALSE
   end repeat
   return TRUE
end
```

The "on isPrime" function tries every number between two and the square root of the number to see whether it can find a case where there is no fractional remainder to the division. It compares the number to itself converted to an integer to see whether there is a remainder.

This process takes several seconds to run on a PowerMac 8500 with a 225 MHz processor. It also does this calculation in 1000 steps, so it is a prime candidate for a progress bar.

Of the two sprites involved in the progress bar, only the filled portion needs a behavior. The other sprite is there for merely cosmetic purposes.

Like the slider marker behavior, this sprite needs to know the size of its final, full rectangle. To make that easy to determine, set the sprite up on the Stage to already be its full size. That way, the *on beginSprite* handler can get the full rectangle size by simply looking at the rect of the sprite when the behavior starts.

```
property pFullRect

on beginSprite me
  pFullRect = sprite(me.spriteNum).rect
end
```

The only other handler needed is the one that will set the progress bar when needed. It will be a custom handler that a process such as "on findPrimeNumbers" calls when it can.

```
on setProgress me, currentVal, highestVal
  -- get amount filled as a value between 0 and 1
  percentFilled = float(currentVal)/float(highestVal)

  -- convert to a pixel width
  pixelRange = pFullRect.right-pFullRect.left
  x = percentFilled*pixelRange

  -- set the rect of the sprite
  r = rect(pFullRect.left, pFullRect.top, ¬
      pFullRect.left + x, pFullRect.bottom)
  sprite(me.spriteNum).rect = r
end
```

The "on setProgress" handler takes two parameters. The first is the current value of the progress bar, and the second is the maximum value of the progress bar. It takes these two values and divides them to get the percentage of fill needed. It then determines the physical width of the progress bar area and determines the point to which the sprite should stretch. Finally, it builds a rectangle from this information and sets the sprite.

To use this behavior, you need to call it from the process taking place. In this case, the "on findPrimeNumbers" handler will use it.

```
on findPrimeNumbers
  list = []
  repeat with i = 1 to 1000
    sendSprite(sprite 2,#setProgress,i,1000)
    updateStage
    if isPrime(i) then add list, i
  end repeat
  return list
end
```

Notice that an *updateStage* is needed because the frame is not looping here. Director is caught inside the *repeat* loop and does not know to update the Stage without you telling it.

You can easily change the color and dimensions of a progress bar such as this. If you prefer a more stylized progress bar, you may want to convert this behavior to use three elements: a left end, a right end, and a stretchable middle piece. Doing so would require the same behavior to control two other sprites, possibly specified as parameters.

CREATING GRAPHIC POP-UP MENUS

Like the check boxes, radio buttons, sliders, and progress bars, another item that can be created with bitmaps and a behavior is the pop-up menu.

Pop-up menus are the little menus that appear in windows and dialog boxes, as opposed to the main menu bar which appears at the top of a screen or window. In the Director authoring environment, you can see examples of these in the Score window and Sprite Inspector. As a matter of fact, just about every window in Director includes some type of pop-up menu.

Creating pop-up menus as interface elements in your movies is possible with a behavior. First, create a series of bitmaps in the Cast to be used. Figure 15.10 shows the cast window with some example bitmaps. A single bitmap represents the pop-up menu when it is not active, and then five other bitmaps that appear under it when it is pressed. All five of these bitmaps have a corresponding hilite state.

To create the pop-up on the Stage, place the sprites as you would want to see them when the pop-up is pressed and active. Never mind that the list under the "Choose One" graphic should not be present when the user first comes to the frame; the behavior will handle that.

For the behavior to do that, it needs to know where these sprites are. So one property of this behavior must be a list of sprites. Another property will be the members that are initially in these sprites. The behavior itself will be attached to the pop-up menu button, which is the "Choose One" graphic in this case:

```
property pSpriteList, pMemberList, pPressed

on getPropertyDescriptionList me
  list = [:]
```

```
    addProp list, #pSpriteList, [#comment: "Sprite List",¬
      #format: #list, #default: []]
    return list
end
```

To start, the behavior needs to record the members used by each of the sprites that are part of the pop-up. This example does not include the pop-up button.

```
on beginSprite me
  pMemberList = [:]
  repeat with i in pSpriteList
    addProp pMemberList, i, sprite(i).member.name
  end repeat
  hidePopup(me)
end
```

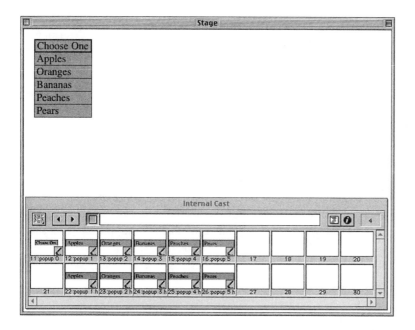

Figure 15.10
The Stage shows a pop-up menu as it appears during creation of the movie. The cast window shows these members, as well as the hilite states.

The call to "on hidePopUp" removes the pop-up items before the user sees them. The best way to do this is to set the *memberNum* property of the sprites to 0:

```
on hidePopup me
  repeat with i = 1 to pSpriteList.count
    sprite(pSpriteList[i]).memberNum = 0
  end repeat
end
```

The mouse click handlers look similar to those used in earlier behaviors. Both *on mouseUp* and *on mouseUpOutside* call a custom handler that calls the "on hidePopup" again as well as an "on select" handler:

```
on mouseDown me
  pPressed = TRUE
end
```

```
on mouseUp me
  liftUp(me)
end

on mouseUpOutSide me
  liftUp(me)
end

on liftUp me
  pPressed = FALSE
  hidePopup(me)
  select(me)
end
```

In the *on exitFrame* handler, a variety of tasks are performed when the pop-up is pressed. First, it calls "on showPopup" which returns the sprites to the members they used when you set up the movie. Then, it uses *the rollover* property to determine over which sprite the mouse is currently hovering. It uses *getOne* on the "pSpriteList" property to determine whether this is one of the pop-up items.

> **Note**
>
> The *getOne* property of a list enables you to find the position of an item in a list. If the item is there, it returns the number of the item, which can also be interpreted as TRUE. If the item is not in the list, a 0 is returned, which is always seen as FALSE.

If the mouse is over a sprite in the list, it then changes the member of that sprite to a member of the same name, except with the word "hilite" appended. (This is just a convention that this behavior uses to figure out which hilite members belong to which normal members.) You could just as easily have placed all the hilite members in the next member over from the normal members, and recorded the member numbers of the sprites, using a +1 to find the hilite member, which will be the very next member in the Cast.

```
on exitFrame me
  if pPressed then
    showPopup(me)
    s = the rollover
    if (pSpriteList.getOne(s)) then
      sprite(s).member = member (pMemberList.getProp(s)&&"hilite")
    end if
  end if
end
```

The result of this handler is that the pop-up items will be shown if the "pPressed" property is true, and any item that the cursor is currently over will show up as the hilite member. Figure 15.11 shows this in action.

Figure 15.11
The pop-up menu has been selected and the cursor is over the second item.

The "on showPopup" handler is similar to the "on hidePopup" handler except that the "pMemberList" is used to assign the correct member to each sprite:

```
on showPopup me
  repeat with i in pSpriteList
    sprite(i).member = member pMemberList.getProp(i)
  end repeat
end
```

Finally, the "on select" handler is called when the user releases the mouse button. It cannot assume that the cursor is over an item in the pop-up list, so it must check in the same way that the *on exitFrame* handler checks:

```
on select me
  s = the rollover
  if (pSpriteList.getOne(s)) then
    alert pMemberList.getProp(s)
  end if
end
```

In this case, a simple *alert* box appears to signify that a choice has been made. However, in your program you will want to set a global, go to a frame, or perform some other action.

This pop-up menu behavior can be customized in a lot of ways. With a little more work you can even have the selected item appear to replace the "Choose One" graphic, or have sounds play as the pop-up is used.

Notice that nothing in the script specifies that the items must be positioned directly below the original sprite. Why not have them line up to the right of the sprite? Or, have them appear above it? The possibilities are many.

→ **See** "Creating Text Pop-Up Menus," Chapter 16, "Controlling Text," for another way to make pop-up menus

TROUBLESHOOTING GRAPHIC INTERFACE ELEMENTS

- Be sure you understand the difference between *the clickLoc* and *the mouseLoc*. The first is the exact location of the mouse when the user clicked. The second is the current location of the mouse, which may have changed since the user clicked.

- When performing calculations where the result will be a number between 0 and 1, as in the slider behavior or the progress bar behavior, it is important to convert the numbers to floats before doing division. Otherwise, a calculation like 3/6 will return a 0, rather than a 0.5.

- The *memberNum* property of a sprite enables you to set the member of a sprite by just referring to it by number. It is good for setting a sprite to the next member or something similar, but should not be used otherwise. You should use the *member* property instead and set the sprite to a specific member by name.

DID YOU KNOW?

- In the *sendSprite* command, the word "sprite" is optional. So you can write *sendSprite(7,#myHandler)* instead of *sendSprite(sprite 7, #myHandler)*.

- There are two forms of syntax for the keyword "rollover". The function *rollover*(x) returns a TRUE if the cursor is over sprite x. The property *the rollover* returns the number of the sprite directly under the cursor.

- The *memberNum* property does not enable you to set the sprite to a member in another cast library. However, you can change the *castLibNum* to do that.

- The obsolete property *castNum* can still be used. It returns the same value as *memberNum* for members in the first cast library, but returns much higher values for members in other cast libraries. For instance, the first member in cast library 2 would have a *castNum* of 131073.

USING LINGO TO CONTROL MEDIA

CHAPTER **16**

CONTROLLING TEXT

In this chapter

Although text may seem primitive compared to images, sounds, and digital video, it is still the primary way in which most computer programs communicate information to the user. Director 7 has two primary cast members that handle text, plus dozens of Lingo commands and functions used to manipulate these members and strings. Using these cast members, commands, and functions is the topic of this chapter.

USING STRINGS AND CHUNKS

Strings, whether they are in variables or as the text inside members such as fields and text members, are controlled with string commands, chunk expressions, and string functions. A group of string constants also enables you to refer to common characters such as returns and tabs.

BUILDING STRINGS

Chapter 13, "Essential Lingo Syntax," provided a brief summary of string commands and functions. Here is a more detailed list of commands and operators used to build strings:

- &—Concatenates two strings.
- &&—Concatenates two strings and inserts a space in between them.
- put ... after—Appends a string onto another string. Can be used with chunk expressions to insert characters into the middle of a string.
- put ... before—Puts a string into another string, before the characters that are already there. Can be used with chunk expressions to insert characters into the middle of a string.
- put ... into—Puts a string into another variable. Can be used with chunk expressions to replace characters in one string with characters from another.
- delete—Removes a chunk from a string.

All the preceding commands can use chunk expressions to modify their functions. Chunk expressions are elements such as *char*, *word*, *line*, and *item*. Although the *delete* command requires a chunk expression, the three variations of the *put* command can use a chunk expression to insert or replace existing text.

For example, if you have a simple string that looks like this: "abcdefg", and you want to insert *xyz* in between the *c* and the *d*, here's what you can do:

```
s = "abcdefg"
put "xyz" after s.char[3]
put s
-- "abcxyzdefg"
```

However, you could have also done this:

```
s = "abcdefg"
put "xyz" before s.char[4]
put s
-- "abcxyzdefg"
```

What if you wanted to replace the letter *c* with an *x*? That is easy:

```
s = "abcdefg"
put "x" into s.char[3]
put s
-- "abxdefg"
```

But what if you wanted to replace the letter *c* with more than one character? The *put* command does not require that the replacement string and the original chunk be the same size.

```
s = "abcdefg"
put "xyz" into s.char[3]
put s
-- "abxyzdefg"
```

You can also replace a larger chunk with a smaller string:

```
s = "abcdefg"
put "xyz" into s.char[2..6]
put s
-- "axyzg"
```

CHUNK EXPRESSIONS

Notice in the preceding section that the *char* chunk can accept a single number parameter to refer to one character, but can also use the a..b notation to refer to a series of characters. The same is true of all chunk expressions.

Chunk expressions were also introduced in Chapter 13. Here is a more detailed list and description of the chunk expressions:

- char—Enables you to specify a single character or group of consecutive characters in a string.

- word—Enables you to specify a word or group of words in a string. Words are delimited by spaces or any non-visible character such as a tab or return. A request for a single word does not include these delimiters, but a request for a group of words includes the delimiters between them.

- item—Enables you to specify an item or group of items in a string. Items are delimited by the character that corresponds to the *itemDelimiter* property. This property is initially set to a comma, but can be changed. A request for a single item does not include the delimiter, but a request for a group of items includes the delimiters between them.

- line—Enables you to specify a line or group of lines in a string. Lines are delimited by returns. Any soft wrapping in fields is ignored. A request for a single lines does not include the returns, but a request for a group of lines includes the returns between them.

- paragraph—A new Director 7 chunk that acts the same as *line*.

Chunk expressions can be combined to create specific descriptions of the position of chunks in a string. For instance: `myString.line[1].word[1..2].char[3..4]`.

You can also use old Director 6 syntax to refer to strings. The preceding example could have been stated: `char 3 to 4 of word 1 to 2 of line 1 of myString`.

COMPARING STRINGS

It will quite frequently be necessary to compare strings in complex programs. You can use the plain old "=" operator to see whether strings match exactly, but you can also use a variety of operators and functions to perform other types of comparisons, as:

- = —Compares two strings and returns TRUE if they are equal. This operator ignores case.
- < —Compares two strings and returns TRUE if the first one comes before the second alphabetically. This operator ignores case.
- <= —Compares two strings and returns TRUE if the first one comes before the second alphabetically, or if they are equal. This operator ignores case.
- > —Compares two strings and returns TRUE if the first one comes after the second alphabetically. This operator ignores case.
- >= —Compares two strings and returns TRUE if the first one comes after the second alphabetically, or if they are equal. This operator ignores case.
- <> —Compares two strings and returns TRUE if they are not the same. This operator ignores case.
- contains—Compares two strings and returns TRUE if the first one contains the second. It ignores case.
- starts—Compares two strings and returns TRUE if the first one starts with the same characters as the second. It ignores case.
- offset—This is not really an operator, but is a function that can be used like *contains*. It returns the character position of one string inside another, or a 0 if the one string is not in the other string.

The *contains* and *starts* operators are used in the same way as the = syntax. Here are some examples:

```
s = "Hello World."
put (s contains "World")
-- 1
put (s contains "Earth")
-- 0
put (s starts "World")
-- 0
put (s starts "Hello")
-- 1
```

The *contains* function works pretty fast even on large strings or fields. It can be used to quickly search hundreds or even thousands of field members for a phrase or keyword. This makes it very useful for database programs.

The *contains* function is also more forgiving than =, which requires an exact match, except for case. If you need to know whether a cast member name has the word "button" in it, *contains* finds members named "button normal", "button down", "button rollover", and so on, whereas = finds only an exact match.

STRING FUNCTIONS

In addition to commands and operators, a variety of functions can be used to get information from strings, convert strings to other variable types, or convert other variable types to strings. Here is a detailed list of these string functions:

- chars—An old function from early versions of Director that enables you to get a series of characters from a string. For example, `chars(myString,3,5)` is the same as `myString.char[3..5]`.

- charToNum—This converts a single character to its ASCII code number. This is the number that the computer uses to store the character.

- count—This word can be used as a property of a chunk, such as *char* or *word*, to return the total number of such chunks in a string. For example, `myString.count`.

- float—This function, when given a string, tries to convert the string to a floating point number. A "4.5" returns a 4.5000.

- integer—This function, when given a string, tries to convert the string to an integer number. A "4" returns a 4.

- length—This function returns the length of a string in characters. It can also be used as a property of the string.

- numToChar—The opposite of *charToNum*, this function takes an integer that represents the ASCII value of a character and converts it into a single-character string.

- offset—This function takes two strings as parameters. It returns a number that corresponds to the character position of the first time the first string appears in the second. If the first string does not appear at all, it returns a 0.

- stringP—This function tests a variable to see whether it is a string. It returns TRUE if it is.

- string—This function takes any other type of variable (integer, float, list, and so on) and returns a string representation of it.

- value—This function takes a string and tries to evaluate it as a Lingo expression. For instance, "4" returns 4, and "4.0" returns 4.0000.

The *charToNum* and *numToChar* functions can be incredibly useful. Every character maps to a corresponding number, called an ASCII code. A list of these numbers appears in Appendix D, "Tables and Charts."

The number that corresponds to a capital "A" is 65. "B" is 66, and so on. The number that corresponds to a lowercase "a" is 97. Lowercase "b" is 98, and so on. Knowing this, you can create a simple handler that converts a mixed-capitalization string to one that is all capitals.

```
on allCaps text
  repeat with i = 1 to text.length
    thischar = charToNum(text.char[i])

    -- check to see if it is a lower case letter
    if thischar >= charToNum("a") and¬
        thischar <= charToNum("z")  then

      -- subtract 32, to make it upper case
      thischar = thischar - 32

      -- replace the character
      put numToChar(thischar) into text.char[i]
    end if
  end repeat
  return text
end
```

Any string passed into this handler returns the same string, but with capital letters replacing the lowercase ones:

```
put allCaps("This is a test.")
-- "THIS IS A TEST."
```

You can easily write a handler that reverses this process and converts a string to all lower-case.

The preceding handler also uses the *length* property. This keyword can be used as either a property or a function. It returns the number of characters in a string:

```
s = "Hello World."
put s.length
-- 12
put length(s)
-- 12
```

You can also use the *count* property to get the number of chunks in a string:

```
s = "Hello World."
put s.word.count
-- 2
put s.line.count
-- 1
```

The *length* function can be combined with chunk expressions to return the number of characters in a chunk as well:

```
s = "Hello World."
put length(s.word[1])
-- 5
```

The *offset* function doesn't offer anything that can't be done with a *repeat* loop and some = comparisons. However, it is very fast. If you need to find the first instance of a string in another very long string, *offset* is the way to go.

It may seem like finding only the *first* instance of a string inside a string is a little limiting. However, you can use the *offset* function to find all the instances of the string inside the string. Here is a handler that does it for you:

```
on findStringInString substring, text

  -- initialize list and character position
  list = []
  currentChar = 1

  repeat while TRUE
    -- find in remaining string
    loc = offset(substring,text.char[currentChar..text.length])

    -- see if none left
    if loc = 0 then exit repeat

    -- add char pos to list
    add list, currentChar+loc-1

    -- move char pointer forward
    currentChar = currentChar+loc
  end repeat
  return list
end
```

In the Message window, the function works in this way:

```
s = "Hello World."
put findStringInString("o",s)
-- [5, 8]
```

The last string function in the preceding list is the *value* function. Even from its short description, you can see how powerful it is.

If you want to convert a string to a number, *value* is often better than *integer* and *float* because it converts the string to whichever of the two is appropriate, rather than forcing it into one type or the other. Also, the capability of *value* to perform math functions on strings, such as returning 2 for the string "1+1", is very powerful.

You can even call Lingo functions with *value*. Suppose you have the following handler in a movie script:

```
on test
  return "testing!"
end
```

Now try this in the Message window:

```
put value("test()")
-- "testing!"
```

You can make an entire "calculator" movie using just *value* to determine the result. Figure 16.1 shows such a calculator. The first field is editable so that the user can alter the equation.

Figure 16.1
Four sprites make up a simple calculator: two text fields, an "=" graphic, and a "calculate" button.

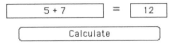

The only Lingo scripting needed is a simple, two-line handler in a behavior attached to the button. This can even be shortened to one line if you prefer:

```
on mouseUp
  answer = value(member("question").text)
  member("answer").text = string(answer)
end
```

STRING CONSTANTS

Although characters such as *a* are easy enough to represent, some characters, such tabs and returns, are not. You could figure out which ASCII numbers they correspond to, and use *numToChar*, but Lingo has some built-in constants that you can use for some characters.

- SPACE—The same as a " ". The main purpose of this is that it looks neater in your code.

- TAB—This corresponds to ASCII character 9, which is the character generated by the Tab key on the keyboard. It comes in handy when you import some text from a spreadsheet that uses tabs as item delimiters.

- RETURN—This corresponds to ASCII character 13, which is generated by the Return key on Macs and the main Enter key in Windows. It is also the character used to separate the *line* chunks from a string.

- QUOTE—Because the quote character is used in Lingo to define strings, you need this character to add actual quote marks into your strings.

- EMPTY—This corresponds to "", or a string with zero length.

- BACKSPACE—This corresponds to ASCII character 8, which is generated by the Delete key on Mac or the Backspace key in Windows. It is handy for interpreting keyboard input by the user.

- ENTER—This corresponds to ASCII character 3, which is generated by the Enter key on the numeric keypad if the keyboard is set to use it properly.

The QUOTE constant is the one that comes in the handiest in day-to-day Lingo programming. If you want to create a string that uses quotes, combine the use of QUOTE with the use of &, as follows:

```
s = "The computer replied, "&QUOTE&"Hello World."&QUOTE
put s
-- "The computer replied, "Hello World.""
```

TEXT REFERENCES

Director 7 has a new variable structure called *ref*. This variable enables you to reuse a reference to a chunk in a text member. For instance, you can say:

```
put member("myText").line[2].word[2]
-- "is"
put member("myText").line[2].word[2].font
-- "Times"
```

Or, you could use the *ref* property to set a variable to be a reference to this chunk. Then, you can use that reference to get other properties.

```
r = member("myText").line[2].word[2].ref
put r.text
-- "is"
put r.font
-- "Times"
```

Currently, only the *text*, *font*, *fontStyle*, and *fontSize* properties are available to *ref* references. All those but for the *text* property can be set to new values, and that change is related in the text member.

→ **See** "Using String Variables," Chapter 13, for more information about using strings

USING TEXT MEMBERS AND FIELDS

Although text members and fields essentially hold just text, they also have lots of other properties that affect how the text appears on the Stage. Text formatting, such as styles, fonts, and sizes, is not a part of strings, but plays a major part in the text used in these members.

FIELDS

A field member's primary property is the text it contains. You can get this text in Lingo with the *text* property of the member. You can also use the Lingo syntax *field* to refer to any field's text as if it were a string.

Using *field*, you can use the *put* commands and chunk expressions directly on the field contents without having to first store them in a string variable. For instance, if a field holds the text "Hello World", you can perform this command:

```
put "-" into char 6 of field 1
```

Notice that you cannot use the new Director 7 dot syntax with this type of functionality. You cannot write put "i" into field(1).char[6], for instance. However, you can write put "i" into member(1).char[6]. This is true because *field* is considered antiquated syntax, so the dot syntax was not implemented for it between Director 6 and 7.

Some things can still be done to field members only using the old syntax, such as setting the font of characters inside the field. If you want to set the font of the entire member, you can do that with dot syntax:

```
member(1).font = "Times"
```

However, if you want to set the font of just a few characters, words, or lines in the field, you need to use the *field* syntax.

```
set the font of word 6 to 9 of field 1 = "Geneva"
```

You can set many properties in a field like this one. Here is a detailed list of such properties:

- font—The typeface of the characters. You should specify the font as you would a string, as in "Times" or "Arial", for example.
- fontSize—The size of the font of the characters. Should be an integer, such as 9, 12, or 72.
- fontStyle—The style of the font. Should be a comma-delimited string that contains all the styles requested. For instance, "bold", or "bold, underline". You can use the styles "plain", "bold", "italic", "underline", "shadow", and "outline". The last two are Mac only. To turn off all styles, use "plain".
- foreColor—The color of the characters. You can set the color of any chunk in the field to a color in the movie's color palette.

In addition to these properties that can be applied to chunks in the field, a variety of properties can be applied to the entire field member. Here is a detailed list:

- alignment—This can be set to either "left", "right", or "center" to change the alignment of the field.
- autotab—Use TRUE or FALSE to change the member property of the same name. When TRUE, and the field is editable, the user can use the Tab key to move quickly between fields.
- bgColor—Enables you to set the background color of the field member. You can use the new *rgb* and *paletteIndex* structures.
- border—Enables you to set or change the border width around the field. A value of 0 removes the border.
- boxDropShadow—Enables you to set or change the drop shadow around the box of the field. A value of 0 removes the drop shadow.
- boxType—Enables you to change the type of field member. The options are #adjust, #scroll, #fixed, and #limit, just as they are in the field member's Properties dialog box.

- color—The same as *foreColor*, but you can use the new *rgb* and *paletteIndex* structures. The entire field has to be set at once.

- dropShadow—Enables you to set or change the drop shadow around the text of the field. A value of 0 removes the drop shadow.

- editable—Enables you to change the editable property of the member. Can be either TRUE or FALSE. When TRUE, and the movie is playing, the user can click and edit the text in the field.

- lineHeight—Enables you to set the line height, in pixels, of the entire text field. Typically, line heights are set to be a few points above the font size.

- margin—Enables you to change the inside margin property of the text field.

- wordWrap—Enables you to turn automatic word wrapping on or off by setting this to TRUE or FALSE.

If a field is set to be a scrolling type, several commands and properties enable you to control the field, as follows

- scrollByLine—A command that forces the field to scroll up or down a number of lines. For instance, `scrollByLine member(1), 2`, scrolls down two lines. Use a negative number to scroll up.

- scrollByPage—The same as *scrollByLine*, except that it scrolls by pages. A page is the number of lines in the field visible on the Stage. Use a negative number to scroll up.

- scrollTop—This property corresponds to the number of pixels that the scrolling field is from the top. If a field uses the line height 12, and it is scrolled one line, *the scrollTop is* 12.

The powerful thing about these three scrolling field commands is that they also work on fields set to be a "fixed" type. This means you can use Lingo to scroll a field even if the scrolling bar elements are not on the screen.

Editable text fields have a special quality in that text can be selected inside them by the user. Some Lingo code relates to this. You can get the position of the selection, the selection itself, and even set the selection.

- hilite—This command enables you to set the selection of an editable text field. For instance: `hilite word 2 of member "myField"`.

- the selection—This property returns the text selected in the currently active editable text field. Do not place a member reference after this property; it stands on its own.

- the selStart—This returns the number of the first character in the current selection. You can use it to set the selection. Do not place a member reference after this property; it stands on its own.

- the selEnd—This returns the number of the last character in the current selection. You can use it to set the selection. Do not place a member reference after this property; it stands on its own.

Lastly, for fields, several functions enable you to find the correlation between a location on the screen and the characters in a field:

- charPosToLoc—This function takes a field member and a number as parameters and returns a point that corresponds to where that character is located in the member. The point is relative to the upper-left corner of the member, regardless of any scrolling that is taking place.

- linePosToLocV—This function takes a field member and a number as parameters and returns the distance, in pixels, from the top of the member to where the line is located.

- locToCharPos—This function takes a member and a point as parameters and returns the number of the character located at that point in the field. The point should be relative to the upper-left corner of the member, regardless of any scrolling that is taking place.

- locVtoLinePos—This function takes a member and a number as parameters and returns the line number that is that distance from the top of the field.

- the mouseChar—Returns the number of the character that is under the cursor, regardless of what field it is.

- the mouseWord—Returns the number of the word that is under the cursor, regardless of what field it is.

- the mouseLine—Returns the number of the line that is under the cursor, regardless of what field it is.

- the mouseItem—Returns the number of the item that is under the cursor, regardless of what field it is.

Although *the mouseChar* and similar properties tell you what chunk number is under the cursor, it does not tell you to which field that chunk belongs. You can use the other functions to get a more accurate reading. Here is a function that tells you what field and chunk is under the cursor at any time, regardless of scrolling:

```
on underCursor
  s = the rollover
  loc = the mouseLoc

  -- is there a sprite under the cursor?
  if (s > 0) then

    -- is there a field attached to that sprite?
    if sprite(s).member.type = #field then

      -- subtract the loc of the sprite to get relative loc
      loc = loc - sprite(s).loc

      -- add any field scrolling
      loc.locV = loc.locV + sprite(s).member.scrollTop

      -- get the character number
      c = locToCharPos(sprite(s).member,loc)
```

```
    -- figure out the character
    ch = (sprite(s).member.text.char[c])
    put "The cursor is over character"&&c&&"("&ch&")"
  end if
end if
end
```

TEXT MEMBERS

Text members have a similar set of properties and functions as fields. However, sometimes the syntax varies.

For instance, you can still set the font, size, style, and color of any chunk in a text member, but you must use the new dot syntax. *Font* and *fontSize* work pretty much as you would expect. For example:

```
member("myText").char[2..5].font = "Times"
member("myText").char[2..5].fontSize = 18
```

However, font style works a little differently. Rather than giving it a string, such as "bold, underline", you need to give it a list, such as [#bold, #underline]. As is the case elsewhere, using [#plain] removes all styles.

Coloring text is also a little different. You can use the *color* property to set the color of the whole text member or just a chunk inside it. Here are some examples:

```
member("myText").color = rgb(40,120,0)
member("myText").char[2..5] = rgb("#6699CC")
member("myText").word[7].color = paletteIndex(35)
```

The text members do not have any border, margin, or drop shadows. However, they do share some of the other properties of fields. Most of these, however, use different values. They also have some new properties, as follows:

- alignment—This can be set to either #left, #right, or #center to change the alignment of the member. Text members also have a #full setting that justifies text.

- autotab—Use TRUE or FALSE to change the member property of the same name. When TRUE, and the member is editable, the user can use the Tab key to move quickly between text members.

- boxType—Enables you to change the type of text member. The options are #adjust, #scroll, and #fixed just as they are in the text member's Properties dialog box.

- editable—Enables you to change the editable property of the member. Can be either TRUE or FALSE. When TRUE, and the movie is playing, the user can click and edit the text in the member.

- fixedLineSpace—The same as the *lineHeight* property of fields, but you can set different lines to different amounts.

- charSpacing—The number of extra pixels to place between characters. The default is 0.

- kerning—Set this to FALSE if you do not want Director to automatically adjust the character spacing in the text member if the text changes.

- kerningThreshold—Set this to the minimum font size that you think that the *kerning* property should default to within that cast member.

- leftIndent—The number of pixels away from the edge that the text should start at the left side of the member.

- rightIndent—The number of pixels away from the edge that the text should start at the right side of the member.

- firstIndent—The number of pixels away from the left edge that the first line of text in a paragraph should start.

- antiAlias—TRUE or FALSE, depending on whether you want the text in the member to display with a smooth, anti-aliased effect.

- antiAliasThreshold—A point size at which the member should display text anti-aliased. Any characters under this point size are displayed normally.

Text members, when set to be editable, can also have a selected area. The Lingo functions to deal with this are different than those that deal with fields.

To get the selected text, use the *selectedText* property. This returns a *ref* structure. From that, you can get the text string of the selected area, and some font information:

```
r = member("myText").selectedText
put r.text
-- "the"
put r.font
-- "Times"
put r.fontSize
-- 12
put r.fontStyle
[#plain]
```

The *selection* property returns a list with the first and last character number of the selected area. You can also set the selected area of a text member, as long as the member is editable, the movie is playing, and the text member has focus. This means you cannot use the Message window to successfully set the *selection*.

```
on preselectText
  member("myText").selection = [6,9]
end
```

Text members also have the capability to tell you what character is at a spot. The functions for this are quite different than with fields. The basic function is *pointToChar* and it tells you what character is under a point. It looks like this: pointToChar(sprite 1, point(x,y)).

> **Tip**
>
> Notice that this function uses the sprite reference, rather than the member reference. To determine what character is under the cursor, use *the mouseLoc* as the point.

This function has several companions: *pointToWord*, *pointToItem*, *pointToLine*, and *pointToParagraph*. They perform basically the same way, but with different chunk expressions.

Unlike the field functions, these text member functions figure things out according to the actual Stage location, calculating differences caused by the sprite location and scrolling automatically.

Text members also differ from fields in how they are represented in memory. Text members can be either rich text or HTML text. Fields have a *text* property that holds the plain, unformatted text of the member. So do text members. However, they also have rich text and HTML properties named *rtf* and *html*. Here is what happens if you create a simple text member, place the word "Testing" in it, and then try to access these properties in the Message window:

```
put member(1).text
-- "Testing"

put member(1).rtf
-- "{\rtf1\mac\deff3 {\fonttbl{\f3\fswiss Geneva;}{\f20\froman
Times;}}{\colortbl\red0\green0\blue0;\red0\green0\blue224;\red224\green0
\blue0;\red224\green0\blue224;}{\stylesheet{\s0\fs24 Normal Text;}}\pard¬
\f3\fs24{\pard \f20\fs36\sl360 Testing\par}}"

put member(1).html
-- "<html>
<head>
<title>Untitled</title>
</head>
<body bgcolor="#FFFFFF">
<font face="Times, Times New Roman" size=5>Testing</font></body>
</html>
"
```

The *rtf* and *html* properties are constantly updated to reflect changes in the text member. What's even better is that you can directly set either of these properties, and the text member recreates itself to match.

Few people are familiar with rich text format, but many know HTML. The capability to create custom HTML text in Lingo and then have it applied to a text member is possibly the most powerful and, so far, underused feature of Director 7.

CREATING TEXT LISTS

A few interface elements use fields and text members. One of these is sometimes called a *text list*. It is similar to a group of radio buttons, but only one sprite is needed. This sprite contains a text field on which the user can click to select a line of text from a list. Figure 16.2 shows an example of such a text list.

Figure 16.2
A small text list that
highlights the text line
selected by the user.

To create one of these text lists, first create the field member. The field in Figure 16.2 has several lines of text, uses a 2-pixel margin, and a 1-pixel border. It is *not* editable, despite the fact that selecting text does highlight it.

The behavior is short and simple. Only one property is needed, and that is one of convenience. You need to reference the member of the sprite several times, so placing it as a property will make it easily available:

```
property pMember

on beginSprite me
  pMember = sprite(me.spriteNum).member
end
```

The selection action can take place on either an *on mouseUp* or an *on mouseDown* handler. It calls one custom handler to determine the line clicked, and then one to select the line:

```
on mouseDown me
  -- get the number of the line clicked
  clickedLine = computeLine(me,the clickLoc)

  -- select that line
  selectLine(me,clickedLine)
end
```

The next handler calculates the line clicked from the click location, the sprite location, and the scrolling position of the field. The field in this example isn't a scrolling one, but this extra line ensures that the behavior will be ready to go in the future if you want to have a scrolling text list:

```
on computeLine me, loc
  -- get the vertical location minus the top of the sprite
  verticalLoc = loc.locV - sprite(me.spriteNum).locV

  -- add any amount that the field has been scrolled
  verticalLoc = verticalLoc + pMember.scrollTop

  -- return the results of locVtoLinePos
  return locVtoLinePos(pMember,verticalLoc)
end
```

You could replace the entire "on computeLine" function with the use of *the mouseLine*, but this can be considered sloppy. If the user clicks one line and then moves the mouse quickly away before Director executes the line that includes *the mouseLine*, the actual line clicked and the line selected differ.

The "on selectLine" handler can be as simple as one line. If you use the command *hilite*, and refer to the member as a *field*, nothing more is needed.

```
on selectLine me, clickedLine
  -- use a simple hilite command to hilite the line
  hilite line clickedLine of field pMember
end
```

If you take another look at the image in Figure 16.2, you can see that the results do not look as nice as they could. Most importantly, the highlight does not go all the way across the line. It just stops with the last character in the line. It would be nicer to have the highlight go from left margin to right margin. This can be accomplished by using *char* references rather than *line* references with the *hilite* command. All that is needed is for the invisible return character at the end of each line to be included in the *hilite*, as follows:

```
on selectLine me, clickedLine
  --figure out the first and last chars for hilite
  if clickedLine = 1 then
    -- first line, start with char 1
    startChar = 1
  else
    -- not first line, count chars before line
    -- and add 2 to go past return to the next line
    startChar = (pMember.text.line[1..clickedLine-1]).length + 2
  end if

  -- for last char, count chars including line,
  -- and then add 1 for the RETURN character
  endChar = (pMember.text.line[1..clickedLine]).length + 1

  hilite char startChar to endChar of field pMember
end
```

The text list can also be accomplished by just using the radio button behaviors and some members that contain one line of text each. Or, you could use text members rather than field members and place a rectangle shape behind the text to act as the highlight. By doing so, you could even add more code and allow for multiple selections in the text list, so the items in the list act like a group of check boxes. You cannot do this using *hilite*, because it only allows for a continuous selection area.

CREATING TEXT POP-UP MENUS

A natural extension of text lists are text pop-up menus. These types of pop-ups are one of those tricks that developers have learned over the years. Because fields can be set to be "Adjust To Fit" and can be updated on-the-fly, you can make them imitate pop-ups pretty convincingly.

Take a look at Figure 16.3. It shows a single text field with one line of text. The field has been set to have a 1-pixel border, a 2-pixel margin, and a 2-pixel box drop shadow to make it look like something that can be clicked.

Figure 16.3
A simple field can be
made to look like an
inactive pop-up menu.

Choose One

The behavior attached to the field changes its appearance by simply placing more lines
of text in it. Because the field is set to "Adjust To Fit", it grows when that happens.
Figure 16.4 shows what the field will look like when clicked. Not only is more text added,
but a *hilite* command is used to show which item would be selected if the mouse was
released at the moment.

Figure 16.4
The field pop-up
expands as more text
is placed in it.

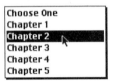

To accomplish this neat trick, the behavior first needs to get the list of items to place in the
field when the field is active. This can be done a number of ways. For this example behavior, the field starts with all the items present. All the lines but the first are hidden from view
when the sprite begins. The field should be set to a frame type of "fixed" and contain an
extra Return at the end of the last line. Here is the start of the behavior:

```
property pMember -- the field used in the popup
property pText -- the complete text of the popup
property pSelection -- the selected text
property pPressed -- whether the user is making a selection
property pLastHilite -- the last line highlighted

on beginSprite me
  -- get some properties
  pMember = sprite(me.spriteNum).member
  pText = pMember.text
  pSelected = pText.line[1] -- assume first line is default
  pPressed = FALSE

  -- set the field to the selected item
  pMember.text = pSelected

  -- set the field rectangle
  setMemberRect(me)
end
```

The action starts when the user clicks on the field. Then the pop-up menu needs to appear.
Here are the handlers for that action:

```
on mouseDown me
  pPressed = TRUE
  openPopup(me)
end
```

```
on openPopup me
  pMember.text = pText
  setMemberRect(me)
  pLastHilite = 0
end

-- This handler will adjust the field to be the size
-- of the text contained in it
on setMemberRect me
  memRect = pMember.rect
  numLines = pMember.text.lines.count
  if pMember.text.line[numLines] = "" then numLines = numLines - 1
  memRect.bottom = memRect.top + (numLines * pMember.lineHeight)
  pMember.rect = memRect
end
```

PART

VI

CH

16

The *on exitFrame* handler now needs to keep checking the mouse location to ensure that the correct item is highlighted:

```
on exitFrame me
  if pPressed then
    -- What line is the cursor over
    thisLine = getLine(me)

    -- is it over a different line than before?
    if thisLine <> pLastHilite then
      selectLine(me,thisLine)
      pLastHilite = thisLine
      pSelection = pText.line[thisline]
    end if
  end if
end
```

When the mouse button is released, the pop-up text needs to go away and the field should be restored to its former self. In addition, if the mouse is released over the sprite, it probably means that a selection has been made:

```
on mouseUp me
  pPressed = FALSE
  closePopup(me)
  makeSelection(me)
end

on mouseUpOutside me
  pPressed = FALSE
  closePopup(me)
end

-- set the popup to the current selection
on closePopup me
  pMember.text = pSelection
  setMemberRect(me)
end
```

The utility handler "on getLine" figures out which line the cursor is currently over. This function is a substitute for *the mouseLine* function, which worked well in older versions of Director, but does not work properly in Director 7 if the cursor is past the return in a line:

```
-- get the line the cursor is over
on getLine me
  if the rollover <> me.spriteNum then
    return 0
  else
    y = the mouseV - sprite(me.spriteNum).locV
    lineNum = y/(pMember.lineHeight)+1
    return lineNum
  end if
end
```

The "on selectLine" handler is the same one used for the text list behavior:

```
on selectLine me, clickedLine
  --figure out the first and last chars for hilite
  if clickedLine = 1 then
    -- first line, start with char 1
    startChar = 1
  else
    -- not first line, count chars before line
    -- and add 2 to go past return to the next line
    startChar = (pMember.text.line[1..clickedLine-1]).length + 2
  end if

  -- for last char, count chars including line,
  -- and then add 1 for the RETURN character
  endChar = (pMember.text.line[1..clickedLine]).length + 1

  hilite char startChar to endChar of field pMember
end
```

Finally, the "on makeSelection" handler is the one that actually does something. In this case, just an *alert* is shown. Note, however, that it must subtract one from the line number to get a corresponding choice number. This is necessary because the choices start at line two of the field.

```
on makeSelection me
  if pLastHilite > 0 then
    alert "You picked number"&&(pLastHilite-1)
  end if
end
```

One last handler needed is the *on endSprite* handler, which will be called when the movie leaves the frame with the sprite. This handler ensures that the original text gets replaced inside the field:

```
on endSprite me
  -- restore the contents of the field
  pMember.text = pText
end
```

Pop-up menus such this are not as pretty as those created with bitmaps. However, they are very easy to create and customize. If you need dozens of different pop-up menus and appearance is not critical, this is the way to go.

→ **See** "Creating Graphic Pop-Up Menus," Chapter 15, "Graphic Interface Elements," for another way to create pop-up menus

→ **See** "Questionnaires," Chapter 28, "Business Applications," for an example of using pop-up menus

USING KEYBOARD INPUT

Although great multimedia presentations and games that use only the mouse can be made, sooner or later you will need the user to use the keyboard, either to enter text or perhaps use the arrow keys to control a game.

KEYBOARD LINGO

Lingo has quite a few functions and events that handle keyboard input. Here is a detailed list:

- the commandDown—Returns a TRUE only if the Command key on the Mac or the Ctrl key in Windows is pressed.

- the controlDown—Returns a TRUE only if the Control key on the Mac or the Ctrl key in Windows is pressed. In Windows, this is the same as *the commandDown.*

- the optionDown—Returns a TRUE only if the Option key on the Mac or the Alt key in Windows is pressed.

- the shiftDown—Returns a TRUE only if the Shift key is pressed.

- on keyDown—An event handler that can be used in editable field or text member sprites, or in the frame or movie script. The message is sent when the user first presses the key. If the user holds down the key, it keeps sending "keyDown"s according to the keyboard repeat settings of the user's computer. When called, the properties *the key* and *the keyCode* are set.

- on keyUp—An event handler that can be used in editable field or text member sprites, or in the frame or movie script. The message is sent when the user lifts his or her finger off a key. It does not repeat if the key is held down. When called, the properties *the key* and *the keyCode* are set.

- keyPressed—A function that tests to see whether a character key is pressed. For instance, `keyPressed("a")` returns TRUE if the *a* key is being held down at the moment.

- the key—This property exists inside an *on keyDown* or *on keyUp* handler and holds the character that was pressed and thus activated the handler.

- the keyCode—This property exists inside an *on keyDown* or *on keyUp* handler and holds the keyboard number of the key that was pressed and thus activated the handler. It is reliable for only arrow keys and function keys.

- the keyboardFocusSprite—This property enables you to change which sprite has text entry focus in case more than one editable field or text member is on the Stage.

The event handlers *on keyDown* and *on keyUp* are used to modify the text input in fields and text members. The new Director 7 *keyPressed* function is primarily used for direct access to the keyboard in games and other real-time applications.

RECOGNIZING THE RETURN

A simple first step to using keyboard Lingo is to build a behavior that recognizes when the user presses the Return key while typing. The purpose would be to "steal" the Return, so that the user cannot type a second line of text, and also to use the Return as a trigger for performing some event.

> **Note**
>
> The Return key is actually labeled "Enter" on most Windows keyboards. This may be confusing because there is also an "Enter" key on the numeric keypad of most keyboards. Macs use a Return key on the main keyboard and an Enter key on the numeric keypad. When this text refers to a Return key, it means the Return key on Mac and the primary Enter key in Windows.

For instance, if you have a screen where you want to have users enter their names, capturing the Return key might be a good idea. First, it prevents users from starting a second line of text, something not ordinarily done when typing a name. Second, it signals the end of the entry, and does not require users to press a special "I have finished typing" button.

Here is a behavior that captures the Return key. You can attach it to an editable field or text member sprite:

```
on keyDown me
  if the key = RETURN then
    alert "You typed:"&&sprite(me.spriteNum).member.text
    dontpassevent
  else
    pass
  end if
end
```

The behavior uses only an *on keyDown* handler. It checks *the key* to see whether it is equal to the constant RETURN. If it is, it performs an action. It also uses the command *dontpassevent* which prevents the "keyDown" message from traveling any farther than this handler. Its next stop would have been to tell the editable member itself that a key was pressed, and the member would have added that key, in this case a Return, to the text in the member.

In the case where *the key* is not a Return, the *pass* command sends the message on its way, where it adds a character to the text. The use of the *dontpassevent* command is implied in this handler, actually, and only the *pass* command is needed. However, using the *dontpassevent* command doesn't hurt, and it makes the handler code a little clearer.

This simple behavior uses only an *alert* command to signify that the Return has been pressed. In a real program, you would want to do something like record the text in a global and go to another frame. If there is more than one editable text field on the Stage, you may want to use *the keyboardFocusSprite* to move the text entry insertion point to another sprite.

RESTRICTING INPUT

Because the *on keyDown* handler can capture any keystroke, you can also use it to restrict the characters that are allowed to pass to the member. Suppose you want the user to enter only digits into a field. You can write a behavior that accepts only digits.

Such a behavior needs to know which characters are allowed. This work is best performed by a parameter:

```
property pAllowed

on getPropertyDescriptionList me
  list = [:]
  addProp list, #pAllowed, [#comment: "Allowed Chars",¬
    #format: #string, #default: ""]
  return list
end
```

The rest of the behavior is an *on keyDown* handler that tests to see whether the character typed is acceptable.

```
on keyDown me
  if pAllowed contains the key then
    pass
  else
    dontpassevent
  end if
end
```

This behavior is not very restrictive. As a matter of fact, even the Backspace key has no effect on it. Creating a behavior that accepts the Backspace key is easy. Plus, the handler can also look for the Return key and process it as well.

```
on keyDown me
  if the key = RETURN then
    alert "You typed:"&&sprite(me.spriteNum).member.text
    dontpassevent
  else if the key = BACKSPACE then
    pass
  else if pAllowed contains the key then
    pass
  else
    dontpassevent
  end if
end
```

This same handler can be used to restrict the text to only letters, or both letters and digits, excluding all symbols. Using the same basic idea, you can even restrict the number of characters accepted in an editable member. Here is a handler that does this:

```
property pMaxChars

on getPropertyDescriptionList me
  list = [:]
  addProp list, #pMaxChars, [#comment: "Maximum Number of Chars",¬
    #format: #integer, #default: 10]
  return list
end

on keyDown me
  if the key = RETURN then
    alert "You typed:"&&sprite(me.spriteNum).member.text
    dontpassevent
  else if the key = BACKSPACE then
    pass
  else if sprite(me.spriteNum).member.text.length < pMaxChars then
    pass
  else
    dontpassevent
  end if
end
```

This handler makes sure that there are fewer than the maximum number of accepted characters present before enabling the user to add another. Note that the BACKSPACE check is handled separately, so that it can still be used even when the maximum length of the member has been reached.

CAPTURING KEYSTROKES

Text entry in editable fields and text members is fine for soliciting information from the users. However, if you just want to capture single keystrokes to enable the user to control something else in the movie, you don't need them.

If an editable member is not present, the keyboard events pass on to the frame, where they can be captured by the frame script. You use the same handlers, *on keyDown* and *on keyUp*, to do this.

The following handler in a frame script captures keystrokes and places a message in the field in sprite 1. The message contains *the key*, *the keyCode*, and also *the key* converted to its ASCII number:

```
on exitFrame
  go to the frame
end

on keyUp me
  sprite(1).member.text =¬
    "You pressed:"&&¬
    the key&&¬
    "("&chartonum(the key)&","¬
    &the keyCode&")"
end
```

The purpose of this behavior is not only to demonstrate how you can capture keystrokes with a frame script, but also how you can test different keys and see what their corresponding key codes are. A little playing around with this script reveals that the key codes for the arrow keys are 123, 124, 125, and 126, which correspond to left, right, down, and up.

With this knowledge, you can write a behavior that captures these keystrokes and then tells a sprite to move relative to them. Here is a frame script that does this:

```
on exitFrame
  go to the frame
end

on keyDown
  case the keyCode of
    123: sendSprite(sprite 1, #move, point(-5,0))
    124: sendSprite(sprite 1, #move, point(5,0))
    125: sendSprite(sprite 1, #move, point(0,5))
    126: sendSprite(sprite 1, #move, point(0,-5))
  end case
end
```

Each arrow key sends a "move" message to sprite 1. It also sends along a point structure that tells it how much to change the position of that sprite. Here is a behavior that can be used to capture these "move" messages for sprite 1.

```
on move me, dist
  loc = sprite(me.spriteNum).loc
  loc = loc + dist
  sprite(me.spriteNum).loc = loc
end
```

> **Note**
>
> The *on keyDown* and *on keyUp* event handlers require that the Stage has focus. This means that it is the active window and receives keyboard events. This may require the user to click on the Stage after playing the movie and before using the arrow keys.

Because the frame script uses *on keyDown* to capture the keys, the user can hold down the arrow keys to keep the sprite moving. This works only because the computer itself sends multiple "keyDown" messages when the user holds down a key. The result is the same as if the user were to press the key down repeatedly.

This sort of movement might work for very basic onscreen activity, but there is a way to create a more fluid movement. You can use the function *keyPressed* to constantly check the keyboard to determine whether a key is being pressed.

Here is a frame script that uses *keyPressed* to check the keyboard and send "move" messages to sprite 1.

```
on exitFrame
  if (keyPressed(123)) then sendSprite(sprite 1, #move, point(-5,0))
  if (keyPressed(124)) then sendSprite(sprite 1, #move, point(5,0))
  if (keyPressed(125)) then sendSprite(sprite 1, #move, point(0,5))
```

```
   if (keyPressed(126)) then sendSprite(sprite 1, #move, point(0,-5))
   go to the frame
end
```

The difference is remarkable. The *on keyDown* method creates a jerky, slow, movement, whereas the *keyPressed* method creates the type of movement that you expect in an arcade game. In fact, the faster the frame rate, the more fluid the movement.

Although *the keyPressed* works great for arrow keys and alphanumeric keys, there is no way to use it to check keys such as the Shift key or Command key. For these, you must use the special properties for each that are described in the preceding bulleted list.

USING RICH TEXT FORMAT

By using the *rtf* property of a text member, you have access to its rich text format version. This is a whole language unto its own and is now maintained by Microsoft. Here are the results of creating a text member with the word "Testing" in 18-point "Times" font, and using the Message window to get the *rtf*:

```
put member(1).rtf
-- "{\rtf1\mac\deff3 {\fonttbl{\f3\fswiss Geneva;}{\f20\froman
Times;}}{\colortbl\red0\green0\blue0;}{\stylesheet{\s0\fs24 Normal Text;}}\pard¬
\f3\fs24{\pard \f20\fs36\sl360 Testing\par}}"
```

Rich text format, as you can see, requires a lot of control structures to define styles and colors. Detailing what each of these structures means would take a whole book. Because RTF is so rarely used nowadays, and is being replaced by HTML as a text standard, it is hardly worth going into.

However, you should know that you do have the power to create your own rich text formatted code and replace the text in a member by setting the *rtf* property. If you took the messy line shown previously and replaced "Times" with "Courier," for instance, you could set the text member to look the same, but with Courier font instead.

USING HTML AND TABLES

The *html* property of text members is much easier to use. You can actually create your own HTML code with Lingo and apply it to the member. The following example illustrates how easy this property is to use.

A SIMPLE HTML APPLICATION

Here is the same "Testing" member's *html* property.

```
put member(1).html
-- "<html>
<head>
<title>Untitled</title>
</head>
<body bgcolor="#FFFFFF">
```

```
<font face="Times, Times New Roman" size=5>Testing<br>
</font></body>
</html>
"
```

You can see that Director likes to make sure the proper "<html>", "<head>", "<body>", and "<title>" are present. The title is always given as "Untitled", but the "bgcolor" actually reflects the background color of the member.

The *html* property is very easy to edit, especially if you already know HTML. You can even ignore some of the tags and Director will fill them in for you. Try this in the Message window with a text member in cast member position one:

```
member(1).html = "Testing"
put member(1).html
-- "<html>
<head>
<title>Untitled</title>
</head>
<body bgcolor="#FFFFFF">
Testing</body>
</html>
"
```

PART

VI

CH

16

You can see that most of the proper tags were added by Director. However, these tags are required if you want to use some of your own HTML tags to modify the text. Try this:

```
member(1).html = "<B>Testing</B>"
put member(1).html
-- "<html>
<head>
<title>Untitled</title>
</head>
<body bgcolor="#FFFFFF">
&lt;B&gt;Testing&lt;&#47;B&gt;</body>
</html>
"
```

You can see that Director did not correctly interpret your bold tag to make the text bold. Instead, it took it as a literal. The resulting text on the Stage would look like "<B>Testing</B>". For Director to recognize the bold tag, it needs to see the "<body>" tag.

```
member(1).html = "<HTML><B>Testing</B></HTML>"
put member(1).html
-- "<html>
<head>
<title>Untitled</title>
</head>
<body bgcolor="#CCCCCC">
<b>Testing</body>
</html>
"
```

Now it correctly identifies the bold tags as tags. However, the background color of the member has been set to gray, which is meant to imitate the default gray background of browsers. To make it something other than gray, you have to set your own body tag as well:

```
member(1).html = ¬
   "<HTML><BODY BGCOLOR=#FFFFFF><B>Testing</B></BODY></HTML>"
put member(1).html
-- "<html>
<head>
<title>Untitled</title>
</head>
<body bgcolor="#FFFFFF">
<b>Testing</body>
</html>
"
```

Now the text member appears as you want it to. You can add font tags with sizes and faces to set the font of the text. You can even add table tags to create tables.

APPLYING TABLES

Creating tables with HTML is an extremely powerful new function of Director. It enables you to create highly formatted text in a way that was nearly impossible in Director 6.

To create a table, all you need to do is construct it in HTML and then apply that to the *html* property of the text member. Here is a simple example. Create a text field, name it "html text", and then place the following text in it:

```
<html>
<body bgcolor="#FFFFFF">
<table border=1>
<TR><TD>
Test1
</TD><TD>
Test2
</TD></TR>
<TR><TD>
Test3
</TD><TD>
Test4
</TD></TR>
</table>
</body>
</html>
```

Now, create an empty text member and place it on the Stage. Name it "html member". Using the Message window, you can apply the HTML text to the text member.

```
member("html member").html = field "html text"
```

The text member on the Stage should appear as shown in Figure 16.5.

Test1	Test2
Test3	Test4

Just about all the special features of HTML tables are available to the text member. Using a movie handler, you can create tables to suit any need. Here is a handler that takes a few lists and creates a table from them:

```
on makeTable memberName, headings, widths, data
  -- start with <HTML> and <BODY> tags
  htmlText = "<HTML><BODY BGCOLOR=FFFFFF>"

  -- beginning of table
  put "<TABLE BORDER=0><TR>" after htmlText

  -- place headings as TH tags
  repeat with i = 1 to count(headings)
    put "<TH WIDTH="&widths[i]&">" after htmlText
    put "<B>"&headings[i]&"</B></TD>" after htmlText
  end repeat
  put "</TR>" after htmlText

  -- add each row
  repeat with i = 1 to count(data)
    put "<TR>" after htmlText

    -- add a row
    repeat with j = 1 to count(data[i])
      put "<TD>" after htmlText
      put data[i][j]&"</TD>" after htmlText
    end repeat

    put "</TR>" after htmlText
  end repeat

  -- close table and html
  put "</TABLE></BODY></HTML>" after htmlText

  member(memberName).html = htmlText
end
```

This handler takes a member name and three linear lists as parameters. The first list contains the column heading text. The second contains the widths of the columns in HTML-based pixels. The third list contains a series of smaller lists, each representing a row in the table. The number of items in these smaller lists should be the same as the number of items in the other two lists. Here is an example handler that uses this "on makeTable" handler:

```
on testTable
  headings = ["Name","Address","Phone","Birthday","City"]
  widths = [100,150,60,60,80]
  data = []
  add data, ["John Doe", "123 Street Road", "555-3456", ¬
```

```
       "7/28/65", "Seattle"]
     add data, ["Betty Deer", "654 Avenue Blvd", "555-1234", ¬
       "9/11/68", "Los Angeles"]
     add data, ["Robert Roberts", "9346 Dead End Pl.", ¬
       "555-9999", "1/8/67", "New York"]
   makeTable("html table",headings, widths, data)
 end
```

The result of using these two handlers is shown in Figure 16.6.

Figure 16.6
This table was generated with Lingo and applied to a text member.

Name	Address	Phone	Birthday	City
John Doe	123 Street Road	555-3456	7/28/65	Seattle
Betty Deer	654 Avenue Blvd.	555-1234	9/11/68	Los Angeles
Robert Roberts	9346 Dead End Pl.	555-9999	1/8/67	New York

One of the strengths of tables like this is that text can wrap inside a column. This is far superior to using multiple lines with tabs to form a table. You can even place tables like this into scrolling text members when they are too long to fit on the screen all at once.

USING HTML AND HYPERTEXT

Another new feature of Director 7 is the capability to easily add hypertext to text members. In fact, it is so simple, you hardly need any Lingo at all.

SETTING AND USING HYPERLINKS

Indicating that some text represents a link only requires the use of the member and the Text Inspector. You can edit the text on the Stage or in the Text Cast Member editing window. Just select some text, and then type the hyperlink data in the bottom text field of the Text Inspector.

Figure 16.7 shows this process in action. The Stage contains a text member, with the word "dog" selected. The Text Inspector has been used to place "man's best friend" as the hyperlink data for that text. The result is that the word "dog" in the text member is now underlined and colored blue, as hypertext in Web browsers is typically styled. The word "quick" has already been set as hypertext.

After the hypertext has been set, the hyperlink data is accessible through Lingo whenever the text is clicked. The styling of the text is automatic. Also, the cursor automatically changes to a finger cursor.

Tip

You can turn off the automatic styling and cursor change by setting the member property *useHyperlinkStyles*. Then you can color and style the text independently.

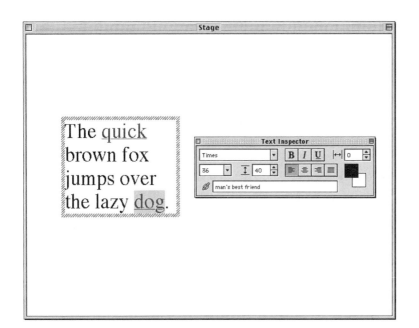

Figure 16.7
The Text Inspector is
used to set hypertext
in text members.

In order for hypertext to actually do anything, you need to create a simple behavior to capture the messages sent when the user clicks a hyperlink. An *on hyperlinkClicked* handler gets this message as well as the hyperlink data stored for that specific link. Here is an example:

```
on hyperlinkClicked me, data
  put data
end
```

This simple handler places the hyperlink data in the Message window. That line of code is not very useful by itself, but can be used instead to place the data in another field. A handler like this can be used to create a simple glossary function. The user can click a hyperlinked word, and the definition appears at the bottom of the Stage.

```
on hyperlinkClicked me, data
  member("Glossary").text = data
end
```

You can also have this script do something, such as make the movie jump to another frame. The frame name would be the *data* parameter.

```
on hyperlinkClicked me, data
  go to frame data
end
```

If you were creating a Shockwave applet, the hypertext could be used to make the browser go to another location. This would then act just like a normal hyperlink on a Web page. The hyperlink data would have to be a valid location, such as http://clevermedia.com.

```
on hyperlinkClicked me, data
  gotoNetPage(data)
end
```

One more parameter can be used with the *on hyperlinkClicked* handler. It returns a small list with the first and last character positions of the hyperlink that was clicked. You can use this to get the actual text of the hyperlink by using a normal chunk expression. Here is a modified version of the hyperlink glossary script:

```
on hyperlinkClicked me, data, pos
  definition = data
  hyperword = sprite(me.spriteNum).member.char[pos[1]..pos[2]]
  member("Glossary").text = hyperword&":"&&definition
end
```

MODIFYING HYPERLINKS WITH LINGO

In addition to setting hyperlinks with the Text Inspector, you can also set them with Lingo. The *hyperlinks* and *hyperlink* properties of text members enable you to add, modify, and delete hyperlinks and their data.

The *hyperlinks* property returns a list of small lists that contain the first and last character positions of each link. For instance, the example in Figure 16.7 shows two hyperlinks. If you use the Message window to get the *hyperlinks*, this is the result:

```
put member(1).hyperlinks
-- [[5, 9], [41, 43]]
```

Although this property is useful for determining what hyperlinks are present in the text, you cannot actually set hyperlinks this way. Instead, use the *hyperlink* property. Here is an example:

```
put member(1).char[5..9].hyperlink
-- "fast, speedy"
```

You can set the hyperlink data to something new in a similar manner.

```
member(1).char[5..9].hyperlink = "no definition"
put member(1).char[5..9].hyperlink
-- "no definition"
```

Setting the hyperlinks in this manner without specifying the exact character positions of the hypertext is not a good idea. However, Director does behave in a logical way when this happens. If you try to set a subset of the hyperlink, like characters 6 to 8 of the previous example, the entire hyperlink is changed.

To remove a hyperlink, set its hyperlink data to "", or the empty string.

```
member(1).char[5..9].hyperlink = EMPTY
```

Setting the hyperlink on a set of characters that does not already have a hyperlink applied to it creates one. Here is a script that searches for a word in a text member and sets all instances of it to act as hyperlinks.

```
on makeHyper memberName, hyperword, hyperdata
  text = member(memberName).text
  repeat with i = 1 to text.word.count
    if text.word[i] = hyperword then
      member(memberName).word[i].hyperlink = hyperdata
```

```
      end if
    end repeat
  end
```

USING TEXT FILES AND THE FILEIO XTRA

Using text files has always been more difficult in Director than it should be. Director 7 is no different. It requires you to use the FileIO Xtra. This is an Xtra that adds Lingo commands to handle reading and writing files.

Using an Xtra such as this is like using a behavior, except that the Xtra is referenced through a variable, not a sprite. Here is an example. To read a text file, use the following series of commands:

```
fileObj = new(xtra "FileIO")
openFile(fileObj, "myfile.txt")
text = readfile(fileObj)
closeFile(fileObj)
```

The variable "fileObj" is used to store an instance of the Xtra. The *new* command in the first line creates this instance, and a pointer to it is placed in the variable "fileObj". You can think of "fileObj" as the *me* in a behavior. It is now needed to refer to this instance of FileIO.

An instance of FileIO is capable of opening, creating, writing, reading, and deleting files. In the preceding example, the object is used to open a file with the *openFile* command, read the contents of the file with the *readFile*command, and then close the file with the *closeFile* command.

Here is a complete list of commands used with the FileIO Xtra:

- new—Creates a new instance of the Xtra.
- fileName—This function returns the name of the file currently being controlled by this instance of the Xtra.
- status—This function returns the error code of the last command used on the Xtra. A 0 means that there was no error.
- error—This function takes the object and an integer as parameters. It returns a string with the description of the error number passed in as the integer.
- setFilterMask—This function takes the object and a string as parameters. The string defines the type of files to be shown in the Open and Save dialog boxes. On the Mac, pass a string that contains one or more four-letter file types, such as "TEXT" or "JEPGGIFF". In Windows, the string should be a comma-delimited list alternating file descriptions and types, such as "Text Files,*.txt,GIF Files,#.gif".
- openFile—This function opens the file for reading, writing, or both. You need to call this function before performing most other file functions. It takes an additional parameter, which should be a 1 to read, a 2 to write, or 0 for both.

- closeFile—This function closes the file associated with the file object. You must call this when you are finished with the file.

- displayOpen—A function that displays a Mac or Windows Open dialog box and enables the user to browse and select a file. It returns that file path.

- displaySave—A function that displays a Mac or Windows Save dialog box and enables the user to browse and select the destination of that file. It returns that file path.

- createFile—Give this command the object and a string that represents the filename or full path of the file. You must call this before *openFile* in cases where the file does not yet exist.

- setPosition—This function takes an integer as an extra parameter. It sets the position in the file where the next read will take place.

- getPosition—This function returns the current reading position in the file.

- getLength—This function returns the length of the currently opened file.

- writeChar—This function writes a single character to the file.

- writeString—This function writes a complete string into the file.

- readChar—This function reads a single character from the file.

- readLine—This function reads from the current position in the file to the next return character. It includes the return in the returned value.

- readFile—This function reads from the current position in the file until the end.

- readWord—This function reads from the current position in the file until the next space or non-visible character.

- readToken—This function takes three parameters: the object, a skip character, and a break character. It reads from the current position in the file until the break character, and it skips the skip characters whenever it encounters them.

- getFinderInfo—This Mac-only function gets the file type and creator of the currently opened file. It returns it as a nine-character string with a space between the file type and creator. For example: "TEXT ttxt".

- setFinderInfo—This Mac-only command enables you to set the file type and creator of the currently open file. You must use a nine-character string, such as "TEXT ttxt".

- delete—This command removes the currently opened file.

- version—This function returns the version of the Xtra. Use it in this manner:
  `put version(xtra "FileIO")`.

- getOSDirectory—This function is part of the Xtra, but does not require a reference to it. Use it in this manner: `put getOSDirectory()`. It returns the path to the Mac system folder or the Windows directory.

Reading and writing files takes many lines of code. However, a handler that does this can be reused many times. Here is a handler that prompts the user for a text file to read, and then returns that text file's contents:

```
on openAndReadText
  -- create the FileIO instance
  fileObj = new(xtra "FileIO")

  -- set the filter mask to text files
  if the platform contains "mac" then
    setFilterMask(fileObj,"TEXT")
  else
    setFilterMask(fileObj,"Text Files,*.txt,All Files,*.*")
  end if

  -- open dialog box
  filename = displayOpen(fileObj)

  -- check to see if cancel was hit
  if filename = "" then return ""

  -- open the file
  openFile(fileObj,filename,1)

  -- check to see if file opened ok
  if status(fileObj) <> 0 then
    err = error(fileObj,status(fileObj))
    alert "Error:"&&err
    return ""
  end if

  -- read the file
  text = readFile(fileObj)

  -- close the file
  closeFile(fileObj)

  --return the text
  return text
end
```

PART

VI

CH

16

If you want to use this handler to read a file that you already know the name of, just pass in the "filename" variable as a parameter to the handler, and remove the references to the *setFilterMask* and *displayOpen* commands.

The opposite of this handler is one that saves any text to a file. This handler takes care of it all, down to setting the file type of the new file to a SimpleText file for the Mac. The text placed in the file is passed in as a parameter.

```
on saveText text
  -- create the FileIO instance
  fileObj = new(xtra "FileIO")

  -- set the filter mask to text files
  if the platform contains "mac" then
    setFilterMask(fileObj,"TEXT")
```

```
    else
      setFilterMask(fileObj,"Text Files,*.txt,All Files,*.*")
    end if

    -- save dialog box
    filename = displaySave(fileObj,"","")

    -- check to see if cancel was hit
    if filename = "" then return FALSE

    -- create and open the file
    createFile(fileObj,filename)
    openFile(fileObj,filename,2)

    -- check to see if file opened ok
    if status(fileObj) <> 0 then
      err = error(fileObj,status(fileObj))
      alert "Error:"&&err
      return FALSE
    end if

    -- write the file
    writeString(fileObj,text)

    -- set the file type
    if the platform contains "Mac" then
      setFinderInfo(fileObj, "TEXT ttxt")
    end if

    -- close the file
    closeFile(fileObj)
    return TRUE
end
```

The "on saveText" and "on openAndReadText" can be customized in many ways to suit many purposes. You can use *getOSDirectory()*, for instance, to find the path to the operating system and store files in the preferences folder. You can also use the Lingo property *the pathname* to get the path of the Director application or Projector to store files there.

TROUBLESHOOTING TEXT AND STRINGS

- Remember that when comparing strings or using comparison functions such as *contains* or *offset*, Lingo is not case-sensitive. So "AbC" is the same as "aBc".

- ASCII codes for normal letters and numbers are exactly the same for all non-symbol fonts on both Mac and Windows. As a matter of fact, almost all ASCII characters between 32 and 127 are the same for all fonts. However, characters above 127 can be very different in different fonts and be different even on the same fonts from different platforms. These are special symbols, such as currency symbols and accent marks. See "Fonts" in Chapter 35, "Cross-Platform Issues," for information on font mapping.

- If you used *the mouseLine* in Director 6.5 or before, note that it has a very different behavior in Director 7.0 (initial release). If the cursor is to the right of the Return character on the line, it registers as being over the next line.

- If you used the *hilite* command with fields in Director 6.5 or before, note that you get a slightly different result with Director 7.0 (initial release). If you try to highlight the last line of a field, only the characters in the line are highlighted. The highlighting does not stretch the whole width of the field.

- If you are restricting the input of an editable field or a text member, remember to allow the BACKSPACE character. Otherwise, users may not be able to erase what they are typing if they make mistakes.

Did You Know?

- You can force Director to be your own RTF-to-HTML converter by importing RTF files and then getting the *html* property of that member. The same would work in reverse.

- Use `put interface(xtra "FileIO")` in the Message window to get a list of all the FileIO commands and functions. The same function works with most Xtras.

- Rather than using *put* to place text before, after, or into a text member, you can use some undocumented Lingo: *setContentsBefore*, *setContentsAfter*, and *setContents*. For instance, you can write: `member("myText").setContentsBefore("abc")` to place "abc" before the text in the member, or `member("myText").char[7].setContentsAfter("abc")` to place "abc" after character 7 of the member, or just plain `member("myText").setContents("abc")` to replace the contents of the member completely.

- If you import a text file that was created on Windows, you might see extra block characters at the start of each line. These are *newline characters*. Director and most modern word processors do not use them. To get rid of them, simply write a *repeat look* that checks each character against numToChar(10) and deletes it if it matches. Or, you can use the *offset* function in a *repeat look* to quickly hunt down and remove them.

CONTROLLING SOUND

In this chapter

Although the Score can handle background sounds, and behaviors from the library can add sounds to buttons and other simple elements, understanding the Lingo commands that control sound is necessary to use sounds in more advanced Director programs. All three main types of sounds—internal cast members, external files, and compressed Shockwave audio—can be controlled using Lingo. This chapter discusses the ways to control sound using Lingo.

USING LINGO'S SOUND COMMANDS

The main Lingo command used to play cast member sounds is *puppetSound*. The basic idea is that you are taking over one of the sound channels in the Score. A typical use for this looks like this:

```
puppetSound 1, "mySoundMember"
```

The number 1 represents the first sound channel. The word "mySoundMember" represents a cast member. If a sound is already being played in sound channel 1 of the Score, it is replaced by the sound in that member. The sound plays immediately; it does not wait for the frame to loop or an for an *updateStage* command to begin.

You can also play sounds in sound channel 1 with a plain *puppetSound* command:

```
puppetSound "mySoundMember"
```

Using this command differs in two ways from using the *puppetSound* command including a channel number. First, the sound does not begin playing until the next frame starts, or an *updateStage* command is used. The second difference is that the first available sound channel is used. Therefore, if sound channels one and two are busy, channel 3 will be used.

> **Note**
>
> You can safely use sound channels 1 through 8, even though only the first two are available in the Score. If you are using more than one sound channel at a time, there may be a delay when you play a sound on Windows, because it takes a while for the two sounds to be mixed. Macs can play multiple sounds simultaneously, so there is no delay. This delay in Windows can be avoided if the playback machine has QuickTime 3.

To stop a sound from playing and to return control of the sound channel to the Score, just issue a *puppetSound* command with a 0 as the member, as follows:

```
puppetSound 1, 0
```

Many other sound commands provide even more control. The *soundBusy* function, for example, returns a TRUE if the sound channel specified is being used, and a FALSE if it is not being used. The following handler plays a sound and freezes the movie until the sound is done:

```
on playAndFreeze soundName
  puppetSound 1, soundName
  repeat while soundBusy(1)
  end repeat
end
```

If you want to find out how much of a sound has been played, the *currentTime* property of the sound channel returns the time since the start of the sound in milliseconds. Try this in the Message window after you have imported a long sound and named the cast member "mySound":

```
puppetSound 1, "mySound"
put sound(1).currentTime
-- 6966
put sound(1).currentTime
-- 9009
```

Of course, the results vary depending on when you type the lines in the Message window.

You have two properties that enable you to set the volume of a sound. The first is *the soundLevel*, which actually controls the volume of the playback computer. You can set it to values from 0 (silence) to 7 (max):

```
the soundLevel = 7
```

PART

VI

CH

17

This property is useful for creating volume controls for the entire movie. You can use the slider behavior described in Chapter 15, "Graphic Interface Elements," with the range of 0 to 7, to create a quick volume control.

If you want to control the volume for one sound only, you can set its *volume* property. The values here range from 0 to 255:

```
sound(1).volume = 128
```

In addition to *volume*, there are also a number of other sound properties. The following is a complete list:

- channelCount—Returns the number of sound channels in a sound member. For instance, a value of 2 tells you that the sound is in stereo.
- currentTime—The current time, in milliseconds, of a sound.
- loop—A member property. This is the equivalent to the loop property in the Sound Cast Member dialog box. You can change its value with this Lingo property.
- sampleRate—Returns the sample frequency rate of the sound member.
- sampleSize—Returns the sample size, in bits, of the sound member. Typical values are 8 or 16.
- volume—Enables you to set the volume, from 0 to 255, of a playing sound.

There are also several properties for determining the computer's capability to play sounds, as follows:

- the multiSound—This is TRUE if the computer can support playing more than one sound at a time.

- the soundDevice—This property tells you which system device is being used to play sounds. The property can currently have three values: "MacSoundManager," "Macromix," and "QT3Mix." The first is available only on the Mac, and it works quite well. "Macromix" is available only on a Windows machine without QuickTime 3, and it is very slow. If the movie is playing back on Windows and QuickTime 3 is present, you should set this property to "QT3Mix" for best performance.

- the soundDeviceList—This property returns a list of the sound devices currently available.

- the soundEnabled—Thisproperty provides you with a mute function. If you set it to FALSE, the sound shuts off, but the value of the volume property does not change, so the same volume level is used when *the soundEnabled* property is reset to TRUE.

→ **See** "Using Sound In Director," Chapter 5, "Sound Members," for more information about using sounds

PLAYING EXTERNAL SOUNDS

Playing most external sounds is actually exactly like playing Internet sound members. All you need to do is import them as linked files. The sound member refers to this external file for the sound data, but all the Lingo commands treat it like an internal sound.

However, you can also play a sound file that is not linked as a cast member. Just one two-word command performs this action: *sound playFile*. Here is an example:

```
sound playFile 1, "mySound.aif"
```

This sound will play the file specified in channel 1. If the file is not in the same folder as the movie, you should specify a full pathname.

Note

The main advantage to playing external sound files is that Director streams them off the hard drive or CD-ROM. This means that the entire sound does not have to be loaded into memory before being played.

The *sound playFile* command can play AIFF or wave sounds, the most common formats for Mac and Windows, respectively. It can also play Shockwave audio files. "AU" formatted sounds can be played as long as the "Sun AU Import Export" Xtra is present.

To stop a sound that was started with the *sound playFile* command, you can use the *puppetSound* command, with the sound channel and a 0 for the sound name, such as:

```
puppetSound 1, 0
```

There is also the obsolete *sound stop* command that does the same thing, but which may not be supported in the future.

→ **See** "External Sounds," Chapter 5, for more information about using external sounds

USING SHOCKWAVE AUDIO

Playing Shockwave audio is a little different than playing regular sounds. To play Shockwave audio, you need to create a Shockwave audio cast member. You can do this by choosing Insert, Media Element, Shockwave Audio.

The result is a new member that has a Properties dialog box like the one shown in Figure 17.1. The most important part of this dialog box is the Link Address, which specifies the full or relative path of the Shockwave audio file. If the path is relative and the movie is play-ing in Director or a projector, the path can specify a file on the hard drive or CD-ROM rather than on the Internet.

> **Note**
>
> You can use the Import dialog box to completely import a SWA sound so that it is con-tained in the internal Cast. However, this defeats the purpose of streaming, which is to play very large sounds without requiring that they be loaded completely into memory first. Internal SWA sounds also do not work in Shockwave.

Figure 17.1
The SWA Cast Member Properties dialog box enables you to set the location of the Shockwave audio file.

After a Shockwave audio member has been created, you can also use the *url* property to change the location of the file in Lingo. This means that only one member is needed to play multiple files, as long as the files play at separate times.

To start a Shockwave audio member playing, just use the *play* command, as follows:

```
play member "mySound.swa"
```

The *stop* command halts playback, as follows:

```
stop member "mySound.swa"
```

It is just that simple. The *pause* command enables you to halt a sound, but then use the *play* command to resume playing it again at that same point, rather than at the beginning of the sound.

If you want to get more information from a playing Shockwave audio member, there are many properties that you can access. Here is a complete list of member properties:

- bitRate—This property returns the bit rate, in Kbps, of the file.
- bitsPerSample—This property returns the size, in bits, of each sample. Typical values are 8 and 16.
- copyrightInfo—This property returns the copyright information set when the Shockwave audio file was created.
- duration—This property returns the length of the sound in *ticks* (1/60th of a second).
- numChannels—This property returns the number of channels in the sound. For example, 2 would mean it is in stereo.
- percentStreamed—This property returns a value between 0 and 100 that corresponds to how much of the file has been read from the Internet.
- percentPlayed—This property returns a value between 0 and 100 that corresponds to how much of the file has been played.
- preloadTime—This is the amount of the file that should be loaded into memory before playback begins. It is displayed in seconds.
- sampleRate—This is the frequency rate of the sound.
- soundChannel—This is the member property that determines which sound channel is used to play back the sound. If the value 0 is given, Director chooses the first available sound channel.
- state—This returns a value that tells you what the member is doing at any given time. A list of values is given in Table 17.1.
- streamName—Same as the *url* property.
- url—The location of the Shockwave audio file. You can set and reset this many times to use one member over and over. This way, you can play different audio files but only use one member.
- volume—The volume of the sound. A value between 0 and 255.

TABLE 17.1   VALUES FOR THE STATE OF A SHOCKWAVE AUDIO MEMBER

State	Definition
0	Cast streaming has stopped.
1	The cast member is reloading.
2	Preloading ended successfully.
3	The cast member is playing.
4	The cast member has paused.
5	The cast member has finished streaming.
9	An error occurred.
10	There is insufficient CPU speed.

The *percentStreamed* and *percentPlayed* properties are prime candidates for the progress bar behavior in described in Chapter 15. The *volume* property can be set with the slider behavior discussed in that same chapter.

→ **See** "Shockwave Audio," Chapter 5, for more information about making Shockwave audio files

TROUBLESHOOTING SOUND

- Remember that when you use *puppetSound* to take control of a sound channel, it cuts off any sound being played in the Score using that channel. It is often a good idea to use channel 3 and above for *puppetSounds* if you are using Score sounds also.

- Using a relative path to a Shockwave audio file can be tricky. It does not work until the movie is located on a server and running from Shockwave. Instead, use *the pathname* and the relative path to construct a string for the *url* if *the runMode* is "Author." Also, remember that you need to use different pathnames for Mac and Windows, because Mac uses a colon (:) as a path delimiter and Windows uses a backslash (\).

PART

VI

CH

17

DID YOU KNOW?

- There is no need to create more than one SWA cast member unless you are planning to play more than one sound at a time. Instead, just create one SWA member and use Lingo to set the *url* property to the sound you want to play.

- You can use cue points for more than just synchronization. You can set the cue points to different lyrics, and then display them in a text member as they go by. Use the *on cuePointPassed* event handler for this.

CONTROLLING BITMAPS

In this chapter

Director offers many commands, functions, and properties that enable you to modify the appearance of bitmap sprites on the Stage. Director 7, in fact, has many new features not available in its predecessors, such as rotation and skewing. These features are the subject of this chapter.

DISTORTING SPRITES

So far, you have used the *loc*, *locH*, and *locV* properties to change the location of a sprite. Many additional properties determine the appearance of bitmaps.

THE rect PROPERTY

The *rect* property was used in the slider and progress bar behaviors in Chapter 15, "Graphic Interface Elements," to redefine the shape of rectangles. This same property can be used to stretch or shrink sprites.

For instance, if you place a sprite on the Stage and use the Message window, you can check its initial *rect*. Here is an example:

```
put (sprite 1).rect
-- rect(200, 150, 400, 400)
```

You can then set the *rect* to something else. It doesn't even have to have the same relative dimensions. For instance, you can squeeze the sprite horizontally by moving only the left and right portions of the *rect*. Try this:

```
(sprite 1).rect = rect(250,150,350,400)
updateStage
```

The *rect* really gives you all the power of the *loc* property, plus much more. You are essentially controlling the locations of all four sides of the sprite, so you can move it, stretch it, or shrink it. This works for all bitmap sprites, plus shapes, and vector graphics. It even works for text and field members to a limited extent; these are truly adjustable only if the frame property of the member is not set to "Adjust To Fit."

> **Note**
>
> The first number represents the position of the left side of the rectangle. The second is the top of the rectangle. The third is the right side location. The last is the bottom location. So it goes: left, top, right, bottom.

THE ROTATION PROPERTY

One of Director 7's new powerful features is the capability to rotate sprites. You have complete Lingo control over this sprite attribute with the *rotation* property. Bitmaps and text can be rotated, but shapes cannot.

The values of *rotation* are in degrees. They range from 0 to 360, but you can use numbers outside of that range and Director can translate them to a number in that range. A new sprite is always set to a *rotation* value of 0.0.

```
put (sprite 1).rotation
-- 0.0000
```

You can set the *rotation* just as easily, as follows:

```
(sprite 1).rotation = 45
updateStage
```

The following shows a one-line behavior that makes a sprite rotate around its center. It rotates one degree every frame:

```
on exitFrame me
  (sprite 1).rotation = (sprite 1).rotation + 1
end
```

A more complex behavior is one that aligns the rotation of the sprite to always point to the cursor. The behavior assumes that the "point" of the bitmap is normally pointing to the right side of the Stage. It reorients it to point toward the cursor, as follows:

```
on exitFrame me
  -- get the mouse location
  p = the mouseLoc
  x1 = p.locH
  y1 = p.locV

  -- get the sprite location
  x2 = (sprite me.spriteNum).locH
  y2 =  (sprite me.spriteNum).locV

  -- use atan to compute the angle
  angle = atan(float(y2-y1)/float(x2-x1))

  -- correct the angle
  if x1 < x2 then angle = pi()+angle

  -- convert the angle to degrees
  angle = angle*360.0/(2.0*pi())

  -- set the sprite
  (sprite me.spriteNum).rotation = angle
end
```

PART

VI

CH

18

You can use this behavior just as easily with other points, as well. For instance, it can align a sprite to the location of another sprite. As that sprite moves, either through user interaction or animation, the controlled sprite follows.

The *atan* function is at the heart of this behavior. Its purpose is to convert a slope, made by two points, into an angle. The results are limited to only one half of a circle, so an adjustment is made to deal with angles on the left side of the circle. The angle resulting from this is in radians, so there needs to be a conversion into degrees before the angle can be applied to the *rotation* property.

> **Note**
>
> Radians, if you remember your high school trigonometry, are another way to measure the size of an angle. Whereas there are 360° in a circle, there are two times pi, or 6.2832, radians in a circle.

THE FLIPH AND FLIPV PROPERTIES

Bitmap sprites can also be flipped along either the horizontal or vertical axis. Flipping takes place around the registration point of the member. Lingo controls this feature through the *flipH* and *flipV* properties. They can be set to either TRUE or FALSE. If the setting is TRUE the sprite is displayed flipped.

Here is an example. This example flips a sprite horizontally:

```
(sprite 1).flipH = TRUE
updateStage
```

However, if the sprite is already flipped, this last example does nothing. Here is an example that reverses the horizontal flip of a sprite:

```
(sprite 1).flipH = not (sprite 1).flipH
updateStage
```

Here is a behavior that controls a sprite's flip properties according to where the cursor is located relative to the sprite. It flips whenever the cursor crosses one of the sprite's axes:

```
on exitFrame me
  -- get the cursor location
  cLoc = the mouseLoc

  -- get the sprite location
  sLoc = (sprite me.spriteNum).loc

  -- flip horizontally if needed
  if cLoc.locH > sLoc.locH then
    (sprite me.spriteNum).flipH = TRUE
  else
    (sprite me.spriteNum).flipH = FALSE
  end if

  -- flip vertically if needed
  if cLoc.locV > sLoc.locV then
    (sprite me.spriteNum).flipV = TRUE
  else
    (sprite me.spriteNum) .flipV = FALSE
  end if
end if
```

THE SKEW PROPERTY

The *skew* property can also be set with Lingo. The result is a change in the angle of the vertical sides of the sprite's rectangle. Angles from 0 to 90° tilt the vertical sides to the right, whereas angles from 0 to -90° tilt it to the left. Angles between 90° and 180° and -90° and -180° appear to flip the sprite. Any change of 360° places the skew back where it started, which is the same as a skew of zero.

Here is a simple behavior that repeatedly adds 10° to the skew of a sprite:

```
on exitFrame me
  (sprite 1).skew = (sprite 1).skew + 10
end
```

The results of the behavior are shown in Figure 18.1.

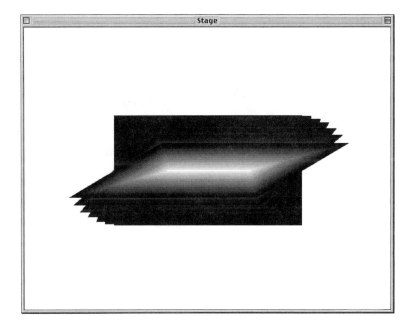

Figure 18.1
The result of changing the skew of a sprite by 10° several times, and having trails turned on to record each step.

PART

VI

CH

18

THE QUAD PROPERTY

The last and greatest of the sprite manipulation properties is the *quad* property of the sprite. This is a list of four items, like *rect*, but it contains points, not numbers. Each of these points represents one of the corners of a sprite. Here is an example:

```
put (sprite 1).quad
-- [point(184.0000, 126.0000), point(463.0000, 126.0000), point(463.0000, ¬
302.0000), point(184.0000, 302.0000)]
```

The beauty of the *quad* property is that you can set the four points to whatever you want. You can essentially "pull" on any of the corners using Lingo.

For instance, if you take a rectangular image, and then push the upper-left corner of the sprite down and to the right, and the upper-right corner of the sprite down and to the left, you can imitate perspective on the Stage and create the illusion of 3D. Figure 18.2 shows this effect.

Note

The difference between using *quad* and *skew* is that with *quad* you have total control over the four corners of a sprite. With *skew*, you control just the angle of the sides of the sprite's rectangle.

Figure 18.2
The Stage shows two sprites, both with the same bitmap member. However, one sprite's quad has been changed to imitate 3D perspective.

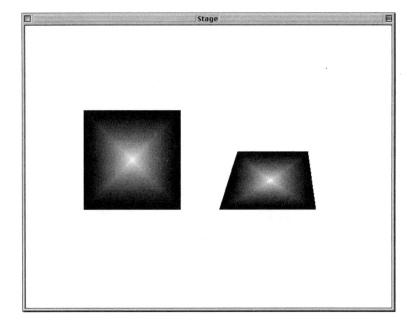

You have no way of altering a sprite's *quads* on the Stage, but this handler enables you to do it while the movie is playing. It enables you to click and grab any corner of the sprite and drag the corner:

```
property pCorner

on beginSprite me
  pCorner = 0
end

on mouseDown me
  pCorner = 0
  repeat with i = 1 to 4
    if distance(me,the clickLoc,sprite(me.spriteNum).quad[i]) < 10 then
      pCorner = i
      exit repeat
    end if
  end repeat
```

```
      put pCorner
  end

  on mouseUp me
    pCorner = 0
  end

  on mouseUpOutside me
    pCorner = 0
  end

  on exitFrame me
    if pCorner > 0 then
      q = sprite(me.spriteNum).quad
      q⁰pCorner] = the mouseLoc
      sprite(me.spriteNum).quad = q
    end if
  end

  on distance me, p1, p2
    return sqrt (power(p1.locH-p2.locH,2)+power(p1.locV-p2.locV,2))
  end
```

OTHER DISTORTION PROPERTIES

Many other properties affect bitmap sprites at a less dramatic level than the properties previously discussed. Many of these are newly available in this version of Director. Here is a complete list:

- *useAlpha*—Determines whether alpha channel information included with 32-bit bitmaps is used in displaying the member. When TRUE, the alpha channel is used to vary the level of transparency of the bitmap.

- *alphaThreshold*—If an alpha channel is present, this property can be set to a value between 0 and 255. 0 means that all pixels in the sprite can respond to mouse clicks. Any other setting determines the degree of nontransparency required for a pixel to register a click.

- *blend*—This corresponds to the "blend" property in the Score. You can set it to values between 0 and 100, but the ink of the sprite must be one that supports blends.

- *color*—The foreground color of the sprite. This property can be set to either a *paletteIndex* structure, such as `paletteIndex(255)`, or a *color* structure, such as `color(255,255,255)` or `color("#FFFFFF")`. The difference is most dramatic with 1-bit members that use their *color* property for all used pixels. It is also used by sprites set to Lighten or Darken inks.

- *bgColor*—The background color of the sprite. This can be set to either a *paletteIndex* structure, such as `paletteIndex(255)`, or a *color* structure, such as `color(255,255,255)` or `color("#FFFFFF")`. The difference is most dramatic with 1-bit members that use their *bgColor* property for all unused pixels. Results vary according to ink. The *bgColor* property is also used by sprites set to Lighten or Darken inks.

→ **See** "Bitmap Member Properties," Chapter 3, "Bitmap Members," for more information about bitmaps

→ **See** "Sprite Inks," Chapter 10, "Properties of Sprites and Frames," for more information about inks

→ **See** "Sprite Blend," Chapter 10, for more information about sprite blends

→ **See** "Sprite Color," Chapter 10, for more information about sprite color

→ **See** "Sprite Shape," Chapter 10, for more information about sprite shapes

→ **See** "Other Sprite Properties," Chapter 10, for more information about sprite properties

ADDING 3D EFFECTS

Director is not a 3D authoring environment. But then again, neither are computer 3D programs. The fact is, computer screens are flat. By nature, 3D computer graphics are just illusions that trick the users into seeing 3D on what is really only a flat screen. This section discusses how to use Lingo to make those illusions as realistic as possible.

SHRINKING SPRITES

The shrinking sprite illusion is a special effect that Director and Lingo can easily handle. The basic idea is that real-life objects that are farther away look smaller to the eye. So if you have two objects that are the same size, but one is twice as far away, the farther one appears to be half as big.

Figure 18.3 shows a Stage with two sprites. The sprite on the left is shown at 100%, whereas the sprite on the right is shown at 50%. The result is that one appears closer than the other.

Figure 18.3
Setting the sizes of sprites can create the illusion of depth.

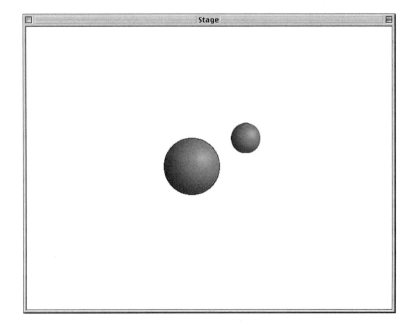

The illusion becomes even stronger when used with animation. Imagine, for instance, an object that appears as a small dot at first, and then grows to full size. It looks as if it the object is moving toward the viewer.

The following code shows a behavior that does just that. It assumes that the center of the screen is 320, 240, and that it is the origination point for the sprite. It gets the *quad* of the sprite and manipulates all four points according to the scale and the center of the screen. It stops when the scale reaches 1.0, as follows:

```
property pOrigQuad, pScale

on beginSprite me
  pOrigQuad = sprite(me.spriteNum).quad
  pScale = 0.0
end

on exitFrame me
  if pScale < 1.0 then
    -- increase scale 1%
    pScale = pScale + .01

    -- copy the quad
    newQuad = duplicate(pOrigQuad)

    -- set new quad points
    repeat with i = 1 to 4
      newQuad[i] = newPoint(me,newQuad[i],pScale)
    end repeat

    -- set the sprite
    sprite(me.spriteNum).quad = newQuad
  end if
end

-- this handler will take a point and a scale
-- and return a new point based on the
-- center of 320, 240
on newPoint me, p, scale
  centerPoint = point(320,240)

  -- find relative location
  p = p - centerPoint

  -- multiply by the scale
  p = p*scale

  -- add back center point
  p = p + centerPoint

  return p
end
```

A script such as this can be used to make objects come from a distance to their positions on the screen. It can also be a good effect for creating text that flies "toward" the user, rather than just moving left, right, up, or down.

SHRINKING SPRITES WITH MOVEMENT

Another way to create a feeling of depth is to resize the sprite as it moves around the Stage. If, for instance, the left side of the Stage is supposed to be farther back than the right side, you can shrink the object depending on how far from the left side of the Stage it is.

The following code shows a behavior that has the center of a sprite follow the mouse. The closer the user brings the sprite to the left side of the Stage, the smaller the scale gets:

```
property pWidth, pHeight

on beginSprite me
  pWidth = sprite(me.spriteNum).rect.width
  pHeight = sprite(me.spriteNum).rect.height
end

on exitFrame me
  -- get the new location
  x = the mouseH
  y = the mouseV

  -- figure the size as a number between 0 and 1
  if x = 0 then  percent = the maxInteger
  else percent = 640.0/x

  -- figure the new height and width
  w = pWidth/percent
  h = pHeight/percent

  -- make a rectangle with the point at the center
  newRect = rect(x-w/2,y-h/2,x+w/2,y+w/2)

  -- set the sprite
  sprite(me.spriteNum).rect = newRect
end
```

An illusion such as this becomes even easier to see when the background graphic hints toward it. In the preceding example, you may want to include a background graphic of a wall that recedes back toward the left.

USING THE QUAD PROPERTY TO CREATE ILLUSIONS

Yet another way to create 3D illusions is to play with the *quad* of sprites to form 2D representations of 3D shapes. A cube is a good example. Figure 18.4 shows a cube on the Stage. It is actually drawn with six sprites, one for each side. It uses 3D trigonometry and *quads* to figure out where each side goes.

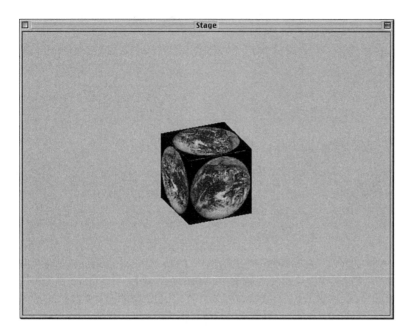

Figure 18.4
Six sprites are used to draw this 3D cube.

Here is the code that makes this 3D cube. There are actually many different ways to pull this off, but this example uses the following movie script:

Note

This code can be considered very complex. If you don't understand exactly what is going on, don't worry. Try the demo file on the CD-ROM to get a better understanding of this example.

```
global gCorners, gCenter, gRectList, gRotate, gPlane

on startMovie
  -- initialize lists for a cube
  initBox
end

on frameScript
  -- add to rotation based on mouse location
  gRotate = gRotate - (float(the mouseH-320)/30)*pi()/100

  -- calc plane tilt based on mouse location
  gPlane = - (float(the mouseV-240)/30)*pi()/20
  drawSides
end

on initBox
  -- list of corners with x, y and z coordinates
  gCorners = [[-60,-60,-60],[60,-60,-60],[60,60,-60],¬
    [-60,60,-60],[-60,-60,60],[60,-60,60],[60,60,60],[-60,60,60]]

  -- the screen center
  gCenter = point(320,240)
```

```
      -- list of sides
      -- each side has four corners
      gRectList = [[1,2,3,4],[1,2,6,5],[3,4,8,7],[2,3,7,6],¬
        [1,4,8,5],[5,6,7,8]]
end

on drawSides
   -- generate a list of screen points and depths based on the
   -- gCorners list and the transformation to 2d screen coordinates
   list = []
   repeat with i = 1 to count(gCorners)
     temp = plotPoint(gCorners[i])
     add list,temp
   end repeat

   -- create a quad list that takes 4 points to display side of cube
   quadList = [:]
   repeat with i = 1 to count(gRectList)

     -- get the four corners that make this side
     thisRect = gRectList[i]

     -- get the four screen points to draw
     q = [list[thisRect[1]][2],list[thisRect[2]][2],¬
         list[thisRect[3]][2],list[thisRect[4]][2]]

     -- get the closest (depth) screen point
     z = min(list[thisRect[1]][1],list[thisRect[2]][1],¬
           list[thisRect[3]][1],list[thisRect[4]][1])

     -- add to list, with closest screen point as the property name
     addProp quadList, z, q
   end repeat

   -- sort list by property name so closest
   -- sides get drawn on top of farther ones
   sort quadList

   -- draw each side
   repeat with i = 1 to count(gRectList)
     sprite(i).quad = quadList[i]
   end repeat
end

on plotPoint objectInfo
   -- get x, y, and z from objectInfo list
   x = getAt(objectInfo,1)
   y = getAt(objectInfo,2)
   z = getAt(objectInfo,3)

   -- TRANSFORM BY ROTATION AROUND Z

   -- compute the radius
   radius = sqrt(x*x+y*y)

   -- compute the angle
   if x = 0.0 then angle = atan(the maxInteger)
```

```
    else angle = atan(float(y)/x)
    if y < 0 then angle = angle + pi()

    -- rotate
    set angle = angle+gRotate

    -- compute new x, y, and z
    realX = radius*cos(angle)
    realZ = radius*sin(angle)
    realY = Z

    -- TRANSFORM BY ROTATION AROUND X

    -- compute then radius
    radius = sqrt(realY*realY+realZ*realZ)

    -- compute the angle
    if realZ = 0 then angle = atan(the maxInteger)
    else angle = (atan(realY/realZ))
    if realZ < 0 then angle = angle + pi()

    -- rotate
    angle = angle - gPlane

    -- compute then new x, y and z
    screenX = realX
    screenY = radius*sin(angle)
    screenZ = radius*cos(angle)

    -- return both z, and the x and y point
    return  [screenZ,point(screenX,screenY)+gCenter]
end
```

For this movie script to have any effect, it also needs six square-shaped bitmaps in the first six sprites, plus a frame script:

```
on exitFrame
  frameScript
  go to the frame
end
```

The code uses the mouse position to determine the plane and rotation of the cube. However, you can remove this code and include buttons that enable the user to move the cube. You could even have it rotate at a constant rate.

MAPPING SPRITES

When you use the *quad* property to distort a sprite, Director still keeps track of the original member's appearance. In fact, you can use two special functions in Lingo to convert between screen locations and the relative locations of pixels in the original bitmap.

Figure 18.5 shows a good example of why you will need to do this conversion. The chessboard has been distorted with quads to appear as if it has depth. In reality, the board is a simple 160×160 square with 64 spaces.

Figure 18.5
The chessboard
bitmap is actually a
straight-down image
that has been altered
using quads to appear
to have depth.

Here is the *on beginSprite* handler that takes the plain, square board and turns it into the 3D one you see in Figure 18.5. It simply moves the top two quad points. No special math is used, just estimated, hard-coded points for simplicity in this example:

```
on beginSprite me
  q = sprite(me.spriteNum).quad
  q[1] = q[1]+point(-30,100)
  q[2] = q[2]+point(30,100)
  sprite(me.spriteNum).quad = q
end
```

When the movie runs, this sprite looks as it does in Figure 18.5. When it was just a plain rectangle, it would have been easy to get the column and row of a mouse click. Each space on the board is 20×20, so you could just divide the horizontal and vertical location by 20, and add one to get a number between one and eight. However, with the board distorted as shown in Figure 18.5, you need to map the click location with Lingo.

The function needed to map the click location is *mapStageToMember*. It takes a sprite number and a Stage location and then converts these to a location relative to the bitmap member.

So if the user clicks the upper-left corner of the distorted sprite, the function returns point (0,0). Here is an *on mouseUp* handler that uses the *mapStageToMember* function to calculate where the user clicked:

```
on mouseUp me
  p = mapStageToMember(sprite 1, the clickLoc)
  x = 1+p.locH/20
  y = 1+p.locV/20
  put "Row:"&&x&&"Column:"&&y
end
```

The flip side of the *mapStageToMember* function is the *mapMemberToStage* function. You can use it to find any Stage location based on a location in the member. Here is a handler that returns the Stage location when given a space on the chessboard:

```
on getPos me, x, y
  p = point(x*20-10,y*20-10)
  return mapMemberToStage(sprite 1, p)
end
```

To position the queen as seen on Figure 18.5, you can use this behavior. It assumes that the board is in sprite channel 1.

```
on beginSprite me
  p = getPos(sprite 1, 4, 5)
  sprite(me.spriteNum).loc = p
end
```

Mapping sprites in this way enables you to distort one sprite and then position other sprites relative to this distortion. It can be used along with the cube example to place an object on the face of a cube. Or, it can be used with the shrinking sprite example to map one sprite onto another, or provide valid clicks on the sprite as it changes size.

→ **See** "Advertising," Chapter 31, "Shockwave Applets," for an example that uses the 3D cube script

MANIPULATING BITMAP MEMBERS

You cannot do much with bitmap members. They do not have an editable component as text members or fields do. You can, however, crop members with the *crop* command.

This command takes a member name and a *rect* as parameters and places the cropped image back into the same cast member slot. So if you have a bitmap that is 100 pixels wide by 100 pixels high, and you want only the bottom right corner of it, you might use the command:

```
crop(member "mybitmap", rect(75,75,100,100))
```

The numbers in the *rect* define the rectangle inside the bitmap member that you want to retain. The rest is removed.

You are likely to want to keep your original bitmap member around. You can duplicate bitmap members by creating a new cast member and then copying the image into it.

The *new* command can be used to create a new cast member of any type. For bitmaps, just use it in this manner:

```
myNewMember = new(#bitmap)
```

The variable "myNewMember" now holds a reference to the new cast member. You can now set its name with this reference:

```
myNewMember.name = "New Bitmap"
```

If you want to create this member in a cast library other than the internal one, just use a second parameter:

```
myNewMember = new(#bitmap, castLib "pictures")
```

Or, you can specify the exact cast member location, with or without a *castLib* reference, as follows:

```
myNewMember = new(#bitmap, member 18)
myNewMember = new(#bitmap, member 18 of castLib "pictures")
```

After you have a new member, you can place information in it by referring to the main property of the cast member. For instance, for fields, you can use the *text* property:

```
myNewMember.text = "Some text"
```

For text members, you can use either the *text*, *rtf*, or *html* properties. For bitmaps, however, you must use the *picture* property. You cannot create a picture in Lingo, however; you must take it from another member. To copy a bitmap from one member to another, do this:

```
myNewMember.picture = member("my picture").picture
```

You can also use the property *media*. This property acts like *picture* for a bitmap member, *html* for a text member that uses HTML, *rtf* for a text member that uses RTF, a sound for a sound cast member, and so on. It simply represents whatever type of media the member contains.

> **Tip**
>
> Text members also contain a *picture* property. This property represents the bitmap of the text that is displayed on the Stage. You can grab that *picture* and place it in a bitmap member.

The Stage, along with bitmap members, has a *picture* property. You can grab a screenshot of the Stage and store it in a bitmap as follows:

```
member("myBitmap").picture = (the Stage).picture
```

You can then use *crop* to crop this image. Here is a short handler that grabs the Stage image and then crops it to match a rectangle:

```
on grabArea intoMember, screenArea
  member(intoMember).picture = (the stage).picture
  crop(member(intoMember),screenArea)
end
```

> **Note**
>
> The preceding example does not work as expected if the Stage has white space to the left or top. When the image is grabbed and placed in the cast member, any white space is ignored. So the *rect* you grab has to take into account that the *rect* of the Stage and the *rect* of the image are different.

You can easily grab a section of the Stage that has a background rectangular sprite, such as a shape, by using the *rect* of that sprite as the crop *rect*, as follows:

```
grabArea(member "myMember", sprite(1).rect)
```

All the properties in this chapter provide you with ultimate control over the bitmap members and sprites in your movie.

TROUBLESHOOTING BITMAPS

- Nothing is free. When you rotate, skew, or stretch sprites, you take a speed hit. You cannot expect to have dozens of constantly rotating sprites on the Stage and others stretched with *quad* and still have your animation running as fast as an animation without all that. Keep this in mind when designing.

- If a 32-bit image is displayed incorrectly, or it looks different in the Paint window than on the Stage, try turning off the "Use Alpha" property. Sometimes bad alpha channels creep into 32-bit images.

- Using straight Photoshop documents with an alpha channel produces a "pre-multiplied" alpha channel. This just means a white halo appears around the images. One easy way to correct this is to open the file in Macromedia Fireworks first, save it as a PNG file, and then import that file.

DID YOU KNOW?

- You can use the undocumented function *getPixel*, with an x and y coordinate in a bitmap to get an integer representation of a color pixel in a bitmap. For instance:

```
getPixel(member("myBitmap"), 50, 100)
```

You can use the also undocumented *setPixel* to change its color:

```
setPixel("myBitmap"),50,100,65535)
```

Because these functions are unsupported, they are not reliable and it is hard to determine what the numbers correspond to. The numbers you need to use depend on the bit depth of the member and the presence of an alpha channel.

- An undocumented system property is *the useFastQuads*. Set this to TRUE and sprites stretched with the *quad* property draw more quickly, but are not stretched quite the same. The result is not as good for simulating 3D.

- To convert degrees to radians, divide the number by 360.0 and multiply by 2.0×pi. To convert radians to degrees, divide by 2.0×pi and then multiply by 360.0. Make sure your original number is a floating point number, not an integer.

CHAPTER **19**

CONTROLLING VIDEO

In this chapter

Whereas most digital video used in Director is simply placed on the Stage with the default control bar, sometimes it is necessary to control video with Lingo. Digital video is not as easy to manipulate as bitmaps are, but a variety of properties can be used to affect how video is displayed. These properties are the subject of this chapter.

USING VIDEO COMMANDS

There are more member and sprite properties for digital video than for any other media type. Because some of the properties are for the member, and others for the sprite, it can get very confusing. There are even functions involving QuickTime tracks that act like properties. For the sake of clarity, this section separates the properties for the members from the properties for the sprites.

MEMBER PROPERTIES

Two groups of member properties are for digital video members. The first group corresponds exactly to the properties shown in the video's Properties dialog box. The following is a brief list of the most common digital video member properties:

- center—A TRUE or FALSE value that determines whether the video is centered in the sprite's rectangle. This only works if the *crop* property is set to TRUE.

- controller —A TRUE or FALSE value that determines whether the default QuickTime or AVI controller is shown.

- crop —If this value is set to TRUE, the movie remains the same scale, even if the sprite's rectangle is changed. If it is set to FALSE, the movie adjusts to fit in the sprite's rectangle.

- directToStage —This property determines whether the video is drawn directly to the screen, covering and ignoring other sprites. If the video is drawn directly to the screen you get a smoother display, but you do not have the capability to use as many special effects.

- frameRate —This property can be set to a number that is then the playback frame rate of the video. Using the special value -2 causes the video to play back as fast as it can, whereas the value -1 causes it to play back at normal speed. Playing a video with this property set disables the sound for the video. Set the *frameRate* to 0 to return the video member to the "Sync To Soundtrack" normal state.

- loop —This property determines whether the video is to automatically loop back to the beginning when it reaches the end.

- pausedAtStart —This property determines whether the movie starts playing as soon as it appears on the Stage, or whether it waits for the controller or Lingo to tell it to play.

- sound —This property determines whether the sound is played or silent.

- video —This property determines whether the video is displayed.

In addition to these member properties that can be controlled with or without Lingo, a few properties can be accessed, but not set, with Lingo:

- digitalVideoType —Returns either #quickTime or #videoForWindows.
- duration—Returns the length in ticks (1/60th of a second) of the video.
- isVRMovie —Returns a TRUE if the video is a QuickTime VR movie.

SPRITE PROPERTIES

There are also several sprite properties that can be set with Lingo. These are useful for creating video controls and effects. Here is a complete list:

- loopBounds —This property enables you to set the start and end times of a looping video. Use a short, two-item list, like [0,240].
- movieRate —This property represents the speed of forward movement of the video. A value of 0 means the video has stopped. A value of 1 means it is playing normally. A value of 2 means it is going at double-speed. You can also use negative values to make the video go backward.
- movieTime —This property represents the current time, in ticks, of the video. You can set this to 0 to go to the start, or to the member's *duration* to go to the end.
- rotation —Believe it or not, you can rotate a QuickTime video. Set this property to the angle, in degrees, of rotation. This property works best when the video member is not set to "Direct To Stage".
- scale —You can also scale the video by setting this property to a small list with the horizontal and vertical scale values, such as [1.5, 1.5].
- volume —This works just as it does for sound members, enabling you to change the sound level of the video.

PART

VI

CH

19

MASKS

Digital video members can also have masks. A *mask* is a 1-bit bitmap that tells Director which pixels of the video to show and which pixels to throw away. Figure 19.1 shows three images: a video, a 1-bit bitmap, and the same video with the 1-bit bitmap applied as a mask.

Figure 19.1
A 1-bit bitmap can be used as a mask for a digital video member.

The best part about masks is that they can be used when the video is in "Direct to Stage" mode. This means that the video is not slowed by the mask effect.

To apply a mask, create the 1-bit bitmap and name it. Then use the *mask* property to apply it to the member. You can even do it in the Message window to test it out. The property *mask* is a member property, but this command uses the sprite to figure out the member:

```
sprite(1).member.mask = member("myMask")
```

You can also use the *invertMask* property to have white pixels, rather than black, represent visible pixels in the movie. Keep in mind that the registration point for the mask should be set to the upper-left corner rather than the center.

→ **See** "Digital Video Settings," Chapter 6, "Digital Video," for some background on using digital video in Director

BUILDING VIDEO CONTROLS

Using the video properties explained previously, it is easy to build your own custom controls. As a matter of fact, one behavior can handle 10 different types of controls.

The following behavior needs to know which sprite contains the digital video. It also needs to know for what type of control it is being used.

```
property pControlType, pVideoSprite

on getPropertyDescriptionList me
  list = [:]
  addProp list, #pControlType, [#comment: "Control",¬
    #format: #symbol,¬
    #range: [#play, #stop, #pause, #stepForward, #stepBackward,¬
      #start, #reverse, #fastForward, #fastReverse, #end, #loop],¬
    #default: #stop]
  addProp list, #pVideoSprite, [#comment: "Video Sprite",¬
    #format: #sprite, #default: 1]
  return list
end
```

Although a more complex behavior might also include button handler-like effects, such as down states and rollovers, this behavior sticks to doing only what is necessary to control the video sprite.

In the case of a "play" button, all that is needed is for the *movieRate* to be set to 1.

```
on mouseUp me
  case pControlType of
    #play:
      sprite(pVideoSprite).movieRate = 1
```

A stop button does the opposite, setting the *movieRate* to 0. The same can be done for the "pause" button. To make the "play" button different, it can also set the *movieTime* back to 0, which stops and rewinds the video, rather than just stopping it.

```
    #stop:
        sprite(pVideoSprite).movieRate = 0
        sprite(pVideoSprite).movieTime = 0
    #pause:
        sprite(pVideoSprite).movieRate = 0
```

A "start" or "end" will take the video to the beginning or end and pause it. Note that this means the "start" button and "stop" button actually do the same thing!

```
    #start:
        sprite(pVideoSprite).movieRate = 0
        sprite(pVideoSprite).movieTime = 0
    #end:
        sprite(pVideoSprite).movieRate = 0
        sprite(pVideoSprite).movieTime = sprite(pVideoSprite).duration
```

A "reverse" button plays the video at normal speed, but backward.

```
    #reverse:
        sprite(pVideoSprite).movieRate = -1
```

There are two types of "step" buttons: forward and reverse. If the digital video is set to play at a typical 15 frames per second, that means that there is one frame every 4/60 of a second, or 4 ticks.

```
    #stepForward:
        sprite(pVideoSprite).movieTime = sprite(pVideoSprite).movieTime + 4
    #stepBackward:
        sprite(pVideoSprite).movieTime = sprite(pVideoSprite).movieTime - 4
```

A "fast forward" or "fast reverse" button can make the video travel at speeds greater than 1 or less than -1. In this case, 3 is used.

```
    #fastForward:
        sprite(pVideoSprite).movieRate = 3
    #fastReverse:
        sprite(pVideoSprite).movieRate = -3
```

PART

VI

CH

19

One last button type is the loop switch. This determines whether the movie loops at the end. It is usually a good idea to make this a separate behavior and use some of the same code from the check box behaviors, so that the button can change from a looping to non-looping state. However, to simplify the coding, this button just toggles the *loop* property and does not give any feedback to the user.

```
    #loop:
        sprite(pVideoSprite).member.loop = ¬
            not sprite(pVideoSprite).member.loop
    end case
end
```

Other video buttons can be made as well. For instance, you could use the *loopBounds* to switch between different loops within the same video. A slider can be used as a volume control. Or, you can even use a slider to set the *movieTime* property. Such a slider is just like the one used by QuickTime's default controller, but you can use your own custom graphics.

→ **See** "Digital Video Settings," Chapter 6, for more information on digital video properties

USING OTHER VIDEO TECHNIQUES

These video properties can also be used to make video sprites perform tricks. For instance, the following behavior uses the *blend* property of the sprite to cause a video sprite to fade in:

```
property pSpeed

on getPropertyDescriptionList me
  list = [:]
  addProp list, #pSpeed, [#comment: "Speed", #format: #integer,¬
    #range: [#min: 1, #max: 20], #default: 7]
  return list
end

on beginSprite me
  sprite(me.spriteNum).member.directToStage = FALSE
  sprite(me.spriteNum).member.crop = TRUE

  sprite(me.spriteNum).blend = 0
end

on exitFrame me
  if sprite(me.spriteNum).blend < 100 then
    sprite(me.spriteNum).blend = ¨
        min(sprite(me.spriteNum).blend+pSpeed,100)
  end if
end
```

Notice that the handler also sets the *directToStage* and *crop* properties of the video sprite. Although this is usually not necessary, it makes sure that any changes to these properties from other behaviors are not still in effect.

The same things can be done in reverse. Here is a behavior that fades a video sprite to a *blend* of 0.

```
property pSpeed

on getPropertyDescriptionList me
  list = [:]
  addProp list, #pSpeed, [#comment: "Speed", #format: #integer,¬
    #range: [#min: 1, #max: 20], #default: 7]
  return list
end

on beginSprite me
  sprite(me.spriteNum).member.directToStage = FALSE
  sprite(me.spriteNum).member.crop = TRUE

  sprite(me.spriteNum) .blend = 100
end

on exitFrame me
  if sprite(me.spriteNum).blend > 0 then
    sprite(me.spriteNum).blend = ¬
        max(sprite(me.spriteNum).blend-pSpeed,0)
  end if
end
```

These behaviors can, of course, be combined into one that provides either function. Note that they can be used for bitmaps and even text members, too.

For a more complex effect, the following behavior causes the video to start off as a small point. It then grows lengthwise until it is a line. Then it grows up and down until it is the original shape of the video. The result looks something like an old-fashioned television warming up.

```
property pOrigRect, pSpeed

on getPropertyDescriptionList me
  list = [:]
  addProp list, #pSpeed, [#comment: "Speed", #format: #integer,¬
    #range: [#min: 1, #max: 20], #default: 7]
  return list
end

on beginSprite me
  sprite(me.spriteNum).member.directToStage = TRUE
  sprite(me.spriteNum).member.crop = FALSE

  pOrigRect = sprite(me.spriteNum).rect

  -- set rect to center point
  x = pOrigRect.left+(pOrigRect.width/2)
  y = pOrigRect.top+(pOrigRect.height/2)
  r = rect(x,y,x,y+1)
  sprite(me.spriteNum).rect = r
end

on exitFrame me
  if sprite(me.spriteNum).rect.width < pOrigRect.width then
    r = sprite(me.spriteNum).rect
    r.left = max(r.left-pSpeed, pOrigRect.left)
    r.right = min(r.right+pSpeed, pOrigRect.right)
    sprite(me.spriteNum).rect = r

  else if sprite(me.spriteNum).rect.height < pOrigRect.height then
    r = sprite(me.spriteNum).rect
    r.top = max(r.top-pSpeed, pOrigRect.top)
    r.bottom = min(r.bottom+pSpeed, pOrigRect.bottom)
    sprite(me.spriteNum).rect = r

  end if
end
```

Digital video can also be rotated. This next behavior probably has no real use, but is a good demonstration.

```
property pSpeed

on getPropertyDescriptionList me
  list = [:]
  addProp list, #pSpeed, [#comment: "Speed", #format: #integer,¬
    #range: [#min: 1, #max: 20], #default: 7]
  return list
end
```

```
on beginSprite me
  sprite(me.spriteNum).member.directToStage = TRUE
  sprite(me.spriteNum).member.crop = TRUE
end

on endSprite me
  sprite(me.spriteNum).rotation = 0
end

on exitFrame me
  sprite(me.spriteNum).rotation = ¬
        sprite(me.spriteNum).rotation + pSpeed
end
```

Here is a very different effect. The following behavior takes the video, shrinks it, and then places it on the left side of the screen. It turns on the *trails* property of the sprite so that the image is left behind. It then moves over to the right and leaves another image. It continues to do this, leaving behind what looks like a film strip. When it gets to the right side of the screen, it starts replacing the images to the left.

```
property pOrigRect, pSize, pSpacing, pStart, pDirect

on getPropertyDescriptionList me
  list = [:]
  addProp list, #pSize, [#comment: "Size (%)", #format: #integer,¬
    #range: [#min: 5, #max: 100], #default: 25]
  addProp list, #pSpacing, [#comment: "Spacing", #format: #integer,¬
    #range: [#min: 0, #max: 25], #default: 5]
  addProp list, #pStart, [#comment: "Start X", #format: #integer,¬
    #default: 0]
  addProp list, #pDirect,  [#comment: "Direct To Stage", #format: #boolean,¬
    #default: TRUE]
  return list
end

on beginSprite me
  sprite(me.spriteNum).member.directToStage = pDirect
  sprite(me.spriteNum).member.crop = FALSE
  sprite(me.spriteNum).trails = FALSE

  pOrigRect = sprite(me.spriteNum).rect
  r = sprite(me.spriteNum).rect
  r = (r*pSize)/100.0
  sprite(me.spriteNum).rect = r
  sprite(me.spriteNum).locH = pStart
  sprite(me.spriteNum).trails = TRUE
end

on endSprite me
  sprite(me.spriteNum).trails = FALSE
  sprite(me.spriteNum).rect = pOrigRect
end

on exitFrame me
  x = sprite(me.spriteNum).locH
  x = x + sprite(me.spriteNum).rect.width + pSpacing
```

```
   if x > the stageRight then x = pStart

   sprite(me.spriteNum).locH = x
end
```

Figure 19.2 shows the effects of this code in action.

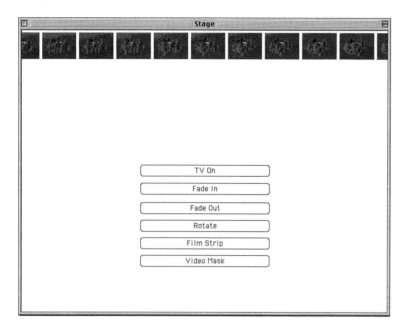

Figure 19.2
The Film Strip behavior places images of the video in different positions on the Stage.

These are only simple examples of what can be accomplished with the digital video member and sprite properties. You can combine and expand on them depending on your needs. Experimentation is the best way to find what works best for you.

→ **See** "Working with Digital Video," Chapter 6, for more information on using digital video

TROUBLESHOOTING VIDEO

■ If you are using the built-in QuickTime controller, check the size on both Mac and Windows; they may be slightly different. It depends on the version of QuickTime. The Windows controller was slightly taller than the Mac in QuickTime 2.1.

DID YOU KNOW?

■ You can use the video control scripts to control MIDI-only or sound-only QuickTime video. This way, you can build a jukebox that uses MIDI or super-compressed QuickTime audio.

■ When you set the *movieRate* property to a negative number, not only does the movie play backward, but so does the sound!

PART
VI

CH
19

CHAPTER 20

CONTROLLING VECTOR GRAPHICS

In this chapter

Because vector shape cast members are new to Director 7, they require a whole new set of Lingo properties and commands. Actually, many of these were borrowed from the Flash cast member, which was introduced in Director 6.5, largely because the vector shape cast member uses the Flash engine in the Flash Asset Xtra. This chapter discusses the Flash member and vector shape member Lingo you need to understand to use these members.

USING FLASH MEMBER LINGO

Flash cast members are, no doubt, the most complex type of cast member. After all, they are created in Macromedia Flash, a program all to itself. Flash creates mostly vector-based animations that are streamlined for the Internet. The program even warrants a few books all to itself and there are several to choose from.

Flash members are made up of frames, just like Director movies. Each frame can contain different elements such as shapes, bitmaps, buttons, and sounds. So rather than being a still media like bitmaps, Flash members are a time-based media like digital video. Most of the Lingo for Flash movies reflect that fact.

The following is a list of properties that control the speed at which the Flash movie plays while it is on the Stage:

- playBackMode—You have three options: #normal, #lockstep, and #fixed. The #normal option tells the Flash movie to rely on the settings established when it was created in Flash. The #lockstep setting causes one frame of the Flash movie to play for every one frame of the Director movie. The #fixed setting uses the *fixedRate* property of the member to determine the Flash movie's frame rate.

- fixedRate —Set this only when you are using the #fixed setting for the *playBackMode*. It enables you to specify the frame rate for the Flash movie. You can even change it during playback.

- frameRate —This property tells you what the Flash movie's original frame rate was.

- frameCount —This property tells you the number of frames in the Flash movie.

You can also use Lingo to navigate within the Flash movie, as follows:

- goToFrame—This command enables you to specify a frame number or frame label in the Flash movie. An example looks like this: goToFrame(sprite 5, "intro"). The sprite must contain a Flash member.

- findLabel —This function takes a sprite number and a frame label and tries to return a frame number that corresponds to the frame in the Flash movie contains that label. If it is not found, a 0 is returned.

- pausedAtStart—This TRUE or FALSE property determines whether the Flash movie automatically starts playing when it appears on the Stage.

- playing—This property tells you whether the Flash movie is currently playing.

- rewind —This command takes the sprite number as its one parameter. It takes the Flash movie back to its first frame.

- stop —This command stops the Flash movie in the sprite specified.

- play —This command enables the Flash movie in the specified sprite to continue playing.

You can also control how much like a Flash movie a Flash member should act. Because Flash movies have their own buttons and actions, you will sometimes want to disable those elements in the Flash member when using it in Director.

- actionsEnabled—Determines whether any of the actions in a Flash sprite or member should work.

- buttonsEnabled—Determines whether buttons in the Flash sprite or member work.

You can also establish when you want to have mouse events, such as clicks and rollovers, be passed to your Lingo behaviors attached to the sprite.

- clickMode—This property of a sprite or member can be set to one of three things: #boundingBox, #opaque, or #object. The #boundingBox option enables clicks and other mouse events to be detected over the entire sprite's rectangle. The #opaque option enables clicks to be detected only when the cursor is over an opaque portion of the Flash member. The #object option detects mouse events only when the cursor is over a filled shape in the Flash member. The #opaque option works only when the sprite is set to the Background Transparent ink.

- eventPassMode —Determines whether clicks are passed on to Lingo behaviors. The four modes are: #passAlways, #passButton, #passNotButton, and #passNever. The #passAlways setting is the default.

An additional two functions tell you when a point is over something in a Flash movie sprite:

- hitTest—This function takes two parameters: the sprite and a point. The point should be relative to the sprite's location. It returns #background, #normal, or #button, depending on what the point is over. #normal means that it is over a shape in the Flash movie.

- mouseOverButton—Returns a TRUE if the cursor is over a button in the specified Flash movie sprite.

→ **See** "Flash Members," Chapter 7, "Vector Members," for some background on using Flash members in Director

PART
VI

CH
20

USING VECTOR SHAPE LINGO

Vector shape members have one major difference from Flash members: they are static images, rather than time-based media. However, unlike Flash members, they can be completely controlled with Lingo. You can even create a vector shape from scratch in Lingo and design it to look however you want.

Tip

Because vector shape members use the Flash engine in Director to draw themselves, many of the properties of Flash members are available to vector shapes and vice versa.

The combined vector shape properties enable you to change every aspect of a vector shape. Here is a complete list:

- antiAlias—Determines whether the member is drawn anti-aliased. When off, the member may draw a little faster, but the lines do not look as smooth.

- backgroundColor—The member's (not the sprite's) background color.

- broadcastProps—Determines whether changes to the member are immediately reflected on the Stage. If not, the sprite shows changes to the member only after it leaves and then reappears on the Stage.

- centerRegPoint—If set to TRUE, the registration point of the member changes automatically when the sprite is resized. If you are changing the vector shape with Lingo while the member is visible on the Stage, you should set this property to FALSE to prevent the sprite from jumping around.

- closed—Determines whether the first and last point in the vector shape are joined. It must be set to TRUE for the shape to be filled.

- defaultRect—A configurable property that can be used, in conjunction with *defaultRectMode*, to change the default rectangle for new sprites that use the vector shape member.

- defaultRectMode —This property can be set to either #flash or #fixed. The #flash setting sets all new sprites that use the member to the normal rectangle of the member. The #fixed mode instead uses the *defaultRect* property to set the initial rectangle of the sprite. This setting also affects any existing sprites that have not yet been stretched.

- directToStage—Determines whether the member is drawn on top of all other sprites, ignoring the sprite's ink effects. Drawing members in this manner improves performance.

- endColor—The destination color of a gradient fill in a vector shape member. Use an *rgb* or *paletteIndex* structure to set this. The *fillMode* must be set to gradient and the *closed* property must be TRUE.

- fillColor —The color of the interior of a vector shape member if the *fillMode* is set to #solid, or the starting color if the *fillMode* is set to #gradient. Use a *rgb* or *paletteIndex* structure to set this. The *closed* property must be TRUE.

- fillCycles —The number of fill cycles in a vector shape member that have the *fillMode* set to #gradient. Should be a number from 1 to 7.

- fillDirection —The direction of the fill, in degrees. The *fillMode* must be set to #gradient and the *gradientType* should be set to #linear.

- fillMode —This can be set to #none, #solid, or #gradient.

- fillOffset —This property is a point that corresponds to the horizontal and vertical offsets for the fill. This only works when the *fillType* is set to #gradient.

- fillScale —This corresponds to the "spread" in the vector shape editing window. The *fillMode* must be set to #gradient for this to work.

- flashRect—The original size of the vector member as a member, not as a sprite.

- gradientType—Can be set to #linear or #radial. Only works when the *fillMode* is #gradient.

- originMode—This is the relationship between the vertex points and the center of the sprite. It can be set to #center, #topLeft, or #point. The #center option makes the vertex points relative to the center of the member, whereas the #topLeft option makes them relative to the top left corner. The #point option uses the *originPoint* property. Set the *originMode* to #center if you plan to adjust a vertex while the movie is playing.

- originPoint —A point indicating the relationship between the vertex points and the member's location. This is used only if *originMode* is set to #point. You can also use the *originH* and *originV* properties.

- scale—Enables you to scale the member, using a list such as [1.000, 1.000], where the first item is the horizontal scale and the second is the vertical scale. This is an alternative to simply stretching the sprite.

- scaleMode —This is the equivalent to the member property in the vector shape's Properties dialog box. It can be set to #showAll, #noBorder, #exactFit, #noScale, and #autoSize. You can also use this as a property of a sprite that contains a vector shape.

- strokeColor—The color of the line used by the vector shape. The *strokeWidth* must be greater than 0 for this to work.

- strokeWidth —The width of the line used by the vector member.

- vertexList—The main property of a vector shape. It is a list of all of the points that make up the shape.

- viewPoint—This point enables you to change the point of the vector shape that appears at the center of the sprite.

- viewScale —Another way to scale the size of the vector shape on the Stage.

There are a lot of vector shape properties, as you can see. These don't even include the many sprite properties that also work on vector shapes, such as *rotation*, *flipH*, *flipV*, and *skew*.

The key property of any vector shape member is the *vertexList*. Taking a look at one using the Message window will help you understand how it works. Create a new vector shape and draw a rectangle in it. Then, use the Message window to see the *vertexList*.

```
put member(1).vertexList
-- [[#vertex: point(-104.0000, -40.0000)], [#vertex: point(104.0000, -40.0000)],¬
[#vertex: point(104.0000, 41.0000)], [#vertex: point(-104.0000, 41.0000)]]
```

The *vertexList* is a list of lists. Each small list is a property list with one property: #vertex. The value of #vertex is a point. Each point corresponds to a corner of the vector shape.

You can alter the *vertexList* in a few different ways. The *addVertex*, *deleteVertex*, and *moveVertex* commands enable you to do so without dealing with the member's properties directly. For instance, to add a new vertex, just use a command like this:

```
addVertex(member(1),3,point(0,0))
```

This command adds a point at 0,0 after the second vertex point and before the third. You can move an existing vertex by using a relative point and the *moveVertex* command:

```
moveVertex(member(1),3,100,10)
```

This command moves the third vertex point over to the right by 10 pixels. You can also delete a vertex, as follows:

```
deleteVertex(member(1),3)
```

Rather than using these commands, you could simply replace the entire vertex list. This next series of commands moves the third vertex over to the right 10 pixels:

```
vl = member(1).vertexList
v = vl[3].vertex
v = v + point(10,0)
vl[3].vertex = v
member(1).vertexList = vl
```

This is a lot more involved than just using *moveVertex*. However, resetting the entire vertex list actually makes sense in many cases. If you are using Lingo to create a vector shape from scratch, and then you want to replace it with another, slightly different, shape, you can use the same handler to create both shapes. This handler uses parameters to make the two shapes different, by simply replacing the entire vertex list each time, rather than trying to figure out what points differ. Tests show that there is no difference in drawing speed either way.

Tip

The *vertexList* items actually have two elements other than the #vertex. These are #handle1 and #handle2. They are points as well. However, they correspond to the curve handles of the point. These are the same handles that you can see when you edit a point in the vector shape editing window. The values in the *vertexList* are points that are relative to the actual #vertex point.

→ **See** "Vector Members," Chapter 7, for some background on using Vector members in Director

BUILDING VECTORS WITH LINGO

By simply setting the *vertexList* property of a vector member, you can create all sorts of interesting things with Lingo. For instance, here is a handler that creates a new, simple line:

```
on makeLine
  mem = new(#vectorShape)
  mem.name = "Line"
  mem.vertexList = [[#vertex: point(0,0)], [#vertex: point(200,100)]]
end
```

This handler uses the *new* command to create a new member. It names it, and then sets its *vertexList* to two simple points. You could also use the *strokeWidth* and *strokeColor* to set the line's thickness and color.

Here is a more complex handler that creates a curve using the *sin* function. Figure 20.1 shows the results of this handler, placed on the Stage.

```
on makeSine
  mem = new(#vectorShape)
  mem.name = "Sine"

  list = []
  repeat with x = -100*pi() to 100*pi()
    y = sin(float(x)/100.0)*100
    add list, [#vertex: point(x,y)]
  end repeat
  mem.vertexList = list
end
```

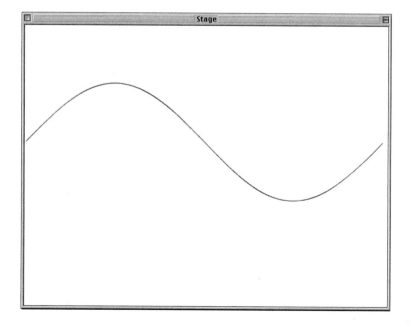

Figure 20.1
This sine curve is a single vector shape member created with Lingo.

PART

VI

CH

20

Only a little more work is needed to create a circle. Unlike the circle created with the vector shape editing window, this circle consists of 63 individual points with lines attaching them. The result actually looks very round, despite being made up of little lines. Figure 20.2 shows the result.

```
on makeCircle
  mem = new(#vectorShape)
  mem.name = "Circle"

  radius = 100

  list = []
  repeat with angle = -10*pi() to 10*pi()
    x = cos(float(angle)/10.0)*radius
    y = sin(float(angle)/10.0)*radius
    add list, [#vertex: point(x,y)]
  end repeat
  mem.vertexList = list
  mem.closed = TRUE
end
```

Figure 20.2
This circle is made up of 63 small lines in a single vector shape member created by Lingo.

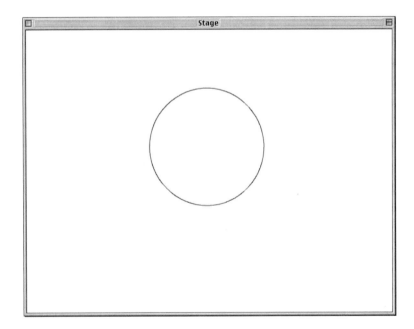

Notice that the *closed* property of the vector shape member is set to TRUE. This enables you to also set the *fillMode* property to #solid and set the *fillColor* property to the color you want to use. You could also use a gradient by setting the *fillMode* to #gradient and then set the whole collection of fill properties to specify the color, type, direction, scale, and type of gradient fill.

Simple shapes are not where Lingo vector creation shines. Complex ones, such as polygons, really show off the power of creating vectors with Lingo. Here is a behavior that sets a vector graphic in a sprite to a polygon. You can even choose the number of sides in the polygon:

```
property pNumPoints, pRadius

on getPropertyDescriptionList me
  list = [:]
  addProp list, #pNumPoints, [#comment: "Number of Points",¬
    #format: #integer, #default: 5]
  addProp list, #pRadius, [#comment: "Radius",¬
    #format: #integer, #default: 100]
  return list
end

on beginSprite me
  mem = sprite(me.spriteNum).member

  -- how many degrees apart is each point
  angleDiff = 360/pNumPoints

  -- build vertex list
  list = []
  repeat with angle = 0 to pNumPoints-1
    p = circlePoint(angle*angleDiff,pRadius)
    add list, [#vertex: p]
  end repeat

  -- set the member
  mem.vertexList = list
  mem.closed = TRUE
end

-- the following handler returns the point on any circle
-- given the angle and radius
on circlePoint angle, radius
  a = (float(angle-90)/360.0)*2.0*pi()
  x = cos(a)*radius
  y = sin(a)*radius
  return point(x,y)
end
```

Figure 20.3 shows the use of this behavior. It resets the member used by the sprite as a polygon. If the same member is used in more than one sprite, the behaviors interfere with each other. Instead, create multiple copies of a vector shape and place each one on the Stage only once. The initial vector shapes can be anything, such as small rectangles or circles. The behavior resets the *vertexList* of the sprite, and makes sure it is closed. However, the fill color and type remain as they were before. A more complex behavior can set these, too.

Figure 20.3
These polygons were created with a polygon behavior which takes any vector shape and molds it into a polygon.

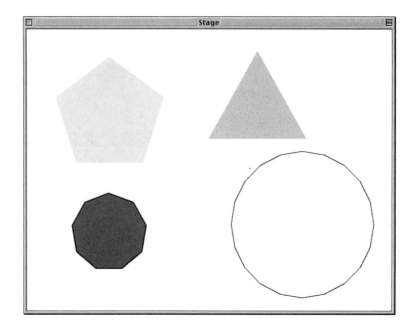

A little modification to this behavior gives you a handler that creates a star rather than a polygon. It just needs to set alternative outer and inner points. Figure 20.4 shows the result of this behavior.

```
property pNumPoints, pRadius

on getPropertyDescriptionList me
  list = [:]
  addProp list, #pNumPoints, [#comment: "Number of Points",¬
    #format: #integer, #default: 5]
  addProp list, #pRadius, [#comment: "Radius",¬
    #format: #integer, #default: 100]
  return list
end

on beginSprite me
  mem = sprite(me.spriteNum).member

  -- how many degrees apart is each point
  angleDiff = 360/pNumPoints

  -- build vertex list
  list = []
  repeat with starPoint = 0 to pNumPoints-1

    -- outer point location
    p = circlePoint (starPoint*angleDiff,pRadius)
    add list, [#vertex: p]
```

```
     -- inner point location
     p = circlePoint((starPoint+.5)*angleDiff,pRadius*.5)
     add list, [#vertex: p]
  end repeat

  -- set the member
  mem.vertexList = list
  mem.closed = TRUE
end

-- the following handler returns the point on any circle
-- given the angle and radius
on circlePoint angle, radius
  a = (float(angle-90)/360.0)*2.0*pi()
  x = cos(a)*radius
  y = sin(a)*radius
  return point(x,y)
end
```

Figure 20.4
These stars were created with a star behavior, which takes any vector shape and molds it into a star.

PART

VI

CH

20

All the previous handlers and behaviors draw a shape once, usually *on beginSprite,* and leave the vector shape alone. However, Lingo can just as easily redraw the vector shape each and every frame to create animated vector shapes.

A simple example draws a random shape. The following behavior draws a vector between 20 random points. The result is a messy scribble. However, it recreates itself on each frame to create a unusual animated effect. Check the movie on the CD-ROM to see it in action.

```
on exitFrame me
  mem = sprite(me.spriteNum).member

  list = []
  repeat with i = 1 to 20
    x = random(100)
    y = random(100)
    add list, [#vertex: point(x,y)]
  end repeat
  mem.vertexList = list
end
```

The same idea can be applied to the star shape behavior. Stars are sometimes known to twinkle. The following behavior redraws the star every frame, but with a different random point stretched slightly. The result, if done with the right color and size, is an animated twinkling star:

```
property pNumPoints, pRadius, pPointToMove, pPointMoveDiff, pPointMoveAmount,¬
pTwinkleSpeed, pTwinkleAmount

on getPropertyDescriptionList me
  list = [:]
  addProp list, #pNumPoints, [#comment: "Number of Points",¬
    #format: #integer, #default: 5]
  addProp list, #pRadius, [#comment: "Radius",¬
    #format: #integer, #default: 25]
  addProp list, #pTwinkleSpeed, [#comment: "Twinkle Speed",¬
    #format: #integer, #default: 1]
  addProp list, #pTwinkleAmount, [#comment: "Twinkle Amount",¬
    #format: #integer, #default: 3]
  return list
end

on beginSprite me
  moveNewPoint(me)
  mem = sprite(me.spriteNum).member
  mem.centerRegPoint = FALSE
  mem.originMode = #center
  mem.closed = TRUE
end

-- this handler decides which new point of the star
-- to twinkle
on moveNewPoint me
  repeat while TRUE
    r = random(pNumPoints)
    if r <> pPointToMove then exit repeat
  end repeat
  pPointToMove = r
  pPointMoveDiff = 0
  pPointMoveAmount = pTwinkleSpeed
end
```

```
on exitFrame me
  mem = sprite(me.spriteNum).member

  -- how many degrees apart is each point
  angleDiff = 360/pNumPoints

  -- build vertex list
  list = []
  repeat with starPoint = 1 to pNumPoints

    -- move twinkling point in or out
    if starPoint = pPointToMove then
      pPointMoveDiff = pPointMoveDiff + pPointMoveAmount
      if pPointMoveDiff > pTwinkleAmount then pPointMoveDiff = -pTwinkleSpeed
      if pPointMoveDiff <= 0 then moveNewPoint
      p = circlePoint(starPoint*angleDiff,pRadius+pPointMoveDiff)
    else

      -- keep non-twinkling point normal
      p = circlePoint(starPoint*angleDiff,pRadius)
    end if

    add list, [#vertex: p]
    p = circlePoint((starPoint+.5)*angleDiff,pRadius*.5)
    add list, [#vertex: p]
  end repeat

  -- set the member
  mem.vertexList = list
end

-- the following handler returns the point on any circle
-- given the angle and radius
on circlePoint angle, radius
  a = (float(angle-90)/360.0)*2.0*pi()
  x = cos(a)*radius
  y = sin(a)*radius
  return point(x,y)
end
```

The result looks just like the previous star shape behavior, but one point at a time is animating. First it moves a little bit out from the center, and then it moves back into place.

A more dramatic behavior is one that uses the handles of each vertex point. Because these handles measure the curve of the line coming into and going out of the vertex, they are very difficult to use. Changing the handles is easy enough, but getting them to do what you want is another matter. Even illustrators who have used vector editing programs for years can sometimes be at a loss to explain exactly how to use handles. They simply use them intuitively. There are mathematics behind these handles, but the complexities are beyond the scope of this book.

The following code shows a behavior that uses the #handle1 to create a curved look to many points along the bottom of a vector shape. The behavior then moves the vertex points downward to create a "curtain" or "dripping blood" effect. Figure 20.5 shows the result in mid-animation.

PART

VI

CH

20

```
property pNumPoints, pRadius, pVlist

on getPropertyDescriptionList me
  list = [:]
  addProp list, #pNumPoints, [#comment: "Number of Points",¬
      #format: #integer, #default: 25]
  addProp list, #pRadius, [#comment: "Radius",¬
      #format: #integer, #default: 12]
  return list
end

on beginSprite me
  pVlist = []

  -- space between drips
  spacing = 640/pNumPoints

  -- add top and sides
  add pVlist, [#vertex: point(640+spacing,0)]
  add pVlist, [#vertex: point(640+spacing,0)]
  add pVlist, [#vertex: point(0-spacing,0)]

  -- add drip spots along bottom
  repeat with i = 0 to pNumPoints
    add pVlist, [#vertex: point(i*spacing,0), ¬
#handle1: point(spacing/2,spacing)]
  end repeat

  -- set member
  mem = sprite(me.spriteNum).member
  mem.vertexList = pVlist
  mem.centerRegPoint = FALSE
  mem.originMode = #center
  mem.closed = TRUE
end

on exitFrame me
  -- change 20 vertex points at a time
  repeat with i = 1 to 20
    r = random(pNumPoints+1)+3
    pVlist[r][#vertex] = pVlist[r][#vertex] + ¬
      point(0,random(pRadius))
  end repeat
  sprite(me.spriteNum) .member.vertexList = pVlist
end
```

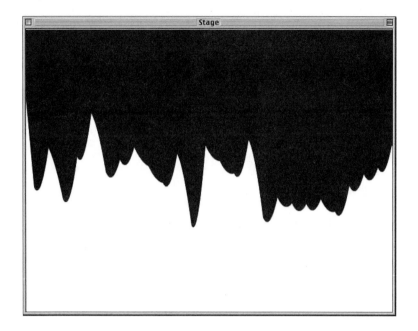

Figure 20.5
The dripping blood effect was created with a vector shape and a Lingo behavior that moves the vertex points down over time.

Another effect uses both the #handle1 and #handle2 properties to direct the curve of many points along a line. With each frame, the angle of the curve changes to make the point appear to roll over, like a wave. The final result, seen in Figure 20.6, is a sea-like graphic.

```
property pNumPoints, pRadius, pList, pOffset, pAngle

on getPropertyDescriptionList me
  list = [:]
  addProp list, #pNumPoints, [#comment: "Number of Points",¬
    #format: #integer, #default: 25]
  addProp list, #pRadius, [#comment: "Radius",¬
    #format: #integer, #default: 12]
  return list
end

on beginSprite me
  pOffset = 0
  pAngle = 0
end

on exitFrame me
  pList = []
  spacing = 680/pNumPoints
  pOffset = pOffset + 2
  if pOffset > spacing then pOffset = 0

  -- create bottom and sides
  add pList, [#vertex: point(680+spacing,0)]
  add pList, [#vertex: point(680+spacing,100)]
  add pList, [#vertex: point(0-spacing,100)]
```

```
  -- add wave points
  repeat with i = 0 to pNumPoints

    -- move the waves
    pAngle = pAngle - 1
    if pAngle < -90 then pAngle = 90

    -- get the handle
    h = circlePoint(pAngle,pRadius)
    h2 = circlePoint (pAngle+180,pRadius)

    add pList, [#vertex: point(i*spacing-pOffset,0), ¬
#handle1: h, #handle2: h2]
  end repeat

  -- set the member
  mem = sprite(me.spriteNum).member
  mem.vertexList = pList
  mem.centerRegPoint = FALSE
  mem.originMode = #center
  mem.closed = TRUE
end

-- the following handler returns the point on any circle
-- given the angle and radius
on circlePoint angle, radius
  a = (float(angle-90)/360.0)*2.0*pi()
  x = cos(a)*radius
  y = sin(a)*radius
  returnpoint(x,y)
end
```

Figure 20.6
The changing loca-
tions of the handles
for each vertex point
create animated
waves.

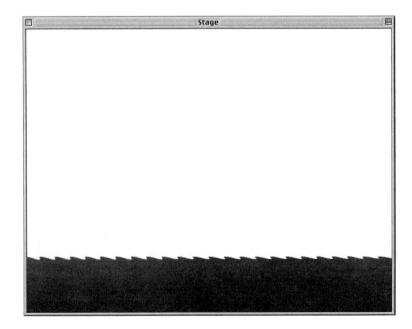

LEARNING ADVANCED VECTOR TECHNIQUES

One of the ways in which vector shape members are different from bitmaps is that, with vector shapes, you can actually tell whether a point is inside or outside a vector shape. You can do this with bitmaps and *the rollover* property, but only when the ink is set to matte and the mouse is at the location you are trying to detect.

The function *hitTest* enables you to specify a sprite and a Stage location. The returned value is either #background, #normal, or #button. The last value can be returned by only a Flash movie, not a vector shape. However, the other two values can be used to determine whether any point is inside or outside a shape, no matter how complex that shape is.

The following code shows a behavior that takes advantage of this feature. It assumes that there is a shape in sprite 1 that the behavior cannot move its sprite over. It looks for key presses and then moves its sprite accordingly. If it finds that the new location is inside the shape in that sprite, it does not allow the move to take place.

```
property px, py

on beginSprite me
  -- get initial location
  px = sprite(me.spriteNum).locH
  py = sprite(me.spriteNum).locV
end

on exitFrame me

  -- assume x doesn't change
  newx = px

  -- see if it does
  if keyPressed(123) then newx = px - 1
  if keyPressed(124) then newx = px + 1

  -- see if new x will hit the shape
  if hitTest(sprite(1),point(newx,py)) <> #normal then
    px = newx
  end if

  -- assume y doesn't change
  newy = py

  -- see if it does
  if keyPressed(125) then newy = py + 1
  if keyPressed(126) then newy = py - 1

  -- see if new y will hit the stage
  if hitTest(sprite(1),point(px,newy)) <> #normal then
    py = newy
  end if

  -- new location for the sprite
  sprite(me.spriteNum).loc = point(px,py)
end
```

A more complex behavior might have a parameter that specifies at which sprite the behavior should be looking. Or perhaps the behavior can specify a whole range of sprites.

TROUBLESHOOTING VECTOR LINGO

- When setting the *vertexList* with Lingo, be sure that it is a valid vertex list, with all the properties spelled correctly and the values in the proper format.
- If you are animating by using Lingo to change the *vertexList* while the movie is playing, the *centerRegPoint* should be set to FALSE, the *originMode* set to "center", and the vector's scale mode set to "auto-size". Otherwise, the sprite appears to move around the Stage as the shape changes.
- If you are trying to apply a fill color to a vector shape, make sure that the *closed* property is set to TRUE. Otherwise, there is no area to fill.
- The more vertex points in a vector shape, the more slowly it draws. Anti-aliased vector shapes also draw slower than non–anti-aliased shapes.
- You usually want to set a vector shape's sprite ink to Background Transparent. Leaving it as Copy applies the background color of the member to the whole rectangle on the Stage.

DID YOU KNOW?

- Although vector shape members have only one continuous curve per member, you can create more complex Freehand or Illustrator-like images by using several vector shapes on top of each other.
- EPS files are actually lists of vertex points and handles. If you get to know the EPS file format well enough, you could write a Lingo script that reads these files and creates vector shape members based on the data.
- Vector shapes and Flash members, when placed in a sprite, can be rotated, skewed, and scaled like bitmaps. However, because they are made of curved lines, enlarging them does not degrade the image resolution.
- You can use the Lingo command *put showProps(member x)* in the Message window, where x is a vector shape member, to get a complete list of all its properties. The same is true for Flash members.

PART **VII**

USING ADVANCED LINGO

CHAPTER **21**

CONTROLLING THE DIRECTOR ENVIRONMENT

In this chapter

Lingo provides many ways to control and react to the playback environment. You can create your own menus and change the cursor. You can detect when the computer has been left alone for a period of time and do something when that happens. You can even determine what type of computer the user has or what time it is, and have the movie react accordingly.

USING MENUS

When you create a projector, it runs inside a plain window. On the Mac, it is a simple rectangle. In Windows, it looks like a typical Window, but without a menu bar. In order to make your Projector look and act more like a normal program, you have to add a menu bar.

CREATING MENUS

You can add a menu bar to any projector with the *installMenu* command. This command places the standard Mac menu bar at the top of the screen on Macs, but only with the items you specify. In Windows, it places a standard menu bar at the top of the Projector's window.

While you are authoring, the *installMenu* command replaces Director's menu bar from the time the command is issued until the movie stops. This makes it very easy to test. In Shockwave, *installMenu* has no effect at all.

To use *installMenu*, you first need to create a field cast member that contains the menu description. Here are the typical contents of such a field:

```
menu: @
menu: File
Open/O¦myOpenHandler
(-
Quit/Q¦halt
menu: Edit
Cut(
Copy(
Paste(
Clear(
menu: Navigation
Main Menu/M¦go to frame "main"
Chapter 1/1¦go to frame "one"
Chapter 2/2¦go to frame "two"
Chapter 3/3¦go to frame "three"
```

The first line of this text, "menu: @", tells Director to place the Apple menu, with all its contents, in the menu bar. This is for Macs only. In Windows, this command results in a small menu labeled with a block character.

The second line creates a menu labeled "File". The next three lines place three items in this menu. The first is the item "Open". The character after the forward slash is the command key shortcut. So a Command+O on the Mac or a Ctrl+O in Windows acts as a shortcut for selecting this menu item. After the vertical bar, created while holding down the Shift and the backslash key, is the Lingo command that will execute. In this case it is a custom movie handler called "myOpenHandler". The next line, a simple "(-" places a dividing line in the menu. The third item in the menu is "Quit", which uses "Q" as a shortcut and executes the Lingo *halt* command.

The next menu is the "Edit" menu. All the items in this menu are grayed out, or inactive, and made so by the "(" at the end of each line.

> **Note**
>
> It is always a good idea to include a "File" and "Edit" menu every time you make custom menus. Almost all programs use them, even when the commands in them are grayed out. Having them there provides user interface consistency.

The last menu is called "Navigation" and contains four lines that take the users to four different frames. The resulting menu looks like the menu shown in Figure 21.1.

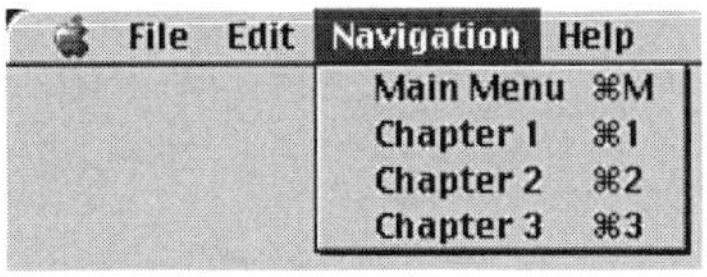

Figure 21.1
This custom menu was created with a field member and the *installMenu* command.

To actually use this menu, you just need to specify its member in the *installMenu* command. A likely place for this is the *on startMovie* handler:

```
on startMovie
  installMenu member("menu")
end
```

All the special characters in the menu field can be quite confusing. There are actually a lot more of them. Table 21.1 lists them all and describes what each one does.

TABLE 21.1   MENU DEFINITION SYMBOLS

Symbol	Example	Description
@	menu: @	Creates the Apple menu on the Mac, complete with the existing Apple menu items.
!v	!vMusic	Places a check mark next to an item.
<B	Copy<B	Sets the item to bold.
<I	Copy<I	Sets the item to italic.
<U	Copy<U	Sets the item to underlined.
<O	Copy<O	Sets the item to outlined.
<S	Shadow	Sets the item to shadow styled.

continues

Symbol	Example	Description
TABLE 21.1	CONTINUED	
|	Quit|halt	Associates a Lingo handler or command with the item.
/	Quit/Q	Adds a Command/Ctrl key shortcut.
(	Copy(	Grays out the item and makes it unselectable.
(-	(-	Creates a dividing line in the menu.

The styling items listed in Table 21.1 are available on the Mac only. Windows menus do not accommodate this sort of styling.

CONTROLLING MENUS

You can also use Lingo commands to control the custom menu after it exists. The menu bar itself is treated like an object, and is referred to by the keyword *menu* and the name or number of the menu. For instance, to get the name of the second menu from the left:

```
put the name of menu 2
-- "File"
```

Note that you must use the old syntax with a "the" rather than the new Director 7 dot syntax. The menu functionality in Director was not updated with the new version, so the dot syntax is not recognized.

To get the total number of menus in the menu bar, use *the number of menus*:

```
put the number of menus
-- 4
```

You can also get the name of any menu item in a menu by using the *menuitem* keyword:

```
put the name of menuitem 1 of menu 4
-- "Main Menu"
```

As you might expect, you can use *the number of menuitems* to get the total number of items of any menu. The next example also demonstrates how you can refer to a menu by its name:

```
put the number of menuitems in menu "Navigation"
-- 4
```

You can also set the name of a menu item. However, you cannot set the name of a menu:

```
the name of menuitem 3 of menu 2 = "Exit"
```

Three more properties—*the checkMark*, *the enabled*, and *the script* —enable you to change three other aspects of individual menu items. The first property enables you to place a check mark next to the item. The second enables you to dim an item and make it unusable. The last property enables you to alter the script for an item.

Another method for changing the menu is to update your menu description field by using Lingo string and text member commands and then reapplying the *installMenu*.

→ **See** "Using Text Members and Fields," Chapter 16, "Controlling Text," for more information on using fields

Using Cursors

There are three ways to change the cursor in Director 7. The first is to use the *cursor* command with a built-in cursor. The second is to use the *cursor* command with one or two bitmaps that represent a black-and-white cursor. The third is to use the Cursor Xtra to make colored or animated cursors.

Using Built-In Cursors

Using one of the 30 built-in cursors is simple with the *cursor* command. All you need to do is give the *cursor* command one of the cursor numbers to use. For instance, to change the cursor to a watch on the Mac or an hourglass in Windows, use the following:

```
cursor(4)
```

A simple behavior that changes the cursor to a finger when the user rolls over a sprite looks like this:

```
on mouseEnter me
  cursor(280)
end

on mouseLeave me
  cursor(0)
end
```

Use the cursor number 0 to return control of the cursor to normal. Usually this means that the cursor will return to the arrow.

Table 21.2 shows all the available cursors. Figure 21.2 shows what these cursors look like on the Mac. Windows cursors appear slightly different. For instance, the watch cursor appears as an hourglass cursor in Windows. You should test your cursors in a cross-platform environment if consistency is important.

TABLE 21.2 CURSOR NUMBERS

Cursor Name	Cursor Number
Arrow	-1
I-Beam	1
Crosshair	2
Crossbar	3

PART

VII

CH

21

continues

Table 21.2   Continued

Cursor Name	Cursor Number
Watch/Hourglass	4
Blank	200
Help	254
Finger	280
Hand	260
Closed Hand	290
No Drop Hand	291
Copy Closed Hand	292
Pencil	256
Eraser	257
Select	258
Bucket	259
Lasso	272
Dropper	281
Air Brush	301
Zoom In	302
Zoom Out	303
Vertical Size	284
Horizontal Size	285
Diagonal Size	286
White Arrow (Mac)	293
Black Arrow with white outline (Windows)	293
Magnify	304
Wait Mouse 1 (Mac)	282
Wait Mouse 2 (Mac)	283

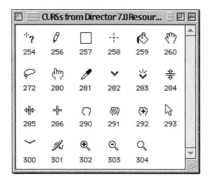

Figure 21.2
Some of the cursors Director uses, taken from the Director resource file using ResEdit.

CUSTOM BITMAP CURSORS

The second way to create cursors is to use bitmaps. With bitmaps you can define the cursor any way you want, as long as it is black and white and static.

The key to doing this is to create two bitmap members. Each member should be no more than 16 by 16 pixels in size, and be 1-bit in bit depth. The first member is the actual cursor. The second member is the mask for the cursor. In that second member, the black pixels are the mask for the cursor, whereas the white pixels are transparent.

The two bitmaps should line up with each other according to their registration points. The location of the registration point is the actual hot spot of the cursor, so be careful where you place it. Figure 21.3 shows two Paint windows, one with the cursor and one with the mask.

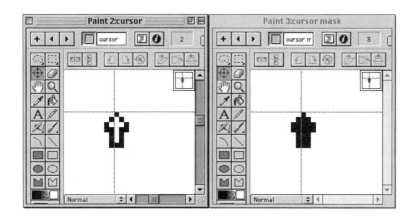

Figure 21.3
Two Paint windows show each of the two parts of a custom cursor. The registration points show the hot spot for the cursor.

After you have these two members, you can use the *cursor* command, as before, but with a list as the parameter. Here is an example:

```
cursor([member "cursor", member "cursor mask"])
```

If the bitmaps are not 1-bit, or a member name is wrong, the *cursor* command simply does nothing.

CURSOR XTRA

The Cursor Xtra, which was introduced with Director 6.5, enables you to build custom cursors from one or more 8-bit color bitmaps. The way you create this type of cursor is by using the Cursor Properties Editor, shown in Figure 21.4.

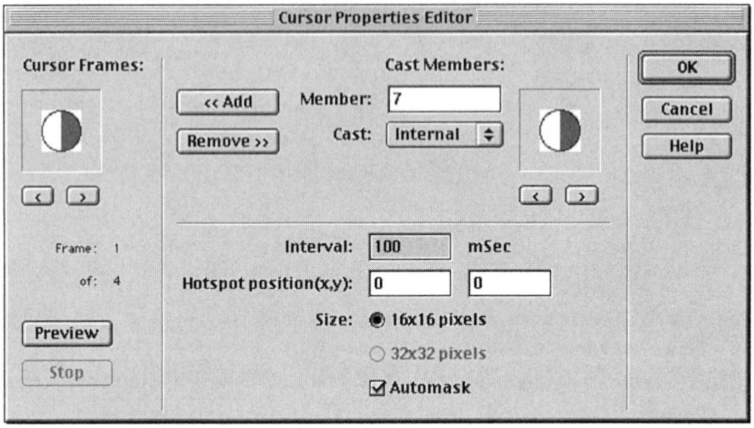

Figure 21.4
The Cursor Properties Editor enables you to create and modify animated cursors.

Adding cast members to a cursor is quite easy. Just use the Cast Members section of the dialog box to find the right member, and then use the Add button to add it. You can also set the speed of the animation and the hotspot location. Check the Automask feature if you do not want the cursor to be transparent.

After you have created the cursor, you can use the *cursor* command, but this time with a single cast member as the parameter:

```
cursor(member("Custom Cursor"))
```

→ **See** "Adding Cursors," Chapter 8, "Other Member Types," for some background on creating custom cursors

USING TIMEOUTS

Suppose you are making a kiosk that sits in a public place. Users are meant to walk up to the kiosk and start on screen one. However, it is impossible to get users to press an "I'm Done!" button when they are finished using the kiosk. You just can't rely on it. The result usually is that the next user walks up and sees the middle of the presentation.

One way to handle this is for the movie to detect when the computer has been idle for some time, and then automatically return to the beginning of the movie.

Director has some Lingo commands to handle this request. The primary one is the handler *on timeOut*. This handler is called after three minutes of inaction. If the handler does not exist, nothing happens. Here is a typical *on timeOut* handler:

```
on timeOut
  go to frame "intro"
end
```

> **Note**
>
> This handler needs to be placed in a movie script. It does not work if it is in a behavior.

Some movie properties can be used to alter how the *on timeout* script is called. For instance, if you want the timeout to happen after two minutes rather than three, use *the timeoutLength* property. Its value is in ticks, or 1/60ths of a second:

```
the timeOutLength = 60*60*2
```

The timeout timer can be accessed with *the timeoutLapsed* property. It tells you how much time has passed since the last action. This timer is reset whenever the mouse is moved or a key on the keyboard is pressed. However, you can turn either or both of these conditions off by setting *the timeoutMouse* or *the timeoutKeyDown* properties to FALSE.

One further modification you can make to timeouts is the handler that is called. Usually it is the *on timeout* handler. However, you can set it to something else with *the timeoutScript* property. Just set it to a string that is the name of a movie script handler:

```
the timeOutScript = "myTimeOutHandler"
```

For most uses, you won't need to set *the timeOutScript* and can just use *on timeOut*. However, you can use it if you have several different ways in which you want to handle timeouts, depending on where in the program the user left the computer.

LEARNING ABOUT THE COMPUTER

Many other movie properties can be accessed to tell you something about the computer on which Director, a Projector, or a Shockwave applet is currently running. The following is a list of these properties:

- the platform—This returns either "Macintosh,PowerPC" or "Windows,32" depending on which platform the movie is running on.
- the runMode—This returns either "Author", "Projector", "Plugin", or "Java Applet". The first tells you that the movie is running in Director, the second when it is running as a Projector, the third option refers to Shockwave, and the fourth tells when it is running as a Java Applet.
- the colorDepth—This returns the bit depth of the current monitor being used by the movie. Examples are 8, 16, 24, or 32.
- the environment—Returns a list with the values for the three preceding properties.
- the desktopRectList—Returns a list of rectangles that correspond to the one or more monitors connected to the computer.
- quickTimeVersion()—Not a property, but a function that returns the version of QuickTime on the computer. It returns only "2.1.2" if the version is before version 3.0.
- version—Not a property either, but actually a persistent global variable automatically created when Director starts. It contains the version number of the Director engine, whether it is Director, a Projector, or Shockwave. An example would be "7.0".

PART

VII

CH

21

You can use these properties to make decisions about what the movie should do if the user does not have a computer capable of performing the tasks you want it to. For instance, to test whether the computer is set to 16-bit color or better, you might do this:

```
on startMovie
  if the colorDepth < 16 then
    alert "Please set your monitor to 16-bit."
    halt
  end if
end
```

Or, if you want to make sure that the user's monitor is at least 800 pixels wide, you can test *the deskTopRectList*'s first item's width. Because most users have only one monitor, and those with two will rarely have their primary monitor set smaller than 800 pixels across, this is a good test.

```
on startMovie
  if (the deskTopRectList)[1].width < 800 then
    alert "Please set your monitor to 800 pixels across."
    halt
  end if
end
```

→ **See** "Designing for a Target Machine," Chapter 34, "Performance Issues," for examples that use machine information

TELLING TIME

Lingo has several ways to tell the date and time. First, there is *the date* property. This system property is a little different, in that you can preface it with the terms *short, long,* or *abbr.*

```
put the date
-- "12/9/98"
put the short date
-- "12/9/98"
put the long date
-- "Wednesday, December 9, 1998"
put the abbr date
-- "Wed, Dec 9, 1998"
```

The *abbr* prefix can also be spelled *abbrev* or *abbreviated.* You can use the returned strings as is, or use chunk expressions to get pieces of them:

```
put (the long date).item[1]
-- "Wednesday"
put (the long date).item[2].word[1]
-- "December"
the itemDelimiter = "/"
put integer((the date).item[2])
-- 9
```

There is also a *the time* property that works in a similar way. However, only the *long* prefix makes any difference in the result:

```
put the time
-- "9:18 PM"
put the short time
```

```
-- "9:18 PM"
put the long time
-- "9:18:43 PM"
put the abbrev time
-- "9:18 PM"
```

Note

> The string format of *the date* depends on your computer's settings. If you check in the control panels in both Mac and Windows, you can see that the user has many options as to how dates will be displayed. Director reflects these preferences in *the date*.

You can also use chunk expressions to get interesting parts of *the time*:

```
put (the time).word[1]
-- "9:20"
the itemDelimiter = ":"
put integer((the time).word[1].item[2])
-- 20
put integer((the long time).word[1].item[3])
-- 57
```

While *the time* and *the date* are great for getting ready-to-use strings and occasionally an integer, there is a better way to work with dates. The property *the systemDate* returns a new type of structure: a *date*.

```
put the systemDate
-- date( 1998, 12, 9 )
```

As you might expect, this *date* structure has three properties that you can extract: the *year*, the *month*, and the *day*:

```
d = the systemDate
put d.day
-- 9
put d.year
-- 1998
put d.month
-- 12
```

What is even more impressive about the *date* structure is that you can add integers to it and it does all the calculations for you. Here are some examples:

```
put the systemDate
-- date( 1998, 12, 9 )
put the systemDate + 1
-- date( 1998, 12, 10 )
d = the systemDate
put d + 10
-- date( 1998, 12, 19 )
put d + 30
-- date( 1999, 1, 8 )
put d + 365*3
-- date( 2001, 12, 8 )
put d - 365
-- date( 1997, 12, 9 )
```

Using the *date* structure, you can perform all sorts of interesting calculations. Here is a handler that computes the number of days since a certain date. Give it your birth date, as a *date* structure, and it computes the number of days you have been alive:

```
on daysAlive birthDate
  t = 0
  repeat while TRUE
    birthDate = birthDate + 1
    t = t + 1
    if birthDate = the systemDate then
      return t
    end if
  end repeat
end
```

In addition to dates and times, there is the very important *the ticks* property. This is the amount of time, in 1/60ths of a second, since Director, the Projector, or the Shockwave applet started.

Although it is not very useful information to display to the user, it is very useful for timing animation. Here is a short handler that creates a pause for two seconds:

```
on pauseForTwo
  t = the ticks + 120
  repeat while (the ticks < t)
  end repeat
end
```

Director 7 has a new companion for *the ticks*: *the milliseconds*. This measures the same amount of time, but with 1000ths of a second instead.

Another property, called *the timer*, also uses ticks. The difference between this property and *the ticks* is that you can use *startTimer* at any time to reset *the timer*. This is more of a convenience, rather than an added feature. There is really nothing that you can do with *the timer* that you cannot do with a variable, some math, and *the ticks*. Here is a handler that pauses for two seconds, but uses *the timer*:

```
on pauseForTwo
  startTimer
  repeat while (the timer < 120)
  end repeat
end
```

MEMORY MANAGEMENT

Several Lingo commands and properties enable you to see and control how memory is used. Controlling memory mostly has to do with loading and unloading cast members from memory.

MEMBER LOADING

All cast members are present in either the Director movie's internal Cast, an external Cast, or an external file that is linked in a Cast. This simply means that they are in a file on the hard drive or CD-ROM. For cast members to be displayed on the Stage, they first have to be loaded into the computer's memory.

Director takes care of this automatically. If a sprite needs a cast member, Director checks to see whether it is present in memory, and if not, load it into memory. As Director uses up more and more memory, it occasionally removes a cast member from memory if it is no longer present on the Stage. This clears room for other members to be loaded.

Although this is automatic, you do have a set of Lingo commands and properties that give you control over this loading and unloading. This can come in handy when speed is critical. After all, it takes time for Director to do this loading and unloading. If you know you will need a cast member soon, and have the time to load it now, a Lingo command forces the load and the member will be ready to go when needed.

Before looking at the Lingo commands, take a look at a typical Member Properties dialog box. Figure 21.5 shows one for a bitmap member.

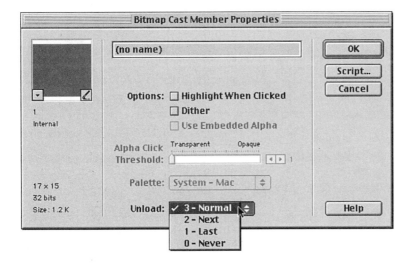

Figure 21.5
The Member Properties dialog box for almost all member types includes an Unload setting as a pop-up menu.

The Unload setting can be set to one of four options: 0-Normal, 1-Next, 2-Last, or 3-Never. The last option, 0-Never, keeps the member in memory, after it is loaded the first time, and ensures that it is never unloaded. The next setting, 1-Last, keeps the member in memory as long as possible. The 2-Next setting flags the member for removal as soon as it is not needed. The 3-Normal setting removes the member after all 2-Next members are removed, but before 1-Last members are removed.

It is almost never worthwhile to use any setting other than 3-Normal. However, if you have a member that is constantly being put on and pulled off the Stage, and the speed of the movie seems to be affected by the loading and unloading, setting this member to 1-Last might be a good idea.

You can set this property with the Lingo *purgePriority* property. Just use the number, such as 0, 1, 2, or 3:

```
member("large image").purgePriority = 2
```

The Lingo commands to control loading and unloading are pretty straightforward. To load a member into memory, simply issue a *preLoadMember* command:

```
preLoadMember "large image"
```

You can also specify a range of members to preload. This command loads both members specified by the range numbers, plus any members that are in between them in the Cast:

```
preLoadMember "large image 1", "large image 7"
```

You can even use the *preLoadMember* command by itself. In this case, Director attempts to load all members in the Cast until it runs out of memory.

There is also a *preLoad* command. This takes frame numbers rather than member names. By itself, it tries to load all the members used in the current frame of the movie to the last frame of the movie. This includes only members actually in the Score. Any members not in the Score, but used by Lingo, such as button state images, are not loaded.

You can also specify two frames in the *preLoad* command, and it will load all the members used in those two frames and any in between. Specifying only one frame loads all the members from the current frame to the one specified.

But what if you are about to jump to another movie with the *go* or *play* command? Because those members are not in the current movie, you cannot use the *preLoadMember* or *preLoad* commands. However, you can use the *preLoadMovie* command. This command loads all the members in the first frame of the new movie.

The commands *unLoad*, *unLoadMember*, and *unLoadMovie* work the opposite of the previous commands by unloading members from memory.

A good rule of thumb with manually loading and unloading members is to experiment. Try running the movie with no special memory management commands, and then try it with your commands. See whether it really makes a difference.

MEMORY INFORMATION

Several functions can tell you how much memory is available. The simple *freeBytes()* function returns the number of available bytes in Director or the Projector's memory space.

A more useful function is the *freeblock()*, which returns the size of the largest contiguous block of memory. Because cast members need to be loaded in a continuous block of memory, you can use this to make sure that such a block exists.

The *size* property of a member returns the size, in bytes, of a member. You can combine this with *freeblock()* to determine whether there is enough room for the member in memory. For instance, if you find that a huge sound member is having trouble playing on a machine with low memory, you can also have a smaller sound ready to play in its place. The following bit of code can decide which one to use:

```
if freeBytes() > member("large sound").size then
  puppetSound "large sound"
else
  puppetSound "small sound"
end
```

You can also use the function *ramNeeded* to determine how much memory is needed for a series of frames. This handler measures how much memory is available to determine whether the movie will jump over a set of frames:

```
if ramNeeded(10,14) > the freeBytes then
  go to frame 15
else
  go to frame 10
end
```

A system property, *the memorySize*, returns the number of total bytes available to Director or the Projector. You can use this to test that the program is running with enough memory to perform a memory-intense function.

You can also get the movie's file size using the *movieFileSize* property. Another property, *the movieFileFreeSize*, returns the amount of space in the file that is not in use. This extra space is what is thrown away when you choose File, Save And Compact.

→ **See** "Improving Performance," Chapter 34, for examples of loading and unloading cast members

LAUNCHING OTHER APPLICATIONS

You can use Director to launch other applications on the user's computer system. Doing this is easy. All you need to do is use the *open* command:

```
open "Macintosh HD:Applications:SimpleText"
```

It seems simple enough, but note that you have to give the full pathname of the application. This can be inconvenient, even if you are trying to run something as simple as Mac SimpleText or Windows NotePad. Sometimes simple Windows applications, such as NotePad, can be launched without a pathname, but you cannot count on that.

You can use *open* to launch an application with a pre-defined starting document. For instance, you can launch SimpleText with the document "text file" in this manner:

```
open "Macintosh HD:text file" with "Macintosh HD:Applications:SimpleText"
```

PART

VII

CH

21

However, there are problems with this form of the *open* command as well. On the Mac, if SimpleText is already running, and you try to use the *open* command to open a file with SimpleText, SimpleText simply ignores the command. SimpleText appears, but the document does not open. In Windows this is not a problem because you cannot have NotePad running with no Windows open.

The news is better when it comes to Web browsers, because the *gotoNetPage* command actually launches the user's default browser and goes to a pre-defined Web location. You can read more about this command in Chapter 22, "Shockwave and Internet Access."

→ **See** "Controlling the Web Browser with Lingo," Chapter 22, for more information about launching browsers

OTHER ENVIRONMENT LINGO

Director also has the capability to turn itself off. As a matter of fact, on Macs, it can even turn the computer off. The *quit* command does just what you would expect: it acts just like choosing File, Quit or Exit from a typical application. The Projector instantly quits. In Shockwave, the movie stops.

The *quit* command works very well. As a matter of fact, it works too well. If you issue a *quit* command while in Director, the command tries to quit Director. This can be annoying while you are authoring.

Instead, the *halt* command should be used in place of *quit*. In Director, the *halt* command stops the movie. In Projectors, the *halt* command acts just like the *quit* command and will quit the Projector.

If you are building a kiosk on a Mac, you may want to also use the *restart* or *shutDown* commands. They perform the same actions as the menu items in the Mac Finder's Special menu. You can use these to enable a store owner or museum curator to shut down the computer at night, or restart it. This way, users don't have to exit the Projector and then use the Finder.

You can also use these commands in association with code that reads the time. This way, you can automatically shut down or restart the computer at a certain time, or after a period of inaction. Here is a handler that shuts the computer down at 9:00 p.m. It can be called periodically from an *on exitFrame* handler:

```
on checkTimeShutDown
  if the time = "9:00 PM" then
    shutDown
  end if
end
```

TROUBLESHOOTING ENVIRONMENT LINGO

- Don't rely on the playback computer using the same time settings as yours. Months and days can easily be reversed in *the date* and different item delimiters can easily be set by the user. Even if the target machines are in the same country, users sometimes play with the settings. Use *the system date* when you can.

- Developers waste a lot of time loading and unloading Lingo. Determine whether and precisely where you are having a speed problem before trying to solve it with one of these commands. Director is probably already performing optimally.

- Make sure any custom cursor cast members conform to the required bit depths. Plain custom cursors need to be 1-bit and animated cursor members need to be 8-bit. They will not work otherwise.

- Double-check the text in your menu description fields if you are having trouble. The *installMenu* command is very literal and does not forgive many mistakes.

- Don't forget that adding an Apple menu on the Mac means that a Windows Projector will have a strange menu added as well. You might want to keep separate Mac and Windows menu description fields. In Windows, place any "About" menu item in the traditional "Help" menu, rather than in the Apple menu.

DID YOU KNOW?

- You can build the menu description field with Lingo. Just use string commands and other string Lingo to create or alter the field, and then use *installMenu* to make the changes take effect. This way, you can have a dynamically changing menu bar.

- If you want a cursor of unusual size, you can simply use cursor number 200 to turn off the cursor, and then a sprite in the highest channel can be set to follow the mouse around. The user won't be able to tell that the sprite is not a cursor; it will behave just like one.

- You can use the *version* global with Shockwave to redirect users who have various versions of Shockwave. For instance, you can make a Director 5 Shockwave movie that checks the version and uses *gotoNetMovie* to run a Director 5, Director 6, or Director 7 movie.

- Many more functions exist in the Buddy API Xtra that tell you about the user's system, and even control parts of it. See Chapter 25, "Xtras," for details.

CHAPTER 22

SHOCKWAVE AND INTERNET ACCESS

In this chapter

When Shockwave was introduced in 1995, it was simply a plug-in for Netscape Navigator that enabled the browser to play compressed Director movies. Since then, the term "Shockwave" has grown to encompass just about anything that has to do with both Director and the Internet.

At the same time, Director has grown to incorporate all aspects of Shockwave into the authoring environment and Projectors. Early on, only movies running under a Web browser had capabilities such as accessing Internet information or controlling browser locations. Now, anything made with Director can do this.

This means that all Shockwave commands work while you are authoring in Director and in Projectors. In cases where commands are supposed to control the Web browser, a Projector even launches the user's default Web browser automatically.

Shockwave Lingo can be divided into four parts. The first deals with controlling the Web browser. The second is about getting and sending information over the Internet. The third is about communicating with the HTML page. Finally, the last part is about communicating directly with the server and other Shockwave clients.

CONTROLLING THE WEB BROWSER WITH LINGO

The primary command for forcing the Web browser to go to another Web page is *gotoNetPage*. This command can be used with a relative location, or with an absolute location if the location starts with `http://`. For instance, if the user is already at `http://clevermedia.com`, the two commands are identical:

```
gotoNetPage("http://clevermedia.com/resources/")
gotoNetPage("resources/")
```

You can also use a target frame or window with *gotoNetPage*. Web developers are familiar with how to use targets. Basically, every browser window, and every frame inside a window, has a name. A target tag modifier can specify which of these targets should receive the *gotoNetPage* signal.

If you have developed your own set of windows or frames with HTML, you already know the names of these targets. However, there are a few names, such as "_blank" and "_top" that are reserved for special purposes. Table 22.1 shows their usage.

TABLE 22.1   RESERVED HTTP TARGET NAMES

Name	Action
_blank	Creates a new, blank window without a name.
_self	The new page loads in the current frame. This works even if the HTML pages use the BASE structure.
_parent	Loads the new page one level up in the frame set, replacing the current frame and all its siblings.
_top	Loads in the current window, replacing any and all frames there.

Here are examples of a *gotoNetPage* commands that use a target:

```
gotoNetPage("mypage.html","_blank")
gotoNetPage("http://clevermedia.com","_top")
gotoNetPage("http://clevermedia.com","mainframe")
```

If you are planning to use this command in a Projector, you may want to have more control over which browser is launched. Director uses the browser specified in the network preferences, or the system's default browser if none is specified. You can check the path of the browser with the *browserName()* function:

```
put browserName()
-- "Macintosh HD:Netscape Communicator Folder:Netscape Communicator"
```

You can also set this path with the *browserName* command:

```
browserName "Macintosh HD:Other Browser"
```

You can let the user select the browser application if you use the *displayOpen* function of the FileIO Xtra, and then use the *browserName* command with the results.

If, for some reason, you want to disable the Projector's capability to launch a browser, use the *browserName* command with this odd syntax:

```
browserName(#enabled, FALSE)
```

Use a TRUE in place of the FALSE to enable browser launching.

In addition to telling the browser which page to display, you can replace the current Shockwave movie with a new one. The *gotoNetMovie* command is the network equivalent to *go*. It loads a new movie from the network and replaces the current one directly in the page:

```
gotoNetMovie("newmovie.dcr")
gotoNetMovie("http://clevermedia.com/newmovie.dcr")
```

You can use both relative and absolute pathnames, as you can see. You can even specify a frame in the new movie to jump to. Just place a "#" after the filename and then the name of the frame label.

```
gotoNetMovie("newmovie.dcr#intro")
```

When the *gotoNetMovie* command is used, the current movie continues to play until the new movie has been loaded. If you issue another *gotoNetMovie* command, it cancels the first command and replaces the current movie.

→ **See** "Text Files and the FileIO Xtra," Chapter 16, "Controlling Text," for information on save and reading files from the hard drive

GETTING TEXT OVER THE INTERNET

Shockwave Lingo enables you to get many forms of media over the Internet or an intranet. For bitmaps, getting an external image is as easy as specifying its location. Getting text, however, is a little more complex.

You might get text from another file on the Internet to store textual data in an external file so that non-Director users in your company can update this data. This technique would work with the numbers that make up a chart, for example. You might also import text data from another source, such as a weather report or a small text database.

The primary command for getting text over the Internet is *getNetText*. But this command cannot stand alone. It simply initiates the call to the network. You have to use a series of commands and functions to perform the whole operation.

After the *getNetText* is issued, a *netDone* function tells you when the text has been received. Then, you use *netTextResult* to get the text and store it in a variable or member.

However, you cannot use *getNetText* and then simply lock the movie in a *repeat* loop until *netDone* returns TRUE. A *repeat* loop monopolizes the computer and limits its capability to actually get the text. It will be so busy running the *repeat* loop that it will never have the time to do the network functions.

The proper way to get text is to issue the *getNetText* call, and then let the movie run. It can even loop on a frame to appear paused. Remember that looping on a frame is completely different than using a *repeat* loop inside a handler. While looping, the movie will allow the network functions to complete and the text to be received.

Here is an example in two frames. Each frame has an *on exitFrame* script placed in the frame script channel. The first one initiates the network call:

```
on exitFrame
  global gNetID
  gNetID = getNetText("http://clevermedia.com")
end
```

As you can see, *getNetText* is actually a function. It returns a number that corresponds to the network identification number for this network function. Because Director can perform more than one network function—such as *getNetText*—at a time, these ID numbers are needed to refer to them in the future. This number is likely to be 1 in this case, unless you have already performed a network function.

The next frame contains code that checks to see whether the network function corresponding to the variable "gNetID" is complete. If so, it gets the text, and then moves on. If not, it keeps looping on the frame:

```
on exitFrame
  global gNetID

  -- check to see if text has arrived
  if netDone(gNetID) then
```

```
      -- it has, so get it
      text = netTextResult(gNetID)
      put text

      -- move the movie forward
      go to the frame + 1
   else

      -- text is not here yet, keep looping
      go to the frame
   end if
end
```

It might also be a good idea to check to make sure that the system did not experience any problems in getting the text. You can use the *netError* function immediately after you have confirmed that the operation has been completed with *netDone*. For instance, you can add this code:

```
if netError(gNetID) <> 0 then
   alert "An error occurred trying to get the text."
   halt
end if
```

A 0, obviously, means there is no error. However, any other number means there is a problem. Table 22.2 shows all the possible errors.

TABLE 22.2 THE NETERROR CODES

Code	Meaning
0	Operation completed successfully.
4	The required network Xtras are not installed.
5	Bad MOA Interface. Probably same as 4.
6	Bad location. Or, could be same as 4.
20	Browser detected an error.
4146	Connection could not be established with the remote host.
4149	Data supplied by the server was in an unexpected format.
4150	Unexpected early closing of connection.
4154	Operation could not be completed due to timeout.
4155	Not enough memory available to complete the transaction.
4156	Protocol reply to request indicates an error in the reply.
4157	Transaction failed to be authenticated.
4159	Invalid URL.
4164	Could not create a socket.
4165	Requested object could not be found.

continues

Table 22.2	Continued
Code	**Meaning**
4166	Generic proxy failure.
4167	Transfer was intentionally interrupted by client.
4242	Download stopped by a *netAbort* command.
4836	Download stopped for an unknown reason, possibly a network error, or the download was abandoned.

→ **See** "Information Processing and Display," Chapter 31, "Shockwave Applets," for an example that uses text on the Internet

Sending Text

Since the introduction of Shockwave in 1995, movies have been able to send text over the Internet. However, until Director 7, there were no commands to do this. Instead, a trick was used to send information to server CGI scripts using *getNetText*. This trick is still a great way to communicate with the server. Director 7 also includes a new command that enables the movie to *post* information to a server in the same manner as an HTML page form.

Using *getNetText* to Send Text

It seems confusing, but you can send text by getting text. The *getNetText* command is used to get text information from a server. However, in doing so, you can give information to the server. It is similar to the way that Lingo functions work. A function returns information, but it can also accept information as a parameter.

Here is a typical *getNetText* call. It is asking for an HTML page on a Web server:

```
getNetText("http://clevermedia.com/test.txt")
```

You can also use *getNetText* to call a CGI program. A CGI program is a small computer program, usually written in a language called Perl, that resides on the server. The output of a Perl program is usually text, such as an HTML page:

```
getNetText("http://clevermedia.com/cgibin/echo.cgi")
```

In this case the CGI program returns text, just as the call to "test.txt" did previously. Neither the browser nor Director cares that the server had to run a program rather than just serve up a text file.

CGI programs can do much more than just serve up static text. They can actually take some data and then use it. For instance, they can store data in a file on the server. Information can be given to a CGI program by simply placing a "?" after the Web location, followed by text:

```
getNetText("http://clevermedia.com/cgibin/echo.cgi?gary")
```

In this case the information "gary" was sent to the server. The Perl program on the other end just needs to look for it, get it, and then do something with it. Here is the Perl program that sits on the server:

```
#!/usr/bin/perl
$invar = $ENV{'QUERY_STRING'};
print "Content-type: text/html\n\n";
print "Input: $invar <BR>\n";
```

Although it is beyond the scope of this book to go into Perl, which has many books of its own, here is how this script works:

1. The first line tells the server that this is a Perl program, so that when it is called, the server knows to run Perl, which is a program like Director, and then use this file as the source code.

2. The second line gets the data from after the question mark in the server call. In this case, that information is "gary".

3. The third line starts the output. It places the line Content-type: text/html plus two new line characters into the output stream. This is needed to tell the server and the Web browser what type of output is coming. This line and the extra newline character will never appear in the text you get back. However, everything after it will.

4. The last line outputs the word Input: followed by the text. So the result is an echo of what was sent. It is a good test and shows that the server can get information as well as send it. In this case, the server got "gary", processed it, and sent it back. It could also have opened a file and stored the information. It could have even opened another file, such as a database, and used this information to look up other information.

USING *POSTNETTEXT* TO SEND TEXT

The *postNetText* is new to Director 7 and enables you to perform the same function as an HTML form with "METHOD=POST". The main advantage of using this command is that it can send much more information than the *getNetText* method, which is limited to about 4,000 characters in most situations. The information also arrives in a different format than the *getNetText* method, which many CGI programmers prefer.

The two required arguments of a *postNetText* command are the location of the CGI script and the data. The data, in this case, is a list. Here is an example:

```
postNetText("http://clevermedia.com/echopost.cgi", ["name": "Gary", "ID": 1])
```

The list should be a property list. Each property corresponds to the name of an item, whereas each value is the value of the item. All properties should be strings, but Director translates them to strings if they are not.

After a *postNetText* call, the same process as used for the *getNetText* function has to be followed. You must use the function's return value as an ID number, check *netDone*, and then use *netTextResult* to get the returned text.

> **Note**
>
> Even if no text is meant to be returned, or you do not need the text, you should go through these steps. Otherwise, the call to the server is never ended and you can only have so many open-ended calls before network calls stop working.

Getting *postNetText* to work in Lingo is the easy part. Getting a CGI program that receives and deals with the data is a little more difficult. Hopefully, if you do not know about server programming, you will have the opportunity to work with someone who does. Otherwise, a good book on Perl or maybe some Web research into the subject will help.

WORKING WITH BROWSERS

Shockwave movies placed in Web pages have the capability to communicate with the HTML page and the Web browser. They can read information from the EMBED and OBJECT tags of which they are a part, and also talk to JavaScript and VBScript.

EMBED AND OBJECT TAG PARAMETERS

Movies shown in Netscape Navigator are part of the EMBED tag in the HTML. Movies shown in Microsoft Internet Explorer are part of the OBJECT tag. Both these tags are explained in full detail in Chapter 36, "Delivering the Goods."

These tags look very different, but have a lot in common. For one, they accommodate the use of extra parameters. These parameters can be used to pass information into the Shockwave movie.

The following is an EMBED/OBJECT tag that uses the extra parameter "sw1". Notice that the EMBED tag is actually inside the OBJECT tag. Microsoft Internet Explorer uses the OBJECT tag and ignores the EMBED tag inside it, whereas Netscape Navigator ignores the OBJECT tag and uses the EMBED tag:

```
<OBJECT classid="clsid:166B1BCA-3F9C-11CF-8075-444553540000"
codebase="http://download.macromedia.com/pub/shockwave/cabs/director/¬
sw.cab#version=7,0,0,0" ID=Credits WIDTH=512 HEIGHT=384 ID="shock">
<PARAM NAME=src VALUE="mymovie.dcr">
<PARAM NAME=sw1 VALUE="testing!">
<EMBED SRC="mymovie.dcr" NAME="shock" WIDTH=512 HEIGHT=384 sw1="testing!">
</OBJECT>
```

Notice that the sw1 parameter needed to be added to the code twice: once for Explorer and once for Navigator. This is an unfortunate necessity.

The Shockwave movie can get the parameters from this tag by using the *externalParamValue* function. The function takes either a name, such as "sw1", or a number. You can use the *externalParamName* function to get the name of a parameter, given its number. You can also use the *externalParamCount()* function to get the total number of parameters.

Although you can name parameters anything you want with Navigator, Explorer demands that parameter names come from a preset list. The following is a complete list:

> sw1, sw2, sw3, sw4, sw5, sw6, sw7, sw8, sw9, swURL, swText, swForeColor, swBackColor, swFrame, swColor, swName, swPassword, swBanner, swSound, swVolume, swPreloadTime, swAUdio, swList

None of these parameter names needs to be used for any particular purpose. This collection is just a convenient list of names that the Macromedia engineers came up with, faced with the task of having to decide what sort of parameters developers would want. You could pass a sound name in with the "swURL" parameter, for instance. It doesn't really matter.

Because Explorer requires that you use one of these preset parameter names, it is a good idea to stick to them if you are on the Navigator side as well. This way, you won't have to read one parameter for one platform and one for another.

→ **See** "Making Shockwave Movies," Chapter 36, for more information on using Shockwave

TALKING WITH JAVASCRIPT

JavaScript is the programming language of Netscape Navigator. It is also available on Microsoft Internet Explorer, in addition to Explorer's own language, VBScript. These languages are embedded into the HTML page. They are both very complex, object-oriented programming languages. Learning them is a task for a whole book, and indeed there are many more JavaScript books than Director and Lingo books in existence.

However, the commands used to enable these languages to talk to a Shockwave movie are pretty simple. They just basically send a message to the movie.

Showing examples of JavaScript-to-Shockwave communication is difficult because browsers are constantly changing. At the time of this writing, Netscape Navigator 4.5 and Microsoft Internet Explorer 4.0 are the primary browsers being used. However, by the time you read this, both browsers will probably be at version 5.0.

Be prepared to use these examples as a guide to help you formulate your code, not as verbatim code samples. Also keep in mind that some users will still be working with older browsers. With browser differences and the lack of good documentation for JavaScript, using JavaScript with Director or alone is something you may want to avoid if at all possible.

To send a message to Shockwave, you first need to name your Shockwave object in the OBJECT/EMBED tag. In the example earlier in this chapter, the object was named "shock" by using the ID parameter in the OBJECT tag and the NAME parameter in the EMBED tag.

Now you need to assign the object to a JavaScript variable. This is also different for each browser. This JavaScript code takes care of this difference and stores the object reference in myShock:

```
if (navigator.appName == "Netscape") {
  myMovie = document.shock;
} else {
  myMovie = shock;
}
```

Now, to send a message to the applet, you just need to use the object, followed by the message. For example:

```
myMovie.GotoFrame(42)
```

This code issues a command to the Shockwave movie to jump to frame number 42. You can use eight different message types. The following list includes them all. Remember that these commands are for use in the HTML code of the browser, not in the Director movie.

- Stop()—Halts the movie.
- Play()—Starts the movie from the current position.
- AutoStart()—Given a TRUE or FALSE, determines whether the movie starts playing after it is loaded or after a *Rewind()*.
- Rewind()—Takes the movie back to frame 1.
- GotoFrame(x)—Jumps the movie to frame number x.
- GotoMovie(location)—Loads another movie in place of the current one.
- GetCurrentFrame()—Returns the number of the current frame.
- EvalScript(string)—Sends a text string into a movie to be used by the Lingo *on EvalScript* handler.

EvalScript is the most useful of all of these commands. It can pass any string into the movie. At the other end should be a *on EvalScript* handler. Here is a simple example:

```
on EvalScript text
  alert("Message From JavaScript:"&&text)
end
```

Of course, a handler that actually takes the text and does something with it is far more useful. You can even have the movie execute any Lingo command or handler call by using the *do* command:

```
on EvalScript text
  do text
end
```

Tip

The *do* command takes a text string and runs it as if it were typed into the Message window. You can call handlers, set globals, or even issue direct commands.

TALKING TO SHOCKWAVE

The opposite of the *EvalScript* handler is the *externalEvent* command. It sends a string that represents a command to JavaScript. Here is an example:

```
externalEvent("myJavaScriptFunction('param')")
```

If the user has Netscape Navigator, this command simply runs the JavaScript function named, with the parameter included. However, Microsoft Internet Explorer attempts to send the command to VBScript, *not* to JavaScript. If you know how to use VBScript, you can write a function that does the same thing as the Netscape JavaScript, or even calls out to the same JavaScript handler, passing the parameter information along. Here is such a script. It assumes that the OBJECT tag set the ID of the applet to "shock":

```
<script language="vbscript">
sub shock_ExternalEvent(byVal aMessage)
  call myJavaScriptFunction(aMessage)
end sub
</script>
```

USING SHOCKWAVE PREFERENCE FILES (COOKIES)

Suppose that a Shockwave movie were to ask the user for his or her name and then use that name throughout the presentation. It would be nice if, when the user returns to the page later, the movie remembered the user's name. This sort of thing can be done with preference files.

A preference file is just a small text file that can be stored on the user's computer. It is actually placed in the user's browser's file space, separate from the user's other files for security reasons.

You can create a preference file with the *setPref* command. For instance, to store a user's name, you can do this:

```
setPref("cmprefname.txt", gUserName)
```

In this example, "cmprefname.txt" is the preference filename, and the text of the variable "gUserName" is the contents of that file. The reason that such a complex name is given for the file is that the preference file area must be shared by all Shockwave movies. If you simply named the file "name.txt", and some other developer made a Shockwave applet with "name.txt", one file would overwrite the other.

It is a good idea to pick a file prefix that another developer is unlikely to use. "cmpref" seems to be a good one if your company is "CleverMedia". If you are working for "Joe's Multimedia and Burgers," you might want to start the name of the preference file "jmb" or something similar. You should also use ".txt" as the suffix for the file, because Windows requires this sort of suffix and at least some, if not most, of your users will be using Windows. If you try to use a suffix other than ".txt," you get an error message.

The contents of the preference file can be anything, as long as it is a string. If you need to store a lot of information, you may want to consider converting a property list to a string, and then converting it back with the *value* command when you read the file.

To read a preference file, you use the *getPref* command:

```
text = getPref("cmprefname.txt")
```

If the preference file does not exist, you get a VOID as a value. You can test for this to see whether a user has ever used that particular movie before.

One use for the preference file is to store a local high score for a game. If your movie is a game that uses a scoring system, you can simply have it write the user's score after a game, and then retrieve it when the user returns. It can be displayed as "Your best score" or something similar. This score is in no way compared to other users' on other computers, but that is how home and mall arcade games work because they are not connected to each other either.

You can also use *getPref* and *setPref* in Director and Projectors. Doing so creates a preference folder in the same location as the application. Any preference files will be stored there. This folder is primarily for testing purposes, but if it is used correctly it can replace simple uses of the FileIO Xtra for storing some text and information.

→ **See** "Using Text Files and the FileIO Xtra," Chapter 16, for another way to save and read text

COMMUNICATING WITH SERVERS AND CLIENTS

Director 7 includes a new Xtra called the Multiuser Xtra. This enables Shockwave movies, Director, and Projectors to communicate with the Director 7 Multiuser Server program. This Xtra comes with Director 7.

You can also use this Xtra to communicate directly with other users on the Internet, provided that they are also using a Shockwave movie or Projector with the same Xtra.

The Multiuser Xtra deserves a whole book of its own. More than 40 commands, functions, and properties are related to its use. Plus, the Xtra is likely to change and grow as time goes by. Refer to the online Director documentation for more information and lots of examples. Several behaviors in the Library Palette can provide a jump start on using this exciting, new feature.

TROUBLESHOOTING SHOCKWAVE LINGO

- When you upload a Director movie, make sure that you are using the binary setting on your FTP program. Using the ASCII setting results in an invalid file at the other end.
- If you are trying to use JavaScript communication, be sure to test your movie on all browsers and versions that you expect your audience to use. It is a lot of work, but there is no other way to ensure that all browsers will handle your commands correctly.

- When using preference files, you should always use the ".txt" suffix. Using another suffix will be considered a security problem by Shockwave and an error message will be shown to the user.

- When a movie attempts to get text from a different server with *getNetText*, a security alert will appear. To avoid this alert, place both text and the movie on the same server and use a relative pathname.

- In the past, using a target with *gotoNetPage* sometimes did not work in Microsoft Internet Explorer if the *gotoNetPage* command was issued by an *on exitFrame* handler or a handler called by an *on exitFrame* handler. Test to make sure your targets work in Internet Explorer; if they don't, use *on mouseUp* handlers instead.

- For most developers, using Perl scripts means either controlling your own Web server so that you can create any type of Perl scripts you want, or contacting the Internet Service Provider who hosts your site/domain to find out what you are allowed to do.

- Using Perl scripts can be very frustrating if you have never used them before. You can test out your Perl scripts by typing the CGI calls in your browser. Do this to confirm that they work before trying to use Shockwave movies to call them.

DID YOU KNOW?

- You can place multiple lines of text in a preference file. Store as much information as you want.

- You can use a second parameter with *getNetText* to specify a different server character set: "JIS" or "EUC". The default for this parameter is "ASCII" and the setting "AUTO" attempts to automatically determine the server character set.

- The *netMIME* function can be used to determine the file's MIME type after the *netDone* command returns TRUE.

- The function *netLastModDate* can be used to determine the server's time stamp for the file after the *netDone* returns TRUE.

- You can use network Lingo over HTTPS (secure servers). This functionality is new to Director 7.

- An *on EvalScript* handler can use *return* to send information back to JavaScript.

- Global variables persist from movie to movie when you use the *gotoNetMovie* command.

OBJECT-ORIENTED PROGRAMMING

In this chapter

Object-oriented programming, also known as *OOP*, is a term that may scare some non-programmers. It sounds mysterious and complex. In reality, it is what you have been doing all along in Director. OOP is simply programming that marries code to data. A behavior, attached to a sprite, is OOP. The code is the Lingo in the behavior, and the data is the properties of the sprite: the member, location, and custom properties of the behavior.

OOP enables you to write one piece of code, and then reuse that code for different objects. In Director, those objects are usually sprites, but they don't have to be. An object can just be an invisible set of data, such as an entry in a database or an enemy ship in a game.

WHAT IS AN OBJECT?

Behaviors are object-oriented scripts customized to fit Director's sprite-oriented nature; you can use parent scripts to create non-sprite-oriented objects, sometimes called *code objects*.

> **Tip**
>
> A code object is a self-contained unit of code in memory that keeps track of its own internal data. Code objects share some traits with other Director objects. Code objects have internal variables called *properties*, and they respond to messages just as behaviors do. But unlike the other objects in the Lingo environment, you can't see code objects and they don't come ready-made.

In Lingo, you define an object template by writing a parent script. You then create an object from that parent script by sending a new message to the parent script. You can create as many objects as you want from the same template. The Director manuals call the objects created from a parent object *child objects*.

You get a Lingo object to respond by sending it a message. The object's methods (*method* is a fancy word for *handler*) determine to which messages it responds. An object can have a method for just about anything you can program in Lingo. Director objects also have a built-in data management system, similar to structures in more traditional programming languages. Other than the messages sent to and from an object, the objects are completely isolated from each other. The OOP word for code that manages its own data and shields its internal workings from the outside is *encapsulation*. By this standard, Lingo objects are encapsulated.

If you are coming to Lingo with experience in an OOP language such as C++, it may take you some time to get your bearings. Lingo does not have a ready-made class library, nor does it impose many rules about object structure, but it uses its own unique terminology. Table 23.1 shows the OOP terms and their Lingo equivalents.

TABLE 23.1   OBJECT-ORIENTED PROGRAMMING VERSUS LINGO TERMS

OOP Term	Lingo Equivalent
Base class	Ancestor script
Class	Parent script
Instance variable	Property variable
Class instance/object	Child object
Method/member function	Method

→ **See** "Controlling a Single Sprite," Chapter 14, "Creating Behaviors," for more information about behaviors as objects

REASONS TO USE OBJECTS

Almost everything you can do with objects in Lingo can be done without much difficulty using Director's Score-based environment. So why use objects? Objects offer advantages of efficiency, flexibility, and optimal use of processing and memory resources. Following are five reasons to use objects.

OBJECTS ORGANIZE YOUR CODE

Better organization is achieved with objects because the parent contains both the code and the variables on which the code relies. If all your code and variables related to printing a report or playing digital video are in the same place, it's easier to maintain them using objects.

OBJECTS PRESERVE THE GLOBAL SPACE

Like globals, an object's property variables maintain their state over time; unlike globals, the properties are known only to the object maintaining them. This keeps the properties out of the global pool.

Suppose that you have a catalog application. In each product section, such as Electronics or Clothing, for example, you are keeping track of the number of products users have bought, the number of items for which they have looked, and how long each user has spent in each section. This enables you to track the users' buying preferences. All these variables must be globals, or part of a global list, to be capable of maintaining their contents over time. In this case, you would end up with a lot of global variables all named with some variation of a product section name and counter or timer, all available everywhere in the project. How long before you accidentally use the same global name twice for two different purposes?

Alternatively, you could make an object for each section with property variables for the number of products bought, the number of items looked at, and the time spent in that section. The Electronics object can have a "productsBought" property variable, and so can the Clothing object. Neither of these variables is part of the global pool because its scope is restricted to the object to which it belongs. This way, you don't have to worry about using a variable name multiple times for different purposes; you can instead reference the properties of each object.

OBJECTS ARE EASY TO TEST

An object is self-contained. Because it is not dependent on any code outside of itself, an object can be tested before other parts of the project are finished. After an object is coded, you should be able to test it by sending messages to all its methods. If the methods set the correct property variables or return the correct values, you know that the object is functioning properly and can be integrated into the larger project. Easy unit testing is another benefit of encapsulation.

OBJECTS MAKE CODING EASIER AND MORE EFFICIENT

Using objects makes coding easier and more efficient through the concept of inheritance. *Inheritance* is an OOP term that refers to the capability of one script to incorporate the methods and properties of another script. Inheritance is a way of reusing existing code for similar programming problems, rather than writing code completely from scratch every time.

In Lingo, inheritance works in this manner: A parent script defines the methods and properties any object created from it will have. The created object inherits the methods and properties of the parent. Multiple objects can be created from the same parent, and if appropriate, individualized with their own additional properties and methods.

An ancestor script is another level of script in Lingo that utilizes the concept of inheritance. A parent script can link to an ancestor script. In this way, all the ancestor script's methods and properties become part of the parent script and are, in turn, passed on to the child object. The child object inherits the ancestor's methods and properties, plus any of the parent's methods and properties that are also needed. Ancestor scripts are discussed in more detail in the "Using Ancestors" section later in this chapter.

OBJECTS CAN BE REUSED

If you create objects with reuse in mind, eventually you will have a library of objects that you can put together to handle much of your routine coding. Director has the capability to link a movie to more than one Cast; this capability enables you to maintain a code library containing library objects that you can easily link to any movie. Almost any object you create has the potential to be reused, and if it is an external cast library, reuse is easy. If you create an object to handle grading a quiz, for example, the same object can be used in any quiz by simply changing a few of the properties.

CREATING AN OBJECT IN LINGO

To create an object, you must first create a parent script. As mentioned in the previous section, a parent script defines the methods and properties of objects created from it. The programming problem you are trying to solve determines the methods and properties that you should include in your parent script. The basic method required by all parent scripts is the *new* handler.

The *new* handler creates a new object from a parent script. A parent script is like a template document in a word processing program. Just as you can create any number of identical documents from one template, you can create any number of identical objects by calling the *new* method of a parent script. Each time you send a parent script a *new* message, it creates a new object from that parent script.

The syntax for the *new* method is as follows:

```
on new me
    return me
end
```

It is important to use the word *me* in the line beginning with *on*. The word *me* holds a pointer to the location in memory of the object created from the parent script. It is also important to include the *return* line inside the *new* method. This returns a pointer to the object. If you don't include this *return*, you have no way of communicating with the object after you create it.

Director has a parent script type, available through the Script window, which is the proper place for creating parent scripts. If you accidentally create an object from a movie script and send it a message, Director looks through all the movie scripts for a handler for that message. If you have a movie script handler with the same name as one of your object methods, the movie script handler, rather than your object, gets the message.

When you create objects from a parent script, it's a good idea to store them in globals so that the objects are available to code anywhere in the movie where you want to use them.

Global objects, like any other globals, persist across movies. After an object is created from a parent script, it exists independently in memory. The object no longer references the parent script. If you go to another movie that does not contain the object's parent script, the object still works. The object is using its own copy of the code defined in the parent script that it has stored in memory. If you change a parent script's code after you have created an object from it, you do not change the object already in memory. You must create a new object from the edited parent script; if you want to update multiple objects created from the same parent script, you must create new objects to replace each of the older ones.

With these background facts in mind, you can turn to building an object. Create a new, empty parent by first creating a script cast member. Click the Info button in the Script window and use the Type pull-down menu to change the script's type property to Parent. Enter the name "minimal" in the script's Name field. A name is not optional for a parent script; it is required because you need to refer to it in other Lingo code.

Enter the following code into your minimalist parent script and name the script member "minimal":

```
on new me
   return me
end
```

Create a new object by typing the following Lingo into the Message window:

```
minimalObj = new(script "minimal")
```

The code line you entered created a new object from the minimal script and put it in the global "minimalObj". It's a good idea to store your objects in globals so that they will be available to code anywhere in your movie that they are needed.

Enter the following in the Message window and press Return or Enter to see whether you created an object. Director returns the contents of the object variable, which confirms that the object was successfully created:

```
put minimalObj
-- <offspring "minimal" 2 8daa90>
```

The object "minimalObj" was created successfully, but it can't really do anything yet. It cannot receive any messages other than *new*, and it has no property variables to store data.

Add a script to make the button the vehicle for creating a new object, so that you will not have to do so by typing commands in the Message window every time you play the movie. Make an *on mouseUp* handler that handles creating the object, as follows:

```
on mouseUp
  global gObj
  set gObj = new(script "minimal")
end
```

Rewind and play your movie and create a new object by clicking the button on the Stage. Check to see whether the object was properly created by typing put gObj in the Message window and pressing Return or Enter.

Create an "on hello" method for the object that makes the object beep. Edit the parent script to contain the following code:

```
on new me
   return me
end

on hello me
   beep
end
```

Rewind and play your movie and create a new instance of the object by clicking the button you created on the Stage. You should now be able to type the following code into the Message window. If everything worked correctly, your computer should beep.

```
hello(gObj)
```

→ **See** "Creating Simple Behaviors," Chapter 14, for more information about behaviors

CREATING OBJECT PROPERTIES

So far, you have created a simple object that beeps if you send it the hello message. This object isn't terribly functional, however. To add greater functionality to an object, it needs more than methods. The minimal object is missing the second component of truly functional objects in Director: properties. The property variables of an object can be used to hold any type of data and are unique to each instance of the object.

You declare an object's property variables at the top of the parent script in the same manner as you declare globals and properties in behaviors:

```
property pProp1, pProp2, pProp3...
```

You can refer to the property inside the parent script by just its name. Outside the parent script, you can refer to it using the dot syntax. For instance, if an object is referenced by the variable "gObj" and you want to get the value of its property "pProp1", then "gObj.pProp1" gives you that value.

Here is a simple parent script that sets a property during the *new* handler. You can then use the "on test" handler to see that the property is there:

```
property pTest

on new me
  pTest = "Hello World."
  return me
end

on test me
  put pTest
end
```

You can try it out in the Message window:

```
gObj = new(script "Test Object")
test(gObj)
-- "Hello World."
```

As noted earlier in this chapter, you can produce multiple identical objects from the same parent script. You can then individualize the objects by giving them different properties. In this way, you can enjoy the efficiency of not rewriting code for methods and properties that are the same from object to object. Yet, you still have the flexibility to create unique objects as your programming problem demands.

Here is a script parent similar to the last one. In this case, however, it sets the property "pTest" in the *new* handler according to a parameter:

```
property pTest

on new me, val
  pTest = val
  return me
end
```

```
on test me
  put pTest
end
```

Now, try this in the Message window. It demonstrates the creation of two separate objects from one parent script and how the values of the properties inside each object can be different:

```
gObj1 = new(script "Test Object 2", "Hello World.")
gObj2 = new(script "Test Object 2", "Testing...")
put gObj1
-- <offspring "Test Object 2" 2 4abfdac>
put gObj2
-- <offspring "Test Object 2" 2 4abfe24>
test(gObj1)
-- "Hello World."
test(gObj2)
-- "Testing..."
```

→ **See** "Controlling a Single Sprite," Chapter 14, for more information about properties

USING OOP

In Director 7, using OOP is so automatic that you can hardly avoid doing it. Every behavior is OOP code that controls a sprite or frame.

In the past, parent scripts were created to take control of sprites and make them behave in certain ways. Behaviors have taken over this responsibility. As a result, the usefulness of parent scripts has decreased.

You can still use parent scripts for non–visually-oriented tasks. For instance, if you want to create a vocabulary program, you can store words as objects. After all, a word can many properties: spelling, definition, synonyms, and so on. Here is a simple parent script that can be used to create a word object:

```
property pWord
property pDefinition

on new me, theword
  pWord = theword
  return me
end

on setDefinition me, def
  pDefinition = def
end

on define me
  return pDefinition
end
```

Using the Message window, you can see how this can be applied:

```
gWord = new(script "Word Object", "Clever")
put gWord.pWord
```

```
-- "Clever"
setDefinition(gWord,"Skillful in thinking.")
put define(gWord)
-- "Skillful in thinking."
```

Now you can add more properties, such as synonyms, antonyms, homonyms, anagrams, common misspellings, and so on. You can add more handlers to accept and process these properties, or create universal ones that accept and return any property.

This same sort of OOP logic can be applied to any type of data. You can have a database of employees, for instance. Each object can have properties such as the employee's name, address, phone number, date of birth, Social Security number, and so on.

In turn, the handlers in the parent script would be custom built to work with this data.

→ **See** "Creating Simple Behaviors," Chapter 14, for more information about behaviors

USING ANCESTORS

Parent scripts can use a special property, called an *ancestor*, which is a reference to another parent script.

When you define and use the *ancestor* property, you give the object access to all the handlers and properties in that ancestor parent script. In this way, you can have objects created with different parent scripts, but using the same ancestor script. In other words, they can share some handlers, but not others.

Suppose you want to use objects to track items in a store. One of the problems with items in a store is that they have different properties. A piece of fruit, for instance, has an expiration date. A can of food, on the other hand, may not have an expiration date, but does have a size property: It can fit on some shelves but not others.

Here is an ancestor script that has all the properties shared by both types of items. It also has a handler that does something with them:

```
property pProductName
property pIsleNumber

on new me
  return me
end

on whereIs me
  return pProductName&&"is in isle"&&pIsleNumber
end
```

The shared item is the aisle number. This is the way the store keeps track of where things are. In addition, all products have a name. An "on whereIs" handler returns a string that contains both.

The first type of product that the store stocks is fruit. It is a product, so it uses the ancestor script, and from that gets the use of the "pProductName" and "pAisleNumber" properties, as well as the "on whereIs" handler. In addition, it has an expiration date. Here is a parent script for a piece of fruit:

```
property ancestor
property pExpires

on new me
  ancestor = new(script "Product Ancestor")
  return me
end

on expiration me
  return me.pProductName&&"expires"&&pExpires
end
```

The first property in the fruit parent script is the *ancestor*. In the *on new* handler, this is set to be a new instance of the ancestor script. In addition, this parent script has a "pExpires" property and a handler that uses it. This handler also accesses the "pProductName" property from the ancestor script by using the *me* property and dot syntax.

In the Message window you can see how all this works. When an object is created from the fruit parent script, the ancestor is attached to it. You can then assign the object with properties from both its own parent script and its ancestor script. Then you can access handlers from both as well.

```
gApple = new(script "Fruit Parent")
gApple.pProductName = "Apple"
gApple.pIsleNumber = 14
gApple.pExpires = "12/31/98"
put expiration(gApple)
-- "Apple expires 12/31/98"
put whereIs(gApple)
-- "Apple is in isle 14"
```

The power from this technique comes when you need to create another type of product, such as canned food, for instance. Here is a parent script for cans:

```
property ancestor
property pSize

on new me
  ancestor = new(script "Product Ancestor")
  return me
end

on size me
  return me.pProductName&&"is size"&&pSize
end
```

This script looks similar to the fruit parent script, but has a different property. Things such as product name and aisle number are already taken care of because you used the same ancestor script.

```
gYams = new(script "Can Parent")
gYams.pProductName = "Canned Yams"
gYams.pIsleNumber = 9
gYams.pSize = "Medium"
put size(gYams)
-- "Canned Yams is size Medium"
put whereIs(gYams)
-- "Canned Yams is in isle 9"
```

You can now go on to create dozens or hundreds of different types of parent scripts that all use the same ancestor script. If you then want to add another shared property, such as an order number, you can add it to the ancestor script and all the objects that use that ancestor script inherit the property when you run the movie again.

TROUBLESHOOTING OOP

- A common error is to forget the *return me* at the end of the *on new me* handler.

- When you use the *new* command to create an object, it takes the code as it currently exists. If you change the script member, you have to recreate the object with the *new* command before the change takes effect.

- If you use a handler name in a parent script, be sure not to use that same handler name somewhere else.

- Creating parent scripts may seem natural to OOP programmers, but in many cases a behavior is really what is needed. A good rule of thumb is to use parent scripts only when there is no visual component to the object, or possibly when more than one sprite needs to be controlled by an object.

DID YOU KNOW?

- When you create an object and then examine it in the Message window, the strange-looking result is actually the name of the script, the number of references to the script, and the member location of the object. It might look like this: <offspring "Can Parent" 2 4abfeec>.

- There is a system property called *the actorList*. If you use *add* to add objects to this list, the objects begin to receive *on stepFrame* handler calls exactly once per frame.

- You can use parent scripts to store handlers in memory to be used when the Projector or Shockwave changes movies. Because the code resides in a global variable, it persists beyond the movie. You can use that global to call the handlers that existed in the parent script, even though the script is not present in the current movie.

CHAPTER 24

MOVIES IN A WINDOW AND ALTERNATIVES

In this chapter

Movies in a window, usually referred to as *MIAWs*, are an unusual part of Director. They enable you to open other windows, besides the Stage, that contain Director movies.

The uses for MIAWs are many. Because they play independently of each other and of the Stage, they are useful for functions that don't fit into the Stage's window. You can create your own custom dialog boxes or message windows with MIAWs. You can even create your own application using several different windows, just as Director and almost every other professional computer application does.

USING MIAWs

MIAW Lingo can be simple or complex. If you just want to open a window to display some information, only a few lines of code are needed. On the other hand, a whole set of commands, functions, properties, and special event handlers exist to support further use of MIAWs. In any case, you first need to create an MIAW, which is covered in the following section.

CREATING AN MIAW

To use MIAWs, you first need to have another movie file. In cases where you want to create a small window, the Stage size for that movie should be set accordingly. Save that file as `miaw.dir` and open another new movie. You can actually use the Message window to show the MIAW.

```
miaw = window("Test MIAW")
miaw.filename = "miaw.dir"
miaw.visible = TRUE
```

The new window appears over the Stage. It shows a title of "Test MIAW". The global variable that is created, "MIAW", holds the reference to that window. You can get its value:

```
put miaw
-- (window "Test MIAW")
```

You can refer to this MIAW using both the global variable and the structure *window("Test MIAW")*. To close and remove that MIAW, you can also use the Message window:

```
close(miaw)
forget(miaw)
```

A handler that opens an MIAW for you looks similar to the preceding Message window code. Here is that handler, and one that closes the MIAW:

```
on startMIAW
  global gTestMIAW
  gTestMIAW = window("Test MIAW")
```

```
    gTestMIAW.filename = "miaw.dir"
    gTestMIAW.visible = TRUE
end

on endMIAW
    global gTestMIAW
    close(gTestMIAW)
    forget(gTestMIAW)
end
```

Notice that closing an MIAW takes two commands. The first, *close*, actually just makes the window invisible. The second command, *forget*, erases it from memory. If you issue only the first command, the MIAW is really still there, taking up memory and causing potential problems if you plan on using more MIAWs later.

MIAW PROPERTIES

The simple example described in the preceding section shows some of the basic properties of an MIAW. It has the *filename* and the *visible* property. You can also infer the *name* property from the above example. The following is a complete list of the MIAW properties:

- visible—Determines whether the window is visible or hidden. Even hidden windows can execute Lingo code.

- filename—The filename that corresponds to the Director movie used for the MIAW. If the computer is connected to the Internet, a URL can be used.

- name—The name of the MIAW. This is used as a default title for the window, and used to refer to it with the *window* structure.

- title—Can be used to override the *name* of the window in the visible title bar.

- titleVisible—When the MIAW type is set to -1, this determines whether the MIAW shows the title bar.

- windowType—You can set this to -1, 0, 1, 2, 3, 4, 5, 8, 12, 16, or 49. Tables 24.1 and 24.2 show what is included with each type.

- drawRect—This powerful property can be used to scale the MIAW, including bitmaps in it.

- rect—This property enables you to crop or expand the MIAW, with no scaling.

- sourceRect—Returns the original coordinates for the MIAW, before changes to the *drawRect* or the *rect*.

- modal—When this property of a window is set to TRUE, the window takes over all input and prevents other windows, including the Stage, from receiving clicks or key presses until the MIAW is gone or the *modal* is set to FALSE.

TABLE 24.1 MIAW TYPES FOR WINDOWS

Type Number	Description	Movable	Close Box	Maximize	Minimize
0	Standard	Yes	Yes	No	No
1	Alert Box	No	No	No	No
2	Rectangle	No	No	No	No
3	Rectangle	No	No	No	No
4	Document	Yes	Yes	No	No
5	Document	Yes	Yes	No	No
8	Document	Yes	Yes	Yes	No
12	Document	Yes	Yes	Yes	No
16	Document	Yes	Yes	No	No
49	Palette (Not in Projectors)	Yes	Yes	No	No

TABLE 24.2 MIAW TYPES FOR MAC

Type Number	Description	Movable	Close Box	Stretch Box	Resize Box
0	Standard	Yes	Yes	Yes	No
1	Alert Box	No	No	No	No
2	Rectangle	No	No	No	No
3	Rectangle with Drop Shadow	No	No	No	No
4	Document	Yes	Yes	No	No
5	Document	Yes	No	No	No
8	Document	Yes	Yes	Yes	Yes
12	Document	Yes	Yes	No	Yes
16	Curved Border Box	Yes	Yes	No	No
49	Palette (Not in Projectors)	Yes	Yes	No	No

Although Tables 24.1 and 24.2 give you a good idea of what each window type should look like, keep in mind that the look is determined both by your Director version and the version of your operating system. A window type looks different in Mac OS 8.1 than it does in Mac OS 8.5, and different in Windows 95 than it does in Windows 98.

WINDOW COMMANDS

The *open*, *close*, and *forget* commands are the primary ones used with MIAWs. Two others, however, are designed to work when more than one MIAW is open at once. Some additional commands enable MIAWs to talk to the Stage and to each other. The important window commands are described as follows:

- *open*—Creates a new MIAW and returns a reference to it.
- *close*—Makes an MIAW invisible, although the MIAW is really still present.
- *forget*—Unloads the MIAW from memory.
- *moveToFront*—Takes the MIAW and makes it the frontmost window.
- *moveToBack*—Takes the MIAW and places it behind all others.
- *tell*—Sends a Lingo command or handler call to an MIAW. It can also be used to direct a set of Lingo commands to an MIAW.

PART

VII

CH

24

The *tell* command is what MIAWs and the Stage use to communicate. You can use it to send a single command like this:

```
tell window("Test MIAW") to myHandler
```

You can also send a whole set of lines to the MIAW:

```
tell window("Test MIAW")
  myHandler
  myOtherHandler
  go to frame "x"
end tell
```

MIAW SYSTEM PROPERTIES

In addition to the individual window properties available in Lingo, some system properties relate to windows. This is a complete list of properties that tell you which windows are present, which window is active, and which window is at the front.

- *the windowList*—Returns a list of all the current MIAWs, including ones that are invisible. If no windows are present, it returns an empty list.
- *the activeWindow*—Returns a reference to the currently active window. If the Stage is the active window, (the stage) is returned.
- *frontWindow*—Returns a reference to the front-most window. If this is the Stage, (the stage) is returned.
- *windowPresent()*—This function, when given a string with a window name, tells you whether a window with that name is present. It works only with window names, not window references in variables.

You can get good use out of *the windowList* property by creating a script that closes any and all MIAWs. It determines the number of windows from *the windowList* and then closes and forgets all of the windows, as follows:

```
on closeAllMIAWs
  n = count(the windowList)
  repeat with i = 1 to n
    close window(1)
    forget window(1)

  end repeat
end
```

MIAW EVENT HANDLERS

MIAWs can also use many special event handlers. They involve typical window events, such as opening, closing, and moving the window.

Each of these handlers can be used in movie scripts in the MIAW's Director movie. Here is a complete list:

- on activateWindow—This handler is called if the window is not currently the active one and the user clicks it to make it active.
- on closeWindow—This handler is called if the user uses the close box to close the window, or if the window is closed with the *close* command.
- on deactivateWindow—This handler is called if the window is the active one, and the user clicks another window, thus making this one not active.
- on moveWindow—This handler is called every time the MIAW is dragged around the screen by the user. The call comes when the user releases the mouse button.
- on openWindow—This handler is called immediately after the MIAW opens for the first time.
- on resizeWindow—This handler is called whenever the user uses the corner or sides of the window to resize it.
- on zoomWindow—This handler is called whenever the user clicks a zoom, maximize, or minimize box.

→ **See** "Using Handlers," Chapter 13, "Essential Lingo Syntax," for some background about creating handlers

CREATING DIALOG BOXES

With MIAWs, you don't have to be stuck with plain, ordinary alert boxes and dialog boxes. After all, if the artwork on your Stage is strange and unusual, why should your dialog boxes look like standard Mac and Windows interfaces? Instead, you can make use of the window properties and event handlers to construct your own custom dialog boxes and alert boxes. This section shows you how.

CONFIRMATION DIALOG BOXES

Confirmation dialog boxes usually ask a yes or no question. In most programs, yes or no is usually expressed as OK and Cancel. However, you can make them anything you want with MIAWs.

Figure 24.1 shows the Stage with an MIAW confirmation dialog box. It is simply a normal MIAW, like the one used in the example earlier in this chapter. The *windowType* has been set so that the window is a non-movable rectangle. The *modal* property has been set to TRUE so that the user must interact with it.

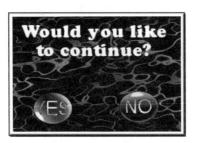

Figure 24.1
Out-of-the-ordinary dialog boxes can be easily created with MIAWs.

Here is the script that opens this MIAW with the correct window type and modal:

```
on mouseUp
  global gFunkyDialog
  gFunkyDialog = window("Funky Dialog")
  gFunkyDialog.filename = "24funkydialog.dir"
  gFunkyDialog.windowType = 1
  gFunkyDialog.modal = TRUE
  gFunkyDialog.visible = TRUE
end
```

Inside the MIAW, the two buttons can be wired up with code that closes the dialog box and also tells the Stage what to do. For instance, here is the code for the Yes button:

```
on mouseUp
  close(the activeWindow)
  forget(the activeWindow)
  tell (the Stage) to continueYes
end
```

The handler "on continueYes" should be in the main movie. You can also have an "on continueNo" that is called by the No button.

In the preceding script, *the activeWindow* is used as a convenient way to determine which MIAW to close. After all, if the user is clicking it, it should be the active window. Using this function is more convenient than passing a global variable around.

ALERT DIALOG BOXES

Alert dialog boxes are as simple as MIAWs get. However, you may want to create an MIAW that can handle many types of alerts. To do this, you can use a *tell* command to place different pieces of text in a field in the MIAW so that it shows a different message each time. Figure 24.2 shows such a dialog box.

Figure 24.2
MIAWs can be used to create custom alert boxes.

A handler that creates such an MIAW could look like this:

```
on mouseUp
  global gAlertBox
  gAlertBox = window("Alert Box")
  gAlertBox.filename = "24alertbox.dir"
  gAlertBox.windowType = 0
  gAlertBox.modal = TRUE

  tell gAlertBox
    member("Text").text = "Danger Will Robinson!"
  end tell

  gAlertBox.visible = TRUE
end
```

This code is just like the other handlers that open MIAWs, but the *tell* command is used to change the text in a field in the MIAW. This is done just before the MIAW is made visible so that the user doesn't see the change.

TEXT INPUT DIALOG BOXES

Another type of MIAW dialog box is one that asks the user for more information. You can have radio buttons, check boxes, and even text input fields in these input dialog boxes.

Here is an example of an MIAW that asks the user to type her name. Figure 24.3 shows what this could look like. The field in the middle is a simple editable text field member.

The MIAW in the main movie is created in the same way as the other MIAWs. However, the code executed when the user clicks the OK button is a little more complex. It takes the text in the field and passes it back to the Stage through a *tell* command:

```
on mouseUp
  text = member("Text Input").text
  close(the activeWindow)
```

```
    forget(the activeWindow)
    tell (the Stage) to textInputDone(text)
end
```

Figure 24.3
MIAWs can gather information through text input and other interface devices.

The code for the Cancel button is similar, but this button is intended to pass just a VOID constant back rather than text. Then, the main movie handles the input with something like this:

```
on textInputDone text
  if text = VOID then
    put "Cancelled."
  else
    put "Text Entered:"&&text
  end if
end
```

Of course, in real life, the "on textInputDone" is likely to store the user's name in a variable or place it in a field. It probably also uses a *go* command to proceed to the next part of the movie.

→ **See** "A Complete Button Behavior," Chapter 14, "Creating Behaviors," for more information about creating buttons

→ **See** "Using Keyboard Input," Chapter 16, "Controlling Text"

OTHER USES FOR MIAWs

Confirmation dialog boxes, alert boxes, and input dialog boxes are just three of the many possible uses for MIAWs. Just about anything you can do in Director, you can do in MIAWs, so the sky is the limit.

Some developers use MIAWs as the primary screen in projectors. They make the Stage as small as possible, and even stick it out of the monitor's screen area, perhaps at a negative horizontal and vertical location. This way, you can have a movable window as the main screen, even in Mac projectors which insist on a non-movable rectangular Window for the Stage.

Here are some other uses for MIAWs:

- A Shockwave Player—Because you can use Internet locations as well as filenames for MIAWs, why not open up some Shockwave content in your projectors this way?

- Hyperlinks—In educational programs, MIAWs can be used as glossary windows or windows with additional information. Use hyperlinks in text members to activate them.

- Multiple Movies—If you need to have more than one movie playing at a time, you can do so with a single projector that opens two MIAWs.

- Debugging—You can have an MIAW that contains extra information about the main movie that is meant for your eyes only. It can be updated with the *tell* command. When the project is done, just remove the MIAW or make it invisible.

- Stage Overlay—If you create a plain rectangle MIAW, it can be placed on top of the Stage and the user will not even know it is a separate window. You can use this to place animations or other external pieces "in" your movies.

USING LINKED MOVIES

An alternative to the "Stage Overlay" idea is to use linked movies rather than MIAWs. A linked movie is simply a cast member that has been imported into the main movie. The linked movie can be placed on the Stage and the user will not know it is a separate movie. The Score and Cast for this linked movie still exist as independent files, but they are represented in your main movie as members.

After you have such a member, you can place it on the Stage and position it. You can even animate its position over a series of frames.

> **Note**
>
> The difference between a linked movie and a film loop is that all the scripts in the linked movie are still active and working. In a film loop, only behaviors and some other scripts work. Film loops are really meant more for animation, whereas linked movies are for more complex interactive movies.

→ **See** "Film Loops and Linked Movies," Chapter 11, "Advanced Techniques," for some basic information about film loops

USING MUI XTRA DIALOG BOXES

The MUI Xtra that comes with Director is used by various parts of the authoring environment to create dialog boxes similar to the ones that behaviors bring up when dropped onto a sprite. MUI stands for *Macromedia User Interface*, which is a set of guidelines that Macromedia follows for all its software products.

Macromedia also provided a straight Lingo interface for this Xtra, which enables you to create some standard and custom dialog boxes. All the elements in the dialog boxes look like Macromedia standard interface elements, but that is not necessarily a bad thing. Macromedia has created a good set of cross-platform elements that look like standard dialog boxes.

There are actually five ways to call the MUI Xtra. The first four represent some standard dialog box types: file open, file save, get URL, and an alert. The alert box is very customizable. The fifth way to use the MUI Xtra is to create a custom dialog box from scratch.

CREATING A FILE OPEN DIALOG BOX

Creating a file open dialog box is very simple. All you need to do is create an instance of the Xtra, use its *FileOpen* method to generate the dialog box, and then retrieve its results. Figure 24.4 shows an example. Here is a handler that does just that:

```
on muiFileOpen
  gMUI = new(xtra "mui")
  filename = FileOpen(gMUI,the pathname)
  gMUI = 0
  return filename
end
```

The only other parameter for *FileOpen* is the default pathname of the file. The function returns the resulting filename. After that, you should dispose of the Xtra instance by setting it to VOID or 0.

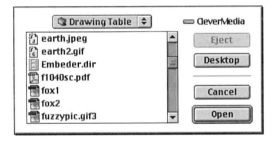

Figure 24.4
The file open dialog box created with the MUI Xtra.

CREATING A FILE SAVE DIALOG BOX

The *FileSave* method for the MUI Xtra works in a similar way. You need to give it two parameters: the default name for the file, and a piece of text to be displayed in the dialog box. Figure 24.5 shows an example.

```
on muiFileSave
  gMUI = new(xtra "mui")
  filename = FileSave(gMUI,"myfile", "Save Game")
  gMUI = 0
  return filename
end
```

The *FileSave* command returns the pathname to the location of the file to be created.

Figure 24.5
The file save dialog box created with the MUI Xtra.

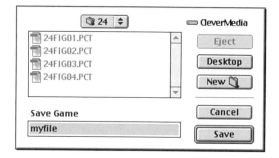

CREATING A GET URL DIALOG BOX

The *GetURL* method displays a dialog box with the name Open URL. You can specify a default location, and whether the dialog box is movable. Figure 25.6 shows an example.

```
on muiGetURL
  gMUI = new(xtra "mui")
  default = "http://clevermedia.com"
  moveable = TRUE
  filename = GetURL(gMUI, default, moveable)
  gMUI = 0
  return filename
end
```

Figure 24.6
The Open URL dialog box created with the MUI Xtra.

CREATING ALERT BOXES

Creating alert boxes is much more complex because so many more options are available. This handler creates the alert box shown in Figure 24.7. It is a simple alert with a "caution" icon and an OK button:

```
on muiAlert
  gMUI = new(xtra "mui")
  list = [:]
  addProp list, #buttons, #Ok
  addProp list, #default, 1
  addProp list, #title, "Alert!"
  addProp list, #message, "Danger Will Robinson"
  addProp list, #icon, #caution
  addProp list, #moveable, FALSE
  res = Alert(gMUI,list)
  gMUI = 0
  return res
end
```

Figure 24.7
A simple alert dialog box created with the MUI Xtra.

As you can see in the handler, a list is passed into the *Alert* function. This list contains various options that describe how the alert box is to look.

The first property, #buttons, can be set to #OK, #OKCancel, #AbortRetryIgnore, #YesNoCancel, #YesNo, or #RetryCancel. Each of these options determines how many buttons the alert box has, and what they are named.

The #default property determines which of the buttons is the default one. This button looks different than the others and also reacts to a Return or Enter key press.

The #title property allows you to customize the label in the title bar of the alert window. The #message and #icon property allow you to determine the contents of the box. The options for #icon are #stop, #note, #caution, #question, or #error.

The #moveable property allows you to determine whether the alert box window is moveable.

This type of dialog box returns the number of the button pressed. So if the buttons are #OKCancel, it can return a 1 or a 2.

PART

VII

CH

24

CREATING CUSTOM MUI DIALOG BOXES

Custom MUI dialog boxes are even more complex than alert boxes because you can specify every aspect of the window as well as the interface elements inside it.

The best way to learn how to use the custom dialog boxes is to take a look at an example. But even a short example has a lot of Lingo lines associated with it. Figure 24.8 shows a simple custom dialog box that the following handler creates.

Figure 24.8
A custom handler dialog box created with the MUI Xtra.

```
on muiCustom
  global gMUI
  gMUI = new(xtra "mui")
```

Next, the properties for the window must be defined. Rather than requiring you to build the lengthy window properties list from scratch, the MUI Xtra enables you to get a copy of a default property list with the *getWindowPropList* function. This default list contains all the properties needed to define a window, plus their default settings. So all you have to do is change the settings for the properties you want to alter:

```
windowProps = getWindowPropList(gMUI)
windowProps.type = #normal
windowProps.name = "Custom MUI Dialog"
windowProps.callback = "myCallbackHandler"
windowProps.width = 160
windowProps.height = 230
windowProps.mode = #pixel
```

In this case, the *name, callback* handler, *width, height,* and *mode* of the window were changed. The callback handler is the name of the movie handler that is called each time the dialog window is touched by the user. The *mode* can be set to #data, #dialogUnit, or #pixel. The first attempts to do the layout of the dialog box for you, whereas the other two enable you to specify locations for items.

After the window properties are set, you need to start creating interface elements to be added to the dialog box. Create a list to which these items should be added:

```
list = []
```

Now you can create your first element. Like the window properties, the element properties are so complex that the MUI Xtra includes a special function, *getItemPropList*, that returns a default item property list. Customize this list to become a specific interface element. Here is a label element:

```
element = getItemPropList(gMui)
element.type = #label
element.value = "What size burger do you want?"
element.locH = 10
element.locV = 10
element.width = 140
element.height = 40
add list, element
```

Next, you can add a pop-up menu. This element needs a special #attributes property that includes some information specific to that interface element type.

```
element = getItemPropList(gMui)
element.type = #popupList
element.locH = 10
element.locV = 45
element.width = 140
element.height = 20
element.attributes = ¬
   [#popupStyle: #tiny, #valueList: ["Small", "Medium", "Large"]]
add list, element
```

After another label, the three check boxes can be added.

```
element = getItemPropList(gMui)
element.type = #label
element.value = "What do you want with your burger?"
element.locH = 10
element.locV = 70
element.width = 140
element.height = 40
add list, element

element = getItemPropList(gMui)
element.type = #checkBox
element.title = "Fries"
element.locH = 10
element.locV = 110
element.width = 140
element.height = 20
add list, element

element = getItemPropList(gMui)
element.type = #checkBox
element.title = "Chips"
element.locH = 10
element.locV = 140
element.width = 140
element.height = 20
add list, element

element = getItemPropList(gMui)
element.type = #checkBox
element.title = "Onion Rings"
element.locH = 10
element.locV = 170
element.width = 140
element.height = 20
add list, element
```

The last element needed is the OK button.

```
element = getItemPropList(gMui)
element.type = #defaultPushButton
element.title = "OK"
element.locH = 40
element.locV = 200
element.width = 80
element.height = 20
add list, element
```

PART

VII

CH

24

After all the elements are ready, a call to *Initialize* creates the dialog box. You need to pass it the window properties and the element properties. Then, use *Run* to create the dialog box.

```
Initialize(gMUI, [#windowPropList: windowProps, #windowItemList: list])
Run(gMUI)
end
```

Unlike the other MUI dialog boxes, a custom one does not return a simple value. Instead, it uses the callback handler defined to send any activity information. It sends every click or item change. It passes this information back as three parameters: what happened, which item it affected, and the property list for that item.

Here is a handler that receives these messages. It is a very simple handler that just sends messages to the Message window:

```
on myCallbackHandler action, elementNumber, elementList
  global gMUI
  put "Action Reported:"&&action
  if action = #itemClicked and elementList.title = "OK" then
    put action, elementList.title
    put gMUI
    Stop(gMUI,0)
    gMUI = VOID

  else if action = #itemChanged then
    newval = elementList.value
    itemName = elementList.title
    put itemName&&"changed to"&&newval
  end if
end
```

In real life, you should record the information provided to this handler in global variables or fields. Each time an item is changed you can record the change. Or, alternatively, you can reference the values of all the interface elements through the "gMUI" global.

The scope of custom MUI dialog boxes does not end with pop-ups, labels, and check boxes. You can have radio buttons, sliders, bitmaps, editable text fields, dividers, and other types of buttons as well.

To see all the possibilities, try this in the Message window:

```
put Interface(Xtra "Mui")
```

What you will see is a huge listing of all the possibilities in the MUI dialog box. This listing is also the most up-to-date one. The MUI Xtra is constantly being updated by Macromedia to accommodate new needs in the software. Just about every update of Director has a slightly different MUI Xtra.

TROUBLESHOOTING MIAWS AND ALTERNATIVES

- Always make sure that you *forget* MIAWs when you want to get rid of them. Closing them only makes them invisible.

- Be sure to test all your code in an MIAW. If a Lingo error occurs in the code in an MIAW while it is running as an MIAW, Director may return bad information about what is wrong and where the problem is.

- Test your MIAWs on both platforms, and in various versions of operating systems (Windows 95 and 98, for instance), to make sure they look okay.

- The MUI Dialog Xtra was not designed for developers to use. Instead it was made for Macromedia to use for future Director and Xtra development. It is a very advanced technique and should not be attempted by beginners. It is also not fully supported by Macromedia.

- Errors in MUI Xtra property lists can cause Director to crash. Save your movies often when you are working with the MUI Xtra.

- MIAWs can position themselves differently for different screen sizes. Be sure to test your MIAWs with different monitor settings and adjust the *rect* property accordingly.

DID YOU KNOW?

- You can use one MIAW file to create many MIAWs. Just use *tell* to make the MIAW go to another frame in the MIAW movie file before making it visible. You can even use the same movie file that the Stage is using!

- You can use the *drawRect* property to scale the MIAW, including all bitmaps and other scalable sprites. You can use this to display an MIAW as double-pixel size, for instance.

- You can change items in a custom MUI dialog box while the dialog box is on the screen so that you can have a bitmap in the MUI dialog box that changes in reaction to another interface element.

- You can take the picture of an MIAW just as you can take the picture of the Stage. Just use *(the stage).picture* in a piece of code in the MIAW, or use the *tell* command. The MIAW doesn't even have to be visible.

XTRAS

In this chapter

Even with all the features in Director 7, most developers will, at one time or another, need to use an Xtra. Xtras are small files that extend Director capabilities, either by adding cast member types, Lingo commands, or authoring tools. In fact, many standard items in Director, such as vector members, network Lingo, and bitmap importing, are made possible by Xtras already installed in Director.

WHAT ARE XTRAS?

Xtras serve three purposes. First, they give Macromedia a way to develop pieces of Director independently, without requiring it to make a whole new version of Director. Features such as Java export, animated cursors, image filters, and vector graphics are all made possible by Xtras, not anything inside the Director program itself.

Xtras are also used by Macromedia to add features that not all developers may need in their finished products. Network Lingo, for instance, is not needed in a Projector that does not communicate with the Internet. Because network Lingo is enabled through Xtras, these Xtras can be left out when a Projector is created and the resulting Projector is smaller.

Finally, Xtras can be developed by third parties to add functionality to Director that Macromedia has not provided. Many companies produce Xtras commercially, and you can purchase them. At other times, companies develop Xtras for their own use in a single product.

XTRAS THAT COME WITH DIRECTOR 7

Many Xtras are installed with Director in the Xtras folder inside the Director folder. Still more are on the Director 7 CD-ROM in the Xtra Partners folder.

Macromedia provides many Xtras that come pre-installed with Director. You can find these in the Xtras folder. Most are Xtras that add functionality to the authoring environment, but some can be used in Projectors as well.

The following list includes most of the Xtras that come with Director:

- ActiveX—Also known as the Control Xtra, this Windows-only Xtra enables you to access and use ActiveX controls, such as the Internet Explorer browser engine, or custom-built ActiveX programs.
- Beatnik Xtra Lite—This Xtra, provided by a third-party company, enables you to play MIDI files, Beatnik music files, and even single notes from a bank of sounds.
- MacroMix—This Windows-only Xtra enables Director movies to play more than one sound at a time in Windows.
- Photoshop Filters—This Xtra enables you to use Photoshop-compatible filters on bitmap cast members.
- Flash Asset—This Xtra enables you to import Flash movies as cast members. It is also used as the engine for vector shape members.

- Intel Effects—These Windows-only Xtras enable you to perform a variety of processor-intensive special effects.

- Animated GIF Asset—The Xtra enables you to import and use Animated GIFs.

- FileIO—This Xtra adds Lingo commands to enable you to open, save, and modify text files.

- Font Asset—This is the Xtra that enables you to import fonts as cast members.

- Import Xtra for PowerPoint—This Xtra enables you to import Microsoft PowerPoint files. It converts the file to a Score and Cast, complete with all the items in the original presentation.

- MUI—This Xtra contains code to generate many of the dialog boxes used in Director. You can also use it to create your own dialog boxes.

- SWA Xtras—These Xtras enable you to import and create Shockwave audio files and use them in your movies. They also enable you to compress internal sounds with Shockwave audio compression.

- Text Asset—This Xtra drives the text member, as well as all the text-based authoring windows, such as the script window.

- XMLParser—This Xtra contains additional Lingo commands for dealing with XML code, such as HTML.

- Mix Xtras—These Xtras enable you to import all sorts of different file types, including images and sounds.

- MultiUser—This Xtra enables you to communicate with the Director MultiUser server program. It also communicates with other Director Projectors or Shockwave applets as long as they are networked.

- Net Support Xtras—These Xtras add the network Lingo commands and the protocols to support them.

- Photocaster 2—With this Xtra you can import a single layer of a Photoshop document. The full version enables you to import all the layers of a Photoshop document.

- QuickTime 3—This Xtra enables you to use any QuickTime 3 movie, including QuickTime VR movies, as a cast member.

- Save As Java—This Xtra, and its supporting files, takes your current Director movie and creates a Java applet that emulates it.

Many of the Xtras in the Director Xtras folder are not meant to be used in Projectors. They are simply things that extend the authoring environment. The MIX Xtras, for instance, are used only to import images and sounds. However, sometimes this Xtra is required if you are importing new images in your Projector while it is running on the user's machine.

Some Xtras cannot be used in Projectors. The QuickTime 3 Asset Options Xtra, for instance, supplies the Options dialog box that the author uses during authoring. There are also "options" Xtras for the Flash and Animated GIF Xtras. Including these with a

Projector results in an error message. These three Xtras are all named with the word "options", so you know not to include them.

→ **See** "Using Text Files and the FileIO Xtra," Chapter 16, "Controlling Text," for more information about using the FileIO Xtra

→ **See** "MUI Xtra Dialog Boxes," Chapter 24, "Movies in a Window and Alternatives," for more information about using the MUI Dialog Xtra

→ **See** "Making Projectors," Chapter 36, "Delivering the Goods," for more information about including Xtras in your Projector

Third-Party Xtras

The Xtra Partners folder on the CD-ROM includes many Xtras that are not installed with Director initially. Many are only demos or restricted versions. To use these Xtras, you will have to register or purchase the full product from the individual companies.

However, the versions on the CD-ROM are very useful in themselves. The Buddy API Xtra, for instance, enables you to use any two functions that you choose at a time for free, and the Print-O-Matic Lite Xtra is very powerful in itself.

Buddy API Xtra

The Buddy API Xtra adds a bunch of Lingo functions that deal with the computer operating system. Because the Mac and Windows operating systems differ so much, many of these functions work on only one platform or the other.

To be available for use, the Buddy API Xtra merely needs to be present in the Xtras folder. You don't have to create an instance of the Xtra or do anything else. Just use the functions as you would any other Lingo syntax.

A basic example uses this Xtra to get the operating system version. For instance, on a Mac, in the Message window, you can do this:

```
put baVersion("mac")
-- "8.5.1"
```

All functions of the Buddy API Xtra start with "ba" to distinguish them from other Lingo functions. Here are some more useful functions:

```
put baVersion("os")
-- "Mac8"
```

The other possible values for this function are "Win16," "Win95," "Win98," "WinNT," and "Mac7". The following function tests to see whether a font is installed:

```
put baFontInstalled("Arial","Plain")
-- 1
```

On Windows, you can even use Buddy API to install a font. You can also get Windows registry information, .ini files, or command line arguments to Windows Projectors, restart Windows, set the default DOS directory, restrict the cursor to an area, and set screensaver information.

Buddy API can also create a folder and copy and rename files—tasks that are sadly missing from the FileIO Xtra.

Take a look at the Buddy API documentation on the CD-ROM to see a complete list of commands and functions. It is a truly impressive list.

PRINT-O-MATIC LITE

Director's printing functionality is restricted to the *printFrom* command. Although this is a nice feature for animators who want a frame of animation printed to help with development, it has little use in Projectors.

All that the *printFrom* command can do is print a screenshot of the Stage. You can set a reduction amount, or choose to print one frame or a series of frames.

The Print-O-Matic Lite Xtra adds the *print* command to Lingo. You can use this command to print any cast member or text string.

Although this is already an improvement over the *printFrom* command, Print-O-Matic does a lot more when you create an instance of the Xtra and use more of its commands. A typical handler looks like this:

```
on printPage
  gPrintDoc = new(xtra "PrintOMatic_Lite")
  if not objectP(gPrintDoc) then
    alert "Unable to use Print-O-Matic"
    exit
  end if
  setDocumentName gPrintDoc, "My Document"
  setMargins gPrintDoc, Rect(36,36,36,36)
  setLandscapeMode gPrintDoc, TRUE
  append gPrintDoc, member "myMember"
  if doJobSetup(gPrintDoc) then print gPrintDoc
  gPrintDoc = 0
end
```

PART

VII

CH

25

The handler first needs to create the Xtra instance. Then it checks to make sure that it was created. It then uses the *setDocumentName* command to name the print job. It uses the *setMargins* and *setLandscapeMode* commands to set the margins to about a half an inch and to print in landscape mode rather than vertically.

The *append* command is used to add items to the print job. In this case, just one member is added. However, you can add members, sprites, and even plain text.

Finally, the *doJobSetup* command is used to bring up the operating system's print dialog box. This function returns TRUE if the user clicks the OK button. Then, the *print* command sends the whole thing to the printer.

The full version of Print-O-Matic enables you to perform more functions and even draw lines directly to the print buffer.

PHOTOCASTER 2

PhotoCaster has been some developers' best friend since Director 5. This Xtra enables you to import PhotoShop files. No big deal, right? After all, you can import PhotoShop files normally. However, Photocaster enables you to import *layers* from a PhotoShop file.

With the unregistered version that comes with Director, you can only import layers one at a time, but with the full version you can import an entire file with each layer as a separate cast member. Even better, the registration points in the members will match up perfectly when you are finished.

Using this tool, an artist can create a many-layered document in PhotoShop, and a Director developer can import the file as layers. This means that these layers can all be placed on the Stage together. They can be made background transparent so higher layers show through to lower ones. The result looks just like the original PhotoShop document, but each layer is still independent and can be moved or removed as the developer wants.

This technique is often used so that an artist can create a whole array of art—backgrounds, buttons, animated actors, and so on—all in one PhotoShop document. This makes the art very easy for the artist to maintain, and also easy for the Director developer to import.

Figure 25.1 shows the PhotoCaster import dialog box. This is just to give you an idea of what options are available. Try it out yourself to get more precise information about how it works.

Figure 25.1
The PhotoCaster Xtra enables you to import individual layers of PhotoShop documents.

> **Tip**
>
> PhotoCaster also takes 32-bit images and converts them to 8-bit ones. It can actually take a set of images and convert them all to a new 8-bit color palette that is optimized for use across all the images.

BEATNIK

The Beatnik Lite Xtra is a new addition to Director 7. Beatnik is also a plug-in for Internet browsers. It includes small files, similar to MIDI, that play music, plus a file that represents a bank of instruments.

The Xtra and Director 7 come with several demos. The sound quality is truly impressive. Plus, the Xtra is cross-platform, which is even more impressive.

You can use Beatnik to play simple MIDI files, if you like. The Lingo code is pretty typical for an Xtra. First, you have to create an instance of the Xtra. Then, you have to give it some initial information. In this case, the Xtra needs to know the location of the instrument bank it is to use.

When the Xtra instance is ready, a simple *play* command will kick off a MIDI file. To stop it, the *stop* command is used, and setting the Xtra instance to 0 clears memory.

```
global gBeatnik

-- This handler will initialize Beatnik
on startBeatnik
  -- create Xtra instance
  gBeatnik = new(xtra "beatnik")
  if not objectP(gBeatnik) then
    alert "Could not access Beatnik."
    exit
  end if

  -- initialize it
  setSliceSize (gBeatnik,2)
  if the platform contains "mac" then
    setSampleLibrary(gBeatnik, the applicationPath &¬
      "xtras:Beatnik Xtra Lite:Patches.hsb")
  else
    setSampleLibrary(gBeatnik, the applicationPath &¬
      "Xtras\Beatnik Xtra Lite\Patches.hsb")
  end if
  setReady(gBeatnik)

  -- check to make sure it is ready
  if not isReady(gBeatnik) then
    alert "Could not initialize Beatnik."
    exit
  end if
end

on playMIDI
  play(gBeatnik,0,the pathname&"MYMIDI.MID")
end
```

```
on stopBeatnik
  stop(gBeatnik)
  gBeatnik = 0
end
```

In the preceding example, the location of the song bank is specified as the location of Director, plus the Patches.hsb file that is included in the Beatnik folder in the Xtras folder. Your Projectors, of course, will use a different path.

> **Tip**
>
> Beatnik also includes Lingo commands, such as *noteOn* and *playNote,* which enable you to play one note at a time, even from different instruments.

The documentation that comes with Beatnik is pretty comprehensive. Check it out for more information. This Xtra looks like it will finally bring high-quality music into Director.

3D GROOVE

The 3D Groove Xtra is the one that Director developers have been waiting for for years. This Xtra enables you to import and manipulate 3D environments. This is the real thing, not a slow VRML Xtra or a panoramic or object-based 3D display engine. This Xtra is meant for creating 3D games and similar applications.

Two demos of this Xtra appear on the Director 7 CD, so you can see for yourself. Figure 25.2 shows a screenshot of one of these demos.

Figure 25.2
The 3D Groove Xtra enables the user to navigate through 3D space, as in some popular games.

One of the best features of 3D Groove is that it is cross-platform. You can develop and deploy on both Mac and Windows.

The beta versions I have played with show that this Xtra is really meant for the Director experts. It includes a huge list of Lingo commands for manipulating 3D objects and the camera. Look for the final version of this Xtra to be ready by the time you read this.

Using Xtra Lingo

A few Lingo properties and functions help you work with Xtras. You can, for instance, determine whether an Xtra is working simply by trying to use it. If the initial *new* command does not return a valid object, you know there has been an error. Use the *objectP* function to determine whether you have a valid object:

```
xObj = new(xtra "FileIO")
put objectP(xObj)
-- 1
```

If you want to determine whether an Xtra is present before you try to use it, you can take a look at each Xtra present by using the *name* property, as well as the *number* property, of the *xtras* object. Here is a handler that checks for the existence of an Xtra:

```
on checkForXtra xtraname
  repeat with i = 1 to the number of xtras
    if the name of xtra i = xtraname then
      return TRUE
    end if
  end repeat
  return FALSE
end
```

You can test this handler in the Message window:

```
put checkForXtra("FileIO")
-- 1
put checkForXtra("xxx")
-- 0
```

Two other properties also tell you about what Xtras are available. The *the xtraList* property returns a long list of what Xtras are available. Each item in the list contains a #name and #version property.

There is also a *the movieXtraList* property that corresponds to the dialog box you get when you choose Modify, Movie, Xtras. Each item is a list that contains either a name, and/or a #packageFiles list. The #packageFiles list contains a #name and a #version that gives the movie the information it needs to download the Xtra from the Internet for use in Shockwave.

For most Xtras, you can use the *interface* function to get a list of all of the possible commands, properties, and usage guidelines. The results vary from Xtra to Xtra, depending on what the developer decided this function should return. You can use it in the Message window by typing something like this: `put interface(xtra "FileIO")`.

OTHER XTRAS

Appendix H, "Guide to Xtras," of this book lists most, but not all, of the Xtras available at the time of printing. Because Xtras are developed independently of versions of Director, new ones come out all the time. Xtras are also updated constantly.

It is possible, maybe even likely, that a new Xtra will be announced by some company the day after this book is published. Another developer will decide to retire an Xtra as well. For these reasons, trying to compile a list of available Xtras is difficult.

It is also unnecessary. Several online resources list the locations of Xtras on the Internet. These are usually updated fairly frequently, so they will always be more up-to-date than a book. Check Appendix C, "Online Resources," of this book for a list of Web locations.

TROUBLESHOOTING XTRAS

- Remember that Xtras require different files for different platforms. If you use the Buddy API Xtra, for instance, you have to bundle the Mac version with your Mac Projectors and the Windows version with Windows Projectors.

- After you decide to use an Xtra with a movie, you must include it with the Projector when you are finished. You can do this in several ways. See Chapter 37, "Creating Java Applets," for detailed information.

- Xtras can be used with Shockwave movies, but the Xtra must have a downloadable counterpart on the Web that has been approved by Macromedia. Check the Macromedia site for an updated list. This means a major Xtra such as QuickTime 3 is available in Shockwave, whereas a rare custom Xtra is not.

- If you are thinking about making your own Xtra, beware of the trap into which many developers fall: They often assume that a task cannot be done with Lingo alone when it can. Director 7 Lingo is so powerful that you should always carefully consider the option of using Lingo before commissioning an Xtra.

- If you ever get the message "A duplicate Xtra has been found…" when starting Director, this means that you have to go to your Xtras folder and find the duplicate. Unfortunately, Director does not point you in any direction. Because the same Xtra can have different filenames, it might be hard to find the culprit. Many times, you have to remove one Xtra at a time and restart Director until the mystery is solved.

DID YOU KNOW?

- The xtrainfo.txt file contains information that determines what Xtras are bundled with Projectors by default. You can change this each time you make a Projector, or edit this file to change the defaults.

- While authoring, you can use the *showXlib* command in the Message window to see a simple list of all the Xtras present. It is not as detailed as *put the xtraList*, but most of the time it is what you need to see which Xtras are there.

- If you want to access an Xtra that is not in the Xtras folder, you can open it with the *openXlib* command, followed by the full or relative pathname. You can also use *closeXlib* to free up memory when you are finished with the Xtra.

CHAPTER 26

DEVELOPING FOR DEVELOPERS

In this chapter

Many times, the Lingo programmer's job in a company is not to develop content directly, but to build templates and tools for others, usually referred to as "multimedia authors." These tools can take the form of Lingo-based Xtras, a behavior library, or even a set of Director movie templates. This chapter is all about creating those tools, either by Score recording, by creating Xtras, or by making behavior libraries.

SCORE RECORDING

Although behaviors can change the properties of a sprite while the movie is running, these properties all return to their default Score settings when the movie is done. Lingo does have the capability, however, to affect real changes in the Score.

To make changes in the Score you need to use Score recording commands. You can define the beginning of a Score recording session, and then make changes to sprites. These changes then become "real," because the Score is permanently changed. You can even insert and delete frames.

Animators can use this technique to build Score-based animations, rather than just having Lingo control the animation during playback. This enables Lingo developers to make tools for animators that will result in visible Score changes.

WRITING TO THE SCORE

Creating or modifying sprites in the Score is pretty simple. First, you must use the *beginRecording* command. Every change to a sprite between that and the *endRecording* command effects a change in the Score.

After a Score recording session begins, you can use regular Lingo commands, such as *go to* jump around in the Score. It is when you start using sprite properties that you effect change.

The following is a handler that adds the member number 1 to the Score in sprite 7. It uses *go* to make sure that it is placing it in frame 1:

```
on simpleChange
  beginRecording
    go to frame 1
    sprite(7).member = member(1)
    sprite(7).loc = point(100,100)
    updateFrame
  endRecording
end
```

The command *updateFrame* is actually where the change is made. You need to issue either an *updateFrame* or an *insertFrame* command. The first command places all your changes in the current frame, and advances the movie to the next frame. The *insertFrame* command places the movie in the current frame, makes a copy of that frame, changes and all, and then inserts it after the current frame. The playback head is now in the inserted frame.

Here is a handler that performs a more complex task. It inserts frames, beginning with the current one, and moves sprite 1 over to the right 10 pixels each time. It does this until the sprite reaches the horizontal location of 600:

```
on recordMove
  sNum = 1
  minX = 0
  maxX = 600
  stepSize = 10

  beginRecording
    x = minX
    repeat while TRUE
      sprite(sNum).locH = x
      insertFrame
      x = x + stepSize
      if x > maxX then exit repeat
    end repeat
  endRecording
end
```

Although this handler doesn't really do anything that a behavior can't while the movie is running, it demonstrates creating animation in the Score with Score recording. A tool such as this can enable animators to easily add common animations to the Score, while also using traditional Score animation techniques in other sprites.

SCORE RECORDING TOOLS

A more useful Score recording handler is one that takes existing sprites and manipulates them in a way that no other tool can. Director includes the Align Tool, which enables you to lock horizontal and vertical positions of sprites to each other. However, what is missing is a tool that evenly spaces sprites.

The next handler does just that. It takes three or more sprites in the same frame, finds the minimum and maximum horizontal and vertical positions, and then uses that information to evenly space them. For simplicity, it assumes that the first sprite should be positioned first, the second should be positioned second, and so on. Therefore, it does not work in cases where you have the sprites out of order.

The first thing that this handler does is get *the scoreSelection*. This is a list of lists that tells you what the author has selected in the Score. For instance, if sprite 7 of frame 5 is selected, you get [[7,7,5,5]]. The first two numbers of each item are the sprite, and the third and fourth numbers represent the frame range.

```
on evenlySpace
  set ss = the scoreSelection

  if ss.count < 3 then
    alert "You must select at least 3 items"
    exit
  end if

  -- find max and min locations
```

```
minX = sprite(ss[1][1]).locH
maxX = minX
minY = sprite(ss[1][1]).locV
maxY = minY
repeat with i = 2 to ss.count
  x = sprite(ss[i][1]).locH
  y = sprite(ss[i][1]).locV

  if x < minX then minX = x
  if x > maxX then maxX = x
  if y < minY then minY = y
  if y > maxY then maxY = y
end repeat

-- figure out spacing
spaceX = (maxX - minX)/(ss.count-1)
spaceY = (maxY - minY)/(ss.count-1)

-- record all changes
beginRecording

  -- space in order ofsprite number
  x = minX
  y = minY
  repeat with i = 1 to ss.count
    sprite(ss[i][1]).loc = point(x,y)
    x = x + spaceX
    y = y + spaceY
  end repeat

  -- set changes and end recording
  updateFrame
endRecording

end
```

You can also use *the selection of castLib* to determine what members are selected in the cast window. If the author has selected members 2 through 5 and member 8, for instance, you get this result:

```
put the selection of castLib 1
-- [[2, 5], [8, 8]]
```

Using *the selection of castLib* and *the scoreSelection* you can determine what members and sprites the author is pointing to at any time. This property can be used to build tools that react to different author selections.

CREATING MIAW XTRAS

After you have built a handy routine like the *on evenlySpace* handler described previously, it can be used to create an Xtra. These are not the sort of Xtras that were discussed in Chapter 25, "Xtras." Instead of creating an Xtra using C or some other programming language, you are simply creating a Director movie and then placing it in the Xtras folder.

After a Director movie is in the Xtras folder, it appears in the Xtras menu. When selected, it is brought up in a Movie In a Window (MIAW). It can then *tell* the Stage to do things, such as initiate Score recording.

The *on evenlySpace* handler can be turned into a simple Xtra by placing it in its own movie. Make the Stage size of that movie very small, maybe 240×160. Then, add a button that calls the *on evenlySpace* handler. This handler needs one change: the *tell the stage* command must be added before the first line, and an *end tell* at the end. With this change, this handler directs all the commands at the Stage, not the MIAW Xtra itself.

All that is left is to place the Director movie in the Xtras folder. You can even compress it into a .dcr file before doing this. Doing so makes the Xtra available to be used, but makes the scripts unavailable to other developers. Therefore, you can produce Lingo-based Xtras for distribution without worrying about someone stealing your code.

→ **See** "Using MIAWs," Chapter 24, "Movies in a Window and Alternatives," for more information on using MIAWs

USING BEHAVIOR LIBRARIES

Just as a Director movie can be placed in the Xtras folder, a Director cast library file can be placed in the Libs folder. This makes it available in the Library Palette.

Director 7 already comes complete with a large set of behavior libraries that appear in this palette. Take a look at the Libs folder in the Director folder to see how these are arranged. Some cast libraries are just sitting in the folder, whereas others are in subfolders. This structure determines how the libraries appear in the Library Palette pop-up menu.

You can use this structure by creating a new folder in the Libs folder for your own custom behaviors. The same structure relates the Xtras folder to the Xtras menu.

PART

VII

CH

26

Tip

A lot of developers have a behavior library that they constantly update as needed. The Libs folder is the perfect place to keep this cast library so that the behaviors are always accessible.

You are not restricted to just behaviors. You can also place any other type of cast member in a library Cast. You can store clip art, common sounds, and even movie scripts. Depending on the type of member, you can drag these members from the library palette onto the Stage, Score, Cast, or all three.

You can even provide custom icons for cast members in a library. When you are building the members of the cast library to be used as a library, you can open up the Member Properties dialog box and use a small pop-up menu on the left, under the member's icon, to copy, cut, and paste icons. The special icons with the behaviors in Director's built-in libraries were given their special icons in this way.

TROUBLESHOOTING DEVELOPING FOR DEVELOPERS

- Score recording always requires an *insertFrame* or *updateFrame* command to make the changes stick. Forgetting this is a common mistake.

- Score recording has been known to correctly update the Score, but to not show the changes in the Score window until the movie has been rewound and played again. Keep this in mind if it doesn't seem to work at first.

- MIAW Xtras are easy to create and open, but not so easy to eliminate. If you permit the user to click the close box in the window to make it go away, the window is actually still there. You can even see it in *the windowList*. A good idea is to place a *forget(the activeWindow)* in the *on closeWindow* handler. This forces the window to be discarded when the user clicks the close button.

DID YOU KNOW?

- If you don't want the user to see each change in a Score recording session as it occurs, you can set *the updateLock* to FALSE at the beginning of the session. This causes the Stage to freeze while changes are made.

- You can set *the windowType* of a MIAW Xtra after it has been opened. The programmer will see this change occur, however.

- You can also set the MIAW Xtra's screen position after it has been opened.

PART VIII

USING DIRECTOR TO CREATE PROFESSIONAL APPLICATIONS

CHAPTER **27**

EDUCATIONAL APPLICATIONS

In this chapter

Using a single Director command, function, or property is easy for novice and advanced users alike. However, putting syntax together to make a useful program is a much harder task.

This chapter, and the ones that follow it, give examples of typical types of programs created with Director. An overview of each program is given, followed by the Lingo required to put it together. All this code, and in fact a complete demonstration movie, is included on the CD-ROM that accompanies this book. To get the most out of these chapters, look at the movie on the CD-ROM to see how the Lingo code, Score, Cast, and Stage all work together.

This first applications chapter focuses on educational programs. Five typical programs were selected. The first is a simple matching game where the user must click and drag items on the right to items on the left. The second is a drawing program that gives users the opportunity to create their own artwork. The third program is a simple example of using Lingo to turn on and off overlay sprites like transparent overlays in a textbook. The fourth program is a geography quiz, where users must answer questions by clicking a map. The last program is one that simulates a standardized test.

CREATING A MATCHING GAME

A matching game is fairly common in most educational CD-ROMs. Users see two lists of words, names, or phrases. If they were working on paper, they would then draw lines between the two lists, matching up those items that are related.

For instance, users can be asked to match up inventors and their inventions. The two lists appear as this:

```
Benjamin Franklin     Cotton Gin
Thomas Edison         Telegraph
Eli Whitney           Electricity
Alfred Nobel          Light Bulb
Samuel Morse          Rocket Engine
Robert Goddard        Dynamite
```

The two lists do not match up directly, of course; such a game would be very simple.

When this type of activity is done as a computer program, drawing lines is no longer necessary. Instead, users can drag one item over to the other. Sometimes graphics are drawn to show that items fit together, like puzzle pieces.

Figure 27.1 shows a screen of a matching game program. It includes two columns of six words each. The items are drawn so that they appear to be pieces that have been ripped apart from each other. The user's task is to drag the pieces on the right over to match the pieces on the left.

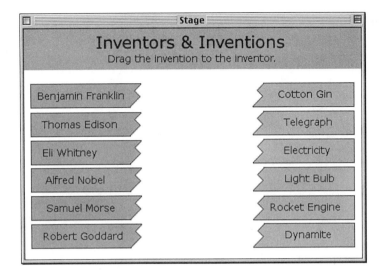

Figure 27.1
The matching game uses two columns of items. The user must drag items on the right over to their matches on the left.

To start a project like this, which requires many similar cast members, you should first come up with a logical naming scheme for the members. In this case, all the members on the left are named "left X," where the X stands for a number. All the members on the right are named "right X." The number assigned as the X signifies which left and right elements match up. So "Benjamin Franklin" is "left 1" and "Electricity" is "right 1".

The left elements do not move, so they do not need to have any behavior attached to them. The right elements, however, need a behavior. In fact, this behavior can take care of the entire game.

The behavior starts off with the declaration of the properties:

```
property pDrag    -- is the sprite currently being dragged
property pOffset  -- the cursor offset used in the drag
property pOrigLoc -- the starting location of the sprite
property pLocked  -- is the sprite locked in place
```

When the behavior starts, it needs to record the original location of the sprite, plus set some other properties. The original location is needed so that if a user drags the item, but does not successfully match it to the correct item, it snaps back in place.

```
-- set all of the properties that need it
on beginSprite me
  pOrigLoc = sprite(me.spriteNum).loc
  pDrag = FALSE
  pLocked = FALSE
end
```

When the user clicks the sprite, the dragging begins. But first, the *on mouseDown* handler checks to see whether the sprite is already locked in place. If it is, dragging is not allowed any more. The *on mouseDown* handler also determines the offset between the mouse and the sprite location, so that it can be used to make it possible to drag a sprite from any location on the sprite, not just the center.

```
on mouseDown me
  -- don't allow to drag if already in place
  if pLocked = TRUE then exit

  -- set to drag
  pDrag = TRUE

  -- record offset between cursor and sprite
  pOffset = sprite(me.spriteNum).loc - the mouseLoc
end
```

When the user releases the mouse button, the dragging comes to an end. It also means that the behavior must check to see whether the item has found its match. The *on mouseUpOutside* handler is also called, in case the user has moved so quickly that the mouse is not over the sprite when it is released.

```
-- turn off dragging and check for correct placement
on mouseUp me
  pDrag = FALSE
  checkLock(me)
end
on mouseUpOutside me
  pDrag = FALSE
  checkLock(me)
end
```

This behavior uses the *on prepareFrame* handler to reposition the sprite as it is being dragged. This keeps the sprite location as close as possible to the mouse location. However, handlers such as *on exitFrame* or *on enterFrame* would have produced virtually identical results.

```
-- reposition sprite if being dragged
on prepareFrame me
  if pDrag then
    sprite(me.spriteNum).loc = the mouseLoc + pOffset
  end if
end
```

The "on checkLock" handler takes the name of the member and determines which other member it should match. It then searches all the sprites for that matching member. When it finds it, it checks to determine whether the two sprites are close enough to be locked together. If a lock is called for, the sprites are set to be at the same location. Then, the "on checkForDone" handler is called to see whether the game is complete.

Because matching sprites are intended to lock together with their locations being equal, the two bitmaps need to be drawn so that their registration points determine how the two sprites appear on the Stage relative to each other. In the case of the images in Figure 27.1, the registration points for the left side pieces are at the right side, and the registration points of the right side pieces are on the left side. Therefore, when they are placed in the same location on the Stage, they appear to lock together, side by side. Check the movie on the CD-ROM to see exactly where the registration points are.

```
--check to see if there is a match
on checkLock me

  -- determine match member's name
  memName = sprite(me.spriteNum).member.name
  memNum = memName.word[2]
  matchName = "left"&&memNum

  -- check all the sprites
  repeat with i = 1 to the lastChannel

    -- is it the matching sprite?
    if sprite(i).member.name = matchName then

      -- is it close enough to lock in place?
      if closeEnough(me, sprite(i).loc,sprite(me.spriteNum).loc) then

        -- place sprite in exact location
        sprite(me.spriteNum).loc = sprite(i).loc

        -- set lock
        pLocked = TRUE

        -- change colors
        sprite(me.spriteNum).bgColor = rgb("#CCCCCC")
        sprite(i).bgColor = rgb("#CCCCCC")

        -- see if all are locked in place
        checkForDone(me)

        -- leave this handler
        exit
      end if
    end if
  end repeat

  -- never found a matching member close enough
  -- return to original position
  sprite(me.spriteNum).loc = pOrigLoc
end
```

This next handler is used by the "on checkLock" handler to determine whether two pieces are close enough to each other to lock. It basically checks to see whether both the horizontal and vertical locations are within 10 pixels of each other:

```
-- determine if two locations are close
on closeEnough me, loc1, loc2
  maxdistance = 10 -- use 10 pixels as max distance
  if abs(loc1.locH - loc2.locH) < maxdistance then
    if abs(loc1.locV - loc2.locV) < maxdistance then
      -- close enough, return TRUE
```

```
      return TRUE
    end if
  end if
  return FALSE
end
```

This handler, which will be called by the "on checkForDone" handler, returns a TRUE if the item has been locked in place:

```
-- simply report on condition of pLocked
on amIDone me
  return pLocked
end
```

To determine whether all the pieces have been locked in place, a "amIDone" message is sent to every sprite. Sprites that do not have this behavior attached to them return a simple VOID. The rest return a TRUE or FALSE. If a FALSE is encountered, the handler ends, because the game is not complete. If no FALSE is found in all the sprites, the movie jumps to the payoff, or final, frame:

```
-- check all sprites to see if all are locked
on checkForDone me
  repeat with i = 1 to the lastChannel

    -- ask a sprite if it is done
    done = sendSprite(sprite i,#amIDone)

    -- sprite did not know about #amIDone
    if voidP(done) then next repeat

    -- sprite returned that it was not locked
    if done = FALSE then exit
  end repeat

  -- if they got here, then all are done
  -- go to another frame
  go to frame "payoff"
end
```

The only other Lingo script needed to make this program work is a simple looping frame script. The rest is taken care of by one behavior. This means that you can easily add more items to the game. The trick is to create two matching members, both left and right items, and name them correctly. Then put them both on the Stage and drop this behavior onto the right-side item. You don't even have to worry about which sprites these members are in.

Tip

If you want to use text members, rather than bitmaps, there is only one thing to consider. Text members always have their registration points set to the upper left of the member. So to match them up, you need to come up with a new way of determining when items "lock" and a new standard of how to position the items when they are locked. For instance, you might want to make the items lock to the upper-right corner of the rectangle of the sprite, instead of the location of the sprite, which is really the upper-left corner.

When this game is done, the movie moves to the "payoff" frame. Here, you can place any sort of sound or animation that you want. You can even have the matching items animate, because you already know exactly where they must be positioned for the game to end.

Another consideration is sound. Using the *puppetSound* command, you can add sounds that activate when the items lock in place and sounds that activate when there is a mismatch.

→ **See** "Dragging Sprites," Chapter 15, "Graphic Interface Elements," for more information on behaviors that drag sprites

MAKING A DRAWING ACTIVITY

A common activity in educational computer programs for younger kids is one in which they can draw. These programs are usually based on the early simple draw programs made for the computers in the '70s and '80s.

Basically, the user can click the screen and draw while moving the mouse. The example used in this section includes different colors that the user can choose, as well as different brushes.

Using a sprite to draw is actually pretty simple. All you have to do is make it follow the cursor, and at the same time turn its *trails* property on, so that impressions of the sprite's member are left behind as the user moves. However, this method is flawed. If the user moves the mouse too quickly, subsequent impressions of the sprite can be far apart, leaving a gap in the drawing. This is not what happens when you are drawing with a marker or crayon on paper. Therefore, this program must handle cases where the mouse is moved quickly, and place smooth lines between the two points.

Figure 27.2 shows the sample movie. On the left are some colors, with the current color outlined. Under that are some brushes with the current brush outlined. The main area starts off blank, and the user can draw in it.

Figure 27.2
With this simple drawing applet, users can change colors and brushes. They can use the color white, along with a larger brush, to "erase."

PART
VIII

CH
27

This movie also has one large behavior driving it. However, it is not on a sprite, but in the frame script channel. This is necessary because the user is not clicking a sprite to draw, but clicking an empty area of the Stage to draw. Therefore, the frame script channel is the logical place to put the handlers.

A sprite must still be used for drawing, however, so whether drawing is in progress is one of the properties. In addition, the properties include one that determines whether drawing is happening at the moment, one that records the location of the last draw impression, and the member to use for drawing, which can be considered the "brush."

```
property pDrawSprite -- which sprite to use
property pDraw -- drawing in progress
property pLastDrawLoc -- last spot drawn on
property pBrush -- member to use to paint

on beginSprite me
  pDrawSprite = 7 -- use sprite 7
  pLastDrawLoc = 0 -- no last drawing loc
  pBrush = sprite(pDrawSprite).member
end
```

When the user clicks the Stage, the drawing begins. All that is really needed is to set the "pDraw" property to TRUE. However, it is also useful to show users a representation of the brush currently in use. Because all the brushes are 1-bit members that are less than 16×16 in size, they can also be used as cursors with the *cursor* command:

```
on mouseDown me
  pDraw = TRUE
  cursor([member pBrush, member pBrush])
end
```

When the user lifts up the mouse button, drawing should end. Not only should the "pDraw" property be reset, but the brush should be removed from the screen. Because the next place the user starts to draw might be a totally different spot, the "pLastDrawLoc" is reset so that a line is not drawn connecting the end point of this brush stroke with the starting point of the next. The cursor is also reset.

```
on mouseUp me
  sprite(pDrawSprite).loc = point(-100,-100)
  pDraw = FALSE
  pLastDrawLoc = 0 -- forget last drawing loc
  cursor(0)
end
```

The drawing is actually done with the *on exitFrame* handler. This means that the drawing is updated exactly once per frame. Because you want the program to run as smoothly as possible, you should turn the frame rate for the movie up to the maximum: 999fps.

This handler also checks to make sure that the mouse location is within a certain boundary. After it does that, it takes both the last point drawn to and the current point, and calls the "on drawLine" handler, which fills in the brush stroke between these two points:

```
on exitFrame me
  if pDraw then

    -- get current location
    curLoc = the mouseLoc

    -- restrict draw area
    if curLoc.locH < 60 then curLoc.locH = 60
    if curLoc.locH > 480 then curLoc.locH = 480
    if curLoc.locV < 35 then curLoc.locV = 35
    if curLoc.locV > 320 then curLoc.locV = 320

    -- if there is a last location
    if (pLastDrawLoc <> 0) then
      drawLine(me,pLastDrawLoc,curLoc)

      -- if not, then just draw a point
    else
      drawLine(me,curLoc,curLoc)
    end if

    -- new last location
    pLastDrawLoc = curLoc
  end if

  go to the frame
end
```

The "on drawLine" handler is simple, but includes some scary-looking math. It uses the "distance" function to determine how many pixels apart the two points are. Then it loops over that distance amount divided by two, so that it draws at every other point. If the brushes were only one-pixel in size, this would create a dotted line, but because the brushes are all larger than that, covering only every other point makes very little difference in the resulting line, but speeds up the drawing.

With every step of the loop, the location of the sprite is brought closer to the most recent mouse location and farther from the end of the previous location. The *updateStage* command is used to place the impression of the sprite on the Stage:

```
-- this handle will draw a line of dots from one point to the next
on drawLine me, loc1, loc2
  sprite(pDrawSprite).trails = TRUE

  -- how many dots to draw
  numSteps = float(distance(me,loc1,loc2))/2+1

  -- repeat and place dots
  repeat with i = 1 to numSteps
    sprite(pDrawSprite).loc = loc1*(numSteps-float(i))/numStep¬
      + loc2*(float(i)/numSteps)
    updateStage
  end repeat
end
```

This simple distance function takes two points and returns the distance between them, in pixels. It is used in the "on drawLine" handler to determine the number of steps in between brush points:

```
-- calculate the distance between two pixels
on distance me, loc1, loc2
  return sqrt(power(loc1.locH-loc2.locH,2)+power(loc1.locV-loc2.locV,2))
end
```

Because this frame script behavior seems to be in control of the function in this movie, it is a good idea to keep auxiliary operations in it as well. This next handler takes a color object as a parameter and sets the drawing sprite to that new color. Because the brushes are all 1-bit members, they take on the color of the sprite, and use that color to draw from that point on. However, it is up to an external handler to call this handler and institute the color change. This will be the scripts that are attached to the color chips seen in Figure 27.2.

```
-- accept a color and change to it
on changeColor me, color
  sprite(pDrawSprite).color = color
end
```

Using the same idea, this next handler accepts a new brush member from a script attached to one of the brushes on the left. In addition to changing the member's number, it also needs to set the "pBrush" property.

```
-- accept a brush member and change to it
on changeBrush me, brush
  sprite(pDrawSprite).member = brush
  pBrush = brush
end
```

This ends the main behavior for the movie. The whole thing works now, except that nothing will happen when the user wants to change colors or brushes. To do this, you need small behaviors on the color chips and brush icons. Here is one for the color chips. It takes the color assigned to that sprite and sends it to the main drawing behavior in the frame script, also known as sprite 0. It also issues a #changeColorSprite message to all sprites. This message is used to reset the outline that shows the user what color is currently in use.

```
on mouseDown me
  color = sprite(me.spriteNum).color
  sendSprite(sprite 0, #changeColor, color)
  sendAllSprites(#changeColorSprite,me.spriteNum)
end
```

The "on changeColorSprite" handler should be in a small behavior attached to the little outline box that surrounds the current color. When the *sendAllSprites* message is sent, all sprites get it, but only this one uses it. This means that the sprite can be located anywhere, without requiring you to hard-code some global variable with its sprite number.

The handler takes the rectangle of the current color chip and expands it by three pixels on all sides. The outline box is set to this new rectangle so that it surrounds the color chip:

```
on changeColorSprite me , colorSprite
  sprite(me.spriteNum).rect = ¬
    sprite(colorSprite).rect + rect(-3, -3, 3, 3)
end
```

Here is a behavior meant for the brushes. It tells the main behavior that the brush has changed, and also sends a #changeBrushSprite message out to all other behaviors so the brush outline box sprite can recognize it and react:

```
on mouseDown me
  brush = sprite(me.spriteNum).member
  sendSprite(sprite 0, #changeBrush, brush)
  sendAllSprites(#changeBrushSprite,me.spriteNum)
end
```

The behavior for the brush outline box is almost the same as for the color outline box sprite:

```
on changeBrushSprite me , colorSprite
  sprite(me.spriteNum).rect = ¬
    sprite(colorSprite).rect + rect(-3, -3, 3, 3)
end
```

The Clear button is easily scripted. It needs to do away with all the drawing created by the trails. This is done in an odd way: by resetting the Stage color. The best way is to actually set the Stage color without changing it at all. The result is that the trails are removed.

```
on mouseDown
  the stageColor = the stageColor
end
```

Lastly, there should be a way to prevent users from clicking the title bar or toolbar areas while drawing. Because the frame script behavior receives "mouseDown" messages only after a sprite has, all you need is a simple script that eats all "mouseDown" messages so the main behavior never gets them:

```
on mouseDown
  -- no action
end
```

Assign this behavior to anything that should be considered inactive, such as the shaded boxes at the top and left sides of the screen.

Take a look at the example on the CD-ROM to see how all these pieces of code work together. You should be able to make modifications very easily. You can change brushes by editing their bitmaps. Changing colors is even easier, because you can change the colors of the color chips on the Stage. You can also add more colors and brushes by adding more sprites and attaching the proper behaviors.

One major improvement to this program would be to add a way for users to save their work. You can do this by *using (the stage).picture* to place the image in a member and the *crop* command to remove the title and tool area. You can use the *saveMovie* command to save this change to the movie file or the *save castLib* command to save an external cast library with the image and bring it back in to the program later.

PART

VIII

CH

27

→ **See** "Manipulating Bitmap Members," Chapter 18, "Controlling Bitmaps," for more information on Lingo commands that affect bitmap members

→ **See** "Trails" in "Other Sprite Properties," Chapter 10, "Properties of Sprites and Frames," for some background information on trails

CREATING OVERLAYS

Remember your high school biology textbook? It had lots of drawings of the human body with the organs and skeleton all exposed. Sometimes you can lift up transparent sheets to "remove" organs; one might have shown the skeleton, one the circulatory system, one the digestive system, and so on. This way, you were able to see where things were in relation to each other.

The same "overlay" technique can be used in other subjects as well. An astronomy book might show a picture of the night sky. Then an overlay can show the star names. Another can show drawings of the constellations, and so on.

Doing this in Director is fairly easy. After you create the layers of artwork as different bitmap images, you only need to place them in the Score in the order you want them to overlay each other. Then you can use the visibility switches on the left side of the Score to test them out.

Figure 27.3 shows such a screen. An outline of the human body is used as a background. On top of that are four other sprites, each showing a different organ.

Figure 27.3
A simple overlay application has a background sprite, several overlays, and simple buttons to match each layer.

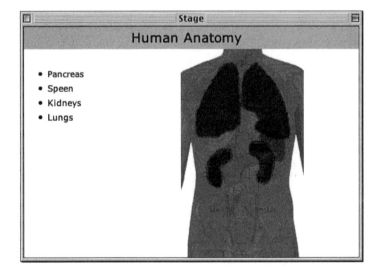

Only one simple behavior is needed to turn the overlay sprites on and off. This should be attached not to the overlays, but to the buttons that activate them. In this case, these buttons are the text members on the left side of the screen.

When the user clicks one of these text member buttons, the overlay should appear or disappear, depending on its current state. The buttons should also reflect the change. In this case, the bullet character to the left of each word will change color. A black color means that the layer is on, whereas white makes the layer invisible on the white background, signifying that the layer is off.

When the behavior begins, it tries to determine whether the bullet character should be black or white. It checks the corresponding overlay sprite. You can therefore set the sprites to be visible or not at startup, and the text buttons will reflect that state:

```
on beginSprite me
  setDot(me)
end

-- takes the first character of the text member and makes
-- it either black or white to reflect the state
on setDot me
  if sprite(me.spriteNum+1).visible = TRUE then
    sprite(me.spriteNum).member.char[1].color = rgb("#000000")
  else
    sprite(me.spriteNum).member.char[1].color = rgb("#FFFFFF")
  end if
end
```

Notice that this behavior assumes that the next sprite (me.spriteNum+1) is the overlay sprite. By making this assumption, and then setting up the Score as shown in Figure 27.4, you can avoid any special behavior parameters that identify the overlay sprite manually.

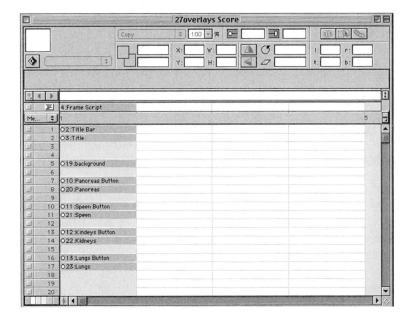

Figure 27.4
The Score shows that each overlay sprite is in the next sprite channel after its corresponding button sprite. This makes it easy for the button to know which sprite to affect.

The last part of the behavior determines whether the sprite is visible or invisible. Because the "on setDot" handler is already able to change the state of the button according to the visibility of the overlay sprite, there is no need to write more code to do this here:

```
-- will change the visible property of the next sprite
on mouseUp me
  sprite(me.spriteNum+1).visible = ¬
    not sprite(me.spriteNum+1).visible
  setDot(me)
end
```

This behavior is simplified by the use of text member buttons. You could use bitmaps instead. In that case, you would need members to represent on and off states. The check box behaviors in Chapter 15 can be adapted for this purpose.

Another thing to consider is the inks of the overlay sprites. Copy ink does not work because it hides anything under the sprite's rectangle with white. Background Transparent and Matte inks are obvious choices. They keep the overlay sprite's current colors, and enable white pixels to show through. In the preceding example, Transparent ink was used so that the edges would be smoother. However, this also altered the colors of the overlays.

> **Tip**
>
> One technique to consider is using 32-bit members with alpha channels. You can then define the level of transparency throughout the image.

→ **See** "Using Check Boxes," Chapter 15, for a review of the check box behavior

CREATING A GEOGRAPHY QUIZ

Although quizzes and tests in school are traditionally done with pencil and paper, with each question taking up a different space on the paper, computer quizzes can be far more interactive. A geography quiz, in fact, can present an interactive map that responds as the student rolls over it and clicks.

Figure 27.5 shows such a quiz. It is a map of the United States. The actual movie is made up of 51 sprites. There is a large, outlined map that overlays the entire thing, and is what is always visible. Under that are 50 individual bitmap sprites, one for each state.

As the user moves the cursor around the map, the state under the cursor lights up. It actually just changes color from white to blue. The behavior used to do this is fairly simple. It uses the *on mouseEnter* handler to signify that the cursor has entered a state, and then changes its color. It also places the name of the state, which is the name of the cast member in the sprite, into a text member. Although this gives away the "answer" during the quiz, it is useful later on as a "payoff" screen activity. Therefore, the text member that shows the name of each state is not present on the quiz frame, and appears only after the student is finished with the quiz.

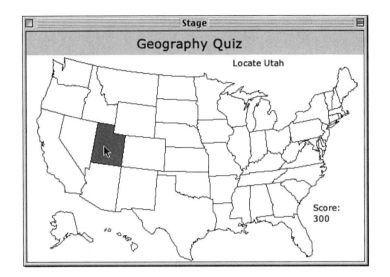

Figure 27.5
A geography quiz. Each state lights up as the user rolls over it so he knows what he is about to select.

```
property pState

-- get the state name
on beginSprite me
  pState = sprite(me.spriteNum).member.name
end

on mouseEnter me
  -- on rollover, change state color
  sprite(me.spriteNum).color = rgb("#336699")

  -- set the text member
  member("State Name").text = pState
end

on mouseLeave me
  -- change state color back to white
  sprite(me.spriteNum).color = rgb("#FFFFFF")

  -- reset text member
  member("State Name").text = " "
end

on mouseUp me
  -- see if answer is right
  answerQuestion(pState)
end
```

This behavior needs to be attached to all 50 state sprites. The state sprite behavior also calls the movie handler "on answerQuestion" when the state is clicked. Be sure that the outlined map that is on top of the state sprites does not have a behavior attached to it that will eat these "mouseUp" messages and never let this behavior receive them.

PART

VIII

CH

27

Running the quiz is actually done via a movie script. It uses several globals to keep track of all the questions, the number of the question the user is being asked, and the score. The way the scoring system in this quiz works is that the user gets 100 points for every correct answer. If the answer is wrong the user is given another chance, but can only score half. So if a user guesses wrong once, and then gets the correct answer the second time, the answer scores 50. For three guesses, the score is 25, and so on. The "gPoints" global keeps track of how many points the user can score for a correct answer. It is set to 100 at the start of each question, and then cut in half every time the user answers incorrectly.

```
global gQuestionNum -- which question is being asked
global gQuestions -- list with all the questions
global gScore -- keep track of score
global gPoints -- keep track of potential points to be scored
```

To start the movie, the "on initQuiz" is called to determine the questions to be asked. Then some other globals are reset. The "on showScore" handler places the score, which starts at 0, in a text member. Finally, the "on askQuestion" kicks off the quiz with question number 1:

```
on startMovie
  initQuiz
  gQuestionNum = 1
  gScore = 0
  showScore
  askQuestion
end
```

The "on initQuiz" handler's job is to come up with 10 random states to use in the quiz. It first gets a list of states by reading the member names of the "States" Cast library, which is where all the state bitmaps are located. After it gets that list, it selects 10 states at random. Each time one is selected, it is tested to see whether it is already used in the quiz. The result of this handler is that the "gQuestions" list is populated with 10 random and unique state names.

```
-- this handler will come up with 10 random and unique states
-- to make up the quiz
on initQuiz

  -- get a list of all states from the cast library member names
  listOfStates = []
  repeat with i = 1 to the number of members of castLib "States"
    add listOfStates, member(i,"States").name
  end repeat

  -- add 10 random names to quiz
  gQuestions = []
  repeat with i = 1 to 10

    repeat while TRUE

      -- get a random state
      r = random(listOfStates.count)
      state = listOfStates[r]

      -- see if the state is already in quiz
```

```
      if getOne(gQuestions,state) then next repeat

      -- add state, go on to add next
      add gQuestions, state
      exit repeat

    end repeat
  end repeat
end
```

This next handler places the text of the next question into a text member that is on the Stage. It also resets "gPoints" to 100:

```
on askQuestion
  -- set text member
  member("Question").text = "Locate"&&gQuestions[gQuestionNum]

  -- set potential points
  gPoints = 100 -- potential points to earn
end
```

When the user clicks a state, this handler is called to determine whether the state is correct. It compares the name of the member clicked to the name in the "gQuestions" list that corresponds to this question number. If they don't match, an alert box is used to send a message. You might want to use a sound or some other method of signifying that the answer is wrong.

If the answer matches, "gScore" is changed, the new score is shown, and a beep is played. Again, you might want to develop a custom sound and use the *puppetSound* command. The question number is incremented, and if all 10 questions have been answered, the movie jumps to another frame. Otherwise, the next question is asked.

```
-- this handler will check to see if a state name matches
-- the expected answer
on answerQuestion state
  -- make sure we are not done
  if gQuestionNum > gQuestions.count then exit

  if state <> gQuestions[gQuestionNum] then
    alert "Wrong. Try Again."

    -- divide potential points in half when a wrong answer
    gPoints = gPoints/2

  else

    -- add to score
    gScore = gScore + gPoints
    showScore
    beep() -- replace with better sound

    -- next question
    gQuestionNum = gQuestionNum + 1

    -- are we done?
    if gQuestionNum > gQuestions.count then
```

```
        member("Question").text = "All done! Use the mouse to explore."
        go to frame "Done"
      else
        askQuestion
      end if
   end if
end
```

One last movie handler is the one that places the current score in a text member on the Stage:

```
-- this handler places the current score in a member
on showScore
  member("Score").text = "Score:"&RETURN&gScore
end
```

When the game is over, the movie jumps to the "Done" frame. This frame can be anything, such as a payoff animation. However, in this example, it is the same map used in the quiz, but this time the user can explore at random. The state behavior is already placing the name of the state in a text member. This member is actually present on the "Done" frame and has another behavior attached to it so that it follows the cursor around.

```
on prepareFrame me
  -- determine sprite width
  textwidth = sprite(me.spriteNum).width

  -- set the location of the sprite to be just above the cursor
  sprite(me.spriteNum).loc = the mouseLoc+ ¬
     point(-textwidth/2,-16)
end
```

This "Done" frame can be used as a payoff, but it also can be used as an application all to itself. Rather than just display the state name in one member, it can also display information about the state elsewhere on the screen. Such information can come from text members or fields in another cast library. You can even wire the "on mouseUp" handlers to go to a frame specific to a state, or to a page on the Web with the *gotoNetPage* command.

→ **See** "Creating Display Rollovers," Chapter 15, for more information about rollover behaviors

CREATING STANDARDIZED TESTS

Although computer geography quizzes and matching games are much more interactive than old-fashioned paper and pencil tests, sometimes all you want is to have the users answer questions. A lot of aspects of paper-and-pencil tests, however, are not easy to duplicate on the computer.

Tests usually have many questions, too many to fit on one sheet of paper. As you can imagine, it makes no sense trying to fit all the questions onto one computer screen, either. Instead, one question per screen is more appropriate. However, this brings up the issue of navigating between questions. After all, paper and pencil tests enable users to skip questions and go back to change answers on previous questions.

Figure 27.6 shows one screen of a standardized test program. It looks similar to tests such as the SAT, GRE or ACT. The question is the central focus of the screen, and under it are several possible answers. The top and left sides of the screen are reserved for the title and some navigation buttons.

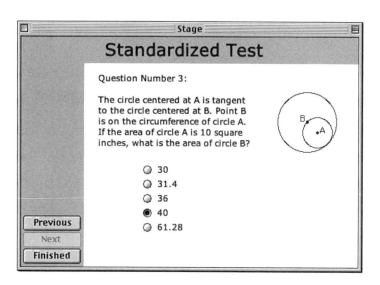

Figure 27.6
One screen of a standardized test program.

To create a test like this, you will rely on two behaviors from earlier chapters. The first is the radio button behavior from Chapter 15. This behavior is applied to the small radio buttons that appear to the left of each possible answer. The navigation buttons use the complete button behavior from Chapter 14, "Creating Behaviors."

Like the geography quiz, this program relies on a movie script for all the important handlers. This movie script needs only one global: a list of answers that the user has so far selected. The movie starts by resetting this global, and going to frame "question 1":

```
global gAnswerList

on startTest
  gAnswerList = []
  go to frame "question 1"
end
```

The movie relies on frame labels to determine on which question the user is currently working. So frame "question 1" is question number 1, frame "question 2" is question number 2, and so on.

The three buttons on the left side of the screen, Next, Previous, and Finished, all have the complete button behavior attached. The example movie on the CD-ROM has both normal and down states for the buttons. The behavior is set to execute the movie handlers "on nextQuestion," "on previousQuestion," and "on finishedTest" for each button.

The "on nextQuestion" and "on previousQuestion" buttons call the "on recordAnswer" handler, which stores the current radio button selection, the one the user has chosen, in the global. It then uses *go next* or *go previous* to go to the next or preceding question, and, if it is one the user has already answered, uses the "on setAnswer" to set the radio buttons.

```
on nextQuestion
  recordAnswer
  go next
  setAnswer
end

on previousQuestion
  recordAnswer
  go previous
  setAnswer
end
```

To record the answer, the program gets the question number from the frame label. Then, it takes the state of the radio buttons from the "on selected" handler in the radio button behavior. Because the radio buttons are in sprites 11 through 15, 10 is subtracted to get an answer between 1 and 5. This is then recorded in the global "AnswerList".

```
on recordAnswer
  -- get question number from frame label
  q = word 2 of the frameLabel
  q = value(q)

  -- get answer from radio buttons
  a = sendSprite(sprite 11, #selected)
  a = a - 10

  -- remember answer
  setAt gAnswerList, q, a
end
```

If the user answers a question, moves on, and then returns to the already-answered question, you want to show the earlier choice. The "on setAnswer" handler takes care of this. It looks up the current value of the question in the "gAnswerList" and sets the radio buttons accordingly:

```
on setAnswer
  -- get question number from frame label
  q = word 2 of the frameLabel
  q = value(q)

  -- get answer from radio buttons
  if gAnswerList.count >= q then
    a = gAnswerList[q]
    sendSprite(sprite (a+10), #turnMeOn)
  end if
end
```

When the user presses the finished button, she is taken to the "finished" frame. Just before that, the program evaluates her results with the "on computeResults" handler. This handler relies on a field named "Correct Answers". This field should contain a line-by-line list of correct answers by number. Each correct answer is compared to the user's answers stored in "gAnswerList" and a total is calculated. The result is placed in a text member visible on the "finished" frame:

```
on finishedTest
  recordAnswer
  computeResults
  go to frame "finished"
end

on computeResults

  -- get list of correct answers
  correct = member("Correct Answers").text

  -- find the number that matches up correctly
  numright = 0
  repeat with i = 1 to correct.line.count
    if value(correct.line[i] = gAnswerList[i]) then
      numright = numright + 1
    end if
  end repeat

  -- put results in Results member
  member("Results").text = "Test complete."&RETURN&RETURN&¬
    "You got"&&numright&&¬
    "correct out of"&&correct.line.count&"."
end
```

The rest of the work you need to do is in setting the behaviors for the radio buttons and navigation buttons. Figure 27.7 shows a Score with a three-question test. The start frame has a "begin" button in it that executes the "on startTest" handler. There are then three frames with questions. The radio buttons are in sprites 11 through 15 in all cases. Therefore, the behavior for each of these radio buttons needs to be set to show that. Use the Behavior Inspector to check out these behavior properties.

The navigation buttons also have grayed-out states that are used when the buttons are not active. For instance, the "Previous" button is not active on the first question and the "Next" button is not active on the last question. These inactive buttons have no behavior attached, whereas the active buttons call one of the movie handlers: "on nextQuestion," "on previousQuestion," and "on finishedTest."

Figure 27.6 showed that you can also include other elements besides text on the screen. Some questions are likely to be just text, and others can use bitmaps, vectors, or even Flash members as additional material. You can even place film loops that animate on these frames. You can't do that with pencil and paper tests!

Figure 27.7
The Score is set up for a short standardized test with three questions.

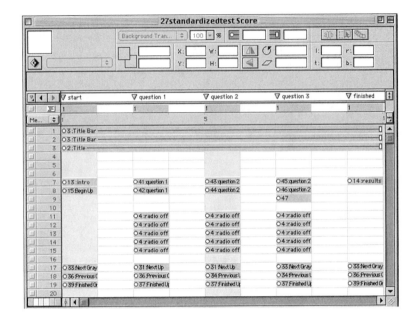

Another improvement that you can try to add is a more comprehensive scoring report. You can tell the user what he got wrong and what he got correct by keeping track of that information in a list. You might want to even let him walk through the questions again and show him explanations of how each should be solved.

→ **See** "A Complete Button Behavior," Chapter 14, for more information about button behaviors

→ **See** "Using Radio Buttons," Chapter 15, for more information about radio button behaviors

TROUBLESHOOTING EDUCATIONAL APPLICATIONS

■ A global is commonly used to record answers in quizzes and tests. To make sure that your program really works, use *clearGlobals* in the Message window often to make sure you are starting off fresh. You might even want to place it in your "on startMovie" handler.

■ In the geography quiz program, make sure that the inks for the states are set to Matte and the behaviors are attached.

■ All the aforementioned programs require that a simple *go to the frame* be placed in the "on exitFrame" script on each frame. Forgetting to do so is a common mistake.

■ Remember to test educational programs as much as you can. A student may click an area of the screen or perform an action that you may not think of. Make sure the program works even when it is misused.

DID YOU KNOW?

- You can combine all these educational applications to make one large test. One question can be matching, one geography, one can involve overlays, and a creative section can enable users to draw their own pictures.

- You can build a test that keeps questions and answers as a separate text file. At the start of the program, the text file is read from disk or over the Internet. Each question can be a single line in the file ("What is the fastest animal?;Duck,Pig,Cheetah;3"). This way you can build a test that a non-programmer can change.

- The geography quiz doesn't have to use a map. You can have a periodic table of the elements, a diagram of the human body, or even a list of potential answers to questions. You can keep the "feel" of the application, without limiting your test to geography as the subject matter.

PART

VIII

CH

27

BUSINESS APPLICATIONS

In this chapter

Although they are not as fun as educational programs or games, many types of business applications can also be created in Director. Most presentations fall into this category, such as the example in Chapter 1, "Animation with Director," which showed a simple slide show presentation.

Some higher-end movies can also handle or present data. This chapter shows you how to make a simple database program in Director, how to build graphs and charts, how to make a survey-like questionnaire, and how to develop training programs.

CREATING DATABASE APPLICATIONS

Building a database in Director is easy. However, creating an interface that a non-programmer can use to interact with the database is a tougher task.

You may have already noticed that property lists look like small databases. If you create a linear list that contains several property lists, you actually have a database. Look at this example:

```
[[#name: "Gary", #title: "Chief Engineer", #company: "CleverMedia"]¬
, [#name: "Bill", #title: "CEO", #company: "Microsoft"]]
```

The property names in this list represent the field names, and the property values are the fields themselves. Each item in the linear list is then a record. This example contains a database with two records and three fields in each record.

THE MAIN MENU SCREEN

Creating a database application is merely a matter of creating screens that manipulate a list database like the one shown previously. Such a program might use a global to store the database. A good name would be "gDatabase". It also needs to know which database record is currently being edited. That information can be a stored in a global called "gCurrentRecord".

A main menu screen enables the users to perform various tasks. Figure 28.1 shows what this might look like.

To begin, the users will need to create a new database. They will do this by clicking the "New Database" button. This handler will clear out the "gDatabase" global and go to the data entry screen:

```
on newDatabase
  gDatabase = [newRecord()] -- database with one record
  go to frame "Entry"
  gCurrentRecord = 1
  showRecord
end
```

The function "on newRecord" returns a new, blank record. This function is handy for adding records to the database or replacing them.

```
on newRecord
  record = [:]
  addProp record, #item, ""
  addProp record, #id, ""
  addProp record, #category, ""
  addProp record, #number, ""
  addProp record, #price, 0.0
  addProp record, #description, ""
  return record
end
```

The "on newRecord" function defines the fields that the database is to contain. You can see that this database has six fields.

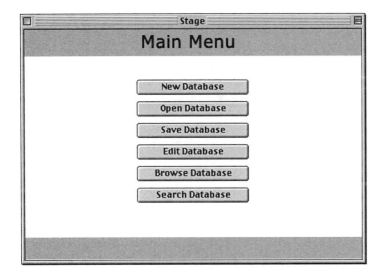

Figure 28.1
The main menu screen contains buttons for all the functions of the database.

THE DATABASE ENTRY SCREEN

Next, you need a database entry screen so that users can enter new records and edit old records. The "on newDatabase" handler ends by calling the "on showRecord" handler. This handler populates the fields on the database entry screen:

```
on showRecord
  -- get current record
  record = gDatabase[gCurrentRecord]

  -- place fields into members on stage
  member("Entry - Item").text = record.item
  member("Entry - ID").text = record.id
  member("Entry - Category").text = record.category
  member("Entry - Number").text = record.number
  member("Entry - Price").text = string(record.price)
  member("Entry - Description").text = record.description

  -- show the record number
  member("Record Number").text = "Record"&&gCurrentRecord
end
```

PART

VIII

CH

28

Figure 28.2 shows what the database entry screen looks like.

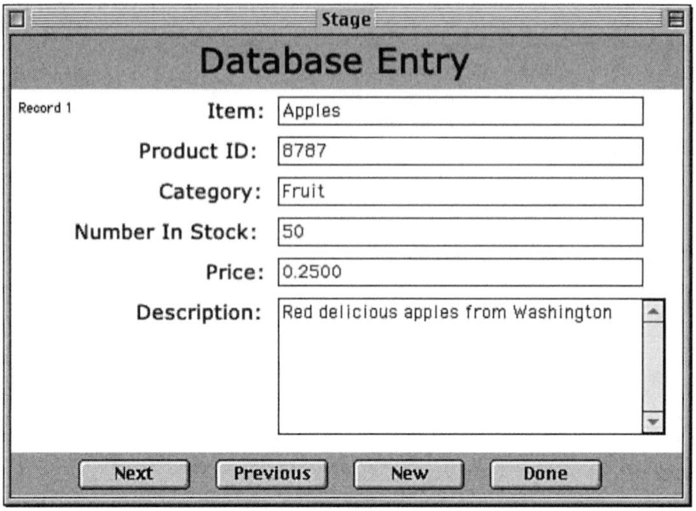

Figure 28.2
A database entry
screen for a simple
supermarket inventory
database.

In the database entry screen, the six editable fields are the active elements. Most of the rest of the screen, such as the field labels to the left, are just static text. A record number field is in the upper-left corner. This is not editable, and displays the record number for the current entry.

Users can enter any text into any field on the screen. All fields are set to editable and "Tab to Next Editable Item" so that they respond to the tab key as other programs do.

The buttons at the bottom of the screen use the complex button behavior described in Chapter 14, "Creating Behaviors." The Next and Previous buttons bring up the following or preceding record. The Done button brings up a main menu screen. The New button, of course, creates a new entry at the end of the database and makes that the current entry.

Whenever one of these buttons is pressed, the information in the fields on the screen needs to be recorded and placed in the database before the action is performed.

The "on recordRecord" handler takes the text from all fields and places it in a new, empty record. It then replaces the old record in the database global:

```
on recordRecord
  -- get empty record to use
  record = newRecord()

  -- change all fields of record to reflect screen data
  record.item = member("Entry - Item").text
  record.id = member("Entry - ID").text
  record.category = member("Entry - Category").text
  record.number = member("Entry - Number").text
  record.price = value(member("Entry - Price").text)
  record.description = member("Entry - Description").text
```

```
  -- replace record in database
  gDatabase[gCurrentRecord] = record
end
```

NAVIGATING THROUGH THE DATABASE

In addition to starting a new database, users should be able to return to the database entry screen to edit records. The "Edit Database" button calls the "editDatabase" handler. This handler needs to make sure that a database exists before allowing the users to edit it. If a database is not present, it creates one rather than giving an error message:

```
on editDatabase
  -- check to see if any database exists
  if not listP(gDatabase) then
    nextDatabase
  else
    go to frame "Entry"
    gCurrentRecord = 1
    showRecord
  end if
end
```

The "Next" and "Previous" buttons also have movie handlers that take care of recording changes to the current item and move forward or backward in database:

```
-- move forward in the database
on nextRecord
  -- accept all changes in current record
  recordRecord

  -- go to the next record
  gCurrentRecord = gCurrentRecord + 1

  -- if past the end of the database, loop around
  if gCurrentRecord > gDatabase.count then
    gCurrentRecord = 1
  end if

  -- display the new record
  showRecord
end


-- move backward in the database
on previousRecord
  -- accept all changes in current record
  recordRecord

  -- go to the previous record
  gCurrentRecord = gCurrentRecord - 1

  -- if user tries to move back past 1, loop around
  if gCurrentRecord < 1 then
    gCurrentRecord = gDatabase.count
  end if

  -- display the new record
  showRecord
end
```

When the user presses the "New" button, a handler must find the last item in the database and add one past that:

```
-- create a new record in the database
on createRecord
  -- accept all changes in current record
  recordRecord

  -- go to the record one past the last in database
  gCurrentRecord = gDatabase.count + 1

  -- set this new record to a blank record
  gDatabase[gCurrentRecord] = newRecord()

  -- display the new record
  showRecord
end
```

The "Done" button enables the users to exit the database entry screen and return to the main menu. Like the other handlers in this section, this button must first record changes to the current entry before performing its action:

```
-- finished entering data, return to main menu
on doneEntry
  recordRecord
  go to frame "Main"
end
```

The next two items to be dealt with are the "Save Database" and "Open Database" buttons. These both call handlers that use the FileIO Xtra to save or load the global database variable to a file.

The "on saveDatabase" handler creates a file and saves a string version of the list to it. In a more advanced application, this would be known as a "Save As..." function. In that case, you would also need a handler that would act as a "Save" function, where the database would be saved to the same file each time, without prompting the user for a file location. For simplicity, this program has only one handler:

```
-- save the current database to a text file
on saveDatabase
  -- ask user for a file name
  fileObj = new(Xtra "FileIO")
  filename = displaySave(fileObj, "Save Database", "database.txt")
  if filename = "" then exit

  -- create file and write to it
  createFile(fileObj,filename)
  openFile(fileObj,filename, 2)
  writeString(fileObj, string(gDatabase))
  closeFile(fileObj)
end
```

To open a file, you must write a handler similar to the one that writes a file. In addition, you must perform some verification on the type of file that the user has selected. The users are enabled to open any kind of file in this case, but the text read is tested to make sure it is a valid Lingo list. If it is, it is considered a valid database file. You can perform a stricter test by making sure it is a linear list that contains only similar property lists if you like:

```
-- open an existing database file
on openDatabase
  -- ask user for a file
  fileObj = new(Xtra "FileIO")
  filename = displayOpen(fileObj)
  if filename = "" then exit

  -- open the file and read the text
  openFile(fileObj, filename, 1)
  text = readFile(fileObj)
  closeFile(fileObj)

  -- try to convert the text to a list
  database = value(text)
  if not listP(database) then
    -- not a list
    alert "Not a valid database file."
  else
    -- is a list, set database
    gDatabase = database
  end if
end
```

So now you can create a database, add items to it, edit items, save it to your hard drive, and then load it back in at a later time. That takes care of building the database; now it would be nice to have the database actually do something.

LISTING RECORDS IN THE DATABASE

Here is a handler that creates a scrolling text field with all the items in the database. It uses HTML formatting to create a table in a text member. Figure 28.3 shows the screen with this list.

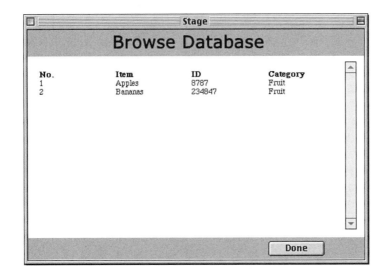

Figure 28.3
The browse database screen shows a list of all the items in the database in an HTML-formatted text member.

```
-- display a list of all the records using HTML
on browseDatabase

  -- html header
  htext = "<HTML><BODY BGCOLOR=#FFFFFF>"&RETURN

  -- put the table headings
  put "<TABLE><TR><TH>No.</TH><TH>Item</TH><TH>ID</TH><TH>Category</TH></TR>"¬
    &RETURN after htext

  -- loop through database and create table rows
  repeat with i = 1 to gDatabase.count
    put "<TR>" after htext
    put "<TD>"&i&"</TD>" after htext
    put "<TD>"&gDatabase[i].item&"</TD>" after htext
    put "<TD>"&gDatabase[i].id&"</TD>" after htext
    put "<TD>"&gDatabase[i].category&"</TD>" after htext
    put "</TR>"&RETURN after htext
  end repeat

  -- close out table and HTML
  put "</TABLE></BODY></HTML>" after htext

  -- place HTML in text member
  member("Database List").html = htext

  go to frame "Browse"
end
```

Although it is nice to be able to see each item of the database in one list, it is better to be able use some criteria to narrow the list. Here is a similar handler to the preceding that performs a simple search on the database. The result is an HTML-formatted list.

This handler gets the search term from an editable text member. The user is first taken to a search screen and asked for a search term:

```
-- display a list of records that are found in search
on performSearch

  -- get search term from field
  searchText = member("Search Text").text

  -- HTML header
  htext = "<HTML><BODY BGCOLOR=#FFFFFF>"&RETURN

  -- put the table headings
  put "<TABLE><TR><TH>No.</TH><TH>Item</TH><TH>ID</TH><TH>Category</TH></TR>"¬
    &RETURN after htext

  -- loop through all records
  repeat with i = 1 to gDatabase.count
    record = gDatabase[i]

    -- see if the record contains the search text
    -- search all properties for it
    if (record.item contains searchText) or¬
      (record.id contains searchText) or¬
```

```
        (record.category contains searchText) or¬
        (record.number contains searchText) or¬
        (record.price contains searchText) or¬
        (record.description contains searchText) then

      -- a match was found, add a row to table
      put "<TR>" after htext
      put "<TD>"&i&"</TD>" after htext
      put "<TD>"&record.item&"</TD>" after htext
      put "<TD>"&record.id&"</TD>" after htext
      put "<TD>"&record.category&"</TD>" after htext
      put "</TR>"&RETURN after htext
    end if
  end repeat

  -- close out table and HTML
  put "</TABLE></BODY></HTML>" after htext

  -- put HTML into text member
  member("Database List").html = htext

  go to frame "Search Results"
end
```

While every field in the database is searched for the search term, you might want to narrow the search a bit. You can search only the description and item name, for instance. You can also search only the category field and get lists of similar items, such as all fruits or all meats. You can even perform a search on the price field for items that are less than or greater than an amount, rather than those that are exactly the same.

It is these searches that make databases powerful. Another common database function is computation. You can have a function that reads through the whole database, multiplies price by quantity for each item, and then sums to get the total value of the inventory.

→ **See** "Using List Variables," Chapter 13, "Essential Lingo Syntax,"for an introduction to lists

→ **See** "Using Text Files and the FileIO Xtra," Chapter 16, "Controlling Text," for more information about FileIO

→ **See** "Using HTML and Tables," Chapter 16, for more information about using HTML in text members

CREATING GRAPHS AND PIE CHARTS

Graphs and pie charts are often simply another type of bitmap image. You can easily create these with graphing programs such as Microsoft Excel or Lotus and then you can cut and paste bitmaps of these graphs into Director as cast members.

However, another option is to create these graphs in Director using various Director elements such as shapes, text members, and lines.

BAR GRAPHS

Figure 28.4 shows a bar graph created in Director. It uses different shape sprites for all the bars, lines for the x and y axes, and text members for the x and y axis labels.

PART

VIII

CH

28

Figure 28.4
This graph was made with different Director elements, and then a Lingo handler was used to adjust the bars to the correct height.

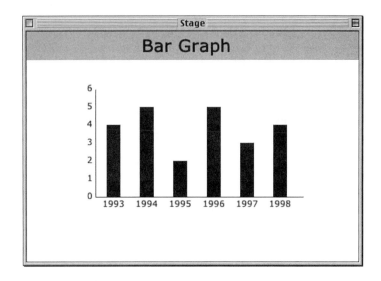

Although you can easily lay out all the pieces of the graph shown in Figure 28.4 manually, a Lingo handler is used to adjust the bars to the proper height. Here is that handler:

```
-- adjust a 6-bar graph
on adjustGraph valueList
  repeat with i = 1 to 6

    -- bar sprites start at 6
    sNum = 5+i

    -- get the rectangle of the sprite
    r = sprite(sNum).rect

    -- reset the rectangle top
    r.top = r.bottom - valueList[i]*25

    -- set the sprite
    sprite(sNum).rect = r
  end repeat
end
```

This handler assumes that the bars are in sprites 6 through 11. It also uses 25 pixels as the measurement between one number and the next. You call the handler in this manner:

```
on startMovie
  adjustGraph([4,5,2,5,3,4])
end
```

This handler sets the bars to the heights that you see in Figure 28.4. You could call the same handler again, but with different numbers, to set the bars differently. Now you can develop a movie that contains several graphs, but uses Lingo to create them, instead of using different bitmap images each time.

For instance, the numbers on the left can indicate sales in millions of dollars. The numbers on the bottom are, of course, years. Then, you can have several different graphs that show the sales for different companies, or for different departments within the same company. Each frame with a graph has the same sprite elements used in the graph, but the "on adjustGraph" handler is called with different numbers each time.

A more complex handler can actually adjust the number of bars, the labels at the bottom and left of the graph, and maybe even add color to the bars. Doing this is far more complex, because creating the labels, and spacing them the proper distance apart, can be difficult. You may want to actually place each label in a separate text member and position it accordingly.

PIE CHARTS

Another type of visual aid is a pie chart. Before Director 7, these were difficult to do, because the pie slices had to be drawn pixel by pixel. However, with vector shape members, you can now create a pie chart from a single member. Recall that these members enable you to create shapes from a curved line and optionally fill that shape with a color or gradient.

Figure 28.5 shows such a member on the Stage. The chart shown was generated from a single vector shape member with a behavior attached to it. The behavior shaped the member into the pie chart during the "on beginSprite" handler.

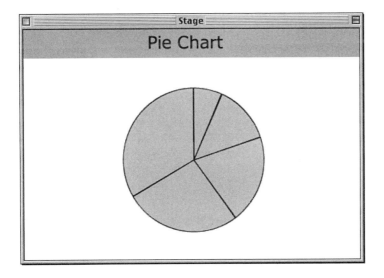

Figure 28.5
A pie chart made up of a single vector shape member.

The behavior uses two parameters: the values of the pie slices and the radius of the pie. It then creates a pie chart, piece by piece, by drawing a circle and connecting a line to the center at the appropriate places.

```
property pValues, pRadius

on getPropertyDescriptionList me
  list = [:]
```

```
    addProp list, #pValues, [#comment: "Value List", ¬
      #default: [], #format: #list]
    addProp list, #pRadius, [#comment: "Radius", ¬
      #default: 100, #format: #integer]
    return list
end

on beginSprite me

  -- determine total value of pie
  total = 0.0
  repeat with i = 1 to pValues.count
    total = total + pValues[i]
  end repeat

  -- start new vertextList
  vlist = []

  -- start 1/4 circle, back
  oldAngle = -pi()/2

  -- start at 0
  swing = 0.0

  repeat with i = 1 to pValues.count

    -- begin slice at center
    add vlist, [#vertex: point(0,0)]

    -- calculate angle for end of piece
    swing = swing + pValues[i]
    newAngle = 2.0*pi()*(swing/total)-pi()/2

    -- move from start to end of piece
    repeat with a = 100*oldAngle to 100*newAngle

      -- add point on circumference
      x = pRadius*cos(a/100)
      y = pRadius*sin(a/100)
      add vlist, [#vertex: point(x,y)]
    end repeat

    -- set start for next piece
    oldAngle = newAngle
  end repeat

  -- use vertexList on this sprite
  sprite(me.spriteNum).member.vertexList = vlist
end
```

By dropping this behavior onto any vector shape member, you can create quick and easy pie charts. However, they don't look as nice as most pie charts because each slice is the same color. Because vector shape members can only have one fill color, it is impossible to create a multicolored pie chart from one vector shape. However, you can do so using multiple shapes.

The following behavior is very similar to the last one, but it draws only one slice of the pie. You can attach this to multiple shape members, all placed at the same location on the Stage, and it creates a pie chart that looks just like the last. However, each slice is actually a different vector shape member. Make sure that each sprite is using a different cast member. If it is using the same vector shape member for each sprite, this process will not work.

The behavior includes a new parameter, "pPiece". This parameter determines which piece of the pie the sprite should represent. When applying the behavior, you can drop it on all six pie piece sprites at once, set the "pValues" and "pRadius" for all of them at once, and then go back and use the Behavior Inspector to reset the "pPiece" property for each one, as follows:

```
property pValues, pRadius, pPiece

on getPropertyDescriptionList me
  list = [:]
  addProp list, #pValues, [#comment: "Value List", ¬
    #default: [], #format: #list]
  addProp list, #pRadius, [#comment: "Radius", ¬
    #default: 100, #format: #integer]
  addProp list, #pPiece, [#comment: "Piece Number", ¬
    #default: 1, #format: #integer]
  return list
end

on beginSprite me

  -- determine total value of pie
  total = 0.0
  repeat with i = 1 to pValues.count
    total = total + pValues[i]
  end repeat

  -- start new vertextList
  vlist = []

  -- start 1/4 circle, back
  oldAngle = -pi()/2

  -- start at 0
  swing = 0.0

  repeat with i = 1 to pValues.count

    -- begin slice at center
    add vlist, [#vertex: point(0,0)]

    -- calculate angle for end of piece
    swing = swing + pValues[i]
    newAngle = 2.0*pi()*(swing/total)-pi()/2

    -- only draw my own piece
    if pPiece = i then
      -- move from start to end of piece
      repeat with a = 100*oldAngle to 100*newAngle
```

```
      -- add point on circumference
      x = pRadius*cos(a/100)
      y = pRadius*sin(a/100)
      add vlist, [#vertex: point(x,y)]
    end repeat
  end if

  -- set start for next piece
  oldAngle = newAngle
end repeat

-- use vertexList on this sprite
sprite(me.spriteNum).member.centerRegPoint = FALSE
sprite(me.spriteNum).member.originMode = #center
sprite(me.spriteNum).member.vertexList = vlist
end
```

After the pie chart has been created, you can edit each of the individual members and change its color. The result is a multicolored pie chart like the one shown in Figure 28.6. You could also add a "pPieceColor" parameter to the behavior and have it set the *fillColor* property of the member for you.

Figure 28.6
This multicolored pie chart was created with six vector members and a single behavior applied to each.

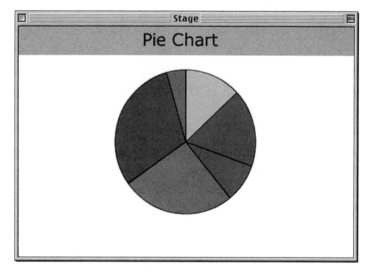

Like the bar graph, the pie chart behavior is only semiautomatic. You can easily change the values of the six pie pieces, without altering the Score or Stage by hand. However, if you want to add a seventh piece, you have to add another sprite and alert all the behavior properties.

A more complex pie chart behavior would create the pie pieces for you using a *new* command to create new members and then set up empty sprites with these members. That way, you could have pie charts created on-the-fly, with no pre-existing sprites or members.

→ **See** "Building Vectors with Lingo," Chapter 20, "Controlling Vector Graphics," for more information about building vector shape members

CREATING QUESTIONNAIRES

Surveys are rarely taken on paper anymore. Probably the most common way to take a survey is over the phone. Of course on the other end of the phone is a person with a computer, entering the answers as you give them. Surveys are also taken on the Web and in standalone computer kiosks.

Creating a survey in Director is very similar to creating the standardized test example shown in Chapter 27, "Educational Applications." The only real difference is that a survey might use more than just radio buttons to enable the respondent to provide answers. Check boxes and pop-up menus are also good options, as well as blank text fields in which users can type whatever they want. Another difference between a test and a survey is that a survey does not require any answer-checking because there are no "wrong" answers.

In the example on the CD-ROM, a simple survey with four questions is given. The user starts by pressing a "Begin" button the screen. This starts the survey by clearing out the global "gAnswers" and resetting any radio button or check box members in the Cast:

```
global gAnswers -- list to store all responses

on beginQuestions
  -- clear list
  gAnswers = []

  -- remove previous selections
  repeat with i = 1 to the number of members
    if member(i).type = #button then
      member(i).hilite = FALSE
    end if
  end repeat

  -- start
  go to frame "question 1"
end
```

The first question uses five radio buttons, just as the standardized test program did in Chapter 27. It looks like Figure 28.7.

The code to control these radio buttons is similar to the radio button behavior described in Chapter 15, "Graphic Interface Elements." However, the behavior calls a movie handler named "on addAnswer" each time a radio button is clicked. Here is that handler:

```
property pState, pGroupList

on getPropertyDescriptionList me
  list = [:]
  addProp list, #pState, [#comment: "Initial State",¬
    #format: #boolean, #default: FALSE]
  addProp list, #pGroupList, [#comment: "Group List",¬
    #format: #list, #default: []]
  return list
end
```

```
on beginSprite me
  if pState then turnMeOn(me)
end

on turnMeOn me
  pState = TRUE
  sprite(me.spriteNum).member.hilite = TRUE
  repeat with i in pGroupList
    if i <> me.spriteNum then
      sendSprite(sprite i,#turnMeOff)
    end if
  end repeat
  addAnswer(sprite(me.spriteNum).member.text)
end

on turnMeOff me
  pState = FALSE
  sprite(me.spriteNum).member.hilite = FALSE
end

on mouseUp me
  turnMeOn(me)
end
```

In the movie script for this movie, the "on addAnswer" takes a string and adds it to the "gAnswers" global. It figures out the question number from the frame label:

```
on addAnswer text
  -- get question number from frame label
  question = value((the frameLabel).word[2])

  -- set the item in the list
  setAt(gAnswers, question, text)
end
```

Figure 28.7
The first question in the survey uses radio buttons to ensure that the user picks one, and only one, item.

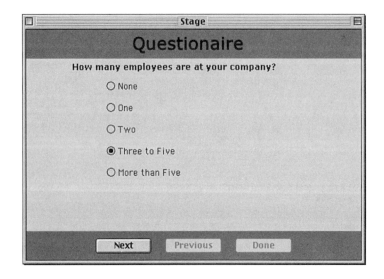

The second question in the movie uses check boxes. This enables the user to select none, one, some, or all of the choices on the screen. Figure 28.8 shows this screen.

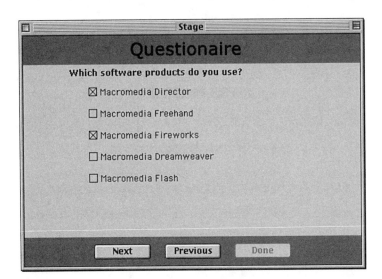

Figure 28.8
Check boxes are used to ask questions when multiple answers are possible.

Check box buttons work on their own, switching on and off as the user clicks. However, a behavior is needed to alter the "gAnswers" global. This behavior calls the same "on addAnswer" handler that the radio button behavior did.

```
on mouseUp me
  text = ""
  repeat with i = 11 to 15
    if sprite(i).member.hilite = TRUE then
      if text <> "" then put "," after text
      put sprite(i).member.text after text
    end if
  end repeat
  addAnswer(text)
end
```

The third screen has another type of interface element. This one is a pop-up menu that enables the user to select a single item from a list. Radio buttons can do this as well, but pop-up menus accommodate longer lists of items. Figure 28.9 shows this screen.

The pop-up menu can be run with the same script that was used in Chapter 16. The action to be performed by this script is to call "on addAnswer" with the behavior property "pSelected" as the parameter.

Finally, a questionnaire might also need an editable text field, such as the one shown in Figure 28.10.

Figure 28.9
Pop-up menus are an alternative to radio buttons.

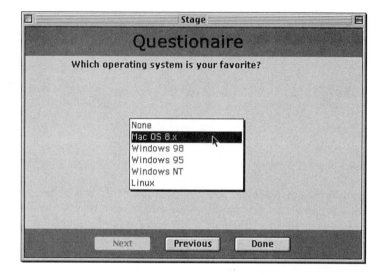

Figure 28.10
An editable text field enables users to enter comments and other information.

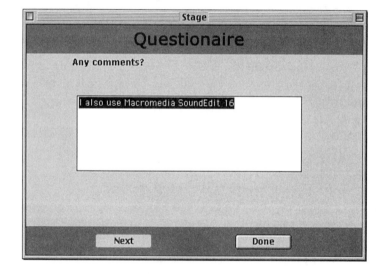

The editable field needs a behavior as well. The following simple behavior clears the text from the field when the sprite appears, and then sends the text to the "on addAnswers" handler when the frame is left.

```
on beginSprite me
  sprite(me.spriteNum).member.text = ""
end

on endSprite me
  addAnswer(sprite(me.spriteNum).member.text)
end
```

In the end, the list "gAnswers" can be converted to a string and saved to a file. You can even append it to the end of a file that already exists and thereby compile the results of multiple surveys. If this is an applet on the Web, you might want to take the data and use *postNetText* to send it back to a CGI program on your server.

→ **See** "Using Radio Buttons," Chapter 15, for more information about using radio buttons

→ **See** "Using Check Boxes," Chapter 15, for more information about using check boxes

→ **See** "Creating Graphic Pop-up Menus," Chapter 15, for more information about making pop-up menus

→ **See** "Using Keyboard Input," Chapter 16, for more information about accepting keyboard input

CREATING COMPUTER-BASED TRAINING PROGRAMS

Quizzes and tests are good for testing knowledge, but if done correctly, they can actually teach as well. Computer-based training programs are those that teach concepts using a computer. They use human-computer interaction to reinforce ideas or processes.

As an example, computer-based training may be used to teach employees at a company how to use the new phone system. If the phone system has lots of different codes that perform different tasks, a beginner can get confused easily and have to look up the codes in a book or on a reference chart. However, it would be far more efficient to have the employees memorize the codes so they can use the phone system without a hassle.

A computer-based training program can show the users a picture of the phone and ask them questions such as, "How do you forward a call?" The users must then use the picture of the phone and press the buttons on it to type that code. If they get it wrong, they have to start again. If they are correct, they move on to the next code. Figure 28.11 shows what such a program could look like.

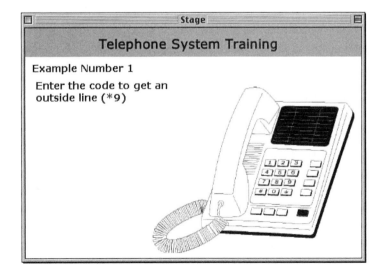

Figure 28.11
A computer-based training program screen that teaches users different telephone codes.

The idea is that people who use this program a few times a day will quickly get up to speed and memorize the codes. Plus, they can learn the codes before they actually need to use them.

The Lingo code for this movie is similar to the code used to create the questionnaire in this chapter. This program requires three globals: the current question number, the correct answer for the current question, and the answer the user has given so far.

```
global gQuestionNum -- which question number
global gCorrectAnswer -- correct for current question
global gAnswer -- the user's answer, so far
```

The movie starts by setting the "gQuestionNum" to 1 and then calling "on askQuestion". This handler grabs the question and correct answer from a text field, sets the question text on the Stage, and records the correct answer in "gCorrectAnswer".

```
-- reset questions and ask first
on startMovie
  gQuestionNum = 1
  askQuestion
end

-- get question info and ask it
on askQuestion
  -- data uses ; as separator
  the itemDelimiter = ";"

  -- get the data from a field
  text = member("Questions").text.line[gQuestionNum]

  -- set the question
  member("Question").text = text.item[1]

  -- get the answer
  gCorrectAnswer = text.item[2]

  -- reset user's answer
  gAnswer = ""

  -- set message
  member("Message").text = "Example Number"&&gQuestionNum
end
```

The text field that contains the questions and answers has to be very carefully formatted. It uses a semicolon as the item separator:

```
Enter the code to get an outside line (*9);*9;
Enter the code to forward the current call (22#);22#;
Enter the code to turn auto answer on (#7);#7;
Enter the code to turn auto answer off (*3);*3;
Enter the code to get an operator (*072952#4);*072952#4;
```

The correct answers can use any of the 10 digits, plus the "#" and "*" characters. These characters correspond to the keys on a telephone. The picture of the telephone in Figure 28.11 actually contains small buttons that are hovering over the keypad. Each one has a cast member that is named appropriately. For example, the member over the "1" key is named "1". When one of these buttons is pressed, it sends a message to a movie handler.

```
on mouseUp me
  -- gets the character from the member name
  k = sprite(me.spriteNum).member.name

  -- send along to movie script
  addToAnswer(k)
end
```

The movie handler "addToAnswer" maintains the "gAnswer" string. It places the new character after all the characters already there. It then compares the whole string to the correct answer. If it matches, the program moves to the next question. If it doesn't match, but corresponds to the beginning characters of the correct answer, it means the user has not strayed from the correct answer—if the user has typed "*6" so far, and the answer is "*69", for instance.

However, if the answer is different in any way from the beginning of the correct one, a message is displayed and the user must try again.

```
on addToAnswer k

  -- add to answer
  put k after gAnswer

  put gAnswer, gCorrectAnswer

  if gAnswer = gCorrectAnswer then
    gotItRight
  else if gCorrectAnswer starts gAnswer then
    -- one step closer, nothing to do here
  else
    gotItWrong
  end if
end
```

The "on gotItRight" and "on gotItWrong" handlers take care of the messages and other post-question functions.

```
-- move on to next question
on gotItRight

  -- next question
  gQuestionNum = gQuestionNum + 1

  -- all done?
  if gQuestionNum > member("Questions").line.count then
    member("Message").text = "Finished."
    beep(3)
  else
    beep()
    askQuestion
  end if
end
```

```
-- wrong answer message
on gotItWrong
  member("Message").text =  "Wrong. Try again."
  gAnswer = ""
end
```

Notice that the questions in the program give the answers away. This is done simply to make the program easier to test. The real program will probably not give this information to the user.

This program is very simple. Real computer-based training programs can get much more complicated. You could ask the questions in a random order, for example. You could also record which questions were answered incorrectly and then retest users on questions they got wrong.

TROUBLESHOOTING BUSINESS APPLICATIONS

- When enabling users to type text, as shown in the database program and the questionnaire, make sure that it is not possible to type a RETURN character in the field. Doing so works, but you cannot convert the data list to a string and then back again. Solutions are using a "on keyDown" script to not enable RETURNs to pass, or converting RETURNs to another character before saving.

- When you build pie charts, or any multiple vector shape-based image, make sure that the members are set to use "Auto-Size" in the member's Properties box. Also set the *centerRegPoint* to FALSE and the *originMode* to #center. If you do not, the members may not line up on the Stage.

DID YOU KNOW?

- When creating bar graphs, you can set the shape members to use a pattern as well as a color. Do this by selecting the member on the Stage and using the tool palette.

- When you save a database file on the Mac, you can use the FileIO setFinderInfo to set a file type for the database file. You can then use *setFilterMask* for both Mac and Windows to restrict users to opening only those files.

- If you write a short handler that saves the questionnaire data as a tab-delimited list, rather than a Director list, you can import it into a spreadsheet or statistical analysis program to process the results of a survey.

CHAPTER **29**

GRAPHICS APPLICATIONS

In this chapter

Although graphics are almost always used in every Director movie, sometimes they are more than just a part of it. Sometimes, they are the whole point of the movie.

For instance, a slide show presentation of different images places a set of graphics as the central focus of a movie. Sometimes the purpose of the movie is to display just one image. Often, this image exceeds the screen size, as in a large map or diagram. In that case, the user needs to pan, scroll, or zoom into the image.

Another possibility is a movie that continually changes an image or images, as in a montage. With inks and colors, Director can alter an image easily.

CREATING SLIDE SHOWS

It is very easy to make a slide show movie like the one created in Chapter 1, "Animation with Director." A simple movie doesn't even require any Lingo. You can just import the images into the Cast, and then create frames in the Score to show each screen.

However, what if you don't know what images will be a part of the slide show until the last minute? Or, what if the images are likely to change? Maybe the images need to be added by someone who does not even know how to use Director or doesn't have access to it.

You can make an intelligent Director movie that compiles a slide show out of any collection of images in a folder. The user can even swap out the files in the folder with new ones to create a completely different slide show.

Such a movie might look like Figure 29.1. The image is one cast member that is actually a linked member, not an imported one. To do this, use the standard import method, but be sure to select "Link to File" in the Import dialog box before importing.

Figure 29.1
A simple slide show presentation can import images one by one, rather than requiring them to all be present in the movie at the start.

All the images for the slide show should be placed in a folder named "Images." This folder should appear in the same location as the movie itself, and eventually in the same folder as the Projector. To make things simpler, link the initial image cast member to the first image of the slide show inside this "Images" folder.

The movie first needs to read the contents of the "Images" folder and store the names of the files in a list. The *getNthFileNameInFolder* function performs this task.

Note

> The *getNthFileNameInFolder* function takes a pathname and a number as its two parameters. It returns the name of the file matching that number in the specified folder. If the number given is greater than the number of files in that folder, an empty string is returned. It has been known to be reliable only for folders with 255 or fewer files.

The list of files is stored in a global. Also, the folder path is stored in a global. It will be needed again when each image is imported. The folder path is determined by the location of the movie or Projector, plus the word "Image". In addition, an extra file separator is needed at the end. This file separator is a ":" on the Mac, but a "\" in Windows.

Here are the global declarations needed, as well as the "on startMovie" handler and the "on getImageList" handler that compiles the list of image files:

```
global gImageFolder -- where the images are located
global gImageList -- a list of all image file names
global gImageNum -- the number of the current image

on startMovie
  -- determine the location of the images
  gImageFolder = the pathname & "Images"
  if the platform contains "mac" then
    gImageFolder = gImageFolder & ":"
  else
    gImageFolder = gImageFolder & "\"
  end if

  -- set other globals
  getImageList
  gImageNum = 1

  -- show first image
  showImage
end

-- this handler looks at each file in the folder and gets the
-- filename of that image
on getImageList
  gImageList = []
  repeat with i = 1 to 255
    filename = getNthFileNameinFolder(gImageFolder,i)
    if filename = "" then exit repeat
    add gImageList, filename
  end repeat
end
```

After the file names have been stored in a list, the task of importing the file into the cast member is simple. You just need to set the *filename* property of the member. The program will set it to the full path of the image, including the previously compiled "gImageFolder" global:

```
-- this handler resets the filename of the image to a new file
on showImage
  member("Image").filename = gImageFolder & gImageList[gImageNum]
end
```

Notice that no changes are needed to the sprites or Score. The Score does not change, it just keeps on displaying the same member. It is the member itself that changes.

The example in Figure 29.1 shows Next and Previous buttons. Scripting these is not hard. You just have to make sure the user does not go past the end or back up past the beginning of the slide show.

```
on nextImage
  gImageNum = gImageNum + 1
  if gImageNum > gImageList.count then
    gImageNum = 1
  end if
  showImage
end

on previousImage
  gImageNum = gImageNum - 1
  if gImageNum < 1 then
    gImageNum = gImageList.count
  end if
  showImage
end
```

The two buttons in the example movie on the CD-ROM are wired up with the complex button behavior from Chapter 14, "Creating Behaviors." In addition, the frame has a simple *go to the frame* placed in the *on exitFrame* handler.

> **Note**
>
> If the images being loaded are large, there will be a delay between the display of each image because the file needs to be read from the disk. You can minimize this by making the images smaller: Use GIFs or JPEGs rather than larger file formats.

The order in which the images are shown is alphabetical. Director actually has no say in the matter. The *getNthFileNameInFolder* function just returns the files in the order that the operating system has them.

Tip

A simple way to get your images to appear in the order that you want is to place charac-ters, such as numbers, at the beginning of each file name. For instance, you can have a file called "0010zebra.jpg" that will appear before "0020elephant.jpg." By leaving some leading zeroes, you ensure that you can represent at least 1,000 images and order them correctly. By adding the last zero, you ensure that you can easily insert images between others, like "0015gorilla."

The *getNthFileNameInFolder* technique is restricted to Director and Projectors. You cannot use this technique in quite the same way with Shockwave because you do not have access to the *getNthFileNameInFolder* function. However, you can still import images by resetting the *filename* property of a linked bitmap member. This property accepts Internet locations as readily as it accepts local disk locations.

The problem then becomes one of determining which files are present. You can maintain a separate list of image filenames in a text file on the server. This file can be read with the *getNetText* series of commands. You just have to update that file every time you add or remove an image.

Some servers even return a list of files in a directory as a simple HTML page, called an index. If your sever does this, you can get an up-to-date list by using "getNetText" with the path to the folder itself. However, the text returned is not a straight list and you might find it difficult to extract the filenames from it.

PANNING LARGE IMAGES

Sooner or later, every Director developer has to face the situation where an image that needs to be displayed is larger than the Stage. Quite frequently these are huge images of maps, diagrams, or even a detailed photograph.

If the detail in the image needs to be preserved, shrinking the image to fit is not an option. The only solution is to display only a portion of the image at a time, and enable users to pan around the image to see whatever portions they need to examine.

Creating functionality like this can be as easy as setting the sprite's *movable* property to TRUE in the Score window. However, doing so enables users to move the image off the screen altogether. It also does not give you a way to provide additional functionality, such special grab-and-drag cursors.

Figure 29.2 shows a movie that represents only a portion of an image. The entire image is actually there, in its single sprite channel, but only the portion centered on the Stage can be seen. Some gray box-shape sprites cover the four edges of the screen as well. These box shapes could serve as places for additional buttons, instructions, or commentary.

Figure 29.2
Only part of a large image can be seen in this movie. However, users can click and drag the image around to see any portions they want.

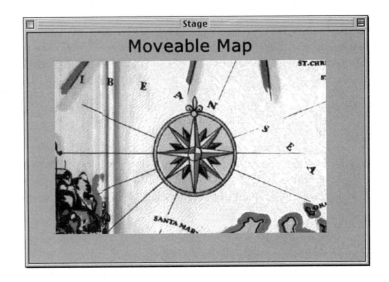

The desired functionality of this movie is to enable users to click the image and drag it around. Users should not, however, be able to drag the image past its edges. To prevent that, the script, which is a behavior in this case, needs to know the coordinates of the visible area. It knows this by creating a sprite with a shape rectangle that is one sprite behind the image. Its dimensions fall directly behind the visible portion of the image. The behavior takes the *rect* of this sprite so that the sprite cannot be dragged past its limits.

The "on beginSprite" handler gets the *rect* of this underlying sprite and uses it to compute the "pBounds" property. This *rect* represents the limits within which the registration point of the image can be moved so that the image still fits inside the visible area. This math is very tricky. Play around with the example on the CD-ROM to see it in action.

```
property pDrag, pOffset, pBounds, pCursor

on beginSprite me
  pDrag = FALSE

  -- get rectangle of display area
  spr = sprite(me.spriteNum)
  mem = sprite(me.spriteNum).member
  screen = sprite(me.spriteNum-1).rect
  pBounds = rect(0,0,0,0)
  pBounds.left = screen.right - (mem.width - mem.regPoint.locH)
  pBounds.right = screen.left + (mem.width - mem.regPoint.locH)
  pBounds.top = screen.bottom - (mem.height - mem.regPoint.locV)
  pBounds.bottom = screen.top + (mem.regPoint.locV)
end
```

When the user clicks the sprite, the "pDrag" property signals that dragging is taking place. In addition, the offset between the click location and the registration point of the sprite is recorded to enable the user to drag the sprite from the point of the click, rather than the center.

```
-- when the image is clicked, enable dragging
on mouseDown me
  pDrag = TRUE
  pOffset = the clickLoc - sprite(me.spriteNum).loc
end
```

In addition to the dragging, this behavior also uses the cursor to show the user what is happening. The *on mouseWithin* handler is called once per frame. It checks to see what is going on, and displays closed and opened hand cursors when appropriate. To make sure that the *cursor* command is not constantly being applied every frame, the "on changeCursor" handler first compares the desired cursor with its record of the cursor's last change. It uses the *cursor* command only when a change is necessary.

```
-- when the cursor is over the image, see if a cursor is needed
on mouseWithin me
  -- check to make sure that the cursor is directly over sprite
  if the rollover = me.spriteNum then
    if pDrag = TRUE then
      -- closed hand for dragging
      changeCursor(me,290)
    else
      -- open hand if not dragging
      changeCursor(me,260)
    end if
  else
    -- normal cursor if not directly over sprite
    changeCursor(me,0)
  end if
end

-- if cursor leaves image area, reset it
on mouseLeave me
  changeCursor(me,0)
end

-- change the cursor only if not the same as last time
on changeCursor me, cursorNum
  if cursorNum <> pCursor then
    pCursor = cursorNum
    cursor(pCursor)
  end if
end
```

Dragging is stopped when the user releases the mouse button:

```
-- stop dragging
on mouseUp me
  pDrag = FALSE
end
on mouseUpOutside me
  pDrag = FALSE
end
```

The "on exitFrame" script is where the action takes place. A new location is calculated, based on the mouse location. That location is then checked to make sure it does not place one of the edges of the image past a boundary. It limits the location to this boundary if it does.

```
-- set the new location if dragging
on exitFrame me
  if pDrag then
    newloc = the mouseLoc - pOffset

    if newloc.locH < pBounds.left then newloc.locH = pBounds.left
    if newloc.locH > pBounds.right then newloc.locH = pBounds.right
    if newloc.locV < pBounds.top then newloc.locV = pBounds.top
    if newloc.locV > pBounds.bottom then newloc.locV = pBounds.bottom
    sprite(me.spriteNum).loc = newloc
  end if
end
```

You can use this behavior very easily by just dragging it on top of any sprite. However, you need to have a rectangle in the sprite channel below it that determines the visible area. Check the example on the CD-ROM to see exactly how this is set up.

You can show images that are very wide or tall with this same behavior. If one dimension fits on the screen, but the other doesn't, set up the underlying rectangle to exactly match the smaller dimension. The users will not be able to drag in that direction at all, because there is nothing more to show. However, they will be able to drag in the longer dimension.

MAKING SCROLL BARS FOR LARGE IMAGES

Although panning enables the user to see any part of a large image, there is no way for them to tell, at any particular time, where they are in the image. In addition, dragging with the cursor can be clumsy at times. If the image is very large, users might have to click and drag many times to get all the way across the image.

Scroll bars solve these problems. They are used so commonly throughout computer applications that even novices can use them without difficulty.

Figure 29.3 shows the movie from Figure 29.2. It has a large image that is only partially visible. The scrolling bars at the right and bottom of the image enable users to get around inside the image. The marker in the middle of each scrolling bar not only shows the relative position of the visible portion of the image, but it also can be dragged.

Scrolling bars are similar to the slider interface element described in Chapter 15, "Graphic Interface Elements." There is a marker, a background graphic, and two arrow buttons. However, there is really no need for the "shadow" used in the slider examples.

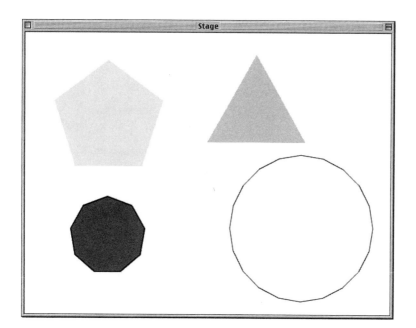

Figure 29.3
Scrolling bars can be used to enable users to decide which portion of a large image to view at any one time.

The behaviors that need to be developed for a program such as the one seen in Figure 29.3 need to work for both horizontal and vertical scroll bars. Whether a behavior controls a horizontal or vertical scroll bar can be decided by parameters. In addition, a parameter needs to link the marker to the background sprite and another needs to link it to the image's sprite:

```
property pPressed -- whether the sprite is being pressed
property pBounds -- the rect of the shadow sprite at start
property pBGSprite -- the number of the shadow sprite
property pImageSprite -- the image to manipulate
property pValue -- actual value of the slider
property pOrientation -- horiz or vert scroll bar

on getPropertyDescriptionList me
  list = [:]
  addProp list, #pBGSprite, [#comment: "Scroll Background Sprite",¬
    #format: #integer, #default: 0]
  addProp list, #pOrientation, [#comment: "Orientation",¬
    #format: #symbol, #default: #horizontal,¬
    #range: [#horizontal, #vertical]]
  addProp list, #pImageSprite, [#comment: "Image Sprite",¬
    #format: #integer, #default: 0]
  return list
end
```

When the sprite starts, it needs to figure out some things. First, it uses the background sprite to determine the marker's movement limit. So the background sprite acts in a fashion similar to that of the "shadow" sprite described in Chapter 15. It also sends the initial location of the scroll bar marker to the image's sprite, where a new handler called "on newImagePos" adjusts the position of the image accordingly.

```
on beginSprite me
  -- get the bounds on all four sides
  pBounds = sprite(pBGSprite).rect
  pBounds.right = pBounds.right - sprite(me.spriteNum).member.width/2
  pBounds.left = pBounds.left + sprite(me.spriteNum).member.width/2
  pBounds.bottom = pBounds.bottom - sprite(me.spriteNum).member.height/2
  pBounds.top = pBounds.top + sprite(me.spriteNum).member.height/2

  -- get initial value and send to image sprite also
  if pOrientation = #horizontal then
    pValue = sprite(me.spriteNum).locH - pBounds.left
    sendSprite(sprite pImageSprite,#newImagePos,getValue(me),VOID)
  else if pOrientation = #vertical then
    pValue = sprite(me.spriteNum).locV - pBounds.top
    sendSprite(sprite pImageSprite,#newImagePos,VOID,getValue(me))
  end if

  setMarker(me)
end
```

The movement of the marker is achieved through the typical handlers used for dragging behaviors.

```
on mouseDown me
  pPressed = TRUE
end

on mouseUp me
  pPressed = FALSE
end

on mouseUpOutside me
  pPressed = FALSE
end

on exitFrame me
  if pPressed then
    moveMarker(me)
  end if
end
```

When the marker is being dragged, the "on moveMarker" handler positions the marker to move with the mouse. The scrolling bar boundaries are always checked to make sure that the marker is not moved too far. The "on newImagePos" handler in the image's sprite behavior is also called each frame so that the image's position is constantly updated to match the marker as it is being dragged.

```
on moveMarker me
  if pOrientation = #horizontal then
```

```
      pValue = the mouseH - pBounds.left
      -- check to make sure it is within bounds
      if pValue > pBounds.width then
        pValue = pBounds.width
      else if pValue < 0 then
        pValue = 0
      end if
      sendSprite(sprite pImageSprite,#newImagePos,getValue(me),VOID)
    else if pOrientation = #vertical then
      pValue = the mouseV - pBounds.top
      -- check to make sure it is within bounds
      if pValue > pBounds.height then
        pValue = pBounds.height
      else if pValue < 0 then
        pValue = 0
      end if
      sendSprite(sprite pImageSprite,#newImagePos,VOID,getValue(me))
    end if

  setMarker(me)
end
```

Like the slider behaviors in Chapter 15, the arrow buttons call a handler inside the marker's behavior. The handler moves the scrolling bar one pixel at a time. It performs the same boundary checking as the preceding handler, and also sends a message to the image's sprite to update it.

```
-- this handler moves the marker one value left or right
on moveMarkerOne me, direction
  if direction = #left or direction = #up then
    pValue = pValue - 1
  else if direction = #right or direction = #down then
    pValue = pValue + 1
  end if

  -- check to make sure it is within bounds
  if pOrientation = #horizontal then
    if pValue > pBounds.width then
      pValue = pBounds.width
    else if pValue < 0 then
      pValue = 0
    end if
    sendSprite(sprite pImageSprite,#newImagePos,getValue(me),VOID)
  else
    if pValue > pBounds.height then
      pValue = pBounds.height
    else if pValue < 0 then
      pValue = 0
    end if
    sendSprite(sprite pImageSprite,#newImagePos,VOID,getValue(me))
  end if

  setMarker(me)
end
```

The behavior needs the supporting handler "on setMarker", which sets the marker according to the value of the scrolling bar. This is used by the "on moveMarkerOne" handler so that the marker moves as the user clicks on the arrow buttons.

```
-- this sets the marker sprite
on setMarker me
  if pOrientation = #horizontal then
    sprite(me.spriteNum).locH = pBounds.left + pValue
  else
    sprite(me.spriteNum).locV = pBounds.top + pValue
  end if
end
```

The "on getValue" handler returns the value of the slider. This handler can be called by a movie handler, or a handler in another behavior. Rather than returning the marker's pixel position, it returns a value between 0 and 1, representing the position of the marker in the scrolling bar.

```
-- this handler returns the value of the slider between 0 and 1
on getValue me
  if pOrientation = #horizontal then
    return float(pValue)/float(pBounds.width)
  else
    return float(pValue)/float(pBounds.height)
  end if
end
```

Finally, the last handler in the scrolling bar marker behavior enables an outside handler to set the position of the marker. It passes in a value between 0 and 1, and the handler figures out the pixel position of the marker from that. This handler enables the user to drag the image around with the cursor, and the markers are updated as the image moves.

```
-- this sets the marker according to a number between 0 and 1
on setValue me, percent
  if pOrientation = #horizontal then
    pValue = percent*pBounds.width
  else
    pValue = percent*pBounds.height
  end if
  setMarker(me)
end
```

The scroll bar marker behavior is now complete, but it does not have the direct capability to move the image. It calls the handler "on newImagePos", which exists in the image sprite's behavior, several times. The following handler, which can be added to the same image sprite behavior used in the last section, repositions the image based on values from 0 to 1.

```
-- this handler receives messages from the scroll bars telling it
-- to change the position of the image
on newImagePos me, hPercent, vPercent
  if not voidP(hPercent) then
    -- message from horizontal scroll bar
    newH = pBounds.left + pBounds.width*(1.0-hPercent)
    sprite(me.spriteNum).locH = newH
```

```
    end if
    if not voidP(vPercent) then
      -- message from vertical scroll bar
      newV = pBounds.top + pBounds.height*(1.0-vPercent)
      sprite(me.spriteNum).locV = newV
    end if
end
```

The image sprite's behavior also needs to reciprocate by sending the scrolling bars information any time the user drags the image around. It does this with the "on sendPosition" handler. This handler needs to be called near the end of the "on exitFrame" script, immediately after the location of the sprite is set.

```
-- this handler sends the new position of the image to the scroll bars
-- so they can adjust their markers accordingly
on sendPosition me
  horizScrollSprite = 18
  vertScrollSprite = 25
  hPercent = 1.0-float(sprite(me.spriteNum).locV-pBounds.top)/pBounds.height
  sendSprite(sprite horizScrollSprite,#setValue,hPercent)
  vPercent = 1.0-float(sprite(me.spriteNum).locH-pBounds.left)/pBounds.width
  sendSprite(sprite vertScrollSprite,#setValue,vPercent)
end
```

The next items to work on are the scrolling bar buttons. They use a script similar to the arrow buttons with the sliders described in Chapter 15. The behavior needs to know what direction each button represents and what marker it relates to. Each button also needs a down state.

```
property pDownMember, pOrigMember -- down and normal states
property pPressed -- whether the sprite is being pressed
property pMarkerSprite -- the number of the marker sprite
property pArrowDirection -- 1 or -1 to add to slider

on getPropertyDescriptionList me
  list = [:]
  addProp list, #pMarkerSprite, [#comment: "Marker Sprite",¬
    #format: #integer, #default: 0]
  addProp list, #pDownMember, [#comment: "Arrow Button Down Member",¬
    #format: #bitmap, #default: ""]
  addProp list, #pArrowDirection, [#comment: "Arrow Direction",¬
    #format: #symbol, #range: [#left,#right,#up,#down], #default: #right]
  return list
end

on beginSprite me
  pOrigMember = (sprite me.spriteNum).member
end

on mouseDown me
  pPressed = TRUE
  (sprite me.spriteNum).member = member pDownMember
end
```

```
on mouseUp me
  liftUp(me)
end

on mouseUpOutside me
  liftUp(me)
end

on liftUp me
  pPressed = FALSE
  (sprite me.spriteNum).member = member pOrigMember
end

on exitFrame me
  if pPressed then
    sendSprite(sprite pMarkerSprite, #moveMarkerOne,¬
      pArrowDirection)
  end if
end
```

This completes the scrolling image program. There are a lot of complex handlers. Most of this complexity has to do with figuring out the moving boundaries of the scrolling bar markers and of the image itself.

You could easily leave out one of the two scrolling bars and create an image that scrolls in only one dimension. You could also remove the handlers that enable the users to control the image by dragging it, leaving the scrolling bars as the only option.

Also remember that the scrolling bar graphics are totally up to you. The ones used in this example look very much like standard scrolling bars. However, you can create colorful creative ones that fit your particular interface style.

ZOOMING IN ON LARGE IMAGES

A third way to enable users to view portions of a large image is to enable them to see the entire thing at first, and then click a spot on the image to zoom in to full size. This is particularly useful for maps, where the shrunken, zoomed-out view of the map is still somewhat viewable.

A program that does this starts out looking like Figure 29.4. The entire image is visible on the screen. The user then clicks a spot and the result looks very much like Figure 29.2. The only difference is that you need to use some extra cursors, such as a magnifying glass, to let users know what is going on.

After the user clicks a spot on the image, the image is enlarged to full size. The spot where the user clicked is centered on the screen, unless it needs to be adjusted near the edges. Then, the user can click and drag the image as before. To return to the zoomed-out image, the user holds down the Shift key and clicks.

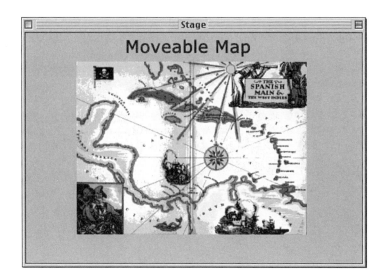

Figure 29.4
When the user clicks
the image, it enlarges
to full size.

The behavior to do this is built from the panning image behavior discussed in the section of
this chapter entitled "Panning Large Images." This time, it needs to keep track of two
modes. The first mode is the fully zoomed-out image, on which the user can click to zoom
in. The second mode is the full size image, which the users can click to drag it around, or
Shift+click to zoom back out.

```
property pMode, pDrag, pOffset, pBounds, pScreen, pOrigRect, pCursor

on beginSprite me
  pDrag = FALSE
  pMode = #zoom

  -- get rectangle of display area
  spr = sprite(me.spriteNum)
  mem = sprite(me.spriteNum).member
  pScreen = sprite(me.spriteNum-1).rect
  pBounds = rect(0,0,0,0)
  pBounds.left = pScreen.right - (mem.width - mem.regPoint.locH)
  pBounds.right = pScreen.left + (mem.width + mem.regPoint.locH)
  pBounds.top = pScreen.bottom - (mem.height - mem.regPoint.locV)
  pBounds.bottom = pScreen.top + (mem.regPoint.locV)

  -- remember original "zoomed out" rect
  pOrigRect = sprite(me.spriteNum).rect
end
```

The "gOrigRect" global is needed for the program to remember how the sprite looked on
the Stage before the behavior started changing it. This original state is the "zoomed out"
view. You need to set the sprite up on the Stage by scaling it down and making it fit in the
area to be used. You can even scale it differently horizontally and vertically if you want.
This behavior works either way.

The next handler takes care of all mouse clicks. If the "pMode" property is #zoom, it uses the *mapStageToMember* function to determine the real point in the image that was clicked. It then centers this point on the Stage, using point (240, 160) as the center of the Stage. It checks to make sure that the image is within the dragable boundaries, and then changes "pMode" to #drag.

If the "pMode" is set to #drag to begin with, the "pDrag" property is set to TRUE and the "pOffset" property is calculated. The "on exitFrame" handler takes care of the dragging until the mouse is lifted.

This handler also looks for the case where the "pMode" is set to #drag and if the user Shift+clicks. It then restores the sprite to its original size.

```
-- when the user clicks, perform one of three actions
on mouseDown me

  -- zoom in on location
  if pMode = #zoom then

    -- get real point clicked
    clickPoint = ¬
      mapStageToMember(sprite(me.spriteNum), the clickLoc)

    -- set sprite to full size
    mem = sprite(me.spriteNum).member
    sprite(me.spriteNum).rect = mem.rect

    -- center on the point clicked
    newloc = point(240,160) + ¬
      sprite(me.spriteNum).member.regPoint - clickPoint
    if newloc.locH < pBounds.left then newloc.locH = pBounds.left
    if newloc.locH > pBounds.right then newloc.locH = pBounds.right
    if newloc.locV < pBounds.top then newloc.locV = pBounds.top
    if newloc.locV > pBounds.bottom then newloc.locV = pBounds.bottom
    sprite(me.spriteNum).loc = newloc

    -- now enable dragging
    pMode = #drag

    -- zoom out to original view
  else if pMode = #drag and the shiftDown then

    -- set to original rect
    sprite(me.spriteNum).rect = pOrigRect

    -- ready for next zoom
    pMode = #zoom

    -- drag
  else if pMode = #drag then

    -- start drag
    pDrag = TRUE
    pOffset = the clickLoc - sprite(me.spriteNum).loc

  end if
end
```

The "on mouseWithin" handler, and the supporting "on changeCursor" handler work the same way they did in the two preceding sections. However, two more cursors are needed. A magnifying glass with a "+" in it is used when the user is over the image and the image is zoomed out. This means that the user can click the image to zoom in. Also, a magnifying glass with a "-" in it is used when the user is over the full-sized image and is holding down the Shift key. This cursor means that the user can zoom out. Here is the code to take care of this:

```
-- when the cursor is over the image, see if a cursor is needed
on mouseWithin me
  if the rollover = me.spriteNum then
    if pMode = #zoom then
      changeCursor(me,302) -- magnifying glass with +
    else if pMode = #drag and the shiftDown then
      changeCursor(me,303) -- magnifying glass with -
    else if pMode = #drag and pDrag = TRUE then
      changeCursor(me,290) -- closed hand
    else if pMode = #drag then
      changeCursor(me,260) -- opened hand
    end if
  else
    changeCursor(me,0)
  end if
end

-- if cursor leaves image area, reset it
on mouseLeave me
  changeCursor(me,0)
end

-- change the cursor only if not the same as last time
on changeCursor me, cursorNum
  if cursorNum <> pCursor then
    pCursor = cursorNum
    cursor(pCursor)
  end if
end
```

The "on mouseUp," "on mouseUpOutside," and "on exitFrame" handlers are identical to the ones used earlier.

```
-- end dragging
on mouseUp me
  pDrag = FALSE
end
on mouseUpOutside me
  pDrag = FALSE
end

-- set the new location if dragging
on exitFrame me
  if pDrag then
    newloc = the mouseLoc - pOffset

    if newloc.locH < pBounds.left then newloc.locH = pBounds.left
    if newloc.locH > pBounds.right then newloc.locH = pBounds.right
```

```
      if newloc.locV < pBounds.top then newloc.locV = pBounds.top
      if newloc.locV > pBounds.bottom then newloc.locV = pBounds.bottom
      sprite(me.spriteNum).loc = newloc
   end if
end
```

This zoom and pan behavior can be used without the panning action as well. You may just want to enable users to click and zoom in, and then click and zoom out. You may also want to use the "on changeCursor" handler to place some instructions in a text member on the Stage. For instance, when the user is in #zoom mode, it could say "Click on the image to zoom in." When the user is in #drag mode, it could say, "Click and drag the image to pan; Shift+click to zoom out."

→ **See** "Creating Sliders," Chapter 15, for more information on making sliders

UTILIZING INK AND COLOR MANIPULATION

Most of the time, images in Director are displayed as-is. However, with the wide variety of inks and the capability to change foreground and background colors, you can take an image and adjust its appearance in many ways.

Practical applications for this are not immediately apparent. The lighten and darken inks, for instance, can change the color of an image in all sorts of different ways. But why would you want to do that? One reason is to enable you to reuse the same image several times and have it look different each time.

When you are manipulating the color of an image, it is sometimes hard to find the settings you are looking for. That is why a program such as the one shown in Figure 29.5 is very useful. It enables you to change both the *color* and *bgColor* properties of the sprite by their red, green, and blue components. These color changes have a great effect on sprites that use the lighten and darken inks.

Figure 29.5
This program enables you to play with the colors used for the lighten and darken inks.

The program itself borrows a lot from behaviors earlier in the book. For instance, the sliders use the slider behaviors in Chapter 15. The two radio buttons also use behaviors from Chapter 15.

The image itself has a simple behavior that reads the values of the radio buttons and sliders and sets the ink and colors of the sprite accordingly. It does this constantly, so changes are shown as you make them.

```
on exitFrame me
  -- read radio buttons to set ink
  if selected(sprite 3) = 3 then
    ink = 40
  else
    ink = 41
  end if
  sprite(me.spriteNum).ink = ink

  -- read first set of sliders to set color
  c = rgb(0,0,0)
  c.red = sprite(7).pValue
  c.green = sprite(12).pValue
  c.blue = sprite(17).pValue
  sprite(me.spriteNum).color = c

  -- read second set of sliders to set bgcolor
  c = rgb(255,255,255)
  c.red = sprite(23).pValue
  c.green = sprite(28).pValue
  c.blue = sprite(33).pValue
  sprite(me.spriteNum).bgColor = c
end
```

You can expand a program such as this to test even more kinds of inks, although the color changes will not have quite as dramatic an effect on most. You can also include a button that enables you to import a new image into the member being shown. You can use the FileIO Xtra or the MUI Xtra to get the image filename, and then set the *filename* property of the image to import it. However, the member must start out as a linked image, not an internal one.

Another possibility for this program is to create your own Xtra with it. You can do this by placing the movie in your Director Xtras folder. You can add some interesting functionality, such as having it use the *selection of castLib* property to see whether the user has selected a bitmap, and then take its *picture* property and replace the *picture* property of the image in the Xtra. This way, you can select an image in the Cast, and then launch the Xtra, which shows you a copy of the image you have selected and lets you play with its inks and colors.

→ **See** "Sprite Inks," Chapter 10, "Properties of Sprites and Frames," for some background information about sprite inks

→ **See** "Sprite Color," Chapter 10, for some background information about sprite color

→ **See** "Sprite Blend," Chapter 10, for some background information about sprite blend

→ **See** "Creating Sliders," Chapter 15, for some more information about making sliders

→ **See** "Using Radio Buttons," Chapter 15

TROUBLESHOOTING GRAPHICS APPLICATIONS

- If your slide show cannot seem to find the image files, it may be because the pathname is not being compiled correctly. Try placing the pathname in the Message with a *put* command each time the *filename* property is set. This way, you can check it.

- In a slide show, you need to have the image member initially linked to some image. Make sure this image is present when you deliver your final product; otherwise, an error dialog box comes up when the movie is launched. It's a good idea to make sure the filename is set to link to the first image in the slide show, or to have it linked to some very small placeholder image file.

- When creating scrolling bar graphics for the scrolling image behaviors, the placement of the background graphic determines the range of movement of the marker. So be sure to test it out at both maximum and minimum values.

- Not all inks are affected by the *color* and *bgColor* properties of a sprite. If the image is 8-bit color or higher, these settings have little effect on the image for most inks.

DID YOU KNOW?

- Another way to create a slide show is to simply have all the images in an external cast library. You can then swap out this library with a new one for a different slide show. This works on the Web as well as in a Projector, and makes the images harder to "steal" because they are not in plain image formats such as JPEG or GIF.

- To complete the scrolling bar behavior, you may want to enable users to click the background bar itself. If they click above the marker, the scrolling area should page up, whereas if they click below the marker, it should page down. This is how most scrolling bars work.

SOUND APPLICATIONS

In this chapter

Sound is the neglected medium in multimedia. Pictures and text are used in just about everything, and video and animation get all the glory. However, sound can be used to create compelling multimedia experiences as both supporting media and as the central focus.

PIANO KEYBOARD

Creating a musical note is an easy task for anyone familiar with computer sound programs. In fact, you can just record a piano or other instrument. Then, you can wire that sound up to a Director button.

It is as easy as that to create a one-note keyboard program. Adding additional notes, enough to enable users to play music, is the tricky part.

First, you want to create the sound files themselves. Macromedia's SoundEdit 16 on the Mac gives you an easy way to do this. Other programs can be used to do this as well, but only SoundEdit 16 makes it this easy.

The first step is to get a sample sound. Make it a middle C note if possible. You can record this using a microphone and a musical instrument, an electronic instrument plugged directly into your computer, or a sound sample from a sound effects CD. Make this sample note as small as possible and save it as C3. The *C* is for the note and the *3* is for the octave of the piano. You could name it anything you want, but this file-naming structure works well.

Tip

It is important to make the sounds as small as you can when building a keyboard. A difference of 5K may not seem like much when creating one sound, but if you are going to have 20 notes, 5K quickly becomes 100K. That's more than a minute of download time for 28.8 modem users if you put these notes in a Shockwave applet.

After you have your C3 sound, you can vcreate other notes from it. Select the entire sound by pressing Command+A. Then, choose Effects, Pitch Shift. A dialog box with a small keyboard appears as shown in Figure 30.1.

Simply select the note you want to convert to, D above middle C for instance, and click the Shift button. The sound is converted to play at that pitch. Then, save the sound as a new file, such as D3.

You can continue to make notes this way. Always start with the original C3 sound to create each note. Name the black keys using the # character to denote a sharp, as in C3#, for instance.

The number of sounds you need depends on how many keys you have on your piano. The program in Figure 30.2 has 20 keys: 12 white and 8 black. It starts at middle C and goes up more than an octave and a half to a higher G.

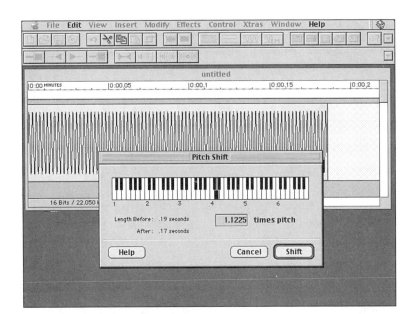

Figure 30.1
SoundEdit 16's Pitch Shift effect helps you build entire keyboards from just one sound.

PART

VIII

CH

30

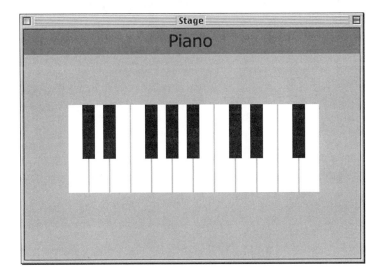

Figure 30.2
A simple keyboard contains keys made of rectangle shapes, colored white and black.

Now that you have all the sounds, import them into Director. The names of the cast members reflect the names of the files. Figure 30.3 shows the complete Cast for this movie.

To create the simple keyboard shown in Figure 30.2, all that is needed is a single shape member. This rectangle is used for all the sprites. Some sprites are colored black and others, white. Because the black keys need to be in front of the whites, they should be in higher sprite channels.

Figure 30.3
The cast window shows all the sounds needed by the keyboard.

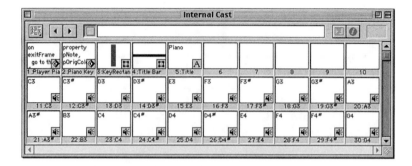

A behavior is what turns these rectangles into piano keys. The following behavior uses a parameter to determine which sound goes with which key. It also reacts to the key press by changing the color to red.

```
property pNote, pOrigColor

on getPropertyDescriptionList me
  list = [:]
  addProp list, #pNote, ¬
    [#comment: "Sound", #format: #sound, #default: VOID]
  return list
end

on beginSprite me
  -- remember original color
  pOrigColor = sprite(me.spriteNum).color
end

on mouseDown me
  press(me)
end

on mouseEnter me
  -- consider it a press when mouse button is down
  -- and the user rolls over to the key
  if the mouseDown then
    press(me)
  end if
end

on mouseUp me
  unpress(me)
end

on mouseUpOutside me
  unpress(me)
end

on mouseLeave me
  unpress(me)
end
```

```
on press me
  -- make key red
  sprite(me.spriteNum).color = rgb(255,0,0)
  -- play note
  puppetSound 1, pNote
end

on unpress me
  -- restore key to black and white
  sprite(me.spriteNum).color = pOrigColor
end
```

This script takes into account some special behavior that normal buttons don't use. If a user presses down on the mouse button outside of a key, and then rolls over it, the note plays. This makes it possible to press down once and "roll" over the keys to play them all.

This keyboard works well, but it could use some graphical improvement. You can go ahead and create your own piano keys with a graphics program. Create up and down states for each. You can even place the keys at an angle to create a 3D effect.

→ **See** "Using Lingo's Sound Commands", Chapter 17, "Controlling Sound," for more information on using sounds

PLAYER PIANO

Another possibility for a piano program is to have it play all by itself. You can provide it with a series of notes and durations, and feed them to the key behaviors at the proper time.

The first step is to come up with a simple notation scheme. Specifying the notes by their member names is a good start, but you also need to specify their duration. A good idea might be to measure this in 1/10ths of a second, or 6 ticks.

Here is an example:

```
F3.3 0.1 G3#.3 0.1 C4.3
```

This notation uses spaces to separate notes. Each note contains a sound member name and a duration, with a period in between. A *0* for a note simply means silence.

You can store notation such as this in a plain text field. Name it "Note List" or something similar.

To play this list of notes, a frame script behavior can be used. This behavior needs to keep track of the list of notes, the current note, the time to play the next note, and the sprite of the key being played.

```
property pNoteList -- a text list of notes and durations
property pNoteNumber -- the position of the current note
property pEndNoteTicks -- when the current note is done
property pNoteSprite -- the sprite with the current note's key
```

To begin, the behavior grabs the list of notes from the field. It keeps this list as a string because there is no advantage to converting it to a list. It then sets the song to the beginning.

```
on beginSprite me
  -- get the list of notes
  pNoteList = member("Note List").text

  -- start at the first note
  pNoteNumber = 1
  pEndNoteTicks = the ticks
end
```

With every frame loop that goes by, the behavior checks "pEndNoteTicks." This is the time when the note currently being played is over, and another note needs to be played.

Before it does that, it needs to turn off the current key by sending an #unpress message to the key. This calls the very same "on unpress" handler used in the preceding section.

```
on exitFrame me
  -- ready for next note?
  if the ticks >= pEndNoteTicks then

    -- if there was a previous note, end it
    if not voidP(pNoteSprite) then
      sendSprite(pNoteSprite, #unpress)
    end if

    -- play new note
    playNote(me)
  end if

  go to the frame
end
```

The "on playNote" handler locates the note in the list and plays it. The part before the period is the sound member and the part after is the duration. It then uses the duration to set the new "pEndNoteTicks."

It then searches through the sprites that are known to contain keys with the piano key behavior. In this case it is sprites 5 to 24. After it finds the sprite that represents the correct key, it sends a #press message.

```
on playNote me
  -- check to see if done
  if pNoteNumber > pNoteList.word.count then exit

  -- get new note and duration
  noteWord = pNoteList.word[pNoteNumber]
  the itemDelimiter = "."
  note = noteWord.item[1]
  duration = noteWord.item[2]

  -- set end time for note
  pEndNoteTicks = the ticks + 8*value(duration)

  -- if a "0", then just silence, else play note
```

```
  if note <> "0" then
    -- find the piano key sprite
    repeat with i = 5 to 24
      if sprite(i).pNote.name = note then
        pNoteSprite = i
        exit repeat
      end if
    end repeat

    -- play it
    sendSprite(pNoteSprite, #press)
  end if

  -- next note
  pNoteNumber = pNoteNumber + 1
end
```

This behavior can now handle a string of notes as long as you want. The problem is converting your favorite song to this notation. The example movie on the CD-ROM contains a relatively long song, just to give you an idea.

There is nothing to prevent you from going further with this movie. For instance, you could have two tracks running at once, one in sound channel 1 and one in sound channel 2. You can even have notes that are not represented by keys. Those notes can just play a sound rather than send a message along to a key sprite.

DYNAMIC STEREO SOUND

Not too long ago, most computers came with a small, low-quality speaker hidden inside the case. Now, it is hard to find even a budget-priced machine that does not come with a sound card and a set of speakers.

However, this stereo sound is an underused feature. As a Director developer, you can take advantage of it without too much trouble.

For instance, if you have a noisy element on the Stage, such as a helicopter, it will probably make a helicopter noise. However, if the user moves the helicopter to the left or right side of the screen, the sound doesn't shift from speaker to speaker as the image moves from side to side.

Because you can play multiple sounds in Director, and control the volume of each sound, it makes sense that you should be able to control the volume in each stereo channel as well. However, you can't. At least not directly.

The way around this is to create two separate sounds, both in stereo. However, the first has the helicopter sound in only the left channel, whereas the second has the sound in only the right channel. Figure 30.4 shows the left sound as seen in the SoundEdit 16 editing window.

Figure 30.4
This sound editing window shows a stereo sound, with both left and right channels. Only the left sound channel, however, contains noise, whereas the other is silent.

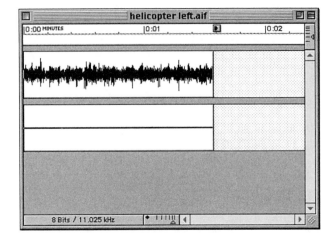

When the helicopter appears on the Stage, the two sounds are started with the *puppetSound* command. Then, the *volume* property of the two sound channels changes depending on the horizontal location of the sprite.

```
on beginSprite me
  -- start sounds
  puppetSound 3, "helicopter left"
  puppetSound 4, "helicopter right"
  setSoundVolumes(me)
end

on setSoundVolumes me

  -- calculate horizontal position
  x = sprite(me.spriteNum).locH
  percent = float(x)/(the stage).rect.width

  -- calculate volumes
  leftVolume = (1.0-percent)*255
  rightVolume = (percent)*255

  -- set volumes
  the volume of sound 3 = leftVolume
  the volume of sound 4 = rightVolume
end


on exitFrame me

  -- sprite follows the cursor
  sprite(me.spriteNum).loc = the mouseLoc

  -- change volumes
  setSoundVolumes(me)
end
```

Note

> Note that the old "the" syntax is used to set the *volume* of a sound channel. It appears that *sound(3).volume* does not work with version 7.0. If you have a newer version of Director, you may want to try it.

You need to make sure that your two sounds are set to loop. Because the sounds are started with, and controlled by, the sprite's behavior, you can even have a behavior such as this attached to multiple sprites at the same time. Because this one is using channels 3 and 4, you would want to have the other sprite use two different channels.

3D SOUND

True 3D sound would mean a set of surround-sound speakers or some similar setup. However, you can easily simulate depth by setting the volume of a sound channel.

Rather than using two different sound channels as shown in the preceding example, this example just uses one simple sound. The sound gets louder as the cursor approaches an object, and quieter as it moves away.

The behavior to do this is relatively simple. It uses the fact that the *volume* property ranges from 0 to 255. It computes the distance from the cursor to the sprite. If the distance is greater than 255, the volume is set to zero. If the distance is closer, it reverses it, so that a distance of 0 plays the sound at full volume (255) and a distance of 254 plays the sound at a volume of 1.

```
on beginSprite me
  -- start sounds
  puppetSound 3, "static"
  setSoundVolume(me)
end

on setSoundVolume me

  -- calculate distance
  d = distance(me,sprite(me.spriteNum).loc,the mouseLoc)

  -- calculate volume
  vol = 255-d
  if d < 0 then d = 0

  -- set volumes
  the volume of sound 3 = vol
end

on exitFrame me
  -- change volumes
  setSoundVolume(me)
end

on distance me, p1, p2
  return sqrt(power(p1.locH-p2.locH,2)+power(p1.locV-p2.locV,2))
end
```

Although the example movie on the CD-ROM uses a television set and a static noise, you can find far more constructive ways to use this behavior. For instance, you can place several objects that have some sort of spoken narration on the Stage. As the cursor moves closer to an object, the looping audio gets louder.

This simulates the experience that you might have at a museum, where audio information is given at each exhibit. As you approach one, the audio become clearer, whereas the audio from the previous exhibit fades.

ADJUSTING VOLUME CONTROLS

If your Director movie uses any sort of sound, it is usually a good idea to offer users a chance to control the overall volume. It is true that every operating system has a sound or volume control panel, but you can imagine that plenty of people don't know that it exists. It is also unreasonable to expect people to have to leave your program to adjust the volume.

Adding a volume control is not hard. Using *the soundLevel* system property, you can set the volume to a number from 0 to 7. This changes the overall volume, independently from any *volume* properties you set. It even controls the volume of the system beep.

VOLUME SLIDER

The first step in adding a volume control is deciding which type of control you want. A slider is commonly used. Figure 30.5 shows a slider control and also a single-button control that you will learn more about later in this section.

Figure 30.5
This figure shows two different volume controls: a slider and a single-button control.

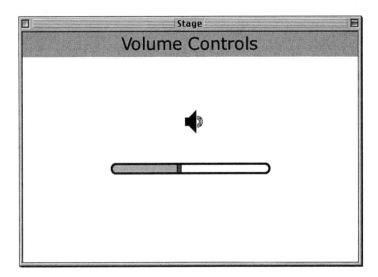

The slider control uses a behavior that is very similar to the slider behavior in Chapter 15, "Graphic Interface Elements." It includes a marker, a shadow, and a background graphic. The behavior is attached to the marker. It tells the shadow's sprite to follow it.

You will recognize most of the code in this behavior from the slider behavior. However, some parameters are not present. The maximum and minimum values of the volume are always 0 and 7, so there is no need to make them parameters. This behavior also has no initial value parameter, because the behavior gets that from the current sound level to which the computer is set.

In fact, there is no need to store the current value of the slider at all. When the user moves the slider, it sets *the soundLevel* system property, which can be used in place of the "pValue" property.

```
property pPressed -- whether the sprite is being pressed
property pBounds -- the rect of the shadow sprite at start
property pShadowSprite -- the number of the shadow sprite
property pMinimumValue, pMaximumValue -- use by the marker sprite only

on getPropertyDescriptionList me
  list = [:]
  addProp list, #pShadowSprite, [#comment: "Shadow Sprite",¬
    #format: #integer, #default: 0]
  return list
end

on beginSprite me
  pBounds = sprite(pShadowSprite).rect
  pMinimumValue = 0
  pMaximumValue = 7
  setMarker(me)
  setShadow(me)
end

on mouseDown me
  pPressed = TRUE
end

on mouseUp me
  pPressed = FALSE
end

on mouseUpOutside me
  pPressed = FALSE
end

on exitFrame me
  if pPressed then
    moveMarker(me)
  end if
  setMarker(me)
  setShadow(me)
end

-- this handler takes the mouse position and figures the
-- value of the slider
on moveMarker me
  -- compute the position as a number between 0 and 1
  x = the mouseH - pBounds.left
  sliderRange = pBounds.right-pBounds.left
```

```
    pos = float(x)/sliderRange

    -- translate to a value
    valueRange = pMaximumValue - pMinimumValue
    val = pos*valueRange + pMinimumValue
    val = integer(val)

    -- check to make sure it is within bounds
    if val > pMaximumValue then
      val = pMaximumValue
    else if val < pMinimumValue then
      val = pMinimumValue
    end if

    the soundLevel = val
end


-- this sets the marker sprite
on setMarker me
  -- compute the value as a number between 0 and 1
  valueRange = pMaximumValue - pMinimumValue
  sliderPos = float(the soundLevel)/float(valueRange)

  -- translate to a screen position
  sliderRange = pBounds.right-pBounds.left
  x = sliderPos*sliderRange + pBounds.left

  -- set marker
  sprite(me.spriteNum).locH = x
end

-- this handler lets the marker sprite set the shadow sprite
on setShadow me
  x = (sprite me.spriteNum).locH
  r = rect(pBounds.left, pBounds.top, x, pBounds.bottom)
  sprite(pShadowSprite).rect = r
end
```

Note that the *on exitFrame* handler in this behavior sets the volume regardless of whether the slider is currently being moved. This means that the slider reacts to changes in *the soundLevel*, even if the slider did not affect those changes. You can test this by running the movie and using the Message window to set *the soundLevel*. The slider reacts to the change. This also happens if the user decides to change the volume manually with the computer's control panel. It ensures that the slider always displays the current sound setting.

→ **See** "Creating Sliders," Chapter 15, for more information about creating sliders

VOLUME BUTTON

Although a volume button does its job well, it is sometimes hard to implement. Perhaps you don't have the screen space, or a slider doesn't match your interface design.

I like to use a simpler option. You can place a single sprite on the Stage that the user can press to change the volume. If it is pressed once, the volume goes up one level. If the volume is at a maximum, it goes to 0.

Such a button can use a set of eight graphics to represent the eight levels of *the soundLevel*. Figure 30.5 showed this button just above the slider. Figure 30.6 shows the Cast that contains all eight variations of this button.

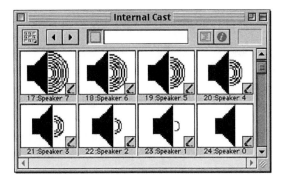

Figure 30.6
The cast window shows eight images that represent the eight sound levels for a volume button.

PART

VIII

CH

30

The behavior that controls this button is much simpler than the slider behavior. But like it, it sets the member of the button every frame, regardless of whether the button was pushed. This ensures that the button reflects the current sound level even if the user changes it manually.

In fact, you can place both volume controls on the Stage at once, as shown in Figure 30.5. If you change the volume with one control, the other reflects the change. You can even wire up the button to be used to change the sound, whereas the slider could show the change, but could not be clicked.

```
on beginSprite me
  setIcon(me)
end

on setIcon me
  val = the soundLevel
  sprite(me.spriteNum).member = member("speaker"&&val)
end

on mouseDown me
  val = the soundLevel
  if val < 7 then
    val = val + 1
  else
    val = 0
  end if
  the soundLevel = val
  setIcon(me)
end

on exitFrame me
  setIcon(me)
end
```

You can use any of the eight members to represent the eight sound states. You can get very creative with this by using different size audio speakers or pictures of people whispering to pictures of them yelling.

TROUBLESHOOTING SOUND APPLICATIONS

- Does there seem to be a large delay in playing sounds when you are mixing more than one? Always check to see whether the movie is running on a Windows machine with *the platform*. If it is, try to set *the soundDevice* to "QT3Mix." If users have QuickTime 3 installed, this results in much better sound mixing. If they do not, *the soundDevice* reverts to "MacroMix."

- Windows machines have a history of difficulty in supporting good multi-channel audio playback. It is especially important that developers test early and often on the machines they plan to support, and to document the system requirements for their users. Macromedia's Tech Support Web site is an important source of information in troubleshooting sound issues.

- If you are trying to use stereo sounds, and the sound ends up being mono after you make a Shockwave movie, check your Shockwave Audio Settings in the Xtras menu. It may be set to convert all stereo sounds to mono to make them smaller.

DID YOU KNOW?

- If you don't like sliders or the single-button volume control, you have plenty of other options. You can use a text-based pop-up menu like the behavior described in Chapter 16, "Controlling Text." You could also use a set of radio buttons. Even a dial is possible: Just have eight dial graphics, one for each sound level, and have the volume increase when the users click on the right side of the dial, and decrease when they click the left side.

- You can create a mute button that uses some of the code from the check box behavior described in Chapter 15. Just have the behavior remember the current sound level and start in the "on" position. If users click the check box, set *the soundLevel* to 0. When they click again, reset *the soundLevel* to its original value. Or, better yet, use *the soundEnabled* property. This enables you to turn off sound without changing *the soundLevel*.

- You can use the *volume* property of a sound to gradually fade a sound in or out. However, Lingo has two commands, *sound fadeIn* and *sound fadeOut*, that do exactly this. You can even cross fade between sounds in two channels by having both play at the same time.

- Sound placed in QuickTime 3 tracks offers you even more control over what is playing and what is not. You can have multiple tracks, all synchronized, and turn off and on individual ones with *setTrackEnabled*.

SHOCKWAVE APPLETS

In this chapter

Just about any Director movie can be a Shockwave applet. Most of the examples in the previous four chapters, plus the examples in the next chapter, can be placed on the Web or an intranet for viewing in a browser.

However, a few types of programs work only in the world of the Web. Navigation tools, such as navigation pages and navigation bars, are built specifically to enable the users to navigate through a Web site. There are also Web advertisements, which can be made very interesting by creating them in Director. There are even programs that draw on other sources of information on the Web.

CREATING NAVIGATION PAGES

Just about every Web site has a front end. Although this can be a plain HTML page, you can also do something more complex, such as using a Shockwave applet.

Macromedia's site, for instance, uses Shockwave Flash to create an interactive experience right at the front door. Shockwave for Director is even more capable of producing interaction.

Although you can use any one of the many techniques discussed earlier in this book to make interactive movies, the basic difference between those movies and ones that are meant to be Shockwave navigation pages is the actual Web navigation.

Web navigation is achieved through the use of the *gotoNetPage* command. This replaces the current HTML page with another one. It enables you to turn Shockwave buttons into links just like standard HTML "A HREF" tags.

Figure 31.1 shows a typical Shockwave applet navigation page in the Director Stage window. It contains six buttons, plus some extra graphics. The three color swipes at the top animate from left to right.

The behavior attached to each Web button is pretty simple. It takes one parameter: the Web location that the button will use. It doesn't even use the traditional "down" states like the complex button behavior discussed in Chapter 14, "Creating Behaviors."

```
property pURL

on getPropertyDescriptionList me
  list = [:]
  addProp list, #pURL, [#comment: "URL", #format: #string, #default: ""]
  return list
end

on mouseUp me
  gotoNetPage(pUrl)
end
```

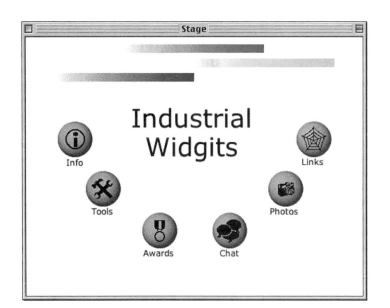

Figure 31.1
A simple Director movie that can be used as the front end of a Web site.

The purpose of this behavior is to highlight what is needed to create a Web navigation button, which is the ability to specify a URL and then use the *gotoNetPage* command to execute the jump.

It is recommended that you use a behavior such as the complex button behavior described in Chapter 14. You can actually use that behavior as-is by just placing a Lingo command such as gotoNetPage("info.html") in the parameter for "Lingo to Execute."

After the movie is done, it can be embedded in an HTML page and placed on your Web site. For more information on how to do this, see "Making Shockwave Movies" in Chapter 36, "Delivering the Goods." Figure 31.2 shows what the embedded movie might look like in Netscape Navigator.

The examples shown in Figures 31.1 and 31.2 are not all that they could be. Because you have so many power features in Director, it is a shame to use it only to display buttons and a simple animation. A more sensible use of the applet would be to provide rollovers, as described in Chapter 15, "Graphic Interface Elements." Or, perhaps you would want to include sounds and sprites with behaviors that make them react to the mouse position. These are all things that are easy to do in Director, but much harder in HTML.

Figure 31.2
The Shockwave navigation movie has been embedded into a plain white Web page.

→ **See** "Rollovers," Chapter 15

→ **See** "Shockwave Lingo," Chapter 22, "Shockwave and Internet Access"

→ **See** "Making Shockwave Movies," Chapter 36

CREATING NAVIGATION BARS

Many Web sites use frames. Frames enable you to divide the browser's window into smaller parts, each of which contains a separate HTML page.

One use for frames is to have one large frame be a central area where information is displayed, while another small frame contains buttons that control what is in the large frame. Although you could place some plain HTML in this small frame, you could also make a Shockwave movie for it.

Such a movie might look like Figure 31.3. This is a narrow little applet that appears in a frame to the left of the main one.

Figure 31.3
A narrow navigation bar applet to control the HTML location of another frame in the browser.

PART

VIII

CH

31

The buttons in this applet are only a little more complex than the buttons in the previous program. This time, however, they need to specify the frame that the *gotoNetPage* command should affect. This is done with a second parameter:

```
property pURL, pTarget

on getPropertyDescriptionList me
  list = [:]
  addProp list, #pURL, ¬
    [#comment: "URL", #format: #string, #default: ""]
  addProp list, #pTarget, ¬
    [#comment: "Target", #format: #string, #default: "main"]
  return list
end

on mouseUp
  gotoNetPage(pUrl,pTarget)
end
```

The "pTarget" property should be set, for every button, to the name of the target frame. This name is determined by the HTML code in the parent page. Here is an example:

```
<HTML><HEAD>
<TITLE>Navigation Bar Demo</TITLE>
</HEAD>
```

```
<FRAMESET Cols="100,*">
<FRAME Name="bar" SRC="navbar.html" Scrolling="Auto">
<FRAME Name="main" SRC="info.html" Scrolling="Auto">
</FRAMESET>

</HTML>
```

It is the "navbar.html" page that has the Shockwave applet on it. The other frame is called "main" and starts off with "info.html", the same content that might be displayed when users press the "Info" button in the applet.

Figure 31.4 shows the frames displayed in Netscape Navigator. The "info.html" page is shown, but there would obviously be more to it if this were not just a simple example.

Figure 31.4
The browser window is broken up into two frames. The one on the left contains a page with a Shockwave applet that controls the one on the right.

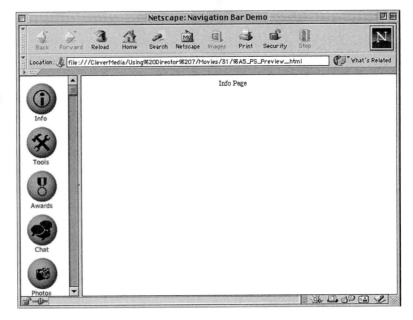

Like the navigation page applet described earlier, this navigation bar is only an example. To make it worthwhile to use Shockwave, rather than just plain HTML images and links, you should add some animation or interaction.

→ **See** "Controlling the Web Browser with Lingo," Chapter 22

→ **See** "Making Shockwave Movies," Chapter 36

CREATING ADVERTISING

Advertising is everywhere on the Web nowadays. At first, these were just static images. Now, Web advertisements are usually animated GIF images.

Sometimes, however, ads are Java applets, dynamic HTML, or Shockwave. Although Shockwave Flash movies as ads are more common than Shockwave for Director, it is not unheard of to have a movie as an ad. This is especially true because JavaScript can be used to determine whether users have Shockwave, and simply display a less-rich ad, such as an animated GIF, if they do not.

Making an ad in Director is another task that is relatively simple, but it does not have to be. Because Web ads are usually just animation, it is tempting to just do that in Director, too. But you can do so much more.

One idea is to use Lingo and behaviors to make animation that is not possible to make with animated GIFs or Flash. For instance, take a look at the 3D cube script in Chapter 18, "Controlling Bitmaps." This script produced a 3D cube by manipulating six square bitmaps by their *quad* property. The cube rotated and changed angles depending on the mouse's location.

You can place that same script into a small advertising applet. Because it reacts to the mouse location, it is something that cannot be made in a simpler medium such as GIFs or Flash. The different angles that are possible also make it hard to do in other mediums, because the cube can be displayed in an almost infinite number of ways.

Figure 31.5 shows such a Web applet. It is set to 468 pixels by 60 pixels, a common Web advertisement size.

PART
VIII
CH
31

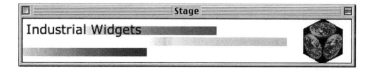

Figure 31.5
A small Shockwave applet can be used as an advertisement. This ad contains an interactive 3D cube on the right.

The only changes made to the 3D cube script were to make it a radius of 20 pixels, rather than 60, and to center it in a new position. The movie itself is several frames, rather than just one, so that the three color swipes can animate from left to right without any extra Lingo.

→ **See** "Using Quad," Chapter 18

PROCESSING AND DISPLAYING INFORMATION

An often overlooked feature of Director is the power of the *getNetText* series of commands. With them, you can get any Web page from the Internet and process its raw HTML. You can also get a plain text file in the same way.

Because the Internet is full of information, there are plenty of uses for this. For instance, you can read in stock price information and display it in a ticker-like interface. You can even process the text of an HTML page to remove tags and find the information you want.

A good example of information retrieval is a Shockwave movie that reads reports from the National Weather Service, which provides simple conditions and forecasts on its Web site at `http://iwin.nws.noaa.gov`. Checking out the site further, you can see that the forecasts are broken up by state. So Colorado's forecast is at `http://iwin.nws.noaa.gov/iwin/co/` `state.html`, and California's forecast is at `http://iwin.nws.noaa.gov/iwin/ca/state.html`. The "co" and "ca" refer to the two-letter abbreviations for the states. Figure 31.6 shows a page with the forecast.

Figure 31.6
The browser window shows a forecast from the National Weather Service.

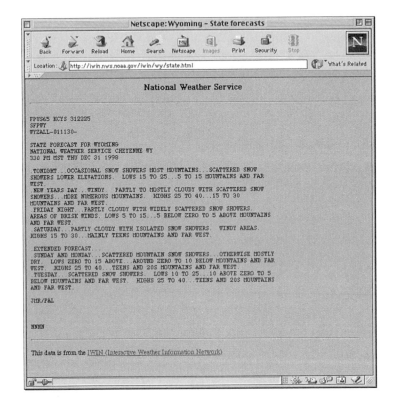

Figure 31.7 shows a small applet that presents weather forecasts in a "stock ticker" format. The buttons enable the users to specify which forecast the applet should retrieve.

Figure 31.7
This applet retrieves the text of a weather forecast and presents it like a stock ticker.

The following is the behavior for the buttons in Figure 31.7. Each button has two states, the down state representing that the button has been pressed, and an up state. The down state stays down until another button is pressed. So a set of buttons such as these act like radio buttons.

```
property pStateCode, pUpMember, pDownMember, pNetID

on getPropertyDescriptionList me
  list = [:]
  addProp list, #pStateCode, [#comment: "State Code", #format: #string, ¬
#default: "XX"]
  return list
end

on beginSprite me
  pUpMember = sprite(me.spriteNum).member
  pDownMember = member(pUpMember.number + 1)
  gNetID = 0
end

on mouseDown me
  sendAllSprites(#reset)
  sprite(me.spriteNum).member = pDownMember
  pNetID = getNetText¬
    ("http://iwin.nws.noaa.gov/iwin/"&pStateCode&"/state.html")
  sendSprite(sprite 12, #newData, "Loading a new forecast...")
end

on exitFrame me
  if pNetID > 0 then
    if netDone(pNetID) then
      text = netTextResult(pNetID)
      text = processReport(text)
      pNetID = 0
      sendSprite(sprite 12, #newData, text)
    end if
  end if
end

on reset me
  sprite(me.spriteNum).member = pUpMember
  pNetID = 0
end
```

PART
VIII

CH
31

This button behavior also starts a network operation with *getNetText* when the button is pressed. It checks every frame to see whether the information has been received. When that document has been received, the button behavior passes it along to the behavior attached to sprite 12, which is the stock ticker. The button behavior also gives that sprite a message immediately after the network operation begins.

There are many ways to make a stock ticker. You can make the sprite itself move from right to left, or you can simply replace the characters in the text member every frame. Because these weather reports are very long, it is probably best to replace the text every frame, giving the text member just enough characters to make it across the screen.

```
property pText, pChar, pSpaces

on beginSprite me
  pSpaces = ""
  repeat with i = 1 to 70
    put SPACE after pSpaces
  end repeat

  pText = pSpaces&"Click on a state button below to select a forecast."
  pChar = 1
end

on newData me, text
  pText = pSpaces&text
  pChar = 1
end

on exitFrame me
  text = pText.char[pChar..pChar+70]
  sprite(me.spriteNum).member.text = text
  pChar = pChar + 1
  if pChar > pText.length then pChar = 1
end
```

This stock ticker behavior pads every piece of text it gets with 70 spaces. This forces the text to start off blank, and then the first character moves in from the right. It basically displays a different sub-string each frame. So when the behavior starts, it displays characters 1 to 70, and then 2 to 71, and then 3 to 73, and so on.

When this behavior starts, it places some default text in the ticker. It also starts the ticker over again when the text runs out. You could handle this differently, by having it start with a forecast of a default state, or none at all. You could also have it return to the default message to select a state when it is done.

Notice that the ticker calls a movie handler named "on processReport" to change the HTML text it receives before passing it along to the stock ticker. This handler is needed because the text at that Web location is certain to have some HTML tags and also some Return characters in it. To display it properly in the ticker, the tags and Returns should be removed. They are actually replaced with spaces to prevent pieces of information from appearing next to each other.

```
on processReport text
  text = removeTags(text)
  text = removeReturns(text)
  return text
end

on removeTags text
  inTag = FALSE
  newText = ""
  repeat with i = 1 to text.length
    if text.char[i] = "<" then
      inTag = TRUE
      put " " after newText
```

```
        else if text.char[i] = ">" then
          inTag = FALSE
        else if inTag = FALSE then
          put text.char[i] after newText
        end if
    end repeat
    return newText
  end

  on removeReturns text
    repeat while TRUE
      c = offset(RETURN, text)
      if c < 1 then exit repeat
      put " " into text.char[c]
    end repeat
    return text
  end
```

The actual function of the "on processReport" handlers depends on the content of the HTML page you are trying to read. Another page might present information in a table, and you might want to write a complex handler to extract it.

This program gives just an example of what can be done with the *getNetText* series of commands. You don't have to use a stock ticker to display information; you could just have it appear. Or, you could use graphics to show information, such as a line graph of stock prices. You could even have *getNetText* read in information from several pages and compile a report.

→ **See** "Getting Text over the Internet," Chapter 22
→ **See** "Making Shockwave Movies," Chapter 36

TROUBLESHOOTING SHOCKWAVE APPLETS

- If you are working with Director 6 and Director 6 Shockwave, *gotoNetPage* commands with a target frame specified do not work properly in Microsoft Internet Explorer. Explorer sometimes creates a new window rather than repopulating the target window or frame. This happens when *gotoNetPage* is called in a handler such as *on exitFrame*, rather than a handler such as *on mouseUp*. It is too early to tell whether this bug will persist into Shockwave 7.

- To quickly test a movie in Shockwave, choose File, Preview in Browser. This tests the movie in your machine's default browser. You still need to test it in three other browsers. These should include both Netscape and Internet Explorer on both Windows and Mac. You may also want to check it in various versions of the browsers.

- Microsoft Internet Explorer 4.0 for the Mac had many problems that prevented Shockwave movies from working correctly. Developers should plan to support only version 4.01 and above on the Mac.

DID YOU KNOW?

■ You don't necessarily need to embed a Shockwave applet inside an HTML page. You can point a browser directly to a Shockwave applet just as you can point it directly to a GIF or JPEG. The movie will fill the window, starting at the upper-left corner. It will not scale, however.

■ Although *getNetText* can be used to retrieve data from a server stored in .html or .txt format, you can also use full CGI-like pathnames to access scripts. You can use *postNetText* to access scripts that respond only to posts.

■ Use the Lingo function *netError* to determine whether something has gone wrong with a *getNetText* command, and what the problem is.

■ You can use *getNetText*, *netDone*, and *netTextResult* without a network ID stored in a variable just as the examples in this book show. In that case, the program assumes that you mean the most recent network operation. It will work fine as long as you only have one network operation going on at a time.

GAMES

In this chapter

Probably the most common use for Director is making games. Games can be used for many things. They can be used both to entertain and teach. You can even use them to demonstrate a point, or simply make information more fun.

Some games seem to be favorites among Director developers because they are fairly straightforward to make and can be used for a variety of purposes. Matching games are a good example.

Other games are more difficult to do in Director, but they are popular types of games, so Director developers have learned to make them anyway. Card games, such as blackjack, are examples of these types of games. This chapter shows you how to create various types of games.

CREATING A MATCHING GAME

The basic object of a matching game is to correctly connect pairs of items on the screen. Each item is hidden, or face down, to use a card metaphor. You turn over one item, and then try to turn over its match. If you succeed, the two items are taken off the screen. If they do not match, both items are turned back over. This type of matching game is a memory game, where you need to remember where items are located as you turn them over.

To make a game such as this, you first need a set of bitmaps to represent the items. Figure 32.1 shows a cast library with such a set. It includes 18 items. Because each is to be used in a pair of sprites, the Stage will include 36 sprites that form a six-by-six grid.

Figure 32.1
The cast window shows a cast library with 18 items to be used in a matching game.

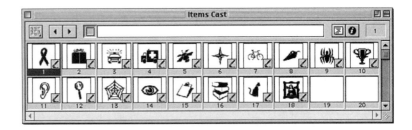

After you have the bitmaps for each item, you then need a bitmap to represent the items as they appear when they are laid face down. This should be a bitmap of the same size, but just be plain black. Name this member "Blank."

A movie script is used to control the whole game. You need two globals, one to contain a list of all the items according to the sprites in which they are placed. The other global needs to contain the sprite number of the one face-up sprite. The movie starts by randomizing the locations of the items in the sprites.

```
global gItemList, gSelected

on startMovie
  -- randomize items
```

```
  gItemList = createList()

  gSelected = 0
end
```

The items need to be placed in random sprites on the Stage, of course, or the game will be the same every time it is played. First, each item is added to the list twice, making a full set of pairs of items. Then, the list is shuffled into a new one.

```
on createList
  -- create ordered list
  templist = []
  repeat with i = 1 to 18
    add templist, i
    add templist, i
  end repeat

  -- shuffle list
  list = []
  repeat while templist.count > 0
    r = random(templist.count)
    add list, templist[r]
    deleteAt templist, r
  end repeat

  return list
end
```

All the sprites on the Stage should show the "Blank" member, so there is no need to set up the sprites in any way. The movie's Score has them as "Blank" members and they remain so until the user clicks them.

When the user clicks one of the images, the "on clickItem" handler is called. The sprite number clicked is passed into this handler. The movie has the 36 items placed in sprites 11 to 46. So, to get the location of each item in the "gItemList" global, 10 needs to be subtracted from this number, giving you a number between 1 and 36.

When an item is clicked, the "Blank" member changes to the member corresponding to the item in the list. Then the handler checks to see whether this is the first item selected. If so, it sets the "gSelected" global to the sprite number. If not, it compares the items of the last sprite clicked with the current sprite. If they match, both are removed. If not, the previous sprite is turned back to "Blank" and the current sprite is stored in the "gSelected" global.

```
-- this handler is called by the item sprites when the user clicks
-- 10 is subtracted from the sprite number because the items
-- start with sprite 11
on clickItem sNum
  -- take control of sprite and turn over, use members from "items" cast
  puppetSprite sNum, TRUE
  sprite(sNum).member = member(gItemList[sNum-10],"Items")

  if gSelected = 0 then
    -- first item turned over
    gSelected = sNum
```

```
    else if gSelected = sNum then
      -- user clicked on selected item
      -- do nothing

    else if gItemList[sNum-10] = gItemList[gSelected-10] then
      -- user clicked on matching item
      -- make both go away
      sprite(sNum).memberNum = 0
      sprite(gSelected).memberNum = 0

      -- set items in list to 0
      gItemList[sNum-10] = 0
      gItemList[gSelected-10] = 0

      -- reset selection
      gSelected = 0

      -- check for end of game
      if checkForDone() then
        go to frame "done"
      end if

    else
      -- user clicked on wrong item
      -- turn last item back over
      sprite(gSelected).member = member("Blank")

      -- item clicked in now one selected
      gSelected = sNum
    end if
end
```

The "on clickItem" handler also calls the "on checkForDone" handler if a match is found. This handler looks at the member numbers of all the sprites where items should be. If all have been set to 0, then it knows that the game is over. In that case, the movie jumps to another frame.

```
on checkForDone
  repeat with i in gItemList
    -- found an item still there
    if gItemList <> 0 then return FALSE
  end repeat

  -- all were 0, so game is over
  return TRUE
end
```

Figure 32.2 shows this game in action. Often, an image is placed behind the game, so that it is revealed as the users eliminate items. Because the item sprites start at 11, plenty of sprites in which to place this image are under the items.

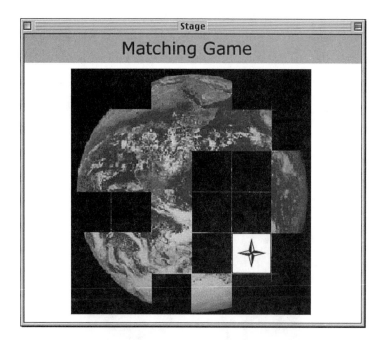

Figure 32.2
The matching game in progress. As the user finds pairs, a picture is revealed.

CREATING A SLIDING PUZZLE GAME

Another game that reveals an image as it is played is a sliding puzzle game. This is also played with squares on the screen. This time, all the items are shown, but they are all out of order. In addition, one piece is missing. The user can move any adjacent piece into the open spot. The user manipulates pieces in this way to try to put the image in order. Figure 32.3 shows this type of puzzle.

This puzzle was created with 15 different cast members, one for each piece. Because they will be randomized on the screen, the members need to know where they really belong. In order for them to know, each member needs a name that is also the correct horizontal and vertical positions of the pieces in the puzzle. Look at Figure 32.4 to see an example.

Like the matching game, this game consists mainly of a movie script. It needs to keep track of only one piece of information: the location of the blank spot in the puzzle. It stores this as two numbers, representing the horizontal and vertical location of the spot. The movie starts by setting this spot to position 1, 1. It also uses the *puppetSprite* command to give Lingo control of the sprites with the pieces. This enables the movie script, as opposed to individual behaviors, to control the sprites.

```
global gOpenSpotX, gOpenSpotY

on startMovie
  gOpenSpotX = 1
  gOpenSpotY = 1
  repeat with i = 11 to 25
    puppetSprite i, TRUE
```

```
      end repeat
      scramble
   end
```

Figure 32.3
A partially-solved sliding puzzle with 15 pieces.

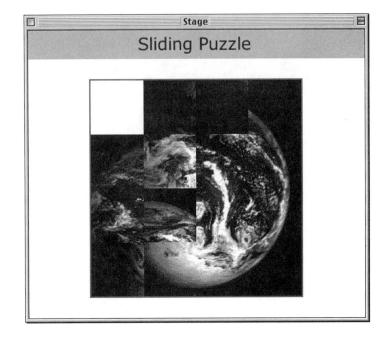

Figure 32.4
A cast library with 16 puzzle pieces. Each is named according to its real position in the solved puzzle.

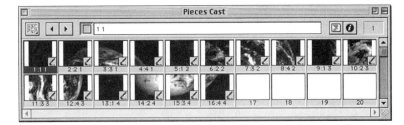

The scramble can be done in a way similar to how the shuffle in the matching game was accomplished. The "on scramble" handler takes a more visual approach, however. It selects two sprites at random, and then switches them. It uses the *updateStage* command to make this switch visible to the users because it is an interesting effect.

```
on scramble
  repeat with i = 1 to 100
    -- pick two sprites at random and switch them
    s1 = random(15)+10 -- sprites between 11 and 25
    s2 = random(15)+10
    loc = sprite(s1).loc
    sprite(s1).loc = sprite(s2).loc
    sprite(s2).loc = loc
    updateStage
  end repeat
end
```

When a sprite with a piece is clicked, the "on clickOnPiece" handler is called. The sprite number is passed into it. The location of that piece in the puzzle is calculated by dividing the location of the sprite by 75. This is the number of pixels separating each piece from its neighbors. A 90 and 70 are subtracted horizontally and vertically because the puzzle's upper-left piece is located at 90, 70.

After the piece's position is established, all four sides are checked to see whether any contains the empty spot. If the empty spot is found, the "on slide" handler is called.

```
on clickOnPiece sNum
  h = sprite(sNum).locH
  v = sprite(sNum).locV
  x =  (h-90)/75+1
  y = (v-70)/75+1

  -- check all surrounding spots
  if (gOpenSpotX = x-1) and (gOpenSpotY = y) then
    slide(sNum,-1,0)
  else if (gOpenSpotX = x+1) and (gOpenSpotY = y) then
    slide(sNum,1,0)
  else if (gOpenSpotX = x) and (gOpenSpotY = y-1) then
    slide(sNum,0,-1)
  else if (gOpenSpotX = x) and (gOpenSpotY = y+1) then
    slide(sNum,0,1)
  end if
end
```

The "on slide" handler moves the current piece up, down, left, or right, 75 pixels in 20 steps. You can add more steps to slow down the animation or fewer, to speed it up.

```
on slide sNum, dx, dy
  step = 20
  x1 = sprite(sNum).locH
  y1 = sprite(sNum).locV
  x2 = x1+(dx*75)
  y2 = y1+(dy*75)
  repeat with i = 0 to step
    p = float(i)/step
    sprite(sNum).locH = (p*x2)+((1.0-p)*x1)
    sprite(sNum).locV = (p*y2)+((1.0-p)*y1)
    updateStage
  end repeat
  gOpenSpotX = gOpenSpotX-dx
  gOpenSpotY = gOpenSpotY-dy
  if checkDone() then alert "You got it!"
end
```

At the end of each slide, the "on checkDone" handler compares all the sprite's positions with the location specified by the name of the member. If one does not match, it means that the puzzle is not complete. If they all match, then the user has solved the puzzle.

```
on checkDone
  repeat with i = 11 to 25
    x = sprite(i).locH
    y = sprite(i).locV
    x = (x-90)/75+1
```

```
    y = (y-70)/75+1
    name = sprite(i).member.name
    if (value(name.word[1]) <> x) or (value(name.word[2]) <> y) then
      return FALSE
    end if
  end repeat
  return TRUE
end
```

The sliding puzzle game can be done with more or fewer pieces. You can also change the size of the pieces and their spacing. Just make sure that you adjust the numbers in the script accordingly. Another task might be to standardize all the handlers so that they do not rely on hard-coded numbers such as 75, 90, and 70. Instead, they can use the member's width and the smallest horizontal and vertical positions in the puzzle.

CREATING A FALLING OBJECTS GAME

Another type of game that seems to be popular with Director developers is one that involves falling objects. The user controls something at the bottom of the Stage, such as a baseball glove or a cartoon character. Objects then fall from the top of the screen. Users must "catch" some of these objects and avoid others. Figure 32.5 shows a game such as this.

Figure 32.5
A falling objects game with baseball objects. The user moves the glove left and right and must catch balls while avoiding other objects.

The game is made up of several behaviors and a short movie script. The behavior that controls the glove movement is simple. It sets the horizontal location of the sprite to match the mouse.

```
on exitFrame me
  -- move glove with mouse
  sprite(me.spriteNum).locH = the mouseH
end
```

The falling object behavior is a little more complex. It uses a "pMode" property to determine whether the sprite is currently falling or awaiting instructions. It also enables itself to fall at different speeds, specified by the "pSpeed" property.

```
property pMode, pSpeed

on beginSprite me
  pMode = #none
  pSpeed = 10
end
```

In the *on exitFrame* handler, the "pMode" is checked. If it is set to #fall, the object's vertical position is changed. It then checks to see whether the sprite intersects the glove, which is in sprite 5.

PART

VIII

CH

32

Tip

> The *intersects* keyword in Lingo is an unusual one. It is not exactly a function, but it does compare two objects. The syntax looks like this: `if sprite a intersects b then`.... The word *sprite* appears before the first sprite number, but not the second. The whole structure returns TRUE if the sprite rectangles intersect, and FALSE otherwise.

If the two sprites intersect, another test is performed. This makes sure that the center of the object is close to the center of the glove. Registration points are used to determine the center, so the registration point of the glove is set a little farther down than center, so it represents the "pocket" of the glove.

If this test proves true, the object is considered to be "caught." If it is the baseball, a point is added. If not, a point is subtracted. Either way, the sprite is reset.

```
on exitFrame me
  if pMode = #fall then
    -- move object down
    sprite(me.spriteNum).locV = sprite(me.spriteNum).locV + pSpeed

    -- see if it intersects the glove
    if sprite me.SpriteNum intersects 5 then

      -- see if it is close to the center of the glove
      if distance(me,sprite(me.spriteNum).loc,sprite(5).loc) < 20 then

        -- add points
        if sprite(me.spriteNum).member.name = "Baseball" then
          addPoint
```

```
        else
          subtractPoint
        end if

        -- reset object sprite
        pMode = #none
        sprite(me.spriteNum).locV = -100
      end if

    else if sprite(me.spriteNum).locV > 400 then
      -- went past bottom, reset
      pMode = #none
      sprite(me.spriteNum).locV = -100
    end if
  end if
end


-- utility handler
on distance me, p1, p2
  return sqrt(power(p1.locH-p2.locH,2)+power(p1.locV-p2.locV,2))
end
```

Because all the sprites start with the "pMode" of #none, something is needed to set it to #fall. The "on startFall" handler performs this task. It is called by the frame script. It specifies a speed and a member. If the sprite is already falling, the message is passed on to the next sprite.

```
on startFall me, speed, type
  if pMode <> #none then
    -- this sprite being used, go to next
    sendSprite(sprite(me.spriteNum+1), #startFall, speed, type)

  else
    -- set member, location, speed and mode
    sprite(me.spriteNum).member = member(type)
    sprite(me.spriteNum).loc = point(40+random(400),-20)
    pSpeed = speed
    pMode = #fall
  end if
end
```

In the "on startFall" handler, the horizontal location of the sprite is set randomly. Because the Stage in this example is 480 pixels across, a random number between 1 and 400 is chosen, and 40 is added. This gives a random number between 41 and 440, which keeps the object away from the edges.

The frame script is responsible for randomly telling sprites to drop. On a 1-in-10 chance, the script tells the first object sprite to drop. If that sprite is busy, it tells the next to drop, and so on.

The frame script also picks a random object, either a "baseball" member or one of three "object" members. It chooses a speed between 6 and 15, as follows:

```
on exitFrame

  -- drop object on 10% chance
  if random(10) = 1 then

    -- decide what type of object
    r = random(4)
    if r = 4 then type = "Baseball"
    else type = "Object"&&r

    -- send message to sprite(s)
    sendSprite(sprite 8, #startFall, 5+random(10), type)
  end if

  go to the frame
end
```

The movie script is present only to keep track of the score. It resets the score to 0 at the start of the movie, and then handles increasing or decreasing the score. It makes sure that the score does not go below 0, because a point is subtracted each time the user catches something that is not a baseball, but is one of the three other "object" types.

```
global gScore

on startMovie
  gScore = 0
  showScore
end

on addPoint
  gScore = gScore + 1
  showScore
end

on subtractPoint
  gScore = gScore - 1
  if gScore < 0 then gScore = 0
  showScore
end

on showScore
  member("Score").text = "Score:"&&gScore
end
```

The only thing that this example game does not have is an ending. There are a lot of possibilities. You could have the game end when the user's score reaches a certain value. Or, you could count each object as it falls, and have the game end after a certain number of objects. You could also keep track of correct catches and incorrect catches, and stop the game after a certain number of incorrect catches. Another possibility is to set a timer and give the user a certain amount of time to collect as many points as possible.

EMULATING A SHOOTING GALLERY

Yet another common game that is easily done in Director is a shooting gallery. This is meant to emulate the shooting games at carnivals. Objects appear and move on the Stage, and the user tries to "shoot" them.

Figure 32.6 shows a typical setup. Some rectangles represent boxes or some other barrier. Ducks rise from them, and then descend back behind them. The cursor is changed to a cross-hairs and the user clicks to shoot. If the user clicks on a duck, the shot is recorded.

Figure 32.6
A shooting gallery game that challenges the user to shoot wooden ducks.

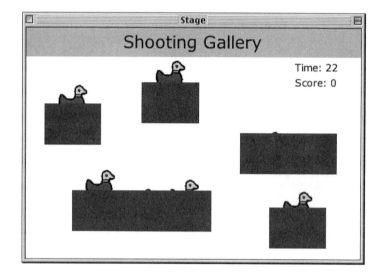

The movie consists mostly of a single behavior. This behavior controls the ducks. These ducks exist as sprites on the Stage, hidden behind rectangle sprites.

The behavior uses "pMode" to determine whether the duck is rising, falling, or not moving. If the duck is not moving, "pMode" is set to #down. Then, on a 1-in-30 chance, the duck begins to rise. A speed of 1 to 3 is chosen for this movement.

If the "pMode" is #rise, the duck moves up. If the pMode is #fall, the duck moves down. When the duck is rising, the behavior checks to see whether it has risen 30 pixels. If so, it changes the "pMode" to #fall.

A fourth mode is #hit, which means that the user has recently hit the duck. In that case, it resets to its original position and stops moving.

```
property pMode, pOrigLocV, pSpeed

on beginSprite me
  pMode = #down
  pOrigLocV = sprite(me.spriteNum).locV
end
```

```
on exitFrame me
  if pMode = #down then
    -- see if it is time to pop up
    if random(30) = 1 then
      pMode = #rise
      pSpeed = random(3) -- random speed
    end if

  else if pMode = #rise then
    -- move duck up
    sprite(me.spriteNum).locV = sprite(me.spriteNum).locV - pSpeed

    -- see if at highest point
    if sprite(me.spriteNum).locV < pOrigLocV-30 then
      pMode = #drop
    end if

  else if pMode = #drop then
    -- move duck down
    sprite(me.spriteNum).locV = sprite(me.spriteNum).locV + pSpeed

    -- see if at the lowest point
    if sprite(me.spriteNum).locV >= pOrigLocV then
      pMode = #down
    end if

  else if pMode = #hit then
    -- if recently hit, reset locV and member
    sprite(me.spriteNum).locV = pOrigLocV
    sprite(me.spriteNum).member = member("Duck")
    pMode = #down
  end if
end
```

The duck behavior also has a *on mouseDown* behavior. When the user clicks a duck, the duck is considered to be "hit." The following handler changes the member of the sprite to one that shows a duck being hit. In the example, the duck turns red. The movie handler "addScore" is called, and the "pMode" is changed to #hit so that the *on exitFrame* handler can know that the duck has been hit.

```
on mouseDown me
  -- if already hit, then ignore
  if pMode = #hit then exit

  -- use other member
  sprite(me.spriteNum).member = member("Duck Hit")
  updateStage

  -- add point
  addScore
  pMode = #hit
end
```

This duck behavior comprises most of the game. All that is left is to position the duck sprites behind the rectangles on the Stage. These rectangles block mouse clicks, so that the user cannot shoot "through" them. A simple behavior "eats" these mouse clicks.

```
-- block mouseDowns with boxes
on mouseDown
  nothing
end
```

The "on addScore" handler called by the duck behavior is in a movie script. In addition, some handlers are needed to take care of the game timer. This timer ticks down from 30 seconds. It actually works by noting the time, in ticks, when the movie starts. It adds 30 seconds to that time to determine the time when the game should end. It then subtracts the current time from that time to get the time remaining in the game.

The time remaining is displayed every frame, if needed. The handler also checks to see whether the game is over and then goes to another frame.

```
global gScore, gEndTime

on startMovie
  -- use sight cursor
  cursor([member "Sight",member "Sight"])

  -- reset score
  gScore = 0

  -- game ends 30 seconds from now
  gEndTime = the ticks + 30*60

  showScore
  showTime
end

on showScore
  member("Score").text = "Score:"&&gScore
end

on showTime
  -- convert ticks to seconds remaining
  timeLeft = (gEndTime - the ticks + 30)/60

  -- use this text
  text = "Time:"&&timeLeft

  -- if text is different than text displayed
  if member("Time").text <> text then
    member("Time").text = text
  end if

  -- time up?
  if timeLeft <= 0 then
    cursor(0)
    go to frame "Done"
  end if
end
```

```
on addScore
  gScore = gScore + 1
  showScore
end

on stopMovie
  cursor(0)
end
```

Another function that the movie handlers perform is the use of the *cursor* command to change the cursor to a cross-hair. This cursor is stored as member "Sight". The program turns this cursor on during *on startMovie*, and turns it off when the game ends, or alternatively, when the game is interrupted through the *on stopMovie* handler.

The frame script completes the game. It just needs to call "on showTime" every frame to check the current time, display it if necessary, and end the game when the time comes.

```
on exitFrame
  showTime
  go to the frame
end
```

The game play is determined by the duck behavior. For instance, if you want to make a game where the ducks travel from side to side, you alter that behavior to make the ducks move that way, rather than rise and fall. You can even create several different behaviors that make targets move in different ways. You could combine these behaviors into one movie that has many different types of targets.

Another improvement would be to increase the speed of the sprites according to the time, or to the user's score. This makes the game more challenging for experienced players.

PART

VIII

CH

32

CREATING SPRITE INVADERS

The most classic of all games, Space Invaders, has given rise to hundreds, maybe thousands, of imitators. Some of these were done with Director. The following example is a very simple version of a game of this genre. Figure 32.7 shows the game during play.

Making an invaders game is more involved than making any of the previous games in this section. It boils down to four behaviors: one for the invading sprites, one for the ship, one for bullets fired from the invaders, and one for bullets fired from the ship.

Figure 32.7
An "invaders" game
that uses very silly
bitmaps as invaders.

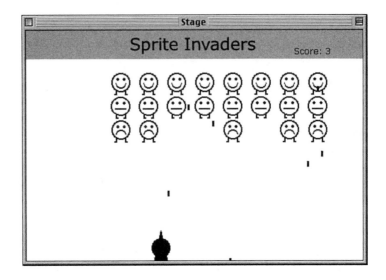

CREATING THE INVADING SPRITES

The game play is mostly dominated by the movement of the invaders. They move from side to side, all together. When they hit one side of the screen, they drop down, closer to the bottom.

A behavior for this kind of movement needs to worry about only one invader. The same behavior can be attached to all the invader sprites on the screen. However, two globals, "gHitWall" and "gHitBottom," are used so that when at least one sprite reaches a side of the screen or the bottom, the globals are set to TRUE and the frame script handles the situation.

The behavior begins by the direction and speed being set to 2, which means that the invader moves two pixels to the right every frame. It also records the member number of the sprite. The Cast is set up so that each invader has two members. They are essentially the same, but the feet reverse to give a "marching" feel. The invader behavior switches between these two members every frame.

```
global gHitWall, gHitBottom
property pDirection, pMemNum

on beginSprite me
  -- start moving 2 pixels to right
  pDirection = 2
  pMemNum = sprite(me.spriteNum).memberNum
end

on exitFrame me
  -- freeze if not on play frame
  if the frameLabel <> "Play" then exit
```

```
  if pDirection = 0 then
    -- no direction, must have been hit
    sprite(me.spriteNum).memberNum = 0 -- remove sprite

else
    -- move
    sprite(me.spriteNum).locH = sprite(me.spriteNum).locH + pDirection

    -- hit a wall?
    if pDirection > 0 and sprite(me.spriteNum).locH > 460 then
      gHitWall = TRUE
    else if pDirection < 0 and sprite(me.spriteNum).locH < 20 then
      gHitWall = TRUE
    end if

    -- toggle to other member to create animation
    if sprite(me.spriteNum).memberNum = pMemNum then
      sprite(me.spriteNum).memberNum = pMemNum + 1
    else
      sprite(me.spriteNum).memberNum = pMemNum
    end if

    -- fire 1 out of 200 times
    if random(200) = 1 then
      sendSprite(sprite 55, #fire, sprite(me.spriteNum).loc)
    end if
  end if
end
```

The *on exitFrame* handler also triggers an invader bullet to fire on a 1-in-200 chance. It sends a #fire message to sprite 55, which is where the invader bullets are located.

The *on exitFrame* handler sets the "gHitWall" global to TRUE if that sprite is too close to a side. The example shown in Figure 32.7 uses 24 invaders. It takes only one of the invaders being close to the wall to set this global. If it does become TRUE, the frame script handles it by sending a #changeDirection message to all sprites. Only the invader sprites use this message. The following handler is what is called. It moves the invaders down, and also reverses the direction of movement. It also checks to see whether any sprite has gone down too far.

```
on changeDirection me
  -- got change direction message

  -- move down
  sprite(me.spriteNum).locV = sprite(me.spriteNum).locV + abs(pDirection)

  -- hit bottom?
  if sprite(me.spriteNum).locV > sprite(5).rect.top then gHitBottom = TRUE

  -- reverse direction
  pDirection = -pDirection
end
```

Another message that can be sent to the invader is #hit. In this case, the member is changed to a bitmap that shows an explosion. The Stage is updated, so the explosion is shown right away. Then, the "pDirection" property is set to 0. This is used to let the *on exitFrame* handler know that the invader is dead, and it removes the sprite altogether in the next frame by setting its member number to 0.

```
on hit me
  -- got the message I was hit

  -- change to hit graphic
  sprite(me.spriteNum).member = member("Invader Hit")

  -- show me, since I will disappear next frame
  updateStage

  -- dead, so no direction
  pDirection = 0
end
```

Along with the invader behavior is the behavior for the invader bullets. These are assigned to a block of sprites from 55 to 75. You can assign more sprites if you want to enable the invaders to fire more at once, or fewer if you want the invaders to be able to fire less.

The invader bullet behavior has a "pMode" property that tells it whether it is currently firing. The "on fire" handler causes the bullet to fire, or passes along the message to the next sprite if the bullet is already firing. The *on exitFrame* handler moves a firing bullet and also checks to see whether it hit anything or fell past the bottom.

```
property pMode

on beginSprite me
  pMode = #none
end

on fire me, loc
  if pMode = #fire then
    -- busy, send to next sprite
    sendSprite(sprite(me.spriteNum+1),#fire,loc)
  else
    -- set loc, mode
    sprite(me.spriteNum).loc = loc
    pMode = #fire
  end if
end

on exitFrame me
  -- freeze unless on play frame
  if the frameLabel <> "Play" then exit

  if pMode = #fire then
    -- move down
    sprite(me.spriteNum).locV = sprite(me.spriteNum).locV + 8
    if sprite(me.spriteNum).locV > 320 then
      -- hit bottom
      pMode = #none
```

```
      else
        -- hit gun?
        didIHit(me)
      end if
    end if
  end
```

The *on exitFrame* handler calls "on didIHit" to determine whether the bullet ran into the ship. The ship, or gun, is in sprite 5.

```
on didIHit me
  -- hit gun?
  if sprite 5 intersects me.spriteNum then
    -- gun explodes
    sprite(5).member = member("Invader Hit")
    updateStage

    -- game over
    go to frame "Done"
  end if
end
```

CREATING THE SHIP

Now that the invaders and the invader bullets are working, the next task is to get the ship to work. This is a fairly simple behavior that makes the ship move left and right with the left and right arrow keys. If the spacebar is pressed, a #fire message is sent to the block of sprites with the ship bullets.

```
property pFiredLastFrame

on exitFrame me
  if the frameLabel <> "Play" then exit

  if keyPressed(123) then
    -- left arrow
    sprite(me.spriteNum).locH = sprite(me.spriteNum).locH - 5
  end if

  if keyPressed(124) then
    -- right arrow
    sprite(me.spriteNum).locH = sprite(me.spriteNum).locH + 5
  end if

  -- check spacebar, plus check to make sure did not fire last frame
  if keyPressed(SPACE) and not pFiredLastFrame then
    -- space, fire
    sendSprite(sprite 6, #fire, sprite(me.spriteNum).loc)
    pFiredLastFrame = TRUE
  else
    pFiredLastFrame = FALSE
  end if
end
```

The ship behavior uses a property called "pFiredLastFrame", which prevents the user from holding down the spacebar and creating a stream of bullets that would spell certain death for the invaders. Instead, bullets can be fired only every other frame. To space bullets even farther apart, you can use this property to count how many frames since the last bullet was fired, and only allow a new bullet every 3, 4, or more frames.

The ship's bullets have a behavior very similar to the invader bullets. The differences are that the bullet moves up, and it checks to see whether it hit any invader sprites.

Because a hit is scored every time a bullet hits an invader, the "gScore" global is referenced. The user's score is increased when a hit is determined.

```
global gScore
property pMode

on beginSprite me
  pMode = #none
end

on fire me, loc
  -- got signaled to fire
  if pMode = #fire then
    -- busy, send to next sprite
    sendSprite(sprite(me.spriteNum+1),#fire,loc)
  else
    -- fire
    sprite(me.spriteNum).loc = loc
    pMode = #fire
  end if
end

on exitFrame me
  -- freeze if not on play frame
  if the frameLabel <> "Play" then exit

  if pMode = #fire then
    -- move bullet up
    sprite(me.spriteNum).locV = sprite(me.spriteNum).locV - 16

    if sprite(me.spriteNum).locV < 0 then
      -- reached top of screen
      pMode = #none
    else
      -- check for hit
      didIHit(me)
    end if
  end if
end

on didIHit me
  -- loop through invader sprites
  repeat with i = 30 to 53
    -- see if it hit
    if sprite i intersects me.spriteNum then
```

```
      -- send hit message
      sendSprite(sprite i, #hit)

      -- get rid of bullet
      sprite(me.spriteNum).locV = -100
      pMode = #none

      -- add to score
      gScore = gScore + 1
      showScore
    end if
  end repeat
end
```

The movie script takes care of a few things, such as resetting the user's score and displaying a new score when needed:

```
global gScore

on startMovie
  gScore = 0
  showScore
  go to frame "Play"
end

on showScore
  member("Score").text = "Score:"&&gScore
end
```

CREATING THE FRAME SCRIPT

Finally, the game needs a frame script. This script does more than your typical frame script. For one, it sends a #changeDirection to all sprites when a "gHitWall" flag is found. It also ends the game when a "gHitBottom" is found. These tasks are taken care of in the *on enterFrame* handler, which ensures that the tasks will execute before the *on exitFrame* handlers of all the behaviors attached to sprites.

```
global gHitWall, gHitBottom

on enterFrame me
  if gHitWall then
    -- an invader hit the wall
    sendAllSprites(#changeDirection)

  else if gHitBottom then
    -- an invader hit the bottom
    go to frame "Done"

  end if

  -- reset wall hit flag for this frame
  gHitWall = FALSE
end

on exitFrame
  go to the frame
end
```

This completes the scripts needed for the game. Many numbers, such as the speed of the ship, bullets, and invaders, can be changed. You can place as many or as few invaders as you want on the screen. You can also make them any bitmap image you want, but remember that every invader consists of two members which constantly switch to create animation.

Take this example movie on the CD-ROM and try altering it. You can place the invaders in any formation you want. You can create a "shield" by adding some more sprites and writing a "shield" behavior script. You can go a lot of ways with this game to improve it.

CREATING TRIVIA GAMES

Trivia games can be found everywhere. They include popular board games, arcade machines, and even games you can play in bars. The hardest part of making a trivia game is coming up with the questions. The Director movie that asks the questions and keeps track of the score is fairly straightforward.

This example uses a movie script to do most of the work. The result is a game that looks like Figure 32.8. One question is asked at a time, and the user has to click one of four buttons to answer. A timer ticks down, so the longer the user takes to answer, the fewer points are rewarded. If the answer is incorrect, a full 100 points are removed from the timer.

Figure 32.8
A simple trivia game that asks one question at a time and provides four possible answers.

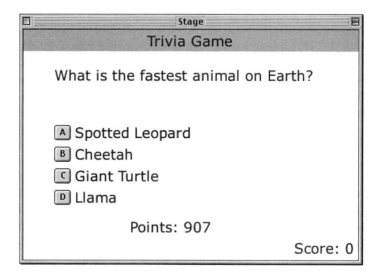

The movie script is needed to keep track of a few things in globals. It needs to know the question number that the user is on, the number of points possible if the answer is correct, the current score, and which answer is the correct one for the current question. The game starts by resetting these globals.

```
global gQuestionNum, gPossiblePoints, gScore, gCorrectAnswer

on startGame
  gQuestionNum = 1
  gScore = 0
  showScore
  askQuestion
  go to frame "Play"
end
```

The questions are stored in a field named "Data." This field holds one question per line. Each line contains three items, separated by a semicolon. The first item is the question; the second is the four possible answers, separated by commas; and the third is the number of the correct answer.

The "on askQuestion" handler takes care of retrieving all this information from the field and setting up the text on the screen.

```
on askQuestion
  text = member("Data").text.line[gQuestionNum]

  the itemDelimiter = ";"
  question = text.item[1]
  answers = text.item[2]
  gCorrectAnswer = value(text.item[3])

  member("Question").text = question
  the itemDelimiter = ","
  repeat with i = 1 to 4
    member("Answer"&&i).text = answers.item[i]
  end repeat

  gPossiblePoints = 1000
  showPossiblePoints
end
```

The "on gameTimer" handler is called every frame loop by the frame script. It subtracts one point from the number of points that the user can earn by answering the question correctly. The speed at which it does this depends on the frame rate. It calls "on showPossiblePoints" to change the text member on the Stage.

```
on gameTimer
  gPossiblePoints = gPossiblePoints - 1
  showPossiblePoints
end

on showPossiblePoints
  member("Possible Points").text = "Points:"&&gPossiblePoints
end
```

The "on showScore" handler changes the score text member on the Stage after the user answers a question.

```
on showScore
  member("Score").text = "Score:"&&gScore
end
```

To answer a question, the user must click one of four buttons on the Stage. They are all wired up with the complex button behavior discussed in Chapter 14, "Creating Behaviors." Each one is set to execute the Lingo handler "on clickAnswer" with the number 1, 2, 3, or 4 as the parameters, depending on the button.

This handler adds the potential points to the score if the user gets the question right, and then asks the next question. However, if the user answers wrong, it just subtracts 100 points from the potential points and does nothing. The user must try again.

```
on clickAnswer n
  if n = gCorrectAnswer then
    gScore = gScore + gPossiblePoints
    showScore
    nextQuestion
  else
    gPossiblePoints = gPossiblePoints - 100
    showPossiblePoints
  end if
end
```

The "on nextQuestion" handler advances the "gQuestionNum" global by one. If all the questions in the field have been asked, it jumps the movie to another frame.

```
on nextQuestion
  gQuestionNum = gQuestionNum + 1
  if gQuestionNum > member("Data").text.line.count then
    go to frame "done"
  else
    askQuestion
  end if
end
```

This movie can definitely benefit from sound. It should make a positive sound when the user clicks the correct answer, and a negative sound when the wrong answer is clicked. Maybe there should even be a ticking sound while the movie awaits the user's answer.

You can also try to take care of a lot of unusual situations that could arise in the game. For instance, what if the user continues to click wrong answers, or lets the clock run out? Should there be negative potential points? Or, should users just be advanced to the next question automatically?

Some popular trivia games use a lot of animation between the questions. Director can certainly do this easily enough. You may want to have a long movie with animated sequences between frames that ask a single question.

CREATING A BLACKJACK GAME

Implementing a card game, such as blackjack, is a far more difficult task than the creating the games in the previous examples in the chapter. Even the following program, which does not take into account common blackjack rules such as splitting and doubling down, has a lot more Lingo code to it.

Figure 32.9 shows how this game can be very complex. Two sets of cards are shown: the dealer's, at top, and the player's immediately below. Six decks are used, and any number of cards can be in each hand—up to 11 if the player or dealer draws all 2s. Below the cards, several text fields show the player's total cash, the player's bet, the player's hand value, the dealer's hand value, and an additional message. There are also three buttons (Deal, Hit, and Stay), as well as an editable text field that enables the player to enter a bet.

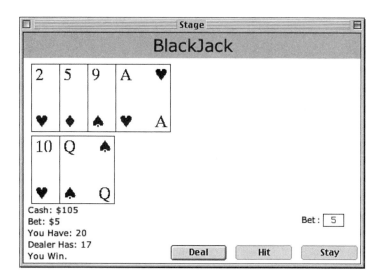

Figure 32.9
Even a simple black-jack program has many parts to it.

This example uses a movie script to control the game. The globals include a list that contains the cards in the game, a list for the dealer's cards, a list for the player's cards, the total amount of cash the player has, and the current bet.

The movie uses two frames. The first has an active Deal button, and enables the user to enter a bet. A click to the Deal button takes the user to the second screen, which has active Hit and Stay buttons.

The movie starts by shuffling the cards with the "on shuffle" handler. This handler creates an ordered list of the six decks of cards and then randomizes it. Each card is represented by a short string, such as "5c" for the five of clubs or "Qh" for the queen of hearts.

Also notice that *the floatPrecision* is set to 2, which causes all dollar amounts in the game to display in a nicer format than with four digits after the decimal point.

```
global gDeck, gNextCardSprite, gDealer, gPlayer, gCash, gBet

-- Shuffles Deck, resets cash
on startMovie
  the floatPrecision = 2
  shuffle
  gCash = 100
```

```
  member("bet field").text = "5"
  clearScreen
  go to frame "Bet"
end

-- Set up deck list
on shuffle
  gDeck = []
  tempList = []
  suit = ["c","s","h","d"]
  number = ["2","3","4","5","6","7","8","9","10","J","Q","K","A"]

  -- create an ordered deck
  repeat with i = 1 to 6 -- six decks of cards
    repeat with s = 1 to 4
      repeat with n = 1 to 13
        card = getAt(number,n)&getAt(suit,s)
        add tempList, card
      end repeat
    end repeat
  end repeat

-- pick cards out of tempList and place them in the deck
  repeat while tempList.count > 0
    r = random(tempList.count)
    add gDeck, getAt(tempList,r)
    deleteAt tempList,r
  end repeat
end
```

Another handler called from "on startMovie" is one that sets up all the text members on the Stage. It also clears the members from sprites 10 through 40, which can be used for playing cards later in the game.

```
on clearScreen
  -- reset all text
  member("Cash").text = "Cash: $"&gCash
  member("Bet").text = ""
  member("Player Value").text = ""
  member("Dealer Value").text = ""
  member("Message").text = ""

  -- clear out sprites 10 to 40
  repeat with i = 10 to 40
    sprite(i).memberNum = 0
  end repeat
end
```

Every time a hard is dealt, several things happen. First, the text members are reset. Then, the "gDeck" list is checked to make sure that at least half of the deck remains in the list. If less than that amount remains, another shuffle is performed to create a new six-deck stack of cards.

Then, both the dealer's and the player's hands are reset to empty lists. Two cards are dealt to each, in the order that they are usually dealt in blackjack. The "on dealCard" handler is called to take care of selecting and placing a card on the Stage and in the dealer or player list. The first card dealt is dealt face down, signified by a second parameter to the "on dealCard" handler.

After the cards are dealt, the bet is deducted from the player's cash and several text members are updated to reflect this deduction.

In blackjack, if the player draws 21 to begin with, the player wins and the hand is over. So the handler checks for this situation. An "on figureHand" handler is called to determine the value of any hand. It can return a list of either one or two values. A hand has two possible values if it contains an ace, because an ace is worth either 1 or 11.

Because it is undesirable for a hand to be worth more than 21, the program does not need to check for the case where there is more than one ace in a hand. Having both aces equal to 11 would mean a hand of at least 22, which is never desirable.

If the player initially draws blackjack, the player's score is increased by a total of 2.5 times the bet and the hand ends. The program shows the dealer's face-down card, and then returns to the "bet" screen.

```
-- Clears screen and deals initial hand
on dealHand
  clearScreen

  -- if less than half a deck left, shuffle before deal
  if gDeck.count <= 26 then
    shuffle
  end if

  -- start with sprite 10
  gNextCardSprite = 10

  gDealer = []
  gPlayer = []

  -- initial deal
  dealCard #dealer,TRUE -- deal face down
  dealcard #player
  dealcard #dealer
  dealCard #player

  -- deduct bet from cash
  gBet = value(member("bet field").text)
  gCash = gCash-gBet

  -- set screen text
  member("Cash").text = "Cash: $"&gCash
  member("Bet").text = "Bet: $"&gBet
  playerVal = figureHand(gPlayer)
  member("Player Value").text = "You Have:"&&displayVal(playerVal)
  go to frame "Play"
```

```
-- Check for inital Blackjack
if getLast(figureHand(gPlayer)) = 21 then
  member("Message").text = "BlackJack!"
  gCash = 2.5*gBet+gCash
  member("Cash").text = "Cash: $"&gCash
  sprite(10).member = member(gDealer[1])
  go to frame "bet"
end if
end
```

The "on dealCard" handler takes the first card in the "gDeck" list and uses it. It deletes this item from "gDeck". If the "toWho" parameter is #dealer, it adds the card to the "gDealer" list and sends a message to "on drawCard" to place it at vertical position 90. For #player, it adds it to the "gPlayer" list and places it at vertical position 190.

```
-- Pick the next card off the deck
on dealCard toWho, faceDown
  c = gDeck[1]
  deleteAt gDeck, 1
  if toWho = #dealer then
    add gDealer, c
    drawCard(90,gDealer.count,c,faceDown)
  else
    add gPlayer, c
    drawCard(190,gPlayer.count,c,faceDown)
  end if
  updateStage
end
```

The "on drawCard" handler takes care of creating the sprite that shows each card. It uses *puppetSprite* to take control of a sprite specified by "gNextCardSprite." It then sets the vertical position of that sprite according to the "y" parameter, and the horizontal position according to the "n" parameter. If the "faceDown" parameter is TRUE, it shows the member "back" as opposed to the card member.

For this handler to work, it needs 53 bitmap members: one for each card, and a card "back" for the card facing down. The cards can look like those in Figure 32.9, or be of your own design.

```
-- Draw the card on the stage by assigning it to the next sprite
on drawCard y, n, card, faceDown
  -- control next sprite and set it to card location
  puppetSprite gNextCardSprite, TRUE
  sprite(gNextCardSprite).locV = y
  sprite(gNextCardSprite).locH = n*40+10

  -- Card up or down
  if not faceDown then
    sprite(gNextCardSprite).member = member(card)
  else
    sprite(gNextCardSprite).member = member("back")
  end if

  gNextCardSprite = gNextCardSprite+1
```

```
   -- Delay a bit
   startTimer
   repeat while the timer < 15
   end repeat
end
```

The "on figureHand" handler takes a list of cards and computes its numerical value. It recognizes the cards with a "10," "J," "Q," or "K" as a value of 10. It also recognizes when the hand contains at least one ace, and then computes two values for it, one with the ace worth one, and one with it worth 10. It returns the value or values in a short list.

```
-- Calculate the value of a hand and return a list
on figureHand list
   total = 0

   -- Loop through hand, and add up cards
   repeat with i = 1 to list.count
     card = list[i]
     if "1JQK" contains card.char[1]  then
       total = total + 10
     else if card.char[1]  = "A" then
       total = total + 1
       haveAce = TRUE
     else
       total = total + value(card.char[1])
     end if
   end repeat

   -- If an ace is present, then there are two values
   if haveAce then
     if total+10 > 21 then return [total]
     else return [total,total+10]
   else
     return [total]
   end if
end
```

Although the "on figureHand" handler computes the value of a hand and returns a list, you will not want to display that list to the user. Instead, it is a good idea to break the list apart and display the hand value as either a number or two numbers.

```
-- Take the returned value list and display it in English
on displayVal val
   if val.count = 1 then return string(val[1])
   else return val[1]&&"or"&&val[2]
end
```

The three buttons on the Stage use the complex button behavior described in Chapter 14. The Deal button calls "on dealHand." The Hit button, however, calls the following "on hitMe" handler, which deals a new card to the player. It checks to see whether the player busts. It also displays the new value of the hand.

```
-- Give the player another card
on hitMe
  dealCard #player
  playerVal = figureHand(gPlayer)
```

PART

VIII

CH

32

```
  if playerVal[1] > 21 then
    member("Player Value").text = "Bust."
    dealerWins
  else
    member("Player Value").text = "You Have:"&&displayVal(playerVal)
  end if
end
```

The Stay button calls the "on doDealer" handler. First, it turns over the face-down card. Then, this handler creates a loop and adds cards to the dealer's hand. It does this only as long as the dealer has a 16 or less. If the dealer has 17 or more busts, the dealer is finished. The "on decideWhoWins" handler is called for the next step.

```
-- Dealer hits until 17 or above
on doDealer
  -- Show face down card first
  sprite(10).member = member(gDealer[1])
  dealerVal = figureHand(gDealer)
  member("Dealer Value").text = "Dealer Has:"&&displayVal(dealerVal)
  updateStage

  -- Keep adding cards
  repeat while TRUE
    -- See if dealer is done
    if (dealerVal[1] > 16) or ((getLast(dealerVal) > 16) and ¬
(getLast(dealerVal) < 22)) then
      decideWhoWins
      exit repeat
    else
      dealCard #dealer

      dealerVal = figureHand(gDealer)
      member("Dealer Value").text = "Dealer Has:"&&displayVal(dealerVal)
      updateStage

      -- wait a second
      startTimer
      repeat while the timer < 60
      end repeat
    end if

  end repeat
end
```

To decide who wins, first the dealer's hand is examined to see whether it is over 21. If not, the two hand values are compared. In this program, if the player and dealer tie, the dealer wins.

```
-- Figure out who has highest valid hand
on decideWhoWins
  -- Get hand values
  dealerVal = figureHand(gDealer)
  playerVal = figureHand(gPlayer)
```

```
  -- Dealer busts
  if (dealerVal[1] > 21) then
    member("Message").text = "Dealer busts. You Win."
    playerWins

    -- Dealer and player have valid hands
  else
    -- Decide highest possible value of each hand, given aces present
    if (dealerVal[dealerVal.count] < 22) then dval = dealerVal[dealerVal.count]
    else dval = dealerVal[1]
    if (playerVal[playerVal.count] < 22) then pval = playerVal[playerVal.count]
    else pval = playerVal[1]

    -- Who wins
    if pval > dval then
      member("Message").text =  "You Win."
      playerWins
    else
      member("Message").text =  "You Lose."
      dealerWins
    end if
  end if
end
```

The "on decideWhoWins" calls two handlers to finish the hand. The first rewards the player with twice the bet, and the second returns to the bet screen.

```
-- Double money back
on playerWins
  gCash = 2*gBet+gCash
  member("Cash").text = "Cash: $"&gCash
  go to frame "bet"
end

-- No money back
on dealerWins
  go to frame "bet"
end
```

In addition to the movie script, a small script is attached to the bet amount field. It prevents users from entering a number greater than the amount of cash they have. It also prevents them from typing anything other than number keys.

```
on keyDown
  if "0123456789" contains the key then
    pass
  end if
end

on keyUp
  global gCash
  if value(field "bet field") > gCash then
    put string(gCash) into field "bet field"
  end if
end
```

Check the example movie on the CD-ROM to see how the whole thing fits together. Try adding some more features to it. You might want to add card shuffling and dealing sounds, maybe even a "cheer" when the player gets a blackjack.

A much harder task is to enable users to split. With splitting, the user plays two separate hands. You can show both hands on the screen at the same time, or you can have them play each hand one at a time. Double-down is an easier rule, in which users double their bet and get one, and only one, extra card. You can deduct the same amout as the original bet from the user's cash and then deal them one card. To complete the game, you should deal with situations in which users run out of cash.

TROUBLESHOOTING GAMES

- Many games combine behaviors and movie scripts. Remember to check to make sure that each type of script is set correctly, so that a behavior is not set to be a movie script and a movie script is not set to be a behavior.

- The new Director 7 function *keyPressed()* has many game applications because it tells you exactly what is happening on the keyboard whereas *on keyDown* sends only a single message at a given time. However, watch out for the reality that users can have more than one key pressed at a time. Make sure your games can handle it when users press *both* the left and right arrow keys.

- Don't just worry about bugs and obvious errors when it comes to games. Also think about playability and fun. Games are supposed to be enjoyable entertainment. Consider it a bug if your game is not fun.

DID YOU KNOW?

- Many games use a shuffle to randomize playing pieces or cards. Shuffling uses the *random* function to pick cards out of the first list and place them in the second. If you want to keep the shuffle the same every time you play, which is good for testing, try setting *the randomSeed* property to a specific number, such as 1, 2, 3, on so on. This ensures that the same random numbers are generated each time and makes your shuffle the same for each game.

FINISHING A PROJECT

CHAPTER **33**

DEBUGGING

In this chapter

If you create a Director movie that has more than a few lines of Lingo in it, chances are that you will have to do some debugging. This means, literally, getting rid of bugs. Bugs can be as obvious as error messages generated by a faulty Lingo line, or as vague as "something just not working right."

Note

> The reason program errors are called "bugs" is that the first bug was actually, well, a bug. An early computer produced an error when a moth flew in and short-circuited it. The name stuck.

WRITING GOOD CODE

An ounce of prevention goes a long way when programming. This means commenting your code, using descriptive handler and variable names, and dividing your code into sensible script members.

Well-written code has much less chance of containing an error. If it does contain bugs, well-commented code increases the chance that these bugs can be located and fixed.

COMMENTING YOUR CODE

Knowing when to comment in your code is the trick. You can't add code comments for every line, because it clutters up your script window and makes it even harder to read. At the same time, no commenting at all makes it very hard to debug or to alter your code in the future.

A comment is anything on a line that follows a double dash: "- -". You can place comments in lines by themselves, or follow lines of actual code with a comment.

You can add three types of comments to your code. You can write blocks of comments before a handler or a section of code, write comment lines before a line or group of lines, or write a short comment at the end of a line of code.

BLOCK COMMENTS

Writing several lines of commentary before a handler is a common technique in Lingo and other programming languages. As shown in the following commentary, you can state what the handler does, talk about what parameters it needs and what type of value it returns, and specify when and how the handler is used.

Here is an example:

```
-- This handler will add a number to the gScore global
-- and place the global in the text member. It will
-- also check to make sure that the score is not less
-- than 0, and make it 0 if it is. The number passed in
-- should be an integer.
```

```
-- INPUT: integer
-- OUTPUT: none
-- EFFECTS: gScore, member "score"

on changeScore n
  gScore = gScore + n
  if gScore < 0 then gScore = 0
  member("score").text = string(gScore)
end
```

The main advantage of the block comments is that they stay out of the way of actual code. Because Lingo code is written in English anyway, individual line comments are not always necessary.

Block comments are also good for situations where other programmers will take your code and use it in their programs. They can read the block comment rather than the code itself. In these cases, the block comments should include information about the parameters, the return value, and perhaps a list of globals, members, and sprites that are affected by the handler.

COMMENT LINES

Placing a single line of commentary before important lines is another technique commonly used. The idea is to use the comments to clarify what the following line does and why it does it.

Here is an example:

```
on changeScore n

  -- add n to the score global
  gScore = gScore + n

  -- make sure score isn't less than 0
  if gScore < 0 then gScore = 0

  -- place score in text member on Stage
  member("score").text = string(gScore)
end
```

PART

IX

CH

33

Although the preceding example used a comment line before each code line, a more typical example would use a comment line only before some of the lines. This way the code doesn't get too cluttered with comments.

Comment lines are useful to remind you of what is going on inside the handler. This helps in debugging, and in altering the handler in the future.

SHORT LINE COMMENTS

Line comments appear on the same line as the code and explain what is going on in that line. Sometimes the comment points out a specific piece of information about a variable or function in that line.

Here are some examples:

```
on changeScore n
  gScore = gScore + n -- gScore is a global
  if gScore < 0 then gScore = 0 -- make sure it is less than 0
  member("score").text = string(gScore) -- show on screen
end
```

The first line of the handler demonstrates using a short line comment to point out something specific about a part of the line. The other comments serve the same purpose as the full comment lines.

Line comments are useful when you don't feel that full explanations are needed, but would rather just use short, helpful "hints" for the person reading the code. Like comment lines, they are useful when you need to go back and alter the code later on.

The best strategy for commenting is often to combine all three types of comments. You may place a block comment at the start of a behavior, or before each handler in a movie script, and then use comment lines and line comments in tricky parts of the code.

→ **See** "Writing Lingo Code," Chapter 12, "Learning Lingo," for more information about writing code

USING DESCRIPTIVE NAMES

Chapter 12 contains some information about using descriptive handler and variable names. I cannot stress the importance of this enough. Several techniques that you can use to make your names more descriptive are described next.

USE MULTIPLE WORD NAMES

A convention among Lingo coders has been to use multiple words, all run together, as handler names. Each word, except the first, is capitalized.

Here is an example:

```
on addNumberToScore numberToAdd
  gTotalScore = gTotalScore + 1
end
```

The handler name and both variable names are descriptive little phrases all run together. You can see that this makes additional commenting almost unnecessary. It is obvious what the handler does and how it does it.

It may seem that using the long word has the disadvantage of taking up more space in your script window and taking longer to type. However, if it eliminates the need for a comment on that line or before it, if more than pays for itself in keystrokes.

USE FIRST LETTER CONVENTIONS

Throughout this book you may have noticed the letter g at the beginning of all global variables and a p in front of all property variables. This sort of convention makes it easier to remember where a variable originated and the range through which it is available.

You can use other conventions for the first letter of a variable. Sometimes the letter *l* is used in front of local variables. Most developers prefer to make local variables the only variable types without a letter prefix, however.

You might also see the letter *i* used in front of property variables in parent scripts. The *i* stands for "instance."

You can also use a single letter prefix in front of handler names. This used to be common in parent scripts, where *m* would be used to mean meaning "method," another term for a handler in a parent script. You can use *m* in front of handlers in behavior scripts as well.

If you are the only one to look at your code, or you have a small team that can agree on standards, you might want to implement your own prefixes. A *b* for behavior handlers, an *m* for movie handlers, and a *p* for parent script handlers might be a helpful combination. A custom set of prefixes such as this should be explained in your documentation somewhere, in case other programmers work on the code.

USE DESCRIPTIVE MEMBER NAMES

If you are being descriptive when it comes to variable names, you should apply the same techniques to member names. The only difference is that you can actually use separate words, not divided by spaces.

It is very tempting to not use any name for a member. After all, a member placed on the Score and referenced by its sprite number doesn't need to be referenced by name in Lingo code. However, you can still benefit from naming that member. Just try cleaning up a cast window that has dozens of unnamed members and you will learn why.

Member names should be descriptive, and should be unique. It is useless to have a bunch of text members named "text." You can mention where and how these members are used in a name. For instance, if one text member shows the score during a game and another shows it in the "game over" frame, name the first "Score Text in Game" and the other "Score Text for Game Over."

Also, it is very helpful to arrange your members in the Cast in a useful manner. You can arrange them by member type, or by how or when they are used in the Score.

→ **See** "Preferences," Chapter 9, "The Director Environment," for more information on cast window preferences

PART

IX

CH

33

USE VARIABLE CONSTANTS

Another way to make your code more usable and readable is to use variables to represent commonly used numbers and objects. For instance, if the number 2 is used several times in your code for similar reasons, you might want to set a variable to 2, and then use that variable. Look at this example:

```
on moveFromKeyPress charPressed, position
  case charPressed of
    "i": position.locV = position.locV - 2
    "m": position.locV = position.locV + 2
```

```
    "j": position.locH = position.locH - 2
    "l": position.locH = position.locH + 2
  end case
  return position
end
```

This handler is used in a program to change the position of sprite on the Stage when a key is pressed. It makes the position change by 2 in any direction. However, if you want to change this code to make the position differ by three, you need to change it in four places. Instead, the following handler enables you to make the change in only one place:

```
on moveFromKeyPress charPressed, position
  diff = 2
  case charPressed of
    "i": position.locV = position.locV - diff
    "m": position.locV = position.locV + diff
    "j": position.locH = position.locH - diff
    "l": position.locH = position.locH + diff
  end case
  return position
end
```

As another example, consider the need to refer to a sprite several times. You can place a sprite object in a variable and use that instead. For instance, you can code:

```
thisSprite = sprite(34)
```

Then, anywhere in that handler, you can refer to "thisSprite" rather than sprite(34). If you ever need to change the code to refer to sprite 33, for example, you have to change it in just one place.

You can also use this technique with globals. You can set a global to a constant number, string, or object, and then refer to that global throughout your code. If you want to change that constant later, you need to change it in only one place. The disadvantage of using this method with globals, however, is that you must declare the global variable with the *global* command in every script where it is used.

→ **See** "Writing Lingo Code," Chapter 12, for more information on writing code

WRITING ERROR-PROOF CODE

Impossible, you say? Well, maybe. But you can get awfully close. Many Lingo handlers can be changed in such a way as to catch errors before users are affected by them.

Many times this involves writing code that recognizes that something is wrong, tells the users about it if they can do anything, and stops the code before it can do any harm.

BUG-FREE FILEIO CODE

If you want to write some code to create a file and place some text in it, all that is required is a few short commands that use the FileIO Xtra. Here is an example:

```
on writeFile name, text
  fileObj = new(Xtra "FileIO")
```

```
    fileName = displaySave(fileObj, "Save"&&name, name&".txt")
    createFile(fileObj,fileName)
    openFile(fileObj,fileName,2)
    writeString(fileObj,text)
    closeFile(fileObj)
    fileObj = 0
end
```

This code works well most of the time. But what if there is a problem? For instance, what if the user clicks the Cancel button when the save dialog box appears? In the preceding handler, the code marches directly to the *createFile* command with a bad filename. The result is that the file is never created and nothing happens. But the user does not know that.

It would be better to check to see whether the Cancel button has been pressed. If it has, the variable "filename" will contain an empty string. You can test for that, and report it to the user. You can then *exit* the handler before the other commands are used.

But what if the movie cannot create the file for some reason? Imagine that the user chooses a file that has the same name as one already present. You can check for this as well.

FileIO has two functions that enable you to test for errors. The first is the *status* function, which returns a number. If that number is 0, everything is fine; otherwise, there has been an error. You can then take the error number and feed it into the second function, the *error* function, to get a string that represents the error in plain English.

Here is the same handler as previously shown, but with comprehensive error checking. Every step of the file-creation process is checked to see whether there is a problem, and is handled accordingly.

```
on writeFile name, text
  fileObj = new(Xtra "FileIO")

  -- check to make sure object was created
  if not objectP(fileObj) then
    alert("FileIO failed to initialize")
    return FALSE
  end if

  fileName = displaySave(fileObj, "Save"&&name, name&".txt")

  -- check to see if a filename was returned
  if filename = "" then
    alert "File not created."
    return FALSE
  end if

  createFile(fileObj,fileName)

  -- check to see if file was created ok
  errorNum = status(fileObj)
  if errorNum <> 0 then
    alert "Error:"&&error(fileObj,errorNum)
    return FALSE
  end if
```

```
  openFile(fileObj,fileName,2)

  -- check to see if file was opened ok
  errorNum = status(fileObj)
  if errorNum <> 0 then
    alert "Error:"&&error(fileObj,errorNum)
    return FALSE
  end if

  writeString(fileObj,text)

  -- check to see if file was written to ok
  if errorNum <> 0 then
    alert "Error:"&&error(fileObj,errorNum)
    return FALSE
  end if

  closeFile(fileObj)

  -- check to see if file was closed ok
  if errorNum <> 0 then
    alert "Error:"&&error(fileObj,errorNum)
    return FALSE
  end if

  fileObj = 0
  return TRUE
end
```

Notice that every error found will return a FALSE from the handler. However, if the handler completes its task, it will return a TRUE. This doesn't need to be present, but it is a nice feature. Any handler that calls this "on writeFile" handler can then call it as a function and get an answer back as to whether the file was actually saved.

About 18 different error messages can be returned. Table 33.1 shows a complete list of errors that can be returned by the FileIO Xtra. If the *error* function is used, and the error number does not correspond to one of the numbers listed here, the text Unknown Error is returned.

TABLE 33.1   A LIST OF ERROR CODES USED BY THE FILEIO XTRA

Code	Message
124	File is opened write-only
-123	File is opened read-only
-122	File already exists
-121	Instance has an open file
-120	Directory not found
-65	No disk in drive
-56	No such drive

-43	File not found
-42	Too many files open
-38	File not open
-37	Bad file name
-36	I/O Error
-35	Volume not found
-34	Volume full
-33	File directory full
0	OK
1	Memory allocation failure

→ **See** "Text Files and the FileIO Xtra," Chapter 16, "Controlling Text," for more information on reading and writing files

BUG-FREE SHOCKWAVE CODE

Although FileIO has the *status* and *error* functions, other categories of Lingo commands also have error handling functions. Shockwave Lingo commands have the *netError* function. You can use this function to determine what has happened after the *netDone* function returns TRUE.

Here is an *on exitFrame* script that replaces the one from the section "Getting Text over the Internet" in Chapter 22, "Shockwave and Internet Access." It checks the *netDone*, as it did before, but then goes a step further and checks *netError*. This function returns an OK if the operation was successful. If not, it returns a number. That number corresponds to the numbers in Table 33.2.

PART

IX

CH

33

```
on exitFrame
  global gNetID
  if netDone(gNetID) then
   err = netError(gNetID)
    if err = "OK" then
      text = netTextResult(gNetID)
      put text
      go to the frame + 1
      exit
    else
      if err = 4165 then
        alert "Could not find that URL."
      else
      -- handle error somehow
      end if
    end if
  end if
  go to the frame
end
```

This example looks for error code 4165, which usually happens if a file is not found. You might want to replace the comment line with some code that handles other errors too.

TABLE 33.2 SHOCKWAVE LINGO netError CODES

Number	Definition
0	Everything is okay.
4	Bad MOA class. The required network or nonnetwork Xtras are improperly installed or not installed at all.
5	Bad MOA interface. See 4.
6	Bad URL or Bad MOA class. The required network or nonnetwork Xtras are improperly installed or not installed at all.
20	Internal error. Returned by *netError()* in the Netscape browser if the browser detected a network or internal error.
4146	Connection could not be established with the remote host.
4149	Data supplied by the server was in an unexpected format.
4150	Unexpected early closing of connection.
4154	Operation could not be completed due to timeout.
4155	Not enough memory available to complete the transaction.
4156	Protocol reply to request indicates an error in the reply.
4157	Transaction failed to be authenticated.
4159	Invalid URL.
4164	Could not create a socket.
4165	Requested object could not be found (URL may be incorrect).
4166	Generic proxy failure.
4167	Transfer was intentionally interrupted by client.
4242	Download stopped by netAbort(url).
4836	Download stopped for an unknown reason, possibly a network error, or the download was abandoned.

→ **See** "Getting Text over the Internet," Chapter 22, for more information about getting text from the Internet

SHOCKWAVE AUDIO ERROR LINGO

Error codes can also be returned by Shockwave Audio members. They return errors through use of the *getError()* function. The on parameter that it takes is the name of the SWA member.

Whereas *getError* produces a number, *getErrorString* returns a string that you can display to the users. Table 33.3 shows a list of these errors.

TABLE 33.3   SHOCKWAVE AUDIO ERROR CODES

GetError code	*getErrorString* message	Meaning
0	OK	No error
1	memory	Not enough memory available to load the sound
2	network	A network error occurred
3	playback device	Unable to play the sound
99	other	

→ **See** "Using Shockwave Audio," Chapter 17, "Controlling Sound," for more information about Shockwave audio

FLASH ERROR LINGO

You can also use *getError* with Shockwave Flash members that stream over the Internet. Rather return than a number, these return symbols. Table 33.4 shows them all.

TABLE 33.4   FLASH MEMBER ERRORS WITH getERROR

Symbol Returned	Meaning
FALSE or 0	No error
#memory	Not enough memory available to load the member
#fileNotFound	Could not locate the file
#network	A network error occurred
#fileFormat	File is not a Flash movie
#other	Some other return error occurred

→ **See** "Flash Member Properties," Chapter 20, "Controlling Vector Graphics," for more information about using Flash members

OTHER ERROR LINGO

In return addition to those functions that relate to a specific type of media or Lingo category, some functions can be used to test variables to make sure that they are a certain type. For instance, suppose you treat a number like a list. This generates an error message. However, you can check to see whether a variable is, in fact, a list, before you try to use it.

Most of these functions end with the letter *P*. This stands for "predicate." Here is a list of functions and what they test for:

■ listP()—Is the variable a list?

■ integerP()—Is the variable an integer?

- floatP()—Is the variable a floating point number?
- stringP()—Is the variable a string?
- symbolP()—Is the variable a symbol?
- objectP()—Is the variable an object, such as a member, sprite, list, or Xtra instance?

Here are some examples in the Message window:

```
x = 1
put integerP(x)
-- 1
put floatP(x)
-- 0
put listP(x)
-- 0
put stringP(x)
-- 0
put objectP(x)
-- 0
x = [1,2,3]
put integerP(x)
-- 0
put listP(x)
-- 1
put objectP(x)
-- 1
x = "abc"
put integerP(x)
-- 0
put stringP(x)
-- 1
put objectP(x)
-- 0
x = member(1)
put listP(x)
-- 0
put objectP(x)
-- 1
```

The *listP* function is useful, but it doesn't tell the full story. Is the list a property list or a linear list? Another function, called *ilk*, tells you what type of list a variable is. Possible values are #color, #date, #list, #proplist, #point, and #rect.

Here are some examples in the Message window:

```
x = [1,2,3]
put ilk(x)
-- #list
put x.ilk
-- #list
x = [#a: 1, #b: 2, #c: 3]
put x.ilk
-- #propList
x = point(100,150)
put x.ilk
-- #point
```

```
x = rect(0,0,10,10)
put x.ilk
-- #rect
x = the systemDate
put x
-- date( 1999, 1, 5 )
put x.ilk
-- #date
x = rgb(0,0,0)
put x.ilk
-- #color
```

You can also use *ilk* to compare a variable and a type. The variable is the first parameter, and the type is the second. In this case, the function returns TRUE for more than one type per list, because some list types can be used in more than one way. A color, for instance, is a list, a linear list, and a color list. In addition to the symbols used by the one-parameter *ilk* function, you can also use *#linearlist* to test to see whether a variable is that specific type of list.

```
x = [1,2,3]
put ilk(x,#list)
-- 1
put ilk(x,#linearlist)
-- 1
put ilk(x,#proplist)
-- 0
x = [#a: 1, #b: 2, #c: 3]
put ilk(x,#list)
-- 1
put ilk(x,#linearlist)
-- 0
put ilk(x,#proplist)
-- 1
x = rgb(0,0,0)
put ilk(x,#list)
-- 0
put ilk(x,#linearlist)
-- 0
put ilk(x,#proplist)
-- 0
put ilk(x,#color)
-- 1
```

→ **See** "Using List Variables," Chapter 13, "Essential Lingo Syntax," for more information about lists

ERROR-HANDLING LINGO

Even after implementing error checking along every step of the way, there is always a chance that a bug will persist and end up in your final product. There is one way you can minimize the effects of these nasty things, though. Director enables you to intercept errors when they happen.

You can use this power to send your own error message instead of the standard Director one. You can also use this power to display no error message at all. In many cases, the program can continue with little problem after a non-serious error.

The way it works is a little complicated. First, you set a system property called *the alertHook*. You set this to a parent script. A good place to set it is during the *on prepareMovie* or *on startMovie* handlers. In this case, *the alertHook* is set to a parent script that has the member name "Error Handling."

```
on prepareMovie
  the alertHook = script("Error Handling")
end
```

Then, you need to create the parent script itself. This script needs to contain an "on alertHook" handler. Here is an example:

```
on alertHook me, error, message
  alert "Error:"&&error&RETURN&message
  return 1
end
```

The "on alertHook" handler should have a first parameter of *me*, and then it can accept two more: the error and the message. They are actually both messages. They correspond to the two pieces of information displayed with every Director Lingo error. The first message is usually something like "Script runtime error" and is very general. The second message contains specific information about the error, such as "Handler not defined" or "Cannot divide by zero."

You can use these two strings to determine what to do next. For instance, if you want to handle an "Index out of range" error a specific way, you can look for that error and handle it one way, and then handle other errors another way.

The one last thing that the *on alertHook* handler needs to do is to return a value. If a value of 0 is returned, Director proceeds to display the error Message that it wanted to show in the first place. A value of 1 suppresses the error Message as long as it is not a fatal error.

If you plan to suppress error Messages completely, it might be a good idea to at least check whether *the runMode* is "author" and handle that by returning 0. Otherwise, you could be getting errors while creating or altering the movie, and not know about it.

If you need to turn off the alertHook error handling, just set *the alertHook* to 0.

USING LINGO DEBUGGING TOOLS

The best thing to do when you find a bug, of course, is to fix it. Fixing bugs is actually a major part of coding. A Lingo program of any size is certain to need some debugging. It doesn't matter how experienced you are. Expert Lingo programmers tend to write more code, and this code is more complex. Thus, they have just as many bugs as beginning programmers, who are more conservative in their programming.

When a bug appears, it is usually in the form of an error message. Figure 33.1 shows a typical error message dialog box. The important items to notice are the Debug and Script buttons. These buttons take you to the two most powerful debugging tools: the debugger and the script window.

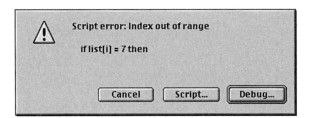

Figure 33.1
A typical error message dialog box in Director shows the error type, the error message, and the Script, Debug, and Cancel buttons.

In addition to the debugger and the script window, there is a watcher window that displays the values of variables in your movies as they change. The Message window is also a valuable debugging tool.

USING THE DEBUGGER

The debugger can be used on two occasions. The first is when you get an error message, and then press the Debug button in that message dialog box to bring up the debugger. The result looks like Figure 33.2.

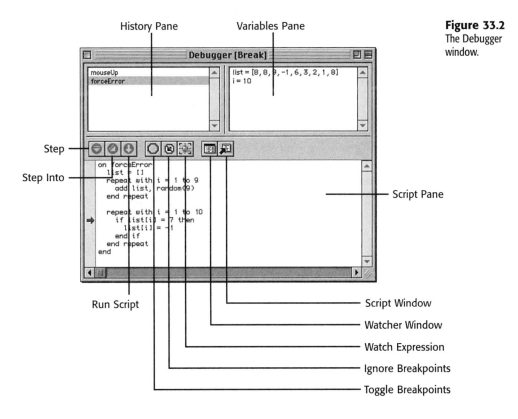

Figure 33.2
The Debugger window.

PART
IX

CH
33

The debugger window contains three panes and a set of buttons that enable you to examine the current state of the movie or walk through code step by step. You can see the code of a handler called "on forceError" in the Debugger window, in Figure 33.2. This is the code that was executed at the time the error occurred. The error message was the one seen in Figure 33.1.

The upper-left pane in the Debugger window shows a list of handler names. The last one in the list is the handler currently executing, in this case "on forceError." The handlers listed above it are the handlers called that lead to the current situation. In this case, *on mouseUp* initiated the action, and that called "on forceError."

The upper-right pane contains a list of local and global variables used in the current handler. Next to each is its value.

The largest pane in the Debugger window is the script pane. This displays the script that contains the current handler, along with a green arrow next to the line that was just executed.

In this case, you can see that the Debugger has stopped on the line if list[i] = 7 then. The error was "Index out of range," so the first suspect would be that the "i" used to reference the "list" is a larger number than the number of items in "list." Sure enough, that is the case because "i" is 10, but "list" has only nine items.

Another way to use the debugger is to set a breakpoint. You can see the Toggle Breakpoints button in Figure 33.2. The same button appears in the script window. You can also set breakpoints in the script window by clicking in the gray area to the left of any line of Lingo code.

Setting a breakpoint causes a movie to stop and open the Debugger window when the line containing the breakpoint is executed. This is different from using the Debugger when an error occurs, because you can start to step through the code, line by line.

The three arrow buttons shown in Figure 33.2, labeled Step, Step Into, and Run Script, enable you to continue. The first simply advances you to the next line. The Lingo code executes normally, changing variables and objects on the Stage. You can use this to slowly watch the progress of your code as it runs.

If, as you are stepping through code, you encounter a line that calls another handler, it executes that handler all as one step. However, if you use the Step Into button instead, it enables you to step, line by line, through that handler as well.

The last arrow button, Run Script, enables the program to run again at full speed. The Debugger does not track it anymore. However, if it encounters another breakpoint, it stops again.

This is why there is a Toggle Breakpoint button in the Debugger itself, so you can set a new breakpoint further down in the code, and hit the Run button to have the program advance to that point.

USING THE WATCHER

In addition to the Debugging window, you can also use the Watcher to check on the values of expressions and variables. Figure 33.3 shows the Watcher window.

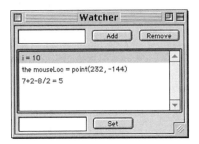

Figure 33.3
The Watcher window enables you to track changes in expressions as the movie runs.

The main area in the Watcher window lists the expressions you want to watch. Above that is an area for you to type new expressions and add them to the list. Below, you can type a number, string, or other value, select a variable in the list, and set it to that value.

You can actually type in any Lingo code that evaluates to a value and see it change as your program runs. This means you can use operations like addition and subtraction, and movie properties such as *mouseLoc*.

The main use for the Watcher window is to enable you to track variables that you think may be causing a problem. You can watch them as the movie runs and see where they go wrong.

The Watcher window is so easy to use that it is sometimes more convenient to use it rather than to type *put* statements into the Message window to test values.

USING THE SCRIPT WINDOW

The importance of the Script window shouldn't be overlooked in any discussion on debugging. A lot of bugs can be squashed just by reading over your code.

In fact, it is my first stop when I find a new bug. When I see the error dialog box appear, as shown in Figure 33.1, I press the Script button and have a look. Most of the time I can see the bug right away and fix it without having to go to the Debug window or using some other technique.

Usually, a question mark appears in the dialog box that tries to point out the exact location of the bug. However, because Director is not privy to what you were actually thinking when writing the script, it is not always correct.

The Script window is also where you can set breakpoints for the Debugger, and, of course, place helpful comments to help you quickly and easily find and kill the trickier bugs.

PART

IX

CH

33

USING THE MESSAGE WINDOW

The Message window can serve many purposes when it comes to writing error-free code and debugging code that is not so error-free.

First, you can use the Message window to test short bits of Lingo code that you are not quite sure about. It is what is known as a command line interpreter in other programming environments. So, for instance, rather than just assume that a text member's *type* is *#text*, you can test it.

```
put member("score").type
-- #text
```

Forget what the items in *the systemDate* are? Just try it out:

```
put the systemDate
-- date( 1999, 1, 5 )
```

Now you can program with confidence.

In addition, you can use the Message window to test out individual movie handlers. Just type their names, add any parameters, and press Enter. If the handler is a function, you can place *put* before it to have the result placed in the next line of the Message window.

```
put addToNumbers(4,5)
-- 9
```

You can also test global variables in the Message window. So if you want to see what the global *gScore* is currently set to, just try it:

```
put gScore
-- 405
```

You can even set globals in the Message window:

```
gScore = 10000000
```

Another way to use the Message window is to place the *put* command inside scripts. You can send variable contents to the Message window. This is similar to using the Watcher window, but you get to keep a record of values.

Note

> Make sure that you comment out or delete debugging *put* statements before finishing your movie. Sending lots of information to the Message window slows down your movie considerably.

USING TRACE

The Message window is also the primary tool for using a debugging method known as *tracing*. With tracing, Director sends a message to the Message window every time a line of Lingo executes, and every time a variable changes. Figure 33.4 shows a sample trace session.

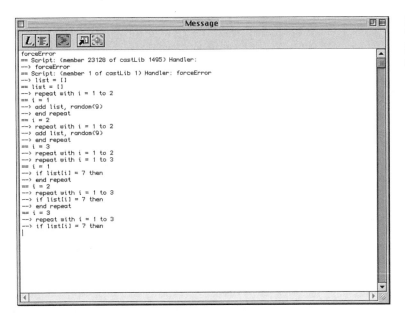

Figure 33.4
The Message window is where trace information is displayed.

Note

Note that the first line in the Message window is one actually typed. After you press Enter, the trace begins. Director incorrectly states that the "forceError" message came from member 23128. However, this does not affect the rest of the trace which starts on the next line.

To turn tracing on, simply click the Trace button at the top of the Message window. It is the middle button of the five shown in Figure 33.4.

In addition, you can set *the trace* to TRUE or FALSE, to turn tracing on or off. You can do this in the Message window, or you can insert it in your handlers. Doing either one enables you to start the trace before a sensitive piece of code, and stop it afterward.

PART

IX

CH

33

USING OTHER DEBUGGING METHODS

Debugging works great in Director, but what if the bug only appears when the movie is running as a Projector or in Shockwave?

There is no debugger for these situations, but you can still output messages at points in your code to let you know the settings for your variables, or at what point in the code your movie currently is.

In projectors, the *alert* command comes in handy for this. You can use *alert* at a sensitive part of your code to figure out what is going on. For instance, if your program isn't working correctly after a *getNetText* series of commands, you might want to check to see whether the text that your Shockwave movie is getting is actually the text you expect. Rather than just getting the text and moving on, you may want to try this:

```
text = netTextResult(gNetID)
alert text
```

Now, you can see the text and check to make sure it is what you expect. Of course, you should remove the *alert* command after the testing is done.

Shockwave also offers you the chance to use the *netStatus* command. This command places a message in the Netscape Navigator message space at the bottom of the browser window.

You can also use *netStatus* to display useful information to users, such as the potential destination or action of a button over which the user's cursor is hovering. This is similar to how it is used by plain HTML and JavaScript code.

TESTING YOUR CODE

It is a sad fact that most major pieces of software released today are released with bugs in them. Maybe it is not so much sad as unavoidable. After all, how do you thoroughly test software? Thousands of different computer configurations are available that vary by one item or another: processor type, processor speed, operating system type, operating system version, video card manufacturer, video card driver version, video settings, hard drive speed, CD-ROM speed, RAM size, system settings, system extensions, and so on.

It is impossible to test on every machine available. However, you can test on a variety of machines and find a majority of the problems.

TEST EARLY AND OFTEN

Any computer science professor or software project manager will tell you: Test early and test often. Take these words to heart.

Start your testing as soon as you have something that can be tested. If you are writing handlers, test each one individually if you can. For instance, if you write a handler that takes two points and finds the distance between them, why not use the Message window to try it out? Did you get an error? Did the result come out as expected?

Although this method of testing may seem tedious, consider the alternative. A large Lingo program may have a few dozen movie handlers, many behavior scripts, and lots of named (or misnamed) members. If you try programming it all at once, never testing any piece individually, chances are very slim that it will work when you are initially finished. However, if you perform a minute of testing here and there, the program could work as soon as you write your last line of code.

TESTING IN-HOUSE

In-house testing is sometimes called *alpha testing*. It starts when the program is "done" and you give it a thorough test yourself. Run the program through its paces. Most of your bugs actually show up right away.

The next step is to let others in your company or organization test it. In a classroom situation, this can be lab partners or classmates. Maybe some of your friends, too.

This level of testing gives you a lot more control than the next stage. You can personally talk to people who use the software, and maybe even have them show you, first hand, what was going wrong.

You may even want to use the *alertHook* Lingo to give detailed reports when errors occur. This makes it easier for you to track down the problem, but it does not affect the final product because you can remove this code before the product is finished.

BETA TESTING

After your program seems to work for you, and everyone in your company has tested it, you can start a beta test. This means that you can give out a copy of your program to people outside of your company or organization. Many times these are people you don't even know.

Some developers do a private beta test, whereby only a few selected individuals get to test. These individuals can be found among the company's loyal customers, or among applications received from simply advertising.

Some companies do a public beta test, where anyone can download and test the software. This usually results in many people downloading, but few actually reporting errors. It does give you the widest range of testers, however.

Although I recommend that beta tests occur after the product is fully developed and somewhat tested, there are many companies that hold beta tests during development. This enables them to test out new features and get feedback from actual users while they develop.

Beta testing can be overkill if you have a small project, however. Also, if you are developing a Shockwave applet, consider how easy it is to update your movie after you make it live. The applet really only exists in one place: your Web site. If an error, even a big one, is found, you can correct it and upload a new version immediately.

DID YOU KNOW?

- Try using the Lingo command *nothing* as a place to put breakpoints. *nothing* does just that. You can place *nothing* inside a conditional statement and set a breakpoint on it to have the debugger start at only a particular time. For instance:
```
if i = 8 then
  nothing
end if
```

- You can also place *nothing* inside a conditional statement that looks for a keyboard function, such as *the shiftDown*. This way you can have the debugger start when the code is at a certain spot, but only when you want it.

```
if the shiftDown then
  nothing
end if
```

■ You can click in the handler history pane of the Debugger window to see the previous handlers and the point to which the program will return as soon as the more recent handler is done. This also changes the variables in the second pane to reflect the state of the handler selected.

CHAPTER 34

PERFORMANCE ISSUES

In this chapter

Performance can be the difference between a good Director movie and a great one. Issues that you may not think about can sometimes spoil a multimedia experience for a user. For instance, issues such as a long download over the Internet, too long of a pause before a digital video starts, poor color quality in a picture, or a sound that isn't synchronized with the animation can spell disaster for your product.

Solving performance issues is usually about fine-tuning. Most of the time it is left for the last stage of development. However, at some point, performance issues must be examined and solved before a project can be considered done.

DESIGNING FOR A TARGET MACHINE

Every time you create a Director movie, you should think about the type of computer that will run it when it is done. You not only need to decide what a typical system will be, but what the minimum system requirements are.

COMPROMISE

Kiosk builders have it easy. They know on exactly what computers the movie will run, and usually even get to test it on that machine during development.

If you are developing a project for yourself, a co-worker, or even a movie that will be seen by only a few co-workers and friends, it also makes the job easier. The best situation is when you are creating a presentation and plan to run the finished product only on your own computer, the same one on which you are developing it.

However, most developers are not that fortunate in a typical situation. If you are creating a CD-ROM, you will usually have to decide what the minimum specifications are for a computer that can use the CD-ROM. That information usually goes on the packaging.

The operative word is "minimum". You can expect most of your users to have pretty fast computers, but you always have to think of that one user who buys the product and has a machine with the bare minimum.

Shockwave developers have it even tougher. People use all sorts of computers to surf the Web. You have to think about your target audience and what they might have. Even if you specify minimum requirements, users with less powerful computers are still going to try to use your movie.

On the one hand, you probably want to make the Shockwave experience available to as many people as possible. On the other hand, you don't want to build something that lacks quality, just so the movie works for a few more people with five-year-old computers. It is definitely a situation for compromise.

SAMPLE REQUIREMENTS

The computer industry is moving amazingly fast. A system that would have been typical two years ago is almost unacceptable today. Knowing that this book will be on shelves for many years makes it hard to talk about specifics.

In the beginning of 1999, computers are less expensive than ever. For less than $1,000, you can get a Windows machine running at 233MHz, with a video card and monitor capable of supporting millions of colors. Stereo speakers are almost always included.

However, that doesn't mean that everyone who bought a computer in 1997 ran out and upgraded. People hang on to old machines that work just fine for most things.

Worse, educational institutions often get hand-me-down computers. So a 1997 machine will find its way into a school in 2001. A student might sit down and use that computer to try and run a movie made by you. It is up to you to decide whether it will work reasonably well on those machines.

Macromedia has made this a little easier for Director 7 developers. Director 7 Projectors can be made for only a 32-bit Windows system or a Macintosh PowerPC. Shockwave runs on only these two platforms as well. Windows 95, 98, or NT are the only 32-bit Windows systems.

So this eliminates any worry about having to create movies for Windows 3.1 or Macintosh 68K machines.

> **Note**
>
> If you need to create for Windows 3.1 and Mac 68K, have no fear. Director 6.5 is an excellent program that can be used to make Projectors and Shockwave for these computers.

So what should the minimum requirements be? If I were to make a mass-market CD-ROM right now, the minimum requirements would be as follows:

- Pentium 133MHz Processor
- CD-ROM Drive
- 640×480 Monitor with 8-bit color
- 16MB of RAM
- 750MB hard drive
- Windows 95

On the Mac side, the requirements would be as follows:

- PowerPC Processor
- CD-ROM Drive
- 16MB RAM

- 640×480 monitor with 8-bit color
- 750MB hard drive
- System 7.5

These requirements are pretty conservative. But the idea is that the CD-ROM is supposed to be mass-market, possibly even educational. If I were creating something that contained a lot of digital video and other high-end effects, such as maybe an adventure game, my requirements might be

- 166MHz Pentium MMX Processor
- 4× or better CD-ROM Drive
- 32MB of RAM
- 800×600 monitor with 24-bit color
- 1GB hard drive
- Windows 95

On the Macintosh side, my requirements would be

- 603, 604 or G3 Processor
- 4× or better CD-ROM drive
- 32MB of RAM
- 800×600 monitor with 32-bit color
- 1GB hard drive
- System 8.0 or better

In early 1999, either a PC or an iMac that meets these requirements costs less than $1,000.

One very important difference between my first set of requirements and my second is the high resolution color. If you have 8-bit color as your minimum requirement, it forces you to constantly think about 256-color palettes throughout the development process. Using a higher color depth, even if your graphic members are still only 8-bit, really frees you up and enables you to accomplish a lot of nice visual effects.

Sometimes, a client or boss will specify the system requirements. Usually they are pretty conservative: 8-bit color, 640×480 screen, and so on. It is important that you tell them about how much those specifications will degrade the movie for a majority of users. Sometimes, when a client or boss finds out that the colors will be poor and the screen will look tiny for most users, they decide to revise their minimum requirements.

ISSUES AFFECTING PERFORMANCE

Many things affect performance on a computer. You should think about all these issues when developing your movie, and when writing the system requirements, if any.

To do this, it helps to understand each part of a computer system that could affect performance. You can break these into the categories of hardware, software, and network.

To really get into these issues, you need a knowledge of computer engineering. However, it helps to understand the basics. This way, you can know what to look for when testing, and have some idea of what might be happening in situations where performance varies from machine to machine.

HARDWARE

The term "hardware" represents the computer itself. Just about everything except the case can affect performance.

PROCESSOR

All computer manufacturers love to talk about the processor speed of their latest machines in their ads. In early 1999, these speeds have topped 400MHz for both Mac and Windows computers. More importantly, low-priced consumer versions are usually above 200MHz.

Processor speed, of course, does affect the performance of your movies. Higher processor speeds enable you to attain higher frame rates and smoother transitions. Lingo computes faster.

Also, keep in mind that there are different types of processors. You can get a standard Pentium, a Pentium with MMX, and a Pentium II, each one offering a little bit of a speed boost beyond just the MHz number. On the Mac side, the 601 chip, the 603e, and the 604 series of chips offer increasing speeds as well. The new G3 processors include a backside processor cache discussed in the following section.

PROCESSOR CACHE

A cache is memory chip that is super-fast, usually much faster than normal RAM. It is used to store things, such as code or data, that were recently accessed in memory. The idea is that something recently accessed in memory is likely to be accessed again soon. If it is, and it is still stored in the cache, it can be retrieved from the cache, rather than the slower RAM memory.

The larger the cache and the faster it is, the faster the computer can process commands. It will appear as if the processor is even faster, and have a positive effect on the speed of your movie.

In early 1999, a good cache size is one megabyte. Slower machines will have 512K or 256K caches, and many machines have none at all. The PowerMac G3 machines are specifically designed with large, fast caches called "backside caches." They are located on the back side of the processor card, placing them that much closer to the processor and thereby increasing speed.

RAM

Random Access Memory is usually just referred to as "memory." The more a computer has, the more programs it can run at one time. Also, for memory-intensive things such as movies with large cast members, RAM is very important.

Director stores all cast members in the file. However, as each one is used, it loads that cast member into memory. The more memory that is available to Director, the more cast members can be stored in memory. When no more memory is left, a cast member that has not been used recently is erased to make room for more. If the erased member is needed again, it has to be loaded again. This repeated loading slows things down.

VIRTUAL MEMORY

Virtual memory is something used by just about every home computer. The idea is for the computer to pretend that it has more RAM than it really does. It uses hard drive space to pull this off.

The hard drive stores a large file that is actually the total contents of the virtual memory that the computer thinks it has. The real RAM is used as a cache to store the most recently used parts of this virtual memory. Because recently used parts of memory are the most likely parts to be used again soon, a slowdown is only caused when new parts of memory need to be loaded into RAM.

Virtual memory therefore makes a computer slower, but it also increases the amount of memory, at least virtually. For many users, virtual memory is the only option, because their computers came with only 16 or 32MB of RAM.

DISK SPEED

All hard drives are not equal. Some hard drives read and write data faster than others. Although this is usually not an issue for consumer-based products, it can be for kiosks. If your kiosk includes media that needs to stream from the hard drive, such as full-screen video, you will need to take this under consideration.

CD-ROM SPEED

Although this is not an issue for more recent machines, older ones came with single-speed (1×) or 2× CD-ROM drives. 1× CD-ROMs read data off the CD at the same rate as audio CD players.

At 1×, you can only hope to get to 150 megabits per second (Mbps), which means an average of more like 90. This is too slow for decent digital video, and you will definitely see a performance hit in loading large cast members. 2× CD-ROMs double these numbers, but still make it hard to deliver high-quality video or fast-loading movies. At speeds above that, however, you can expect decent performance. In early 1999, even budget computers come with 16× CD-ROM drives, which perform very nicely for Director movies.

However, CD-ROM drives are still slower than regular hard drives. One way to compensate for this is to require users to install the Projector onto their hard drives before running it.

Bus Speed

Although processor speed is the subject most frequently discussed when it comes to buying a new computer, bus speed is another concern. A bus is the vehicle through which the various parts of the computer, such as the processor, the cache, the keyboard, the video, and the sound cards and other pieces, communicate. It is usually set to match the speed of the processor.

Video Cards

Video cards also have different capabilities. Director does a lot of drawing to the screen. Drawing occurs as a result of communication between the software and the video card. If the video card is slow, drawing a frame takes longer and the frame rate suffers.

Sound Cards

Although a slow sound card may not slow down the frame rate, it could mean that sounds are delayed in starting. More commonly, a bad sound card just makes sounds not sound very good. Also, remember that on PCs, MIDI sounds are processed by the sound card. Cheap sound cards can make music as if it is being played on a child's toy keyboard. Some high-end sound cards, on the other hand, can make MIDI sound as if the music is being played on professional keyboards.

Speakers

This point is easy to overlook. If your movie has CD-quality sound in it, it will still sound only as good as the user's speakers. If the user has the cheap speakers that come with so many bargain computers, you can expect the worst.

Many developers have a great set of speakers, complete with sub-woofers and a good range. They design sound for these speakers because that is what they have. Then, the end user's machine tries to play these sounds, which come out like mere noise. This usually occurs because the sound relies too much on the low- or high-end frequencies.

It is worth the $14.95 to buy a pair of cheap speakers to use for testing if you expect to make movies for users who have them.

PART
IX
CH
34

SOFTWARE

Hardware is only half the picture when it comes to an individual computer. The software is the other half. Your Projector, or Shockwave, is what will be running your movie. It talks to the operating system, which in turn talks to the hardware. Every step of the way is the place for a potential performance problem.

OPERATING SYSTEM

PCs will be using Windows 95, 98, or NT to play back Director movies. There were two major releases of Windows 95, known as A and B. There are also many different versions of Windows NT. As of early 1999, PowerMacs are using everything from System 7.5 to System 8.5.1.

Each upgrade of the operating systems incorporates better performance. Upgraded operating systems handle memory better, handle disk drive access better, and display your graphics better.

EXTENSIONS

Beyond the basic operating system, extensions add more functionality to a computer. Typically, the more extensions, the worse performance is. Extensions take up disk space, increase the amount of memory needed by the operating system, and slow down the machine with more information to process on a regular basis.

However, some extensions are designed specifically to increase the performance of the computer. QuickTime 3, for instance, makes QuickTime media available to the computer, and also gives Director movies a better way to mix sound on PCs. An extension such as DirectX enables a Windows machine to process graphics better and faster.

DRIVERS

Unlike extensions, drivers are a necessary part of the operating system. They tell it how to communicate with various pieces of hardware, such as video cards, sound cards, and printers.

What most users do not know is that drivers have updates. The driver that comes installed on their machines is usually the original driver for the hardware, such as a sound card. A few months later, the hardware company may release a newer version of the driver and make it available for download on the Web. The new version fixes bugs and increases performance.

Sometimes developers are savvy enough to know about driver upgrades and install them on their machines. But you cannot assume that about the end user. Testing with lowest-common-denominator drivers is a good idea for a mass-market product.

DISPLAY SETTINGS

The two main display settings are screen resolution and color depth. One user may have the display set to 640×480 at 8-bit color, while another has the display set to 1024×768 and 32-bit color.

The difference? Well, the first user can see only one palette of 256 colors at a time, cannot fit a Projector larger than 640×480, or a Shockwave movie larger than 640×480 minus the 200 pixels vertically and the 50 pixels horizontally that the browser uses.

However, the 640×480 8-bit setting is usually *faster* than the 1024×768 32-bit setting. Why? Because there is less display information to process. Multiplying 640 times 480, and then by 8, you get 2.5 million bits of information. On the other hand 1024 times 768 times 32 gives you 25 million bits, or 10 times the first number.

On Macs, you can use *the colorDepth* property to change the user's color depth. A few Windows machines enable you to do this too, but most do not. However, on both Mac and Windows, you can use the Buddy API Xtra to change the color depth and screen resolution. You may want to consider that for super-fast, arcade-style movies.

NETWORK ACTIVITY

Although this is no longer much of a problem, it used to be that computers hooked up to a network were slowed down by the overhead of staying in touch with the network. Processors are so fast now that this is not a problem. However, if the hard drive on a computer is being accessed by the network, it does slow down a Projector or Shockwave movie currently running.

BROWSERS

Browsers stand between your Shockwave movie and the rest of the computer. Although Shockwave draws most graphics and sounds directly to the portion of the browser window it owns—making it pretty fast—some activity does need to pass through the browser.

Internet text retrieval and media linking, for instance, rely on the browser for the connection. Browsers vary in their performance for this task. In some cases, such as in older Microsoft Internet Explorer versions on the Mac, they will not even allow you to use network Lingo.

Basically, the newer the browser version, the more compatible it is with the complex features of Shockwave.

NETWORK

Hardware and software describe what is inside a computer, but many factors outside a computer can also affect performance. This is especially true if the movie is a Shockwave movie that needs to be loaded from the Web. Keep in mind that Projectors also sometimes call on the Internet for information or media.

PART

IX

CH

34

MODEMS

In early 1999, a 28.8 modem is still the lowest common denominator. There are a lot of them out there. For these users, movies load at the top rate of about 2Kbps, which means that a 120Kbps movie takes a full minute to download.

Even people with digital subscriber line modems or cable modems still have limits. They can expect a normal rate of maybe 20Kbps. This means that a 1MB file still averages about a minute to download.

THE INTERNET

In a perfect network situation, the user's computer and your server with the Shockwave movie on it would be directly connected. This is not true on the Internet. Chances are the data routes through all sorts of systems, and probably comes in and out of other servers. This is true even if the client and server are in the same town.

Data can even travel in different paths at different times. So a user might experience a great connection to your server one time, and then a very slow one the next.

You can't do much about this as a Director developer. However, you can plan for it, and make sure that the movie loading process works well at slow speeds.

→ **See** "Making Shockwave Movies," Chapter 36, "Delivering the Goods"

SERVERS

If you or your company own your own servers, then you will want to consider performance on those as well. Can your server handle 20 users? A hundred? A thousand? What happens when it goes down in the middle of the night? Although these are not issues that can be solved with Lingo, they are still important to the end user looking for your Shockwave game.

IMPROVING PERFORMANCE

Plenty of things can degrade the performance of your movie. But how can you improve performance? There are many ways.

MEMBER LOADING

In the section called "Member Loading" in Chapter 21, "Controlling the Director Environment," you learned how to use the different load settings for different members. You also learned how to use Lingo to preload members. Careful use of this can improve performance.

For instance, suppose you have an animation that takes the movie through many frames. Somewhere in the middle of the animation, the background art changes. At first it is a 640×480 8-bit graphic of one image, and then it changes to a whole different 640×480 8-bit graphic.

The movie is supposed to move smoothly through the frames, but instead it pauses for a time just before the frame where the background is replaced. This happens because Director has to suddenly load that large graphic into memory.

But what if you use *preloadMember* to request that the member be in memory before the animation begins? Then, when that critical frame hits, the movie does not have to load the graphic into memory; it is already there.

Also, consider the Unload member settings in the member's Properties dialog box. Chapter 21 has more detail about it in the section titled "Member Loading."

SHOCKWAVE FILE SIZE AND STREAMING

If the movie is playing from the Web in Shockwave, you should always take the download time of the movie into account. Does the value of the movie to the end user make the download time worth it?

Consider a Shockwave movie that introduces a Web site. You want it to look very cool, so it has all sorts of bitmap images and sounds. It is 300KB in size. But, the movie is really nothing more than an animated introduction. There is very little information for the users; that is all further down in the site.

Well, if a 28.8Kbps modem user is coming into the site wondering what is there, he is going to be forced to wait for about three minutes to see the Shockwave movie. Then, he is going to be disappointed to learn that the movie does not tell him anything he wants to know. The movie is clearly not worth the download time for the user. However, a 30KB movie might have been just fine.

On the other hand, if the Shockwave movie is a real program, such as a game, a business application, or a presentation of some information, it might be worth a 300KB download.

The first thing you should do with Shockwave movies that are too large is to use some trimming techniques to get the file size down to something more reasonable. See the section called "Trimming Media" later in this chapter.

After trimming, you should look at streaming techniques. The section "Shockwave Streaming" in Chapter 11, "Advanced Techniques," goes into detail about this.

COMPENSATING WITH ALTERNATIVES

Another method of improving performance is to have alternatives to items that may not work well on some systems. A simple example is to create two Shockwave movies, one that uses some very small 1-bit graphics and plain-colored backgrounds, and one that is a much larger movie with sounds and all the images you wish.

Then, just ask the users to choose to look at the "slim" movie, which you can recommend for 28.8 modem users, or the "full" version, which is recommended for people with faster connections. This also gives 28.8 users the option to select the full version if they really want. In that case, they will expect the long download time rather than be upset by it.

PART

IX

CH

34

> **Note**
>
> There is no way to tell the speed of a user's connection. Some developers have tried a method wherein they have the user load a small movie or external sound first, and the movie times how long it took to download. The results can easily be misleading, however.

You can also offer alternatives at a smaller level. For instance, you can have a 32-bit image and an 8-bit image in your Projector, and use the first if the user's monitor is set to 32-bit color depth, and the second otherwise. This maximizes performance for both users.

The same is true with sound and video. You can have alternate versions of these kinds of media in your movie, and play the appropriate one based on information you have about the user's system. You can check the *freeBlock* for instance, and see whether it is too small to fit a large, stereo sound, and instead play the smaller, mono sound. This way, both types of users can hear the sound at levels that their machines support.

→ **See** "Other Memory Information," Chapter 21

TRIMMING MEDIA

Of course you always want to trim your media as much as possible in a Shockwave movie to make the file size smaller. Even if you are delivering your product on a CD-ROM, you should pay attention to this. Smaller bitmaps and sounds load and display more quickly.

BITMAPS

The first item to check with bitmaps is to make sure that you are using every part of every image. For instance, if you have a background image that is 700 pixels wide, but only 640 of those pixels are visible on the Stage, 60 pixels worth of data in the image will never be seen by users. Cut the excess out.

Next, check to see whether the color depth you are using for an image is as low as it can be. If you expect the end user to be at 32-bit color, you may be using 32-bit color images for your bitmaps. However, in most cases you can use 8-bit color with a custom palette. An image of a forest might have a palette that is mostly greens and browns, whereas an ocean view might use blues and grays. You can display as many graphics as you like on the screen in as many different palettes as you like if the user is in 32-bit color. These 8-bit images with custom palettes are smaller and draw quicker.

Also, consider 1-bit images in cases where the image contains only one or two colors. Remember that you can set the foreground and background colors of a 1-bit image after it is placed on the Stage. Just select the sprite and use the color chips in the Tool Palette.

→ **See** "Bitmap Member Properties," Chapter 3, "Bitmap Members"
→ **See** "Sprite Color," Chapter 10, "Properties of Sprites and Frames"
→ **See** "Sprite Blend," Chapter 10
→ **See** "Distorting Sprites," Chapter 18, "Controlling Bitmaps"

SOUNDS

With sounds, consider whether the sound is of too high a quality. Did you try it at a lower quality to see whether it was acceptable? If you are using Shockwave audio compression, which is recommended, try different settings. Try it at 32bps. This is acceptable for many uses.

Make sure that you are using compact, trim sounds. Many developers make the mistake of leaving a second or two of silence at the start or end of a sound. They probably do so because many sound effects collections store their sounds in this manner. Trim away this excess and your sounds will start when you want them to and only use as much file space as needed.

VIDEO

The same is true for video and any other time-based media. Does a digital video sequence have excess seconds at the beginning or end? Also, is it stored at too high a quality setting for the use that you need? Consider these issues.

CUTTING OUT DEAD WOOD

One obvious thing to do to reduce the file size of your movie is to look for unused cast members. While developing, you may have created or imported members that didn't end up being used. You should cut away these useless members.

One way to make these cuts is to use the Find Cast Member window, shown in Figure 34.1. You can access this window by choosing Edit, Find, Cast Member, or by using Command+; on the Mac or Ctrl+; in Windows.

If you use the "Usage" setting in this window, a list of all the members not used in the Score is shown. If you select one or more of these member names, you can use the "Select All" button to return to the cast window and have all the unused members selected for you automatically.

But don't click Delete right away. The Find Cast Member window does not take into account any members that are referenced strictly in Lingo scripts. So down states for buttons, for instance, may not be selected. You will have to look at each member on a case-by-case basis.

Figure 34.1
The Find Cast
Member window
enables you to search
for members using all
sorts of criteria.

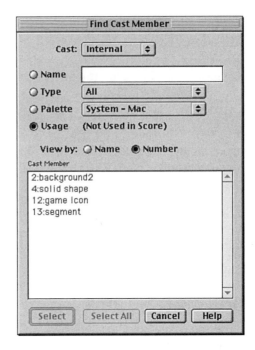

OPTIMIZING LINGO PERFORMANCE

If your movie is Lingo-intensive, you might want to consider looking at the performance of your Lingo handlers. There is almost always more than one way to do tasks in Lingo, but that does not mean that different tasks are equal. Some methods take longer, and use more system resources, than others.

For instance, if you have a handler that runs many times in your movie, and refers to all the cast member names in a cast library, you may want to consider placing these names in a list when the movie starts, and referring to the list, rather than to the members themselves.

There are as many ideas for optimizing Lingo as there are tasks that can be accomplished with Lingo. The best way to learn how to optimize is to test.

Benchmark tests compare two different methods of accomplishing the same task. Benchmarks are commonly used by expert Lingo programmers to determine the fastest method of doing something.

The idea is that you set up a fake handler that accomplishes a task. Chances are that it takes only a fraction of a tick to accomplish the task, so the task is repeated many times to get a better reading of how long it takes.

The following handler benchmarks a simple *if* statement. It runs the *if* statement 10,000 times, and marks the time before it began and then reports the total time to the Message window.

```
on testIf
  startTime = the ticks
  repeat with i = 1 to 10000
    r = random(3)
    if r = 1 then
    else if r = 2 then
    else if r = 3 then
  end repeat
  totalTime = the ticks - startTime
  put totalTime
end
```

Of course the *random* function takes up a large chunk of the time in this handler. However, the handler that you race this script against should also use the same *random* function, as well as the same *nothing* commands. The only difference between the two handlers will be the Lingo syntax used to branch on the value of "r".

This next benchmark handler tests the *case* statement.

```
on testCase
  startTime = the ticks
  repeat with i = 1 to 100000
    r = random(3)
    case r of
      1: nothing
      2: nothing
      3: nothing
    end case
  end repeat
  totalTime = the ticks - startTime
  put totalTime
end
```

You can see that the two handlers are identical, except the first uses *if* and the second, *case*. This is important, because any other difference, other than the command you are testing, could skew the results.

When the first handler is run on my computer, it takes 72 ticks. I actually ran the handler several times from the Message window and averaged the results.

The second handler averaged out to about 80 ticks. This means that it is a little more than 10% slower to use a *case* statement rather than an *if* statement.

However, remember that the handlers were testing the commands 10,000 times a piece. So don't stop using the *case* statement based on this. However, if a *case* statement is being executed in a *on exitFrame* script in a behavior that is attached to hundreds of sprites on the Stage, you might want to consider this sort of optimization.

The purpose of this example is not to show the speed difference between *if* and *case*, but to demonstrate how to do your own benchmark tests. If you are trying this on something that will have a larger effect, such as using different inks to draw animating sprites, chances are that you will see a much larger difference.

DID YOU KNOW?

- There are companies that specialize in taking your nearly-finished product and testing it on different machines in a testing lab. They then report back on bugs and performance issues.

- A cheap way to test your Projector or Shockwave movies on other machines is to find public computers that you can use. For instance, you can find older machines in libraries. You can also use computers in Internet cafes.

- On Macs, you can use the Extensions Manager to set up an alternate set of system extensions to use for testing. Such a set may not include some of the performance-enhancing extensions that your development machine normally uses.

- If you are a serious Shockwave developer, you may want to pay for a few $19.95-per-month dial-up Internet connections, even if you have a faster connection available. Then, every once in a while, try the applets on your site using these various services to see what your users are seeing.

CHAPTER 35

CROSS-PLATFORM ISSUES

In this chapter

If you are developing for just the Mac or just Windows, you may not have to worry about cross-platform compatibility. However, this is usually not the case. Most of the time you need to consider both platforms.

The same is true for Shockwave and browsers. This time the competitors are Microsoft, again, with Internet Explorer, and Netscape Navigator. Your Shockwave movies can be run in both, so you must keep this in mind when developing your programs.

DEVELOPING FOR MAC AND WINDOWS

A typical Director movie is developed for both platforms. For Shockwave, you almost have no choice, unless you want to tell users of one platform or another that they cannot look at your site.

Even with Projector-based products that are originally created for one platform only, you should take cross-platform issues into account. I have been in the situation many times where a project that started as a single-platform delivery product suddenly expanded cross-platform when a demo CD-ROM was needed for a concern that used the other platform.

The issues that you need to consider for cross-platform compatibility are the differences in the two operating systems: fonts, system palettes, display brightness, non–cross-platform Lingo commands, and so on. Each of these issues is discussed in more detail in the following sections.

FONTS

Although the issue of Font compatibility across platforms was very important in Director 6.5 and before, the new font cast member type makes this less of an issue.

If you import all the fonts that your movie needs, and then use only text members that use these font members as fonts, you will not run into a cross-platform font problem.

However, if you use any fields, you have to worry about fonts. After all, the same fonts don't appear across the two operating systems.

For instance, Arial is a very popular font in Windows. However, there is no Arial on the Mac. The Mac uses a font named Helvetica instead. Many users still have Arial on their Macs, probably because they have installed a Microsoft program such as Word. However, you cannot rely on this.

The Font Map is how Director decides which fonts on one operating system map to which fonts on the other. To access the Font Map, choose Modify, Movie, Properties. At the bottom of this dialog box are two buttons, Save Font Map and Load Font Map.

To make a change to the Font Map, you need to use the Save Font Map button to create a text file. Then you can edit it in a program such as SimpleText on the Mac or Notepad in Windows. Then you must use the Load Font Map button to implement the change.

The Font Map file contains a lot of comment lines, all starting with a semicolon. It basically explains how to use the active part of the file, which consists of lines that map Mac fonts to Windows fonts, and vice versa. Here is the first set:

```
Mac:Chicago        => Win:System
Mac:Courier        => Win:"Courier New"
Mac:Geneva         => Win:"MS Sans Serif"
Mac:Helvetica      => Win:Arial
Mac:Monaco         => Win:Terminal
Mac:"New York"     => Win:"MS Serif"
Mac:Symbol         => Win:Symbol  Map None
Mac:Times          => Win:"Times New Roman" 14=>12 18=>14 24=>18 30=>24
Mac:Palatino       => Win:"Times New Roman"
```

Each line consists of a three-letter abbreviation for the name of the system, followed by a colon and the name of a the font. The name of the font should be surrounded by quotes if it is more than one word. Then any number of spaces separate the instructions for the first system from the three-letter abbreviation for the other system, and the name of the font to which it should map.

So, for instance, the font Helvetica on the Mac is mapped to Arial on Windows. If you make a movie on the Mac and you have a text field in your movie that contains text using Helvetica, and you run it on a Windows, it is converted to Arial. If you want it, instead, to map to MS Sans Serif, you can just replace the "Helvetica" text with "MS Sans Serif" and then load the font map into your movie.

Also note the numbers listed after the Times to Times New Roman mapping. These numbers identify specific font sizes of text that uses that font and changes them. So not only is text using Times converted to Times New Roman, but any of that text that is 14-point is converted to 12-point at the same time. You just need to specify the two sizes, with the "=>" between them.

In addition to this mapping from Mac to Windows, the file also contains a mapping from Windows to Mac. Here it is:

```
Win:Arial             => Mac:Helvetica
Win:Courier          => Mac:Courier
Win:"Courier New"     => Mac:Courier
Win:"MS Serif"        => Mac:"New York"
Win:"MS Sans Serif"   => Mac:Geneva
Win:Symbol            => Mac:Symbol  Map None
Win:System            => Mac:Chicago
Win:Terminal          => Mac:Monaco
Win:"Times New Roman" => Mac:"Times" 12=>14 14=>18 18=>24 24=>30
```

You can see that this is just the opposite of the other mapping. It is important that you coordinate the two mappings. If not, you could end up in an odd situation. Suppose you map Times on the Mac to Times New Roman on Windows. Then, you take your movie and move it to a Windows machine and open it to test. The conversion takes place. Then, if you take that movie back to the Mac, and have the conversion of Times New Roman to New York, you do not end up with the same fonts as before.

The Font Map file also includes character mappings, which is necessary because special characters, such as Yen signs and other symbols, are not in the same locations in Mac and Windows fonts. This mapping converts characters appropriately so that your symbols match up.

Some lines also deal with Japanese fonts. Comments around these lines explain their use if you need to alter them.

COLOR PALETTES

The issue of cross-platform color palettes is another that is slowly going away. Because most computers are capable of displaying at greater than 8-bit color depth, you no longer have to worry about palettes as much.

However, if you are developing for 8-bit screens, you do need to know some things.

Both Mac and Windows use a default system palette when set to 8-bit color. These are the 256 colors that the screen uses when nothing but the operating system is running. They include the colors used by the different buttons, icons, menus, and other items seen on the desktop.

You can use your Director movie to change the screen's palette to the one being used by your movie. This happens automatically in a Projector.

However, if the desktop is still visible around the edges of the Projector, consider that the palette may not be providing the correct colors for the rest of the desktop—or any other running program—to display. As a result, your movie looks fine, but the rest of the screen does not.

There are some ways around this:

- You can set the Projector to occupy the whole screen. This is the default setting when you make a Projector. This hides everything else and makes it easy for you to use any palette you want.

- You might also want to consider using 16-bit or higher color depth. Computers capable of only 8-bit color depth see a badly drawn Stage, but it is somewhat useable. You can use the *colorDepth* to detect this situation and add a message to users that strongly suggests they change their monitor settings if possible.

- You can also place all your bitmap cast members in an external Cast. Then, build a second version of this Cast with the same cast members in the same slots. One cast file uses bitmaps all set to the Mac system palette, and the other uses them set to the Windows system palette. Then, place the correct cast library on the correct partition of a cross-platform CD-ROM.

With this last technique, you must also use Lingo to tell the Stage to use a different color palette depending on the system. Use *puppetPalette* to set this.

You can also try playing with the *paletteMapping* property, which tries to map bitmap images that use a different palette than the Stage is currently using.

DISPLAY BRIGHTNESS

One common cross-platform mistake is made by Mac developers. The Macintosh display is much brighter than a typical Windows display. Developers working in dark colors are surprised by how much darker they appear in Windows.

You can adjust for this by using your Mac's Monitors and Sound control panel and changing the Gamma setting. Then compare a dark image on both Mac and Windows platforms before you get too far into your development.

DIGITAL VIDEO

Although QuickTime 3 is available on both Mac and Windows platforms, you may want to consider the situation in which Windows users do not have QuickTime. You can certainly ask them to install it, or you can simply have a substitute Video for Windows movie waiting to be played instead.

Use *the quickTimeVersion* property to determine whether users have QuickTime installed.

FILE PATHNAMES

If you are using FileIO to read any text files, or you are using Lingo to set the *filename* property of a linked member, you need to think about pathnames. On the Mac, the character that goes between folder names in a path is a colon. On Windows, it is a backslash.

If you have a image in a folder that is at the same level as your projector, you might use a command like this one the Mac:

```
member("linkedimage").filename = "images:newimage.jpg"
```

However, in Windows, you might use this command:

```
member("linkedimage").filename = "images\newimage.jpg"
```

If you try to use the wrong one on the wrong platform, the image cannot be found. Instead, first determine on which platform the movie is running and use the appropriate command, as follows:

```
if the platform contains "mac" then
  member("linkedimage").filename = "images:newimage.jpg"
else
  member("linkedimage").filename = "images\newimage.jpg"
end if
```

You can also use a variable to store an item delimiter character, and then refer to that character later on. This works best if you need to set multiple pathnames.

```
if the platform contains "mac" then pathDel = ":"
else pathDel = "\"
member("linkedimage1").filename = "images"&pathDel&"newimage1.jpg"
member("linkedimage2").filename = "images"&pathDel&"newimage2.jpg"
member("linkedimage3").filename = "images"&pathDel&"newimage3.jpg"
```

NON–CROSS-PLATFORM LINGO

Many Lingo commands are just not available in both platforms or work differently in different platforms. The following list includes some of the most common ones:

- *shutdown*—Exits a Projector on Windows, but exits the Projector and shuts down the computer on Mac.

- *restart*—Exits a Projector on Windows, but exits the Projector and restarts the computer on Mac.

- *optionDown*—Examines the state of the Option key on a Mac, but the Alt key on Windows.

- *commandDown*—Examines the state of the Command (Apple) key on the Mac, but the Ctrl key on Windows.

- *controlDown*—Examines the state of the Ctrl key on Windows, but only the Control key on Mac, not the Command key.

- *colorDepth*—Can be tested in both platforms, but set only on the Mac.

Also, all commands that depend on the operating system for execution behave differently on different platforms. So the *alert* command brings up a different-looking alert box for each platform (and does not beep in Windows). The FileIO and MUI Dialog Xtra dialog boxes look slightly different to reflect the different systems.

→ **See** "Learning About the Computer," Chapter 21, "Controlling the Director Environment"

DEVELOPING FOR NETSCAPE NAVIGATOR AND MICROSOFT INTERNET EXPLORER

The biggest difference between Shockwave in the two browsers is the way that the Shockwave plug-in is installed. Netscape users have to download a Shockwave installer program and run it. This places a plug-in in their browser's plug-in folder that prompts them to download (and automatically install) all of Shockwave's components the next time they browse over to a Shockwave movie.

In Internet Explorer, the plug-in is wrapped inside an ActiveX control. ActiveX controls are files that extend the functionality of the operating system or of a program somehow. In this case, the ActiveX control adds Shockwave to the browser. The way users get this control is better than the downloading scenario for Netscape users. It actually looks for and loads the ActiveX control for Shockwave the first time the user browses over to a Shockwave movie. It therefore is automatic.

In addition to installation differences, you need to prepare your HTML pages that contain Shockwave to send the correct signals to both Netscape and Internet Explorer. Netscape needs an EMBED tag, whereas Internet Explorer needs an OBJECT tag. See "Making Shockwave Movies" in Chapter 36, "Delivering the Goods," for detailed information about these tags.

If you want to talk to the browser through JavaScript, you also have to do it differently with each browser. In Internet Explorer, JavaScript cannot receive messages from Lingo. Instead, you have to route these messages through VBScript, Internet Explorer's alternate browser language. See "Talking with JavaScript" in Chapter 22, "Shockwave and Internet Access," for examples.

One final consideration might be screen size. As Netscape and Internet Explorer change, they have different elements at the top, bottom, and sides that take away screen space from the content. If you want your Shockwave movies to fit on the screen, you have to take into account a lot of different potential configurations by the users.

Experiment with different Stage sizes and how they look inside both browsers on both platforms. Try the 640 × 480 monitor setting, the 800 × 600 monitor setting, and any others that you think your users may have. There is no ideal solution, because people with large monitors will think a 600 × 300 applet is too small, whereas people with small monitors will barely be able to fit it in their browsers.

→ **See** "Making Shockwave Movies," Chapter 36
→ **See** "Talking With JavaScript," Chapter 22

THE CROSS-PLATFORM CHECKLIST

It is useful for developers to have a checklist of potential problem areas for cross-platform development. Don't use this checklist only when the project is finished. Review it before you begin, and occasionally as the development continues.

- Lingo—Are you using any commands that may not work on another platform? Will commands that work differently on another platform still perform adequately?

- Xtras—Are you using Xtras that may not be available on another platform? Do all your Xtras behave the same on each platform?

- Pathnames—Are you using the colon or backslash (":" or "\") item delimiters to describe pathnames in your code? If so, does the code recognize when it is running on each platform and adjust as needed?

- Color Palettes—If you are making an 8-bit color presentation, does it work cross-platform if it is set to 8-bit?

- Fonts—Are you using fields? If so, are the fonts that you are using properly mapped to fonts on the other platform?

- Screen Size—Does your Stage fit in the screen? How about with the Windows taskbar at the bottom? Do you want it to fit inside both browser windows without requiring the users to scroll? Does it?

- Digital Video—Are you using digital video that may work on only one platform? How do you deal with situations in which the users do not have the correct extensions, like QuickTime?

- Transitions—Some transitions are slower on Windows than on Mac. It is a good idea to test all your animations for speed.

DID YOU KNOW?

- If you are developing for the Mac, and you have a fast one, you can buy an emulator that runs Windows. These are commonly used by Mac developers to test Windows Projectors. The ones that emulate an actual Pentium chip, and then run Microsoft's version of Windows on top of that, are very reliable testing devices because they are usually more "typical" of a Windows configuration than a randomly selected Windows machine can be.

- When you create a new movie, the fontmap.txt file is read in from the Director folder and used as the font map. You can change that file so that the default font map settings for any new movie you create also change.

CHAPTER 36

DELIVERING THE GOODS

In this chapter

Once you are all done creating a movie, you always have to take those final steps to create a deliverable product. In some cases, these steps require you to create a Projector. In others, they require you to make a compressed Shockwave movie. You may also want to export your Director movie as a Java applet. This chapter covers the steps you need to take to deliver the final product.

MAKING PROJECTORS

The section called "Creating a Standalone Projector" in Chapter 2, "Presentations with Director," goes into detail about creating a Projector. In addition, there are many options to choose from when building a Projector, and it is recommended that you carefully examine each setting before you build one.

You also have some alternatives to the simple Projector. You can build what is called a *stub Projector*, which can run any Director movie. Director 7 also enables you to build *Light Projectors*, which rely on Shockwave components on the user's system.

STUB PROJECTORS

The need for a Stub Projector is obvious once you think about it. Rather than creating a new Projector each time you make a change to a movie, just create a simple Projector that runs your movie as an external file.

The Projector can simply be a Projector with one movie that contains a *go to movie* command as the sole command of an *on exitFrame* script. This script is placed in the first frame of the movie:

```
on exitFrame
  go to movie "myrealmovie.dir"
end
```

Take this one-frame, one-member movie and create a Projector from it. Then, when you run it, it jumps directly to the first frame of the external movie, which is the main (or first) movie of your presentation or program.

If you make a change to your movie later, you don't have to rebuild the Projector. Just run it again and it will use the new, modified version of your movie.

You can even make more complicated Stub Projectors by having your Lingo code read in the name of the Stub Projector with *movie* property, removing a ".exe" if there is one, and then appending a ".dir" to the end. This will then be the name of the movie it should run.

This way, a Projector named "present.exe" will look for and run "present.dir." If you then create a movie called "program.dir," you can copy the "present.exe" Projector, change its name to "program.exe," and it can run the new movie.

Here is a script that does just this:

```
on exitFrame
  moviename = findMyMovie()
  go to movie moviename
end

on findMyMovie
  myname = the movie
  if myname contains ".exe" then
    myname = myname.char[1..offset(".",myname)-1]
  end if
  moviename = myname&".dir"
  return moviename
end
```

A more complex Projector script can even check to make sure the file is there before running it. You use the *getNthFileNameInFolder* command to do this. Look for a ".dcr" file first, a ".dxr" file next, and then a ".dir" file if neither of the first two is there. This way, the Projector works while you are testing and will also work when you decide to create a protected version of your movie.

Some Projectors check to see what the user's machine is like, and run a movie that is appropriate to the power of that machine. So it may run "myMovie640.dir" if the user's monitor is 640 480, or "myMovie800.dir" if the monitor is larger. The same can be done for platform, memory, screen depth, and so on.

→ **See** "Slide Show," Chapter 29, "Graphics Application," for more information on using getNthFileNameInFolder

LIGHT PROJECTORS

Light Projectors, also called Shockwave Projectors, are smaller than full-sized projectors, but are not really stand-alone. They require users to have Shockwave 7 on their computers. A Projector uses Shockwave 7 as the core engine to play the movie.

If the users do not have Shockwave, the Light Projector prompts them to download it first.

→ **See** "Finishing a Project," Chapter 2, for more information about creating projectors

MAKING SHOCKWAVE MOVIES

Making a Shockwave movie requires almost no effort. Actually, it can be said to require no effort at all because any Director movie, compressed or not, can be run in Shockwave.

However, most uses of Shockwave require that the movie be saved as a Shockwave movie, so that it is compressed. "Showing Your Presentation" in Chapter 2 also goes into creating a basic Shockwave movie. Doing so is simply a matter of choosing File, Save As Shockwave.

However, after the Shockwave movie has been created, you usually want to make an HTML page to hold the movie. This means that you have to write some HTML.

There are two main browsers: Netscape Navigator and Microsoft Internet Explorer. Shockwave has versions for both. For Navigator, Shockwave is a plug-in that handles Director movies inside a Web page. For Explorer, Shockwave is an ActiveX control, which is like an extension to the browser.

The result is the same: The Director movie appears in the browser directly on the Web page. However, the information needed to place the movie on the page differs for each browser.

NETSCAPE NAVIGATOR EMBED TAG

With Navigator, a movie is placed in a page with the *EMBED* HTML tag. Here is an example:

```
<EMBED SRC="mymovie.dcr" WIDTH="400" HEIGHT="200">
```

This tag simply states that the movie file is named "mymovie.dcr" and the size of the movie is 440×200. You could use a more complex path for the file if the movie is not in the same directory as the HTML page.

Tip

If you want, you never have to deal with the EMBED or OBJECT tag. The AfterShock program that comes with Director can build HTML pages that contain all the necessary tags.

In addition to the SRC, WIDTH, and HEIGHT parameters shown in the previous piece of code, you can also include several others. Here is a complete list:

- SRC—The relative or absolute location of the movie.
- WIDTH, HEIGHT—The screen size of the movie. The actual movie can be larger or smaller, but this parameter reserves a rectangle exactly this size on the page.
- PALETTE—Set to "Foreground" or "Background." The "Foreground" value forces. the computer screen to use the palette of the movie. The "Background"" value forces the movie to use the palette of the computer screen. This setting matters only in situations where the users have monitors set to 256 colors.
- TEXTFOCUS—Set to "never," "onstart," or "mouseUp." These parameters determine whether the Shockwave movie receives key presses. Different versions of different browsers, however, do not use the "onstart" setting properly. The users may have to click the Shockwave movie before typing.
- NAME—This parameter is more for the HTML page and JavaScript than for use by the movie itself. It is how you will refer to the movie object in HTML code.
- TYPE—Some versions of Netscape enable you to specify the MIME type of the object in the EMBED tag. You should set this to "application/x-director." This way, if your server is not set up for Shockwave movies, some users can still see the movie.
- PLUGINSPAGE—You can set the location of the download page for Shockwave here. Newer versions of Netscape use this to direct users to the place where they can get the plug-in. A good URL to use is http://www.macromedia.com/shockwave/download/.

MICROSOFT INTERNET EXPLORER OBJECT TAG

To achieve the same result as a Netscape EMBED tag, you need to write a very different type of tag for Internet Explorer.

The OBJECT tag is used to embed an object for which an ActiveX control provides the engine. In this case, the ActiveX control is Shockwave.

The OBJECT tag specifies the identification code for the ActiveX control. This number was assigned by Microsoft to Shockwave. The browser will use the number to determine whether it already has this ActiveX control. If not, the browser will use an Internet address, also specified in the tag, to download and install it.

Here is a sample OBJECT tag:

```
<OBJECT classid="clsid:166B1BCA-3F9C-11CF-8075-444553540000"
codebase="http://download.macromedia.com/pub/shockwave/cabs/director/¬
sw.cab#version=7,0,0,0"
ID=Credits WIDTH=512 HEIGHT=384>
<PARAM NAME=src VALUE="Credits.dcr">
</OBJECT>
```

The first part of the OBJECT tag is the "classid," which is the identification code mentioned earlier. The second part is the location on the Internet where the browser can get this ActiveX control if it is not already installed.

Notice that the last part of the location contains "version=7,0,0,0.", which tells Macromedia's Web site which version of the control is needed.

After those two pieces, the ID parameter is used in the same manner as the NAME parameter in the EMBED tag. It identifies the Shockwave movie object to any JavaScript or VBScript that needs to know about it.

The WIDTH and HEIGHT are next, and they serve the same purpose as the equivalent parameters in the EMBED tag. This ends the first part of the OBJECT tag.

However, this is not the end of the OBJECT tag as a whole. It requires an "</OBJECT>" tag to really end it. In between, there can and should be some PARAM tags. You can see one in the preceding example. Each PARAM tag specifies a parameter name and a value. In the example, the parameter is "src" and the value is "Credits.dcr." This of course, denotes the location of the Shockwave movie itself.

You can also include other PARAM tag parameters such as "textfocus" and "palette" that do the same things as their EMBED counterparts.

USING BOTH THE EMBED AND OBJECT TAGS

Most of the time, you want to build an HTML page for both browsers. This requires you to use both the EMBED and OBJECT tags.

This works fine for Netscape Navigator, where the EMBED tag is used and the OBJECT tag is ignored.

However, Internet Explorer recognizes both tags. The OBJECT tag is used to show the Shockwave movie as you expect. But Internet Explorer can also use the EMBED tag to use Netscape Navigator plug-ins. So it attempts to display the Shockwave movie a second time with the EMBED tag. Chances are that the browser does not have the Shockwave plug-in available, but the rectangular area for the Shockwave movie is still reserved for its use and users may even be prompted for a download.

Fortunately, there is a simple solution for this. Just place the EMBED tag inside the OBJECT tag. Microsoft Internet Explorer is smart enough to ignore EMBED tags inside OBJECT tags, so the movie will not be displayed twice.

Here is an example:

```
<OBJECT classid="clsid:166B1BCA-3F9C-11CF-8075-444553540000"
codebase="http://download.macromedia.com/pub/shockwave/cabs/director/¬
sw.cab#version=7,0,0,0"
ID=Credits WIDTH=512 HEIGHT=384>
<PARAM NAME=src VALUE="Credits.dcr">
<EMBED SRC="Credits.dcr" swLiveConnect=FALSE WIDTH=512 HEIGHT=384¬
TYPE="application/x-director"
PLUGINSPAGE="http://www.macromedia.com/shockwave/download/¬
index.cgi?P1_Prod_Version=ShockwaveDirector">
</OBJECT>
```

→ **See** "Working with Browsers," Chapter 26, "Developing for Developers," for more information about building HTML tags

BUILDING CD-ROMs

Next to the Internet, the most common way to deliver Director content is on CD-ROMs. The steps involved in making a CD-ROM depend on the CD-ROM burner you have, and the CD-ROM burning software you have. Usually the software comes with documentation. Because software varies greatly, it is impossible to go into complete detail here.

If you are making a cross-platform CD-ROM, this usually involves building two descriptions of the CD-ROM contents. The popular CD-ROM burning software, Adaptec Toast, requires you to make the Mac description first by creating a temporary hard drive partition and copying all the files to it.

Next, you can describe the Windows side of the CD-ROM to it, pointing to files both on the Mac temporary partition and elsewhere. The program is then smart enough to place shared files on the CD-ROM once, in such a way that both platforms can read them.

This way, if you have a 650-MB CD-ROM, you might have just a few MB of Mac-only data and a few MB of PC-only data. The Mac-only data and PC-only data can be the Projector and all the Xtras. The rest can be nearly 650MB of shared data.

Optimization used to be an important topic for CD-ROM creators. Today's software is so advanced that it does a good job of optimizing the positions of the files on the CD-ROM even without more information from you. Check your software's documentation for more information.

TROUBLESHOOTING DELIVERING THE GOODS

- Some computers, especially laptops, do not recognize CD-ROMs that have been created in one-off CD-ROM burners. They still work well with CD-ROMs created in factories.

- If a Shockwave movie still does not appear on a page after you upload it to a server, it may be because the MIME type for Shockwave is not set on the server. MIME types enable the server to tell the browser what a media element is. Search the Macromedia Web site for "MIME" for the latest information about setting MIME types for different servers.

- Check your browser cache settings before testing. Many browsers come with a default setting that has the movie check for new content only once per session. If you are uploading new versions constantly and then testing, you may actually be looking at the cached version of your old movie. Set the cache to check the server every time.

- More about caches: Even when you have the browser set to check the server each time for a new version, it still sometimes uses a cached version. Versions of both Internet Explorer and Navigator have exhibited this behavior for developers in the past. To make absolutely sure that you are using a new version of the Shockwave movie on your server, you must go to another page, clear the cache, and then return to the Shockwave page.

DID YOU KNOW?

- You can place an IMG tag inside an OBJECT tag for Internet Explorer users. If the browser is unable to display the Shockwave movie, the image appears instead.

- Director 7 comes with a wonderful program called AfterShock. It can take your Shockwave movie and create the OBJECT/EMBED tag for you, depending on your specifications. It can even add JavaScript to handle other options as well.

CHAPTER 37

CREATING JAVA APPLETS

In this chapter

A new way to distribute Director movies, introduced with Director 6.5, is the Save As Java function. This function is actually an Xtra that takes a Director movie and translates it, Lingo and all, to a Java applet.

This means that you can create Java applets, which are a series of small files that make up a computer application. These applets require the Java playback engine to run. The most common use for Java applets is to place programs in Web pages. Both Netscape Navigator and Microsoft Internet Explorer have the Java playback engine and are capable of playing Java applets.

Java applets will almost always perform more poorly than a Shockwave equivalent. They usually require larger download times, and exported applets support only a small subset of the features in Director. In fact, the only reason to use Java applets rather than Shockwave is that Netscape and Explorer can play back Java applets without requiring users to install extra software.

UNDERSTANDING SAVE AS JAVA BASICS

Creating a Save As Java function was an incredible feat for Macromedia's engineers. They had to basically rewrite the Director engine in Java, and then provide a translator that would take the Score, Cast, and Lingo scripts and translate them into a Java applet and data files.

Most developers have still not realized the power of the Save As Java Xtra. Basically, it gives a Director developer or development shop the chance to say "yes" when asked whether they can develop a Java applet.

There are two ways to go about creating a Java applet. The first is to take a movie that you have already created and make changes to it so that the features not supported by the Save As Java Xtra are not present.

The second way to work is to build a movie from the ground up with the Save As Java Xtra in mind. This means programming around all its limitations. Both methods are described in more detail in the following two sections.

TRANSLATING AN EXISTING MOVIE INTO AN APPLET

Developers who have tried this method have been disappointed when they cannot create Java applets from their old Director movies. A lot of Director features are not supported by the Save as Java Xtra. There are workarounds for most of them, however, but you have to do a lot of work to get an old movie working in Java.

For instance, you have to strip out all sprites except for those that use bitmaps, shapes, or fields. This means translating text members into static bitmaps or making them into fields if they change while the movie is playing.

You can't use any vector or Flash members, either, so these members have to be made into standard bitmaps.

Then, you need to get into your Lingo code. Many commands do not translate, but there are workarounds for the most common. Chunk expressions in strings, for instance, do not work. But you can use the *chars* and *offset* functions to write handlers to simulate things such as *line*, *word*, and *char*. You can also use *length*, and utility functions such as *numToChar* and *charToNum*. The *string()* and *value()* functions work as well. They can be used for converting numbers to strings, and vice versa.

If you are using some of the behaviors from Director's built-in library, note that they will probably not translate either. However, you can use a whole separate set of behaviors in the library particularly built for export to Java. You should probably restrict yourself to using only the Java behaviors.

If you have some behaviors of your own that you would like to try in Java, you have to examine them, word for word, and look for functions that are not compatible with the Save As Java function. Another way to test your behaviors and other scripts would be to just try to make a Java applet and see what errors appear during the process.

Even though translating an existing movie into Java is a possibility, and eventually works, it is not recommended. A much better way to go about creating Java applets is to build a movie with Java in mind from the start.

BUILDING A MOVIE WITH JAVA IN MIND

If you start from scratch and build a movie with the Save As Java Xtra's restrictions always in mind, you can make some incredible applets.

Even without fancy members such as text and vectors, Director is a great environment for creating complex applications quickly. When you start building a movie to be compiled as a Java applet, just forget about the other features and the Lingo commands that don't work in Java. You'll find that you still have plenty of features and options as you build.

Also, if you are not into programming your own Lingo handlers, you can use the Java behavior library to perform lots of different types of actions.

If you are creating a simple animation, such as something that might be used for a Web ad, you'll find Director is as easy to work with when you consider Java as it is on its own. For Lingo programmers, it will take slightly longer because you have to forget about some of your Lingo tricks and create new ones that use the supported Lingo.

The best way to create Java applets from Director is to start off with a new movie and create it with the Save As Java Xtra's restrictions in mind.

UNDERSTANDING WHAT WORKS AND WHAT DOESN'T IN THE XTRA

Before starting to compose your first movie to be made into a Java applet, you need to familiarize yourself with which features of Director are and are not supported by the Xtra. Some features that are supported do not work as well in Java as they do in Director and Shockwave. Also, many of the features that are not supported have viable workarounds.

MEMBERS

Six types of members are supported: bitmaps, shapes, fields, sounds, transitions, and, of course, scripts. The rest—digital video, text, linked movies, film loops, palettes, buttons, Shockwave audio, font members, and Xtra member types—are not.

The first thing to keep in mind is that you cannot refer to members through a variable reference. You cannot set a variable such as "myMem" to *member(1)* and then say: *myMem.width*. Instead, refer to the member directly: *member(1).width*.

FIELDS

Text members will be converted to bitmaps when the Java applet is created, which means you cannot perform operations on them, such as changing the text while the applet is running. Instead, convert them to fields, which can still be altered.

You should set all your fields to "Fixed" or "Scrolling" frame types. The "Adjust to Size" frame type is not fully supported. The field starts off in the Java applet as a size determined by the amount of text in it, but it does not adjust itself as the text changes.

In addition, you are very limited by what Lingo you can use to access fields. You can replace all the text in the field in one shot, but not parts of it. This works fine as long as you plan ahead for this restriction.

The properties you can use for fields are *text*, *font*, *fontSize*, *foreColor*, *backColor*, *fontStyle*, and *border*. The only styles you can use are bold and italic. You cannot use any Lingo that will help you locate characters in a field, such as *charPosToLoc*.

SOUND

The AU format is the only one that Java supports for sounds, and any internal sounds are converted to this format. Any external sounds should be in that format. You can use external sounds only if they are linked to a cast member. You cannot use a totally external sound with a *sound play* command.

Sounds in Java also do not support streaming Shockwave audio, cue points, fades, and volume control. However, the *puppetSound* command does work.

DIGITAL VIDEO

Short, simple digital video pieces can be translated into animation sequences, but there is no good way to incorporate real video directly into the applet. In addition, linked movies and film loops are not supported.

PALETTES

Palettes are not supported, but GIF images are. As a matter of fact, you can use GIFs as external files. Because each GIF has its own palette, using GIFs is a good way to incorporate 8-bit images into the applet. All internal images are translated into JPEGs, which you can also use as external images.

LINKED MEDIA

If you are using linked media, you have to keep a few more rules in mind. External images need to be GIFs or JPEGs. If you have another type of image, such as a BMP or PCT file, it is converted to an internal member, rather than a linked one.

All linked images and sound need to be in the same folder as the movie or in folders under it. You can use the Lingo *filename* property to switch a member's linked image.

BITMAPS

When you make your <images, avoid 2-bit color depth. It is actually a good idea to use all 8- or 32-bit images and the Save As Java Xtra converts them to JPEG and GIF formats with size optimization in mind.

You can't use any Lingo that alters the Cast, so the Lingo commands *move*, *erase*, *duplicate* and *new* (for creating a new cast member) do not work. In addition, you cannot get the *picture*, *media*, *scriptText*, *scriptType*, or *size* properties of members.

You can't do too much to alter a bitmap image, but you can get and set the *regPoint* property. You have access to, but cannot alter, the *rect* property. You also cannot use the *rotation* or *quad* properties. You cannot rotate or skew bitmap sprites on the Stage either.

SHAPES

Shapes work pretty much as they do in Director and Shockwave. If you are using patterns to fill a shape, you can use only the first 15 patterns.

As for shape Lingo, you can set the *shapeType*, *filled*, and *lineSize* properties.

SPRITES

Of the six member types that the Save as Java Xtra supports, only three can be made into sprites: bitmaps, fields, and shapes.

INKS

You are very restricted on the types of inks you can use. However, the few you can use are the most common. Table 37.1 shows which inks can be used with which sprites.

TABLE 37.1 INK USAGE IN JAVA APPLETS

Ink	Bitmaps	Fields	Shapes
Copy	Yes	Yes	Yes
Matte	Yes	Same as Background Transparent	Yes
Background Transparent	Yes	Yes	Yes
Blend	Yes	No	No

You cannot use the trails and movable properties of sprites. A behavior in the Java Behaviors library simulates the movable property.

SPRITE LINGO

As far as Lingo goes, you can still change the location, size, and shape of a bitmap or shape sprite. To do this, stick to these properties: *loc*, *locH*, *locV*, *rect*, *height*, and *width*. You can also alter the location but not the size or shape of field sprites.

You can change which member a sprite is using with the *member* property. You can also switch inks with the *ink* property, and colors with the *foreground* and *background* properties. The *blend* and *visible* properties also work.

To detect collisions between sprites, the *sprite...intersects* syntax works as it does in normal movies.

Just as with members, you cannot store a reference to a sprite in a variable and refer to it through that variable; instead, always refer to sprites directly, as in *sprite(7).loc*.

FONTS

Java is very particular about which fonts it allows. For this reason, fields can display only a few fonts. Table 37.2 shows their Java names, and what they translate to on the Mac or in Windows.

TABLE 37.2   Fonts That Can Be Used in Java Applets

Java Font Name	Corresponding Windows Font	Corresponding Macintosh Font
Helvetica	Arial	Helvetica
TimesRoman	Times New Roman	Times
Courier	Courier-New	Courier
Dialog	MS Sans Serif	Chicago or Charcoal
DialogInput	MS Sans Serif	Geneva
ZapfDingbats	WingDings	Zapf Dingbats
Default	Arial	Helvetica

To determine which fonts your field will display, just look up the font you are using in the column that corresponds to your development machine, either Mac or Windows. Then, see what font the other platform uses in the same row. Do not try to use fonts not on this list.

CAST LIBRARIES

If you divide your movies into multiple cast libraries, the Save As Java Xtra still works, but none of the advantages of using multiple cast libraries will be present. It really treats all the members as if they were in one large Cast.

You can use multiple internal libraries, just for authoring convenience. It is suggested that you have unique names for all your cast members and that you refer to them by name only, not by cast library.

NETWORK LINGO

Because Java is a language that is at home on the Internet, many network Lingo commands translate into Java ones. The commands *getNetText* and *gotoNetPage* work fine, just as they do in Shockwave. However, *netTextResult* actually returns a composite of the last 10 *getNetText* calls. It is therefore a good idea to call *getNetText* and *netTextResult* for one file at a time, rather than try to load multiple files at the same time.

In addition, the network commands *getLatestNetID*, *netAbort*, *netDone*, *netError*, *netMime* and *netStatus* also work to support *getNetText*.

However, *gotoNetMovie* does not work. Your Java applet can play only the one movie that has been made into an applet, and cannot jump to another. You can use *gotoNetPage* to jump to another Web page that contains another applet.

You also cannot use *downloadNetThing*, *streamStatus* and *tellStreamStatus*, *getPref*, and *setPref*. In addition, *getNetText* and other network commands can access only files that are on the same server. So you cannot set the *filename* of a linked bitmap to a file outside your server, due to security restrictions inside Java.

Communication with the browser seems like something that should work, but it does only somewhat. The *externalEvent* command works to send messages to JavaScript only in Netscape, but not in Internet Explorer. Using EvalScript to communicate with a JavaScript doesn't work at all.

OTHER LINGO

Some Lingo is available to help you determine whether members are ready to be displayed. The *frameReady* and *mediaReady* functions work as they do in Director normally. The *preloadMember* also enables you to load a member into memory, but only if it has been loaded from the Internet onto the user's machine.

You cannot use any Lingo that refers to another movie, such as *go to movie* or *play movie*. In addition, you cannot use *play* at all. However, some behaviors in the Java Behaviors library enable you to do the same thing as *play* and *play done*.

You cannot use the *pause*, *continue*, or *delay* commands. But an experienced Lingo programmer doesn't use those, anyway. The behaviors in the library should give you enough functionality to do basic navigation.

Tempo changes are supported, not only in the Score, but also with the Lingo *puppetTempo* command.

Although behaviors are supported, communication between behaviors is not. So there is no *sendSPrite*, *sendAllSprites*, *call*, *callAncestor*, *ancestor*, or *scriptInstanceList*.

Keyboard Lingo is also only partially supported. The *on keyUp* and *on KeyDown* event handlers work. However, properties such as *shiftDown*, *optionDown*, *controlDown*, or *commandDown* do not work unless they are inside one of those event handlers referring to the moment that the key was pressed. The *keyPressed* property is not available.

When dealing with the keyboard, you need to remember that the browser intercepts all keyboard input first. This means that the applet needs to have focus, which usually requires that the user click the applet first. It also means that keyboard shortcuts that are used by the browser never reach the applet. So a Command+D or a Ctrl+D simply adds a bookmark; it will never register in the applet.

Also, the mouse location is only updated in between handlers, so it does not update inside a *repeat* loop.

In addition, only cursors –1, 0, 1, 2, and 4 are supported. No timeout Lingo works. Also, the *on idle* handler and right mouse event handlers do not work.

TRANSITIONS

Not all transitions are supported in the Save as Java Xtra. The Lingo *puppetTransition* command does not work; only transitions in the Score do. Here is a list of supported transitions:

- Center out (horizontal, vertical, and square)
- Checkerboard
- Dissolve (bits, bits fast, boxy rectangles, boxy squares, patterns, pixels, and pixels fast)
- Edges in (horizontal, vertical, and square)
- Random (column and row)
- Venetian blinds
- Vertical blinds
- Wipe (right, left, down, and up)

A LOOK INSIDE THE PROCESS

The Save As Java Xtra actually converts the Director movie into a series of files. These files include several .class files. These are pure Java. Many of them have names such as "Sprite.class" and "Member.class," so you can get an idea of what is inside.

In addition, there is a ".djr" file. This file contains a version of the media in the movie. The file will be about the size of your original movie.

There is also a ".class" file with the same name as your movie. This contains the translated Lingo code.

The Lingo translation is done almost line for line. You can see it for yourself if you export with the "Source Java" option, rather than the "Compiled Java" option, and look at the source code generated.

Developers should be aware that Java and Lingo differ greatly in how they handle variables. In Lingo, you can use the same variable to hold a number one minute, and a string another. Java can use a variable to hold only one type of value, such as an integer.

To compensate for this difference, the engineers have created the "LVal" variable type. This Java variable type holds a structure that can contain any type of value, such as an integer, string, or even a list.

The disadvantage of the "LVal" structure is that it is slow. After all, it has to take into account a lot of different types of values and be prepared to handle any type at any time. You can create variables that are specifically typed to use only integers and that therefore work much faster.

The way to make a variable a real integer is to "declare" the variable with something simple like "x = 0." Then, set it to only integers throughout the handler or movie.

This is not as simple as it sounds. If you write a piece of code like "x = myFunction( )", the Save As Java Xtra must assume that the function can return a non-integer value, and it will make "x" an LVal type. However, if you use "x = integer(myFunction())", it can assume that "x" will receive an integer value.

The only benefit to using this type of technique is a little speed. But speed is more important than ever in Java applets, because Java is not a very fast environment. If you want to make arcade-style games, you need to optimize wherever you can.

Using the Xtra

Although the Save As Java function is an Xtra, and appears in the Xtras folder, you do not access it from the Xtras menu. Instead, you choose File, Save As Java.

The first thing you are presented with is the Save As Java dialog box. Figure 37.1 shows this dialog box, which has only a few options.

Figure 37.1
The Save As Java dialog box enables you to choose a few options, but most are hidden behind the Options button.

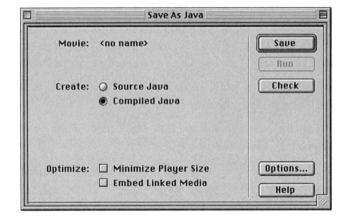

You can choose to export Java source code or a compiled Java applet. If you are a Java programmer, or are just curious, you can export the source code to see your translated Lingo.

However, you will not find the Java code that will perform the amazing tasks that Director does, like manage sprites and so on. That part of the applet is already compiled and unavailable to the developer.

If you choose Minimize Player Size, any parts of Director's Java player that are not used by the movie are automatically removed. With this option selected, the Save As Java function takes a little more time to work, but the file size of the resulting applet is much smaller. You should always choose this option when you generate your final applet.

The "Embed Linked Media" takes any external cast members and brings them into the ".djr" file.

Before making an applet, you should always press the Options button. This button brings up the dialog box shown in Figure 37.2.

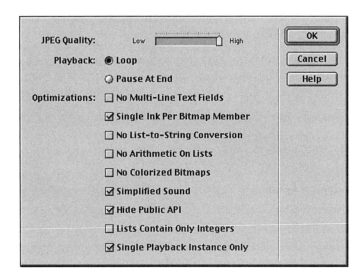

Figure 37.2
In the Save As Java options dialog box, you can make a lot of decisions about what will be supported in the applet.

The first option is the JPEG quality. Because most bitmap members will be converted to JPEGs, you should leave it at its highest setting to get bitmaps that look like your movie's bitmaps. However, you can try it at a lower setting to see how much it reduces the file size.

The Playback options are Loop or Pause At End. These options are self-explanatory.

Next is the No Multi-Line Text Fields option. If you select this, all fields will contain only one line. However, you will see a speed improvement from it.

Most of the remaining options are also for speed improvements, if you are willing to sacrifice features. Many features are rarely used by developers, such as No List-to-String Conversion, No Arithmetic On Lists and No Colorized Bitmaps. If you are not using a feature, check it off.

The Lists Contain Only Integers option gives you a speed boost for list handling. However, all you can have is linear lists with integers. If you can program around that, check that option off.

When you finish selecting your options, click OK to return to the main dialog box. Use Check first to check your Cast, Score, and Lingo for anything that is not supported. You will be presented with a list of unsupported items, if you have any. You need to go back and make changes and implement workarounds before you proceed.

If the check turns up nothing, click Save to make the Java Applet. After it has been compiled, you can click Run to try it out in your browser.

LEARNING JAVA BUILDING TECHNIQUES

In addition to your usual methods of working with Director to create movies, you should learn some unusual techniques before making a Java applet. First, you should familiarize yourself with the special set of Java behaviors in the library.

For more advanced users, you might want to learn how to make movies that can be used both as Shockwave applets and Java applets. When you do this, you can embed Lingo code segments that the Save As Java Xtra ignores.

Also, Java programmers want to know how they can embed lines of real Java code inside their Lingo handlers.

JAVA BEHAVIORS

Although experienced Lingo programmers might shy away from using the canned behaviors that come with Director, you should seriously consider looking at the Java-oriented behaviors in the library.

The library behaviors provide a simple way to get some complex functionality in your movie without having to worry about what Java can and cannot do. These behaviors are written with all the workarounds in mind, and you can simply drag and drop them onto sprites and frames.

Each behavior has a description that you can see in the Behavior Inspector. You can also drag the behaviors to the Cast and then open them in the Script Editor to see how Macromedia wrote the code to work around some of the restrictions.

In addition to behaviors, two movie scripts are included. The first is a handler that converts a string to a list. This is handy because simply using *value* does not convert a string to a list as it does in Director normally.

Two handlers also enable you to simulate the *play* and *play done* commands in Java applets.

HIDING LINGO FROM JAVA

If you are building an applet in Java, you may want to also use it as a Shockwave movie. After all, the Shockwave movie will be faster and more reliable.

To create a Shockwave movie, you simply have to save the movie as a Shockwave file and you are all set. However, you want to add extra features at times in the Shockwave version. These would be features that do not work in Java, or are faster versions of workarounds that you have created for Java.

For this reason, there is a way to hide Lingo from the Save As Java Xtra. You can simply use the comment line, "--Lingo begin" to start such a section, and "--Lingo end" to end it. Here is an example:

```
list = [1,3,2,5,12,6,3,7,3,7,3]
--Lingo begin
sort(list)
--Lingo end
```

In this case, the *sort* command is hidden from the Java Xtra. If it were not, the Save As Java process would have been stopped by an error message because the *sort* command is not supported. In this example, the list is sorted for the Shockwave applet as a "bonus" for users, whereas it is unsorted for the Java applet.

EMBEDDED JAVA CODE

You can also embed real Java code into your movie. This code is ignored by Director because it appears as comment lines. However, it is recognized and used by the Save As Java Xtra. The raw code is placed in the Java source at the exact location where the "comments" appear.

Of course, embedding is for Lingo/Java experts only. The code needs to be between "--Java begin" and "--Java end" lines, and every line should be commented out with a double-dash. Search the Macromedia site for a technote or technotes with examples.

FINISHING A JAVA APPLET

Like a Shockwave movie, the product isn't finished until it is up on a Web site. A few more steps are involved in getting the applet up, including bundling the applet, making sure it's compatible with all possible media, and troubleshooting the applet.

BUNDLING THE APPLET

When you are done, you are left with a lot of small .class files and a .djr file. There will also be a sample HTML file. You could upload all these parts to your server, but this is not the preferred delivery method.

Instead, you should bundle the files up into a compressed format. You need to use an uncompressed ZIP file for older browsers, a JAR file for Netscape 4.x, and a CAB file for Internet Explorer. All three represent the Java applet in a single-file unit.

Although creating these three different types is very time-consuming, Macromedia has made it easy for you. Just use the AfterShock program that comes with Director 7. In addition to performing a lot of other finishing tasks for Director Shockwave movies, this program also creates all three types of Java files for you. It even generates some HTML code that you can use as-is, or copy and paste into your HTML framework.

See the AfterShock documentation for more information, or just try it out. The program is very intuitive.

COMPATIBILITY ISSUES

The Save As Java Xtra outputs pure Java. It should work in anything that supports Java 1.02, which means you can run your Director content even on UNIX-based or Java machines.

In browsers, Director-created Java applets work on both Netscape Navigator and Microsoft Internet Explorer versions 3.0 and above. It also works on both Mac and Windows versions of these browsers.

However, as with Shockwave, it is best to test as much as possible. This is especially true if you plan to have your applets running on anything but standard browsers.

PROBLEMS AND MORE INFORMATION

It is highly recommended that you carefully read Macromedia's documentation about the Save As Java Xtra. Not only will you find more information there, but you might learn about updates.

Because this functionality is added via an Xtra, it is possible that Macromedia might continue to develop it even before another major release of Director. Check the Macromedia site every once in a while to see whether there has been an update.

Creating Java applets with Director is a delicate and sometimes frustrating task. You should be prepared for much longer development times than you would normally face for creating a Shockwave movie.

TROUBLESHOOTING JAVA APPLETS

- Several of the Java behaviors that came with Director 7 have a bug in them. When you try to drag and drop them, you get an error message because they do not use the proper syntax for *member*. The bugs are easy to correct if you know some Lingo, or you can check the Macromedia site for an update.

- Even if the Save As Java Xtra does not detect any problems, the Java compiler might. In those cases, you may have to do some detective work to find out which line of your Lingo code or which member is causing the problem.

- I do not recommend that you use Java in cases where software needs to be 100% error free. Java is still a young language and the many different versions make it tough to produce an applet that works 100% of the time. Short animations and presentations are much more likely to work as opposed to Lingo-intensive movies.

- Some versions of Internet Explorer do not properly run Java Applets unless they have been put on the server and are tested from there, as opposed to being tested from your local hard drive. This is unlike Shockwave movies, which can be locally tested in all browsers.

THE LINGO REFERENCE GUIDE APPENDIXES

WHAT'S NEW IN DIRECTOR 7

Developers talked and Macromedia listened. Director 7 contains a wide array of new features, generated mostly from user feedback.

In addition to features, Director 7 runs with a completely new engine. The Director 6 engine reportedly still had code dating back to the early days of Macromind. After its release, the engineers built Shockwave 6.0.1, which used a new, faster, more compact engine than Shockwave 6.0. This engine was then improved and refined to be used in Director 7 and Shockwave 7.

You will see performance increases in just about every aspect of the program. In addition, the new features list adds incredible power. The following sections include a summary of those new features.

THE SCORE

- The Score now can have up to 1,000 sprite channels. Set the number of sprite channels in the Movie Properties dialog box.
- A new interface is at the top of the Score window. It includes fields for items such as the sprite span, and new features such as rotation and flipping.

THE STAGE

- The Stage is now a movable window in the authoring environment.
- The Stage can be set to any width, not just multiples of 16.

THE CAST

- Each cast member's thumbnail can now be customized.

SPRITES

- You can rotate, skew, and flip sprites.
- Sprites can appear in front of or behind others regardless of their sprite channels, with the use of the *locZ* Lingo property.
- The four corners of a sprite can be set independently with the *quad* property. This enables you to perform odd stretches or simulate a 3D perspective.

PROJECTORS

- You can now build small Projectors that rely on users having the Shockwave plug-in installed. The Projector can automatically download Shockwave if it is not already installed on the user's machines.
- Only Windows 95 (and above) and PowerMac Projectors can be built. Director 7 does not support Windows 3.1 or Mac 68K machines.

SHOCKWAVE AND NETWORK COMMUNICATION

- New and updated components of Shockwave install automatically on the user's machine.
- Xtras certified by Macromedia can be downloaded and installed automatically if the movie needs them.
- There is a new *postNetText* command for submitting information to Internet servers.
- There is now support for HTTPS communication.
- An XML Xtra for parsing XML information is now included.
- Director 7 also includes a multiuser server and an Xtra that enables Projectors or applets to communicate with a server or peer to peer.

VECTOR SHAPES

- A new vector shape member was introduced with Director 7. It can be a line or a closed shape. It can be anti-aliased. It can be filled solid, or with a gradient. It can be totally built and controlled with Lingo.
- Flash 3 movies are now supported as cast members.

BITMAPS

- 32-bit bitmaps can now have alpha channel information that makes them semitransparent.
- JPEG and GIF images are now supported as cast members. If edited in Director, they are converted to normal bitmaps.
- Animated GIFs are also supported and you can control the playback with Lingo.
- You can grab a screen shot of the Stage with the *(the Stage).picture* property.
- You can crop a bitmap with the *crop* command.
- Director 7 includes support for PNG files.

TEXT

- Text members are now editable during playback.
- HTML, including tables, can be imported as text members.
- Hyperlinks can be set in text members that trigger Lingo events.
- A new font member was introduced with Director 7. Fonts can be imported as members and used in text members. The text can then be displayed in this font without the users needing to have the font installed on their own machines.
- Text members and fields can now hold a virtually unlimited amount of text.
- Fields in movies that are saved as Java can now use multiple lines of text.
- You can now use Lingo to detect missing fonts.

COLOR

- Movies now support 32-bit RGB color in Lingo, rather than just 8-bit palette index color.
- The new Lingo types *color*, *rgb*, and *paletteIndex* enable you to use real color or palette colors almost interchangeably.
- The Web palette is included as a built-in palette.

SOUND

- You can now access the *loop* property with Lingo and change it.
- Shockwave audio files can now be imported and used in Projectors.
- There is better Windows sound mixing with the help of QuickTime 3.
- The new Beatnik Xtra plays back MIDI and custom music formats.
- Bias Peak LE is now the sound application included with Director 7 for Macintosh.

LINGO

- The dot syntax replaces the old scripting style of "the" and "of."
- The *set* command is no longer needed. Just use "=."
- Scripts can be automatically colorized.
- The Script window can now hold a virtually unlimited amount of text.
- Finally, the *mouseLoc* property!

OTHER NEW FEATURES

- The *systemDate* property and the new date structure enable you to program around differences in international date formats. You can even add and subtract days from a date structure.
- The new library palette enables you place Casts in the libs folder and easily access common behaviors or media. Director 7 comes with a large behavior library already installed.
- Director 7 supports frame rates up to 999fps.
- Director now has a Preview in Browser menu item with which you can quickly check out a movie in your browser with Shockwave.

DIRECTOR GLOSSARY

ActiveX: ActiveX controls are files that extend the operating system or a program, such as Internet Explorer, somehow. Shockwave is available as an ActiveX control for Microsoft Internet Explorer for Windows. The ActiveX Xtra enables Projectors to use other controls.

AIFF: The Audio Interchange File Format is the most common sound format used on Macs. It is also used in the digital music recording industry. You will see these files on both Mac and Windows machines, usually represented with an .aif extension.

Alpha Channel: An extra channel of information in an image file. (The other channels are usually red, green, and blue color amounts.) This channel determines how transparent each pixel is.

Animated GIF: A file using Graphic Image Format that contains more than one frame of animation.

Anti-Aliasing: A technique that takes the edges of a text graphic and blends them with the background colors to make a smooth edge.

ASCII: American Standard Code for Information Interchange is the number system that corresponds to the 255 characters. In Director, it is used in the *charToNum* and *numToChar* functions.

AVI: See *Video for Windows*

Behavior: A script member that controls a sprite or a frame. You can have only one behavior attached to a frame, but multiple behaviors can be attached to a sprite. You can create one with the Behavior Inspector or by writing raw Lingo, or use one from the Library palette.

Bit Depth: The number of bits used to represent a single unit in a file. In an 8-bit image, for instance, each pixel is represented by eight bits of information. In a 16-bit sound, each sound sample is represented by 16 bits of information. Higher bit depth usually means higher quality.

Bitmap: An image cast member. You can edit most bitmaps in Director by using the Paint window.

BMP: Windows format for plain bitmap files.

Boolean: Math involving only two states: true and false. Used in programming to determine branching, as in *if* statements.

Buttons: This can refer to the quick, simple buttons made in Director with the Tool palette. It is also a term used to describe any bitmap or other member that is assigned a script that reacts to a mouse click.

Cache: When a browser loads a document or a media element, it places it in a folder called the cache. When users want that document again sometime very soon, they can get it from the cache rather than load it again from the Internet. This is much faster. The same principle is applied to computer memory contents when you are using virtual memory on your machine.

Cast: The list of cast members used in a movie. All movies have at least one internal Cast, but movies can have many other internal Casts and external Casts. An external Cast is its own file, usually with a ".cst" extension.

Cell: Sometimes used to refer to the intersection of a frame and a sprite channel.

Channel: A numbered position in the Score. The Score has channels one through 1,000, as well as a few special channels at the top of the Score. Which channel a sprite is in determines whether it gets drawn on top of or under another sprite.

Child: An instance of a parent script, stored in a variable or list. Created with the *new* command.

Chunk: A piece of a string, such as a character or series of characters, word or series of words, line or series of lines.

Codec: A piece of hardware or a software algorithm that converts sound or video to digital code and then back again. You compress audio and video files with codecs.

Color Depth: The amount of information stored per pixel in an image or on the screen. With 8-bit color depth, for example, eight bits (256 possible values) are stored per pixel.

Cue Point: A marker in a sound or digital video file. These markers can be read and reacted to with Lingo.

Digital Video: An external file that is linked to the Director movie. It can display video or a time-based animation such as a 3D rendering. Video members can come in a variety of formats but are usually in Apple QuickTime format or Windows AVI format. The definition can be extended to hold a variety of QuickTime formats such as QuickTime VR and MIDI files.

Dithering: The process whereby pixels in an image are colored with available colors to simulate a color that is not available. For instance, two pixels next to each other might be colored two shades of red to produce the visual effect of the shade of red exactly between the two colors.

Event: Something that affects the computer or Director environment. Examples are a mouse click, a frame advance, a key press, or a window movement. Messages are sent to parts of the Director environment when an event occurs. Handlers can be written to respond to these messages.

Fields: The original text member from before Director 5. It still has a few properties that text members do not, such as borders and drop shadows.

Film Loop: A cast member that contains a complete animation. Any Score selection can be copied and pasted into the Cast as a Film Loop and used as a single cast member.

Flash: A program and the files it creates. Flash is another Macromedia tool that enables you to create mostly vector-based animation for the Web. Flash files can be imported and used as Director members.

Font: The description of how a set of characters appear on the screen. In Director 7, fonts can be imported so that they can be used in the movie even if the font does not exist on the user's computer.

FPS: Frames per second, such as in the tempo of movement through a Director movie.

Frame: An instant of time in Director. Also, a column in the Score. While you are working on a movie, the Stage shows a single frame. While the movie is animating, the Stage moves through frames to create the visual effect of animation.

Frame Script: A script that controls a frame. It appears in the script channel. Only one script can be attached to a frame. In the Cast, frame scripts are shown as behaviors.

GIF: Graphics Interchange Format is an image format that stores 8-bit images with a custom palette.

Global Variable: A variable that can be accessed by any script in Director, as long as it is mentioned in a global command in that script.

Handler: A Lingo function or procedure. Sometimes incorrectly referred to as a "script," which is actually a collection of handlers.

HTML: Hypertext Markup Language is the language used to compose Web pages. It consists of plain text with special tags that are interpreted by Web browsers and other programs. The tags style and position the text, and add elements such as links, images, and other media.

Ink: The rules by which a sprite is drawn on the Stage. Copy ink places the sprite on the Stage as an opaque rectangle. Background Transparent ink treats white pixels as transparent. You can also choose from dozens of other inks.

Inspectors: Small, palette-like Windows in Director that enable to you see and change information about selected items. An example is the Sprite Inspector.

JPEG: The Joint Photographic Experts Group format for images. It takes 32-bit images and compresses them a variable amount, depending on the decisions you make concerning file size versus quality.

Kerning: Modifications made to the spacing of characters in a text member.

Keyframe: A frame in a sprite that denotes a specific position and other properties of the frame that the Stage must show exactly when that frame is reached. Between keyframes, the position and state of a sprite is tweened. See also *Tweening*.

Kiosk: A single computer set up in a public place running a multimedia program.

Label: A label is a name given to a frame in the Score. Frames in the Score can be labeled and referred to by that label. Also called *markers*.

Lingo: The programming language of Director.

Local Variable: A variable available only inside the handler. When the handler is done, the variable ceases to exist, although variables with exactly the same name can be used in other handlers.

Marker: A marker is a name given to a frame in the Score. Frames in the Score can be labeled and referred to by that marker. Also called *labels*.

Member: A single element such as a bitmap, some text, a sound, a shape, a vector drawing, or a piece of digital video.

MIAW: Movie in a Window. A Director movie that exists in a window other than the Stage.

MIDI: Musical Instrument Digital Interface. The means by which computers communicate with keyboards and other instruments. MIDI files contain musical compositions that can be played back with a MIDI device such as a Windows sound card or QuickTime.

Movie: The primary Director file; contains one or more cast libraries and a Score. It is the only Director file you need for most productions.

Movie Script: A script that controls the entire movie. You can have as many movie scripts as you want. They do not appear in the Score.

MPEG: A digital video format (Motion Picture Experts Group) that uses a lot of compression, but still retains high quality.

OOP: Object-Oriented Programming is a method of programming that assigns code to objects, such as sprites or data.

Palette: A list of colors that can be used by an image or by the whole screen to display graphics using only those colors.

Parent Script: A script member that is not used directly, but is instead used to create a script instance or instances. It is used for object-oriented programming.

PICS: A single file that contains multiple images. It can be imported into a variety of programs. It can also be imported into Director as a film loop and series of members. Available on the Mac only.

PICT: The standard image file for Macs.

Pixel: The smallest possible dot on a computer screen. The screen is actually made up of rows and columns of pixels.

Plug-In: A plug-in is an extension to Netscape Navigator that is used to add new media types to the browser. Shockwave for Director is a plug-in that adds to browsers the capability to display Director movies.

PNG: The Portable Network Graphics format is an up-and-coming format that newer browsers support. It is the native format of Macromedia Fireworks.

Projector: A stand-alone application program created from a Director movie.

PART
X

CH
B

QuickTime: The standard video format for Macs and also used by about 50% of all Windows machines. Currently version 3.02.

RAM: Read-Only Memory is usually just referred to as "memory" in the computer.

Registration Point: The location in a bitmap image or other member that is used to position the sprite on the Stage. When the sprite is set to an x, y location, it is the registration point of the image that appears at that exact location.

RTF: Rich Text Format is a old standard format for transferring styled text between word-processing programs. It consists of plain text, with special tags that are interpreted as styles and media elements.

Sample Frequency: In a sound file, the measurement describes how often a sound sample was taken of the original file to build the data that exists in the current file.

Score: A chart showing which members appear on the Stage at what times.

Script: Used to describe a Lingo cast member. Sometimes used to describe a single handler.

Shapes: Director has a few special cast member types called shapes. You can draw lines, ovals, rectangles, and rounded rectangles. All but lines can appear either filled or as outlines. You use these shapes to add quick graphic elements to your movies without having to create bitmaps for them.

Shockwave: Technology that enables Director movies to play back inside Web browsers. "Shockwave" usually means "Shockwave for Director," whereas "Flash" usually means "Shockwave Flash."

Shockwave Audio: A sound file format that can be used by Director to stream sound over the Internet.

Sounds: Director can import many different types of sound formats, but does not really have the capability to create or edit sounds. Sounds can be quick, simple buzzes and beeps, or long music pieces.

Sprite: The description of what member is shown, where it is in the Score, where it appears on the Stage, and many other properties.

Stage: The main Director screen where all the action takes place.

Streaming: The process by which a movie or other media is played for the users while the file is gradually loaded in from a network or the Internet.

String: A variable that contains alphanumeric characters.

Tempo: The speed at which the movie plays. Usually measured in frames per second.

Text Member: A text member contains formatted characters. You can create them in Director with the text-editing window, or you can import files created in word-processing programs. Director has the capability to display very graphically pleasing anti-aliased text. In anti-aliased text, the edges of characters are smooth rather than jagged. Director 7 also has the capability to enable you to create text members that use fonts that don't need to be on the user's machine to display properly.

Thumbnail: A small image that represents the cast member in the cast window.

TIFF: Tagged Image File Format. An older image file format.

Toolbar: The strip of buttons that appears at the top of the Director screen.

Transition: A method of changing the screen, such as a dissolve or wipe.

Tweening: The process whereby you tell Director to place a sprite in a certain location and with certain properties in one frame, and then in a new location and new properties in another (keyframes). Then, Director animates the sprite between the two positions and the property sets in the frames in between. See also *Keyframes*.

URL: Uniform Resource Locator. This is the address of an item on the Internet.

Variables: Storage areas for values. See also *Global variable*, *Local variable*.

Vector Shapes: Vector shape members are similar to the media created with programs such as Macromedia Freehand and Adobe Illustrator. A vector member is one long line that can be bent and curved. A closed loop in a vector member can be filled. Vector members can be scaled to any size and still maintain their shape and clarity.

Video For Windows: The video format built into Windows. Sometimes called AVI files. Available in Windows only.

WAV: A Windows sound format.

XML: Extensible Markup Language. Similar to HTML, but rather than using pre-defined tags like "<P>", it enables you to define your own tags and what they mean. An Xtra that comes with Director 7 enables you to parse such documents.

Xtras: Extensions to Director, developed by Macromedia and by third parties, that add or enhance functionality. Some Xtras enable you to have new types of cast members such as cursor cast members or 3D graphics.

APPENDIX

ONLINE RESOURCES

The Director world is constantly changing. New Xtras are released constantly. Developers discover new techniques and share them with the rest of the community. New updates of Director and Shockwave produce new features.

To keep up to date, developers should be checking Internet sources of Director information frequently.

Here is a list of the 10 best places to find and share information about Director. There are actually more than 100 sites, but because most of these sites have links to others, you are only a few clicks away from all of them.

DIRECTOR WEB

`http://www.mcli.dist.maricopa.edu/director/`

This is an intense, yet well-organized and often-updated site put together by Alan Levine at Maricopa Center for Learning and Instruction. It is sometimes referred to as "the Maricopa site." This resource is completely independent of Macromedia and has different information and technical notes than Macromedia's site. It includes tips and tricks, lists of known bugs, links to other resources on the Web, and a huge list of Shockwave sites.

MACROMEDIA

`http://www.macromedia.com`

This is the official site. Here you will find technical notes, the latest updates, and an excellent list of Xtras. The Director information is mostly at `http://www.macromedia.com/software/director/`.

The most important part of the site for developers is the TechNotes. They are currently located in the support section of the Director product pages. They include some valuable information on how to perform difficult tasks in Director. Just make sure that the TechNote you read is for Director 7, not an earlier version. This is also where to go to get upgrades, the latest Shockwave plug-ins, and some cool free Xtras.

CLEVERMEDIA

`http://clevermedia.com/resources/`

Okay. So I am a little biased with this one. At least I restrained myself from placing it as number one. My site includes all sorts of Director, Lingo, and Shockwave information. It also includes the Director Community Resource (DCR), which is a message board where developers can ask or answer questions and exchange ideas. You can also find a huge collection of Shockwave games at `http://clevermedia.com/arcade/`.

DIRECTOR ONLINE USERS GROUP (DOUG)

`http://www.director-online.com/`

This is a newer site, having been launched in late 1997. However, it has grown quickly. It is possibly the best source for the latest news about Director and Director-related products. It also has a lot of interviews and articles written by developers.

UPDATESTAGE

`http://www.updatestage.com`

The main feature here is a monthly column by Gretchen Macdowell. Each issue features four or five useful tips. You can search the database, too. A lot of developer interaction goes on here, with contributions by other people often appearing in the column. She has a bug-base with workarounds that rivals Macromedia's tech support area. She also has a list of Director quirks and some Xtras and Director-related products.

DIRECT-L

`DIRECT-L@UAFSYSB.UARK.EDU`

This is a mailing list with more than 2,000 subscribers. To subscribe, send email to the above address with "SUBSCRIBE DIRECT-L YOUR_NAME" in the body of the message. Be sure to check out its Web site at `http://www.mcli.dist.maricopa.edu/director/direct-l/manners.html` first. Mailing lists are a great way to stay in touch with the Director community around the world. However, it can be a bit overwhelming, because 2,000 people can generate a lot of email over the course of a day.

To search the archives of this mail list, go to `http://www.mcli.dist.maricopa.edu/director/digest/`. If you are an advanced user, you may want to remember that this list is full of novices, and you might find yourself answering questions, not asking them (which is not all bad—it is a great way to land consulting gigs).

PART

X

CH

C

BEHAVIORS.COM

`http://www.behaviors.com/`

Terry Schussler, of gmatter fame, maintains this site, which is a repository for behaviors and some Xtras. It even includes some Dreamweaver extensions.

DIRECTOREGON

`http://www.moshplant.com/direct-or/`

Darrel Plant, author of a few books on Director and Flash, runs this site. He is also the Technical Editor of the Macromedia User Journal. He likes to play around a lot with new features in Director, and has posted many features, such as his EPS-to-vector-shape converter tool. You can also search the Direct-OR list, an Oregon-based developer mailing list.

GROMMETT.COM

`http://www.grommett.com/`

This is another site run by a Director book author, Kirk Keller. It has some useful tips and techniques, as well as articles on multimedia production. It also includes some useful tools.

YAHOO CLUBS: MACROMEDIA DIRECTOR

`http://clubs.yahoo.com/clubs/macromediadirector`

This site just started up while this book was being written. The Yahoo Club interface accommodates an extended message board system and chat room.

APPENDIX

TABLES AND CHARTS

ASCII Character Chart

These are the numbers used by *charToNum* and *numToChar* functions. Some characters, especially those above 127, vary from font to font and platform to platform.

3	Enter	53	5	84	T		
8	Delete	54	6	85	U		
9	Tab	55	7	86	V		
10	Line Feed	56	8	87	W		
13	Return	57	9	88	X		
27	Clear	58	:	89	Y		
28	Left Arrow	59	;	90	Z		
29	Right Arrow	60	<	91	[		
30	Up Arrow	61	=	92	\		
31	Down Arrow	62	>	93	]		
32	[space]	63	?	94	^		
33	!	64	@	95	_		
34	"	65	A	96	`		
35	#	66	B	97	a		
36	$	67	C	98	b		
37	%	68	D	99	c		
38	&	69	E	100	d		
39	'	70	F	101	e		
40	(	71	G	102	f		
41	)	72	H	103	g		
42	*	73	I	104	h		
43	+	74	J	105	i		
44	,	75	K	106	j		
45	-	76	L	107	k		
46	.	77	M	108	l		
47	/	78	N	109	m		
48	0	79	O	110	n		
49	1	80	P	111	o		
50	2	81	Q	112	p		
51	3	82	R	113	q		
52	4	83	S	114	r		

115	s	148	"	181	µ		
116	t	149	•	182	¶		
117	u	150	–	183	·		
118	v	151	—	184	¸		
119	w	152	˜	185	¹		
120	x	153	™	186	º		
121	y	154	π	187	»		
122	z	155	›	188	¼		
123	{	156	œ	189	½		
124	|	157	∫	190	¾		
125	}	158	Ω	191	¿		
126	~	159	Ÿ	192	À		
127	DEL	160	á	193	Á		
128	≠	161	¡	194	Â		
129	∞	162	¢	195	Ã		
130	‚	163	£	196	Ä		
131	f	164	¤	197	Å		
132	„	165	¥	198	Æ		
133	…	166	¦	199	Ç		
134	†	167	§	200	È		
135	‡	168	¨	201	É		
136	ˆ	169	©	202	Ê		
137	‰	170	ª	203	Ë		
138	ˇ	171	«	204	Ì		
139	‹	172	¬	205	Í		
140	Œ	173	–	206	Î		
141	≤	174	®	207	Ï		
142	≥	175	¯	208	Đ		
143	Σ	176	°	209	Ñ		
144	Π	177	±	210	Ò		
145	`	178	²	211	Ó		
146	'	179	³	212	Ô		
147	"	180	´	213	Õ		

PART

X

Ch

D

continues

continued

214	Ö	228	ä	242	ò
215	×	229	å	243	ó
216	Ø	230	æ	244	ô
217	Ù	231	ç	245	õ
218	Ú	232	è	246	ö
219	Û	233	é	247	÷
220	Ü	234	ê	248	ø
221	Ý	235	ë	249	ù
222	Þ	236	ì	250	ú
223	ß	237	í	251	û
224	à	238	î	252	ü
225	á	239	ï	253	ý
226	â	240	ð	254	þ
227	ã	241	ñ	255	ÿ

MEMBER TYPES

These are the possible values returned by the *type* property of a member.

#animgif	#flash	#shape
#bitmap	#font	#sound
#button	#movie	#swa
#cursor	#ole	#text
#digitalVideo	#palette	#transition
#empty	#picture	#vectorShape
#field	#QuickTimeMedia	
#filmLoop	#script	

TRANSITIONS

The following list shows each transition with its Lingo number, which can be used in *puppetTransition* commands.

1	Wipe right
2	Wipe left
3	Wipe down

4	Wipe up
5	Center out, horizontal
6	Edges in, horizontal
7	Center out, vertical
8	Edges in, vertical
9	Center out, square
10	Edges in, square
11	Push left
12	Push right
13	Push down
14	Push up
15	Reveal up
16	Reveal up, right
17	Reveal right
18	Reveal down, right
19	Reveal down
20	Reveal down, left
21	Reveal left
22	Reveal up, left
23	Dissolve, pixels fast*
24	Dissolve, boxy rectangles
25	Dissolve, boxy squares
26	Dissolve, patterns
27	Random rows
28	Random columns
29	Cover down
30	Cover down, left
31	Cover down, right
32	Cover left
33	Cover right
34	Cover up
35	Cover up, left
36	Cover up, right

PART

X

CH

D

continues

continued

37	Venetian blinds
38	Checkerboard
39	Strips on bottom, build left
40	Strips on bottom, build right
41	Strips on left, build down
42	Strips on left, build up
43	Strips on right, build down
44	Strips on right, build up
45	Strips on top, build left
46	Strips on top, build right
47	Zoom open
48	Zoom close
49	Vertical blinds
50	Dissolve, bits fast*
51	Dissolve, pixels*
52	Dissolve, bits*

Note

Transitions marked with an asterisk (*) do not work on monitors set to 32 bits.

INKS

The following table includes the Lingo number for each ink, which you can use to set a sprite's ink property.

Lingo Ink Number	Ink Name	Description
0	Copy	Displays the cast member as is. The rectangular bounding box of the image appears as white.
1	Transparent	Makes all the colors in a sprite transparent.
2	Reverse	Reverses all color in the sprite; sets white pixels to transparent.
3	Ghost	Changes black to white and white to transparent. Works best on 1-bit cast members.
4	Not Copy	A reverse effect is applied to all colors in the sprite, and then the Copy ink is applied.
5	Not Transparent	A reverse effect is applied to all colors in the sprite, and then the Transparent ink is applied.

Lingo Ink Number	Ink Name	Description
6	Not Reverse	A reverse effect is applied to all colors in the sprite, and then the Reverse ink is applied.
7	Not Ghost	A reverse effect is applied to all colors in the sprite, and then the Ghost ink is applied.
8	Matte	Sets the white pixels within a bounding box of a sprite to transparent.
9	Mask	Uses the next cast member in the cast window to block or unblock background colors. Rules for a Mask are as follows: must be the same size as the masked cast member, next cast member position in the cast window, and must be 1 bit.
32	Blend	Applies a blend to the sprite. The amount used in the blend is set in Sprite Properties from the Modify menu.
33	Add Pin	The same as Add with the exception that if the color value exceeds the maximum visible color, the maximum color is used.
34	Add	Creates a new color. The values of the background and foreground colors are added to one another. The sprite displays the combined values. If the color value exceeds the maximum visible color, the color wraps around the color scale.
35	Subtract Pin	The same as Subtract with the exception that if the color value is less than the minimum visible color, the minimum color is used.
36	Background Transparent	Sets all the white pixels within an image to transparent
37	Lightest	Compares pixels in the foreground and background colors. The Lightest ink effect displays only the lightest pixel found in the background and foreground colors.
38	Subtract	The opposite of Add with the exception that the minimum values are used. If the new value is less than the minimum visible color, the color wraps around the color scale from the top.
39	Darkest	Compares pixels of the foreground and background colors. The Darkest ink effect displays only the darkest pixel found in the background and foreground colors.
40	Lighten	The background color changes the brightness of the sprite: Lighter colors make the sprite darker. The foreground color is applied to the sprite as if you were shining a light of that color on it.
41	Darken	Uses the background color like a color filter. The foreground color is applied to the sprite as if you were shining a light of that color on it.

PART
X
CH
D

COMMON COLORS

Director enables you to set colors using the *rgb* object and a string with a hexadecimal value. Because it is not easy to remember the code for "maroon" (800000), it is handy to have a name-to-color chart. The names used here are the official color names for Netscape Navigator colors.

Color	RGB Hexadecimal Code
aliceblue	F0F8FF
antiquewhite	FAEBD7
aqua	00FFFF
aquamarine	7FFFD4
azure	F0FFFF
beige	F5F5DC
bisque	FFE4C4
black	000000
blanchedalmond	FFEBCD
blue	0000FF
blueviolet	8A2BE2
brown	A52A2A
burlywood	DEB887
cadetblue	5F9EA0
chartreuse	7FFF00
chocolate	D2691E
coral	FF7F50
cornflowerblue	6495ED
cornsilk	FFF8DC
crimson	DC143C
cyan	00FFFF
darkblue	00008B
darkcyan	008B8B
darkgoldenrod	B8860B
darkgray	A9A9A9
darkgreen	006400
darkkhaki	BDB76B
darkmagenta	8B008B

Color	RGB Hexadecimal Code
darkolivegreen	556B2F
darkorange	FF8C00
darkorchid	9932CC
darkred	8B0000
darksalmon	E9967A
darkseagreen	8FBC8F
darkslateblue	483D8B
darkslategray	2F4F4F
darkturquoise	00CED1
darkviolet	9400D3
deeppink	FF1493
deepskyblue	00BFFF
dimgray	696969
dodgerblue	1E90FF
firebrick	B22222
floralwhite	FFFAF0
forestgreen	228B22
fuchsia	FF00FF
gainsboro	DCDCDC
ghostwhite	F8F8FF
gold	FFD700
goldenrod	DAA520
gray	808080
green	008000
greenyellow	ADFF2F
honeydew	F0FFF0
hotpink	FF69B4
indianred	CD5C5C
indigo	4B0082
ivory	FFFFF0
khaki	F0E68C
lavender	E6E6FA

PART

X

CH

D

continues

continued

Color	RGB Hexadecimal Code
lavenderblush	FFF0F5
lawngreen	7CFC00
lemonchiffon	FFFACD
lightblue	ADD8E6
lightcoral	F08080
lightcyan	E0FFFF
lightgoldenrodyellow	FAFAD2
lightgreen	90EE90
lightgrey	D3D3D3
lightpink	FFB6C1
lightsalmon	FFA07A
lightseagreen	20B2AA
lightskyblue	87CEFA
lightslategray	778899
lightsteelblue	B0C4DE
lightyellow	FFFFE0
lime	00FF00
limegreen	32CD32
linen	FAF0E6
magenta	FF00FF
maroon	800000
mediumaquamarine	66CDAA
mediumblue	0000CD
mediumorchid	BA55D3
mediumpurple	9370DB
mediumseagreen	3CB371
mediumslateblue	7B68EE
mediumspringgreen	00FA9A
mediumturquoise	48D1CC
mediumvioletred	C71585
midnightblue	191970
mintcream	F5FFFA

Color	RGB Hexadecimal Code
mistyrose	FFE4E1
moccasin	FFE4B5
navajowhite	FFDEAD
navy	000080
oldlace	FDF5E6
olive	808000
olivedrab	6B8E23
orange	FFA500
orangered	FF4500
orchid	DA70D6
palegoldenrod	EEE8AA
palegreen	98FB98
paleturquoise	AFEEEE
palevioletred	DB7093
papayawhip	FFEFD5
peachpuff	FFDAB9
peru	CD853F
pink	FFC0CB
plum	DDA0DD
powderblue	B0E0E6
purple	800080
red	FF0000
rosybrown	BC8F8F
royalblue	4169E1
saddlebrown	8B4513
salmon	FA8072
sandybrown	F4A460
seagreen	2E8B57
seashell	FFF5EE
sienna	A0522D
silver	C0C0C0
skyblue	87CEEB

PART

X

CH

D

continues

continued

Color	RGB Hexadecimal Code
slateblue	6A5ACD
slategray	708090
snow	FFFAFA
springgreen	00FF7F
steelblue	4682B4
tan	D2B48C
teal	008080
thistle	D8BFD8
tomato	FF6347
turquoise	40E0D0
violet	EE82EE
wheat	F5DEB3
white	FFFFFF
whitesmoke	F5F5F5
yellow	FFFF00
yellowgreen	9ACD32

SHOCKWAVE AUDIO STATES

These numbers are returned from the *state* property of a Shockwave audio member.

0	Cast streaming has stopped.
1	The cast member is reloading.
2	Preloading ended successfully.
3	The cast member is playing.
4	The cast member is paused.
5	The cast member has finished streaming.
9	An error occurred.
10	There is insufficient CPU space.

FLASH MEMBER STATES

These values are returned by Flash members while the movie is running.

0	The cast member is not in memory.
1	The header is currently loading.
2	The header has finished loading.
3	The cast member's media is currently loading.
4	The cast member's media has finished loading.
-1	An error occurred.

MOVIE IN A WINDOW (MIAW) TYPES

The following two tables describe the MIAW types for both Windows and Mac.

MIAW TYPES FOR WINDOWS

Type Number	Description Minimize	Movable	Close	Box	Maximize
-1	Default	Yes	Yes	No	No
0	Standard	Yes	Yes	No	No
1	Alert Box	No	No	No	No
2	Rectangle	No	No	No	No
3	Rectangle	No	No	No	No
4	Document	Yes	Yes	No	No
5	Document	Yes	Yes	No	No
8	Document	Yes	Yes	Yes	No
12	Document	Yes	Yes	Yes	No
16	Document	Yes	Yes	No	No
49	Palette (Not in Projectors)	Yes	Yes	No	No

PART

X

CH

D

MIAW TYPES FOR MAC

Type Number Box	Description Resize Box	Movable	Close	Box	Stretch
-1	Default	Yes	Yes	Yes	No
0	Standard	Yes	Yes	Yes	No
1	Alert Box	No	No	No	No
2	Rectangle	No	No	No	No
3	Rectangle with Drop Shadow	No	No	No	No
4	Document	Yes	Yes	No	No
5	Document	Yes	No	No	No
8	Document	Yes	Yes	Yes	Yes
12	Document	Yes	Yes	No	Yes
16	Curved Border Box	Yes	Yes	No	No
49	Palette (Not in Projectors)	Yes	Yes	No	No

APPENDIX

LINGO BY SUBJECT

In addition to having an alphabetical listing of all Lingo keywords, it is useful to have a list of keywords arranged by subject. This can come in handy when you can't remember the name of a certain command or property. It can also be a good way to familiarize yourself with a set of keywords for a part of Lingo that you may not have used before. This appendix provides just that list.

ANIMATED GIF

directToStage

fixedRate

linked

pause

playBackMode

resume sprite

rewind sprite

BEHAVIORS

beginSprite

endSprite

enterFrame

exitFrame

getBehaviorDescription

getBehaviorTooltip

getPropertyDescriptionList

idle

me

mouseDown

mouseEnter

mouseLeave

mouseUp

mouseUpOutSide

mouseWithin

prepareFrame

property

rightMouseDown

rightMouseUp

runPropertyDialog

scriptInstanceList

scriptList

sendAllSprites

sendSprite

spriteNum

stopEvent

BITMAP

alphaThreshold

centerRegPoint

crop

depth

dither

getPixel

palette

paletteRef

picture

regPoint

setPixel

useAlpha

BUTTONS

buttonType

checkBoxAccess

checkBoxType

font

fontSize

PART

X

APP

E

fontStyle

hilite

text

CASTS

castLib

castLibs

erase

fileName

findEmpty

name

new

number

save castLib

selection

CURSORS

autoMask

castMemberList

cursor

cursorSize

hotSpot

interval

DATE AND TIME

abbr, abbrev, abbreviated

date

day

hour

milliSeconds

minutes

month

startTimer

systemDate

ticks

timer

DEBUGGING TOOLS

alertHook

trace

traceLoad

traceLogFile

DIGITAL VIDEO

center

controller

crop

cuePointNames

cuePointTimes

currentTime

digitalVideoTimeScale

digitalVideoType

directToStage

duration

frameRate

invertMask

isVRMovie

loop

loopBounds

mask

mostRecentCuePoint

movieRate

movieTime

pausedAtStart

preLoad

preloadRam

qtRegisterAccessKey

qtUnRegisterAccessKey

quickTimeVersion

scale

setTrackEnabled

sound

startTime

stopTime

timeScale

trackCount

trackEnabled

trackNextKeyTime

trackNextSampleTime

trackPreviousKeyTime

trackPreviousSampleTime

trackStartTime

trackStopTime

trackText

trackType

translation

video

videoForWindowsPresent

volume

FIELDS

alignment

autoTab

backcolor

bgColor

border

boxDropShadow

boxType

charPosToLoc

color

dropShadow

editable

field

font

fontSize

fontStyle

forecolor

hilite

lineCount

lineHeight

linePosToLocV

locToCharPos

locVToLinePos

margin

mouseChar

mouseItem

mouseLine

mouseWord

pageHeight

scrollByLine

scrollByPage

scrollTop

selection

selEnd

selStart

text

textAlign

textFont

textHeight

textSize

textStyle

wordWrap

FILES

getNthFileNameInFolder

FLASH MEMBERS

ActionsEnabled

antiAlias

broadcastProps

buttonsEnabled

centerRegPoint

clearError

clickMode

defaultRect

defaultRectMode

directToStage

findLabel

fixedRate

flashRect

flashToStage

frame

frameCount

frameRate

frameReady

getError

goToFrame

hitTest

hold

imageEnabled

linked

loop

mouseOverButton

obeyScoreRotation

originH

originMode

originPoint

originV

pausedAtStart

percentStreamed

playBackMode

playing

posterFrame

preLoad

quality

regPoint

rewind sprite

scale

scaleMode

showProps

sound

PART

X

APP

E

stageToFlash

state

static

stop

stream

streamMode

streamSize

viewH

viewPoint

viewScale

viewV

KEYBOARD

commandDown

controlDown

key

keyCode

keyDown

keyDownScript

keyPressed

keyUp

keyUpScript

optionDown

shiftDown

LINKED MOVIES

scriptsEnabled

sound

LISTS

[]

add

addAt

addProp

append

count

deleteAll

deleteAt

deleteOne

deleteProp

duplicate

findPos

findPosNear

getaProp

getAt

getLast

getOne

getPos

getProp

getPropAt

list

listP

setaProp

setAt

setProp

sort

LOGIC

()

<

<=

<>

=

>

>=

and

FALSE

not

objectP

or

TRUE

MATH

*

+

-

/

abs

atan

bitAnd

bitNot

bitOr

bitXor

cos

exp

float

floatP

floatPrecision

inflate

inside

integer

integerP

intersect

log

map

mapMemberToStage

mapStageToMember

max

maxInteger

min

mod

offset

PI

power

random

randomSeed

sin

sqrt

tan

union

MEMBER

castLibNum

copyToClipBoard

duplicate

fileName

height

importFileInto

media

member

modified

move

name

new

number

pasteClipBoardInto

purgePriority

rect

size

thumbnail

type

width

MEMORY

cancelIdleLoad

finishIdleLoad

idleLoadDone

idleLoadMode

idleLoadPeriod

idleLoadTag

idleReadChunkSize

loaded

mediaReady

preLoad

preLoadEventAbort

preLoadMember

preLoadMode

preLoadMovie

ramNeeded

unLoad

unloadMember

unloadMovie

MENU

checkMark

enabled

installMenu

menuItem

name

script

MOVIES IN A WINDOW (MIAW)

activateWindow

activeWindow

close

closeWindow

deactivateWindow

drawRect

fileName

forget

frontWindow

modal

moveToBack

moveToFront

moveWindow

name

number

open

openWindow

picture

rect

resizeWindow

sourceRect

tell

title

titleVisible

visible

window

windowList

windowPresent

windowType

zoomWindow

MISCELLANEOUS

alert

beep

beepOn

bottom

color

colorType

count

framesToHMS

HMStoFrames

left

mci

number

open

paletteIndex

picture

pictureP

point

printFrom

put

recordFont

rect

rgb

right

top

value

zoomBox

MOUSE

clickLoc

clickOn

mouseLoc

mouseH

mouseV

mouseDown

mouseUp

stillDown

MOVIE

centerStage

fixStageSize

frame

frameLabel

framePalette

frameScript

frameSound1

PART

X

APP

E

frameSound2

frameTempo

frameTransition

label

labelList

lastChannel

lastFrame

marker

mouseDownScript

mouseUpScript

movieAboutInfo

movieCopyrightInfo

movieFileFreeSize

movieFileSize

movieName

moviePath

paletteMapping

prepareMovie

puppetPalette

puppetTempo

puppetTransition

savedLocal

saveMovie

score

showGlobals

showLocals

stage

stageBottom

stageColor

stageLeft

stageRight

stageTop

startMovie

stopMovie

updateMovieEnabled

updateStage

NAVIGATION

continue

delay

exitLock

go

go loop

go next

go previous

halt

play

play done

NETWORK

browserName

clearCache

downloadNetThing

getNetErrorString

getNetText

getStreamStatus

gotoNetMovie

gotoNetPage

mediaReady

netAbort

netDone

netError

netLastModDate

netMIME

netPresent

netTextResult

netThrottleTicks

postNetText

proxyServer

streamStatus

tellStreamStatus

OOP

actor

actorList

ancestor

birth

call

callAncestor

me

new

property

stepFrame

PLAYBACK

allowCustomCaching

allowGraphicMenu

allowSaveLocal

allowTransportControl

allowVolumeControl

allowZooming

PROGRAMMING

abort

case

do

dontPassEvent

end

exit

exit repeat

global

if

ilk

next repeat

nothing

on

otherwise

param

paramCount

pass

repeat

result

return

set

to

VOID

voidP

QTVR

enableHotSpot

fieldOfView

getHotSpotRect

hotSpotEnterCallback

hotSpotExitCallback

motionQuality

mouseLevel

node

nodeEnterCallback

nodeExitCallback

nodeType

pan

ptToHotSpot

staticQuality

swing

tilt

triggerCallback

warpMode

SCORE RECORDING

activeCastLib

beginRecording

clearFrame

deleteFrame

duplicateFrame

endRecording

frameLabel

framePalette

frameScript

frameSound1

frameSound2

frameTempo

frameTransition

insertFrame

scoreColor

scoreSelection

scriptNum

tweened

type

updateFrame

updateLock

SCRIPTS

scriptText

scriptType

SHAPE

filled

lineDirection

lineSize

pattern

shapeType

SHOCKWAVE

EvalScript

externalEvent

externalParamCount

externalParamName

externalParamValue

frameReady

getPref

gotoNetMovie

gotoNetPage

netStatus

preLoadNetThing

safePlayer

setPref

SHOCKWAVE AUDIO
bitRate

bitsPerSample

copyrightInfo

duration

getError

getErrorString

numChannels

pause member

percentPlayed

percentStreamed

play member

preLoadBuffer

preLoadTime

sampleRate

sampleSize

soundChannel

state

stop member

streamName

url

volume

SOUND
channelCount

cuePassed

cuePointNames

cuePointTimes

currentTime

isPastCuePoint

loop

mostRecentCuePoint

puppetSound

sound fadeIn

sound fadeOut

sound playFile

sound stop

soundBusy

soundDevice

soundDeviceList

soundEnabled

soundKeepDevice

soundLevel

volume

SPRITES

backcolor

bgColor

blend

blendLevel

bottom

castLibNum

color

constrainH

constraint

constrainV

cursor

editable

endFrame

flipH

flipV

forecolor

ink

height

member

intersects

left

loc

locH

locV

locZ

mapMemberToStage

mapStageToMember

memberNum

moveableSprite

puppet

puppetSprite

quad

rect

right

rotation

skew

sprite

spriteBox

startFrame

top

trails

useFastQuads

visible

width

within

STRINGS

&

&&

..

after

BACKSPACE

before

char

chars

charToNum

contains

count

delete

EMPTY

ENTER

item

itemDelimiter

last

length

line

number

numToChar

offset

paragraph

put after

put before

put into

QUOTE

ref

RETURN

SPACE

starts

string

stringP

TAB

value

word

SYMBOLS

#

symbol

symbolP

SYSTEM

applicationPath

buttonStyle

clearGlobals

colorDepth

colorQD

cpuHogTicks

currentSpriteNum

date

deskTopRectList

doubleClick

emulateMultiButtonMouse

environment

freeBlock

freeBytes

globals

idle

idleHandlerPeriod

lastClick

lastEvent

lastKey

lastRoll

machineType

memorySize

mouseCast

mouseDown

mouseH

mouseLoc

mouseMember

mouseUp

mouseV

multiSound

organizationName

platform

productName

productVersion

quit

restart

rollOver

romanLingo

runMode

searchCurrentFolder

searchPaths

PART

X

APP

E

serialNumber

shutDown

stillDown

switchColorDepth

time

userName

version

TEXT

alignment

antiAlias

autoTab

backcolor

bgColor

bottomSpacing

boxType

charPosToLoc

color

editable

firstIndent

fixedLineSpace

font

fontSize

fontStyle

forecolor

HTML

hyperlink

hyperlinkClicked

hyperlinkRange

hyperlinks

hyperlinkState

kerning

kerningThreshold

leftIndent

linePosToLocV

locToCharPos

locVToLinePos

missingFonts

pageHeight

pointInHyperLink

pointToChar

pointToItem

pointToLine

pointToParagraph

pointToWord

rightIndent

scrollByLine

scrollByPage

scrollTop

selectedText

selection

setContents

setContentsAfter

setContentsBefore

tabCount

tabs

text

useHyperTextStyles

TIMEOUTS

timeout

timeoutKeydown

timeoutLapsed

timeoutLength

timeoutMouse

timeoutPlay

timeoutScript

TRANSITIONS

changeArea

chunkSize

duration

transitionType

VECTOR SHAPES

addVertex

antiAlias

bgColor

broadcastProps

centerRegPoint

closed

color

defaultRect

defaultRectMode

deleteVertex

directToStage

endColor

fillColor

fillCycles

fillDirection

fillMode

fillOffset

fillScale

flashRect

gradientType

hitTest

imageEnabled

moveVertex

moveVertexHandle

originH

originMode

originPoint

originV

regPoint

scale

scaleMode

showProps

stageToFlash

strokeColor

strokeWidth

vertex

vertexList

viewH

viewPoint

viewScale

viewV

XTRAS

closeXLib

interface

movieXtraList

name

new

number

openXLib

showResFile

showXLib

xtra

xtraList

Behavior Library Quick Reference

Director 7 comes with a large collection of behaviors available through the Library Palette. Although you can browse these in Director and view ToolTip information on each one, you might find this printed quick reference guide to them more handy to use.

ANIMATION, AUTOMATIC

Color Cycling: Changes the foreground color of a sprite from one value to another once, many times, or forever.

Cycle Graphics: Cycles through a series of consecutive cast members.

Fade In/Out: Uses a blend to fade a sprite in or out once, many times, or forever.

Random Movement and Rotation: Moves and spins a sprite in a defined area.

Rotate Continuously (frame-based): Rotates a sprite through a certain number of degrees per frame.

Rotate Continuously (time-based): Rotates a sprite at a constant rate, regardless of the tempo.

Rotate to Follow Path: The sprite always faces a certain angle relative to its initial location on the Stage.

Rotation (frame-based): Rotates a sprite a specific number of degrees with speed determined by the tempo.

Rotation (time-based): Rotates a sprite a specific number of degrees over a period of time.

Scale and Clip: Scales a Flash or vector shape sprite from one size to another. Clipping occurs if one of the sizes is greater than 100%.

Slide In/Out: Moves a sprite from one position on the screen to another.

Sway: Rotates a sprite between two angles.

Waft: Uses a random movement to make a sprite zigzag and rise from the bottom of the screen.

Zoom In/Out: Scales the sprite up to the Score size, or down to nothing.

ANIMATION, INTERACTIVE

Avoid Mouse: The sprite moves away from the cursor.

Avoid Sprite: The sprite moves away from another sprite.

Collision Detection: Detects when the sprite collides with another. Sends a "Collision_Newsflash" message when it does.

Constrain to Line: Enables the user to drag the sprite along a line. Useful for sliders.

Constrain to Sprite: Enables the user to drag a sprite around the Stage, but constrained to the rectangle of another sprite.

Drag and Toss: Enables the user to move the sprite around the Stage, and will maintain some momentum when the mouse button is released.

Drag Quad Points: Enables the user to grab a corner of a sprite and drag it.

Drag to Rotate: Enables the user to rotate a sprite around its registration point.

Drag to Scale: Enables the user to grab the sprite and drag it to scale it.

Drag to Stretch and Flip: Enables the user to stretch and flip a sprite by clicking and dragging.

Draggable: Enables the user to reposition the sprite by clicking and dragging.

Move, Rotate, and Scale: Enables the user to click and drag the sprite. If a modifier key is pressed, the sprite scales. Another modifier key enables the user to rotate the sprite.

Multiple Sprite Drag: Enables the user to grab a sprite and drag it, and other sprites will follow.

Rollover Cursor Change: The cursor changes when the mouse is over the sprite.

Rollover Member Change: Changes the sprite's member when the mouse is over the sprite.

Snap to Grid: Enables you to define an invisible grid for the sprite that makes it align itself with the nearest grid point when the grid is active.

Sprite Track Mouse: Moves a sprite so that it is under the cursor.

Turn to Fixed Point: The sprite turns to face a point on the Stage.

Turn Towards Mouse: The sprite turns so that it always faces the cursor location.

Turn Towards Sprite: The sprite turns so that it always faces the location of another sprite, even while that sprite is moving.

Vector Motion: The sprite moves in a straight line.

CONTROLS

Analog Clock: Turns a vector shape into a clock hand.

Display Text: Used by the "ToolTip" or "hypertext—Display Status" behaviors to show a text field.

Draw Connector: Takes a line member and enables the user to draw with it.

Dropdown List: Creates a pop-up menu from a field member.

Jump Back Button: Takes the user back through frames, reversing the "Jump to Marker Button," "Jump to Movie Button," or "Jump Forward Button" behaviors.

Jump Forward Button: Enables the user to go "forward" frames after using "Jump Back Button" to go back.

Jump to Marker Button: Takes the user to another frame. "Jump Back Button" enables the user to go back.

Jump to Movie Button: Takes the user to another movie. "Jump Back Button" enables the user to go back.

Multi-State Button: Creates a graphic check box button.

Push Button: Standard button behavior.

Radio Button Group: Enables you to group graphic radio buttons.

Tooltip: Displays a ToolTip when the user rolls over the sprite.

INTERNET, FORMS

Form Post—Dropdown List: Used to create a pop-up menu to create data to be sent using *postNetText*.

Form Post—Field: Used to enable the user to type data to be send using *postNetText*.

Form Post—Hidden Field: Acts as a hidden text field that is to be sent using *postNetText*.

Form Post—Submit Button: The submit button that works with the posting interface behaviors described previously.

INTERNET, MULTIUSER

Connect To Server: Begins a client/server multiuser session.

Disconnect From Server: Ends a client/server multiuser session.

Chat Input: Used on a field to type chat messages.

Chat Output: Used on a field to display the chat text.

Display Group Member Names: Displays the member in a group from a server connection.

INTERNET, STREAMING

Loop Until Next Frame Is Available: Waits on a frame until the media for the next frame is ready.

Loop Until Member Is Available: Waits on the frame until a specific member is ready.

Loop Until Media in Frame Is Available: Waits on the frame until the specified frame is ready.

PART

X

APP

F

Loop Until Media in Marker Is Available: Waits on the frame for a range of frames to be ready.

Jump When Member Is Available: Jumps to a point in the Score when a specific member is ready.

Jump When Media in Frame Is Available: Jumps to a specific frame when the media in a frame is ready.

Jump When Media in Marker Is Available: Jumps to a specific frame when the media in a range of frames is ready.

Progress Bar for Streaming Movies: Uses the sprite as a progress bar that shows the streaming percentage.

Progress Bar for URL Linked Media: Uses the sprite as a progress bar that shows the streaming percentage.

Show Placeholder: Places a vector in place of a member until the media is available.

MEDIA, FLASH

Set Click Modes: Sets how the Flash sprite responds to clicks.

Set Playback Quality: Enables you to set the quality at which Flash sprites are displayed.

Set Scale, Origin and View: Enables you to set these properties before the sprite appears.

MEDIA, QUICKTIME

QuickTime Control Button: Can turn a sprite into a play, pause, rewind, fast forward, fast rewind, or jump button.

QuickTime Control Slider: Enables the sprite with the "Constrain To Line" behavior to control the position of the QuickTime video.

MEDIA, SOUND

Play Sound File: Plays an external sound file.

Play Sound Member: Starts an internal sound.

Sound Beep: A mouse click produces a system beep.

NAVIGATION

Go Loop: Loops the movie from the current frame to the most recent marker.

Go Next Button: Jumps to the next marker.

Go Previous Button: Jumps the movie to the marker before the current one.

Go to Frame X Button: Jumps to a specific frame.

Go to URL: Uses *gotoNetPage* to jump to a new location in a Web browser.

Hold on Current Frame: Simple looping frame script.

Loop for X Seconds: Loops on a frame for a specific amount of time.

Play Done: Issues a *play done* command.

Play Frame X: Issues a simple *play* command.

Play Movie X: Issues a *play movie* command.

TEXT

Add Commas to Numbers: Automatically inserts commas into large numbers.

Calendar: Creates a calendar in a Text member.

Countdown Timer: Displays numbers, counting backward.

Custom Scrollbar: Can be used on four graphic members to build a custom text scrollbar.

Filter Input Characters: Enables you to limit the characters that a user can input in an editable text or field member.

Force Case: Forces the text typed into editable field and text members to upper or lower case.

Format Numbers: Enables you to display the numbers in a field or text member in a variety of formats.

Get Net Text: Retrieves text from a location on the Internet.

Hypertext—Display Status: Displays the link in a text member when the user rolls over a hyperlink.

Hypertext—General: Enables you to perform a variety of tasks when the user clicks on a hyperlink.

Hypertext—Go to Marker: Jumps to a marker according to the hyperlink data.

Password Entry: Enables the user to type in a field, but the field displays only bullet characters.

Tickertape Text: Scrolls text in a field or text member horizontally.

Typewriter Effect: Slowly types text in a field or text member.

KEYBOARD SHORTCUTS

Director has a very intuitive interface. If you have never used a function before, and are not sure where to find it, just look at the menu names and think about their meanings. You can make a very educated guess.

However, if you use Director eight hours a day, you want to learn all the tricks. There are a ton of shortcuts, and few users know them all. These lists will help you find the items that will help you in your common tasks.

MACINTOSH SHORTCUTS

FILE MENU SHORTCUTS

Command	Shortcut
New Movie	Command+N
New Cast	Command+Option+N
Open	Command+O
Close	Command+W
Save	Command+S
Import	Command+R
Export	Command+Shift+R
Page Setup	Command+Shift+P
Print	Command+P
General Preferences	Command+U
Exit/Quit	Command+Q

EDIT MENU SHORTCUTS

Command	Shortcut
Undo	Command+Z
Repeat	Command+Y
Cut	Command+X
Copy	Command+C
Paste	Command+V
Clear	Delete
Duplicate	Command+D
Select All	Command+A
Find Text	Command+F

Command	Shortcut
Find Handler	Command+Shift+;
Find Cast Member	Command+;
Find Selection	Command+H
Find Again	Command+Option+F
Replace Again	Command+Option+E
Edit Sprite Frames	Command+Option+]
Edit Entire Sprite	Command+Option+]
Exchange Cast Members	Command+E
Launch External Editor	Command+, (comma)

PART

X

APP

G

VIEW MENU SHORTCUTS

Command	Shortcut
Next Marker	Command+right arrow
Previous Marker	Command+left arrow
Zoom In	Command++
Zoom Out	Command+-(hyphen)
Show Grid	Command+Shift+Option+G
Snap to Grid	Command+Option+G
Show Rulers	Command+Shift+Option+R
Show Info	Command+Shift+Option+O
Show Paths	Command+Shift+Option+H
Show Toolbars (Score, Paint window, Cast window, Text window, Vector Shape window)	Command+Shift+H
Keyframes	Command+Shift+Option+K

INSERT MENU SHORTCUTS

Command	Shortcut
Insert Keyframe	Command+Option+K
Insert Frame	Command+]
Remove Frame	Command+[
Insert Frames dialog box	Command+Shift+]

MODIFY MENU SHORTCUTS

Command	Shortcut
Cast Member Properties	Command+I
Xtra Cast Member Options Properties	Command+Shift+O
Cast Member Script	Command+' (apostrophe)
Sprite Properties	Command+Shift+I
Sprite Script	Command+Shift+' (apostrophe)
Movie Properties	Command+Shift+D
Movie Casts	Command+Shift+C
Font	Command+Shift+T
Text style bold	Command+Option+B
Text style italic	Command+Option+I
Text style underline	Command+Option+U
Paragraph	Command+Shift+Option+T
Tweening	Command+Shift+B
Join sprite	Command+J
Split sprite	Command+Shift+J
Extend sprite	Command+B
Bring to Front	Command+Shift+up arrow
Move Forward	Command+up arrow
Move Backward	Command+down arrow
Send to Back	Command+Shift+down arrow
Align	Command+K
Tweak	Command+Shift+K

CONTROL MENU SHORTCUTS

Command	Shortcut
Play	Command+Option+P
Stop	Command+. (period)
Rewind	Command+Option+R
Step Backward	Command+Option+left arrow
Step Forward	Command+Option+right arrow
Loop Playback	Command+Option+L

Command	Shortcut
Volume: Mute	Command+Option+M
Toggle Breakpoint	Command+Shift+Option+K
Watch Expression	Command+Shift+Option+W
Ignore Breakpoints	Command+Shift+Option+I
Step Script	Command+Shift+Option+down arrow
Step Into Script	Command+Shift+Option+right arrow
Run Script	Command+Shift+Option+up arrow
Recompile All Scripts	Command+Shift+Option+C

PART

X

APP

G

WINDOW MENU SHORTCUTS

Command	Shortcut
Toolbar	Command+Shift+Option+B
Tool Palette	Command+7
Behavior Inspector	Command+Option+;
Sprite Inspector	Command+Option+S
Text Inspector	Command+T
Stage	Command+1
Control Panel	Command+2
Markers	Command+Shift+M
Score	Command+4
Cast	Command+3
Paint	Command+5
Vector Shape	Command+Shift+V
Text	Command+6
Field	Command+8
Color Palettes	Command+Option+7
Video	Command+9
Script	Command+0
Message	Command+M
Debugger	Command+' (apostrophe)
Watcher	Command+Shift+' (apostrophe)

STAGE SHORTCUTS

Action	Shortcut
Open cast member editor	Double-click sprite
Inks pop-up	Command+click
Toggle record light on and off	Option+click
Real-time record	Control+Spacebar+drag sprite on the Stage
Display shortcut menu for selection	Control+click
Change contents of stage to black	Keypad - (minus)

SCORE WINDOW SHORTCUTS

Action	Shortcut
Duplicate selected sprites or keyframes	Option+drag
Open cast editor for selected sprite	Double-click cast thumbnail
Select entire range of a cast member	Double-click cell with a sprite in it
Select channel	Double-click channel number
Select multiple channels	Double-click channel number and drag up or down
Toggle record light	Option+click the channel number
Move playback head to end of movie	Tab
Move playback head to frame 1	Shift+Tab
Move playback head to beg/end	Command+Shift+left/right arrow
Open frame settings dialog box	Double-click the tempo, palette, or transition channel
Go to next marker comment (or jump 10 frames)	Command+right arrow
Previous marker comment (or back 10 frames)	Command+left arrow
Shuffle backward/forward	Command+up arrow/down arrow

CAST WINDOW AND CAST EDITOR WINDOW SHORTCUTS

Action	Shortcut
Open cast member editor	Double-click member, or select it and press Return
Cast member script	Command+' (apostrophe)
Open script in new window	Option+Script button
Place selected cast member in center of the Stage	Command+Shift+L

Action	Shortcut
Find selected cast member in the Score	Command+H
Cast to Time	Command+Shift+Option+L
New cast member*	Command+Shift+A
Previous cast member*	Command+left arrow
Next cast member*	Command+right arrow
* same function, in a new window	Command+Option+left/right arrow
Scroll up/down one window	Page Up/Page Down
Scroll to top left of cast window	Home
Scroll to show last occupied cast member	End
Type-select by cast member	Type a number

PAINT WINDOW SHORTCUTS

Action	Shortcut
Undo	~ (tilde)
Next/previous cast member	Keypad left/right arrow keys
Turn selected tool into foreground eyedropper	D, while mouse is pressed
Turn selected tool into background eyedropper	Shift+D
Turn selected tool into destination eyedropper	Option+D
Turn selected tool into hand tool	Spacebar, while mouse is pressed
Nudge selection rectangle or lasso selection	Keypad arrows with rectangle or lasso selected
Change airbrush size	Keypad up/down arrows with airbrush selected
Change airbrush flow (while painting)	Keypad left/right arrows with airbrush selected
Change foreground color (not painting)	Keypad up/down arrows, all tools
Change background color (not painting)	Shift+keypad up/down arrows, all tools
Change destination color (not painting)	Option+keypad up/down arrows, all tools
Draw border with current pattern	Option+shape or line tools
Select background color	Shift+eyedropper
Select destination color	Option+eyedropper

continues

PART X
APP G

continued

Action	Shortcut
Toggle between custom and grayscale patterns	Option+click pattern
Polygon lasso	Option+lasso
Duplicate selection	Option+drag
Stretch	Command+drag
Draw with background color	Option+pencil tool
Open Gradient Settings dialog box rectangle, and set ink to gradient	Double-click paintbrush, paint bucket, or polygon tool
Open Air Brush Settings dialog box	Double-click airbrush
Clear visible part of window	Double-click eraser
Open color palettes window	Double-click foreground, background, or destination color chip
Open Pattern Settings dialog box	Double-click pattern chip
Open Brush Settings dialog box	Double-click paintbrush
Open Paint Window Preferences	Double-click line width selector
Open Transform Bitmap dialog box	Double-click color resolution indicator
Toggle Zoom in/Zoom out	Control+click in window or double-click pencil tool

VECTOR SHAPE WINDOW SHORTCUTS

Action	Shortcut
Circle	O
Filled Circle	Shift+O
Rounded rectangle	P
Filled rounded rectangle	Shift+R
Pen	6
Arrow	0
Hand tool	H
Registration tool	G
Scale with arrow tool	Option+Command+drag
Move bezier handles independently with arrow tool	Command+drag
Drag control handles from square points	Option+drag
Constrain movement to 45° increments	Shift+drag

Action	Shortcut
Add a point to an open curve with the pen	Option+click
Create symmetrical shapes (squares, circles)	Shift+drag

NUMERIC KEYPAD SHORTCUTS FOR MOVIE PLAYBACK CONTROL

Action	Shortcut
Play/Stop	Enter
Play/Stop and show only the Stage	Shift+Enter
Rewind	0
Back one frame	1
Forward one frame	3
Previous marker	4
Center playback head	5
Next marker	6
Mute sounds	7
Loop	8

WINDOWS SHORTCUTS

FILE MENU SHORTCUTS

Command	Shortcut
New Movie	Ctrl+N
New Cast	Ctrl+Alt+N
Open	Ctrl+O
Close	Ctrl+F4
Save	Ctrl+S
Import	Ctrl+R
Export	Ctrl+Shift+R
Preview in Browser	F12
Page Setup	Ctrl+Shift+P
Print	Ctrl+P
General Preferences	Ctrl+U
Exit/Quit	Alt+F4

EDIT MENU SHORTCUTS

Command	Shortcut
Undo	Ctrl+Z
Repeat	Ctrl+Y
Cut	Ctrl+X
Copy	Ctrl+C
Paste	Ctrl+V
Clear	Backspace
Duplicate	Ctrl+D
Select All	Ctrl+A
Find Text	Ctrl+F
Find Handler	Ctrl+Shift+;
Find Cast Member	Ctrl+;
Find Selection	Ctrl+H
Find Again	Ctrl+Alt+F
Replace Again	Ctrl+Alt+E
Edit Sprite Frames	Ctrl+Alt+]
Edit Entire Sprite	Ctrl+Alt+[
Exchange Cast Members	Ctrl+E
Launch External Editor	Ctrl+, (comma)

VIEW MENU SHORTCUTS

Command	Shortcut
Next Marker	Ctrl+right arrow
Previous Marker	Ctrl+left arrow
Zoom In	Ctrl++
Zoom Out	Ctrl+-(hyphen)
Show Grid	Ctrl+Shift+Alt+G
Snap to Grid	Ctrl+Alt+G
Show Rulers	Ctrl+Shift+Alt+R
Show Info	Ctrl+Shift+Alt+O
Show Paths	Ctrl+Shift+Alt+H
Show Toolbars (Score; Paint, Cast, Text, Vector Shape windows)	Ctrl+Shift+H
Keyframes	Ctrl+Shift+Alt+K

Insert Menu Shortcuts

Command	Shortcut
Insert Keyframe	Ctrl+Alt+K
Insert Frame	Ctrl+]
Remove Frame	Ctrl+[
Insert Frames dialog box	Ctrl+Shift+]

Modify Menu Shortcuts

Command	Shortcut
Cast Member Properties	Ctrl+I
Xtra Cast Member Options Properties	Ctrl+Shift+O
Cast Member Script	Ctrl+' (apostrophe)
Sprite Properties	Ctrl+Shift+I
Sprite Script	Ctrl+Shift+' (apostrophe)
Movie Properties	Ctrl+Shift+D
Movie Casts	Ctrl+Shift+C
Font	Ctrl+Shift+T
Text style bold	Ctrl+Alt+B
Text style italic	Ctrl+Alt+I
Text style underline	Ctrl+Alt+U
Paragraph	Ctrl+Shift+Alt+T
Tweening	Ctrl+Shift+B
Join sprite	Ctrl+J
Split sprite	Ctrl+Shift+J
Extend sprite	Ctrl+B
Bring to Front	Ctrl+Shift+up arrow
Move Forward	Ctrl+up arrow
Move Backward	Ctrl+Alt+down arrow
Send to Back	Ctrl+Alt+Shift+down arrow
Align	Ctrl+K
Tweak	Ctrl+Shift+K

PART

X

APP

G

CONTROL MENU SHORTCUTS

Command	Shortcut
Play	Ctrl+Alt+P
Stop	Ctrl+. (period)
Rewind	Ctrl+Alt+R
Step Backward	Ctrl+Option+left arrow
Step Forward	Ctrl+Option+right arrow
Loop Playback	Ctrl+Alt+L
Volume: Mute	Ctrl+Alt+M
Toggle Breakpoint	F9
Watch Expression	Shift+F9
Ignore Breakpoints	Alt+F9
Step Script	F10
Step Into Script	F8
Run Script	F5
Recompile All Scripts	Shift+F8

WINDOW MENU SHORTCUTS

Command	Shortcut
Toolbar	Ctrl+Shift+Alt+B
Tool Palette	Ctrl+7
Behavior Inspector	Ctrl+Alt+;
Sprite Inspector	Ctrl+Alt+S
Text Inspector	Ctrl+T
Stage	Ctrl+1
Control Panel	Ctrl+2
Markers	Ctrl+Shift+M
Score	Ctrl+4
Cast	Ctrl+3
Paint	Ctrl+5
Vector Shape	Ctrl+Shift+V
Text	Ctrl+6
Field	Ctrl+8
Color Palettes	Ctrl+Alt+7

Command	Shortcut
Video	Ctrl+9
Script	Ctrl+0
Message	Ctrl+M
Debugger	Ctrl+' (single quote)
Watcher	Ctrl+Shift+' (single quote)

STAGE SHORTCUTS

Action	Shortcut
Open cast member editor	Double-click sprite
Inks pop-up	Ctrl+click
Toggle record light on and off	Alt+click
Real-time record	Ctrl+Spacebar+drag sprite on the Stage
Display shortcut menu for selection	Right-click
Change contents of stage to black	Keypad - (minus)
Invert everything on stage	Keypad /
Show/hide cursor	Keypad =

SCORE WINDOW SHORTCUTS

Action	Shortcut
Duplicate selected sprites or keyframes	Alt+drag
Open cast editor for selected sprite	Double-click cast thumbnail
Select entire range of a cast member	Double-click cell with a sprite in it
Select channel	Double-click channel number
Select multiple channels	Double-click channel number and drag up or down
Toggle record light	Alt+click the channel number
Move playback head to end of movie	Tab
Move playback head to frame 1	Shift+Tab
Move playback head to beg/end	Ctrl+Shift+left/right arrow
Open frame settings dialog box	Double-click the tempo, palette, or transition channel
Go to next marker comment (or jump 10 frames)	Ctrl+right arrow
Previous marker comment (or back 10 frames)	Ctrl+left arrow
Shuffle backward/ forward	Ctrl+up arrow

CAST WINDOW AND CAST EDITOR WINDOW SHORTCUTS

Action	Shortcut
Open cast member editor	Double-click a paint, text, palette, or script cast member or select the cast member and press Return
Cast member script	Ctrl+' (apostrophe)
Open script in new window	Alt+Script button
Place selected cast member in center of the Stage	Ctrl+Shift+L
Find selected cast member in the Score	Ctrl+H
Cast to Time	Ctrl+Shift+Alt+L
New cast member*	Ctrl+Shift+A
Previous cast member*	Ctrl+left arrow
Next cast member*	Ctrl+right arrow
* same function, in a new window	Ctrl+Alt+left/right arrow
Scroll up/down one window	Page up, Page down
Scroll to top left of cast window	Home
Scroll to show last occupied cast member	End
Type-select by cast member	Type a number

PAINT WINDOW SHORTCUTS

Action	Shortcut
Undo	~ (tilde)
Next/previous cast member	Keypad left/right arrow keys
Turn selected tool into foreground eyedropper	D, while mouse is pressed
Turn selected tool into background eyedropper	Shift+D
Turn selected tool into destination eyedropper	Alt+D
Turn selected tool into hand tool	Spacebar, while mouse is pressed
Nudge selection rectangle or lasso selection	Keypad arrows with selection rectangle or lasso
Change airbrush size	Keypad up/down arrows with airbrush selected
Change airbrush flow (while painting)	Keypad left/right arrows with airbrush selected
Change foreground color (not painting)	Keypad up/down arrows, all tools
Change background color (not painting)	Shift+keypad up/down arrows, all tools

Action	Shortcut
Change destination color (not painting)	Alt+keypad up/down arrows, all tools
Draw border with current pattern	Alt+shape or line tools
Select background color	Shift+eyedropper
Select destination color	Alt+eyedropper
Toggle between custom and grayscale patterns	Alt+click pattern
Polygon lasso	Alt+lasso
Duplicate selection	Alt+drag
Stretch	Ctrl+drag
Draw with background color	Alt+pencil tool
Open Gradient Settings dialog box rectangle, and set ink to gradient	Double-click paintbrush, paint bucket, or polygon tool
Open Air Brush Settings dialog box	Double-click airbrush
Clear visible part of window	Double-click eraser
Open color palettes window	Double-click foreground, background, or destination color chip
Open Pattern Settings dialog box	Double-click pattern chip
Open Brush Settings dialog box	Double-click paintbrush
Open Paint Window Preferences	Double-click line width selector
Open Transform Bitmap dialog box	Double-click color resolution indicator
Toggle Zoom in/Zoom out	Ctrl+click in window or double-click pencil tool

PART

X

APP

G

Vector Shape Window Shortcuts

Action	Shortcut
Circle	O
Filled Circle	Shift+O
Rounded rectangle	P
Filled rounded rectangle	Shift+R
Pen	6
Arrow	0
Hand tool	H
Registration tool	G
Scale with arrow tool	Ctrl+Alt+drag

continues

continued

Action	Shortcut
Move bezier handles independently with arrow tool	Ctrl+drag
Drag control handles from square points	Alt+drag
Constrain movement to 45° increments (handles/points/pen/ arrow)	Shift+drag
Add a point to an open curve with the pen tool	Alt+click
Create symmetrical shapes (squares, circles)	Shift+drag

NUMERIC KEYPAD SHORTCUTS FOR MOVIE PLAYBACK CONTROL

Action	Shortcut
Play/Stop	Enter
Play/Stop and show only the Stage	Shift+Enter
Rewind	0
Back one frame	1
Forward one frame	3
Previous marker	4
Center playback head	5
Next marker	6
Mute sounds	7
Loop	8

GUIDE TO XTRAS

This appendix contains an alphabetical list of Xtras for Director 5, 6, and 7. Most of these will probably be upgraded to work with Director 7 by the time you read this. Some will not. Be sure to check with the company or on the Web to make sure the Xtra works with Director 7.

New Xtras are being created all the time. Check the Web sites listed in Appendix C, "Online Resources," for up-to-date information.

ABSOLUTE PRECISION XTRA

Description: Enables you to receive mouse events at the pixel level.

Developer: Penworks Corporation

Web Address: http://www.penworks.com

Email: sales@penworks.com

Mailing Address: P.O. Box 531, Holderness, NH, 03245-0531

Phone: 1-800-PENWORX

Fax: 1-800-PW-FAX-NUM

ACROVIEWER

Description: Print PostScript-quality PDF files using Adobe Acrobat Viewers.

Developer: XtraMedia International

Web Address: http://www.xtramedia.com/xtras.shtml

Email: productInfo@xtramedia.com

Mailing Address: 1093 East Main Street #502, El Cajon, CA, 92021-6247

ADJUSTCOLORS

Description: Performs color adjustments on graphics. Brightness, saturation, and RGB values of cast members.

Developer: Smoothware Design

Web Address: http://www.smoothware.com

Email: info@smoothware.com

Mailing Address: PO Box 0048, New York, NY, 10023

Phone: 212-595-3190

AlphaMania

Description: A sprite Xtra supporting dynamic alpha-channel compositing of graphics.

Developer: Media Lab, Inc.

Web Address: http://www.medialab.com

Email: xtra-sales@medialab.com

Phone: 800-282-5361 or 303-499-5411

Fax: 303-497-9454

Anecdote Xtra

Description: Multimedia story-boarding tool.

Developer: NEC USA, Inc.

Web Address: http://www.ccrl.neclab.com/Anecdote/

AniRez

Description: Changes monitor resolution and color depth to match the projector.

Developer: Aniware AB

Web Address: http://www.aniware.se/ANIWARE/engpages/download.html

Email: admin@aniware.se

ATI Xtra

Description: Digitizes video, shows overlaid video preview.

Developer: Dirigo Multimedia (Glenn M. Picher)

Web Address: http://www.maine.com/shops/gpicher/

Email: gpicher@maine.com

Mailing Address: 50 Market Street, Suite 1A-338, South Portland, ME, 04106

Phone: 207-767-8015

Attrib Xtra

Description: Manipulates the file attributes of single files or complete file trees.

Developer: Media Connect

Web Address: http://www.mcmm.com/download.htm

Email: ssb@mcmm.com

AUDIO XTRA

Description: Records sound, plays back, and pauses.

Developer: UpdateStage (Gretchen Macdowall)

Web Address: http://www.updatestage.com

Email: support@updatestage.com

Mailing Address: 1341 Massachusetts Ave., Box 124, Arlington, MA, 02476

Phone: 781-641-6043

Fax: 781-641-7068

AUTORUN(PC), AUTOSTART(MAC)

Description: Launches an application or an installer.

Developer: UpdateStage (Gretchen Macdowall)

Web Address: http://www.updatestage.com

Email: support@updatestage.com

Mailing Address: 1341 Massachusetts Ave., Box 124, Arlington, MA, 02476

Phone: 781-641-6043

Fax: 781-641-7068

BEHAVIOR

Description: Automates the process of creating behaviors for Director.

Developer: Ballard Davies Ltd.

Web Address: http://www.ballard.co.uk/xtras/index.html

Email: Mailbox@ballard.co.uk

Mailing Address: 4 High Street, Dorking, Surrey, RH4 1AT, UNITED KINGDOM

Phone: +44-01306-884411

Fax: +44-01306-889911

BinaryIO Xtra

Description: Reads, writes, and edits binary files. No chunk size limit.

Developer: UpdateStage (Gretchen Macdowall)

Web Address: http://www.updatestage.com

Email: support@updatestage.com

Mailing Address: 1341 Massachusetts Ave., Box 124, Arlington, MA, 02476

Phone: 781-641-6043

Fax: 781-641-7068

BitChecker

Description: Finds cast members with incorrect palettes or bit depths.

Developer: Ballard Davies Ltd.

Web Address: http://www.ballard.co.uk/xtras/index.html

Email: Mailbox@ballard.co.uk

Mailing Address: 4 High Street, Dorking, Surrey, RH4 1AT, UNITED KINGDOM

Phone: +44-01306-884411

Fax: +44-01306-889911

bkMixer

Description: Controls CD audio, WAVE and the system master volume on PC.

Developer: UpdateStage (Gretchen Macdowall)

Web Address: http://www.updatestage.com

Email: support@updatestage.com

Mailing Address: 1341 Massachusetts Ave., Box 124, Arlington, MA, 02476

Phone: 781-641-6043

Fax: 781-641-7068

BLINKER XTRA

Description: Makes things blink.

Developer: Penworks Corporation

Web Address: http://www.penworks.com

Email: sales@penworks.com

Mailing Address: P.O. Box 531, Holderness, NH, 03245-0531

Phone: 1-800-PENWORX

Fax: 1-800-PW-FAX-NUM

BLURIMAGE

Description: Enables you to apply filters such as blur, motion-blur, emboss, invert, and find-edges.

Developer: Smoothware Design

Web Address: http://www.smoothware.com

Email: info@smoothware.com

Mailing Address: P.O. Box 0048, New York, NY, 10023

Phone: 212-595-3190

BORDER XTRA

Description: Turns off the borders around the stage window or any MIAW.

Developer: Media Connect

Web Address: http://www.mcmm.com/download.htm

Email: ssb@mcmm.com

BROWSERCONTROLLER

Description: Controls Netscape or Internet Explorer.

Developer: Magister Ludi

Web Address: http://www.magisterludi.com/index.html?/xtras/

Email: info@magisterludi.com

Mailing Address: Via Natale Battaglia 8, 20127, Milan, ITALY

BtV Mediastram Xtra

Description: Enables Director to control BtV MediaStream video playback hardware extensions.

Developer: Brooktree Corporation

Phone: 619-535-3476

Buddy Zip

Description: Zips and unzips files.

Developer: Magic Modules

Web Address: http://www.mods.com.au/default.htm

Email: gary@mods.com.au

Mailing Address: P.O. Box 550, Hamilton, Queensland, AUSTRALIA 4007

Phone: 61-7-3259-4390

Fax: 61-7-3262-6749

CapsLock Xtra

Description: Returns the state of the Caps Lock key.

Developer: Scirius Development

Web Address: http://www.scirius.com/HNorm/index.html

Email: xtras@scirius.com

Mailing Address: Dresdner Stra_e 76a, D-04317 Leipzig, GERMANY

Phone: +49-341-6995741

Fax: +49-341-6995742

CastControl

Description: Controls the attachment and detachment of external cast libraries.

Developer: Paul Farry

Web Address: http://www.magna.com.au/~farryp/director/xtras/

Email: p.farry@poboxes.com

CASTEFFECTS

Description: Enables bitmap and cast manipulation from Lingo. Can transform, rotate, composite, and scale bitmaps and Casts.

Developer: Penworks Corporation

Web Address: http://www.penworks.com

Email: sales@penworks.com

Mailing Address: P.O. Box 531, Holderness, NH, 03245-0531

Phone: 1-800-PENWORX

Fax: 1-800-PW-FAX-NUM

CONVERTDATA XTRA

Description: Enables scripting to convert between integer, hexadecimal, and signature notation, and perform all the usual bitwise logic operations in Lingo.

Developer: Penworks Corporation

Web Address: http://www.penworks.com

Email: sales@penworks.com

Mailing Address: P.O. Box 531, Holderness, NH, 03245-0531

Phone: 1-800-PENWORX

Fax: 1-800-PW-FAX-NUM

CATCUBE

Description: Images can be mapped onto a cube.

Developer: CatEffects S.L.

Web Address: http://www.cateffects.com/xtras.html

Email: cesar@cateffects.com

CATFADE

Description: Smoothes out transitions.

Developer: CatEffects S.L.

Web Address: http://www.cateffects.com/xtras.html

Email: cesar@cateffects.com

CatFlip

Description: Images can be mapped into a plane that spins either horizontally or vertically.

Developer: CatEffects S.L.

Web Address: http://www.cateffects.com/xtras.html

Email: cesar@cateffects.com

CDLink

Description: Manages a Web connection over the PPP-TCP/IP protocol without requiring a browser.

Developer: Ideogram Design

Web Address: http://www.cdlink.com/

Email: developers@cdlink.com

Mailing Address: 15, traverse des Brucs, 06560 Valbonne Sophia Antipolis, FRANCE

Phone: 33-493-65-49-10

Fax: 33-493-65-47-92

CD Pro Xtra

Description: Allows some CD audio control.

Developer: Penworks Corporation

Web Address: http://www.penworks.com

Email: sales@penworks.com

Mailing Address: P.O. Box 531, Holderness, NH, 03245-0531

Phone: 1-800-PENWORX

Fax: 1-800-PW-FAX-NUM

ChartsInMotion Xtra

Description: Enables you to plot standard business charts in a window over a Director Stage.

Developer: XtraMedia International

Web Address: http://www.xtramedia.com/xtras.shtml

Email: productInfo@xtramedia.com

Mailing Address: 1093 East Main Street #502, El Cajon, CA, 92021-6247

COMPONENTS

Description: Reports system components.

Developer: UpdateStage (Gretchen Macdowall)

Web Address: http://www.updatestage.com

Email: support@updatestage.com

Mailing Address: 1341 Massachusetts Ave., Box 124, Arlington, MA, 02476

Phone: 781-641-6043

Fax: 781-641-7068

COMPOSITE XTRA

Description: Composites text and graphics and outputs a composite image. Renders text around a curve.

Developer: Pablo Media

Web Address: http://www.pablomedia.com/products/index.html

Email: info@pablomedia.com

Phone: 650-654-4300

CONVERTDATA

Description: Adds bitwise manipulation of data values to Lingo.

Developer: UpdateStage (Gretchen Macdowall)

Web Address: http://www.updatestage.com

Email: support@updatestage.com

Mailing Address: 1341 Massachusetts Ave., Box 124, Arlington, MA, 02476

Phone: 781-641-6043

Fax: 781-641-7068

COOLXTRA

Description: Allows playback of MPEG2, MPEG1, AC-3 video, and audio.

Developer: E4

Web Address: http://www.e4.com/

Email: info@e4.com

CRYPTO++ SDK

Description: Enables you to add copy to your Director creations.

Developer: Sampson Multimedia

Web Address: http://www.sampson-multimedia.com/banner/

Email: info@sampson-multimedia.com

DATAGRIP

Description: Enables Director to communicate with Microsoft Access databases.

Developer: Sight and Sound Software

Web Address: http://www.datagrip.com/

DATATON

Description: Controls external devices.

Developer: Dataton

Web Address: http://www.dataton.se/

Email: info@dataton.se

DATEMASTER

Description: Enables you to retrieve dates in a consistent format.

Developer: Penworks Corporation

Web Address: http://www.penworks.com

Email: sales@penworks.com

Mailing Address: P.O. Box 531, Holderness, NH, 03245-0531

Phone: 1-800-PENWORX

Fax: 1-800-PW-FAX-NUM

DATETIME XTRA

Description: Returns date- and time-related information.

Developer: Scirius Development

Web Address: http://www.scirius.com/HNorm/index.html

Email: xtras@scirius.com

Mailing Address: Dresdner Stra_e 76a, D-04317 Leipzig, GERMANY

Phone: +49-341-6995741

Fax: +49-341-6995742

Dave's 3D Engine

Description: Positions sprites in 3D, performs translations/rotation/scaling on them, enables you to do sprite sorting, scaling, blending, and member changing of depth cues.

Developer: Dave Cole

Web Address: `http://www.ais.org/~pmethius/3D.html`

Email: `dcole@sigmao.com`

DBXPro Database Xtra

Description: Enables you have some access to Access and ODBC databases.

Developer: MediaDynamics

Web Address: http://www.mediadyn.com/

DDE Xtra

Description: Enables Director to act as a Dynamic Data Exchange client.

Developer: Advanced Technology Center—University of Missouri-Columbia

Web Address: `http://www.atc.missouri.edu/software/`

Email: `ccjr@atc.missouri.edu`

Dervich Pivot

Description: Provides panoramic cast members.

Developer: Volume Deux

Web Address: `http://www.lasociete.com/dvp_us.htm`

Email: `la_societe@compuserve.com`

Mailing Address: 189, rue d'Aubervilliers, ZAC CAP 18 - Case 57, 75018 Paris, FRANCE

Fax: 33-01-53-26-86-19

Dialogs Xtra

Description: Displays Open, Save, and PickFolder file dialog boxes.

Developer: UpdateStage (Gretchen Macdowall)

Web Address: `http://www.updatestage.com`

Email: `support@updatestage.com`

Mailing Address: 1341 Massachusetts Ave., Box 124, Arlington, MA, 02476

Phone: 781-641-6043

Fax: 781-641-7068

DIRECTCOMM XTRA

Description: Provides direct access to communication resources such as serial ports, parallel ports, fax machines, and modems.

Developer: DirectXtras Llc.

Web Address: http://www.directxtras.com/

Email: info@directxtras.com

Mailing Address: P.O. Box 423417, San Francisco, CA, 94142-3417

Phone: 415-505-8249

Fax: 650-938-4633

DIRECTCONTROL

Description: Enables Lingo control of analog and digital joysticks.

Developer: DirectXtras Llc.

Web Address: http://www.directxtras.com/

Email: info@directxtras.com

Mailing Address: P.O. Box 423417, San Francisco, CA, 94142-3417

Phone: 415-505-8249

Fax: 650-938-4633

DIRECTEMAIL XTRA

Description: Enables you to compose and send emails, with attachments.

Developer: DirectXtras Llc.

Web Address: http://www.directxtras.com/

Email: info@directxtras.com

Mailing Address: P.O. Box 423417, San Francisco, CA, 94142-3417

Phone: 415-505-8249

Fax: 650-938-4633

DirectMedia Xtra

Description: Gives developers control over MPEG and AVI files.

Developer: Tabuleiro da Baiana

Web Address: http://www.tbaiana.com/

Email: tbaiana@tbaiana.com

Mailing Address: Rua Conego Eugenio Leite, 1092 Pinheiros, Sao Paulo - SP BRAZIL, 05414 - 012

Phone: 55-11-813-2547

Fax: 55-11-813-2549

DirectOS

Description: Provides access to the Windows operating system.

Developer: DirectXtras Llc.

Web Address: http://www.directxtras.com/

Email: info@directxtras.com

Mailing Address: P.O. Box 423417, San Francisco, CA, 94142-3417

Phone: 415-505-8249

Fax: 650-938-4633

DirectSound Xtra

Description: Enables the use of Microsoft's DirectSound API.

Developer: DirectXtras Llc.

Web Address: http://www.directxtras.com/

Email: info@directxtras.com

Mailing Address: P.O. Box 423417, San Francisco, CA, 94142-3417

Phone: 415-505-8249

Fax: 650-938-4633

DisplayRes Xtra

Description: Controls Window's display devices.

Developer: UpdateStage (Gretchen Macdowall)

Web Address: http://www.updatestage.com

Email: support@updatestage.com

Mailing Address: 1341 Massachusetts Ave., Box 124, Arlington, MA, 02476

Phone: 781-641-6043

Fax: 781-641-7068

DMFade

Description: Provides for fade transitions.

Developer: Dedalomedia Interactive

Web Address: http://www.dmtools.com/

Email: salesdm@dmtools.com

Mailing Address: B.go Padova 170, 35013 Cittadella PD, ITALY

Telephone: +39-049-941-44-11

Fax: +39-049-941-44-30

DM Transition Packs

Description: Provides a variety of transitions.

Developer: Dedalomedia Interactive

Web Address: http://www.dmtools.com/

Email: salesdm@dmtools.com

Mailing Address: B.go Padova 170, 35013 Cittadella PD, ITALY

Telephone: +39-049-941-44-11

Fax: +39-049-941-44-30

DM WAVES EFFECT

Description: Provides realistic ripples.

Developer: Dedalomedia Interactive

Web Address: `http://www.dmtools.com/`

Email: `salesdm@dmtools.com`

Mailing Address: B.go Padova 170, 35013 Cittadella PD, ITALY

Telephone: +39-049-941-44-11

Fax: +39-049-941-44-30

DM STAR FIELD EFFECT

Description: Provides animated star fields.

Developer: Dedalomedia Interactive

Web Address: `http://www.dmtools.com/`

Email: `salesdm@dmtools.com`

Mailing Address: B.go Padova 170, 35013 Cittadella PD, ITALY

Telephone: +39-049-941-44-11

Fax: +39-049-941-44-30

DrawXtra

Description: Enables you to draw lines, shapes, and curves directly to a canvas, and then save that drawing as a cast member.

Developer: Tabuleiro da Baiana

Web Address: `http://www.tbaiana.com/`

Email: `tbaiana@tbaiana.com`

Mailing Address: Rua Conego Eugenio Leite, 1092 Pinheiros, Sao Paulo - SP BRAZIL, 05414 - 012

Phone: 55-11-813-2547

Fax: 55-11-813-2549

EASYBASE

Description: Enables you to create and use a database.

Developer: Klaus Kobald Software Design

Web Address: http://members.EUnet.at/k.kobald/EasyBase/index.htm

Email: k.kobald@EUnet.at

ECD XTRA

Description: Calculates disk space remaining after audio session for enhanced CD.

Developer: Raw i 1

Web Address: http://members.tripod.com/~chief_raw_i/EECD/

EFFECTOR SETS

Description: Provides a library of behaviors.

Developer: Media Lab, Inc.

Web Address: http://www.medialab.com

Email: xtra-sales@medialab.com

Phone: 800-282-5361 or 303-499-5411

Fax: 303-497-9454

ENHANCED CD DEVELOPMENT KIT

Description: Includes two XObjects that provide cross-platform CD audio and file system control from within Director.

Developer: Macromedia

Web Address: http://www.macromedia.com/software/xtras/

ENLIVENXTRA

Description: Provides for Director-to-Java conversion.

Developer: Narrative Communications

Web Address: ww2.narrative.com/enliven20disc.nsf

Email: info@narrative.com

ESCAPE VIDEOSTUDIO

Description: Plays back high-quality full-screen full-motion video sequences.

Developer: Eidos Technologies

Web Address: http://www.eidostechnologies.com/html/escape_info.htm

Email: sales@eidos.co.uk

Mailing Address: Wimbledon Bridge House, 1 Hartfield Road, Wimbledon London, SW19 3RU, UNITED KINGDOM

Phone: +44-181-636-3000

Fax: +44-181-636-3386

FIELDSTYLES XTRA

Description: Controls text field cast members.

Developer: g/matter

Web Address: http://www.gmatter.com/

Email: support@behaviors.com

FILEFLEX

Description: Provides a cross-platform database engine.

Developer: Component Software

Web Address: http://www.fileflex.com

Email: support@fileflex.com

Mailing Address: P.O. Box 201, Rocky Hill, NJ, 08553

Phone: 609-497-4501

Fax: 609-497-4008

FILE IO

Description: Allows for the cross-platform reading and writing of files.

Developer: Macromedia

Web Address: http://www.macromedia.com/software/xtras/

FILEXTRA

Description: Provides a file enhancer.

Developer: Little Planet Publishing

Web Address: `http://www.littleplanet.com/kent/kent.html`

Email: `kent@littleplanet.com`

FOCUS3D XTRA

Description: Enables you to use QuickDraw3D images.

Developer: Focus 3

Web Address: `http://www.umminger.com/focus3/products_and_downloads.html`

Email: `hbdi@dnai.com`

Phone: 510-548-7847

FRACTALDECODER XTRA

Description: Enables Director and Shockwave to support FIF (fractal) images.

Developer: PPC Multimedia

Web Address: `http://www.ppc.mc/xtra/`

FREE ROTATE

Description: Controls the rotation of a cast member in Lingo.

Developer: Smoothware Design

Web Address: `http://www.smoothware.com`

Email: `info@smoothware.com`

Mailing Address: P.O. Box 0048, New York, NY, 10023

Phone: 212-595-3190

FREEPPP CONTROL

Description: Controls connections to the Internet.

Developer: Paul Farry

Web Address: `http://www.magna.com.au/~farryp/director/xtras/`

Email: `p.farry@poboxes.com`

F3EXPORT XTRA

Description: Exports cast members in BMP and JPEG format.

Developer: Focus 3

Web Address: `http://www.umminger.com/focus3/products_and_downloads.html`

Email: `hbdi@dnai.com`

Phone: 510-548-7847

F3SOUNDFX XTRA

Description: Provides sound recording and effects.

Developer: Focus 3

Web Address: `http://www.umminger.com/focus3/products_and_downloads.html`

Email: `hbdi@dnai.com`

Phone: 510-548-7847

F3VIDEOCAPTURE XTRA

Description: Displays live video.

Developer: Focus 3

Web Address: `http://www.umminger.com/focus3/products_and_downloads.html`

Email: `hbdi@dnai.com`

Phone: 510-548-7847

GLU32 XTRA

Description: Calls 32-bit DLLs from Lingo. Provides for direct access to system calls.

Developer: UpdateStage (Gretchen Macdowall)

Web Address: `http://www.updatestage.com`

Email: `support@updatestage.com`

Mailing Address: 1341 Massachusetts Ave., Box 124, Arlington, MA, 02476

Phone: 781-641-6043

Fax: 781-641-7068

GRABBER

Description: Takes snapshots of the screen, stage, or area of the stage. Builds a new cast member by combining existing members either down or across.

Developer: Paul Farry

Web Address: http://www.magna.com.au/~farryp/director/xtras/

Email: p.farry@poboxes.com

HTML XTRA

Description: Enables the display of HTML on the stage.

Developer: Media Connect

Web Address: http://www.mcmm.com/download.htm

Email: ssb@mcmm.com

ICONIZER

Description: Enables you to customize the Projector icon from within Director.

Developer: Penworks Corporation

Web Address: http://www.penworks.com

Email: sales@penworks.com

Mailing Address: P.O. Box 531, Holderness, NH, 03245-0531

Phone: 1-800-PENWORX

Fax: 1-800-PW-FAX-NUM

IMAGE MASTER U32

Description: Displays images in Authorware's presentation window and in separate windows; scrolls images in Authorware.

Developer: MEDIA Shoppe

Web Address: http://www.mediashoppe.com/xtras/

Phone: 806-371-0033

Fax: 806-371-0264

INDEX XTRA

Description: Provides text searches.

Developer: Media Connect

Web Address: http://www.mcmm.com/download.htm

Email: ssb@mcmm.com

INSPECT

Description: Complements the Message window and the debugger in Director.

Developer: codeHorse

Web Address: http://www.codehorse.com/navproducts.html

INSTALL XTRA

Description: Detects hardware and software configurations.

Developer: UpdateStage (Gretchen Macdowall)

Web Address: http://www.updatestage.com

Email: support@updatestage.com

Mailing Address: 1341 Massachusetts Ave., Box 124, Arlington, MA, 02476

Phone: 781-641-6043

Fax: 781-641-7068

INSTALLED FONTS XTRA

Description: Returns a list of the user's installed fonts.

Developer: UpdateStage (Gretchen Macdowall)

Web Address: http://www.updatestage.com

Email: support@updatestage.com

Mailing Address: 1341 Massachusetts Ave., Box 124, Arlington, MA, 02476

Phone: 781-641-6043

Fax: 781-641-7068

INSTANT BUTTONS & CONTROLS

Description: Provides a toolkit containing buttons and controls, including Lingo, sounds, and animation tools.

Developer: Stat Media

Web Address: http://www.statmedia.com

Email: gbirch@statmedia.com

Mailing Address: 7077 E. Shorecrest Drive, Anameim Hills, CA, 92807-4506

Phone: 714-280-0038

Fax: 714-748-0178

LiveCD

Description: Enables movies to import updated media from the Internet.

Developer: ITI

Web Address: http://livecd.iti.gov.sg/

LiveCD PUBLISHER

Description: Enables you to author a CD once and update it anytime.

Developer: New Alloy, Inc.

Web Address: http://www.newalloy.com

Email: info@newalloy.com

LiveCD XTRA

Description: Integrates Netscape-compatible plug-ins and HTML browsing into Director and Authorware.

Developer: g/matter

Web Address: http://www.gmatter.com/

Email: support@behaviors.com

LOADFONT XTRA

Description: Makes a font available to your Director application so that you can know exactly what font will be used on every target machine.

Developer: Pablo Media

Web Address: http://www.pablomedia.com/products/index.html

Email: info@pablomedia.com

Phone: 650-654-4300

MASTERAPP

Description: Enables you to locate, launch, and control other applications from Director and Authorware.

Developer: UpdateStage (Gretchen Macdowall)

Web Address: http://www.updatestage.com

Email: support@updatestage.com

Mailing Address: 1341 Massachusetts Ave., Box 124, Arlington, MA, 02476

Phone: 781-641-6043

Fax: 781-641-7068

MATHXTRAS

Description: Provides educational software support.

Developer: Maxwell Labs

Web Address: http://www.maxwell.com/

Mailing Address: World Headquarters, 9275 Sky Park Court, San Diego, CA, 92123

Phone: 619-279-5100

Fax: 619-277-6754

MHT-CONNECT

Description: Provides launch, connection, and other features for America Online.

Developer: Meetinghouse Tech

Web Address: http://www.meetinghouse.com

Mailing Address: 781 N. Church Rd., Elmhurst, IL, 60126-1413

Phone: 630-941-0600

Fax: 630-941-7777

MHT-Search

Description: Provides a text search engine for Director.

Developer: Meetinghouse Tech

Web Address: http://www.meetinghouse.com

Mailing Address: 781 N. Church Rd., Elmhurst, IL, 60126-1413

Phone: 630-941-0600

Fax: 630-941-7777

MidXtra

Description: Enables you to use MIDI from Lingo.

Developer: Yamaha Corporation

Web Address: http://www.yamaha-xg.com/english/xg/midixtra/midixtra.html

Miles Xtra

Description: Controls any type of audio.

Developer: Rad Game Tools, Inc.

Web Address: http://www.radgametools.com

Email: sales@radgametools.com

Phone: 425-893-4300

Fax: 425-893-9111

MMX Xtra

Description: Provides optimization for Intel's MMX technology within Director.

Developer: Macromedia

Web Address: http://www.macromedia.com/software/xtras/

ModMania

Description: Puts MPEG video into multimedia products.

Developer: Paul Farry

Web Address: http://www.magna.com.au/~farryp/director/xtras/

Email: p.farry@poboxes.com

MpegXtra

Description: PutsMPEG video into your multimedia products.

Developer: Tabuleiro da Baiana

Web Address: http://www.tbaiana.com/

Email: tbaiana@tbaiana.com

Mailing Address: Rua Conego Eugenio Leite, 1092 Pinheiros, Sao Paulo - SP BRAZIL, 05414 - 012

Phone: 55-11-813-2547

Fax: 55-11-813-2549

mPrint

Description: Provides a visual print report Designer and Xtra for codeless printing in Authorware and Director.

Developer: MEDIA Shoppe

Web Address: http://www.mediashoppe.com/xtras/

Phone: 806-371-0033

Fax: 806-371-0264

MUI Maker

Description: Provides a visual dialog layout tool that generates Lingo for MUI Xtra.

Developer: UpdateStage (Gretchen Macdowall)

Web Address: http://www.updatestage.com

Email: support@updatestage.com

Mailing Address: 1341 Massachusetts Ave., Box 124, Arlington, MA, 02476

Phone: 781-641-6043

Fax: 781-641-7068

nCrypt

Description: Provides encryption of text strings and files.

Developer: MEDIA Shoppe

Web Address: http://www.mediashoppe.com/xtras/

Phone: 806-371-0033

Fax: 806-371-0264

OnLooker

Description: Provides for sprite monitoring.

Developer: Yair Sageev

Web Address: yair.sageev@nyu.edu

Email: yair.sageev@nyu.edu

Phone: 718-965-0394

OnStage

Description: Provides full motion video.

Developer: Visible Light

Web Address: http://www.visiblelight.com

Email: sales@visiblelight.com

Phone: 407-327-5700 or 1-800-596-4494

Fax: 407-327-5006

PART

X

APP

H

OpenURL

Description: Opens a URL with the default browser.

Developer: Magic Modules

Web Address: http://www.mods.com.au/default.htm

Email: gary@mods.com.auMailing

Address: PO Box 550, Hamilton, Queensland, AUSTRALIA, 4007

Phone: 61-7-3259-4390

Fax: 61-7-3262-6749

OSUtil

Description: Moves, renames, or copies files from Lingo.

Developer: Paul Farry

Web Address: http://www.magna.com.au/~farryp/director/xtras/

Email: p.farry@poboxes.com

PHOTOCASTER

Description: Imports Photoshop layers into Director as seperate cast members.

Developer: Media Lab, Inc.

Web Address: http://www.medialab.com

Email: xtra-sales@medialab.com

Phone: 800-282-5361 or 303-499-5411

Fax: 303-497-9454

PICKFOLDER XTRA

Description: Enables folders to be chosen.

Developer: Dirigo Multimedia (Glenn M. Picher)

Web Address: http://www.maine.com/shops/gpicher/

Email: gpicher@maine.com

Mailing Address: 50 Market Street, Suite 1A-338, South Portland, ME, 04106

Phone: 207-767-8015

PLANET COLOR XTRA

Description: Uses MCICR reduction technology to create the best color image files from 24-bit images.

Developer: Lizard Tech

Web Address: http://www.lizardtech.com

Email: info@lizardtech.com

Mailing Address: 1520 Bellevue Avenue, Seattle, WA, 98122

Phone: 206-320-9969

Fax: 206-320-0989

PopMenu

Description: Creates custom popup menus on-the-fly.

Developer: UpdateStage (Gretchen Macdowall)

Web Address: http://www.updatestage.com

Email: support@updatestage.com

Mailing Address: 1341 Massachusetts Ave., Box 124, Arlington, MA, 02476

Phone: 781-641-6043

Fax: 781-641-7068

Precision Xtra

Description: Receives mouse events at the pixel level.

Developer: Penworks Corporation

Web Address: http://www.penworks.com

Email: sales@penworks.com

Mailing Address: P.O. Box 531, Holderness, NH, 03245-0531

Phone: 1-800-PENWORX

Fax: 1-800-PW-FAX-NUM

PrintOMatic

Description: Provides a Mac and Windows printing tool.

Developer: Electronic Ink

Web Address: http://www.printomatic.com

Email: ink@crestedbutte.net

Mailing Address: P.O. Box 3473, Crested Butte, CO, 81223

Phone: 970-349-1747

ProgressCopy

Description: Displays a progress bar while it is copying files.

Developer: UpdateStage (Gretchen Macdowall)

Web Address: http://www.updatestage.com

Email: support@updatestage.com

Mailing Address: 1341 Massachusetts Ave., Box 124, Arlington, MA, 02476

Phone: 781-641-6043

Fax: 781-641-7068

PROMIX XTRA

Description: Provides a set of tools targeted directly at sound cards.

Developer: MEDIA Shoppe

Web Address: `http://www.mediashoppe.com/xtras/`

Phone: 806-371-0033

Fax: 806-371-0264

QUICKDRAW 3D

Description: Provides 3D modeling for Director.

Developer: Macromedia

Web Address: `http://www.macromedia.com/software/xtras/`

QUICKTIME SPRITE EXPORT

Description: Converts Director animation to a Quicktime movie.

Developer: Apple Computer, Inc.

Web Address: `http://quicktimevr.apple.com`

REALAUDIO ENCODER XTRA

Description: Exports audio as RealAudio format from SoundEdit 16.

Developer: Progressive Networks

Web Address: `http://www.realaudio.com/`

Email: `sales@real.com`

Phone: 1-800-632-8920

REALAUDIO SDK FOR SHOCKWAVE

Description: Provides a RealAudio stream from Shockwave.

Developer: Progressive Networks

Web Address: `http://www.realaudio.com/`

REALVR XTRA

Description: Combines panoramic viewing and Internet browsing in one.

Developer: RealSpace, Inc.

Web Address: `http://www.rlspace.com`

Phone: 408-261-6262

REARWINDOW

Description: Enables you to display a window behind the Director Stage.

Developer: XtraMedia International

Web Address: `http://www.xtramedia.com/xtras.shtml`

Email: `productInfo@xtramedia.com`

Mailing Address: 1093 East Main Street #502, El Cajon, CA, 92021-6247

REGISTRYREADER

Description: Reads the setup of Windows or applications from the Registry.

Developer: Magister Ludi

Web Address: `http://www.magisterludi.com/index.html?/xtras/`

Email: `info@magisterludi.com`

Mailing Address: Via Natale Battaglia 8, 20127, Milan, ITALY

RELAUNCH

Description: Quits Director application, runs another application, and then restarts original application.

Developer: UpdateStage (Gretchen Macdowall)

Web Address: `http://www.updatestage.com`

Email: `support@updatestage.com`

Mailing Address: 1341 Massachusetts Ave., Box 124, Arlington, MA, 02476

Phone: 781-641-6043

Fax: 781-641-7068

RESERVELAUNCH

Description: A small stub application that dynamically changes the memory size allocated to your Director projector (installed on the hard drive) for best performance.

Developer: Dirigo Multimedia (Glenn M. Picher)

Web Address: `http://www.maine.com/shops/gpicher/`

Email: `gpicher@maine.com`

Mailing Address: 50 Market Street, Suite 1A-338, South Portland, ME, 04106

Phone: 207-767-8015

ROLLOVER TOOL KIT

Description: Attaches button handlers to any sprite, Cast, frame, or movie.

Developer: Penworks Corporation

Web Address: http://www.penworks.com

Email: sales@penworks.com

Mailing Address: P.O. Box 531, Holderness, NH, 03245-0531

Phone: 1-800-PENWORX

Fax: 1-800-PW-FAX-NUM

SCRIPTOMATIC XTRA

Description: Provides a style-sheet driven Lingo script for formatting and printing.

Developer: g/matter

Web Address: http://www.gmatter.com/

SCRNUTIL XTRA

Description: Captures some or all of the screen.

Developer: g/matter

Web Address: http://www.gmatter.com/

SCRNXTRA

Description: Provides a screen capture tool.

Developer: Little Planet Publishing

Web Address: http://www.littleplanet.com/kent/kent.html

Email: kent@littleplanet.com

SETMOUSE XTRA

Description: Sets the mouse to any location on the screen.

Developer: Scirius Development

Web Address: http://www.scirius.com/HNorm/index.html

Email: xtras@scirius.com

Mailing Address: Dresdner Stra_e 76a, D-04317 Leipzig, GERMANY

Phone: +49-341-6995741

Fax: +49-341-6995742

SHOCKTALK

Description: Incorporates spoken user interactions.

Developer: Digital Dreams

Web Address: `http://www.surftalk.com/`

SID6581

Description: Enables you to include Commodore 64 SID music files as Director cast members.

Developer: Paul Farry

Web Address: `http://www.magna.com.au/~farryp/director/xtras/`

Email: `p.farry@poboxes.com`

SMACKER XTRA

Description: Enables playback control of Smacker animation files.

Developer: Rad Game Tools, Inc.

Web Address: `http://www.radgametools.com`

Email: `sales@radgametools.com`

Phone: 425-893-4300

Fax: 425-893-9111

SNAPPY XTRA

Description: Digitizes video from Play, Inc.'s Snappy camera.

Developer: Dirigo Multimedia (Glenn M. Picher)

Web Address: `http://www.maine.com/shops/gpicher/`

Email: `gpicher@maine.com`

Mailing Address: 50 Market Street, Suite 1A-338, South Portland, ME, 04106

Phone: 207-767-8015

SOUNDSPROCKET XTRA

Description: Provides spatial filtering of sound.

Developer: Yair Sageev

Email address: `yair.sageev@nyu.edu`

Phone: 718-965-0394

SPELLER

Description: Spell checks all text cast members.

Developer: Ballard Davies Ltd.

Web Address: `http://www.ballard.co.uk/xtras/index.html`

Email: `Mailbox@ballard.co.uk`

Mailing Address: 4 Highstreet, Dorking, Surrey, RH4 1AT, UNITED KINGDOM

Phone: +44-01306-884411

Fax: +44-01306-889911

SPEECH LINGO XTRA

Description: Incorporates spoken user interactions.

Developer: Digital Dreams

Web Address: `http://www.surftalk.com/`

STYLEUTIL

Description: Takes an editable field and creates the Rich Text Format required to import the Styles field into Director.

Developer: Paul Farry

Web Address: `http://www.magna.com.au/~farryp/director/xtras/`

Email: `p.farry@poboxes.com`

SYSTEM TOOLS

Description: Provides access to many common WIN API functions such as INI files, the Registry, File Open/Save, user's CD-ROM drive, copying, and so on.

Developer: MEDIA Shoppe

Web Address: `http://www.mediashoppe.com/xtras/`

TABLEMAKER XTRA

Description: Enables you to view spreadsheet data over the Director Stage.

Developer: XtraMedia International

Web Address: `http://www.xtramedia.com/xtras.shtml`

Email: `productInfo@xtramedia.com`

Mailing Address: 1093 East Main Street #502, El Cajon, CA, 92021-6247

TABLE XTRA

Description: Enables you to create unlimited-size, scrollable "grids" of Director cast members or text elements on the stage.

Developer: Electronic Ink

Web Address: http://community.crestedbutte.com/ink/

TASKXTRA

Description: Manages automated functions.

Developer: Little Planet Publishing

Web Address: http://www.littleplanet.com/kent/kent.html

Email: kent@littleplanet.com

TEXTCRUNCHER

Description: Provides for text handling.

Developer: Yair Sageev

Email: yair.sageev@nyu.edu

Phone: 718-965-0394

3D DREAMS

Description: Makes it possible to add 3D content to Director movies.

Developer: Shells Interactive Film-Art, Ltd.

Web Address: http://www.shells-ifa.com

Email: info@shells-ifa.com

Mailing Address: 18 A'hail Street, 43317 Ra'anana, ISRAEL

Phone: +972-9-7710205

Fax: +972-9-7741989

TrackThemColors Xtra

Description: Tracks multiple objects in a video according to their color value, brightness, or pattern.

Developer: Smoothware Design

Web Address: http://www.smoothware.com

Email: info@smoothware.com

Mailing Address: P.O. Box 0048, New York, NY, 10023

Phone: 212-595-3190

V-Active

Description: Provides integration of V-Active movies into Director.

Developer: Ephyx Technologies

Web Address: http://www.veon.com/products/index.htm

VCap Xtra

Description: Provides live video capture and priview under Win95/NT.

Developer: Penworks Corporation

Web Address: http://www.penworks.com

Email: sales@penworks.com

Mailing Address: P.O. Box 531, Holderness, NH, 03245-0531

Phone: 1-800-PENWORX

Fax: 1-800-PW-FAX-NUM

Versions

Description: Reports file version numbers.

Developer: UpdateStage (Gretchen Macdowall)

Web Address: http://www.updatestage.com

Email: support@updatestage.com

Mailing Address: 1341 Massachusetts Ave., Box 124, Arlington, MA, 02476

Phone: 781-641-6043

Fax: 781-641-7068

Versions XObject

Description: Determines QuickTime, DOS, and Windows file version numbers.

Developer: Dirigo Multimedia (Glenn M. Picher)

Web Address: `http://www.maine.com/shops/gpicher/`

Email: `gpicher@maine.com`

Mailing Address: 50 Market Street, Suite 1A-338, South Portland, ME, 04106

Phone: 207-767-8015

VolumeController Xtra

Description: Provides smooth control of volume.

Developer: Magister Ludi

Web Address: `http://www.magisterludi.com/index.html?/xtras/`

Email: `info@magisterludi.com`

Mailing Address: Via Natale Battaglia 8, 20127, Milan, ITALY

Volume Control Xtra

Description: Enables volume control of soundcard devices such as CD, WAV, MIDI, and AUX.

Developer: MEDIA Shoppe

Web Address: `http://www.mediashoppe.com/xtras/`

Phone: 806-371-0033

Fax: 806-371-0264

VSnap Xtra

Description: Provides video preview and single frame capture from a Video for Windows capture card.

Developer: Penworks Corporation

Web Address: `http://www.penworks.com`

Email: `sales@penworks.com`

Mailing Address: P.O. Box 531, Holderness, NH, 03245-0531

Phone: 1-800-PENWORX

Fax: 1-800-PW-FAX-NUM

WAVES CONVERT

Description: Enables conversion of sound files for optimized playback.

Developer: Waves

Web Address: http://www.waves.com/

Email: sales-info.us@waves.com

WEBXTRA

Description: Displays HTML and ActiveX content directly on the stage.

Developer: Tabuleiro da Baiana

Web Address: http://www.tbaiana.com/

Email: tbaiana@tbaiana.com

Mailing Address: Rua Conego Eugenio Leite, 1092 Pinheiros, Sao Paulo - SP Brazil, 05414 - 012

Phone: 55-11-813-2547

Fax: 55-11-813-2549

WIND-XTRA

Description: Simplifies creation and use of Movies in a Window.

Developer: North Coast Interactive, Inc.

WINGROUP XTRA

Description: Enables you to create, edit, and delete entries in the Windows Start menu.

Developer: Media Connect

Web Address: http://www.mcmm.com/download.htm

Email: ssb@mcmm.com

XPRESS XTRA

Description: Enables the use of Apples Plaintalk text-to-speech technology.

Developer: DirectXtras Llc.

Web Address: http://www.directxtras.com/

Email: info@directxtras.com

Mailing Address: PO Box 423417, San Francisco, CA, 94142-3417

Phone: 415-505-8249

Fax: 650-938-4633

XTRADRAW

Description: Provides drawing tools for Director and Authorware

Developer: g/matter

Web Address: http://www.gmatter.com/

XTRAGENT

Description: Enables the use of Microsoft's Agent technology in Director applications.

Developer: DirectXtras Llc.

Web Address: http://www.directxtras.com/

Email: info@directxtras.com

Mailing Address: P.O. Box 423417, San Francisco, CA, 94142-3417

Phone: 415-505-8249

Fax: 650-938-4633

XTRANET

Description: Provides connectivity to the Internet.

Developer: g/matter

Web Address: http://www.gmatter.com/

XTRASAFE

Description: Provides for encryption and compression of scripts.

Developer: InterBot, Inc.

YAK XTRA

Description: Adds a "speak" command to Lingo, which speaks any text string using text-to-speech.

Developer: Electronic Ink

Web Address: http://community.crestedbutte.com/ink/

Email: ink@printomatic.com

Phone: 970-349-1747

Mailing address: P.O. Box 3473, Crested Butte, CO, 81224

zLAUNCH

Description: Enables you to launch external applications from Director.

Developer: Zeus Productions

Web Address: http://www.zeusprod.com/

Email: sales@zeusprod.com

Phone: 1-800-797-2968

zOPEN

Description: Opens and prints documents. Locates external applications such as browsers.

Developer: Zeus Productions

Web Address: http://www.zeusprod.com/

Email: sales@zeusprod.com

Phone: 1-800-797-2968

zSCRIPT

Description: Controls AppleScriptable applications.

Developer: Zeus Productions

Web Address: http://www.zeusprod.com/

Email: sales@zeusprod.com

Phone: 1-800-797-2968

APPENDIX

WHAT'S ON THE CD-ROM

Included with this book is a CD-ROM for Mac and Windows. It contains all the programs in the book, plus lots of additional files.

MOVIES FROM THE BOOK

In the "Book Movies" folder are Director 7 movies from all the chapters in the book. It is recommended that you use these as you read through the chapters.

The main purpose of including these movies is to enable you to avoid typos in your code. Even the best typist makes mistakes as he or she types in the Lingo programs. Often, it is hard to track down the mistake. Using the movies on the CD-ROM, however, can help you avoid this problem.

In many cases, the movies simply contain script members with the code, and maybe some supporting graphics and sounds. Some demonstrate themselves by having you press Play, whereas others require you to use the Message window to kick off demo scripts.

BONUS MOVIES AND RESOURCES

The CD-ROM includes some extra movies and behaviors for you to examine and use as you want.

The first is the "Lingo Infinite Possibility Machine." It was originally created in early 1996 for my first book, *The Comprehensive Guide to Lingo*. It was then updated for Director 6 and my second book, *The Director 6 Book*. This new version is for Director 7.

The original was created to demonstrate a whole bunch of advanced Lingo techniques, all being used at the same time. The idea was to include something on the CD-ROM of the book other than shareware and demos. The movie is totally unprotected. You can open it in Director and see the scripts. I added some comments to the script this time, something that the earlier versions were lacking.

I encourage you to try to figure out how each portion of the movie was done. Play with it, examine it, and learn from it.

The second bonus movie is the "Planetary Detective." It is the total output of CleverMedia in one eight-hour work day. We're sort of Multimedia commandos. William Follet, the art director, drew the robot, made the interface, and created nice, anti-aliased planet graphics. Jay Shaffer, the technical director, did the research and generated the audio clips with cue points. I wrote the text and then programmed the Lingo.

It is meant to demonstrate Director's capability to teach. Notice that the game is not just quizzing here. It is actually teaching methods of remembering information. Hopefully, this will result in kids actually learning the stuff, not just getting a grade.

There are a lot of good scripts that you can examine here. Like the Lingo Machine, the movie is completely unprotected so you can see for yourself how it was all done.

Xtra Demos

Another folder contains demos and free versions of some popular and interesting Xtras. Each comes with a Read Me file or similar documentation explaining the use of these Xtras.

Other Demos

The CD-ROM includes some demos of other software that relate to Director or multimedia in general.

Surprises

I have also included a "Free Xtras" folder with some fun extras that I hope you will enjoy.

The "asciiXtra" Xtra enables you to quickly see the full set of ASCII characters for any font on your computer. This can be helpful if you are using the *numToChar* or *charToNum* Lingo commands.

The "colorNameXtra" Xtra takes some standard color names, such as aquamarine, and lets you find the right hex-color code. Director 7 enables you to use these codes to set the colors of sprites and text.

The "Button Maker" Xtra enables you to create some quick button bitmap images to use with button behaviors. You can type in the text to appear on the button and choose from three styles. The result is a set of four images: up state, down state, rollover state, and inactive state. They are placed in your movie's Cast. It is a great way to quickly create lots of buttons that look much better than Director's built-in pushbuttons.

PART

X

APP

I

Third-Party Applications

Adobe

AlienSkin

Aladdin

Application Techniques

Auto F/X

Binary Software

ChromaGraphics

Digital Frontiers

Macromedia

Metacreations

Opcode

PRS

RAYflect

Strata

Vertigo

Browsers

Microsoft Internet Explorer 4

Netscape Communicator 4.5

Graphics

A collection of clipart and photos

Extras

MediaLab

Penworks

UpdateStage

APPENDIX J

LINGO REFERENCE

Whenever you have a large, complex programming language such as Lingo, it is useful to have an alphabetical reference. Every Director 7 owner already has one in the form of the Lingo Dictionary book that comes with the program.

However, because it goes into a fair amount of detail about most commands, functions, and properties, the Lingo Dictionary is only somewhat useful as a quick reference guide.

In contrast, this section is meant for quick reference. Each and every Lingo command is included, and a short description is given for each one. Rather than an example of the syntax in action, a simpler example of what the syntax looks like is included. There are also references to related commands, functions, and properties, and references to chapters that contain more information.

Here is a description of what each column contains:

- Keyword—The Lingo command, function, or property.
- Topic—Which part of Director the keyword relates to. This is truly a "topic," not a "type." For instance, *the systemDate* is shown relating to the topic "Date & Time" rather than as a "system property."
- Type—Command, function, property, and so on.
- Description—A short sentence or paragraph to give you an idea of what the keyword is and how to use it.
- Syntax Sample—A segment of Lingo code that shows the keyword in use. It is usually not a complete example, but will give the intuitive reader a good idea of how to use it. A complete example can usually be found in the Lingo Dictionary.
- See Also—References to other keywords.
- See Chapter/Appendix—If the keyword is specifically talked about in a chapter, that chapter's number is shown here. If it is a basic keyword used throughout Lingo, no reference is shown.

This list also contains many undocumented and obsolete—but still working—keywords. Keep in mind that these are unsupported by Macromedia, which means they could disappear in version 7.0.1 very easily, and may not work in some situations.

Keyword	Topic	Type	Description	Syntax Sample	See Also	See Chapter/ Appendix
#	Symbols	Special Character	Used as the first character of any symbol. Also used as an optional character in front of hexadecimal color values in the rgb function.	`#mySymbol,` `#vectorShape,` `rgb("#FFFFFF")`	symbol, rgb	
&	Strings	Special Character	Concatenates two strings.	`"abc"&"def" =` `"abcdef"`	&&, after, before, into	16
&&	Strings	Special Character	Concatenates two strings and places a space between them.	`"abc"&&"def" =` `"abc def"`	&, after, before, into	16
( )	Logic	Special Character	Used to set order of precedence in operations. Also used to surround parameters with objects or functions calls.	`(5+6)*6, member¬` `("my member"),` `addTwoNumbers(a,b)`		
*	Math	Operator	Multiplies two numbers.	`4*5, a*b`	+, -, /	13
+	Math	Operator	Adds two numbers.	`4+5, a+b`	*, -, /	13
,	Misc	Special Character	Used to separate items in various Lingo syntax such as function calls, handler definitions, global and property statements, lists, and so on.			
-	Math	Operator	Subtracts two numbers.	`4-5, a-b`	+, *, /	13

PART

X

APP

J

continues

Keyword	Topic	Type	Description	Syntax Sample	See Also	See Chapter/ Appendix
.	Misc	Special Character	Used in syntax that refers to the properties of an object.	`text.length, member(1).media, sprite(7).loc`		16
..	Strings	Special Character	Used to refer to a consecutive run of items in chunk expressions.	`text.word[3..7]`		
/	Math	Operator	Divides two numbers.	`4/5, a/b`	+, -, *	13
:	Misc	Special Character	Used in property lists to separate the property name from its value. Used in case statements.	`[#a: 1, #b: 2]`	[], case	
<	Logic	Operator	Less than.	`If 4 < 5 then..., if a < b then...`	<=, >, =, <>	13
<=	Logic	Operator	Less than or equal to.	`If 4 <= 5 then..., if a <= b then...`	<, =, >, <>	13
<>	Logic	Operator	Not equal.	`If 4 <> 5 then..., if a <> b then...`	=, <, <=, >, >=	13
=	Logic	Operator	Equal.	`If 4 = 5 then..., if a = b then...`	<>, <, <=, >, >=	13
>	Logic	Operator	Greater than.	`If 4 > 5 then..., if a > b then...`	<, >=, =, <>	13
>=	Logic	Operator	Greater than or equal to.	`If 4 >= 5 then..., if a >= b then...`	>, <, =, <>	13
[]	Lists	Special Character	Used to surround a list declaration or to refer to an item in a list.	`[4,5,6], [#a: 1, #b: 2], text.char[1], myList[5]`	:	13

Command	Category	Type	Description	Example	See Also	Chapter
¬	Misc	Special Character	Used to continue a command on the next line.			
abbr, abbrev, abbreviated	Date & Time	Modifier	Modifies the date and time properties to return shorter versions.	the abbr date, the abbr time	date, time	21
abort	Programming	Command	Exits the handler and also terminates the handler that called the current one, and so on back to the original event handler, exiting that as well.		exit, halt	
abs	Math	Function	Returns the absolute value of a number. Has the effect of removing the negative sign from negative numbers.	put abs(-7) -- 7		13
activeWindow	MIAW	Event Handler	Called when a window is made active by first appearing, or by a user action such as clicking on the window.		deactivateWindow, openWindow, closeWindow	
activeCastLib	Score Recording	Property	The number of the most recently accessed cast library.	put the activeCastLib	castLib, selectedMembers	
activeWindow	MIAW	Property	The active window object. Returns (the stage) if it is the Stage.	forget(the¬ activeWindow)	close, forget	24

continues

PART

X

APP

J

Keyword	Topic	Type	Description	Syntax Sample	See Also	See Chapter/Appendix
actor	OOP	Function	Undocumented Lingo. It seems that the value of actor(1) returns the memory location of the next object to be added to the actorList. Unconfirmed.	put actor(1)	actorList	26
actorList	OOP	Property	A special list of child objects to which you can make additions. Each object in the list receives a "stepFrame" message each frame.	add the actorList,¬ myChild	new	24
add	Lists	Command	Adds an item to a linear list. If the list has been sorted with the *sort* command, the item will be added in the proper location.	add myList, myValue	append, addProp, deleteAt	
addAt	Lists	Command	Adds an item to a linear list at a specific location.	addAt myList, myValue	add, append, addProp, deleteAt	23
addProp	Lists	Command	Adds a property name and a value to a property list.	addProp myPropList,¬ #name, "Gary"	add, deleteProp	13
addVertex	Vector	Command	Inserts a vertex point into a vector shape member.	addVertex(member¬ ("myVector"), 5,¬ point(50,50))	deleteVertex, moveVertex, vertexList	13
after	Strings	Expression	Enables you to use the *put* command to append a string onto another.	put "." after¬ myString	put, before, into	13

Term	Category	Type	Description	Example	See Also	Page
alert	Misc	Command	Brings up a dialog box that shows a string of text and an OK button. Movie stops while the box is present.	alert "Danger!"		20
alertHook	Debug	Event Handler, Property	Enables you to set a script member as the one that handles error messages when they occur. Also the name of the event handler that must be in that script to receive the error messages.	the alertHook =¬ script("Error¬ Handler") on alertHook me,¬ err, msg		16
alignment	Text, Field	Property	Text or field member property that determines text alignment. Possible for a field at "left," "right," and "center," while the possible values for a text member are #left, #right, #center, and #full.	member("myText").¬ alignment = #center	text, lineHeight, font, fontSize, fontStyle, fixedLineSpace	33
allowCustomCaching	Playback	Property	For future use.			33
allowGraphicMenu	Playback	Property	For future use.			16-
allowSaveLocal	Playback	Property	For future use.			

continues

PART

X

APP

J

Keyword	Topic	Type	Description	Syntax Sample	See Also	See Chapter/Appendix
allowTransportControl	Playback	Property	For future use.			
allowVolumeControl	Playback	Property	For future use.			
allowZooming	Playback	Property	For future use.			
alphaThreshold	Bitmap	Property	A value from 0 to 255 that tells Director when to detect a click on a bitmap according to the value in the alpha channel. A 0 makes all pixels detect hits, where a 255 makes only opaque pixels detect hits.	`member¬ ("my32bitimage").¬ alphaThreshold = 128`	useAlpha	
ancestor	OOP	Property	Defines an ancestor to a parent script. All instances of that parent would have the handlers of its ancestor made available for use.	`the ancestor of me¬ = new(script "ancestor")`	new, me	
and	Logic	Operator	Returns TRUE if both expressions are TRUE and FALSE otherwise.	`if (a = 1) and (b = 2) then...`	or, not	18
antiAlias	Text, Vector, Flash	Property	Determines whether a text, Flash, or vector member is drawn to the screen with anti-aliasing to smooth edges.	`member("myVector").¬ antiAlias = TRUE`	Quality	23

Name	Category	Type	Description	Example	See Also	Chapter
append	Lists	Command	Adds a value to a linear list. Adds the value to the end, even if the list has been sorted.	`append myList, ¬` `myValue`	add	13
applicationPath	System	Property	Returns the full path to the Director application or the Projector.	`put the¬` `applicationPath`	pathName, movie	20
atan	Math	Function	Returns the arctangent of a number in radians.	`put atan(3.0/6.0)`	sin, cos, tan	
autoMask	Cursor	Property	Determines whether the white pixels in an animated cursor are transparent.	`member("cursor").¬` `autoMask = TRUE`	cursor	
autoTab	Text, Field	Property	Determines whether the users can press the Tab key in an editable field or text member and automatically move the insertion point to the next field or text member.	`member("text").¬` `autoTab = TRUE`		13, 18
backcolor	Sprite, Text, Field	Property	Old syntax to enable you to specify the background color of a sprite, or the background color of a text or field member. The color number must be between 0 and 255 and correspond to the movie's palette.	`sprite(1).¬` `backcolor = 35`	forecolor, bgColor	
backgroundColor					bgColor	16
BACKSPACE	Strings	Constant	The equivalent to the character generated by the Delete key on the Mac and the Backspace key in Windows. It is also numtoChar(8).	`if the key = ¬` `BACKSPACE then...`		13

PART

X

APP

J

continues

Keyword	Topic	Type	Description	Syntax Sample	See Also	See Chapter/ Appendix
beep	Misc	Command	Creates a number of system beeps. The sound depends on the user's system settings. If a number is included, that is the number of beeps created; otherwise just one beep is performed.	beep(3)		
beepOn	Misc	Property	If set to TRUE, a beep occurs if the user tries to click where there is no active sprite. Default is FALSE.	the beepOn = TRUE		16
before	Strings	Expression	Enables you to use the *put* command to place a string into another, but at the beginning of the string.	put "He said: " ¬ before myString	put, after into	12
beginRecording	Score Recording	Command	Signifies the start of a Score recording session.		endRecording, updateFrame	
beginSprite	Behaviors	Event Handler	This handler is executed immediately before the sprite first appears.		endSprite	16
bgColor	Sprite, Text, Field, Vector	Property	Enables you to specify the background color of a sprite, or the background color of a text, field, or vector shape member. You can set it to an rgb structure or a paletteIndex.	sprite(1).bgColor¬ = rgb(255,0,0)	rgb, paletteIndex, color	26

Name	Category	Type	Description	Syntax	See Also	Chapters
birth	OOP	Command	Old syntax for creating an object from a parent script. Use *new* instead.		new	14
bitAnd	Math	Function	Takes two numbers and performs a logical AND on the bits and returns the result.	put bitAnd(a,b)	bitOr, bitXor, bitNot	13, 16, 18, 27, 29
bitmap		type				
bitNot	Math	Function	Takes one number and performs a logical NOT on the bits and returns the result.	put bitNot(a)	bitAnd, bitOr, bitXor	
bitOr	Math	Function	Takes two numbers and performs a logical OR on the bits and returns the result.	put bitOr(a,b)	bitAnd, bitXor, bitNot	
bitRate	Shockwave Audio	Property	Returns the bitrate, in Kbps, of a streaming sound. Returns 0 when not streaming.	put member¬ ("mySWA").bitRate	bitsPerSample	
bitsPerSample	Shockwave Audio	Property	Returns the original bit depth of the sound. Works only while streaming. Typical values are 8 and 16.	put member("mySWA").¬ bitsPerSample	bitRate	
bitXor	Math	Function	Takes two numbers and performs a logical EXCLUSIVE OR on the bits and returns the result.	put bitXor(a,b)	bitOr, bitAnd, bitNot	17

continues

PART

X

APP

J

Keyword	Topic	Type	Description	Syntax Sample	See Also	See Chapter/Appendix
blend	Sprite	Property	A value of 0 to 100 determines how much the sprite's pixels should blend with the ones behind it. Works with many inks, particularly the Blend ink.	`sprite(1).blend = 50`	ink, blendLevel	17
blendLevel	Sprite	Property	A value of 0 to 255 determines how much the sprite's pixels should blend with the ones behind it. Same as *blend* but with a different scale.	`sprite(1).` `blendLevel = 50`	ink, blend	
blue					rgb	13, 18, 19, 37
border	Field	Property	The size of the black line around a field member.	`member("myField").¬` `border = 1`	margin, boxType, boxDropShadow, dropShadow	
bottom	Sprite, Misc	Property	The bottom vertical position of the sprite.	`put sprite(1).bottom`	top, left, right, height, rect	13, 29
bottomSpacing	Text	Property	A number indicating any extra spacing after a paragraph in a text member. Also works with negative values.	`member("myText").¬` `line[2].¬` `bottomSpacing = 12`	topSpacing, fixedLineSpace	16, 24
boxDropShadow	Field	Property	The offset of the black drop shadow around a field member. Values from 0 to 255.	`member("myField").¬` `boxDropShadow = 1`	margin, boxType, border, dropShadow	

Name	Type	Members	Description	Example	See Also
boxType	Property	Text, Field	The type of text box used for text members and fields. Possible values are #adjust, #fixed, and #scroll. Field can also be set to #limit.	member("myText").¬ boxType = #fixed	
broadcastProps	Property	Flash, Vector	Determines whether changes made to a Flash or vector shape member are immediately shown in the sprites present on the Stage, or whether they are simply used the next time a sprite appears using that member.	member("myVector").¬ broadcastProps¬ = FALSE	16
browserName	Command, Property, Function	Network	As a command, enables you to set the default browser used by gotoNetPage. As a function, enables you to get the name of the default browser. In an alternate form, enables you to decide whether the browser launches automatically with the gotoNetPage command.	browserName ¬ myNewBrowserPath put browserName() browserName¬ (#enabled, TRUE)	gotoNetPage 16
buttonsEnabled	Property	Flash	Determines whether the buttons in a Flash sprite are enabled.	Sprite(7).¬ buttonsEnabled	actionsEnabled 20

continues

Keyword	Topic	Type	Description	Syntax Sample	See Also	See Chapter/ Appendix
buttonStyle	System	Property	If TRUE, the user can click button members and roll over others and they will highlight. If FALSE, only the button first clicked will highlight.	the buttonStyle¬ = TRUE	checkBoxAccess, checkBoxType, buttonType	22
buttonType	Button	Property	The type of button for a button member. Values can be #pushButton, #checkBox, or #radioButton.	member("myButton").¬ buttonType =¬ #checkBox	checkBoxAccess, checkBoxType, buttonStyle	
call	OOP	Command	Can call a handler in a parent script instance or a sprite behavior instance. Can use a single instance or a list of instances. In the second case, no error message is sent if the handler does not exist. You can also send parameters. You can even use a variable as a reference to the handler.	call(#myHandler,¬ myScriptInstance,¬ param1) call(#myHandler,¬ [myScript1,myScript2],¬ param1,param2)	callAncestor, sendSprite, sendAllSprites	
callAncestor	OOP	Command	Same as call, but sends the message or messages directly to an object's ancestor(s).		call	
cancelIdleLoad	Memory	Command	Cancels loading of members with a specific tag number.	cancelIdleLoad(1)	idleLoadTag	

Term	Programming	Structure	Description	Example	See also	Page

case	Programming	Structure	Starts a case statement. Is followed by a test value and then *of*. Following lines list possible values, followed by a colon. Can use an OTHERWISE statement to deal with all other possible values. The whole structure must end with an END CASE.	`case a of`
				`1: beep 2:`
				`  beep`
				`  go to frame 1`
				`3,4:halt`
				`otherwise:go to ¬`
				`frame 7¬`
				`end case`
					if	

cast			Obsolete syntax for *member*.		member	
castLib	Casts	Object	Defines a cast object. Can accept a name or number.	`put castLib(1)`	castLibNum	13

castLibNum	Member, Sprite	Property	Returns the cast library number of the member or the member used by the sprite. You can set the sprite to use the member in the same position in a different cast library.	`put member(1).¬`
				`castLibNum`
				`sprite(7).¬`
				`castLibNum = 2`
					memberNum	

castLibs	Casts	Function	When used as "the number of castLibs," it returns the number of cast libraries.	`put the number¬` `of castLibs`		18, 26, 27, 29

castMemberList	Cursor	Property	The list of members used by an animated cursor.	`put member¬`
				`("myCursor").¬`
				`castMemberList`
					cursor	

castMembers			Obsolete syntax for "members".		members	

PART

X

APP

J

continues

Keyword	Topic	Type	Description	Syntax Sample	See Also	See Chapter/Appendix
castNum			Obsolete syntax for "memberNum".		memberNum	
castType			Obsolete syntax for "type".		type	
center	Digital Video	Property	A value of TRUE centers the video when the crop property is TRUE.	member("myVideo").¬ center = TRUE	crop	
centerRegPoint	Vector, Flash, Bitmap	Property	When set to TRUE, the registration point is automatically centered when the sprite is resized.	member("myVector") =¬ centerRegPoint =¬ FALSE	regPoint	
centerStage	Movie	Property	When TRUE, the Stage is centered on the monitor when the movie is opened.	the centerStage =¬ TRUE	fixStageSize	
changeArea	Transition	Property	With this property you can set a transition member to affect either the whole Stage or just the changed area.	member¬ ("myTransition").¬ changeArea = TRUE	transitionType, ChunkSize	20, 28
channelCount	Sound	Property	Returns the number of channels in a sound. Typical values are 1 and 2, with 2 usually meaning a stereo sound.	put member¬ ("mySound").¬ channelCount		
char	Strings	Expression	Used to specify a single character or range of characters in a string chunk.	put myString.¬ char[7] put member("myText").¬ text.char[4..7]	word, line, item, chars	

charPosToLoc	Text, Field	Function	Returns the point location of a character in a text or field member. It is relative to the upper-left corner of the member.	`put charPosToLoc¬ (member("myText"),7)`	locToCharPos, locVToLinePos, linePosToLocV, mouseChar	17
chars	Strings	Function	Returns a range of characters in a string. Obsolete, but useful for making Java applets because chunk expressions are not supported.	`put chars¬ (myString,6,9)`	char	13, 16
charToNum	Strings	Function	Converts a character to its ASCII character value.	`put charToNum¬ (myChar)`	numToChar, value	16
checkBoxAccess	Button	Property	A system property. When set to 0 the user can check and uncheck check boxes and radio buttons. When set to 1, the user can only check them. When set to 2, the user cannot do either.	`the checkBoxAccess¬ = 0`	checkBoxType, hilite	16, 37
checkBoxType	Button	Property	A system property. Enables you to determine what a checked checkbox looks like. 0 puts an "X" inside it, 1 puts a small black box inside it, and 2 fills the box completely.	`the checkBoxType = 1`	checkBoxAccess, hilite	16

PART

X

APP

J

continues

Keyword	Topic	Type	Description	Syntax Sample	See Also	See Chapter/ Appendix
checkMark	Menubar	Property	A menu item property. It enables you to check and uncheck a single menu item.	the checkMark of¬ menuitem 1 of¬ menu 1 = TRUE	menuitem, installMenu	
chunkSize	Transition	Property	Determines the smoothness of a transition member. Values are 1 to 128, with 1 being the smoothest, but slowest.	member¬ ("myTransition").¬ chunkSize = 4	transitionType, changeArea	
clearCache	Network	Command	Clears Director's or a Projector's network cache.	clearCache	cacheDocVerify, cacheSize	
clearError	Flash	Command	Resets the error state of a streaming Flash movie	clearError¬ (member("myFlash"))	state, getError	
clearFrame	Score Recording	Command	Clears all the sprites from the current frame during Score recording.	clearFrame	beginRecording, updateFrame	
clearGlobals	System	Command	Sets the value of all globals to VOID.	clearGlobals	global, showGlobals	
clickLoc	Mouse	Property	Returns a point with the location of the last mouse click.	put the clickLoc	mouseLoc, clickOn	

Term	Category	Type	Description	Example	Related	Page
clickMode	Flash	Property	When set to #boundingBox, clicks and rollovers are detected anywhere in a Flash sprite's rectangle. When set to #object, clicks and rollovers are detected when over a filled portion of the sprite. When set to #opaque, the behavior is like #object if the sprite's ink is Background Transparent and #boundingBox if otherwise.	`member("myFlash").clickMode = #object`		12, 27
clickOn	Mouse	Property	Returns the number of the sprite that was last clicked. Returns a 0 if no sprite was clicked.	`put the clickOn`	clickLoc, rollover	15, 29
closed	Vector	Property	TRUE makes the vector shape closed, and fills it with a solid color or a gradient.	`member("myVector").closed = TRUE`		20
close	MIAW	Command	Hides a MIAW. The MIAW is still there; you need to use *forget* to really get rid of it.	`close window ("myWindow")`	open, forget	15
closeWindow	MIAW	Event Handler	Called when the movie is running as a MIAW and the window is closed.	`on closeWindow`	openWindow, activateWindow	20
closeXLib	Xtras	Command	Disposes of an Xtra that has been loaded into memory.	`closeXlib "FileIO"`	openXLib	24

continues

PART

X

APP

J

Keyword	Topic	Type	Description	Syntax Sample	See Also	See Chapter/Appendix
color	Misc, Sprite, Text, Field, Vector	Object	A color object can be either an rgb structure or a paletteIndex structure. You can use the color function to create these objects as well. This keyword is also a property of sprites and of text, field, and vector shape members.	myColor = color¬(#rgb,255,255,255) myColor = color¬(#paletteIndex,35) sprite(7).color¬= rgb(255,0,0)	colorType, rgb, paletteIndex, red, green, blue, bgColor, foreColor	24
colorDepth	System	Property	The current color depth of the user's monitor. Usually 8, 16, 24, or 32. You can set this property on a Mac and some Windows machines.	put the colorDepth	switchColorDepth	25
colorQD	System	Property	Obsolete property that is used to refer to color QuickDraw. Now always returns TRUE.			
colorType	Misc	Property	A property of a color structure. Returns #rgb if it is a rgb structure and #paletteIndex if a paletteIndex structure. The best part is that you can set this property to convert between them.	myColor.colorType¬= #paletteIndex	color, rgb, paletteIndex	21, 34, 35
commandDown	Keyboard	Property	Returns TRUE if the user is holding down the Command key on the Mac or the Ctrl key in Windows.	put the commandDown	controlDown, optionDown, shiftDown, keyPressed	

Term	Category	Type	Description	Example	See Also

constrainH	Sprite	Function	Takes a sprite number and an integer as parameters. If the number is outside the horizontal boundaries of the sprite, it returns the value of the left or right side. Otherwise it returns the integer unchanged.	`sprite(me.spriteNum).¬`
				`locH = constrainH¬`
				`(7, the mouseH)`
					constrainV

constraint	Sprite	Property	A value of greater than 0 constrains the location of a sprite to the bounding box of another sprite. A value of 0 means no constraint.	`sprite(7).¬` `constraint = 6`	16

constrainV	Sprite	Function	Takes a sprite number and an integer as parameters. If the number is outside the vertical boundaries of the sprite, it returns the value of the top or bottom side. Otherwise it returns the integer unchanged.	`sprite(me.spriteNum).¬`
				`locV = constrainV¬`
				`(7, the mouseV)`
					constrainV

contains	Strings	Operator	Determines whether a string is found anywhere inside another.	`if myString contains¬` `".com" then...`	=, offset, starts
continue	Navigation	Command	Obsolete Lingo.		go

PART

X

APP

J

continues

Keyword	Topic	Type	Description	Syntax Sample	See Also	See Chapter/ Appendix
controlDown	Keyboard	Property	Returns TRUE if the user is holding down the Control key on the Mac or the Ctrl key in Windows.	`put the controlDown`	commandDown optionDown, shiftDown, keyPressed	16
controller	Digital Video	Property	Enables you to test for and turn on or off the control strip for a QuickTime video. Does not work for Video for Windows.	`member("myVideo").¬ controller = TRUE`	directToStage	
copyrightInfo	Shockwave Audio	Property	Returns the copyright information embedded into a Shockwave Audio file. Sound must be preloaded or playing first.	`put member("mySWA").¬ copyrightInfo`		16
copyToClipBoard	Member	Command	Copies the media of a member to the computer's clipboard.	`copyToClipBoard¬ (member("myText"))`	pasteClipBoardInto	19
cos	Math	Function	Returns the cosine of an angle. Angle must be in radians.	`put cos(pi()/4)`	sin, tan, atan, pi	
count	List, String, Misc	Property	Returns the number of items in a list. Returns the number of properties in a script object. Returns the number of globals with (the globals), and the number of chunks with strings.	`put myList.count put(the globals).count put myString.word.¬ count`	showGlobals, length	

cpuHogTicks	System	Property	Works on the Mac only. Determines how often Director allows the CPU to process other tasks. Default is 20. Set lower to enable the computer to run more smoothly in general, higher to have Director hog the CPU, thereby producing smoother animation.	`the cpuHogTicks = 40`	13
crop	Bitmap	Command	Crops a bitmap member to a new rectangle relative to upper-left corner of the Stage.	`crop member¬ ("myBitmap",rect¬ (10,10,50,60))`	picture	13
crop	Digital Video	Property	When FALSE, the digital video is scaled to fit the sprite rectangle. When TRUE, the video is presented at 100%, but is cropped by the sprite rectangle.	`member("myVideo").¬ crop = TRUE`	center
cuePassed	Sound	Event Handler	This handler is called when a cue point is passed in a sound.	`on cuePassed¬ channelNum,¬ cuePointNum,¬ cuePointName¬`	cuePointNames, cuePointTimes, isPastCuePoint	18
cuePointNames	Sound, QuickTime	Property	Returns a list of cue point names in a sound member.	`put member¬ ("mySound").¬ cuePointNames`	cuePointTimes, cuePassed, isPastCuePoint	19
cuePointTimes	Sound, QuickTime	Property	Returns a list with the time of each cue point, in milliseconds. Each item corresponds to the same item in the cuePointNames list.	`put member¬ ("mySound").¬ cuePointTimes`	cuePointNames, cuePassed, isPastCuePoint	17

continues

PART

X

APP

J

Keyword	Topic	Type	Description	Syntax Sample	See Also	See Chapter/Appendix
currentSpriteNum	System	Property	Returns the number of the sprite whose script is currently running. Works only in behaviors or cast scripts.	put the¬ currentSpriteNum	spriteNum	
currentTime	Sound, QuickTime	Property	Returns the current time, in milliseconds, of a sound or digital video sprite.	put sound(1).¬ currentTime	movieTime	
cursor	Cursor	Command	Enables you to use a number, 1-bit bitmap, pair of 1-bit bitmaps, or animated cursor member as a cursor.	cursor(4) cursor¬ ([member("myCursor")]) cursor([member("myCursor"),¬ member("myMask")]) cursor(member¬ ("myAnimatedCursor"))		
cursor	Sprite	Property	Enables you to set a cursor to be used when the cursor is over a sprite.	sprite(1).cursor = 3		17
cursorSize	Cursor	Property	For animated cursor members, enables you to set the cursor size to 16 or 32.	member¬ ("myAnimatedCursor")¬ .cursorSize = 32	cursor	21
date	System	Property	Reads the user's computer's clock and returns the date in various formats. You can use "abbr," "long," and "short" as modifiers. The actual result depends on the user's computer's date settings.	put the date put the abbr date put the long date put the short date	abbr, long, short, time, systemDate	

Term	Category	Type	Description	Example	Related	Ch.

date	Date & Time	Object	An object type. Can accept an integer, a string, or three integers initially. Object converts to a series of three integers: year, month, and day.	`d = date(19990506)`
				`d = date("19990506")`
				`d = date(1999,05,06)`
				`put d + 1`
					day, month, year	

day	Date & Time	Property	A property of a date object.	`put myDate.day`	date, month, year	21
deactivateWindow	MIAW	Event Handler	Called when a window is the active window, but is then deactivated because the user clicks on another window or another window opens.		activateWindow, openWindow, closeWindow	21

defaultRect	Flash, Vector	Property	The default size for sprites created using that Flash or vector shape member, or existing sprites that have not been stretched. Only works if the defaultRectMode is set to #fixed. This property automatically changes *defaultRectMode* to #fixed when it is changed.	`member("myFlash").¬`
				`defaultRect =¬`
				`rect(0,0,100,100)`
					defaultRectMode	21

defaultRectMode	Flash, Vector	Property	Either #Flash or #fixed. The first means that the real size of the member will be used in non-stretched sprites. The second means that the defaultRect property will be used.	`member("myFlash").¬`
				`defaultRectMode =¬`
				`#Flash`
					defaultRect	24

continues

PART

X

APP

J

Keyword	Topic	Type	Description	Syntax Sample	See Also	See Chapter/ Appendix
delay	Navigation	Command	Place in an on exitFrame or on enterFrame handler to extend the playback time of a frame by a number of ticks.	delay 60	ticks	20
delete	Strings	Command	Deletes a chunk expression from a string.	delete myString.¬ word[2].char[5]	char, word, line, item	20
deleteAll	List	Command	Removes all items from a list.	deleteAll myList	deleteAt	
deleteAt	List	Command	Removes a single item from a linear or property list.	deleteAt(myList,7)	addAt, getAt	13
deleteFrame	Score Recording	Command	Removes the current frame and moves all frames after it down one during Score recording.		beginRecording, updateFrame	
deleteOne	List	Command	Removes the first value in the list that matches the value given to this command.	deleteOne myList,¬ valueToDelete	deleteAt, deleteProp	13
deleteProp	List	Command	Removes the first property in a property list that matches the property given to this command.	deleteProp myList,¬ propToDelete	deleteAt	
deleteVertex	Vector	Command	Removes a vertex point from a Vector shape member.	deleteVertex(member¬ ("myVector"), 2)	addVertex, moveVertex, vertexList	

Keyword	Category	Type	Description	Example	See Also	Chapter
depth	Bitmap	Property	Returns the bit depth of a bitmap member.	`put member("myBitmap").depth`		13
deskTopRectList	System	Property	Returns a list of rectangles that corresponds to the monitor(s) connected to the computer.	`put (the desktopRectList)[1].width`		20
digitalVideoTimeScale	Digital Video	Property	A system property: units per second timescale that Director uses to track video. A value of 0 means that Director uses the scale of the currently playing video.	`the digitalVideoTimeScale = 0`		18
digitalVideoType	Digital Video	Property	Returns #quickTime or #videoForWindows.	`put member("myVideo").digitalVideoType`		21
directToStage	Flash, Vector, Digital Video, Animated GIF	Property	Whether the member or sprite is drawn directly to the Stage, speeding up playback, but not using sprite inks.	`member("myVideo").directToStage = TRUE` `sprite(7).directToStage = TRUE`		
dither	Bitmap	Property	If TRUE, a 16-bit or higher bitmap will be dithered when shown on an 8-bit screen. This results in a better image, but slower performance.	`member("myBitmap").dither = TRUE`	depth	19
do	Programming	Command	This powerful command takes a string and executes it as a Lingo command. You can include any Lingo syntax, including calls to your own handlers.	`do myString`		19, 20

PART

X

APP

J

continues

Keyword	Topic	Type	Description	Syntax Sample	See Also	See Chapter/Appendix
don'tPassEvent	Programming	Command	Made obsolete by stopEvent. Prevents an event, such as a mouseUp, from passing to the next message level. For instance, a behavior can prevent the message from passing to the movie script. This is considered obsolete because messages are never passed on, unless the *pass* command is used.		stopEvent, pass	
doubleClick	System	Property	Returns a TRUE if the last two mouse clicks were very close together. An odd property, because a true double-click needs to occur on the same object, whereas this property can return TRUE if the two clicks occurred on different sprites.	`if the doubleClick` `then...`	mouseDown, mouseUp	
downloadNetThing	Network	Command	Transfers a file from an Internet location to the local disk. Use netDone to see whether the operation is complete. Does not work in Shockwave for security reasons.	`GNetID =¬` `downloadNetThing¬` `("http://clevermedia.¬` `com/images/cmad3.¬` `gif", "temp.gif")`	netDone	16

Term	Category	Type	Description	Example	See Also	Page

drawRect	MIAW	Property	Returns the rectangle of a window. You can set this property too, which results in the scaling of bitmaps and some other sprites.	`put window("myMIAW").¬`
				`drawRect`
				`put (theStage).drawRect`
					sourceRect	

dropShadow	Field	Property	The offset of the black shadow under text in a field member.	`Member("myField").¬` `dropShadow = 1`	margin, boxType, boxDropShadow, border	

duplicate	Member	Command	Creates a copy of a member. It places it in the next available member slot, or in a specific slot if specified.	`Duplicate member¬`
				`("myMember")`
				`duplicate¬`
				`member("myMember"),¬`
				`member("newMember¬`
				`","otherCast")`
					new, erase	24

duplicate	List	Function	Returns a new list, identical to the one it is given. This is needed because lists are objects, so simply setting a variable equal to a list creates only another pointer to the same list, rather than a new list.	`NewList =¬` `duplicate(myist)`		16
duplicateFrame	Score Recording	Command	During Score recording, this creates a new frame, identical to the current one, and places it after the current one. It also advances the playback head one frame.		beginRecording, updateFrame	

PART

X

APP

J

continues

Keyword	Topic	Type	Description	Syntax Sample	See Also	See Chapter/ Appendix
duration	Transition, Digital Video, Shockwave Audio	Property	The length of the transition (milliseconds), video (ticks), or SWA (ticks, only while streaming).	put member¬ ("myVideo").duration	percentPlayed, movieTime	
editable	Text, Field, Sprite	Property	When TRUE, the text or field member can be edited by the users. If not TRUE as a member property, the member can still be edited if the sprite property is TRUE.	Member("myText"). editable = TRUE sprite(7).editable = TRUE	autoTab	
else					if	17, 19
EMPTY	Strings	Constant	Any empty string with 0 length. Same as "".	if myString =¬ EMPTY then...		16
emulateMultiButton-Mouse	System	Property	If TRUE, a Control+click on the Mac acts like a right mouse button click on Windows.	the¬ emulateMultiButtonMouse¬ = TRUE	rightMouseDown, rightMouseUp	
enabled	Menubar	Property	A menu item property. It enables you to enable or disable a single menu item.	the enabled of¬ menuitem 1 of¬ menu 1 = TRUE	menuitem, installMenu	
enableHotSpot	QTVR	Command	Enables you to enable or disable a hotspot in a QTVR movie.	EnableHotSpot¬ (sprite(7),¬ myHotSpot,TRUE)		

Term	Category	Type	Description	Example	See Also	Chapter
end	Programming	Misc	The line that marks the end of a handler. Also used as END IF, END CASE, and END REPEAT to mark the end of those structures.		on, if, case, repeat	21
endColor	Vector	Property	Destination color of a gradient. Has an effect only if the fillMode is set to #gradient.	Member("myVector").¬ endColor = rgb¬ (255, 0, 0)	fillMode, fillColor, fillCycles, fillDirection, fillOffset, fillScale, closed	
endFrame	Sprite	Property	Returns the last frame of a sprite span.	put sprite(7).¬ endFrame	startFrame	
endRecording	Score Recording	Command	Used to signify the end of a Score recording session.		beginRecording, updateFrame	20
endSprite	Behaviors	Event Handler	This event handler is called when the movie moves out of a frame, and on to one that does not contain the sprite.	on endSprite me	beginSprite	
ENTER	Strings	Constant	Represents the character generated by the Enter key on the numeric keypad.	if the key =¬ ENTER then...	RETURN	26
enterFrame	Frame Scripts, Behaviors	Event Handler	This handler is called just after Director draws the current frame, but before any idle time occurs.	on enterFrame me	prepareFrame, exitFrame, idle	14

continues

PART

X

APP

J

Keyword	Topic	Type	Description	Syntax Sample	See Also	See Chapter/Appendix
environment	System	Property	Returns a list containing platform, runMode, and colorDepth information.	put the environment	platform, runMode, colorDepth	
erase	Casts	Command	Enables you to remove a member from a Cast.	erase member¬ ("myUselessMember")		14
EvalScript	Shockwave	Event Handler	Receives events sent by the browser from JavaScript or VbScript "EvalScript()" functions. Accepts parameters as well. Can also use a return command to send a value back to the browser when it is done.	on EvalScript¬ myParam	externalEvent	
exit	Programming	Command	Exits the current handler without executing any more commands. The handler that called the current one, if any, continues.		abort	
exitFrame	Frame Scripts, Behaviors	Event Handler	This handler is called just before Director leaves the current frame.	on exitFrame me	enterFrame, idle	22
exitLock	Navigation	Property	If this system property is set to TRUE, the user cannot use the keys such as Command+Q, Ctrl+Q, Command+., Ctrl+., or Esc to quit a Projector.	the exitLock = TRUE		

Term	Category	Type	Description	Example	See Also	Page
Exit repeat	Programming	Command	Ends the current repeat loop immediately, skipping any code left in that instance of the loop and picking up with the first line of code after the loop.	exit repeat	repeat	13, 14
exp	Math	Function	Returns the natural logarithm base, e, to the power given.	put exp(3)	log	
externalEvent	Shockwave	Command	Sends a string to the browser, which it interprets with JavaScript or VBScript.	externalEvent¬ ("myJavaScriptFunction¬ ()")	EvalScript	13
externalParamCount	Shockwave	Function	Returns the number of parameters in the EMBED or OBJECT tag for a Shockwave movie.	numParams =¬ externalParamCount()	externalParamName, externalParamValue	13
externalParamName	Shockwave	Function	Returns the name of a specific parameter from the EMBED of OBJECT tag in the browser.	paramName =¬ externalParamName(2)	externalParamCount	22
externalParamValue	Shockwave	Function	Returns the value of a specific parameter from the EMBED of OBJECT tag in the browser.	paramName =¬ externalParamValue¬ (2)	externalParamCount, externalParamValue	22
fadeIn					sound fadeIn	22
fadeOut					sound fadeOut	22
FALSE	Logic	Constant	Logical false. Use in if, repeat, case, or other logic statements. Equivalent to 0.		if, repeat, case, TRUE	

continues

Keyword	Topic	Type	Description	Syntax Sample	See Also	See Chapter/Appendix
field	Field	Object	Old syntax that can be used to refer to field members the same way as member in many cases. It really refers to the text of the member, so it cannot be used as a member reference.	`put field¬ ("myField")`	member	
fieldOfView	QTVR	Property	The current field of view of a QTVR sprite in degrees.	`sprite(7).¬ fieldOfView = 60`		13
fileName	Casts, Member, MIAW	Property	Refers to the external file path of either a cast library, member, or MIAW. In many cases, can also be an Internet location.	`member¬ ("myExternalVideo")¬ .fileName =¬ "newvideo.mov" castLib("myCast").¬ fileName =¬ "newcast.cst"`	url	16
fillColor	Vector	Property	The primary fill color for a closed vector shape member. Also the starting color if a gradient is used.	`member("myVector")¬ .fillColor =¬ rgb(0,0,255)`	endColor, fillMode, fillCycles, fillDirection, fillOffset, fillScale, gradientType, closed	
fillCycles	Vector	Property	The number of cycles in a gradient fill of a closed vector shape member.	`member("myVector").¬ fillCycles = 2`	endColor, fillColor, fillMode, fillDirection, fillOffset, fillScale, gradientType, closed	16, 24

Name	Type	Description	Example	Related	Page
fillDirection	Vector	The number of degrees of rotation of a gradient fill for a closed vector shape member.	`member("myVector"). ¬ fillDirection = 90`	endColor, fillColor, fillMode, fillCycles, fillOffset, fillScale, closed	20, 28
filled	Shape	Whether the shape member is filled or not.	`member("myOval"). ¬ filled = TRUE`	pattern, color	20
fillMode	Vector	The type of fill used by a closed vector shape member. Possible values are: #none, #solid, and #gradient.	`member("myVector"). ¬ fillMode = #gradient`	endColor, fillColor, fillDirection, fillCycles, fillOffset, fillScale, gradientType, closed	20
fillOffset	Vector	The position offset of a fill in a closed vector shape.	`member("myVector"). ¬ fillOffset = ¬ point(100,50)`	endColor, fillColor, fillDirection, fillMode, fillCycles, fillScale, gradientType, closed	20
fillScale	Vector	The scale of a gradient fill for a closed vector shape.	`member("myVector"). ¬ fillScale = 2`	endColor, fillColor, fillDirection, fillMode, fillCycles, fillOffset, gradientType, closed	20

PART
X
APP
J

continues

Keyword	Topic	Type	Description	Syntax Sample	See Also	See Chapter/Appendix
findEmpty	Casts	Function	When given a cast member, returns the next empty member in that Cast.	`put findEmpty¬ (member("myBitmap"))`	erase, duplicate, move	20
findLabel	Flash	Function	Returns the frame number in a Flash movie that is associated with the label name.	`put findLabel¬ (sprite(7), "myLabel")`	frame	20
findPos	List	Function	Returns the position of a property in a property list, and VOID if it is not there.	`put findPos¬ (myList, #myProp)`	findPosNear	
findPosNear	List	Function	Returns the position of a property in a property list, or value in a linear list. If the item is not there, it returns the closest alphanumeric match. The list must be sorted first with the *sort* command.	`put findPosNear¬ (myList, myVal)`	findPos, sort	
finishIdleLoad	Memory	Command	Forces idle loading to complete for members with a specific idle load tag.	`finishIdleLoad 7`	idleLoadTag	
firstIndent	Text	Property	A property of a chunk inside a text member. It provides for a left indent at the start of new lines. Measured in pixels.	`member("myText").¬ line[1..3].¬ firstIndent = 18`	leftIndent, rightIndent	

continues

fixedLineSpace	Text	Property	The line height of a specific line or all the lines in a text member. A value of 0 enables the line height to be determined by the font and size.	`member("myText").¬`
				`line[1..7].¬`
				`fixedLineSpace = 14`
					lineHeight

fixedRate	Animated GIF, Flash	Property	If the playbackMode property of a member or sprite is set to #fixed, this controls frame rate. Default is 15.	`member("myGIF").¬` `fixedRate = 5`	playbackMode 16
fixStageSize	Movie	Property	If TRUE, the Stage remains the same size when a new movie is loaded, even if that movie uses a different Stage size.	`the fixStageSize¬` `= TRUE`	centerStage, drawRect 16

flashRect	Flash, Vector	Property	Returns the original size of a Flash or vector shape member.	`put member¬`
				`("myFlash").¬`
				`flashRect`
					defaultRect, defaultRectMode, state 20

flashToStage	Flash	Property	Returns the point on the Stage that matches a point in a Flash sprite.	`put flashToStage¬`
				`(sprite(7),¬`
				`point(50,30))`
					stageToFlash, hitTest

flipH	Sprite	Property	If TRUE, the sprite appears flipped horizontally on the Stage.	`sprite(7).¬` `flipH = TRUE`	flipV 20
flipV	Sprite	Property	If TRUE, the sprite appears flipped vertically on the Stage.	`sprite(7).¬` `flipV = TRUE`	flipH
float	Math	Function	Converts an integer or string to a floating point number.	`put float(5)` `put float(".5")`	floatPrecision, integer, value 16

PART

X

APP

J

Keyword	Topic	Type	Description	Syntax Sample	See Also	See Chapter/Appendix
floatP	Math	Function	Tests an expression and returns TRUE if it is a floating point number.	`if floatP¬` `(myVal) then...`	integerP	16
floatPrecision	Math	Property	This system property determines how many decimal places are to be returned in any floating point number math. Default is 4. Values can go up to 15. A 0 means that all floating point functions will round to an integer. A negative number is the same as positive, but all floating point math uses absolute (positive) values.	`the¬` `floatPrecision = 2`	float	13
font	Text, Field, Button	Property	The name of the font used by a member, or a chunk in a member.	`member("myText").¬` `font = "Times"`	fontSize, fontStyle	33
fontSize	Text, Field, Button	Property	The size of the font used by a member, or a chunk in a member.	`member("myText").¬` `fontSize = 12`	font, fontStyle	32

fontStyle	Text, Field, Button	Property	The style(s) used by a member, or a chunk in a member. Field and buttons use a string such as "bold, italic," whereas text members use a list, such as [#bold, #italic].	`member("myField").¬`
				`fontStyle = "Bold"`
				`member("myText").¬`
				`fontStyle = [#bold]`
					font, fontSize	14, 16

Name	Type	Description	Example	See Also	Chapter

forecolor	Property	Can be used to set the color of text in a field or text member to a palette index number. Can also be used to set the forecolor of a sprite. Made mostly obsolete by color.	`member("myField").¬`
			`forecolor = 35`
			`sprite(7).¬`
			`forecolor = 215`
				color, backcolor	16

forget	Command	Removes an MIAW from memory. If a variable refers to it, the *forget* command will not work until that variable is set to 0.	`forget window¬` `("myMIAW")`	close	16
frame	Property	The number of the current frame that is playing.	`the frame = 7`	frameLabel, marker, label, go	16
frame	Property	The number of the current frame in the Flash movie sprite.	`put sprite(7).frame`	findLabel, frameCount	24

frameCount	Property	Returns the number of frames in a Flash member.	`put member¬`
			`("myFlash").¬`
			`frameCount`
				frame	

frameLabel	Property	Returns the label of the frame that is currently playing. If there is no label on the current frame, it returns a 0. During Score recording, it can be set.	`put the frameLabel`	frame, labelList	

Movie

MIAW

Movie

Flash

Flash

Movie, Score Recording

continues

PART

X

APP

J

Keyword	Topic	Type	Description	Syntax Sample	See Also	See Chapter/ Appendix
framePalette	Movie, Score Recording	Property	Returns the palette member used in the current frame. Can be set during Score recording.	`put the framePalette`	puppetPalette	20
frameRate	Flash, Digital Video	Property	You can use this to get, but not set, the frame rate of a Flash member. You can set the frame rate of a digital video member from 0 to 255. A value of -1 sets the video to play at normal rate, and a value of -2 sets the video to play as fast as possible.	`member("myVideo").¬` `frameRate = -1`	fixedRate, movieRate, movieTime, playbackMode	
frameReady	Shockwave	Function	Returns TRUE if a frame or range of frames have been loaded in Shockwave streaming.	`if frameReady¬` `(6,10) then...`	mediaReady	

frameReady	Flash	Function	Returns TRUE if a Flash sprite's frame has been loaded and is ready to play.	`if frameReady¬`
				`(sprite(7),25)¬`
				`then...`
						19, 20

frameScript	Movie, Score Recording	Property	Returns the member used in the frame script channel of the current frame. Can be set during Score recording.	`put the frameScript`	scriptInstanceList	37

37

Name	Category	Type	Description	Syntax	Cross-ref
frameSound1	Movie, Score Recording	Property	Returns the sound member used in the first sound channel of the current frame. Can be set during Score recording.	`put the frameSound1`	puppetSound
frameSound2	Movie, Score Recording	Property	Returns the sound member used in the second sound channel of the current frame. Can be set during Score recording.	`put the frameSound2`	puppetSound
framesToHMS	Misc	Function	Takes a number of frames and tempo and returns a string with hours, minutes, and seconds, as in "00:01:30.X." It requires two other parameters: one set to TRUE only if you want to compensate for NTSC video frame timing, and one set to TRUE if the final portion (the X above) is in frames or seconds.	`put framesToHMS¬` `(2000,15,FALSE,FALSE)`	HMStoFrames
frameTempo	Movie, Score Recording	Property	Returns the tempo used in the current frame. Can be set during Score recording.	`put the frameTempo`	puppetTempo
frameTransition	Movie, Score Recording	Property	Returns the transition member used in the current frame. Can be set during Score recording.	`put the¬` `frameTransition`	puppetTransition

continues

PART

X

APP

J

Keyword	Topic	Type	Description	Syntax Sample	See Also	See Chapter/ Appendix
freeBlock	System	Function	Returns the largest free block of memory available to the movie in bytes.	`put the freeBlock()`	freeBytes, memorySize, ramNeeded, size	
freeBytes	System	Function	Returns the total number of bytes available to the movie.	`put the freeBytes()`	freeBlock, memorySize, ramNeeded, size	
frontWindow	MIAW	Property	Returns the window that is frontmost. If it is the Stage, it returns (the stage). If a Director palette is frontmost, it returns VOID.	`put the frontWindow`	activeWindow, moveToFront	34
getaProp	List	Function	Returns the value of a property in a property list. If the property is not present, it returns VOID.	`put getaProp¬ (myList,#a)`	getAt, getProp	21
getAt	List	Function	Returns the value at a specific position in a linear or property list. If position is beyond the end of the list, it generates an error message.	`put getAt(myList,7)`	getProp	24
getBehaviorDescription	Behaviors	Event Handler	The string returned from this behavior is used in the Behavior Inspector.	`on getProperty¬ DescriptionList me`		13

	Behaviors	Event Handler				
getBehaviorTooltip	Behaviors	Event Handler	Used to generate a tool tip when the behavior is made part of a library.	on¬ getBehaviorTooltip me		13
getError	Shockwave Audio, Flash	Function	Returns an error code of a Shockwave audio member. 0 is OK, 1 is a memory error, 2 is a network error, 3 is a playback error, and 99 is another error. For Flash members, it returns symbols: #memory, #fileNotFound, #network, #fileFormat, #other.	if getError(member¬ ("mySWA")) =¬ 0 then...	getErrorString, clearError, state	14
getErrorString	Shockwave Audio	Function	Takes a Shockwave audio error code from getError and returns a string that describes the error.	alert getErrorString¬ (mySWAerror)	getError	14
getHotSpotRect	QTVR	Function	Returns the rectangle of a QTVR hotspot on the Stage.	put getHotSpot¬ (sprite(7),2)		33
getLast	List	Function	Returns the last value in a linear or property list.	put getLast(myList)	getAt	33
getNetErrorString	Network	Function	Takes a network error code from netError and returns a short string description.	alert¬ getNetErrorString¬ (myNetError)	netError	33

continues

PART

X

APP

J

Keyword	Topic	Type	Description	Syntax Sample	See Also	See Chapter/ Appendix
getNetText	Network	Function	Starts retrieving a text file from the Internet. It returns a network ID for the operation.	getNetText¬ ("http://¬ clevermedia.com")	netTextResult, netDone	
getNthFileNameInFolder	Files	Function	When given a valid file path and a number, it returns the filename. If the number is greater than the number of files in the folder, it returns an empty string.	put¬ getNthFileNameInFolder¬ (the pathname,1)	@	
getOne	List	Function	For a linear list, returns the position of the first item that is equal to the given value. For a property list, it returns the property.	put getOne¬ (myList,myValue)	getAt, getProp, getPos	22
getPixel	Bitmap	Function	Undocumented. Returns an integer that corresponds to the color of the pixel at a coordinate in a bitmap image. Type of number depends on the bit depth. 32-bit images return a large integer that corresponds to the hexadecimal color value of the pixel. Sometimes returns bad values, especially if an alpha channel is involved.	put getPixel¬ (member¬ ("myBitmap"),x,y)	setPixel	29, 36

Name	Type	Kind	Description	Example	See Also	Chapter
getPos	List	Function	Like *getOne*, but returns a position for property lists, not a property.	`put getPos¬ (myList,myValue)`	getOne	15
getPref	Shockwave	Function	Gets a preference file's contents. Preference files are used in Shockwave to store "cookies" of information without creating a security risk.	`myPref = getPref¬ ("clevermediaGame1")`	setPref	
getProp	List	Function	Returns the value of a property in a property list. If the property is not present, generates an error message.	`put getProp¬ (myList,#a)`	getAt, getaProp	16, 18
getPropAt	List	Function	Returns the property at a specific position in a property list.	`put getPropAt¬ (myList.,7)`	getProp	22
getPropertyDescriptionList	Behaviors	Event Handler	Called when the behavior is dropped on or added to a sprite. The list returned is used to generate the parameters dialog box.	`on getProperty¬ DescriptionList me`		
getStreamStatus	Network	Function	When given network ID or URL, this function returns a list with information about the progress of streaming. The list includes #URL, #state, #bytesSoFar, #bytesTotal, and #error.	`put getStreamStatus¬ (gNetID)`	tellStreamStatus	

PART

X

APP

J

continues

Keyword	Topic	Type	Description	Syntax Sample	See Also	See Chapter/Appendix
global	Program-ming	Command	Defines variables as globals. Place in handlers, or outside all handlers in a script to declare it for use in all handlers in that script.	`global gMyGlobal, ¬` `gMyOtherGlobal`	property, showGlobals, clearGlobals	14
globals	System	Property	Returns a property list of all globals that are not VOID.	`put the globals`	global	

go	Naviga-tion	Command	Moves the playback head to a new frame or even a frame in another movie. You can use a frame number or label.	`go to frame¬`
				`"newFrame"`
				`go toframe 7`
				`go to frame"into" of ¬`
				`movie"newmovie"`
				`go to movie "newMovie"`
					go loop, go next, go prev, play	13

go loop	Naviga-tion	Command	Sends the playback head back to the most recent frame label.	`go loop`	go, go next, go previous, marker	
go next	Naviga-tion	Command	Sends the playback head to the next frame with a frame label.	`go next`	go, go loop, go previous, marker	13
go previous	Naviga-tion	Command	Sends the playback head to the frame with a frame label that is before the current frame label. This usually means sending the playback head back two labels.	`go previous`	go, go loop, go next, marker	13
goToFrame	Flash	Command	Starts playing a Flash sprite from the frame number or name.	`goToFrame¬` `(sprite(7),"intro")`	frame	13

gotoNetMovie	Shockwave	Command	Gets a new movie from the Internet and replaces the current one with it. The first movie continues playing until the second one loads.	`gotoNetMovie¬`
				`("http://clevermedia.¬`
				`com/arcade/cleverdots`
				`.dcr")`
					netDone	13

gotoNetPage	Shockwave, Network	Command	In Shockwave, it loads a new URL in the current browser window or another window or frame. You can also use a second parameter as a browser target. In Projectors, it launches the user's browser and loads the URL.	`gotoNetPage¬`
				`("http://clevermedia.¬`
				`com")`
				`gotoNetPage(("http://¬`
				`clevermedia.com¬`
				`","_top")`
					netDone, browserName	20, 22

gradientType	Vector	Property	Either #linear or #radial to specify the type of gradient to use. Vector shape member must be closed and have its fillType set to #gradient.	`member("myVector").¬`
				`gradientType =¬`
				`#radial`
					endColor, fillColor, fillDirection, fillMode, fillCycles, fillOffset, fillScale, closed	22

green					rgb	22
halt	Naviga-tion	Command	In Director, the current handler and all other handlers stop and the movie stops. Projectors quit.	`halt`	abort, exit, quit	20

continues

Keyword	Topic	Type	Description	Syntax Sample	See Also	See Chapter/Appendix

height	Sprites, Members	Property	Returns the height of most members and sprites. Can also be used as a property of rect objects.	`put sprite(7).¬`
				`height`
				`put myRect.height`
					width, rect	

hilite	Field	Command	Enables you to select a hunk portion of a field member.	`hilite member¬` `("myField").word[5]`	selStart, selEnd	13

hilite	Button	Property	A radio button or check box property that determines whether the button appears checked.	`if member¬`
				`("myButton").¬`
				`hilite then...`
					checkBoxAccess, checkBoxType	

hitTest	Vector, Flash	Function	Returns either #background, #normal, or #button depending on what the point specified is positioned over.	`if hitTest(sprite(7),¬` `point(50,25)) then...`		16

HMStoFrames	Misc	Function	Opposite of *framesToHMS*, takes a string rather than a number and converts it to a number of frames.	`put HMStoFrames¬`
				`("00:05:20.05",¬`
				`15, FALSE, FALSE)`
					framesToHMS	15

hold	Flash	Command	Stops a Flash sprite.	`hold sprite(7)`		

hotSpot	Cursor	Property	A point that represents the hotspot within an animated cursor.	`member("myCursor")¬`
				`.hotSpot = point¬`
				`(7,13)`
						20

Name	Object	Type	Description	Example	See Also	Chapter

hotSpotEnterCallback	QTVR	Property	Set this to the name of the handler to be called when the cursor enters the hotspot of a QTVR movie. The first parameter is *me*, and the second is the ID of the hotspot.	`sprite(7).¬`
				`hotSpotEnterCallBack`
				`= "myHotSpotHandler"`
					hotSpot
					ExitCallback,
					nodeEnterCallback,
					triggerCallback	

hotSpotExitCallback	QTVR	Property	Set this to the name of the handler to be called when the cursor exits the hotspot of a QTVR movie. The first parameter is *me*, and the second is the ID of the hotspot.	`sprite(7).¬`
				`hotSpotExitCallBack`
				`= "myHotSpotHandler"`
					hotSpot
					EnterCallback,
					nodeExitCallback,
					triggerCallback
						21

HTML	Text	Property	The HTML code that corresponds to the text in a text member.	`put member¬` `("myText").html`	text, rtf	

hyperlink	Text	Property	The hyperlink string for a specific chunk in a text member.	`member("myText").¬`
				`word[6..7].¬`
				`hyperlink = "myLink"`
					hyperlinkClicked,
					hyperlinkRange,
					hyperlinkState	

hyperlinkClicked	Text	Event Handler	Called when a hyperlink is clicked in the text member.	`on hyperlinkClicked¬` `me, data, range`	hyperlink, hyperlinkRange, hyperlinkState	16

hyperlinkRange	Text	Property	Takes the first character of the chunk and returns the full range of any hyperlink that contains it.	`put member¬`
				`("myText").¬`
				`char[123].¬`
				`hyperlinkRange`
					hyperlinkClicked,
					hyperlink,
					hyperlinkState
						16

hyperlinks	Text	Property	Returns a list with all the character ranges for hyperlinks in a text member.	`put member¬`
				`("myText").¬`
				`hyperlinks`
					hyperlinkClicked,
					hyperlinkRange,
					hyperlink
						16

continues

PART
X
APP
J

Keyword	Topic	Type	Description	Syntax Sample	See Also	See Chapter/Appendix
hyperlinkState	Text	Property	Given a chunk, it returns either #normal, #active, or #visited for the hyperlink that contains it.	`put member¬ ("myText").¬ char[241].¬ hyperlinkState`	hyperlinkClicked, hyperlink, hyperlinkRange	
idle	Behaviors, System	Event Handler	The *on idle* event handler is called one or more times between the enterFrame and the exitFrame messages.	`on idle me`	idleHandlerPeriod	16
idleHandlerPeriod	System	Property	The number of ticks between calls to the on idle handler. Default is 1.	`the¬ idleHandlerPeriod¬ = 2`	idle	
idleLoadDone	Memory	Function	Given an idle load tag, it returns TRUE if the loading has been completed.	`if idleLoadDone(7)¬ then...`	idleLoadTag	13
idleLoadMode	Memory	Property	Determines how preload commands will use idle time to load members. 0 = no idle loading, 1 = only in free time between frames, 2 = during idle events, 3 = as frequently as possible.	`the idleLoadMode = 1`	idleHandlerPeriod, idleLoadTag	
idleLoadPeriod	Memory	Property	The number of ticks the movie should wait before doing idle loading. Default is 0.	`the¬ idleLoadPeriod = 1`	idleHandlerMode, idleLoadTag	

Term	Category	Description	Example	See Also
idleLoadTag	Memory	Property	A system property that gives the members cued for loading an ID number that can be used in functions such as *idleLoadDone*.	`the idleLoadTag = 7`	idleLoadDone
idleReadChunkSize	Memory	Property	The maximum size, in bytes, of data that can be read during an idle period. Default is 32768.	`the idleReadChunkSize¬ = 60000`	idleLoadTag
if	Programming	Structure	Checks a statement to see whether it is TRUE. It executes line(s) of code if so. The ELSE IF and ELSE statements can be used to further modify the statement.	```if (a=b) then —run these lines else if (c=d) then —run these lines else —run these lines end if```	case
ilk	Programming	Function	Takes any variable and returns a symbol to describe its type. Possible values include: #integer, #float, #list, #proplist, #color, #date, and so on. Can also be used with two parameters as a test.	```put ilk(myVariable) if ilk(myVariable,¬ #list) then...```	integerP, floatP, stringP, objectP
imageEnabled	Flash, Vector	Property	If set to FALSE, the member or sprite is invisible.	```sprite(7).¬ imageEnabled¬ = FALSE```	
importFileInto	Member	Command	Imports new media from an external file or Internet location into a member.	```importFileInto¬ member("myMember"),¬ "newimage.pct"```	downloadNetThing, 33 filename, preLoadNetThing

continues

Keyword	Topic	Type	Description	Syntax Sample	See Also	See Chapter/Appendix
in			Refers to an element in a chunk expression. Used with other Lingo.		number	
inflate	Math	Function	Takes a rectangle and a width and height change and returns a new rectangle inflated from the center.	`put inflate(rect¬ (10,10,20,20),2,5)`		
ink	Sprite	Property	The ink that is used by that sprite.	`sprite(7).ink = 8`	blend, color, bgColor	
insertFrame	Score Recording	Command	During Score recording, this duplicates the current frame.		beginRecording, updateFrame	
inside	Math	Function	Returns TRUE if the point is inside the rectangle.	`put inside¬ (myPoint,myRect)`	intersects	D
installMenu	Menu	Command	Takes a field member and uses it to create a system menu bar.	`installMenu¬ member("myMenu")`		26
integer	Math	Function	Converts a floating point number or a string to an integer.	`put integer("5.3")`	float	
integerP	Math	Function	Returns TRUE if the number given is an integer.	`put¬ integerP(myNumber)`	floatP	21
interface	Xtras	Function	Returns a string describing the Xtra and its use.	`put interface¬ (xtra "FileIO")`		13

intersect	Math	Function	Takes two rectangles and returns the rectangle intersection. If not intersection, a value of rect(0,0,0,0) is returned.	`put intersect¬ (myRect1,myRect2)`	inside, intersects	33
intersects	Sprites	Function	Determines whether two sprite rectangles overlap. Note the odd syntax.	`if sprite 1¬ intersects 2 then...`	intersect
interval	Cursor	Property	Specifies the delay in milliseconds between frames of an animated cursor member.	`member("myCursor").¬ interval = 1000`
into					put	32
invertMask	Digital Video	Property	If a QuickTime movie is using a mask, setting this to TRUE reverses the mask.	`member¬ ("myQuickTime").¬ invertMask = TRUE`	mask
isPastCuePoint	Sound	Function	Returns TRUE if the cue point (number or name) has been passed. Can use a sprite or sound object.	`if isPastCuePoint¬ (sound 1, "blip")¬ then...`
isVRMovie	Digital Video	Property	TRUE if the QuickTime movie is a QTVR.	`if member¬ ("myQuickTime").¬ isVRMovie then...`		19
item	Strings	Expression	Identifies a chunk in a string, as broken up by the itemDelimiter character.	`put myString.item[7]`	itemDelimiter

PART
X
APP
J

continues

Keyword	Topic	Type	Description	Syntax Sample	See Also	See Chapter/Appendix
itemDelimiter	Strings	Property	This system property determines which character is used by the item chunk expression to break up strings. Default is a comma.	`the itemDelimiter¬ = ";"`	itemDelimiter	19
kerning	Text	Property	If TRUE, the text in a text member is automatically spaced when text is changed.	`member("myText").¬ kerning = FALSE`	kerningThreshold	13
kerningThreshold	Text	Property	If kerning is TRUE, this is the font size where kerning is to begin. Smaller characters will not be adjusted.	`member("myText").¬ kerningThreshold¬ = 14`	kerning	13
key	Keyboard	Property	This system property can be accessed in *on keyUp* and *on keyDown* handlers to determine which key has been pressed.	`if the key =¬ "a" then...`	keyCode, keyDown, keyUp, keyPressed	16
keyboardFocusSprite	Keyboard	Property	Used to set focus for keyboard input on a given text sprite.	`Set the¬ keyboardFocusSprite¬ = 3`		16

keyCode	Keyboard	Property	This system property can be accessed in *on keyUp* and *on keyDown* handlers and returns a keyboard code that can be used to detect arrow keys and function keys. (123 = left, 124 = right, 125 = down, 126 = up).	`if the keyCode¬` `= 123 then...`	key, keyDown, keyUp, keyPressed	16
keyDown	Keyboard	Event Handler	This handler is called when the user presses a key on the keyboard. The properties "the key" and "the keyCode" can be used inside it to determine the key pressed.	`on keyDown`	keyDown, keyUpScript, keyPressed, key, keyCode	16
keyDownScript	Keyboard	Property	Can be set to the name of a handler or a simple Lingo statement. It is executed first when the user presses down on a key, before any *on keyDown* handlers. Set it to an empty string to turn it off.	`the keyDownScript¬` `= "myKeyHandler"`	keyDown	16
keyPressed	Keyboard	Function	This function tests a character or keyboard code to see whether that key is currently being pressed. (123 = left, 124 = right, 125 = down, 126 = up).	`if keyPressed¬` `("a") then...`	keyDown, keyUp	12

continues

Keyword	Topic	Type	Description	Syntax Sample	See Also	See Chapter/Appendix
keyPressed	Keyboard	Property	Returns the character or key code of the last key pressed.	`if the keyPressed¬ = 123 then...`	keyDown, keyUp	
keyUp	Keyboard	Event Handler	This handler is called when the user lifts his finger off a key on the keyboard. The properties "the key" and "the keyCode" can be used inside it to determine the key pressed.	`on keyUp`	keyDown, keyUpScript, keyPressed, key, keyCode	16
keyUpScript	Keyboard	Event Handler	Can be set to the name of a handler or to a simple Lingo statement. It will be executed first when the user lifts up a key, before any on keyUp handlers. Set it to an empty string to turn it off.	`the keyUpScript¬ = "myKeyHandler"`	keyUp	16
label	Movie	Function	Given a frame label, it returns the frame number. If the label does not exist, 0 is returned.	`put label("intro")`	frameLabel, labelList, marker	12
labelList	Movie	Property	Returns a string with each frame label in the Score on a line.	`put the labelList`	frameLabel, label, marker	
last	Strings	Expression	Modifies a chunk expression. Can only be used with old (not dot) syntax.	`put the last¬ word of myString`	char, word, item, line	13, 14

lastChannel	Movie	The number of channels in the Score, as set in the Movie Properties dialog box.	put the lastChannel	
lastClick	System	Returns the number of ticks since the last mouse click.	put the lastClick	lastEvent, lastKey, lastRoll
lastEvent	System	Returns the number of ticks since the last mouse click, rollover, or key press.	put the lastEvent	lastClick, lastKey, lastRoll
lastFrame	Movie	Returns the number of the last frame in the movie.	put the lastFrame	
lastKey	System	Returns the number of ticks since the last key was pressed.	put the lastKey	lastEvent, lastClick, lastRoll
lastRoll	System	Returns the number of ticks since the mouse was last moved.	put the lastRoll	lastEvent, lastClick, lastKey
left	Sprites, Misc	Returns the left side location of a sprite. Can also be used as a property of rect objects.	put sprite(7).left put myRect.left	width, right, top, bottom, rect
leftIndent	Text	Sets the number of pixels for a left indent for a whole text member, or a chunk inside one.	member("myText").¬ line[5..6].¬ leftIndent = 18	rightIndent, firstIndent
length	Strings	Returns the number of characters in a string.	put myString.length	count

continues

Keyword	Topic	Type	Description	Syntax Sample	See Also	See Chapter/ Appendix
line	Strings	Expression	Identifies a chunk in a string, as broken up by the RETURN character.	`put myString.line[7]`	paragraph	16
lineCount	Field	Property	Gives you the number of visible lines, taking into account word wrapping, of a field.	`put member¬ ("myField").¬ lineCount`	wordWrap	16
lineDirection	Shape	Property	A 0 if the line shape goes from upper-left to lower-right, and a 1 if the line shape goes from upper-right to lower-left.	`member("myLine").¬ lineDirection = 1`		
lineHeight	Field	Function	When given a field member and a line number, returns the line height of that line.	`put lineHeight¬ (member("myField"),4)`	fixedLineSpace	
lineHeight	Field	Property	Enables you to set the line height of an entire text field.	`member("myField").¬ lineHeight = 16`	fixedLineSpace	
linePosToLocV	Text, Field	Function	Determines the vertical location of a line in a text or field member. The location is relative to the top of the member.	`put linePosToLocV¬ (member("myText"),7)`	locVtoLinePos, charPosToLoc	16

Name	Category	Type	Description	Example	Related	Chapter
lineSize	Shape	Property	Determines the thickness of the border in a shape member.	member("myShape").lineSize = 2 ¬ sprite(7).lineSize = 2		16
linked	Flash, Animated GIF	Property	Determines whether the member is internal or linked to an external file.	member("myFlash").linked = TRUE	fileName	16
list	Lists	Function	Takes any number of parameters and returns a linear list containing them all.	put list(1,2,3,4,5)	[]	20
listP	Lists	Function	Returns TRUE if the value given is a valid list.	put listP(myVariable)	ilk	
loaded	Memory	Property	Returns TRUE if the member has been loaded into memory.	if member("myMember").loaded then...	preLoad	
loc	Sprites	Property	The location of the sprite on the Stage, as a point.	sprite(1).loc = point(50,20)	rect, locH, locV	33
locH	Sprites	Property	The horizontal location of the sprite on the Stage.	sprite(1).locH = 50	rect, loc, locV	21
locToCharPos	Text, Field	Function	Takes a member and a location and returns the character number at that location. It is relative to the upper-left corner of the member.	put locToCharPos(member("myText"), point(50,0))	charPosToLoc, locVtoLinePos	13
locV	Sprites	Property	The vertical location of the sprite on the Stage.	sprite(1).locV = 50	rect, loc, locH	13

continues

Keyword	Topic	Type	Description	Syntax Sample	See Also	See Chapter/ Appendix
locVToLinePos	Text, Field	Function	Takes a member and a vertical location and returns the line number at that location. It is relative to the top of the member.	`put locVToLinePos¬ (member("myText"),24)`	linePosToLocV, locToCharPos	16
locZ	Sprites	Property	Determines the draw order of a sprite. Each sprite starts with a locZ of its own channel number. You can set it to values from about -2 billion to 2 billion. Lower numbered sprites appear under higher ones. If a tie, the sprite number determines the draw position.	`sprite(7).¬ locZ = 1000`		13
log	Math	Function	Returns the natural logarithm of a number.	`put log(5)`	exp, log10	16
long					date, time	
loop					go loop	
loop	Flash, Digital Video	Property	Whether a Flash movie or video loops back to the beginning when it reaches the end.	`member("myFlash").¬ loop = TRUE`		
loop	Sound	Property	Undocumented property. You can set a sound member to loop.	`member("mySound")¬ = TRUE`		

Term	Category	Type	Description	Example	See Also

loopBounds	Digital Video	Property	The start time and end time for a loop in a QuickTime video. It is a list of two integers, which correspond to time in ticks.	`sprite(7).¬`
				`loopBounds =¬`
				`[60,240]`	

machineType	System	Property	This obsolete system property returns the Macintosh system ID number. For instance, 69 is a PowerMac 8500. For all Windows machines, it returns 256. In almost all cases it is better to use the platform.	`put the machineType`	platform

map	Math	Function	Takes a target rectangle, a source rectangle, and a destination rectangle or point. It returns a new destination rectangle or point that corresponds to the source rectangle mapped to the target rectangle. Used for advanced Lingo positioning.	`put map(myTargetRect,¬`
				`mySourceRect,¬`
				`myDestPoint)`
					19

mapMemberToStage	Sprites, Math	Function	Takes a sprite and a point in the member and returns the location on the Stage that corresponds to the point in the member. Works even with flips, rotation, and skew.	`put mapMemberToStage¬`
				`(sprite(7),¬`
				`point(50,50))`
					mapStageToMember

continues

PART
X
APP
J

Keyword	Topic	Type	Description	Syntax Sample	See Also	See Chapter/Appendix
mapStageToMember	Sprites, Math	Function	Takes a sprite and a point on the Stage and returns the location in the member that corresponds to the point on the Stage. Works even with flips, rotation, and skew.	`put mapStageToMember¬ (sprite(7),¬ the mouseLoc)`	mapMemberToStage	
margin	Field	Property	The size of the space between the edge of a field and the text in the field.	`member("myField")¬ .margin = 1`	border, boxType, boxDropShadow, dropShadow	18
marker	Movie	Function	Returns the frame number of the frame with the current label (0), the preceding label (-1), the next label (1), or any other labeled frame relative to the current frame.	`put marker(0)`	label, labelList, frame	18
mask	Digital Video	Property	Set this to a 1-bit member to be used as a mask for a QuickTime video. Set to 0 to have no mask.	`member("myQuickTime")¬ .mask = member¬ ("Video Mask")`	invertMask	16
max	Math	Function	Compares two or more numbers and returns the highest.	`put max(4,5)` `put max(5,3,8,3,5,12)`	min	13

Term	Category	Type	Description	Example	See Also	Chapter
maxInteger	Math	Property	This system property returns the largest integer supported by the computer. Usually a number just over 2 billion.	put the maxInteger		19
mci	Misc	Command	Sends a command string to the Windows Media Control Interface. This enables you to send commands to PC cards and hardware. This is obsolete, but still works in some cases. Using Xtras is the recommended option.	mci "play midi1"		15
me	OOP, Behaviors	Misc	Special variable name used in parent scripts and behaviors. Enables handlers to be associated with the to which object they belong.		new, ancestor	
media	Member	Property	Represents the contents of a member. For instance, in a bitmap, it represents the image. You can use this property to copy member contents between members.	member("myMember").media = member("other").media	picture, type	
mediaReady	Network, Memory	Property	For a linked member, Cast library, or sprite. Returns TRUE if the member has been loaded from the Internet.	if sprite(7).mediaReady then...	frameReady	14

continues

PART

X

APP

J

Keyword	Topic	Type	Description	Syntax Sample	See Also	See Chapter/Appendix
member	Member	Object	Defines a member object. First parameter is the name or number of the member. The optional second parameter is the name or number of a Cast library.	myMember = member¬ ("this") myMember =member¬ ("this","that")		
member	Sprite	Property	The member associated with the sprite.	sprite(7).member =¬ member("myMember")	memberNum	37
memberNum	Sprite	Property	The number of the member associated with the sprite.	sprite(7).¬ memberNum = 12	memberNum	
members					number	
memorySize	System	Property	The total number of bytes available to the movie.	put the memorySize	freeBytes, freeBlock	
menu					installMenu	
menuItem	Menu	Property	Enables you to refer to a menu item in a menu that was installed with installMenu. Requires old (not dot) syntax.	set menuItem 4 of¬ menu 1 = "Test"	installMenu	
menuItems					number	21
menus					number	21
milliSeconds	Date & Time	Property	Returns the time since the computer was started in milliseconds.	put the milliSeconds	ticks	21
min	Math	Function	Compares two or more numbers and returns the lowest.	put main(4,5) put min(5,3,8,3,5,12)	max	21

Term	Category	Type	Description	Example	See Also	Page
missingFonts	Text	Property	Returns a list of fonts used by a text member that are not available.	`put member("myText").¬ missingFonts`	substituteFont	
mod	Math	Operator	Takes a number and performs a modulus operation with a second number.	`put 6 mod 4`		
modal	MIAW	Property	This window property, when set to TRUE, prevents the user from interacting with any other window, including the Stage, until the current window is gone.	`window("myDialog")¬ .modal = TRUE`	window	
modified	Member	Property	Returns TRUE if the member has changed since the file was last saved.	`put member¬ ("myMember")¬ .modified`		
month					date	24
mostRecentCuePoint	Sound, Digital Video	Property	Returns the name of the most recent cue point that was passed.	`put sound(1).¬ mostRecentCuePoint`	cuePointNames, isPastCuePoint, cuePassed	
motionQuality	QTVR	Property	Enables you to set the motion quality of a QTVR movie. Possible values are #minQuality, #maxQuality, or #normalQuality.	`sprite(7).¬ motionQuality =¬ #normalQuality`		21
mouseCast	System	Property	Returns the number of the member under the cursor on the Stage. Returns a single cast-specific number if not in cast library 1.	`put the mouseCast`	mouseMember	

PART

X

APP

J

continues

Keyword	Topic	Type	Description	Syntax Sample	See Also	See Chapter/Appendix
mouseChar	Field	Property	Returns the number of the character in a field that is currently under the cursor.	`put the mouseChar`	mouseWord, mouseItem, mouseLine	
mouseDown	Behaviors	Event Handler	Responds to events created by the user clicking the mouse down on a sprite (behaviors) or the Stage (frames, movie scripts).	`on mouseDown me`	mouseUp, mouseDownScript	
mouseDown	System	Property	Returns TRUE if the mouse button is currently being pressed.	`put the mouseDown`	mouseStillDown	16
mouseDownScript	Movie	Property	Enables you to set a handler to be called first when the user clicks down.	`the mouseDownScript¬ = "myClickHandler"`	mouseDown, mouseUpScript	
mouseEnter	Behaviors	Event Handler	Responds to the situation where the cursor enters the sprite's area.	`on mouseEnter me`	mouseLeave, mouseWithin	
mouseH	System	Property	Returns the horizontal location of the cursor on the Stage.	`put the mouseLoc`	mouseLoc, mouseV, clickLoc	
mouseItem	Field	Property	Returns the number of the item in a field that is currently under the cursor.		mouseChar, mouseWord, mouseLine	
MouseLeave	Behaviors	Event Handler	Responds to the situation where the cursor leaves the sprite's area.	`on mouseLeave me`	mouseEnter, mouseWithin	

mouseLevel	QTVR	Property	This QTVR sprite property determines how mouse clicks are sent to the QTVR movie. Possible values are #all, #none, #controller (sent only when the control bar clicked on), and #shared (sent to both QTVR and the movie).	`sprite(7).¬` `mouseLevel = #shared`	16	
mouseLine	Field	Property	Returns the number of the line in a field that is currently under the cursor.			mouseChar, mouseWord, mouseItem
mouseLoc	System	Property	Returns the point location of the cursor on the Stage.	`put the mouseLoc`		mouseH, mouseV, clickLoc
mouseMember	System	Property	Returns the member under the cursor on the Stage.	`put the mouseMember`	16	mouseCast

mouseOverButton	Flash	Property	Returns TRUE if the cursor is over a button in the Flash movie sprite.	`if sprite(7).¬`
				`mouseOverButton¬`
				`then...`
						hitTest

mouseUp	Behaviors	Event Handler	Responds to events created by the user clicking the mouse, and then lifting up over a sprite (behaviors) or the Stage (frames, movie scripts).	`on mouseUp me`	20	mouseDown, mouseUpScript

continues

PART

X

APP

J

Keyword	Topic	Type	Description	Syntax Sample	See Also	See Chapter/Appendix
mouseUp	System	Property	Returns TRUE if the mouse button is not pressed.	`put the mouseUp`	mouseStillDown	
mouseUpOutSide	Behav-iors	Event Handler	Responds to events created by the user clicking the mouse down on a sprite, but then lifting up outside the sprite.	`on mouseUpOutside me`	mouseUp	
mouseUpScript	Movie	Property	Enables you to set a handler to be called first when the user clicks down and then releases.	`the mouseUpScript =¬ "myClickHandler"`	mouseUp, mouseDownScript	
mouseV	System	Property	Returns the vertical location of the cursor on the Stage.	`put the mouseLoc`	mouseH, mouseLoc, clickLoc	
mouseWithin	Behav-iors	Event Handler	Called once per frame when the cursor is inside the sprite's area.	`on mouseWithin me`	mouseEnter, mouseLeave, rollover	
mouseWord	Field	Property	Returns the number of the word in a field that is currently under the cursor.		mouseChar, mouseItem, mouseLine	
move	Member	Command	Enables you to move a member from one location in the Cast to another. If no second parameter is used, the member moves to the first vacant spot.	`move member¬ ("myMember"),¬ member¬ (7,"picture cast")`	erase, duplicate, new	

Term	Category	Type	Description	Syntax	See Also	Chapter
moveableSprite	Sprite	Property	Corresponds to the moveable property of the sprite. When TRUE, users can drag the sprite around on the Stage.	`sprite(7).moveableSprite = TRUE`		16
moveToBack	MIAW	Command	Sends a MIAW behind all other MIAWs.	`moveToBack window("myMIAW")`	moveToFront	
moveToFront	MIAW	Command	Moves a MIAW in front of all other MIAWs.	`moveToFront window("myMIAW")`	moveToBack	
moveVertex	Vector	Command	Moves a vertex point by a horizontal and vertical value.	`moveVertex(member("myVector"),5,x,y)`	addVertex, deleteVertex, moveVertexHandle, vertexList	24
moveVertexHandle	Vector	Command	Moves a vertex handle point by a horizontal and vertical value.	`moveVertexHandle(member("myVector",5,1,x,y))`	addVertex, deleteVertex, moveVertex, vertexList	24
moveWindow	MIAW	Event Handler	This event handler is called if the user moves a MIAW.	`on moveWindow`	activeWindow	20
movie					movieName	
movieAboutInfo	Movie	Property	Corresponds to the "about" text entered in the Movie Properties dialog box.	`alert the movieAboutWindow`	movieCopyrightInfo	24
movieCopyrightInfo	Movie	Property	Corresponds to the "copyright" text entered in the Movie Properties dialog box.	`alert the movieCopyrightWindow`	movieAboutInfo	
movieFileFreeSize	Movie	Property	The number of bytes that can be saved by using File, Save And Compact.	`put the movieFileFreeSize`	movieFileSize	

PART

X

APP

J

continues

Keyword	Topic	Type	Description	Syntax Sample	See Also	See Chapter/Appendix
movieFileSize	Movie	Property	The size of the movie's file.	`put the movieFileSize`	movieFileFreeSize	
movieName	Movie	Property	Returns the name of the movie file.	`put the movieName`	moviePath	
moviePath	Movie	Property	Returns the full pathname of the movie file.	`put the movieName`	movieName	
movieRate	Digital Video	Property	Controls the rate at which a digital video sprite plays. 1 is normal, 0 is still, -1 is backward, and 2 is double speed.	`sprite(7).¬` `movieRate = 2`	duration, movieTime	
movieTime	Digital Video	Property	Enables you to get and set the playback position in a digital video sprite. Measured in ticks.	`sprite(7).¬` `movieTime = 0`	duration, movieRate	
movieXtraList	Xtras	Property	Returns a property list with the name and downloadable package information for all the movie's Xtras.	`put the¬` `movieXtraList`	xtraList	19
multiSound	System	Property	Returns TRUE if the computer is capable of playing sound in more than one channel.	`if the¬` `multiSound then...`		19

Name	Category	Type	Description	Example	See also	#
name	Member, Casts, MIAW, Xtras	Property	Returns the name of the member, cast library, window, or Xtra object.	put member(7).name put castLib(2).¬ name put myWindow.name	number	25
name	Menu	Property	Returns the name of a menu installed with installMenu. Cannot be set. Can get and set menuItems, however. Must use old (not dot) syntax.	put the name of menu 1 set the name of¬ menuItem 5 of menu 1¬ = "Test"	menuItem, installMenu	17
netAbort	Network	Command	Cancels a network operation.	netAbort(gNetID)	getNetText, postNetText	
netDone	Network	Function	Returns TRUE if the network operation is complete.	if netDone¬ (gNetID) then...	getNetText, postNetText	
netError	Network	Function	Returns a 0 for no error, and an error code if there is a problem.	if netError(gNetID) ¬ <> 0 then...	getNetText, postNetText	
netLastModDate	Network	Function	After netDone returns TRUE, this function returns the modification date of the item.	modDate =¬ netLastModDate¬ (gNetID)	getNetText, postNetText	22
netMIME	Network	Function	After netDone returns TRUE, this function returns the MIME type (file type) of the item.	mime =¬ netMIME(gNetID)	getNetText, postNetText	22
netPresent	Network	Property	Returns TRUE if the network Xtras are present in a Projector. Does not tell you whether there is a network connection, however.	if the¬ netPresent then...		22

PART

X

APP

J

continues

Keyword	Topic	Type	Description	Syntax Sample	See Also	See Chapter/Appendix
netStatus	Shockwave	Command	Places a string in the message area of Netscape Navigator.	netStatus¬ ("Click here to¬ begin")		22
netTextResult	Network	Function	After netDone returns TRUE, this function returns the text of the item.	myText =¬ netTextResult¬ (gNetID)	getNetText, postNetText	
netThrottleTicks	Network	Property	How frequently network operations are given processing time. Default is 15. Higher means less time spent processing network commands.	the¬ netThrottleTicks¬ = 30		33
new	Member, Casts	Command	Creates a new member at the next empty location in the Cast, or a specific location.	new(#bitmap) new(#text,member¬ 7 of castlib 2)	duplicate, erase, move, media	22
new	OOP	Function	Returns a new instance of a parent script.	myObj = new¬ (script "myParent")	menuItem, installMenu	
new	Xtras	Function	Returns a new instance of an Xtra.	fileObj = new¬ (xtra "FileIO")		
next					go next	
next repeat	Program-ming	Command	Ignores the rest of the lines in a repeat loop and proceeds to the next loop iteration.		repeat	
node	QTVR	Property	The current node being shown by a QTVR sprite.	Put sprite(7).node		

nodeEnterCallback	QTVR	Property	Set this to the name of a handler to get called when the QTVR movie switches nodes. The first parameter is *me*, and the second is the ID of the node.	`Sprite(7).¬`
				`nodeEnterCallback =¬`
				`"myNodeSwitchHandler"`
					HotSpotEnter-Callback, nodeExitCallback, triggerCallback	13

nodeExitCallback	QTVR	Property	Set this to the name of a handler to be called just before the QTVR movie switches nodes. The first parameter is *me*, and the second is the ID of the node.	`Sprite(7).¬`
				`nodeExitCallback =¬`
				`"myNodeSwitchHandler"`
					HotSpotExit-Callback, nodeEnterCallback, triggerCallback	

nodeType	QTVR	Property	Returns the type of node that the QTVR sprite is showing. Possible values are: #object, #panorama, or #unknown (not a QTVR sprite).	`Put sprite(7)¬` `.nodeType`	node	
not	Logic	Operator	Reverses the Boolean value of the expression. TRUE becomes FALSE and FALSE becomes TRUE.	`If not¬` `myCondition then...`	and, or	
nothing	Programming	Command	Performs no action. Useful for filling segments of *if* statements to make them easier to read, or for placing debugging break points.	`Nothing`		

PART

X

APP

J

continues

Keyword	Topic	Type	Description	Syntax Sample	See Also	See Chapter/Appendix
number	Member, Casts, MIAW, Xtras, Strings, Misc	Property	Used throughout Lingo to identify the number of various objects such as members or Cast libraries. Can also be used as an alternative to *count* with old syntax to find the total number of items in string chunks. Can also tell you the number of some objects with syntax, such as "the number of members" or "the number of Xtras". You can use it to tell whether a member exists with "if the number of member("myMember") > 0 then..."	`Put member¬ ("myMember").number put castLib¬ ("myCast").number put the number of¬ words in myString`	name, count	
numChannels	Shockwave Audio	Property	Returns the number of channels used by a Shockwave audio member.	`Put member("mySWA")¬ .numChannels`		
numToChar	Strings	Function	Converts an ASCII character value to a string character.	`put numToChar(65)`	charToNum	
obeyScoreRotation	Flash	Property	If TRUE, the Flash sprite can be rotated on the Stage.	`member("myFlash")¬ .obeyScoreRotation¬ = TRUE`	rotation	17
objectP	Logic	Function	Returns TRUE if the value is some sort of object such as a list, script instance, Xtra instance, or window.	`if objectP¬ (myObject) then...`	ilk, symbolP	16

Name	Type	Description	Example	See Also	
offset	Strings	Takes two parameters: A search string, and a string to search. If it finds the search string in the second string, it returns the position of the first character. Otherwise, it returns 0	`p = offset("wor", "Hello World.")`	contains, starts	
offset	Math	Takes a rectangle, a horizontal offset, and a vertical offset, and returns a rectangle moved by the offset.	`myNewRect = offset(myRect,x,y)`	rect	25, 33
on	Programming	Used before a message name, such as "mouseDown" or "exitFrame" to declare the start of a handler in a script member.			15
open	Misc	Launches an external application from a Projector.	`open "notepad.exe"` `open "mytext.txt" with "notepad.exe"`		
open	MIAW	Opens a MIAW with the movie specified in the filename. Also opens a new window, which must then be assigned a movie by your setting the window's filename property.	`open window ("myMIAW.dir")`	filename, name, visible	
openWindow	MIAW	This event handler is called when the MIAW is first opened.	`on openWindow`	closeWindow, activateWindow	

PART

X

APP

J

continues

Keyword	Topic	Type	Description	Syntax Sample	See Also	See Chapter/ Appendix
openXLib	Xtras	Command	Manually opens an Xtra. Usually Xtras are automatically included by you bundling them with a Projector or placing them in an Xtras folder. This command enables you open Xtra files elsewhere.	openXlib ¬ "Other Xtras:FileIO"	closeXlib	
optionDown	Keyboard	Property	Returns TRUE if the user is holding down the Option key on the Mac or the Alt key in Windows.	put the optionDown	commandDown, controlDown, shiftDown, keyPressed	24
or	Logic	Operator	Returns TRUE if either of two expressions are TRUE and FALSE if neither are.	if (a = 1) or¬ (b = 2) then...	and, not	25
organizationName	System	Property	Returns the company name to which the copy of Director is registered	put the¬ organizationName	serialNumber, userName	16
originH	Flash, Vector	Property	Sets the horizontal location of the point in a vector shape or Flash member or sprite where rotation and scaling occur.	member("myVector")¬ .originH = 45	originMode	
originMode	Flash, Vector	Property	Sets the location in a vector shape or Flash member or sprite where rotation and scaling occur. Possible values are #center, #topleft, and #point. The last relies on originPoint for the location.	member("myVector")¬ .originMode = #point	originPoint, originH, originV	

originPoint	Flash, Vector	Property	Sets the location of the point in a vector shape or Flash member or sprite where rotation and scaling occur.	`member("myVector")` ¬ `.originPoint =`¬ `point(45,34)`	originMode	20
originV	Flash, Vector	Property	Sets the vertical location of the point in a vector shape or Flash member or sprite where rotation and scaling occur.	`member("myVector")` ¬ `.originV = 34`	originMode	20
otherwise	Programming	Structure	An optional final portion of a case statement that execute only if no other case value is matched.		case	20
pageHeight	Field, Text	Property	Returns the height, in pixels, of the visible area of a field or text member.	`put member("myText")` ¬ `.pageHeight`		20
palette	Bitmap	Property	The palette used by a bitmap member. Negative numbers correspond to built-in palettes and positive numbers to palette members.	`put member("myBitmap")` ¬ `.palette`	paletteRef	
paletteIndex	Misc	Object	A color object that is specified by the number in the movie's palette.	`myColor =`¬ `paletteIndex(35)`	color, rgb	

continues

Keyword	Topic	Type	Description	Syntax Sample	See Also	See Chapter/ Appendix
paletteMapping	Movie	Property	Enables Director to remap a member's palette to the closest colors if its palette is different than the one being used by the Stage.	the paletteMapping¬ = TRUE		
paletteRef	Bitmap	Property	Returns the palette symbol, such as #systemMac, for bitmaps that use built-in palettes, and member references for members that use a custom palette.	put member¬ ("myBitmap")¬ .paletteRef	palette	
pan	QTVR	Property	The current viewing angle of a QTVR sprite, in degrees.	put sprite(7).pan		35
paragraph	Strings	Expression	New syntax, equivalent to *line*. It enables you to reference a chunk expression broken up by Return characters.	put myString.¬ paragraph[5]	line	
param	Programming	Function	Enables you to get a parameter of a handler by number.	if param(2) ==¬ #test then...	paramCount	
paramCount	Programming	Property	Returns the number of parameters sent to the current handler.	if the paramCount¬ < 3 then...	param	

continues

Keyword	Programming	Type	Description	Example	See Also
pass		Command	Enables the current event, such as a mouseDown, to be passed to the next level of the message hierarchy when the current handler is done.	`pass`	
pasteClipBoardInto	Member	Command	Takes the current content of the clipboard and places it in the member specified.	`pasteClipBoardInto¬` `member("myMember")`	copyToClipBoard
pathName	Flash cast member	Property	Controls the location of external file where assets of Flash cast member are stored.	`member(myFlashMember)¬` `.pathName`	moviePath, filename
pattern	Shape	Property	The pattern used by the shape. A value of 0 is a solid; other values match positions in the pattern palette of the Tool palette.	`member("myOval")¬` `.pattern = 7`	color, bgColor
pause			Obsolete Lingo. The *go to the frame* works much better anyway.		go 21
pause member	Shockwave Audio	Command	Pauses a Shockwave audio file that is playing.	`pause member("mySWA")`	play, stop
pause	Animated GIF	Command	Pauses an animated GIF sprite.	`pause sprite(7)`	resume, rewind
pausedAtStart	Flash, Digital Video	Property	Determines whether a video or Flash member starts playing when it appears on the Stage.	`member("myVideo").¬` `pausedAtStart¬` `= FALSE`	

PART

X

APP

J

Keyword	Topic	Type	Description	Syntax Sample	See Also	See Chapter/Appendix
pauseState			Obsolete. If the obsolete *pause* command is used, this returns TRUE.	put the pauseState	pause	
percentPlayed	Shockwave Audio	Property	Returns the percentage of a streaming audio sound that has played.	put member("mySWA")¬ .percentPlayed	percentStreamed	19, 20
percentStreamed	Shockwave Audio, Flash	Property	Returns the percentage of a streaming audio sound or Flash member that has loaded.	put member("mySWA")¬ .percentStreamed	percentPlayed	
PI	Math	Constant	Returns pi as a floating point number. Also works as a function: *pi()*.	put PI		17
picture	Bitmap	Property	This property refers to the image inside a bitmap member.	member("myBitmap")¬ .picture = member¬ ("otherBitmap").¬ picture	media	17
picture	MIAW, Misc	Property	The screen image of the Stage or a MIAW. Can be stored in a variable or assigned to a bitmap picture property.	member("myBitmap")¬ .picture =¬ (the stage)¬ .picture		
pictureP	Misc	Function	Returns TRUE if the value is a picture.	If pictureP¬ (myPicture) then...		18
platform	System	Property	Returns either "Macintosh,PowerPC" or "Windows,32". In a Java applet, it returns "Java" plus the version, browser, and operating system.	put the platform	runMode	

Name	Category	Type	Description	Example	See Also	
play	Navigation	Command	Jumps the playback head to a new location. It remembers the current frame, however, and enables the movie to return to it with a *play done* command.	`play frame "myFrame"` `play frame "myFrame" of movie "myMovie"`	play done, go, gotoNetMovie	
playdone	Navigation	Command	After a *play* command has been used, you can use *play done* to return to the frame where the *play* command was issued. You can stack as many *play* and *play dones* as you want.	`play done`	play	21
playBackMode	Flash, Animated GIF	Property	Flash and animated GIF members and sprites can be set to #normal, #lockStep, or #fixed. The #lockStep setting ties the tempo to the Director movie tempo. The #fixed setting uses the *fixedRate* property.	`member("myFlash").playBackMode = #lockStep`	fixedRate	13
playFile					sound playFile	13
playing	Flash	Property	Returns TRUE if the Flash sprite is playing.	`put sprite(7).playing`		20
play member	Shockwave Audio	Command	Starts a Shockwave audio member streaming and playing.	`play member("mySWA")`	pause, stop	17
point	Misc	Object	An object with a horizontal and vertical position. It has the properties *locH* and *locV*.	`put point(50,30).locH`	rect	

PART

X

APP

J

continues

Keyword	Topic	Type	Description	Syntax Sample	See Also	See Chapter/ Appendix
pointInHyperLink	Text	Function	Takes a sprite and a Stage location and returns TRUE if the mouse location is over a hyperlink in that sprite.	put pointInHyperLink¬ (sprite(7),¬ the mouseLoc)		17
pointToChar	Text	Function	Takes a sprite and a Stage location and returns the character number to which the point corresponds, or −1 if the point is not over the text.	put pointToChar¬ (sprite(7),¬ the mouseLoc)	pointToItem, pointToLine, pointToWord	
pointToItem	Text	Function	Takes a sprite and a Stage location and returns the item number to which the point corresponds, or −1 if the point is not over the text.	put pointToItem¬ (sprite(7),¬ the mouseLoc)	itemDelimiter, pointToChar, pointToLine, pointToWord	
pointToLine	Text	Function	Takes a sprite and a Stage location and returns the character number to which the point corresponds, or −1 if the point is not over the text.	put pointToLine¬ (sprite(7),¬ the mouseLoc)	pointToChar, pointToItem, pointToWord	16
pointToParagraph	Text	Function	Same as pointToLine.	put pointToParagraph¬ (sprite(7),¬ the mouseLoc)	pointToLine	

Term	Category	Type	Description	Example	Related	
pointToWord	Text	Function	Takes a sprite and a Stage location and returns the word number to which the point corresponds, or –1 if the point is not over the text.	`put pointToWord¬ (sprite(7),¬ the mouseLoc)`	pointToChar, pointToItem, pointToLine	16
posterFrame	Flash	Property	Determines which frame of a Flash member is the thumbnail image.	`member("myFlash").¬ posterFrame = 20`		
postNetText	Network	Command	This command uses the Internet Post protocol to contact the server and send it information. It accepts a URL and a specially formatted list.	`postNetText¬ (myURL,myList)`	getNetText, netDone, netTextResult, netError	
power	Math	Function	Returns the base number to the power of the exponent.	`put power(12,3)`	sqrt	
preLoad	Memory	Command	Begins loading all the members of a frame, range of frames, or all members in the remaining frames.	`preLoad` `preLoad 3,4`	preLoadMember	22
preLoad	Flash, Digital Video	Property	For video, it determines whether a movie should be preloaded before it starts playing. For Flash members, it determines whether a Flash member must be loaded into RAM before is starts playing.	`member("myVide").¬ preLoad = TRUE`	streamMode	

PART
X
APP
J

continues

Keyword	Topic	Type	Description	Syntax Sample	See Also	See Chapter/Appendix
preLoadBuffer	Shockwave Audio	Command	Pre-streams the first few seconds of a Shockwave audio member.	`preLoadBuffer member¬ ("mySWA")`	preLoadTime	21
preLoadEventAbort	Memory	Property	If this system property is set to TRUE, preloading stops when the user clicks the mouse or presses a key.	`The preLoadEventAbort¬ = TRUE`	preLoad, preLoadMember	21
preLoadMember	Memory	Command	Begins preloading a member, a range of members, or all remaining members.	`preLoadMember preLoadMember¬ "myMember"`	preLoad	
preLoadMode	Memory	Property	This cast library property can be set to 0 (load when needed), 1 (load Cast before frame 1), or 2 (load Cast after frame 1).	`CastLib("myCast")¬ .preLoadMode = 1`		
preLoadMovie	Memory	Command	Preloads the members used in the first frame of another movie. This smoothes the transition when you use *go* or *play* to jump to another movie.	`preLoadMovie¬ ("myOtherMovie.dir")`		21

Name	Category	Type	Description	Example	See Also / Chapter
preLoadNetThing	Shockwave	Command	Tells the browser to load an item into its cache. This can smooth playback when using *gotoNetMovie* or linked media.	`preLoadNetThing¬("http://clevermedia¬.com/sample.dcr/")`	netDone
preloadRam	Digital Video	Property	This system property specifies how much memory is available for preloading video. Measured in KB.	`The preLoadRAM = 300`	21
preLoadTime	Shockwave Audio	Property	The number of seconds of audio that should be buffered before sound starts playing.	`member("mySWA").¬preLoadTime = 15`	preLoadBuffer, play member
prepareFrame	Frame Scripts, Behaviors	Event Handler	This handler is called just before Director draws the current frame.	`on prepareFrame`	enterFrame, exitFrame, idle
prepareMovie	Movie	Event Handler	This handler is called just before Director creates behavior instances and draws the first frame.	`on prepareMovie`	on startMovie 17
previous				`go previous`	12, 14
printFrom	Misc	Command	Enables you to print the Stage. You can specify a range of frames and a percentage (100, 50, or 25).	`printFrom firstFrame, ¬ lastFrame, percent`	12
productName	System	Property	Undocumented Lingo. Returns "Director".	`put the productName`	

continues

PART

X

APP

J

Keyword	Topic	Type	Description	Syntax Sample	See Also	See Chapter/ Appendix
productVersion	System	Property	Undocumented Lingo. Returns "7.0".	put the¬ productVersion		25
property	OOP, Behaviors	Command	Defines variables as properties of behaviors or parent scripts. Place in handlers, or outside of all handlers in a script to declare it for use in all handlers in that script.	property pMyProperty,¬ pMyOtherProperty	globa	
proxyServer	Network	Command	Sets the values for a proxy server to be used in a Projector.	proxyServer¬ serverType,¬ ipAddress, portNum		
ptToHotSpot	QTVR	Function	Returns the ID of a hotspot at a specified point.	put ptToHotSpot¬ (sprite(7),¬ the mouseLoc)		
puppet	Sprites	Property	Returns TRUE if the sprite is under Lingo control.	sprite(7).¬ puppet = TRUE	puppetSprite	
puppetPalette	Movie	Command	Gives Lingo control of the palette channel in the Score and enables it to assign a new palette.	puppetPalette¬ "Rainbow", speed,¬ nFrames	framePalette	

Function	Element	Type	Description	Example	See Also
puppetSound	Sound	Command	Takes control of a sound channel and plays a sound in it. If no sound channel number is given, it uses the next available sound channel, but waits for the next frame to begin, or an *updateStage* command, before it starts.	`puppetSound 1, "mySound"`	frameSound1
puppetSprite	Sprites	Command	If set to TRUE, the sprite is placed under Lingo control and does not respond to changes in the Score until set to FALSE.	`puppetSprite 7, TRUE`	sprite
puppetTempo	Movie	Command	Takes control of the tempo channel and sets it to a speed in frames per second.	`puppetTempo 15`	frameTempo 17
puppetTransition	Movie	Command	Cues up a transition to be used between the current frame and whichever is next.	`puppetTransition 1, time, chunkSize, changeArea`	frameTransition
purgePriority	Members	Property	This sets the purge priority of the member to 0 (Never), 1 (Last), 2 (Next), or 3 (Normal).	`member ("myMember").purgePriority = 1`	
put	Misc	Command	Places the result of the expression into the Message window.	`put myVariable`	alert D

PART

X

APP

J

continues

Keyword	Topic	Type	Description	Syntax Sample	See Also	See Chapter/ Appendix
put after	Strings	Command	Places the contents of one string after the contents of the other.	`put myNewString¬ after myOldString`	put before, put into	21
put before	Strings	Command	Places the contents of one string before the contents of the other.	`put myNewString¬ before myOldString`	put after, put into	
put into	Strings	Command	Places the contents of one string into the contents of the other.	`put myNewString¬ into myOldString`	put after, put before	
qtRegisterAccessKey	Digital Video	Command	Enables you to use the access keys for QuickTime movies.	`qtRegisterAccessKey¬ (categoryString,¬ keyString)`	qtUnRegister-AccessKey	
qtUnRegisterAccessKey	Digital Video	Command	Enables you to use the access keys for QuickTime movies.	`qtUnRegisterAccessKey¬ (categoryString,¬ keyString)`	qtRegister-AccessKey	
quad	Sprites	Property	A list containing the four points that correspond to the four corners of a bitmap or text sprite.	`sprite(7).quad =¬ [point(0,0),point¬ (20,10),point¬ (20,30),point(0,40)]`	rect, rotation, skew	
quality	Flash	Property	Sets the quality for a Flash sprite or member. Possible values are: #autoHigh, #autoLow, #high, or #low.	`member("myFlash")¬ .quality = #high`		

quickTimeVersion	Digital Video	Function	Returns a number, either 3.0 or higher, or 2.12 if before QuickTime 3.	put¬ quickTimeVersion()		18
quit	System	Command	Exits Director or a Projector. Usually better to use *halt* in most situations.	quit	shutdown, restart, halt	
QUOTE	Strings	Constant	Represents the quote character.	myString = QUOTE&¬ "Hello World." &QUOTE	TAB, RETURN, numToChar	
ramNeeded	Memory	Function	Takes a range of frames and returns the number of bytes of free memory needed to display them.	put ramNeeded(1,10)	freeBytes, size	21
random	Math	Function	Returns a random number from 1 to the number given. To get another range or a floating point range, use this command and then add, subtract, or divide the result.	put random(100)	randomSeed	16
randomSeed	Math	Property	Specifies the number seed from which the random function operates. Setting it to a constant number produces an identical series of results from identical random functions.	the randomSeed = 42	random	21

PART

X

APP

J

continues

Keyword	Topic	Type	Description	Syntax Sample	See Also	See Chapter/ Appendix
recordFont	Misc	Command	Embeds a font present on the system into a member.	`recordFont (member¬ ("myFont"), font, face,¬ sizeList,¬ characterString)`		
rect	Misc	Object	An object with four elements, meant to represent a rectangle. It has four direct properties: *left, top, right,* and *bottom.* It also has the indirect properties of width and height.	`myRect = rect¬ (10,10,50,50)`	point	
rect	Members, Sprites, MIAW	Property	Represents the rectangle of the sprite on the Stage, the member size, or the MIAW location and size. Also has the subproperties of *left, top, right, bottom,* width, and height.	`sprite(7).rect =¬ rect(10,10,50,50)`	point	
red	Strings				rgb	
ref	Strings	Property	Provides an object that can be used to refer to a chunk in a member.	`myRef = member¬ ("myText").word[1]`		
regPoint	Bitmap, Vector, Flash	Property	The point in the member that corresponds to the location point on the Stage. It usually defaults to the center, but can be changed in editing windows and with this property.	`put member¬ ("myBitmap")¬ .regPoint`	centerRegPoint	

Name	Category	Structure	Description	Example	Page	Related

repeat	Programming	Structure	Used to create a loop. Needs to use a *while* to repeat until a condition is FALSE, a *with* to repeat through a series of numbers, a *with...down to* to repeat backwards, or a *with...in* to loop through a list of values.	`repeat with i = 1 to 10`
				`  nothing`
				`end repeat`
				`repeat while x < 6`
				`  nothing`
				`end repeat`
				`repeat with¬`
				`i = 10 down to 1`
				`  nothing`
				`end repeat`
				`repeat with I in¬`
				`[5,8,3]`
				`  nothing`
				`end repeat`
					16	exit repeat, next repeat

resizeWindow	MIAW	Event Handler	This handler is called when the MIAW is resized by the user.	on resizeWindow	20	drawRect, sourceRect, moveWindow
restart	System	Command	On the Mac, this restarts the computer. In Windows, it just quits the Projector.	restart		quit, halt, shutDown
result	Programming	Property	This system property contains the return value of the last function called.	put the result	24	return
resume sprite	Animated GIF	Command	Resumes a stopped animated GIF.	resume sprite(7)	21	pause sprite, rewind sprite
return	Programming	Command	In a handler, this exits the handler and returns a value to the command that called it.	return TRUE		

PART

X

APP

J

continues

Keyword	Topic	Type	Description	Syntax Sample	See Also	See Chapter/ Appendix
RETURN	Strings	Constant	Represents the return character. The same as numToChar(13).	myString =¬ "Hello World."¬ &RETURN	TAB, QUOTE, numToChar	
rgb	Misc	Object	A color object that is specified by a red, green, and blue value. It can also take a string, such as "#FFFFFF" or "FFFFFF" and convert it to the normal format. Its properties can also be accessed with *red*, *green*, and *blue* properties.	myColor = rgb¬ (255,255,255) myColor = rgb¬ ("#FFFFFF")	color, paletteIndex,	
rewind sprite	Flash, Animated GIF	Command	Rewinds a Flash or animated GIF to its frame 1.	resume sprite(7)¬	pause sprite, rewind sprite	16
right	Sprites, Misc	Property	Returns the right side location of a sprite. Can also be used as a property of rect objects.	put sprite(7).right put myRect.right	width, left top, bottom, rect	13
rightIndent	Text	Property	Used to set the number of pixels for a right indent for a whole text member, or a chunk inside one.	member("myText").¬ line[5..6].¬ rightIndent = 18	leftIndent, firstIndent	
rightMouseDown	Behaviors	Event Handler	The same as mouseDown, but with the right mouse button in Windows.	on rightMouseDown me	mouseDown, emulateMulti-ButtonMouse	
rightMouseUp	Behaviors	Event Handler	The same as mouseUp, but with the right mouse button in Windows.	on rightMouseUp me	mouseUp, emulateMulti-ButtonMouse	16

Command	Category	Type	Description	Example	See Also	Chapter
rollover	System	Function	When given a sprite number, it returns TRUE if the cursor is in the sprite's area.	put rollover(7)	mouseEnter, mouseLeave, mouseWithin	
rollOver	System	Property	Returns the number of the sprite directly under the cursor.	put the rollover	mouseEnter, mouseLeave, mouseWithin, mouseMember	
romanLingo	System	Property	Usually set to FALSE. Needs to be set to TRUE to deal with special character sets, such as some Mac Japanese fonts.	the romanLingo¬ = TRUE		13, 14
rotation	Sprites	Property	Sets the rotation of a sprite, in degrees. Works with bitmaps, vectors, Flash, text, and some other types.	sprite(7).¬ rotation = 60	skew, rect, quad	13, 14
runMode	System	Property	Returns "Author", "Projector", "Plugin", or "Java Applet".	put the runMode	environment, platform	
runPropertyDialog	Behaviors	Event Handler	This handler is called when the author adds a behavior to a sprite. If this handler is not there, the parameters dialog box is presented instead.	on¬ runPropertyDialog me	getProperty-DescriptionList	18, 19
safePlayer	Shockwave	Property	When set to TRUE, Director simulates the security restrictions imposed on Shockwave in a browser.	the safePlayer¬ = TRUE		21

PART

X

APP

J

continues

Keyword	Topic	Type	Description	Syntax Sample	See Also	See Chapter/ Appendix
sampleRate	Shockwave Audio	Property	Returns the sample frequency of the SWA member. For instance, 22.0100	`put member("mySWA")¬ .sampleRate`	sampleSize	14
sampleSize	Shockwave Audio	Property	Returns the bit depth of the SWA member. Usually 8 or 16.	`put member("mySWA")¬ .sampleSize`	sampleRate	
save castLib	Casts	Property	Saves the external cast library specified. If a second parameter is used, it saves it to a new file.	`save castLib¬ ("myCast"), myPath`	saveMovie	17
savedLocal	Movie	Property	For future use.		allowSaveLocal	17
saveMovie	Movie	Command	Saves the current movie. If a pathname is specified, it saves the movie to a new file.	`saveMovie myNewPath`	save castLib	27
scale	Flash, Vector, Digital Video	Property	For Flash or vector shapes, it uses a floating point number. For QuickTime sprites or members, it uses a list with horizontal and vertical scaling numbers.	`sprite(7).scale = 1.5` `member¬ ("myQuickTime").¬ scale = [1.5,1.5]`	scaleMode, originMode	
scaleMode	Flash, Vector	Property	Controls how Flash and vector shape members scale. Possible values are #showAll, #noBorder, #excatFit, #noScale, and #autoSize.	`member("myFlash")¬ .scaleMode =¬ #autoSize`	scale	27

score	Movie	Property	This property represents the Score itself. It is the same object type as the media property for a film loop member.	`member("myFilmLoop")¬ .media = the Score`	18, 19, 20
scoreColor	Score Recording	Property	Enables you to specify the color used by a sprite in the Score window. Values range from 0 to 5 and match the color chips in the Score window. Can be used during authoring and Score recording.	`sprite(7).¬ scoreColor = 1`	20
scoreSelection	Score Recording	Property	This property returns a list of lists that contain all the sprites selected in the Score window. Channels above channel 1, such as the frame script channel, are represented by numbers -5 to 0.	`put the¬ scoreSelection`	
script	Menu	Property	The script associated with a menu item. You must use old (not dot) syntax to access.	`set the script of¬ menuItem 4 of menu 2¬ = "quit"`	installMenu
scriptInstanceList	Behaviors	Property	Returns a list with all the behaviors attached to a sprite. You can use *add* to add a new behavior. This property is valid only when the movie is running.	`add sprite(7).¬ scriptInstanceList,¬ new(script¬ "myBehavior")`	scriptNum, sendSprite	26

continues

PART
X
APP
J

Keyword	Topic	Type	Description	Syntax Sample	See Also	See Chapter/Appendix
scriptList	Behaviors	Property	Undocumented Lingo. Returns a list with the behaviors attached to a sprite and the parameter values.	put sprite(7)¬ .scriptList	scriptInstanceList	
scriptNum	Score Recording	Property	Enables you to set one script to be used by a sprite during Score recording.	sprite(7).¬ scriptNum = 2		
scriptsEnabled	Linked Movies	Property	If FALSE, the linked movie plays just as an animation, without using any of its scripts.	member¬ ("myLinkedMovie")¬ .scriptsEnabled¬ = FALSE		
scriptText	Scripts	Property	Returns the text of a script member. You can set this too.	put member¬ ("myScript").¬ scriptText		
scriptType	Scripts	Property	Returns the script type, #movie, #score (behavior), or #parent.	put member¬ ("myScript").¬ scriptType		
scrollByLine	Text, Field	Command	Scrolls the text or field member up or down by lines. Use negative numbers to scroll up.	scrollByLine(member¬ ("myText"),2)	scrollTop, scrollByPage	
scrollByPage	Text, Field	Command	Scrolls the text or field member up or down by pages. Use negative numbers to scroll up.	scrollByPage(member¬ ("myText"),2)	scrollTop, scrollByLine	

Term	Type	Kind	Description	Example	See Also	Chapter
scrollTop	Text, Field	Property	The number of pixels in a text or field member that are above the visible area on the Stage. A setting of 0 resets a scrolling member to the top.	`member("myText").scrollTop = 0`	scrollByLine, scrollByPage, pageHeight	16
searchCurrentFolder	System	Property	If TRUE, the current folder will be searched when Director is looking for files.	`the searchCurrentFolder = TRUE`	searchPaths	16
searchPath					searchPaths	16
searchPaths	System	Property	A list of pathnames that Director is to use to look for files such as linked media.	`the searchPaths = [the moviePath, the applicationPath, "c:\mystuff\"]`		
selectedText	Text	Property	Returns a reference to the current selection in a text member.	`put member("myText").selectedText`	ref, selection, selStart, selEnd, hilite	
selection	Text, Field	Property	For text members, returns a two-item list with the first and last character positions selected. Also, as a system property, returns the text of the current selection in a field member.	`put member("myText").selection` `put the selection`	selStart, selEnd, hilite	
selection	Casts	Property	Returns a list of selected items in a cast library. Useful for making developer tools.	`put cast("myCast").selection`		16

continues

PART

X

APP

J

Keyword	Topic	Type	Description	Syntax Sample	See Also	See Chapter/ Appendix
selEnd	Field	Property	This system property returns the position of the last character selected if there is a selection in an editable field.	`put the selEnd`	selStart, selection, hilite	16
selStart	Field	Property	This system property returns the position of the first character selected if there is a selection in an editable field.	`put the selStart`	selEnd, selection, hilite	16
sendAllSprites	Behaviors	Command	Sends a message to all sprites. This message activates event handlers of the same name in behaviors attached to the sprites.	`sendAllSprites¬ (#myHandler,myParam)`	sendSprite	16
sendSprite	Behaviors	Command	Sends a message to a sprite. This message activates event handlers of the same name in behaviors attached to the sprite.	`sendSprite¬ (sprite 7,¬ #myHandler,myParam)`	sendAllSprite	16
serialNumber	System	Property	Returns the serial number of the Director application.	`put the serialNumber`	userName	14
set	Program- ming	Command	Old syntax used to set variable values and property values. In Director 7, it is not required but can still be used.	`set myVariable = 7 set sprite(7).loc¬ = point(40,50)`		14

Name	Type	Description	Syntax	Related
setaProp	Lists	Sets a property value in a property list. If the property does not exist, it creates it instead.	`setaProp myList,¬` `myProperty, myValue`	setProp, addProp, getaProp, getProp
setAt	Lists	Sets an item in a list to a new value.	`setAt myList,¬` `myLocation, myValue`	add, append, getAt

setContents	Text	This undocumented syntax enables you to replace the text in a text member.	`member("myMember").¬`
			`setContents`
			`(myNewString)`
				put into

setContentsAfter	Text	This undocumented syntax enables you to place text after a chunk in a text member.	`member("myMember")¬`
			`.char[2].¬`
			`setContentsAfter¬`
			`(myNewString)`
				put after

setContentsBefore	Text	This undocumented syntax enables you to place text before a chunk in a text member.	`member("myMember")¬`
			`.char[2].¬`
			`setContentsBefore¬`
			`(myNewString)`
				put before

setPixel	Bitmap	This undocumented syntax enables you to set a pixel to a number that corresponds to the color at a coordinate in a bitmap image. Type of number depends on the bit depth. 32-bit images require a large integer that corresponds to the hexadecimal color value of the pixel. Sometimes does not operate properly, especially if alpha channels are involved.	`setPixel(member¬`
			`("myBitmap"),¬`
			`x,y,color)`
				getPixel

continues

PART

X

APP

J

Keyword	Topic	Type	Description	Syntax Sample	See Also	See Chapter/Appendix
setPref	Shockwave	Command	Sets a preference file contents. Preference files are used in Shockwave to store "cookies" of information without creating a security risk.	`setPref¬ ("clevermediaGame1",¬ myPrefString)`	getPref	
setProp	Lists	Command	Sets a property value in a property list. If the property does not exist, it generates an error message.	`setProp myList,¬ myProperty, myValue`	setaProp, addProp, getProp	
setTrackEnabled	Digital Video	Command	Sets whether a video sprite's tracks are enabled.	`setTrackEnabled¬ (sprite 7, myTrack,¬ TRUE)`	trackEnabled	22
shapeType	Shape	Property	Enables you to set the shape type to #rect, #roundRect, oval, or #line.	`member("myShape").¬ shapeType = #rect`	filled	
shiftDown	Keyboard	Property	Returns TRUE if the user is holding down the Shift key.	`put the shiftDown`	controlDown, optionDown, commandDown, keyPressed	
short					date, time	20
showGlobals	Movie	Command	Displays all the global variables and their values in the Message window.	`showGlobals`	clearGlobals, showLocals	16

continues

				showGlobals	showLocals	
showLocals	Movie	Command	When called from inside a handler, this command displays all the local variables and their values in the Message window.			
showProps	Flash, Vector	Command	Displays a list of the properties in a Flash or vector shape member in the Message window.		showProps member¬ ("myVector")	12
showResFile	Xtras	Command	Shows the resources in an open Xtra. Works on only the Mac.	openXlib, showXlib	showResFile "FileIO"	
showXLib	Xtras	Command	Displays a list of all open Xtras in the Message window.	openXlib	showXlib	
shutDown	System	Command	On the Mac, this shuts down the computer. In Windows, it quits just the Projector	quit, halt, restart	shutDown	
sin	Math	Function	Returns the sine of an angle. Angle must be in radians.	cos, tan, atan, PI	put sin(pi()/4)	25
size	Member	Property	Returns the size of the member, in bytes.		put member¬ ("myMember").size	21
skew	Sprites	Property	Returns the skew angle of a sprite.	rotation, quad	put sprite(7).skew	
sort	Lists	Command	Sorts a linear list by value, or a property list by property. After the list is sorted, the add and addProp commands insert the new item at the proper location.		sort myList	

PART

X

APP

J

Keyword	Topic	Type	Description	Syntax Sample	See Also	See Chapter/Appendix
sound	Linked Movies, Digital Video, Flash	Property	If TRUE, the member's sound is enabled. Otherwise, it is silent.	`member("myVideo")¬ .sound = FALSE`		18
soundBusy	Sound	Function	Tests to see whether a sound channel is currently playing a sound.	`if soundBusy(1)¬ then...`		
soundChannel	Shockwave Audio	Property	Specifies the sound channel used by the Shockwave audio member. If the value is 0, the first available channel is used.	`member("mySWA")¬ .soundChannel = 0`		
soundDevice	Sound	Property	This system property determines what computer driver will be used to play and mix sound. In Windows you have a choice: MacroMix or QT3Mix. Always set this to QT3Mix, which mixes better, but requires QuickTime 3. If the user does not have it, MacroMix will be used instead.	`the soundDevice =¬ "QT3Mix"`	soundDeviceList	17
soundDeviceList	Sound	Property	Returns a list of all available sound drivers. If a Windows user has QuickTime 3, it should return ["MacroMix", "QT3Mix"].	`put the¬ soundDeviceList`	soundDevice	17

soundEnabled	Sound	Property	This system property can be set to FALSE to mute all sound.	the soundEnabled ¬ = FALSE	volume, soundLevel	17
sound fadeIn	Sound	Command	Fades in a sound in a channel for a specific number of ticks.	sound fadeIn 1, 60	sound fadeOut, puppetSound	17
sound fadeOut	Sound	Command	Fades out a sound in a channel for a specific number of ticks.	sound fadeOut 1, 60	sound fadeIn, puppetSound	17
soundKeepDevice	Sound	Property	Undocumented system property. Must be set to TRUE (its default) to enable other sound devices to handle sounds.	the soundKeepDevice ¬ = TRUE	soundDevice	
soundLevel	Sound	Property	This system property can have a range of 0 to 7 and controls the volume for the entire computer.	the soundLevel = 5	volume, soundEnabled	
sound playFile	Sound	Command	Plays an external sound file in a specific sound channel. Leave off the second parameter to have it play back in the first available channel.	sound playFile¬ myFile, 1	sound stop, puppetSound	
sound stop	Sound	Command	Stops a sound playing in a specific sound channel.	sound stop 1	sound playFile, puppetSound	17
sourceRect	MIAW	Property	The original Stage rect of a movie playing as a MIAW.	put window¬ ("myMIAW").¬ sourceRect	drawRect	17

continues

PART

X

APP

J

Keyword	Topic	Type	Description	Syntax Sample	See Also	See Chapter/Appendix
SPACE	Strings	Constant	The equivalent to a space character: " " or *numToChar(32)*.	myString =¬ "Hello"&SPACE&"World."	COMMA, QUOTE, TAB, RETURN	17
sprite	Sprites	Object	Defines a sprite object. Sprites can be referenced only by number, but you can then set variables to represent them.	mySprite = sprite(7)	member, spriteNum	24
spriteBox	Sprites	Property	Obsolete Lingo. Use the rect property of a sprite instead.		rect	
spriteNum	Behaviors	Property	The sprite number to which a behavior is attached.	if me.spriteNum¬ = 7 then...		
sprite intersects					intersects	
sprite within					within	
sqrt	Math	Function	Returns the square root of a number.	put sqrt(4)	power, floatPrecision	
stage	Movie	Property	Refers to the Stage itself. You can use it with the *tell* command, or with the *picture* property.	tell the stage to...	tell, picture	
stageBottom	Movie	Property	The vertical position of the bottom of the Stage.	put the stageBottom	stageLeft, stageRight, stageTop	13
stageColor	Movie	Property	The color of the Stage. Use the palette index number.	the stageColor = 255		

Term	Category	Type	Description	Example	See Also	
stageLeft	Movie	Property	The horizontal position of the left of the Stage.	put the stageLeft	stageBottom, stageRight, stageTop	
stageRight	Movie	Property	The horizontal position of the right of the Stage.	put the stageRight	stageBottom, stageLeft, stageTop	27
stageToFlash	Flash, Vector	Function	Returns the coordinates in a Flash sprite that correspond to a location on the Stage.	put stageToFlash¬ (sprite 7, the¬ mouseLoc)	flashToStage	
stageTop	Movie	Property	The vertical position of the top of the Stage.	put the stageTop	stageBottom, stageLeft, stageRight	
startFrame	Sprites	Property	Returns the first frame of a sprite span.	put sprite(7).¬ startFrame	endFrame	
startMovie	Movie	Event Handler	This handler runs just after the first frame of the movie is drawn.	on startMovie	prepareMovie, stopMovie	
starts	Strings	Function	This function compares two strings and returns TRUE if the second is at the very beginning of the first.	if myString starts myOtherString then...	contains, offset	
startTime	Digital Video	Property	Enables you to set the starting time for a digital video sprite.	sprite(7).¬ startTime = 60	stopTime	
startTimer	Date & Time	Command	Resets the timer system property at 0.	startTimer	timer	
state	Flash, Shockwave Audio	Property	Returns the state of the Shockwave audio member or Flash member.	put member("mySWA")¬ .state	clearError, getError	

PART

X

APP

J

continues

Keyword	Topic	Type	Description	Syntax Sample	See Also	See Chapter/Appendix
static	Flash	Property	If set to FALSE, the Flash member redraws only if the sprite moves or changes size. Use for only static Flash members.	`member("myFlash")¬` `.static = TRUE`		21

staticQuality	QTVR	Property	The quality of a panoramic image when it is not moving. Possible values are: #minQuality, #maxQuality, and #normalQuality.	`sprite(7).¬`
				`staticQuality =¬`
				`#maxQuality`
					motionQuality	D

stepFrame	OOP	Event Handler	Any script objects added to the actorList are sent this message once per frame.	`on stepFrame me`	actorList	20

stillDown	System	Property	Returns TRUE inside a mouseDown handler if the mouse is still down, and has not been lifted since the mouse down action that called the handler.	`if the¬`
				`StillDown¬`
				`then...`
					mouseDown	

stop	Flash	Command	Stops a Flash sprite from animating.	`stop sprite(7)`	hold, rewind, play	23
stop member	Shockwave Audio	Command	Stops a Shockwave audio member that is playing.	`stop member("mySWA")`	play member, pause member	

Term	Category	Type	Description	Example	Related
stopEvent	Behaviors	Command	Prevents the current event message from being sent to another behavior attached to a sprite.	stopEvent	pass
stopMovie	Movie	Event Handler	This handler runs when a movie is stopped or ends.	on stopMovie	startMovie 17
stopTime	Digital Video	Property	Enables you to set the end time for a digital video sprite.	sprite(7).¬ stopTime = 60	startTime
stream	Flash	Command	Streams in a number of bytes of a Flash member.	stream(member ("myFlash"), 10240)	
streamName	Shockwave Audio	Property	The Internet location of a streaming Shockwave audio member.	put member ("mySWA").¬ streamName	url
streamMode	Flash	Property	Enables you to stream flash movies in three different modes: #frame (a little each frame), #idle (during idle time), or #manual (must use the *stream* command).	member("myFlash")¬ .streamMode = #manual	stream
streamSize	Flash	Property	The total number of bytes in a streaming Flash member's file.	put member ("myFlash").¬ streamSize	stream
streamStatus	Network	Event Handler	Called periodically while a member is streaming and will be sent information about the streaming.	on streamStatus URL,¬ state, bytesSoFar,¬ bytesTotal, error	getStreamStatus, tellStreamStatus

continues

PART

X

APP

J

Keyword	Topic	Type	Description	Syntax Sample	See Also	See Chapter/Appendix
stretch			Obsolete Lingo. Used to be a sprite property that would tell you whether a sprite had been resized.			
string	Strings	Function	Takes a value such as a list, number, or object and returns a string.	`put string(7)` `put string(myList)`	integer, float, value, numToChar	
stringP	Strings	Function	Returns TRUE if the value is a string.	`if stringP`¬ `(myVariable) then...`	integerP, floatP, listP	
strokeColor	Vector	Property	The color, as an rgb, of the vector shape's line.	`member("myVector")`¬ `.strokeColor =`¬ `rgb(255,0,0)`	strokeColor, fillColor, bgColor	
strokeWidth	Vector	Property	The width of the vector shape's line.	`member("myVector")`¬ `.strokeWidth = 2`	strokeColor, closed	33
swing	QTVR	Command	Moves a QTVR panoramic to a new position.	`swing(sprite(7),`¬ `myPan,myTilt,`¬ `myFieldOfView,`¬ `mySpeedToSwing)`	pan	20
switchColorDepth	System	Property	If TRUE, the Projector attempts to switch the monitor's color depth to match the depth of the movie.	`the switchColorDepth`¬ `= FALSE`	colorDepth	20
symbol	Symbols	Function	Converts a string to a symbol.	`put symbol`¬ `("mySymbol")`	value, string	
symbolP	Symbols	Function	Returns TRUE if the value is a symbol.	`if symbolP`¬ `(myVariable) then...`	ilk	

Term	Category	Type	Description	Example	See Also
systemDate	Date & Time	Property	This system property returns the computer's date using the date format.	put the systemDate	date
TAB	Strings	Constant	Equivalent to the tab character, which is numToChar(8).	myString =¬ "This and"¬ &TAB&"That"	RETURN, QUOTE 33
tabCount	Text	Property	Returns the number of tabs in the ruler of a text member. You can specify the exact chunk within the text member if you want.	put member¬ ("myText").tabCount	tabs 21
tabs	Text	Property	Returns a property list with information about the tab stops in a text member or chunk of a text member.	put member¬ ("myText").tabs	tabCount
tan	Math	Function	Returns the tangent of an angle. Angle must be in radians.	put tan(pi()/4)	cos, sin, atan, pi
tell	MIAW	Command	Sends a message or series of commands to a MIAW or the stage. Can use *to* to send a single line of code, or *end tell* to send many lines.	tell window¬ ("myMIAW") to...	
tellStreamStatus	Network	Function	If you use TRUE, streamStatus messages are sent to the *on streamStatus* handler.	tellStreamStatus¬ (TRUE)	streamStatus, getStreamStatus

continues

PART

X

APP

J

Keyword	Topic	Type	Description	Syntax Sample	See Also	See Chapter/Appendix
text	Text, Field, Button	Property	Returns the text in a text-based member as plain text. You can set it, too.	`put member¬ ("myText").text`	rtf, html	
textAlign	Field	Property	Obsolete field property for alignment.		alignment	
textFont	Field	Property	Obsolete field property for font.		font	
textHeight	Field	Property	Obsolete field property for lineHeight.		lineHeight	
textSize	Field	Property	Obsolete field property for fontSize.		fontSize	
textStyle	Field	Property	Obsolete field property for fontStyle.		fontStyle	
the	Programming	Misc	Used to denote a property.	`put the systemDate`		
then					if	
thumbnail	Member	Property	The picture image used as a thumbnail in the cast window.	`member("myMember")¬ .thumbnail =¬ myPicture`	picture	
ticks	Date & Time	Property	This system property returns the number of ticks (1/60th of a second) since the computer started.	`put the ticks`	milliseconds, timer	
tilt	QTVR	Property	The current tilt, in degrees, of a QTVR movie.	`sprite(7).tilt = 30`		

Term	Category	Type	Description	Example	Related	21
time	System	Property	Reads the user's computer's clock and returns the time in various formats. You can use "abbr", "long", and "short" as modifiers. The actual result depends on the computer's time settings.	put the time put the abbr time put the long time put the short time	abbr, long, short, date	21
timeout	Timeouts	Event Handler	The handler is called when the mouse or keyboard have not been used by the user for timeOutLength.	on timeout	timeOutLength	
timeoutKeydown	Timeouts	Property	Whether key presses will reset timeOutLapsed.	the timeoutKeyDown¬ = TRUE	timeoutLapsed, timeoutLength, timeoutMouse, timeoutPlay, timeoutScript	
timeoutLapsed	Timeouts	Property	The number of ticks that have gone by since the last user action.	put the timeoutLapsed	timeoutLapsed, timeoutKeyDown, timeoutMouse, timeoutPlay, timeoutScript	21
timeoutLength	Timeouts	Property	The amount of time, in ticks, that the timeoutLapsed must reach to trigger a timeout event.	the timeoutLength¬ = 3*60*60	timeoutLapsed, timeoutKeyDown, timeoutMouse, timeoutPlay, timeoutScript	21
timeoutMouse	Timeouts	Property	Whether mouse clicks will reset timeOutLapsed.	the timeoutLMouse¬ = TRUE	timeoutLapsed, timeoutKeyDown, timeoutLength, timeoutPlay, timeoutScript	21

PART

X

APP

J

continues

Keyword	Topic	Type	Description	Syntax Sample	See Also	See Chapter/ Appendix
timeoutPlay	Timeouts	Property	Whether play commands will reset timeOutLapsed.	the timeoutPlay¬ = TRUE	timeoutLapsed, timeoutKeyDown, timeoutLength, timeoutMouse, timeoutScript	21
timeoutScript	Timeouts	Property	The alternative handler to on timeout that gets called when a timeout event occurs. Set to EMPTY to have on timeout called.	the timeoutScript¬ = "myTimeoutHandler"	timeoutLapsed, timeoutKeyDown, timeoutLength, timeoutMouse, timeoutPlay	
timer	Date & Time	Property	This system property returns the number of ticks since the computer started or since the last startTimer command.	put the timer	startTimer, ticks	
timeScale	Digital Video	Property	Returns the unit per second measurement of time for a digital video member. A typical value is 600, meaning 1/600 of a second.	put member¬ ("myVideo").¬ timeScale	digitalVideo-TimeScale	21
title	MIAW	Property	Sets the text to appear in the title bar of a MIAW.	window("myMIAW").¬ title = "My MIAW"	titleVisible, name	21
titleVisible	MIAW	Property	Set to TRUE if you want the title bar visible for a MIAW. Not all window types support a title bar.	window("myMIAW")¬ .titleVisible =¬ TRUE	title	

	Category	Type	Description	Example	See Also	Ch
to	Programming	Expression	Used in old set syntax as a substitute for = and in old chunk statement syntax. Also used in repeat loop statements.	put char 5 to 7 of¬ myString set¬ myVariable to 7 repeat with I =¬ 1 to 10	=, repeat	24
top	Sprites, Misc	Property	Returns the top location of a sprite. Can also be used as a property of rect objects.	put sprite(7).¬ top put myRect.top	width, left right, bottom, rect	24
trace	Debug	Property	If set to TRUE, trace information is sent to the Message window as Lingo executes.	the trace = TRUE	traceLoad, traceLogFile	
traceLoad	Debug	Property	Enables information to be displayed in the Message window about members as they load. Possible values are 0 (no information), 1 (names only), or 2 (names, frame number, movie name, file seek offset).	the traceLoad = 2	trace, traceLogFile	
traceLogFile	Debug	Property	If set to a filename, messages sent to the Message window are also sent to a file. Set to an empty string to close.	the traceLogFile¬ = "trace.txt"	trace, traceLoad	33
trackCount	Digital Video	Function	Returns the number of tracks in a video sprite or member.	put trackCount¬ (sprite(7))	trackType	

PART

X

APP

J

continues

Keyword	Topic	Type	Description	Syntax Sample	See Also	See Chapter/Appendix
trackEnabled	Digital Video	Function	Returns TRUE if the track is enabled.	put trackEnabled¬ (sprite(7),trackNum)	setTrackEnabled	
trackNextKeyTime	Digital Video	Function	Returns the time of the next keyframe.	put trackNextKeyTime¬ (sprite(7),trackNum)	trackType, trackPrevious-KeyTime	
trackNextSampleTime	Digital Video	Function	Returns the time of the next piece of data in a track.	put¬ trackNextSampleTime¬ (sprite(7),trackNum)	trackType, trackPrevious-SampleTime	
trackPreviousKeyTime	Digital Video	Function	Returns the time of the previous keyframe.	put¬ trackPreviousKeyTime¬ (sprite(7),trackNum)		
trackPreviousSampleTime	Digital Video	Function	Returns the time of the previous piece of data in a track.	put¬ trackPreviousSample Time(sprite(7),¬ trackNum)		
trackStartTime	Digital Video	Function	Returns the starting time of a track in a video sprite or member.	put trackStartTime¬ (sprite(7),trackNum)	trackType, trackStoTime	
trackStopTime	Digital Video	Function	Returns the ending time of a track in a video sprite or member.	put trackStopTime¬ (sprite(7),trackNum)	trackType,	
trackText	Digital Video	Function	Returns a string with the text of a digital video text track.	put trackText¬ (sprite(7),trackNum)	trackType	
trackType	Digital Video	Function	Returns the type, whether #video, #sound, #text, or #music, of a video sprite or member track.	put trackType¬ (sprite(7),trackNum)	trackEnabled, trackCount	

Term	Type	Category	Description	Syntax	See Also
trails	Property	Sprites	Indicates whether the sprite leaves a trail behind as it is moved around the Stage.	sprite(7).trails¬ = TRUE	
transitionType	Property	Transition	Returns the number of the transition in a member. This number corresponds to the codes for puppetTransition.	member("myTransition")¬ .transitionType = 34	18
translation	Property	Digital Video	The location offset of a QuickTime video sprite or member from the center or upper-left corner, depending on the *center* property.	sprite(7).¬ translation = [x,y]	center
triggerCallback	Property	QTVR	You can set this to the name of a handle to have that handler called when the user clicks a hotspot.	sprite(7).¬ triggerCallback =¬ "myTriggerHandler"	D
TRUE	Constant	Logic	Logical true. Use in *if*, *repeat*, *case*, or other logic statements. Equivalent to 1.		if, repeat, case, FALSE
tweened	Property	Score Recording	If FALSE, all frames in a sprite are considered keyframes. This is only for Score recording.	sprite(7).tweened¬ = TRUE	beginRecording, updateFrame
type	Property	Member	Returns the type of a member, such as #bitmap or #text.	put member¬ ("myMember").type	

continues

PART

X

APP

J

Keyword	Topic	Type	Description	Syntax Sample	See Also	See Chapter/ Appendix
type	Score Recording	Property	Can be used during Score recording to clear a sprite by setting its type to 0.	`sprite(7).type = 0`	beginRecording, updateFrame	
union	Math	Function	Takes two rectangles and returns the smallest rectangle that contains them both.	`put union(rect¬ (0,0,100,100),¬ rect(50,50,150,150))`	map, rect	D
unLoad	Memory	Command	Removes from memory the cast members used in a frame, range of frames, or all frames.	`unLoad 5, 9 unLoad`	preLoad, unLoadMember	
unloadMember	Memory	Command	Removes a member or range of members from memory.	`unloadMember¬ "myMember"`	preLoadMember, unLoad	
unloadMovie	Memory	Command	Removes from memory the members loaded with the preLoadMovie command.	`unloadMovie¬ "myNewMovie"`	preLoadMovie	21
updateFrame	Score Recording	Command	Makes the changes to the current frame permanent, and moves forward one frame to continue Score recording.	`updateFrame`	beginRecording, updateFrame	
updateLock	Score Recording	Property	If this property is set to TRUE, Score recording does not show changes on the Stage as it works.	`the updateLoc = TRUE`	beginRecording, updateFrame	21

updateMovieEnabled	Movie	Property	If TRUE, changes made to a movie are automatically saved when another movie is loaded.	`the⌐ upodateMovieEnabled⌐ = TRUE`	saveMovie	26
updateStage	Movie	Command	Puts any sprite changes into effect immediately, rather than waiting for the next frame to begin.	`updateStage`	puppetSound	26
url	Shockwave Audio	Property	The Internet location of a streaming Shockwave audio file.	`member("mySWA").⌐ url = "http://⌐ clevermedia.com/⌐ swasample.swa/"`	pathname, filename	
useAlpha	Bitmap	Property	If TRUE, 32-bit bitmaps use the alpha channel information, if available.	`member("myBitmap")⌐ .useAlpha = TRUE`		
useFastQuads	Sprites	Property	Undocumented Lingo. If TRUE, sprites stretched by setting the quad property use a faster method of drawing. The object is not drawn quite correctly for 3D effects, however.	`the useFastQuads⌐ = TRUE`	quad	
useHyperTextStyles	Text	Property	When TRUE, all hyperlinks in the member are blue and underlined. The cursor changes to a finger when over them.	`member("myText").⌐ useHyperTextStyles⌐ = TRUE`	hyperlink	18

continues

PART
X

APP

J

Keyword	Topic	Type	Description	Syntax Sample	See Also	See Chapter/Appendix
userName	System	Property	Returns the username of the registered user of the Director application.	`put the userName`	serialNumber	

value	Strings, Misc	Function	Interprets the string as a Lingo expression and returns its value. The value can even be a list.	`myVal = value("2+2")`
				`myVal = value¬`
				`("[4,5,6]")`
				`myVal =¬`
				`value("myVariable")`
					integer, float, string	

version	System	Property	A global variable that is always present. It contains the version of Director running or the version of Shockwave or the version of Director that created the Projector.	`put version`		

vertex	Vector	Property	Enables you to refer to an individual vertex point.	`put member¬`
				`("myVector").¬`
				`vertex[1]`
				`put member¬`
				`("myVector").vertex.¬`
				`count`
					vertexList	

vertexList	Vector	Property	Returns, or enables you to set, the entire vertex list for a vector shape member.	`put member("myVector")¬` `.vertexList`	vertex	
video	Digital Video	Property	If set to FALSE, the video for a video member is not displayed. Sound and music are still heard.	`member("myVideo").¬` `video = TRUE`	sound	20

Term	Category	Type	Description	Example	See Also	Ch.
videoForWindowsPresent	Digital Video	Property	Returns TRUE if video for Windows is available on the machine.	`if the¬ videoForWindowsPresent`	quickTimeVersion	20
viewH	Flash, Vector	Property	Enables you to shift a Flash or vector shape member from its origin point.	`member("myVector")¬ .viewH = 50`	viewV, viewPoint, viewScale	19
viewPoint	Flash, Vector	Property	Enables you to shift a Flash or vector shape member from its origin point.	`member("myVector")¬ .view = point(50,50)`	viewH, viewV, viewScale	
viewScale	Flash, Vector	Property	Sets the scale amount for a Flash or vector shape member. You must not change this value if you are using the #autoSize scaleMode.	`member("myVector")¬ .viewScale = 2.0`	scaleMode	
viewV	Flash, Vector	Property	Enables you to shift a Flash or vector shape member from its origin point.	`member("myVector")¬ .viewV = 50`	viewH, viewPoint, viewScale	20
visible	Sprites	Property	Hides a sprite, and prevents mouse clicks from reaching it. Other events still occur.	`sprite(7).¬ visible = FALSE`		20
visible	MIAW	Property	Enables you to hide or show a MIAW.	`window("myMIAW")¬ .visible = FALSE`		
VOID	Programming	Constant	Enables you to set a variable to VOID, which is the equivalent to having no value.	`myVariable = VOID`	voidP	

continues

PART

X

APP

J

Keyword	Topic	Type	Description	Syntax Sample	See Also	See Chapter/Appendix
voidP	Programming	Function	Returns TRUE if the value provided is VOID (has no value).	`if voidP(myVariable)¬ then...`	VOID, objectP	
volume	Shockwave audio, Sound, Digital Video	Property	Enables you to set the volume of a Shockwave audio member, the volume of a sound channel, or the volume of a digital video sprite. Possible values are from 0 to 255.	`member("mySWA").¬ volume = 255 sound(1).volume = 255 member("myVideo")¬ .volume = 255`	soundLevel	
warpMode	QTVR	Property	Can be set to #full, #partial, or #none to control QTVR warping.	`sprite(7).warpMode¬ = #partial`		
while					repeat	17
width	Sprites, Members	Property	Returns the width of most members and sprites. Can also be used as a property of rect objects.	`put sprite(7).width put myRect.width`	height, rect	
window	MIAW	Object	Defines a MIAW object.	`myMIAW = window¬ ("myMIAW")`	open window, close window	
windowList	MIAW	Property	This system property returns a list with all the windows present.	`put the windowList`		
windowPresent	MIAW	Function	Tests a MIAW name to see whether it is present.	`if windowPresent¬ ("myMIAW") then...`	windowList	
windowType	MIAW	Property	Returns a number that corresponds to the window type.	`put window("myMIAW")¬ .windowType`		24

Term	Type	Category	Description	Example	See Also	Page
with					repeat	24
within	Sprites	Function	Determines whether the second sprite rectangle is totally within the first. Note the odd syntax.	`if sprite 1¬ within 2 then...`	intersects	24, D
word	Strings	Expression	Used to specify a single word or range of words in a string chunk. Words are separated by spaces or an invisible character such as a Return.	`put myString.word[7]` `put member¬ ("myText").text.¬ word[4..7]`	char line, item, chars	
wordWrap	Field	Property	If TRUE, text automatically wraps in a field.	`member("myField") .wordWrap = TRUE`		
xtra	Xtras	Object	Enables you to define an Xtra as an object.	`fileObj = new¬ (xtra "FileIO")`	new	
xtraList	Xtras	Property	Returns a list with all the Xtras present.	`put the xtraList`		16
year					date	
zoomBox	Misc	Command	Creates a zooming effect between the rectangles of two sprites.	`zoomBox(7,8)`		25
zoomWindow	MIAW	Event Handler	Called if the user presses the Zoom button on the Mac or the Maximize or Minimize	`on zoomWindow`	resizeWindow	21

PART

X

APP

J

INDEX

Y

Z

Shockwave websites grab you by the eyeballs.

Shockwave is on every website
that needs to deliver a captivating experience.
It's on every new Macintosh® and Windows® PC.
It's in your web browser. It's entertaining,
irresistable, effective. Make it with
Director® 7 Shockwave™ Internet Studio™
Use it to add life to the web.
www.macromedia.com

add life to the web

macromedia®

(DIRECTOR)   (SHOCKWAVE) DREAMWEAVER FIREWORKS FLASH FREEHAND GENERATOR

©1999 Macromedia, Inc. All rights reserved. Macromedia, the Macromedia logo, Director, and Shockwave are trademarks or registered trademarks of Macromedia, Inc. All other trademarks or registered trademarks are the property of their respective owners.

READ THIS BEFORE OPENING SOFTWARE

By opening this package, you are agreeing to be bound by the following agreement:

Some of the software included with this product may be copyrighted, in which case all rights are reserved by the respective copyright holder. You are licensed to use software copyrighted by the Publisher and its licensors on a single computer. You may copy and/or modify the software as needed to facilitate your use of it on a single computer. Making copies of the software for any other purpose is a violation of the United States copyright laws.

This software is sold as is without warranty of any kind, either expressed or implied, including but not limited to the implied warranties of merchantability and fitness for a particular purpose. Neither the publisher nor its dealers or distributors assumes any liability for any alleged or actual damages arising from the use of this program. (Some states do not allow for the exclusion of implied warranties, so the exclusion may not apply to you.)

Before using any of the software on this disc, you need to install the software you plan to use. If you have problems with this CD-ROM, please contact Macmillan Technical Support at (317) 581-3833. We can be reached by email at support@mcp.com.

Windows 95 and Windows NT: If you have AutoPlay enabled, insert the CD-ROM and choose installation options from the displayed splash screen.

NOTE: If you have AutoPlay disabled on your computer, the CD-ROM will *not* automatically display the installation splash screen. To browse the CD-ROM manually, double-click My Computer on the desktop, then right-click your CD player icon, and choose Explore from the shortcut menu. By doing this, you can immediately access the files for this CD-ROM. You can run the CD-ROM manually by double-clicking the Start.exe file.

Mac: Use the descriptions of the folder structure in the CD Guide document to locate items on the CD-ROM.